Using Information Technology

Sixth Edition

Using Information Technology

A Practical Introduction to Computers & Communications

Introductory Version

Stacey C. Sawyer

Brian K. Williams

Boston   Burr Ridge, IL   Dubuque, IA   Madison, WI   New York   San Francisco   St. Louis
Bangkok   Bogotá   Caracas   Kuala Lumpur   Lisbon   London   Madrid   Mexico City
Milan   Montreal   New Delhi   Santiago   Seoul   Singapore   Sydney   Taipei   Toronto

 **Technology Education**

USING INFORMATION TECHNOLOGY, INTRODUCTORY EDITION
Published by McGraw-Hill Technology Education, a business unit of The McGraw-Hill Companies, Inc., 1221 Avenue of the Americas, New York, NY 10020. Copyright © 2005, 2003, 2001, 1999, 1997, 1995 by The McGraw-Hill Companies, Inc. All rights reserved. No part of this publication may be reproduced or distributed in any form or by any means, or stored in a database or retrieval system, without the prior written consent of The McGraw-Hill Companies, Inc., including, but not limited to, in any network or other electronic storage or transmission, or broadcast for distance learning.
Some ancillaries, including electronic and print components, may not be available to customers outside the United States.

This book is printed on acid-free paper.

1 2 3 4 5 6 7 8 9 0 QPD/QPD 0 9 8 7 6 5 4

ISBN 0-07-288290-5

Editor in chief: *Bob Woodbury*
Sponsoring editor: *Marc Chernoff*
Developmental editor: *Lisa Chin-Johnson/Burrston House, Ltd.*
Manager, Marketing and Sales: *Andy Bernier*
Media producer: *Greg Bates*
Senior project manager: *Christine A. Vaughan*
Senior production supervisor: *Sesha Bolisetty*
Designer: *Adam Rooke*
Production and Quark makeup: *Stacey C. Sawyer*
Photo research coordinator: *Judy Kausal*
Photo researcher: *Judy Mason*
Senior supplement producer: *Rose M. Range*
Senior digital content specialist: *Brian Nacik*
Cover design and image: *Asylum Studios*
Typeface: *10/12 Trump Medieval*
Compositor: *GTS—Los Angeles, CA Campus*
Printer: *Quebecor World Dubuque Inc.*

Library of Congress Control Number: 2003116359

INTERNATIONAL EDITION ISBN 0-07-1112413
Copyright © 2005. Exclusive rights by The McGraw-Hill Companies, Inc., for manufacture and export.
This book cannot be re-exported from the country to which it is sold by McGraw-Hill.
The International Edition is not available in North America.

www.mhhe.com

Photo and other credits are listed in the back of the book.

Brief Contents

1 INTRODUCTION TO INFORMATION TECHNOLOGY: Your Digital World   1

2 THE INTERNET & THE WORLD WIDE WEB: Exploring Cyberspace   37

3 SOFTWARE: For Productivity & Creativity   85

4 HARDWARE—THE CPU & STORAGE: How to Buy a Multimedia Computer System   139

5 HARDWARE—INPUT & OUTPUT: Taking Charge of Computing & Communications   181

6 TELECOMMUNICATIONS: Networks & Communications—The "New Story" in Computing   215

7 FILES, DATABASES, & E-COMMERCE: Digital Engines for the New Economy   251

8 SOCIETY & THE DIGITAL AGE: Challenges & Promises   277

APPENDIX: SYSTEMS & PROGRAMMING: Development, Programming, & Languages   A1

What Reviewers Said about the 5th Edition of Sawyer & Williams's UIT Introductory Version

"I think the writing style is outstanding. The text is readable yet the tone isn't too casual. The style reflects a respect for the reader. . . . The examples are very good. I think the explanations are clearly presented."

—Lynn Wermers, North Shore Community College, Massachusetts

"[This text] is unique in its readability. The writing style makes the content flow, thus enhancing student focus and concentration. The mix of practical items . . . and conceptual subject matter . . . does indeed distinguish S&W from other texts."

—Edmund Mannion, California State University—Chico

"I'm particularly impressed by the authors' writing style and organization of thought, with smooth segues between sections; emphasis throughout on ethics; key terms AND definitions emphasized; . . . [and] the format of the Summary sections."

—Ken Baldauf, Florida State University

"Sawyer & Williams's writing style is more story-like compared to our current text . . . which reads much more like a book of terminology."

—Tim Pinkelman, Bowling Green State University, Ohio

"This is an easy book to read and use. The depth of the material is right for my course."

—Sandy Week, University of Nevada—Reno

"The text we use at present is [another publisher's] 'complete' edition, with 16 chapters having in-depth coverage. . . . S&W covers most topics and is at par with our current text."

—Khondkar Islam, George Mason University, Virginia

"I like the way that they have presented the main ideas in smaller chunks of information. I follow this same methodology myself. . . . Also, I really like the definition summary listed at the end of each chapter—very practical!"

—Maureen Ellis, Indiana University—Bloomington

"Your pedagogical approach is excellent."

—Arthur Valentine, Sussex County Community College, New Jersey

"Emphasis on practicality is the most important [feature]."

—Mary Kay Tarver, East Central University, Oklahoma

"I especially liked that you have attempted to cover ethical issues throughout, rather than in an isolated unit."

—Ruthann Williams, Central Missouri State University

"The ethics emphasis is one thing that made this book stand out."

—Ruth Schwartz, Indiana University—South Bend

"Critical thinking emphasis is very important and a life-long skill. Students have difficulty in this area, and it's great to see a textbook attempting to deal with the issue."

—Laurie Shteir, Temple University, Pennsylvania

To the Instructor

Introduction

As we embark on our tenth year of publication, we are extremely pleased at the continuing enthusiasm for *USING INFORMATION TECHNOLOGY* as a concepts textbook for the introductory college course on computers. More than half a million students have been introduced to this dynamic and exciting subject through UIT's five earlier editions, and instructors in over 600 schools have selected it for use in their courses.

What are the reasons for this acceptance? One is that UIT was the first textbook to foresee and define the impact of digital convergence—the fusion of computers and communications—as the new and broader foundation for this course. And we have continued to try to pioneer in coverage of new developments. Thus, we are gratified to hear reviewers label UIT as the most up-to-date text published for this course.

The UIT Difference: A Book to Motivate the Unmotivated, & to Teach to a Variety of Students' Computer Backgrounds

But there are two other important reasons, we think, for UIT's frequent adoption. We've often asked instructors—in reviews, surveys, and focus groups—**"What is your most significant challenge in teaching this course?"**

> **Quote**
>
> What instructors say is their most significant challenge in teaching this course
>
> "Motivating the unmotivated is the primary challenge."
> —Lynn Wermers, North Shore Community College, MA
>
> "Coping with the wide disparity of skill levels among the enrolled students."
> —Edmund Mannion, California State University—Chico

- **The first most frequent answer is: "Trying to make the course interesting and challenging."** One professor at a state university seems to speak for most when she says: "Making the course interesting and challenging." Others echo her with remarks such as "Keeping students interested in the material enough to study" and "Keeping the students engaged who know some, but not all, of the material." Said one professor, "Many students take the course because they must, instead of because the material interests them." Another speaks about the need to address a "variety of skill/knowledge levels while keeping the course challenging and interesting"—which brings us to the second response.

- **The second most frequent answer is: "Trying to teach to students with a variety of computer backgrounds."** The most significant challenge in teaching this course "is trying to provide material to the varied levels of students in the class," says an instructor at a large Midwestern university. Another says the course gets students from all backgrounds, ranging from "Which button do you push on the mouse?" to "Already built and maintain a web page with html." Says a third, "mixed-ability classes [make] it difficult to appeal to all students at the same time." And a fourth: "How do you keep the 'techies' interested without losing the beginners?"

As authors, we find information technology tremendously exciting, but we recognize that many students take the course reluctantly. And we also recognize that many students come to the subject with attitudes ranging from complete apathy and unfamiliarity to a high degree of experience and technical understanding.

To address the problem of **motivating the unmotivated and teaching to a disparity of backgrounds,** UIT offers unequaled treatment of the following:

1. **Practicality**
2. **Readability**
3. **Currentness**
4. **Three-level critical thinking system**

We explain these features below.

Feature #1: Emphasis on Practicality

See the list of Practical Action Boxes on the inside <u>back</u> cover.

See the list of Survival Tips on the inside <u>back</u> cover.

This popular feature received overwhelming acceptance by both students and instructors in past editions. **Practical advice,** of the sort found in computer magazines, newspaper technology sections, and general-interest computer books, is expressed not only in the text but also in the following:

- **Bookmark It! Practical Action Box:** This box consists of optional material on practical matters. *Examples:* "Managing Your E-Mail." "Web Research, Term Papers, & Plagiarism." "How to Buy a Notebook." "Preventing Your Identity from Getting Stolen." ***New to this edition:*** "Installing & Reinstalling Software."

BOOKMARK IT!

PRACTICAL ACTION
Choosing an Internet Service Provider

page 76

- **Survival Tips:** In the margins throughout we present utilitarian **Survival Tips** to aid students' explorations of the infotech world. *Examples:* "Recycling Old PCs." "Handling the Annoyance of Spam," "Don't Be Traced," "Urban Legends & Lies on the Internet," "Don't Trash Those Icons," "Decimal to Binary Conversion," "Are Your PC's USB Ports 1.1 or 2.0?," "Data Recovery," "CD Read, Write, & Rewrite Speeds," "Zip vs. Tape," "Temp File Removal," "Your Choice: More Colors or More Resolution?," "Customize Your Sounds."

Survival Tip

Accessing Email While Traveling Abroad

To access your email using a local call while traveling outside North America, get a free email account with Yahoo! (*http://mail.yahoo*), Hotmail (*www.hotmail.com*), or Mail.com (*www.mail.com*).

- **Early discussion of Internet:** Many instructors have told us they like having **"e-concepts" treated earlier and more extensively** in this text compared with other books. Accordingly, the Internet and World Wide Web are **discussed in Chapter 2** instead of in a later chapter, reflecting their importance in students' daily lives.

Chapter 2
THE INTERNET & THE WORLD WIDE WEB: EXPLORING CYBERSPACE 37

- **How to understand a computer ad:** In the hardware chapters (Chapters 4 and 5), we explain important concepts by showing students **how to understand the hardware components in a hypothetical PC ad.**

- 7-Bay Mid-Tower Case
- Intel Pentium 4 Processor 2 GHz
- 128 MB 266 MHz DDR SDRAM
- 512KB L2 Cache
- 2 USB Ports
- 56 Kbps Internal Modem
- 3D AGP Graphics Card (64 MB)
- Sound Blaster Digital Sound Card
- 3.5" Floppy Drive
- Iomega 250 MB Zip Drive
- 80 GB Ultra ATA 7200 RPM Hard Drive
- 4X DVD-RW
- 104-Key Keyboard
- Microsoft IntelliMouse
- 17", .27dp Monitor (16" Display)
- HP DeskJet 970Cse Printer

page 143

Details of this ad are explained throughout this chapter. See the little magnifying glass:

Feature #2: Emphasis on Readability & Reinforcement for Learning

We offer the following features for reinforcing student learning:

- **Interesting writing:** Studies have found that textbooks **written in an imaginative style** significantly improve students' ability to retain information. Both instructors and students have commented on the distinctiveness of the writing in this book. We employ a number of journalistic devices—colorful anecdotes, short biographical sketches, interesting observations in direct quotes—to make the material as interesting as possible. We also use real anecdotes and examples rather than fictionalized ones.
- **Key terms AND definitions emphasized:** To help readers avoid any confusion about which terms are important and what they actually mean, we print each key term in ***bold italic underscore*** and its definition in **boldface**. *Example* (from Chapter 1): "***Data*** **consists of raw facts and figures that are processed into information.**"
- **Material in bite-size portions:** Major ideas are presented in **bite-size form,** with generous use of advance organizers, bulleted lists, and new paragraphing when a new idea is introduced. Most **sentences have been kept short,** the majority not exceeding 22–25 words in length.
- **Key Questions—to help students read with purpose:** We have **crafted the learning objectives as Key Questions** to help readers focus on

essentials. Each Key Question appears in two places: on the first page of the chapter and beneath the section head. Key Questions are also tied to the end-of-chapter summary, as we will explain.

See Ethics examples on pp. 26, 55, 76, 242, 265, 267, 282, 283, 285, 296, 297, 299.

- **QuickChecks:** Appearing periodically throughout the text, **Quick-Checks** spur students to recall facts and concepts they have just read.

- **Summary:** Each chapter ends with a **Summary** of important terms, with an explanation of **what they are and why they are important.** The terms are accompanied, when appropriate, by a picture. Each concept or term is also given a cross-reference page number that refers the reader to the main discussion within the text. In addition, the term or concept is given a Key Question number corresponding to the appropriate Key Question (learning objective).

- **Emphasis throughout on ethics:** Many texts discuss ethics in isolation, usually in one of the final chapters. We believe this topic is too important to be treated last or lightly, and users have agreed. Thus, **we cover ethical matters throughout the book,** as indicated by the special icon shown at right. *Example:* We discuss such all-important questions as copying of Internet files, online plagiarism, privacy, computer crime, and netiquette.

- *New to this edition!* **More Info! icons help students find their own answers** to their questions. The previous edition featured "Click-along" marginal icons that directed readers to the McGraw-Hill website for updates, elaboration, and further examples. This concept was well received, but we realized it didn't enable students to pursue their own range of interests—exactly the kind of thing that makes the World Wide Web such a valuable learning instrument. Accordingly, in this edition we have initiated a **"More Info!" page-margin icon that shows students how to begin their own journey of discovery,** often starting from a particular URL. *Examples:* "More about instant messaging services and products" (p. 52). "More information on web radio" (p. 69). "Researching Linux" (p. 102). See the pages listed on the inside front cover.

info!

If you refuse cookies? Read the article at *http://computer.howstuffworks.com/cookie.htm.*

New readability/reinforcement features!
See inside front cover for pages on which More-Info! and Security icons appear.

- *New to this edition!* In the post 9-11 era, security concerns are of gravest importance. Although we devote several pages (in Chapter 9) to security, we also reinforce student awareness by **highlighting with page-margin Security icons instances of security-related material throughout the book.** *Example:* On p. 55, we use the special icon shown at right to highlight the advice that one should pretend that every email message one sends "is a postcard that can be read by anyone."

SECURITY

Feature #3: Currentness

Reviewers have applauded previous editions of UIT for being **more up to date than other texts.** For example, we have traditionally ended many chapters with a forward-looking section that offers a preview of technologies to come—some of which are realized even as students are using the book. Among the new topics and terms covered in this edition are: *abandonware, Apple Macintosh G4 and G5, Athlon 64 FX-51, baseband transmission, biometric identifier, blog/weblog, DDR-SDRAM, FireWire, flash drive, flatbed* scanner, foreign key, handheld scanners, intelligent hub, keychain memory, Klez worm, LaserCard, Lindows, Lycoris, nanocomputer, national identity card, network-centric computing, Nigerian letter scam, passive hub, personal electronic pen, QXGA monitors, sheetfed scanners, smart mobs, SQL Slammer Code worm, switching hub, USB 1.1 and 2.0, USB hub, Windows CE .NET, Windows Server 2003, Windows XP Service Pack 1, Windows XP Tablet PC Edition.

In addition, in this latest edition, **we have taken the notion of currentness to another level through the "MoreInfo!" feature to encourage students to obtain their own updates** about material. *Example:* The subject of instant messaging is one that changes constantly. Thus, to help students stay current, on p. 52 we give them MoreInfo! advice that enables them to investigate new IM services and products.

Feature #4: Three-Level System to Help Students Think Critically about Information Technology

This feature, which has been in place for the preceding two editions, has been warmly received. More and more instructors seem to have become familiar with **Benjamin Bloom's *Taxonomy of Educational Objectives*,** describing a hierarchy of six critical-thinking skills: (a) two lower-order skills—*memorization* and *comprehension*; and (b) four higher-order skills—*application, analysis, synthesis,* and *evaluation.* Drawing on our experience in writing books to guide students to college success, we have implemented Bloom's ideas in a three-stage pedagogical approach, using the following hierarchical approach in the Chapter Review at the end of every chapter:

- Stage 1 learning—memorization: **"I can recognize and recall information."** Using self-test questions, multiple-choice questions, and true/false questions, we enable students to test how well they recall basic terms and concepts.

- Stage 2 learning—comprehension: **"I can recall information in my own terms and explain them to a friend."** Using open-ended short-answer questions, we enable students to re-express terms and concepts in their own words.

- Stage 3 learning—applying, analyzing, synthesizing, evaluating: **"I can apply what I've learned, relate these ideas to other concepts, build on other knowledge, and use all these thinking skills to form a judgment."** In this part of the Chapter Review, we ask students to put the ideas into effect using the activities described. The purpose is to help students take possession of the ideas, make them their own, and apply them realistically to their own ideas.

Resources for Instructors

The instructor supplements for the last edition UNDERWENT A MAJOR REVISION, with a focus on enhancing instructors' ability to understand and utilize all the resources provided for the text. **We and the publisher have tried to maintain the same respect and care with these supplements in this edition as well.**

- **Instructor's Manual:** The electronic Instructor's Manual, available as part of the Instructor's Resource Kit, now **incorporates all of the resources available to the instructor for each chapter.** Instructors now

Test Table

Learning Level	1	2	3
Key Questions	Knows Basic Terms and Facts	Understands Concepts and Principles	Applies Principles
2.1 What are the means of connecting to the Internet, and how fast are they?	1, 2, 3, 4, 5, 6, 7, 8, 9, 10, 11, 12, 13, 14	15, 16, 17,18, 19, 20, 21, 22, 23, 24, 25, 26, 27	28, 29, 30, 31, 32
	117, 118, 119, 120, 121, 122, 123, 124, 125, 126, 127, 128, 129, 130	**131, 132, 133, 134, 135, 136, 137, 138, 139**	**140, 141, 142, 143, 144, 145**
		<u>**258, 259, 260, 261, 262, 263, 264**</u>	
	<u>**244, 245, 246, 247, 248, 249, 250, 251, 252, 253, 254, 255, 256, 257**</u>		
			329*, 330*, 331*
2.2 What is an Internet service provider, and what kinds of services do ISPs provide?	33, 34, 35	36, 37, 38	
	146, 147	**148**	**149, 150**
	<u>**265, 266, 267**</u>	**332***	

have the ability to harness different visual assets to create effective lectures. The Instructor's Manual works like a web page that is easy to navigate and simple to understand because it provides links to appropriate assets elsewhere on the Web or CD-ROM. Each chapter contains an overview of the changes to this edition, a chapter overview, teaching tips, PowerPoint slides with speaker's notes, group projects, outside projects, web exercises, text figures, and links to appropriate information and games on the book's website.

- **Testbank:** The Testbank format **allows instructors to effectively pinpoint areas of content within each chapter on which to test students.** Each chapter starts off with a "Test Table" that provides a convenient guide for finding questions that pertain to chapter objectives and difficulty level. The Test Table also indicates the type of question so that instructors can create exams using the question types of their choice. The test questions are first organized by chapter objectives and then learning level; they include answers, Key Question numbers, learning levels, page references from the text, and rationales. Following each chapter's test bank questions is a Quick Quiz, designed for use when instructors don't have time to tailor an exam.

  Diploma by Brownstone: Diploma is the most flexible, powerful, and easy-to-use computer-based testing system available for higher education. The Diploma system allows instructors to create an exam as a printed version, as a LAN-based online version, or as an Internet version. Diploma also includes grade book features, which automate the entire testing process.

- **PowerPoint presentation:** The PowerPoint presentation **includes additional material** that expands upon important topics from the text, allowing instructors to create interesting and engaging classroom presentations. Each chapter of the presentation includes important illustrations, and animations to enable instructors to emphasize important concepts in memorable ways. **Each slide of the presentation is integrated into the Instructor's Manual** so that instructors can quickly and effectively determine which slides they would like to use in their presentations.

- **Figures from the book:** All of the photos, illustrations, screenshots, and tables are available electronically for use in presentations, transparencies, or handouts.

- **Online Learning Center:** *(www.mhhe.com/cit/uit6e)* Designed to provide a wide variety of learning opportunities for students, the website for the sixth edition now includes a Web Summary for each chapter, with all of the key terms linked to relevant exercises, games, web links, and self-quizzes. Additional end-of-chapter exercises, web exercises, group projects, outside projects, Instructor's Manual, and Power-Point presentations are also available online for instructors to download.

- **Interactive Companion:** Twenty interactive tutorial labs on some of the most popular topics are available on the Online Learning Center. These tutorials expand the reach and scope of the text by combining video, interactive exercises, animation, additional content, and actual "lab" tutorials. The labs include the following topics:

Using Information Technology Interactive Companion Labs

Lab	Function	Chapter
Binary Numbers	Explore binary numbers including such topics as binary numbers as switches, how to make a binary number, binary addition, and binary logic.	4
Basic Programming	Learn about the thought processes and tools used to instruct computers to perform our work. This lab includes topics on basic computer tasks (input, processing, and output), variables, constants, assignment, mathematical calculations, and reusing code.	App.
Computer Anatomy	Learn the parts that make up a personal computer, including Input, Output, Storage, and Processing devices.	4 & 5
Disk Fragmentation	Understand how data and programs are stored and accessed. Includes concepts such as disk storage, blocks, fragmentation, defragmentation, media types, and data storage.	4
E-mail Essentials	Learn the tools, techniques, and etiquette needed to communicate by e-mail.	2 & 6
Multimedia Tools	Learn the basics of creating a simple multimedia presentation by understanding the types of media, virtual reality, interactivity, multimedia applications, and the uses of multimedia.	2 & 3
Workplace Issues	Learn how Ethics, Privacy, Security, and Time Wasters affect you, either as an employer or as an employee.	All
Introduction to Databases	This lab will introduce you to the many concepts involved in making, maintaining, and using a database to store large amounts of related data. You will have the opportunity to design a database, create the database, and use the information you entered to generate useful reports.	7
Programming II	Learn some of the essentials of visual programming, then implement them to build a working program.	App.
Network Communications	Explore the many types of computer-based communications; how they work and how to use them effectively.	2 & 6

Lab	Function	Chapter
User Interfaces	Learn the basics of user interface elements, key Windows interface features, customizing the Windows interface, key Macintosh interface features, customizing the Macintosh interface, and key Unix (Linux) interface features.	3
Purchasing Decisions	Explore the factors you should consider when deciding what computer to buy, including software, the differences between PCs and Macs, the myths about CPU power, internal upgrades, and external upgrades.	4
File Organization	Learn about the way files are stored on your hard drive and how you can configure this storage to help you work more efficiently.	7
Word Processing and Spreadsheets	Learn the common features of word processing and spreadsheet programs, the basic features of word processing programs, and the basic features of spreadsheet programs.	3
Internet Overview	Explore features of the Internet including communication, browsing, sharing, and how to get connected.	2
Computer Troubleshooting	Learn how to avoid, repair, and troubleshoot computer problems.	All
Presentation Techniques	Learn the tricks for making effective presentations such as focusing your presentation to reach your audience, creating effective graphics, using sound and video in your presentation, and creating auxiliary materials to help augment your presentation or generate discussions.	3
Photo Editing	Learn how to edit digital photos including such topics as capturing digital images, storing devices, resizing and enhancement, and other manipulation techniques.	3
Programming Overview	Learn how code is written and changed into machine language by compilers or interpreters. Learn the different types of languages including object-oriented, procedural, and declarative.	App.
SQL Queries	Learn what a relational database is (RDBMS), what a structured language is (SQL), how to use SQL to build a database, and how to use SQL to retrieve data from a database.	7

Digital Solutions to Help You Manage Your Course

PageOut: PageOut is our Course Web Site Development Center and offers a syllabus page, URL, McGraw-Hill Online Learning Center content, online exercises and quizzes, gradebook, discussion board, and an area for student Web pages.

PageOut requires no prior knowledge of HTML, no long hours of coding, and a way for course coordinators and professors to provide a full-course website. PageOut offers a series of templates—simply fill them with your course information and click on one of 16 designs. The process takes under an hour and leaves you with a professionally designed website. We'll even get you started with sample websites, or enter your syllabus for you! PageOut is so straightforward and intuitive, it's little wonder why over 12,000 college professors are using it. For more information, visit the PageOut website at *www.pageout.net*

The Online Learning Center can be delivered through any of these platforms:

McGraw-Hill Learning Architecture (TopClass)
Blackboard.com
Ecollege.com (formerly Real Education)
WebCT (a product of Universal Learning Technology)

McGraw-Hill has partnerships with WebCT and Blackboard to make it even easier to take your course online. Now you can have McGraw-Hill content delivered through the leading Internet-based learning tool for higher education.

At McGraw-Hill, we have the following service agreements with WebCT and Blackboard:

SimNet Concepts: This is the TOTAL solution for training and assessment in computer concepts. SimNet Concepts offers a unique graphic-intensive environment for assessing student understanding of computer concepts. It includes interactive labs for 77 different computer concepts and 160 corresponding assessment questions. The content menus parallel the contents of the McGraw-Hill text being used for the class, so students can cover topics for each chapter of the text you are using.

SimNet Concepts also offers the only truly integrated learning and assessment program available today. After a student has completed any SimNet Concepts Exam, he or she can simply click on one button to have SimNet assemble a custom menu that covers just those concepts that the student answered incorrectly or did not attempt. These custom lessons can be saved to disk and loaded at any time for review. *Assessment Remediation*, a new feature, records and reports what the student did incorrectly for each question on an exam that was answered incorrectly.

Microsoft Applications Manuals

The following list presents McGraw-Hill Microsoft Applications books that are available for use with *Using Information Technology*. For more information about these books, visit the McGraw-Hill Computer and Information Technology Supersite at *www.mhhe.com/it* or call your McGraw-Hill campus representative.

Windows Applications

Advantage Series by Coulthard, Hutchinson, Miller, and Graves	
Microsoft Office 2003	Microsoft Office Word 2003 (Brief, Intro, Complete)
	Microsoft Office Excel 2003 (Brief, Intro, Complete)
	Microsoft Office Access 2003 (Brief, Intro, Complete)
	Microsoft Office PowerPoint 2003 (Brief, Intro)
	Microsoft Office System 2003
Microsoft Office XP	Microsoft Word 2002 (Brief, Intro, Complete)
	Microsoft Excel 2002 (Brief, Intro, Complete)
	Microsoft Access 2002 (Brief, Intro, Complete)
	Microsoft PowerPoint 2002 (Brief, Intro)
	Microsoft Office XP
	Integrating and Extending Microsoft Office XP
Microsoft Windows	Microsoft Windows XP
	Microsoft Windows 2000
	Microsoft Windows 98

Professional Approach by Juarez, Carter, Stewart, Hinkle, et al.	
Microsoft Office 2003	Microsoft Office Word 2003 (Specialist, Comprehensive)
	Microsoft Office Excel 2003 (Specialist, Comprehensive)
	Microsoft Office Access 2003 (Comprehensive)
	Microsoft Office PowerPoint 2003 (Comprehensive)
	Microsoft Office System 2003 (Specialist)
Microsoft Office XP	Microsoft Word 2002 (Core, Expert)
	Microsoft Excel 2002 (Core, Expert)
	Microsoft Access 2002 (Core, Expert)
	Microsoft PowerPoint 2002 (Comprehensive)
	Microsoft Outlook 2002 (Core)
Microsoft Windows	Microsoft Windows XP

Acknowledgments

Two names are on the front of this book, but a great many others are important contributors to its development. First, we wish to thank our editor-in-chief, Bob Woodbury, and our sponsoring editor, Marc Chernoff, for their support and encouragement during this fast-moving revision process. Thanks also go to our marketing champions, Andrew Bernier and Paul Murphy, for their enthusiasm and ideas. Lisa Chin-Johnson deserves our special thanks for her excellent handling of the supplements program. Everyone in production provided support and direction: Christine Vaughan, Adam Rooke, Sesha Bolisetty, Judy Kausal, Jess Kosic, and Rose Range. We also thank our media technology producer, Greg Bates, for helping us develop an outstanding Instructor's Resource Kit.

Outside of McGraw-Hill we were fortunate—indeed, blessed—to once again have the most professional of all development services, those of Burrston House, specifically the help of Glen and Meg Turner. Jonathan Lippe provided creative ideas for the Chapter Review exercises, especially internet activities. Photo researcher Judy Mason, copyeditor Sue Gottfried, proofreader Martha Ghent, and indexer James Minkin all gave us valuable assistance. Thanks also to all the extremely knowledgeable and hard-working professionals at GTS Graphics, who provided so many of the prepress services.

Finally, we are grateful to the following reviewers for helping to make this the most market-driven book possible.

Ken Baldauf
Florida State University

Maureen Ellis
Indiana University—Bloomington

Khondkar Islam
George Mason University, Virginia

Edmund Mannion
California State University, Chico

Tim Pinkelman
Bowling Green State University, Ohio

Ruth Schwartz
Indiana University—South Bend

Laurie Shteir
Temple University, Pennsylvania

Mary Kay Tarver
East Central University, Oklahoma

Arthur Valentine
Sussex County Community College, New Jersey

Sandy Week
University of Nevada—Reno

Lynn Wermers
North Shore Community College, Massachusetts

Ruthann Williams
Central Missouri State University

Contents

Chapter 1

INTRODUCTION TO INFORMATION TECHNOLOGY: YOUR DIGITAL WORLD 1

1.1 Infotech Is Commonplace: Cellphones, Email, the Internet, & the E-World 3

The Telephone Grows Up 3
"You've Got Mail!" Email's Mass Impact 4
Bookmark It! Practical Action Box:
"Managing Your Email" 5
The Internet, the World Wide Web, & the "Plumbing of Cyberspace" 5
The E-World & Welcome to It 6

1.2 The "All-Purpose Machine": The Varieties of Computers 7

All Computers, Great & Small: The Categories of Machines 7
Servers 11

1.3 Understanding Your Computer: How You Can Customize Your Own PC 11

How Computers Work: Three Key Concepts 12
Pretending to Order a Custom-Built Desktop Computer 14
Input Hardware: Keyboard & Mouse 14
Processing & Memory Hardware: Inside the System Cabinet 15
Storage Hardware: Floppy Drive, Hard Drive, & CD/DVD Drive 17
Output Hardware: Video & Sound Cards, Monitor, Speakers, & Printer 18
Communications Hardware: Modem 19
Software 20
Is Getting a Custom-Built PC Worth the Effort? 21

1.4 Where Is Information Technology Headed? 21

Three Directions of Computer Development: Miniaturization, Speed, & Affordability 22
Three Directions of Communications Development: Connectivity, Interactivity, & Multimedia 23

When Computers & Communications Combine: Convergence, Portability, & Personalization 24
"E" Also Stands for Ethics 25
Onward: Handling Information in the Era of Pervasive Computing 26

Chapter 2

THE INTERNET & THE WORLD WIDE WEB: EXPLORING CYBERSPACE 37

2.1 Choosing Your Internet Access Device & Physical Connection: The Quest for Broadband 38

Telephone (Dial-Up) Modem: Low Speed but Inexpensive & Widely Available 40
High-Speed Phone Lines: More Expensive but Available in Most Cities 41
Cable Modem: Close Competitor to DSL 43
Wireless Systems: Satellite & Other Through-the-Air Connections 43

2.2 Choosing Your Internet Service Provider (ISP) 44

2.3 Sending & Receiving Email 46

Email Software & Carriers 46
Email Addresses 47
Attachments 50
Instant Messaging 50
Mailing Lists: Email-Based Discussion Groups 52
Netiquette: Appropriate Online Behavior 52
Sorting Your Email 53
Spam: Unwanted Junk Email 54
What about Keeping Email Private? 55

2.4 The World Wide Web 55

The Web & How It Works 56
Using Your Browser to Get around the Web 60
Web Portals: Starting Points for Finding Information 64
Four Types of Search Engines: Human-Organized, Computer-Created, Hybrid, & Metasearch 65

Tips for Smart Searching 66
Multimedia on the Web 67
Push Technology & Webcasting 69
The Internet Telephone & Videophone 69
Designing Web Pages 70

Bookmark It! Practical Action Box:
"Web Research, Term Papers, & Plagiarism" 76

Chapter 3

SOFTWARE: FOR PRODUCTIVITY & CREATIVITY 86

3.1 System Software 86

The Operating System: What It Does 87
Utilities: Service Programs 89
The Operating System's User Interface: Your Computer's Dashboard 89
Common Desktop & Notebook Operating Systems: DOS, Macintosh, & Windows 96
Network Operating Systems: NetWare, Windows NT/2000/2003/XP, Microsoft, .NET, Unix, & Linux 98
Operating Systems for Handhelds: Palm OS & Windows CE/Pocket PC/Windows CE .NET 101

3.2 Application Software: Getting Started 102

Application Software: For Sale, for Free or for Rent? 102
Tutorials & Documentation 104
A Few Facts About Files—& the Usefulness of Importing & Exporting 104
The Types of Software 105

3.3 Word Processing 107

Features of the Keyboard 107
Creating Documents 108
Bookmark It! Practical Action Box:
"Installing & Reinstalling Software" 110
Editing Documents 110
Formatting Documents with the Help of Templates & Wizards 111
Printing, Faxing, or Emailing Documents 112
Saving Documents 112
Tracking Changes & Inserting Comments 112
Web Document Creation 113

3.4 Spreadsheets 113

The Basics: How Spreadsheets Work 113
Analytical Graphics: Creating Charts 115

3.5 Database Software 116

The Benefits of Database Software 116
The Basics: How Databases Work 117
Personal Information Managers 119

3.6 Specialty Software 120

Presentation Graphics Software 120
Financial Software 122
Desktop Publishing 123
Drawing & Painting Programs 124
Video/Auditing Editing Software 124
Project Management Software 125
Bookmark It! Practical Action Box:
"How to Buy Software" 126
Computer-Aided Design 126
Web Page Design/Authoring Software 127

Chapter 4

HARDWARE—THE CPU & STORAGE: HOW TO BUY A MULTIMEDIA COMPUTER SYSTEM 179

4.1 Microchips, Miniaturization, & Mobility 140

From Vacuum Tubes to Transistors to Microchips 140
Miniaturization Miracles: Microchips, Microprocessors, & Micromachines 141
Mobility 141
Buying an Inexpensive Personal Computer: Understanding Computer Ads 143

4.2 The System Unit 143

The Binary System: Using On/Off Electrical States to Represent Data & Instructions 143
Machine Language 145
The Computer Case: Bays, Buttons, & Boards 145
Power Supply 146
The Motherboard & the Microprocessor Chip 146
Processing Speeds: From Megahertz to Picoseconds 149
How the Processor or CPU Works: Control Unit, ALU, & Registers 150
How Memory Works: RAM, ROM, CMOS, & Flash 152
How Cache Works: Level 1 (Internal) & Level 2 (External) 153
Ports & Cables 154
Expandability: Buses & Cards 156

4.3 Secondary Storage 159

Floppy Disks 160
Hard Disks 162
Optical Disks: CDs & DVDs 164
Magnetic Tape 166
Smart Cards 166
Flash Memory Cards 168
Online Secondary Storage 168
Bookmark It! Practical Action Box:
"How to Buy a Notebook" 169

Chapter 5
HARDWARE—INPUT & OUTPUT: TAKING CHARGE OF COMPUTING & COMMUNICATIONS 181

5.1 Input & Output 183

5.2 Input Hardware 184

Keyboards 184
Pointing Devices 185
Scanning & Reading Devices 188
Audio-Input Devices 192
Webcams & Video-Input Cards 192
Digital Cameras 193
Speech-Recognition Systems 193
Sensors 194
Radio-Frequency Identification Tags 194
Human-Biology-Input Devices 195

5.3 Output Hardware 195

Traditional Softcopy Output: Display Screens 196
Traditional Hardcopy Output: Printers 199
Mixed Output: Sound, Voice, & Video 201
Bookmark It! Practical Action Box:
"Good Habits: Protecting Your Computer System, Your Data, & Your Health 203

Chapter 6
NETWORKS & COMMUNICATIONS: THE "NEW STORY" IN COMPUTING 216

6.1 From the Analog to the Digital Age 216

The Digital Basis of Computers: Electrical Signals as Discontinuous Bursts 217
The Analog Basis of Life: Electrical Signals as Continuous Waves 217
Purpose of the Modem: Converting Digital Signals to Analog Signals & Back 218
Converting Reality to Digital Form 219

6.2 The Practical Uses of Communications 222

Videoconferencing & Videophones: Video/Voice Communication 222
Workgroup Computing & Groupware 222
Telecommuting & Virtual Offices 222
Home Networks 223
Smart Television: DTV, HDTV, & SDTV 223

6.3 Communications Media & Transfer Rates 224

Wired Communications Media: Transmitting Data by Wires & Cables 225
The Radio-Frequency (RF) Spectrum & Bandwidth 226
Wireless Communications Media: Transmitting Data Through the Air 226
Types of Long-Distance Wireless Communications 228
Short-Range Wireless Communications: Bluetooth & WiFi 233
Compression & Decompression: Putting More Data in Less Space 233

6.4 Networks 235

The Benefits of Networks 235
Types of Networks: WANs, MANs, & LANs 236
Types of LANs: Client/Server & Peer to Peer 237
Components of a LAN 238
Intranets, Extranets, & Firewalls: Private Internet Networks 240
Bookmark It! Practical Action Box:
"How to Create Your Own Simple Website, Easily & for Free" 241

6.5 Cyberethics: Controversial Material & Censorship 242

Chapter 7
FILES, DATABASES, & E-COMMERCE: DIGITAL ENGINES FOR THE NEW ECONOMY 251

7.1 Managing Files: Basic Concepts 252

How Data Is Organized: The Data Storage Hierarchy 252
The Key Field 253
Types of Files: Program Files, Data Files, & Others 254

Two Types of Data Files: Master File &
Transaction File 255
Data Access Methods: Sequential versus Direct
Access 255
Offline versus Online Storage 256

7.2 Database Management Systems 256

Two Main Types of Database Access 257

7.3 Database Models 258

Hierarchical Database 258
Network Database 258
Relational Database 260
Object-Oriented Database 261

**7.4 Databases & the New Economy:
E-Commerce, Data Mining, & B2B
Systems 261**

E-Commerce 261
Data Mining 262
Business-to-Business (B2B) Systems 263

**7.5 The Ethics of Using Storage &
Databases: Concerns about Accuracy &
Privacy 264**

Manipulation of Sound 265
Manipulation of Photos 265
Manipulation of Video & Television 266
Accuracy & Completeness 266
Matters of Privacy 267
Bookmark It! Practical Action Box:
*"Preventing Your Identity from Getting
Stolen"* 269

Chapter 8

SOCIETY AND THE DIGITAL AGE:
CHALLENGES & PROMISES 278

**8.1 The Digital Environment: Is There a
Grand Design? 278**

Internet2: The New Internet 279
The 1996 Telecommunications Act 279
ICANN: The Internet Corporation for Assigned
Names & Numbers 279

**8.2 Security Issues: Threats to
Computers & Communications
Systems 280**

Errors & Accidents 280
Natural & Other Hazards 281
Crimes Against Computers &
Communications 282

Crimes Using Computers &
Communications 283
Worms & Viruses 283
Computer Criminals 284

**8.3 Security: Safeguarding Computers &
Communications 286**

Identification & Access 286
Encryption 287
Protection of Software & Data 287
Disaster-Recovery Plans 288

**8.4 Quality-of-Life Issues: The
Environment, Mental Health, & the
Workplace 289**

Environmental Problems 289
Mental-Health Problems 290
Workplace Problems: Impediments to
Productivity 290

**8.5 Economic Issues: Employment & the
Haves/Have-Nots 291**

Bookmark It! Practical Action Box:
*"When the Internet Isn't Productive: Online
Addiction & Other Time Wasters"* 292
Technology, the Job Killer? 293
Gap between Rich & Poor 293

8.6 Artificial Intelligence 294

Robotics 294
Expert Systems 295
Natural Language Processing 296
Artificial Life, the Turing Test, & AI Ethics 296

**8.7 The Promised Benefits of the Digital
Age 297**

Information & Education 297
Health 298
Commerce & Money 298
Entertainment 299
Government & Electronic Democracy 300

Appendix

SYSTEMS & PROGRAMMING:
DEVELOPMENT, PROGRAMMING, &
LANGUAGES A1

**A1. Systems Development: The Six
Phases of Systems Analysis &
Design A2**

The Purpose of a System A2
Getting the Project Going: How It Starts, Who's
Involved A3

The Six Phases of Systems Analysis & Design A3

The First Phase: Conduct a Preliminary Investigation A4

The Second Phase: Do an Analysis of the System A4

The Third Phase: Design the System A5

The Fourth Phase: Develop the System A6

The Fifth Phase: Implement the System A6

The Sixth Phase: Maintain the System A7

A.2 Programming: A Five-Step Procedure A7

The First Step: Clarify the Programming Needs A9

The Second Step: Design the Program A9

The Third Step: Code the Program A12

The Fourth Step: Test the Program A15

The Fifth Step: Document & Maintain the Program A15

A.3 Five Generations of Programming Languages A16

First Generation: Machine Language A17

Second Generation: Assembly Language A17

Third Generation: High-Level or Procedural Languages A18

Fourth Generation: Very High Level or Problem-Oriented Languages A20

Fifth Generation: Natural Languages A20

A.4 Programming Languages Used Today A20

FORTRAN: The Language of Mathematics & the First High-Level Language A20

COBOL: The Language of Business A22

BASIC: The Easy Language A22

Pascal: The Simple Language A22

C: For Portability & Scientific Use A22

LISP: For Artificial Intelligence Programs A23

A.5 Object-Oriented & Visual Programming Languages A23

Object-Oriented Programming: Block by Block A23

Visual Programming: The Example of Visual BASIC A24

A.6 Markup & Scripting Languages A25

HTML: For Creating 2-D Web Documents & Links A25

VRML: For Creating 3-D Web Pages A26

XML: For Making the Web Work Better A26

JavaScript: For Dynamic Web Pages A27

ActiveX: For Creating Interactive Web Pages A27

Perl: For CGI Scripts A27

Notes N1

Index I1

Credits C1

Using Information Technology

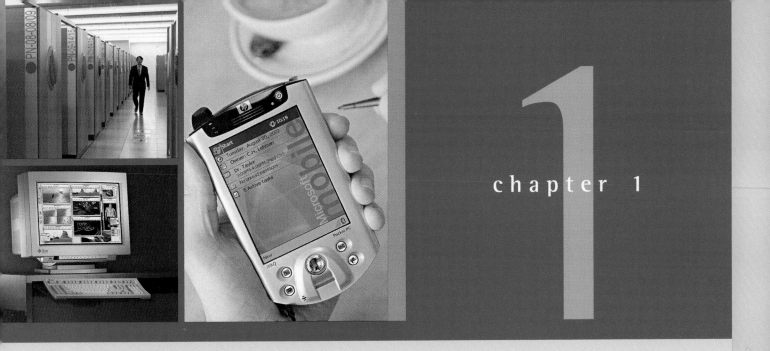

Introduction to Information Technology

Your Digital World

Chapter Topics & Key Questions

1.1 **Infotech Is Commonplace: Cellphones, Email, the Internet, & the E-World** How does information technology facilitate email, networks, and the use of the internet and the web; what is the meaning of the term *cyberspace*?

1.2 **The "All-Purpose Machine": The Varieties of Computers** What are the five sizes of computers, and what are clients and servers?

1.3 **Understanding Your Computer: How Can You Customize Your Own PC?** What four basic operations do all computers follow, and what are some of the devices associated with each operation? How does communications affect these operations?

1.4 **Where Is Information Technology Headed?** What are three directions of computer development and three directions of communications development?

Computers and communications. These are the two powerful wellsprings of the Information Age. From them arises a torrent of technological change.

Consider the following recent innovations:

- Desktop computers—"teleputers"—on which you can watch television as well as check email, write documents, and do calculations.
- Cellphones with digital cameras that allow you to check the news, download videoclips, and participate in multiplayer online games.
- Smart, computerized houses that enable the owners to change window tints, turn on music, control thermostats, monitor security, and from their cars miles away open the front door over the internet and watch via webcam to see who enters.
- Internet refrigerators that make ice, keep track of provisions, and allow you to maintain an address book and calendar, watch television, play music, do email, and surf the web.

Some of these devices might seem merely silly. Who really needs a high-tech icebox, for example? However, in some electricity-starved countries, such as Italy, networked appliances can monitor and adjust to power demands.

More importantly, these devices serve to show that we live in the era of *pervasive computing.* The world has moved on beyond boxy computers that sit on desks or even on laps. Today handheld computers and beefed-up cellphones (not to mention terminals everywhere—libraries, airports, cafés) let us access information anytime anywhere. And not just general information but personal information—electronic correspondence, documents, appointments, photos, songs, money matters, and other data important to us.

Central to this concept is the internet—the "net," that sprawling collection of data residing on computers around the world and accessible by high-speed connections. Everything that presently exists on a personal computer, experts suggest, will move onto the internet, giving us greater mobility and wrapping the internet around our lives.[1] So central is the internet to our lives, in fact, that many writers are now spelling it without the capital "I"— *Internet* becomes *internet,* just as *Telephone* became *telephone*—because both systems belong not to just one owner but to the world. We will follow this new convention in this book.

With so much information available everywhere all the time, what will this do to us as human beings? We can already see the outlines of the future. One result is *information overload:* International Data Corporation (IDC) has forecast that by 2005 more than 36 billion person-to-person emails will be sent daily. Already, the average business user reportedly spends more than 2 hours a day just dealing with email.[2] Another is *less use of our brains for memorizing:* Familiar phone numbers and other facts are being stored on speed-dial cellphones, pocket computers, and electronic databases, increasing our dependence on technology.[3] A third result is a *surge in "multitasking" activity:* People have become highly skilled in performing several tasks at once, such as doing homework while talking on the phone, watching TV, answering email, and surfing the World Wide Web. A fourth, according to technology observer Howard Rheingold, is that *smart mobile devices could produce "smart mobs"*—groups of people who can do things together (in business, politics, and journalism, for example) even if they don't know each other.[4] These four trends pose unique challenges to how you learn and manage information. An important

"Just keeping busy." Multiple electronic devices allow people to simultaneously do multiple tasks—multitasking.

purpose of this book is to give you the tools for doing so, as we explain at the end of this chapter.

First, however, we need to give you an immediate though brief overview of what computing is and how it works. We begin by discussing the internet and some of its features, particularly email. We next describe the varieties of computers that exist. We then explain the three key concepts behind how a computer works and what goes into a personal computer, both hardware and software. Finally, we address how to survive in the new ocean of 24/7/365 information.

1.1 Infotech Is Commonplace: Cellphones, Email, the Internet, & the E-World

KEY QUESTIONS

How does information technology facilitate email, networks, and the use of the internet and the web; what is the meaning of the term cyberspace?

This book is about computers, of course. But not just about computers. It is also about the way computers communicate with one another. When computer and communications technologies are combined, the result is *information technology,* or "infotech." <u>*Information technology (IT)*</u> **is a general term that describes any technology that helps to produce, manipulate, store, communicate, and/or disseminate information.** IT merges computing with high-speed communications links carrying data, sound, and video. Examples of information technology include personal computers but also new forms of telephones, televisions, appliances, and various handheld devices.

Note that there are two important parts to information technology—computers and communications:

- **Computer technology:** You have certainly seen, and probably used, a computer. Nevertheless, let's define what it is. **A <u>*computer*</u> is a programmable, multiuse machine that accepts data—raw facts and figures—and processes, or manipulates, it into information we can use,** such as summaries, totals, or reports. Its purpose is to speed up problem solving and increase productivity.

- **Communications technology:** Unquestionably you've been using communications technology for years. <u>*Communications technology*</u>, **also called *telecommunications technology*, consists of electromagnetic devices and systems for communicating over long distances.** The principal examples are telephone, radio, broadcast television, and cable TV. More recently there has been the addition of communication among computers—which is what happens when people "go online" on the internet. In this context, <u>*online*</u> **means using a computer or some other information device, connected through a network, to access information and services from another computer or information device.**

As an example of a communication device, let's consider something that seems to be everywhere these days—the cellphone.

The Telephone Grows Up

Cellphone mania has swept the world. All across the globe, people have acquired the portable gift of gab; a Japanese industry body estimated that 1.25 billion people worldwide will be using cellphones in 2005.[5] Some cellphone users make 45 calls or more a day. It has taken more than 100 years for the telephone to get to this point—getting smaller, acquiring push buttons, losing its cord connection. In 1964, the * and # were added to the keypad. In 1973, the first cellphone call was processed. In its standard form, the phone is still so simply designed that even a young child can use it. However, it is now becoming more versatile and complex—a way of connecting to the internet and the World Wide Web.

TOP FIVE USES

Percentage of households with PCs that use their computer for each task

Email
████████ 90%

Internet
████████ 87%

Typing letters/
correspondence
███████ 80%

Research
███████ 79%

Games
██████ 76%

Source: The New York Times, September 30, 2002, p. C1.

Why introduce a book that is about computers with a discussion of telephones? Because internet phones, especially "smartphones"—such as the Toshiba 2032, Treo 300, Sanyo SCP-8100, and Kyocera 7135—represent another giant step for information technology. *(See ● Panel 1.1.)* Now you no longer need a personal computer to get on the internet. These infotech phones, with their small display screens, provide a direct, wireless connection that enables you not only to make voice calls and check your daily "to-do" list but also to browse the World Wide Web and receive all kinds of information: news, sports scores, stock prices, term-paper research. And you can also send and receive email. In addition, phones coming on the market now can plug into computer-chip-based sensing devices—from health monitors to automotive diagnostic devices—and translate the data for transmission. For example, if you're having car trouble, you could plug your smart cellphone into a special port under your car's dashboard. The phone's special program would convert engine data and send it to an internet site that could be viewed by mechanics using an auto shop's computer. The mechanics could diagnose your problem, and then you could decide how to deal with it.

"You've Got Mail!" Email's Mass Impact

It took the telephone 40 years to reach 10 million customers, and fax machines 20 years. Personal computers made it into that many American homes 5 years after they were introduced. Email, which appeared in 1981, became popular far more quickly, reaching 10 million users in little more than a year.[6] No technology has ever become so universal so fast. Not surprisingly, then, one of the first things new computer users learn is how to send and receive **_email_—"electronic mail," messages transmitted over a computer network, most often the internet. A _network_ is a communications system connecting two or more computers; the internet is the largest such network.**

Until 1998, hand-delivered mail was still the main means of correspondence. But in that year, the volume of email in the United States surpassed the volume of hand-delivered mail. In 2002, an estimated average of 8 billion messages a day were zipping back and forth across the United States, up from 3.5 billion 3 years earlier.[7] By 2006, the total number of email

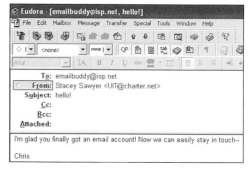

messages sent daily will probably exceed 60 billion worldwide, compared with 31 billion worldwide in 2002.[8] Already, in fact, email is the leading use of PCs. Because of this explosion in usage, suggests a *Business Week* report, "email ranks with such pivotal advances as the printing press, the telephone, and television in mass impact."[9]

How is using electronic mail different from calling on a telephone or writing a conventional letter? Email "occupies a psychological space all its own," says one journalist. "It's almost as immediate as a phone call, but if you need to, you can think about what you're going to say for days and reply when it's convenient."[10] Email has blossomed, points out another writer, not because it gives us more immediacy but because it gives us *less.* "The new appeal of email is the old appeal of print," he says. "It isn't instant; it isn't immediate; it isn't in your face." Email has succeeded for the same reason that the videophone—which allows callers to see each other while talking—has been so slow to catch on: because "what we actually want from our exchanges is the minimum human contact commensurate with the need to connect with other people."[11]

PRACTICAL ACTION BOX
Managing Your Email

For many people, email is the online environment, more so than the World Wide Web. In one study, respondents reported they received an average of 31 email messages a day.[a] But then there are those such as Jeremy Gross, managing director of technology for Countrywide Home Loans, who gets 300 emails a day—and about 200 are junk email (spam), bad jokes, or irrelevant memos (the "cc," previously "carbon copy," now "courtesy copy").[b] Astronomer Seth Shostak gets 50 electronic messages daily, at least half requiring a reply. "If I spend five minutes considering and composing a response to each correspondence," he complains, "then two hours of my day are busied with email, even when I don't initiate a single one."[c]

It's clear, then, that email will increase productivity only if it is used properly. Overuse or misuse just causes more problems and wastes time. The following are some ideas to keep in mind when using email:[d]

- *Do your part to curb the email deluge:* Put short messages in the subject line so recipients don't have to open the email to read the note. Don't reply to every email message you get. Avoid "cc:ing" (copying to) people unless absolutely necessary. Don't send chain letters or lists of jokes, which just clog mail systems.

- *Be helpful in sending attachments:* Attachments—computer files of long documents or images—attached to an email are supposed to be a convenience, but often they can be an annoyance. Sending a 1-megabyte file to a 500-person mailing list creates 500 copies of that file—and that many megabytes can clog or even cripple the mail system. (A 1-megabyte file is about the size of a 300-page double-spaced term paper.) Ask your

recipients beforehand if they want the attachment, and tell them how to open it; they may need to know what word processing program to use, for example.

- *Be careful about opening attachments you don't recognize:* Some dangerous computer viruses—renegade programs that can damage your computer—have been spread by email attachments, which are activated only upon opening.

- *Use discretion about the emails you send:* Email should not be treated as informally as a phone call. Don't send a message electronically that you don't want some third party to read. Email messages are not written with disappearing ink; they remain in a computer system long after they have been sent. Worse, recipients can easily copy and even alter your messages and forward them to others without your knowledge.

- *Don't use email in place of personal contact:* Because email carries no tone or inflection, it's hard to convey personal concern. Avoid criticism and sarcasm in electronic messaging. Nevertheless, you can use email to provide quick praise, even though doing it in person will take on greater significance.

- *Be aware that email you receive at work is the property of your employer:* Be careful of what you save, send, and back up.

- *Realize that deleting email messages doesn't totally get rid of them:* "Delete" moves the email from the visible list, but the messages remain on your hard disk and can be retrieved by experts. Special software, such as Spytech Eradicator and Window Washer, will completely erase email from the hard disk.

From this it is easy to conclude, as *New York Times* computer writer Peter Lewis did, that email "is so clearly superior to paper mail for so many purposes that most people who try it cannot imagine going back to working without it."[12] What is interesting, though, is that in these times when images often seem to overwhelm words, email is actually reactionary. "The internet is the first new medium to move decisively backward," points out one writer, because it essentially involves writing. "Ten years ago, even the most literate of us wrote maybe a half a dozen letters a year; the rest of our lives took place on the telephone."[13] Email has changed all that.

The Internet, the World Wide Web, & the "Plumbing of Cyberspace"

Communications is extending into every nook and cranny of civilization. It has been called the "plumbing of cyberspace." The term *cyberspace* was coined by William Gibson in his novel *Neuromancer* to describe a futuristic computer network into which users plug their brains. (*Cyber* comes from "cybernetics," a term coined in 1948 to apply to the comparative study of automatic control systems, such as the brain/nervous system and mechanical-electrical communication systems.) In everyday use, this term has a rather different meaning.

Today many people equate cyberspace with the internet. But it is much more than that. Cyberspace includes not only the World Wide Web, chat rooms, online bulletin boards, and member-based services such as America Online—all features we explain in this book—"but also such things as conference calls and automatic teller machines," says David Whittler.[14] We may say, then, that **_cyberspace_ encompasses not only the online world and the internet in particular but also the whole wired and wireless world of communications in general**—the nonphysical terrain created by computer and communications systems. Cyberspace is where you go when you go online with your computer.

The two most important aspects of cyberspace are the internet and that part of the internet known as the World Wide Web:

- **The internet—"the mother of all networks":** The internet is at the heart of the Information Age. Called "the mother of all networks," the **_internet_ (the "net") is a worldwide computer network that connects hundreds of thousands of smaller networks. These networks link educational, commercial, nonprofit, and military entities, as well as individuals.**

- **The World Wide Web—the multimedia part of the internet:** The internet has been around for more than 30 years. But what made it popular, apart from email, was the development in the early 1990s of the **_World Wide Web_, usually called simply the "web"—an interconnected system of internet computers (called _servers_) that support specially formatted documents in multimedia form.** The word _multimedia_, from "multiple media," refers to technology that presents information in more than one medium, such as text, still images, moving images, and sound. In other words, the web provides information in more than one way.

There is no doubt that the influence of the net and the web is tremendous. At present, 61% of all Americans go online at least once a month.[15] But just how revolutionary is the internet? Is it equivalent to the invention of television, as some technologists say? Or is it even more important—equivalent to the invention of the printing press? "Television turned out to be a powerful force that changed a lot about society," says _USA Today_ technology reporter Kevin Maney. "But the printing press changed everything—religion, government, science, global distribution of wealth, and much more. If the internet equals the printing press, no amount of hype could possibly overdo it."[16]

Perhaps in a few years we'll begin to know the answer. No massive study was ever done of the influence of the last great electronic revolution to touch us, namely, television. But the Center for Communication Policy at the University of California, Los Angeles, in conjunction with other international universities, has begun to take a look at the effects of information technology—and at how people's behavior and attitudes toward it will change over a span of years.

The E-World & Welcome to It

One thing we know already is that cyberspace is saturating our lives. More than 165.2 million Americans are internet users, according to a recent survey.[17] While the average age of users is rising, there's no doubt that young people love the net. For instance, an amazingly high percentage of American teenagers use the internet, according to Teenage Research Unlimited (TRU), a Chicago market research firm. Why is that? Email is certainly one important reason—it's all about staying connected.

But it has to do with more than just email. Teenagers are also big participants in online commerce. TRU's studies show that when teens want information on a brand, they turn to the internet first. Indeed, teens are voracious consumers of all things electronic.

And not just for teens but for most Americans, the use of the internet's favorite letter, "e"—as in e-business, e-commerce, e-shopping—is rapidly becoming outmoded. "E" is now part of nearly everything we do. As an executive for a marketing research firm says, "E-business is just business."[18] The electronic world is everywhere. The net and the web are everywhere. Cyberspace permeates everything.

QuickCheck

What are the two parts of information technology?

What is email?

What is cyberspace?

How does the World Wide Web differ from the internet?

1.2 The "All-Purpose Machine": The Varieties of Computers

KEY QUESTIONS
What are the five sizes of computers, and what are clients and servers?

When the ★alarm clock blasts you awake, you leap out of bed and head for the kitchen, where you plug in the ★coffee maker. After using your ★electric toothbrush and showering and dressing, you stick a bagel in the ★microwave, then pick up the ★TV remote and click on the ★TV to catch the weather forecast. Later, after putting dishes in the ★dishwasher, you go out and start up the ★car and head toward campus or work. Pausing en route at a ★traffic light, you turn on your portable ★CD player to listen to some music.

You haven't yet touched a PC, a personal computer, but you've already dealt with at least 10 computers—as you probably guessed from the ★s. All these familiar appliances rely on tiny "computers on chips" called *microprocessors.* Maybe, then, the name "computer" is inadequate. As computer pioneer John Von Neumann has said, the device should not be called the computer but rather the "all-purpose machine." It is not, after all, just a machine for doing calculations. The most striking thing about it is that it can be put to *any number of uses.*

What are the various types of computers? Let's take a look.

All Computers, Great & Small: The Categories of Machines

At one time, the idea of having your own computer was almost like having your own personal nuclear reactor. In those days, in the 1950s and '60s, computers were enormous machines affordable only by large institutions. Now they come in a variety of shapes and sizes, which can be classified according to their processing power:

- **Supercomputers:** Typically priced from $500,000 to more than $350 million, **supercomputers** are high-capacity machines with thousands of processors that can perform more than several trillion calculations per second. These are the most expensive but fastest computers

Supercomputer. The NEC Earth Simulator, the world's fastest computer.

available. "Supers," as they are called, have been used for tasks requiring the processing of enormous volumes of data, such as doing the U.S. census count, forecasting weather, designing aircraft, modeling molecules, breaking encryption codes, and simulating explosion of nuclear bombs. More recently they have been employed for business purposes—for instance, sifting demographic marketing information— and for creating film animation. The fastest computer in the world, which cost $350 million and looks like rows of refrigerator-size boxes, is the NEC Earth Simulator in Yokohama, Japan. This supercomputer has 5,120 main processors, each of which consists of 8 subprocessors. It occupies a space the size of four tennis courts and uses 2,800 kilometers of cable. NEC's supercomputer will create a "virtual planet earth" by processing mountains of data sent from satellites, ocean buoys, and other worldwide observation points. The system will analyze and predict environmental activities and changes, including global warming, El Niño effects, marine pollution, rainfall patterns, tectonic plate movement, typhoons, and earthquakes.

Supercomputers are still the most powerful computers. But a new generation is coming: "Imagine a trillion laptops in every drop of water," as one writer puts it.[19] The next generation of computers will be made of DNA and will fit into a single human cell. The biological *nanocomputer* will use DNA as its software and enzymes as its hardware; it will have molecular-sized circuits that will be viewable only through a microscope. (*Nano* means "one-billionth.") This promise of ever smaller, faster, and more powerful computers is an important concept in the realm of pervasive computing, and many companies are working on nanocomputers as you read this, hoping to begin production within 10 years. Some believe that they can create computers the size of a pencil eraser that work 10 times faster than today's fastest supercomputer.[20] Undoubtedly nanotech will first be used by the government, the military, universities, and some private corporate laboratories—but nanotech may eventually show up in every device and appliance in your life!

Who Makes the Most Superfast Computers?			
	Specifications of Fastest Machine		
Company	Name	Speed (gigaflops)	Location
Hewlett-Packard	ASCI Q	7,727	Los Alamos National Laboratory, NM
IBM	ASCI White	7,226	Lawrence Livermore National Laboratory, CA
Sun Microsystems	HPC 4500	420	Swedish Armed Forces, Stockholm, Sweden
Silicon Graphics	ASCI Blue Mountain	1,608	Los Alamos National Laboratory, NM
Cray	T3E 1200	1,166	Unknown (U.S. government)
NEC	Earth Simulator	35,860	Earth Simulator Center, Yokohama, Japan

Source: Claire Tristram, "Supercomputing Resurrected," February, 2003, p. 54; www.technologyreview.com.

Mainframe. In 2003 IBM launched a new mainframe line code-named T-Rex and formally called the z900 models.

Workstation. Sun Ultra450.

- **Mainframe computers:** The only type of computer available until the late 1960s, _**mainframes**_ **are water- or air-cooled computers that cost $5,000 to $5 million and vary in size from small, to medium, to large, depending on their use.** Small mainframes ($5,000 to $200,000) are often called _midsize computers;_ they used to be called _minicomputers,_ although today the term is seldom used. Mainframes are used by large organizations—such as banks, airlines, insurance companies, and colleges—for processing millions of transactions. Often users access a mainframe by means of a _**terminal,**_ **which has a display screen and a keyboard and can input and output data but cannot by itself process data.** Mainframes process billions of instructions per second.

- **Workstations:** Introduced in the early 1980s, _**workstations**_ **are expensive, powerful personal computers usually used for complex scientific, mathematical, and engineering calculations and for computer-aided design and computer-aided manufacturing.** Providing many capabilities comparable to midsize mainframes, workstations are used for such tasks as designing airplane fuselages, prescription drugs, and movie special effects. Workstations have caught the eye of the public mainly for their graphics capabilities, which are used to breathe three-dimensional life into movies such as _The Lord of the Rings_ and _Harry Potter._ The capabilities of low-end workstations overlap those of high-end desktop microcomputers.

- **Microcomputers:** _**Microcomputers,**_ **also called** _personal computers (PCs),_ **which cost $500 to $5,000, can fit next to a desk or on a desktop or can be carried around.** They are either stand-alone machines or are connected to a computer network, such as a local area network. **A** _**local area network (LAN)**_ **connects, usually by special cable, a group of desktop PCs and other devices, such as printers, in an office or a building.**

  Microcomputers are of several types: desktop PCs, tower PCs, notebooks (laptops), and personal digital assistants—handheld computers or palmtops.

  **Desktop PCs** **are microcomputers whose case or main housing sits on a desk, with keyboard in front and monitor (screen) often on top.** _**Tower PCs**_ **are microcomputers whose case sits as a "tower," often on the floor beside a desk, thus freeing up desk surface space.**

Two microcomputers. Compaq Evo desktop microcomputer.   HP Compaq Business d220 tower microcomputer.

Notebook

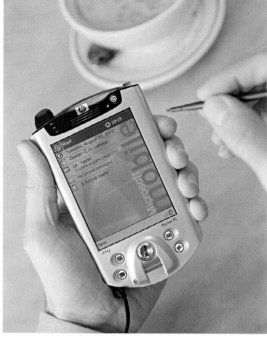

PDA

Notebook computers, also called *laptop computers*, are lightweight portable computers with built-in monitor, keyboard, hard-disk drive, battery, and AC adapter that can be plugged into an electrical outlet; they weigh anywhere from 1.8 to 9 pounds.

Personal digital assistants (PDAs), also called *handheld computers* or *palmtops*, combine personal organization tools—schedule planners, address books, to-do lists—with the ability in some cases to send email and faxes. Some PDAs have touch-sensitive screens. Some also connect to desktop computers for sending or receiving information. (For now, we are using the word *digital* to mean "computer based.")

- Microcontrollers: *Microcontrollers*, also called *embedded computers*, are the tiny, specialized microprocessors installed in "smart" appliances and automobiles. These microcontrollers enable microwave ovens, for example, to store data about how long to cook your potatoes and at what power setting. Recently microcontrollers have been used to develop a new universe of experimental electronic appliances—e-pliances—for example, as tiny web servers embedded in clothing, jewelry, and household appliances such as refrigerators. Microcontrollers are also used in blood pressure monitors, air bag sensors, gas and chemical sensors for water and air, and vibration sensors.

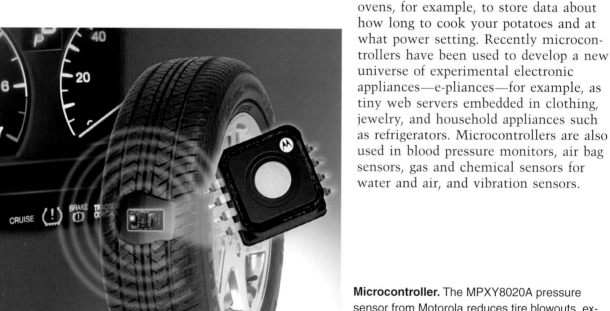

Microcontroller. The MPXY8020A pressure sensor from Motorola reduces tire blowouts, extends tire life, and improves gas mileage. This embedded computer notifies drivers, via a dashboard display, when tire pressure is not optimal.

Server farms. A group of networked servers that are housed in one location is called a *server farm* or a *server cluster.*

Servers

The word *server* describes not a size of computer but rather a particular way in which a computer is used. Nevertheless, because servers have become so important to telecommunications, especially with the rise of the internet and the web, they deserve mention here. (Servers are discussed in Chapter 6.)

A **_server_, or *network server*, is a central computer that holds collections of data (databases) and programs for connecting or supplying services to PCs, workstations, and other devices, which are called _clients_. These clients are linked by a wired or wireless network. The entire network is called a _client/server network._** In small organizations, servers can store files, provide printing stations, and transmit email. In large organizations, servers may also house enormous libraries of financial, sales, and product information.

You may never see a supercomputer or mainframe or server or even a tiny microcontroller. But you will most certainly get to know the personal computer, if you haven't already. We consider this machine next.

QuickCheck

Describe the five sizes of computers.

What are the different types of microcomputers?

Define *servers* and *clients.*

1.3 Understanding Your Computer: How Can You Customize Your Own PC?

KEY QUESTIONS

What four basic operations do all computers follow, and what are some of the devices associated with each operation? How does communications affect these operations?

Perhaps you know how to drive a car. But do you know what to do when it runs badly? Similarly, perhaps you've already been using a personal computer. But do you know what to do when it doesn't act right—when, for example, it suddenly shuts down ("crashes")?

Cars are now so complicated that professional mechanics are often required for even the smallest problems. With personal computers, however, there are still things you can often do yourself—and should learn to do, so that you can be effective, efficient, and employable. To do so, you first need to know how computers work.

How Computers Work: Three Key Concepts

Could you build your own personal computer? Some people do, putting together bare-bones systems for just a few hundred dollars. "If you have a logical mind, are fairly good with your hands, and possess the patience of Job, there's no reason you can't … build a PC," says science writer David Einstein. And, if you do it right, "it will probably take only a couple of hours," because industry-standard connections allow components to go together fairly easily.[21]

Actually, probably only techies would consider building their own PCs. But many ordinary users order their own custom-built PCs. Let's consider how you might do this.

We're not going to ask you to build or order a PC—just to pretend to do so. The purpose of this exercise is to help you understand how a computer works. That information will help you when you go shopping for a new system or, especially, if you order a custom-built system. It will also help you understand how your existing system works, if you have one.

Before you begin, you will need to understand three key concepts.

- **First:** The purpose of a computer is to process data into information. **_Data_ consists of the raw facts and figures that are processed into information**—for example, the votes for different candidates being elected to student-government office. **_Information_ is data that has been summarized or otherwise manipulated for use in decision making**—for example, the total votes for each candidate, which are used to decide who won.

- **Second:** You should know the difference between hardware and software. **_Hardware_ consists of all the machinery and equipment in a computer system.** The hardware includes, among other devices, the keyboard, the screen, the printer, and the "box"—the computer or processing device itself. Hardware is useless without software. **_Software_, or _programs_, consists of all the electronic instructions that tell the computer how to perform a task.** These instructions come from a software developer in a form (such as a CD, or compact disk) that will be accepted by the computer. Examples you may have heard of are Microsoft Windows and Office XP.

- **Third:** _Regardless_ of type and size, all computers follow the same four basic operations: (1) input, (2) processing, (3) storage, and (4) output. To this we add (5) communications.

  1. _Input operation:_ **_Input_ is whatever is put in ("input") to a computer system.** Input can be nearly any kind of data—letters, numbers, symbols, shapes, colors, temperatures, sounds, pressure, light beams, or whatever raw material needs processing. When you type some words or numbers on a keyboard, those words are considered input data.

  2. _Processing operation:_ **_Processing_ is the manipulation a computer does to transform data into information.** When the computer adds 2 + 2 to get 4, that is the act of processing. The processing is done by the _central processing unit_—frequently called just the _CPU_—a device consisting of electronic circuitry that executes instructions to process data.

  3. _Storage operation:_ Storage is of two types—temporary storage and permanent storage, or primary storage and secondary storage. **_Primary storage_, or _memory_, is the internal computer circuitry that temporarily holds data waiting to be processed. _Secondary storage_, simply called _storage_, refers to the devices and media that store data or information permanently.** A floppy disk (diskette) or hard disk is an example of this kind of storage. (Storage also holds the software—the computer programs.)

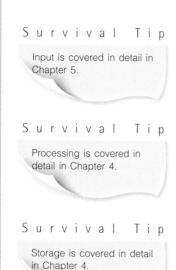

Survival Tip

Input is covered in detail in Chapter 5.

Survival Tip

Processing is covered in detail in Chapter 4.

Survival Tip

Storage is covered in detail in Chapter 4.

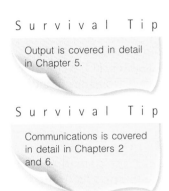

S u r v i v a l   T i p

Output is covered in detail in Chapter 5.

S u r v i v a l   T i p

Communications is covered in detail in Chapters 2 and 6.

4. *Output operation:* **<u>Output</u> is whatever is output from ("put out of") the computer system—the results of processing, usually information.** Examples of output are numbers or pictures displayed on a screen, words printed out on paper in a printer, or music piped over some loudspeakers.

5. *Communications operation:* These days, most (though not all) computers have communications ability, which offers an extension capability—in other words, it extends the power of the computer. With wired or wireless communications connections, data may be input from afar, processed in a remote area, stored in several different locations, and output in yet other places. However, you don't need communications ability to write term papers, do calculations, or perform many other computer tasks.

These five operations are summarized in the illustration. *(See ● Panel 1.2.)*

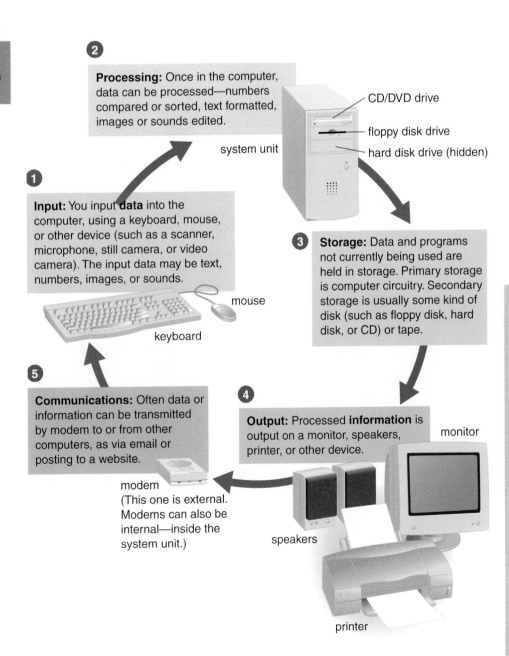

● **PANEL 1.2**
Basic operations of a computer

❷ Processing: Once in the computer, data can be processed—numbers compared or sorted, text formatted, images or sounds edited.

CD/DVD drive
floppy disk drive
system unit
hard disk drive (hidden)

❶ Input: You input **data** into the computer, using a keyboard, mouse, or other device (such as a scanner, microphone, still camera, or video camera). The input data may be text, numbers, images, or sounds.

mouse
keyboard

❸ Storage: Data and programs not currently being used are held in storage. Primary storage is computer circuitry. Secondary storage is usually some kind of disk (such as floppy disk, hard disk, or CD) or tape.

❺ Communications: Often data or information can be transmitted by modem to or from other computers, as via email or posting to a website.

modem
(This one is external. Modems can also be internal—inside the system unit.)

❹ Output: Processed **information** is output on a monitor, speakers, printer, or other device.

monitor
speakers
printer

Introduction to Information Technology

13

Pretending to Order a Custom-Built Desktop Computer

Now let's see how you would order a custom-built desktop PC. Remember, the purpose of this is to help you understand the internal workings of a computer so that you'll be knowledgeable about using one and buying one. (If you were going to build it yourself, you would pretend that someone had acquired the PC components for you from a catalog company and that you're now sitting at a kitchen table about to begin assembling them. All you would need is a combination Phillips/flathead screwdriver, perhaps a small wrench, and a static-electricity-arresting strap for your wrist. [Static electricity can adversely affect some computer components.] You would also need the manuals that come with some of the components.) Although prices of components are always subject to change, we have indicated general ranges of prices for basic equipment current as of late 2003 so that you can get a sense of the relative importance of the various parts. ("Loaded" components—the most powerful and sophisticated equipment—cost more than the prices given here.)

Note: All the system components you or anyone else chooses *must be compatible*—in other words, each brand must work with other brands. If you work with one company—such as Dell, Apple, or Hewlett-Packard—to customize your system, you won't have to worry about compatibility. If you choose all the components yourself—for example, by going to a computer-parts seller such as Aberdeen *(www.aberdeeninc.com)*—you will have to check on compatibility as you choose each component. And you'll have to make sure each component comes with any necessary cables, instructions, and component-specific software (called a *driver*) that makes the component run.

This section of the chapter gives you a brief overview of the components; they are all covered in detail in Chapters 2–7.

S u r v i v a l   T i p

Hardware Info

Go to *www.bizrate.com/ marketplace* for a listing of virtually all types of hardware, their descriptions, ratings, and prices, and the names of sellers.

Input Hardware: Keyboard & Mouse

Input hardware consists of devices that allow people to put data into the computer in a form that the computer can use. At minimum, you will need two things: a *keyboard* and a *mouse*.

Keyboard

Mouse

- Keyboard: Cost: $22–$70. On a microcomputer, a keyboard is the primary input device. **A _keyboard_ is an input device that converts letters, numbers, and other characters into electrical signals readable by the processor.** A microcomputer keyboard looks like a typewriter keyboard, but besides having keys for letters and numbers it has several keys (such as *F* keys and *Ctrl, Alt,* and *Del* keys) intended for computer-specific tasks. After other components are assembled, the keyboard will be plugged into the back of the computer in a socket intended for that purpose. (Cordless keyboards work differently.)

- Mouse: $25–$100. **A _mouse_ is a nonkeyboard input device ("pointing device") that is used to manipulate objects viewed on the computer display screen.** The mouse cord is plugged into the back of the computer or into the back of the keyboard after the other components are assembled. (Cordless mice are also available.)

Processing & Memory Hardware: Inside the System Cabinet

The brains of the computer are the processing and memory devices, which are installed in the case or system cabinet.

Case or system cabinet

- **Case and power supply:** About $80–$160. **Also known as the *system unit*, the *case* or *system cabinet* is the box that houses the processor chip (CPU), the memory chips, and the motherboard with power supply, as well as some secondary storage devices**—floppy-disk drive, hard-disk drive, and CD or DVD drive, as we will explain. The case comes in desktop or tower models. It includes a power supply unit and a fan to keep the circuitry from overheating.

- **Processor chip:** $65–$900 or more. It may be small and not look like much, but it could be the most expensive hardware component of a build-it-yourself PC—and doubtless the most important. **A *processor chip (CPU)* is a tiny piece of silicon that contains millions of miniature electronic circuits.** The speed at which a chip processes information is expressed in *megahertz (MHz)*, millions of processing cycles per second, or *gigahertz (GHz)*, billions of processing cycles per second. The faster the processor, the more expensive it is. For $65, you might get a 1.33-GHz chip, which is adequate for most student purposes. For $350, you might get a 2.13-GHz chip, which you would want if you're running software with spectacular graphics and sound, such as those with some new video games. Only older processors' speed is measured in megahertz now, but if you want a cheap processor—for instance, because you plan to work only with text documents—you could get a 233-MHz processor for $40.

Processor chip. In a cellphone, the chip (shown on fingertip), which does the most important work, is not much bigger than a display screen icon.

- **Memory chips:** $20–$150. These chips are also small. ***Memory chips*, also known as *RAM (random access memory) chips*, represent *primary* storage, or temporary storage; they hold data before processing and information after processing, before it is sent along to an output or storage device.** You'll want enough memory chips to hold at least 128 megabytes, or roughly 128 million characters, of data, which is adequate for most student purposes. If you work with large graphics files, you'll need more memory capacity, 192–256 megabytes or perhaps even 512 megabytes. (We explain the numbers used to measure storage capacities in a moment.)

Memory chips

memory chip (RAM chip)

memory chips mounted on module

- **Motherboard:** About $100–$180. **Also called the *system board*, the *motherboard* is the main circuit board in the computer.** This is the big green circuit board to which everything else—such as the keyboard, mouse, and printer—attaches through connections (called *ports*) in the back of the computer. The processor chip and memory chips are also installed on the motherboard.

  The motherboard has ***expansion slots*—for expanding the PC's capabilities—which give you places to plug in additional circuit boards,** such as those for video, sound, and communications (modem).

Now the components can be put together. As the illustration below shows, ❶ the memory chips are plugged into the motherboard. Then ❷ the processor chip is plugged into the motherboard. Now ❸ the motherboard is attached to the system cabinet. Then ❹ the power supply unit is connected to the system cabinet. Finally, ❺ the wire for the power switch, which turns the computer on and off, is connected to the motherboard.

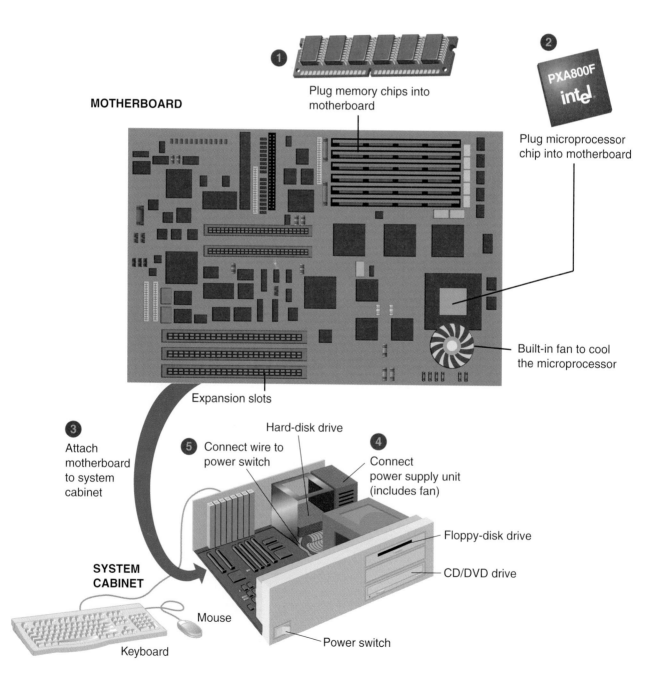

Plug memory chips into motherboard

PXA800F intel

Plug microprocessor chip into motherboard

MOTHERBOARD

Built-in fan to cool the microprocessor

Expansion slots

❸ Attach motherboard to system cabinet

Hard-disk drive

❺ Connect wire to power switch

❹ Connect power supply unit (includes fan)

Floppy-disk drive

CD/DVD drive

SYSTEM CABINET

Mouse

Keyboard

Power switch

Storage Hardware: Floppy Drive, Hard Drive, & CD/DVD Drive

With the motherboard in the system cabinet, the next step is installation of the storage hardware. Whereas memory chips deal only with temporary storage, *secondary storage,* or *permanent storage,* stores your data for as long as you want.

For today's student purposes, you'll need at minimum a floppy-disk drive, a hard-disk drive, and a CD/DVD drive. If you work with large files, you'll also want a Zip-disk drive. These storage devices slide into the system cabinet from the front and are secured with screws. Each drive is attached to the motherboard by a flat cable (called a *ribbon cable*). Also, each drive must be hooked up to a plug extending from the power supply.

A computer system's data/information storage capacity is represented by bytes, kilobytes, megabytes, gigabytes, and terabytes. Roughly speaking:

1 byte = 1 character of data (A character can be alphabetic—A, B, or C—or numeric—1, 2, or 3—or a special character—!, ?, *, $, %.)

1 kilobyte = 1,024 characters

1 megabyte = 1,048,576 characters

1 gigabyte = more than 1 billion characters

1 terabyte = more than 1 trillion characters.

Floppy disk and drive

floppy disk

floppy disk drive

Zip disk and drive

CD/DVD drive

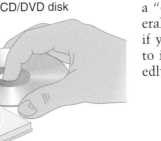

CD/DVD disk

- Floppy-disk and Zip drives: $25 (floppy)–$150 (Zip). **A *floppy-disk drive* is a storage device that stores data on removable 3.5-inch-diameter diskettes.** These diskettes don't seem to be "floppy," because they are encased in hard plastic, but the mylar disk inside is indeed flexible or floppy. Each can store 1.44 million bytes (characters) or more of data. With the floppy-disk drive installed, you'll later be able to insert a diskette through a slot in the front and remove it by pushing the eject button. **A *Zip-disk drive* is a storage device that stores data on removable floppy-disk cartridges with 70–170 times the capacity of the standard floppy.**

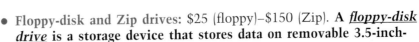

Floppy disk

Zip disk

- Hard-disk drive: $110 for 80 gigabytes of storage (higher-capacity and lower-capacity drives are available). **A *hard-disk drive* is a storage device inside the computer case that stores billions of characters of data on a nonremovable disk platter.** With 80 gigabytes of storage, you should be able to handle most student needs.

Hard disk

- CD/DVD drive: $50. **A *CD (compact-disk) drive,* or its more recent variant, a *DVD (digital video-disk) drive,* is a storage device that uses laser technology to read data from optical disks.** (Some companies call a DVD a "digital versatile disk.") These days new software is generally supplied on CDs rather than floppy disks. And even if you can get a program on floppies, you'll find it easier to install a new program from one CD rather than repeatedly inserting and removing, say, 10 or 12 floppy disks.

The system cabinet has lights on the front that indicate when these drives are in use. (You must not remove the diskette from the floppy-disk drive until its light goes off, or else you risk damage to both disk and drive.) The wires for these lights need to be attached to the motherboard.

Output Hardware: Video & Sound Cards, Monitor, Speakers, & Printer

Output hardware consists of devices that translate information processed by the computer into a form that humans can understand—print, sound, graphics, or video, for example. Now a video card and a sound card need to be installed in the system cabinet. Next the monitor, speakers, and a printer are plugged in.

This is a good place to introduce the term *peripheral device*. **A _peripheral device_ is any component or piece of equipment that expands a computer's input, storage, and output capabilities.** In other words, a peripheral device is not part of the essential computer. Peripheral devices can be inside the computer or connected to it from the outside. Examples include printers and disk drives.

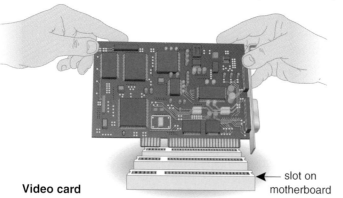
Video card

   ← slot on motherboard

- **Video card:** $50–$500. You doubtless want your monitor to display color (rather than just black-and-white) images. Your system cabinet will therefore need to have a device to make this possible. **A _video card_ converts the processor's output information into a video signal that can be sent through a cable to the monitor.** Remember the expansion slots we mentioned? Your video card is plugged into one of these on the motherboard. (You can also buy a mother board with built-in video.)

- Sound card: $30–$200 and higher. You may wish to listen to music on your PC. If so, you'll need a **_sound card_, which enhances the computer's sound-generating capabilities by allowing sound to be output through speakers.** This, too, would be plugged into an expansion slot on the motherboard. (Once again, you can buy a motherboard with built-in sound.) With the CD drive connected to the card, you can listen to music CDs.

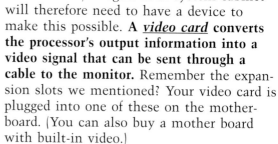
Sound card

Monitor

- **Monitor:** $100–$200 or higher for a 17-inch model, $200–$1,000 for a 19-inch model. As with television sets, the inch dimension on monitors is measured diagonally corner to corner. **The _monitor_ is the display device that takes the electrical signals from the video card and forms an image using points of colored light on the screen.** Later, after the system cabinet has been closed up, the monitor will be connected by means of a cable to the back of the computer, using the clearly marked connector. The power cord for the monitor will be plugged into a wall plug.

Sound speakers

- **Pair of speakers: $25–$250. _Speakers_ are the devices that play sounds transmitted as electrical signals from the sound card.** They may not be very sophisticated, but unless you're into high-fidelity recordings they're probably good enough. The two speakers are connected to a single wire that is plugged into the back of the computer once installation is completed.

- **Printer: $50–$700.** Especially for student work, you certainly need a **_printer_, an output device that produces text and graphics on paper.** There are various types of printers, as we discuss later. The printer has two connections. One, which relays signals from the computer, goes to the back of the PC, where it connects with the motherboard. The other is a power cord that goes to a wall plug. Color printers are more expensive than black-and-white printers, and fast printers cost more than slow ones.

Printer

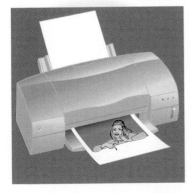

Communications Hardware: Modem

Computers can be stand-alone machines, unconnected to anything else. If all you're doing is word processing to write term papers, a stand-alone system may be fine for you. As we have seen, however, the communications component of the computer system vastly extends the range of a PC. Thus, while the system cabinet is still open, there is one more piece of hardware to install:

Internal modem

- **Modem: $40–$100. A standard _modem_ is a device that sends and receives data over telephone lines to and from computers.** The modem is mounted on an expansion card, which is fitted into an expansion slot on the motherboard. Later you can run a telephone line from the telephone wall plug to the back of the PC, where it will connect to the modem.

Other types of communications connections exist, which we cover in Chapter 6. However, standard modems are still commonly used.

Now the system cabinet is closed up. The person building the system will plug in all the input and output devices and turn on the power "on" button. Your microcomputer system will look similar to the one below. *(See ● Panel 1.3.)* Are you now ready to roll? Not quite.

● **PANEL 1.3**
Completely assembled PC hardware system

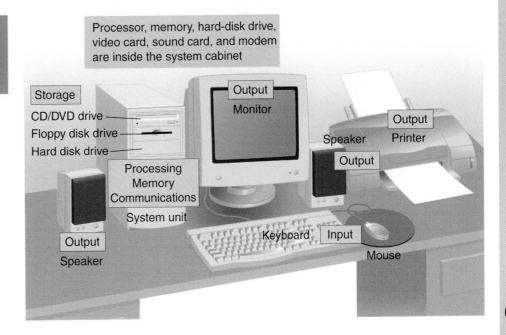

Software

With all the pieces put together, the person assembling the computer needs to check the motherboard manual for instructions on starting the system. One of the most important tasks is to install software, the electronically encoded instructions that tell the computer hardware what to do. Software is what makes the computer worthwhile. There are two types—*system software* and *application software.*

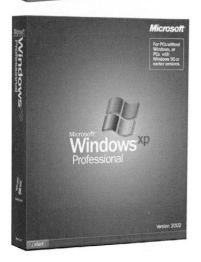

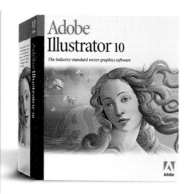

- **System software:** First, system software must be installed. **<u>_System software_</u> helps the computer perform essential operating tasks and enables the application software to run.** System software consists of several electronically coded programs. The most important is the *operating system,* the master control program that runs the computer. Examples of operating system software for the PC are various Microsoft programs (such as Windows 95, 98, Me, XP, and NT), Unix, and Linux. The Apple Macintosh microcomputer is another matter altogether. As we explain in Chapters 4 and 5, it has its own hardware components and software, which, by and large, aren't directly transferable to the Windows PC.

  System software comes most often on CDs. The person building your computer system will insert these into your CD drive and follow the on-screen directions for installation. (*Installation* is the process of copying software programs from secondary storage media—CDs, for example—onto your system's hard disk, so that you can have direct access to your hardware.)

  After the system software is installed, setup software for the hard drive, the video and sound cards, and the modem must be installed. These setup programs (*drivers,* discussed in Chapter 3) will probably come on CDs (or maybe floppy disks). Once again, the installer inserts these into the appropriate drive and then follows the instructions that appear on the screen.

- **Application software:** Now we're finally getting somewhere! After the application software has been installed, you can start using the PC. **<u>_Application software_</u> enables you to perform specific tasks—solve problems, perform work, or entertain yourself.** For example, when you prepare a term paper on your computer, you will use a word processing program. (Microsoft Word and Corel WordPerfect are two brands.) Adobe Illustrator and Photoshop are popular application programs for creating and manipulating graphics. Application software is specific to the system software you use. If you want to run Microsoft Word, for instance, you'll need to first have Microsoft Windows system software on your system, not Unix or Linux.

  Application software comes on CDs or floppy disks packaged in boxes that include instructions. You insert the CDs into your computer, and then follow the instructions on the screen for installation. Later on you may obtain entire application programs by getting them off (downloading them from) the internet, using your modem or another type of communications connection, as we discuss in Chapters 2 and 6.

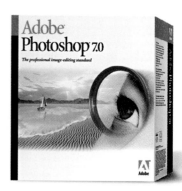

We discuss software in much more detail in Chapters 3 and 4.

Is Getting a Custom-Built PC Worth the Effort?

Does the foregoing description make you want to try putting together a PC yourself? If you add up the costs of all the components (not to mention the value of your time), and then start checking ads for PCs, you might wonder why anyone would bother going to the trouble of building one. And nowadays you would probably be right. "If you think you'd save money by putting together a computer from scratch," says David Einstein, "think again. You'd be lucky to match the price PC-makers are charging these days in their zeal to undercut the competition."[22]

But had you done this for real, it would not have been a futile exercise: By knowing how to build a system yourself, not only would you be able to impress your friends but you'd also know how to upgrade any store-bought system to include components that are better than standard. For instance, as Einstein points out, if you're into video games, knowing how to construct your own PC would enable you to make a system that's right for you. You could include the latest three-dimensional graphics video card and a state-of-the-art sound card, for example. More important, you'd also know how to order a custom-built system (as from Dell, Gateway, or Micron, the mail-order/online computer makers) that's right for you. In Chapters 4 and 5, we'll expand on this discussion so that you can really know what you're doing when you go shopping for a microcomputer system.

Before we end this introductory overview of information technology, let's wrap up the chapter with a look at the future.

QuickCheck

Describe the three key concepts of how computers work.

Name the principal types of input, processing/memory, storage, output, and communications hardware.

Describe the two types of software.

1.4 Where Is Information Technology Headed?

KEY QUESTION

What are three directions of computer development and three directions of communications development?

Today almost every job and profession require computer skills of some sort. Some are ordinary jobs in which computers are used as ordinary tools. Others are specialized jobs in which advanced computer training combined with professional training gives people dramatically new careers. Consider:

- In the hotel business, even front-desk clerks need to know how to deal with computerized reservation systems. Some hotels, however, also have a so-called computer concierge, someone with a knowledge of computer systems who can help guests who have notebooks with their online and other problems.

- In law enforcement, police officers need to know how to use computers while on patrol or at their desks to check out stolen cars, criminal records, outstanding arrest warrants, and the like. However, investigators with specialized computer backgrounds are also required to help solve fraud, computer break-ins, accounting illegalities, and other high-tech crimes.

- In entertainment, computers are used for such ordinary purposes as budgets, payroll, and ticketing. However, there are also new careers in virtual set design, combining training in architecture and 3-D computer modeling, and in creating cinematic special effects

Clearly, information technology is changing old jobs and inventing new ones. To prosper in this environment, you will need to combine a traditional

education with training in computers and communications. And you will need to understand what the principal trends of the Information Age are. Let's consider these trends in the development of computers and communications and, most excitingly, the area where they intersect.

Three Directions of Computer Development: Miniaturization, Speed, & Affordability

One of the first computers, the outcome of military-related research, was delivered to the U.S. Army in 1946. ENIAC (short for "Electronic Numerical Integrator And Calculator") weighed 30 tons and was 80 feet long and two stories high, but it could multiply a pair of numbers in the then-remarkable time of three-thousandths of a second. *(See ● Panel 1.4.)* This was the first general-purpose, programmable electronic computer, the grand-parent of today's lightweight handheld machines.

Since the days of ENIAC, computers have developed in three directions—and are continuing to do so:

Timeline
Overview of some of the historical developments in information technology.

4000–1200 BCE	3000 BCE	1621 CE	1642	1666	1801
Inhabitants of the first known civilization in Sumer keep records of commericial transactions on clay tablets	Abacus is invented in Babylonia	Slide rule invented (Edmund Gunther)	First mechanical adding machine (Blaise Pascal)	First mechanical calculator that can add and subtract (Samuel Morland)	A linked sequence of punched cards controls the weaving patterns in Jacquard's loom

Integrated circuit

- **Miniaturization:** Everything has become smaller. ENIAC's old-fashioned radio-style vacuum tubes gave way after 1947 to the smaller, faster, more reliable transistor. A *transistor* is a small device used as a gateway to transfer electrical signals along predetermined paths (circuits).

  The next step was the development of tiny *integrated circuits*. Integrated circuits are entire collections of electrical circuits or pathways that are now etched on tiny squares (chips) of silicon half the size of your thumbnail. *Silicon* is a natural element found in sand. In pure form, it is the base material for computer processing devices.

  The miniaturized processor, or microprocessor, in a personal desktop computer today can perform calculations that once required a computer filling an entire room.

- **Speed:** Thanks to miniaturization and new material used in making processors, computer makers can cram more hardware components into their machines, providing faster processing speeds and more data storage capacity.

- **Affordability:** Processor costs today are only a fraction of what they were 15 years ago. A state-of-the-art processor costing less than $1,000 provides the same processing power as a huge 1980s computer costing more than $1 million.

These are the three major trends in computers. What about communications?

Three Directions of Communications Development: Connectivity, Interactivity, & Multimedia

Once upon a time, we had the voice telephone system—a one-to-one medium. You could talk to your Uncle Joe and he could talk to you, and with special arrangements (conference calls) more than two people could talk with one another. We also had radio and television systems—one-to-many media (or mass media). News announcers could talk to you on a single medium such as television, but you couldn't talk to them.

There have been three recent developments in communications:

- **Connectivity: _Connectivity_ refers to the connection of computers to one another by a communications line in order to provide online information access and/or the sharing of peripheral devices.** The connectivity resulting from the expansion of computer networks has made possible email and online shopping, for example.

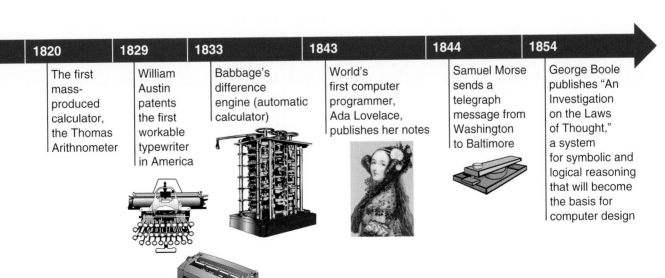

1820	1829	1833	1843	1844	1854
The first mass-produced calculator, the Thomas Arithnometer	William Austin patents the first workable typewriter in America	Babbage's difference engine (automatic calculator)	World's first computer programmer, Ada Lovelace, publishes her notes	Samuel Morse sends a telegraph message from Washington to Baltimore	George Boole publishes "An Investigation on the Laws of Thought," a system for symbolic and logical reasoning that will become the basis for computer design

Interactivity. A dashboard computer allows drivers to request information about their car's operation, geographic location, and nearby services.

- **Interactivity:** _**Interactivity**_ **refers to two-way communication; the user can respond to information he or she receives and modify what a computer is doing.** That is, there is an exchange or dialogue between the user and the computer, and the computer responds to user requests. A noninteractive program, once started, continues without requiring human contact, or interaction. The ability to interact means users can be active rather than passive participants in the technological process. On the television networks MSNBC or CNN, for example, you can immediately go on the internet and respond to news from broadcast anchors. Today, most application software is interactive. In the future, cars may respond to voice commands or feature computers built into the dashboard.

- **Multimedia:** Radio is a single-dimensional medium (sound), as is most email (mainly text). As mentioned earlier in this chapter, _**multimedia**_ **refers to technology that presents information in more than one medium—such as text, pictures, video, sound, and animation—in a single integrated communication.** The development of the World Wide Web expanded the internet to include pictures, sound, music, and so on, as well as text.

Exciting as these developments are, truly mind-boggling possibilities emerge as computers and communications cross-pollinate.

When Computers & Communications Combine: Convergence, Portability, & Personalization

Sometime in the 1990s, computers and communications started to fuse together, beginning a new era within the Information Age. The result was three further developments, which have only just begun.

- **Convergence:** Convergence describes the combining of several industries through various devices that exchange data in the format used by computers. The industries are computers, communications, consumer electronics, entertainment, and mass media. Convergence has led to electronic products that perform multiple functions, such as TVs with internet access, cellphones that are also digital cameras, and refrigerators that allow you to send email.

- **Portability:** In the 1980s, portability, or mobility, meant trading off computing power and convenience in return for smaller size and weight. Today, however, we are close to the point where we don't have to give up anything. As a result, experts have predicted that small, powerful, wireless personal electronic devices will transform our lives far more than the personal computer has done so far. "The

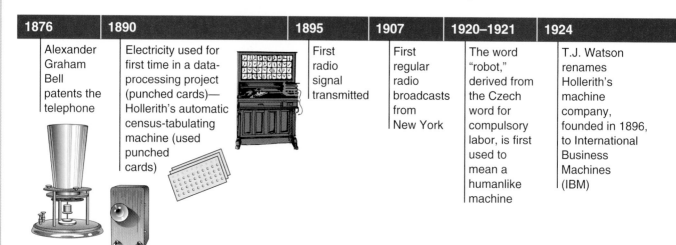

1876	1890		1895	1907	1920–1921	1924
Alexander Graham Bell patents the telephone	Electricity used for first time in a data-processing project (punched cards)—Hollerith's automatic census-tabulating machine (used punched cards)		First radio signal transmitted	First regular radio broadcasts from New York	The word "robot," derived from the Czech word for compulsory labor, is first used to mean a humanlike machine	T.J. Watson renames Hollerith's machine company, founded in 1896, to International Business Machines (IBM)

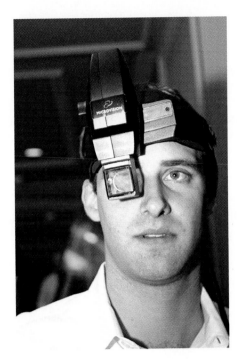

(Left) Micro Vision's Retinal Scanning Display records what the user is seeing and sends the data to a mode worn on the user's belt. *(Right)* The HandsFreeMobile e-Belt wearable computer.

new generation of machines will be truly personal computers, designed for our mobile lives," wrote one journalist back in 1992. "We will read office memos between strokes on the golf course and answer messages from our children in the middle of business meetings."[23] Today such activities are commonplace, and smartphones are taking on other functions. The risk they bring is that, unless we're careful, work will invade our leisure time.

- **Personalization:** Personalization is the creation of information tailored to your preferences—for instance, programs that will automatically cull recent news and information from the internet on just those topics you have designated. Companies involved in e-commerce can send you messages about forthcoming products based on your pattern of purchases, usage, and other criteria. Or they will build products (cars, computers, clothing) customized to your heart's desire.

"E" Also Stands for Ethics

Every computer user will have to wrestle with ethical issues related to the use of information technology. **_Ethics_ is defined as a set of moral values or principles that govern the conduct of an individual or a group.** Because ethical questions arise so often in connection with information technology, we

1927	1930	1944	1945	1946	1952
First demonstration of television in USA	General theory of computers (MIT)	First electro-mechanical computer (Mark I)	John von Neumann introduces the concept of a stored program	First programmable electronic computer in United States (ENIAC)	UNIVAC computer correctly predicts election of Eisenhower as U.S. President

will note them, wherever they appear in this book, with the symbol shown in the margin. Here, for example, are some important ethical concerns pointed out by Tom Forester and Perry Morrison in their book *Computer Ethics*.[24] These considerations are only a few of many; we'll discuss others in subsequent chapters.

ethics

- **Speed and scale:** Great amounts of information can be stored, retrieved, and transmitted at a speed and on a scale not possible before. Despite the benefits, this has serious implications "for data security and personal privacy," as well as employment, Forester and Morison say, because information technology can never be considered totally secure against unauthorized access.
- **Unpredictability:** Computers and communications are pervasive, touching nearly every aspect of our lives. However, at this point, compared to other pervasive technologies—such as electricity, television, and automobiles—information technology seems a lot less predictable and reliable.
- **Complexity:** Computer systems are often incredibly complex—some so complex that they are not always understood even by their creators. "This," say Forester and Morrison, "often makes them completely unmanageable," producing massive foul-ups or spectacularly out-of-control costs.

QuickCheck

Describe the three directions in which computers have developed.

Describe the three recent directions in which communications have developed.

Discuss three effects of the fusion of computers and communications.

Name three ethical considerations that result from information technology.

Onward: Handling Information in the Era of Pervasive Computing

The mountain of information threatens to overwhelm us. How will we cope? Consider the four challenges we mentioned at the start of this chapter:

- **Learn to deal with information overload:** The volume of available information far exceeds the amount of time needed to absorb it. To avoid being buried in an avalanche of unnecessary data, we must

1964	1967	1969	1970	1971	1975	1976
IBM introduces 360 line of computers	Hand-held calculator	ARPANet established by U.S. Advanced Research Project Agency, led to internet	Micro-processor chips come into use; floppy disk introduced for storing data	First pocket calculator	First micro-computer (MIT's Altair 8800)	Apple I computer (first personal computer sold in assembled form)

info!

From now on, whenever you see this icon you'll find information about internet sites to visit and how to search for terms related to the topic just discussed.

learn to distinguish what we really need from what we think we need. Throughout this book, we present suggestions for how to deal with too much information. In this first chapter, these are featured in the Practical Action Box ("Managing Your Email.").

- **Have a strategy for what you memorize and what you don't:** Probably you're already feeling stressed about what you have to memorize. Passing the course for which this book is intended, for example, requires that you absorb and remember a number of facts. Other matters, such as phone numbers, internet addresses, and birth dates, can be stored on a cellphone or handheld computer. But don't entrust such information to just one device. The airlines, for instance, recover thousands of cellphones every month that passengers have misplaced (and that most don't claim because they've already bought a new one).[25] Thus, it's best to have your important phone numbers stored elsewhere as well.

- **Learn how to make your personal "multitasking" efficient:** *Multitasking* refers to a computer's ability to run several programs at once (as we describe in Chapter 4). However, it has also become a popular term for people performing several tasks at once, such as studying while eating, listening to music, talking on the phone, and handling email. You may think you're one of those people who has no trouble juggling all this, but the brain has limits and can do only so much at one time. For instance, it has been found that people who do two demanding tasks simultaneously—drive in heavy traffic and talk on a cellphone, for instance—do neither task as well as they do each alone. Indeed, the result of constantly shifting attention is a sacrifice in quality for any of the tasks with which one is engaged. This clearly has some consequences for studying.

- **Be aware that "smart mobs" could also be dumb mobs:** We mentioned the notion that smart mobile devices could produce groups of people—"smart mobs"—who cooperate in ways never before possible because they carry portable technology that possesses both computing and communications capabilities. Yet there is also the possibility that others—the government, corporate marketers—could transform these devices into weapons against the users. Thus, you need to become aware of how security and privacy can be abridged in ways that could transform you from a member of a smart mob to that of a "dumb mob."

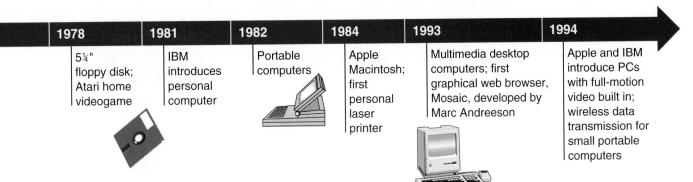

1978	1981	1982	1984	1993	1994
5¼" floppy disk; Atari home videogame	IBM introduces personal computer	Portable computers	Apple Macintosh; first personal laser printer	Multimedia desktop computers; first graphical web browser, Mosaic, developed by Marc Andreeson	Apple and IBM introduce PCs with full-motion video built in; wireless data transmission for small portable computers

Summary

Note to the reader: "KQ" refers to the Key Questions listed on the first page of each chapter and repeated with each numbered main section head.

application software (p. 20, KQ 1.3) Software that has been developed to solve a particular problem, perform useful work on general-purpose tasks, or provide entertainment. Why it's important: Application software such as word processing, spreadsheet, database management, graphics, and communications packages are commonly used tools for increasing people's productivity.

case (p. 15, KQ 1.3) Also known as the *system unit* or *system cabinet;* the box that houses the processor chip (CPU), the memory chips, and the motherboard with power supply, as well as storage devices—floppy-disk drive, hard-disk drive, and CD or DVD drive. Why it's important: The case protects many important processing and storage components.

case

CD (compact-disk) drive (p. 17, KQ 1.3) Storage device that uses laser technology to read data from optical disks. Why it's important: New software is generally supplied on CDs rather than diskettes. And even if you can get a program on floppies, you'll find it easier to install a new program from one CD rather than repeatedly inserting and removing many diskettes. The newest version is called *DVD (digital video disk).* The DVD format stores even more data than the CD format.

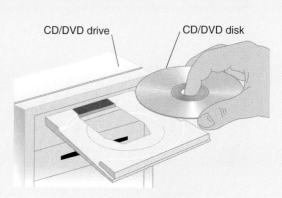

CD/DVD drive   CD/DVD disk

central processing unit (CPU) (p. 15, KQ 1.3) The computer's main chip, consisting of electronic circuitry that executes instructions to process data. Why it's important: The CPU is the "brain" of the computer.

chip *See* **processor chip.**

clients (p. 11, KQ 1.2) Computers and other devices connected to a server, a central computer. Why it's important: Client/server networks are used in many organizations for sharing databases, devices, and programs.

communications technology (p. 3, KQ 1.1) Also called *telecommunications technology;* consists of electromagnetic devices and systems for communicating over long distances. Why it's important: Communications systems using electronic connections have helped to expand human communication beyond face-to-face meetings.

computer (p. 3, KQ 1.1) Programmable, multiuse machine that accepts data—raw facts and figures—and processes (manipulates) it into useful information, such as summaries and totals. Why it's important: Computers greatly speed up problem solving and other tasks, increasing users' productivity.

computer

connectivity (p. 23, KQ 1.4) Ability to connect computers to one another by communications lines, so as to provide online information access and/or the sharing of peripheral devices. Why it's important: Connectivity is the foundation of the advances in the Information Age. It provides online access to countless types of information and services. The connectivity resulting from the expansion of computer networks has made possible email and online shopping, for example.

cyberspace (p. 6, KQ 1.1) Term used to refer to the online world and the internet in particular but also the whole wired and wireless world of communications in general. Why it's important: More and more human activities take place in cyberspace.

data (p. 12, KQ 1.3) Raw facts and figures processed into information. Why it's important: Users need data to create useful information.

desktop PC (p. 9, KQ 1.2) Microcomputer unit that sits on a desk, with the keyboard in front and the monitor often on top. Why it's important: Desktop PCs and tower PCs are the most commonly used types of microcomputer.

DVD (digital video-disk) drive *See* **CD drive.**

email

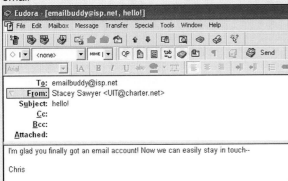

email (electronic mail) (p. 4, KQ 1.1) Messages transmitted over a computer network, most often the internet. Why it's important: Email has become universal; one of the first things new computer users learn is how to send and receive email.

ethics (p. 25, KQ 1.4) Set of moral values or principles that govern the conduct of an individual or a group. Why it's important: Ethical questions arise often in connection with information technology.

expansion slots (p. 16, KQ 1.3) Internal "plugs" used to expand the PC's capabilities. Why it's important: Expansion slots give you places to plug in additional circuit boards, such as those for video, sound, and communications (modem).

floppy-disk drive (p. 17, KQ 1.3) Storage device that stores data on removable 3.5-inch-diameter flexible diskettes encased in hard plastic. Why it's important: Floppy-disk drives are included on almost all microcomputers and make many types of files portable.

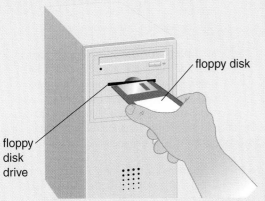

floppy disk

floppy disk drive

hard-disk drive (p. 17, KQ 1.3) Storage device that stores billions of characters of data on a nonremovable disk platter usually inside the computer case. Why it's important: Hard disks hold much more data than diskettes do. Nearly all microcomputers use hard disks as their principal secondary-storage medium.

hardware (p. 12, KQ 1.3) All machinery and equipment in a computer system. Why it's important: Hardware runs under the control of software and is useless without it. However, hardware contains the circuitry that allows processing.

information (p. 12, KQ 1.3) Data that has been summarized or otherwise manipulated for use in decision making. Why it's important: The whole purpose of a computer (and communications) system is to produce (and transmit) usable information.

information technology (IT) (p. 3, KQ 1.1) Technology that helps to produce, manipulate, store, communicate, and/or disseminate information. Why it's important: Information technology is bringing about the fusion of several important industries dealing with computers, telephones, televisions, and various handheld devices.

input (p. 12, KQ 1.3) Whatever is put in ("input") to a computer system. Input devices include the keyboard and the mouse. Why it's important: Useful information cannot be produced without input data.

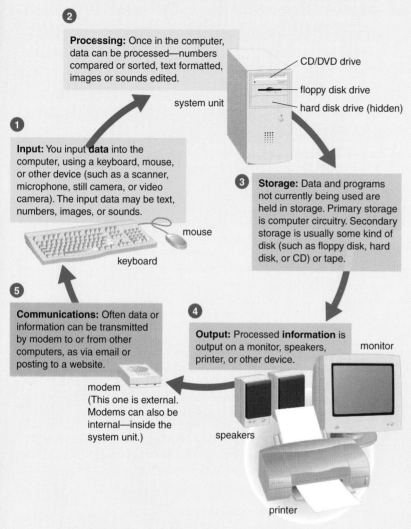

Processing: Once in the computer, data can be processed—numbers compared or sorted, text formatted, images or sounds edited.

CD/DVD drive

floppy disk drive

system unit

hard disk drive (hidden)

Input: You input **data** into the computer, using a keyboard, mouse, or other device (such as a scanner, microphone, still camera, or video camera). The input data may be text, numbers, images, or sounds.

mouse

keyboard

Storage: Data and programs not currently being used are held in storage. Primary storage is computer circuitry. Secondary storage is usually some kind of disk (such as floppy disk, hard disk, or CD) or tape.

Communications: Often data or information can be transmitted by modem to or from other computers, as via email or posting to a website.

Output: Processed **information** is output on a monitor, speakers, printer, or other device.

monitor

modem
(This one is external. Modems can also be internal—inside the system unit.)

speakers

printer

interactivity (p. 24, KQ 1.4) Two-way communication; a user can respond to information he or she receives and modify the process. Why it's important: Interactive devices allow the user to actively participate in a technological process instead of just reacting to it.

internet (the "net") (p. 6, KQ 1.1) Worldwide computer network that connects hundreds of thousands of smaller networks linking computers at academic, scientific, and commercial institutions, as well as individuals. Why it's important: Thanks to the internet, millions of people around the world can share all types of information and services.

keyboard (p. 14, KQ 1.3) Input device that converts letters, numbers, and other characters into electrical signals readable by the processor. Why it's important: Keyboards are the most common kind of input device.

local area network (LAN) (p. 9, KQ 1.2) Network that connects, usually by special cable, a group of desktop PCs and other devices, such as printers, in an office or a building. Why it's important: LANs have replaced mainframes for many functions and are considerably less expensive.

mainframe (p. 9, KQ 1.2) Second-largest computer available, after the supercomputer; capable of great processing speeds and data storage. Costs $5,000–$5 million. Small mainframes are often called *midsize computers*. Why it's important: Mainframes are used by large organizations (banks, airlines, insurance companies, universities) that need to process millions of transactions.

memory chips mounted on module

memory chip (p. 15, KQ 1.3) Also known as *RAM* (for "random access memory") *chip;* represents primary storage or temporary storage. Why it's important: Holds data before processing and information after processing, before it is sent along to an output or storage device.

microcomputer (p. 9, KQ 1.2) Also called *personal computer;* small computer that fits on or next to a desktop or can be carried around. Costs $500–$5,000. Why it's important: The microcomputer has lessened the reliance on mainframes and has provided more ordinary users with access to computers. It can be used as a stand-alone machine or connected to a network.

microcontroller (p. 10, KQ 1.2) Also called an *embedded computer;* the smallest category of computer. Why it's important: Microcontrollers are built into "smart" electronic devices, such as appliances and automobiles.

modem (p. 19, KQ 1.3) Device that sends and receives data over telephone lines to and from computers. Why it's important: A modem enables users to transmit data from one computer to another by using standard telephone lines instead of special communications equipment.

monitor (p. 18, KQ 1.3) Display device that takes the electrical signals from the video card and forms an image using points of colored light on the screen. Why it's important: Monitors enable users to view output without printing it out.

motherboard (p. 16, KQ 1.3) Main circuit board in the computer. Why it's important: This is the big green circuit board to which everything else—such as the keyboard, mouse, and printer—is attached. The processor chip and memory chips are also installed on the motherboard.

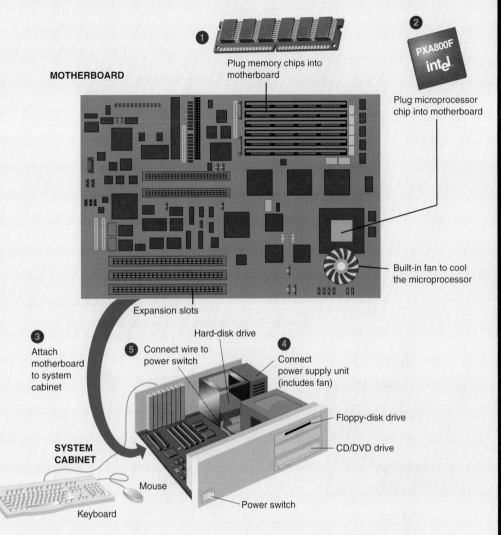

MOTHERBOARD

① Plug memory chips into motherboard

② Plug microprocessor chip into motherboard

PXA800F intel

Built-in fan to cool the microprocessor

Expansion slots

③ Attach motherboard to system cabinet

⑤ Connect wire to power switch

Hard-disk drive

④ Connect power supply unit (includes fan)

SYSTEM CABINET

Floppy-disk drive

CD/DVD drive

Mouse

Keyboard

Power switch

mouse (p. 14, KQ 1.3) Nonkeyboard input device, called a "pointing device," used to manipulate objects viewed on the computer display screen. Why it's important: For many purposes, a mouse is easier to use than a keyboard for inputting commands. Also, the mouse is used extensively in many graphics programs.

multimedia (p. 24, KQ 1.4) From "multiple media"; technology that presents information in more than one medium—including text graphics, animation, video, and sound—in a single integrated communication. Why it's important: Multimedia is used increasingly in business, the professions, and education to improve the way information is communicated.

network (p. 4, KQ 1.1) Communications system connecting two or more computers. Why it's important: Networks allow users to share applications and data and to use e-mail. The internet is the largest network.

notebook

notebook computer (p. 10, KQ 1.2) Also called *laptop computer;* lightweight portable computer with a built-in monitor, keyboard, hard-disk drive, battery, and adapter; weighs 1.8–9 pounds. Why it's important: Notebook and other small computers have provided users with computing capabilities in the field and on the road.

online (p. 3, KQ 1.1) Using a computer or some other information device, connected through a network, to access information and services from another computer or information device. Why it's important: Online communication is widely used by businesses, services, individuals, and educational institutions.

output (p. 13, KQ 1.3) Whatever is output from ("put out of") the computer system; the results of processing. Why it's important: People use output to help them make decisions. Without output devices, computer users would not be able to view or use the results of processing.

peripheral device (p. 18, KQ 1.3) Any component or piece of equipment that expands a computer's input, storage, and output capabilities. Examples include printers and disk drives. Why it's important: Most computer input and output functions are performed by peripheral devices.

PDA

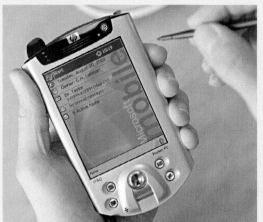

personal digital assistant (PDA) (p. 10, KQ 1.2) Also known as *handheld computer* or *palmtop;* used as a schedule planner and address book and to prepare to-do lists and send email and faxes. Why it's important: PDAs make it easier for people to do business and communicate while traveling.

primary storage (p. 12, KQ 1.3) Also called *memory;* internal computer circuitry that temporarily holds data waiting to be processed. Why it's important: By holding data, primary storage enables the processor to process.

printer (p. 19, KQ 1.3) Output device that produces text and graphics on paper. Why it's important: Printers provide one of the principal forms of computer output.

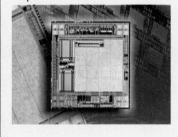

processing (p. 12, KQ 1.3) The manipulation the computer does to transform data into information. Why it's important: Processing is the essence of the computer, and the processor is the computer's "brain."

chip

processor chip (p. 15, KQ 1.3) Also called *central processing unit (CPU);* tiny piece of silicon that contains millions of miniature electronic circuits used to process data. Why it's important: Chips have made possible the development of small computers.

secondary storage (p. 12, KQ 1.3) Also called *storage;* devices and media that store data and programs permanently—such as disks and disk drives, tape and tape drives, CDs and CD drives. Why it's important: Without secondary storage, users would not be able to save their work. Storage also holds the computer's software.

server (p. 11, KQ 1.2) Computer in a network that holds collections of data (databases) and programs for connecting PCs, workstations, and other devices, which are called *clients.* Why it's important: Servers enable many users to share equipment, programs, and data.

software (p. 12, KQ 1.3) Also called *programs;* step-by-step electronically encoded instructions that tell the computer hardware how to perform a task. Why it's important: Without software, hardware is useless.

sound card

sound card (p. 18, KQ 1.3) Special circuit board that enhances the computer's sound-generating capabilities by allowing sound to be output through speakers. Why it's important: Sound is used in multimedia applications. Also, many users like to listen to music CDs on their computers.

speakers (p. 19, KQ 1.3) Devices that play sounds transmitted as electrical signals from the sound card. Speakers are connected to a single wire plugged into the back of the computer. Why it's important: *See* sound card.

supercomputer (p. 7, KQ 1.2) High-capacity computer with thousands of processors that is the fastest calculating device ever invented. Costs up to $350 million or more. Why it's important: Supercomputers are used primarily for research purposes, airplane design, oil exploration, weather forecasting, and other activities that cannot be handled by mainframes and other less powerful machines.

system software

system software (p. 20, KQ 1.3) Software that helps the computer perform essential operating tasks. Why it's important: Application software cannot run without system software. System software consists of several programs. The most important is the operating system, the master control program that runs the computer. Examples of operating system software for the PC are various Microsoft programs (such as Windows 95, 98, NT, Me, and XP), Unix, Linux, and the Macintosh operating system.

terminal (p. 9, KQ 1.2) Input and output device that uses a keyboard for input and a monitor for output; it cannot process data. Why it's important: Terminals are generally used to input data to and receive data from a mainframe computer system.

tower PC (p. 9, KQ 1.2) Microcomputer unit that sits as a "tower," often on the floor, freeing up desk space. Why it's important: Tower PCs and desktop PCs are the most commonly used types of microcomputer.

video card (p. 18, KQ 1.3) Circuit board that converts the processor's output information into a video signal for transmission through a cable to the monitor. Why it's important: Virtually all computer users need to be able to view video output on the monitor.

workstation (p. 9, KQ 1.2) Smaller than a mainframe; expensive, powerful computer generally used for complex scientific, mathematical, and engineering calculations and for computer-aided design and computer-aided manufacturing. Why it's important: The power of workstations is needed for specialized applications too large and complex to be handled by PCs.

World Wide Web (the "web") (p. 6, KQ 1.1) The interconnected system of internet servers that support specially formatted documents in multimedia form—sounds, photos, and video as well as text. Why it's important: The web is the most widely known part of the internet.

Zip-disk drive (p. 17, KQ 1.3) Storage device that stores data on removable floppy-disk cartridges with at least 70 times the capacity of the standard floppy. Why it's important: Zip drives are used to store large files.

workstation

Zip disk and drive

Chapter Review

More and more educators are favoring an approach to learning (presented by Benjamin Bloom and his colleagues in Taxonomy of Educational Objectives) that follows a hierarchy of six critical-thinking skills: (a) two lower-order skills—memorization and comprehension; and (b) four higher-order skills—application, analysis, synthesis, and evaluation. While you may be able to get through many introductory college courses by simply memorizing facts and comprehending the basic ideas, to advance further you will probably need to employ the four higher-order thinking skills.

In the Chapter Review at the end of each chapter, we have implemented this hierarchy in a three-stage approach, as follows:

- *Stage 1 learning—memorization:* "I can recognize and recall information." Self-test questions, multiple-choice questions, and true/false questions enable you to test how well you recall basic terms and concepts.

- *Stage 2 learning—comprehension:* "I can recall information in my own terms and explain them to a friend." Using open-ended short-answer questions, we ask you to reexpress terms and concepts in your own words.

- *Stage 3 learning—applying, analyzing, synthesizing, evaluating:* "I can apply what I've learned, relate these ideas to other concepts, build on other knowledge, and use all these thinking skills to form a judgment." In this part of the Chapter Review, we ask you to put the ideas into effect using the activities described, some of which include internet activities. The purpose is to help you take possession of the ideas, make them your own, and apply them realistically to your life.

stage 1 LEARNING MEMORIZATION

"I can recognize and recall information."

Self-Test Questions

1. The _____ refers to the part of the internet that stores information in multimedia form.

2. _____ and _____ refer to the two types of microcomputer. One sits on the desktop, and the other usually is placed on the floor.

3. _____ technology merges computing with high-speed communications lines carrying data, sound, and video.

4. A _____ is a programmable, multiuse machine that accepts data and processes it into information.

5. Messages transmitted over a computer network are called _____.

6. The _____ is a worldwide network that connects hundreds of thousands of smaller networks.

7. _____ refers to technology that presents information in more than one medium.

8. _____ are high-capacity machines with thousands of processors.

9. Embedded computers, or _____, are installed in "smart" appliances and automobiles.

10. The kind of software that enables users to perform specific tasks is called _____ software.

11. RAM is an example of _____ storage, and a hard drive is an example of _____ storage.

12. A _____ is a communications system connecting two or more computers.

13. The four basic operations of all computers are _____, _____, _____, and _____, and to this we also add communications.

Multiple-Choice Questions

1. Which of the following devices converts computer output into displayed images?
   a. printer
   b. monitor
   c. floppy-disk drive
   d. processor
   e. hard-disk drive

2. Which of the following computer types is the smallest?
   a. mainframe
   b. microcomputer
   c. microcontroller
   d. supercomputer
   e. workstation

3. Which of the following is a secondary storage device?
   a. processor
   b. memory chip
   c. floppy-disk drive
   d. printer
   e. monitor

4. Since the days when computers were first made available, computers have developed in three directions. What are they?

   a. increased expense

   b. miniaturization

   c. increased size

   d. affordability

   e. increased speed

5. Which of the following operations constitute the four basic operations followed by all computers?

   a. input

   b. storage

   c. programming

   d. output

   e. processing

6. Supercomputers are used for:

   a. breaking codes

   b. simulations for explosions of nuclear bombs

   c. forecasting weather

   d. keeping planets in orbit

   e. all of the above

   f. only a, b, and c

7. What is the leading use of computers?

   a. web surfing

   b. email

   c. e-shopping

   d. word processing

8. Which is the main circuit board in the computer?

   a. RAM chip (random access memory)

   b. CPU processor chip (central processing unit)

   c. motherboard (system board)

   d. hard drive

True/False Questions

T F   1. Mainframe computers process faster than microcomputers.

T F   2. Main memory is a software component.

T F   3. The operating system is part of the system software.

T F   4. Processing is the manipulation by which a computer transforms data into information.

T F   5. Primary storage is the area in the computer where data or information is held permanently.

T F   6. The keyboard and the mouse are examples of input devices.

T F   7. The biological nanocomputer will use DNA as its software and enzymes as its hardware.

T F   8. Radio is a form of multimedia.

T F   9. Computers are becoming larger, slower, and more expensive.

 s t a g e **LEARNING**   COMPREHENSION

"I can recall information in my own terms and explain them to a friend."

Short-Answer Questions

1. What does *online* mean?

2. What is the difference between system software and application software?

3. Briefly define *cyberspace*.

4. What is the difference between software and hardware?

5. What is a local area network?

6. What is multimedia?

7. What is the difference between microcomputers and supercomputers?

8. What is the function of RAM?

 s t a g e **LEARNING**   APPLYING, ANALYZING, SYNTHESIZING, EVALUATING

"I can apply what I've learned, relate these ideas to other concepts, build on other knowledge, and use all these thinking skills to form a judgment."

Knowledge in Action

1. Do you wish there was an invention to make your life easier or better? Describe it. What would it do for you? Come up with ideas on how that device may be constructed.

2. Determine what types of computers are being used where you work or go to school. In which departments are the different types of computer used? What are they used for? How are they connected to other computers?

3. Imagine a business you could start or run at home. What type of business is it? What type of computer(s) do you think you'll need? Describe the computer system in as much detail as possible, including hardware components in the areas we have discussed so far. Keep your notes, and then refine your answers after you have completed the course.

4. Has reality become science fiction? Or has science fiction become science fact? Watch a recent science fiction movie, and list all the futuristic technology used.

Categorize according to the operations of input, output, processing, storage, or communications.

5. From what you've read and what you have experienced and/or observed in your life, do you have a positive, negative, or impartial outlook of our rapidly converging technological society? Why? Reevaluate your answers at the end of the course.

Web Exercises

If you are not yet familiar with web surfing, wait until you have finished Chapter 2 to do the following web exercises.

1. Are computers, cellphones, and other electronic devices bad for our health? You may have heard the term *electromagnetic radiation* and dismissed it as an obscure scientific term not worth understanding. Visit the links below to become educated on a topic that will be discussed more seriously and frequently when our society becomes completely wireless.

   www.nzine.co.nz/articles/Electromagnetic_Radiation/
   www.eos.ncsu.edu/eos/info/computer_ethics/social/ workplace/emr/study.html
   www.howstuffworks.com/cell-phone-radiation.htm

2. List the pros and cons of a paperless environment. Do you feel this challenge is something to strive for? Run a web search on what others are doing to implement this idea in their workplaces.

3. Computer pioneer John Von Neumann was one of a group of individuals who conceived the idea of the "stored program." He could also divide two 8-digit numbers in his head. Spend a few hours researching this remarkable man; look up some of the books he wrote at online bookstores and read the reviews. Also search these words: *Tesla, Einstein, Montauk, Bielek, Teller* (you will receive bizarre search results). Had you heard of John Von Neumann before reading this textbook?

4. Looking for legally free programs? Some great places to start:

   www.download.com
   www.shareware.com
   www.freeware.com

5. Visit the following websites to become aware of some topics of interest in the computing world. Full comprehension of these topics isn't necessary at this time; this is only to familiarize you with subject matter you may come in contact with.

   www.siliconvalley.com
   www.zdnet.com/eweek
   www.computeruser.com/
   www.computermarket.com/news/
   http://slashdot.org/

6. So you want to be a millionaire? Visit the web link below for various kinds of interactive calculators that can tell you how much you will need to earn and save to become a millionaire. The website has links that can also calculate other things such as how much you will need to save for retirement and how many tax exemptions you have.

   http://retireplan.about.com/library/weekly/aa_ calculators_a.htm

7. Is there an end to Pi (3.14)? Read the article at the page listed below to see how a Tokyo research team used a supercomputer to calculate Pi to 1.2411 trillion decimal places.

   http://pub39.ezboard.com/fhuntforplanetxfrm49. showMessage?topicID=59.topic
   www.newscom.au/common/story_page/ 0,4057,5638320%5E1702,00.html

8. Go to *www.nec.com/global/features/index9.html www.es.jamstec.go.jp/esc/eng* to see the Earth Simulator, the world's fastest supercomputer. You read in this chapter (p. 8) about some of the things this supercomputer is used for. What other uses are mentioned at this website?

Who's Online?

English language:
About 231 million (36.5% of total world online population)

Non-English language:
About 403.5 million (63.5%)

    Chinese—68.4 million (10.8%)

    Japanese—61.4 million (9.3%)

    Spanish—40.8 million (7.2%)

    German—42 million (6.6%)

    Korean—28.3 million (4.5%)

    French—22 million (3.5%)

    Italian—24 million (3.8%)

    Portuguese—19 million (3%)

    Dutch—12.4 million (2%)

    Arabic—5.5 million (.9%)

Of course, other language groups are also online, and the numbers increase daily.

Source: Global Reach, Global Internet Statistics, January 19, 2003, http://glreach.com/eng/ed/gre/index.php3; "Languages on the I-net."

chapter 2

The Internet & the World Wide Web

Exploring Cyberspace

Chapter Topics & Key Questions

2.1   Choosing Your Internet Access Device & Physical Connection: The Quest for Broadband What are the means of connecting to the internet, and how fast are they?

2.2   Choosing Your Internet Service Provider (ISP) What is an internet service provider, and what do ISPs provide?

2.3   Sending & Receiving Email What are the options for obtaining email software, what are the components of an email address, and what are netiquette and spam?

2.4   The World Wide Web What are websites, web pages, browsers, URLs, and search engines?

2.5   The Online Gold Mine: More Internet Resources What are FTP, Telnet, newsgroups, real-time chat, blogs, distance learning, and e-commerce?

The immensity of the changes wrought—and still to come—cannot be underestimated," says futurist Graham Molitor. "This miraculous information channel—the internet—will touch and alter virtually every facet of humanity, business, and all the rest of civilization's trappings."[1]

Today the world of the internet permits activities hardly imaginable 10 years ago. *(See ● Panel 2.1.)* In 10 more years, pervasive computing will be even more an established fact. By then we will have not only people-to-people connections with cellphones and pagers and wireless personal digital assistants (PDAs). We will also have "everything connected to everything"—for instance, internet-based remote control devices to regulate your home's climate, lighting, security, and home-entertainment systems, as well as your refrigerator and oven and other appliances—even, in fact, your car.[2]

Because of its standard interfaces and low rates, the internet has been the great leveler for communications—just as the personal computer was for computing. Starting in 1969 with four computers linked together by communications lines, the internet expanded to 62 computers in 1974, 500 computers in 1983, and 28,000 in 1987; but it still remained the domain of researchers and academics. Not until the development of the World Wide Web in the early 1990s, which made multimedia available on the internet, and the first browser, which opened the web to commercial uses, did the global network really take off. *(See ● Panel 2.2 starting on p. 40 for an abbreviated history.)* If, as some forecasters believe, in 2005 the internet reaches 1 billion users, that will be big enough, says Molitor, "to dub the virtual world of the internet as the eighth continent!"[3]

How can you become a "citizen of the world," as it were, in this network of networks? To access the internet, you need three things: (1) an *access device,* such as a personal computer with a modem; (2) a *physical connection,* such as a telephone line; and (3) an *internet service provider (ISP).* We cover these subjects in the next two sections. We then describe a little about how the internet works.

2.1 Choosing Your Internet Access Device & Physical Connection: The Quest for Broadband

KEY QUESTIONS
What are the means of connecting to the internet, and how fast are they?

In general terms, **_bandwidth_ is an expression of how much data—text, voice, video, and so on—can be sent through a communications channel in a given amount of time.** The type of data transmission that allows only one signal at a time is called *baseband transmission.* When several signals can be transmitted at once, it's called *broadband transmission.* Broadband includes various kinds of high-speed wired connections (such as coaxial and fiber-optic, described in Chapter 6), as well as DSL, cable, satellite and other wireless connections, discussed shortly. Such high-speed connections are becoming increasingly available to the home user.

A college dormitory wired with coaxial or fiber-optic cable for high-speed internet access will have more bandwidth than will a house out in the country served by conventional copper-wire telephone lines. As a result, access to information will be hundreds of times faster in this kind of dorm. Of course, many students are not privileged to have this kind of **_broadband—_ very high speed—connection.** But so significant is the difference that some students apparently are making decisions about college housing—even choice of college—based on the availability of high bandwidth. And those who are about to graduate wonder how they will ever survive in a narrow-bandwidth world.

Internet user

Internet service provider

**Email &
discussion groups**
Stay in touch worldwide
through electronic mail
and online chat rooms.

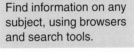

**Research &
information**
Find information on any
subject, using browsers
and search tools.

News
Stay current on politics,
weather, entertainment,
sports, and financial
news.

Entertainment
Amuse yourself with
internet games, music,
and videos.

Download files
Get software, music,
and documents such as
e-books.

E-shopping
Price anything from
plane tickets to cars;
order anything from
books to sofas.

Financial matters
Do investing, banking,
and bill paying online.

Auctions
Sell old stuff, acquire
more stuff, with online
auctions.

**Telephony &
conferencing**
Make inexpensive
phone calls; have online
meetings.

Career advancement
Search job listings, post
résumés, interview
online.

Distance learning
Attend online lectures,
have discussions,
research papers.

E-business
Connect with coworkers,
buy supplies, support
customers.

Let's assume that you have no access to a campus network. What are your choices of a *physical connection*—the wired or wireless means of connecting to the internet? A lot depends on where you live. As you might expect, urban and many suburban areas offer more broadband connections than rural areas do. Among the principal means of connection are (1) telephone (dial-up) modem; (2) several high-speed phone lines—ISDN, DSL, and T1; (3) cable modem; and (4) wireless—satellite and other through-the-air links.

Data is transmitted in characters or collections of bits. A *bit*, as we will discuss later, is the smallest unit of information used by computers. Today's data transmission speeds are measured in bits, kilobits, megabits, and giga-bits per second:

- **bps:** A computer with an older modem might have a speed of 28,800 bps, which is considered the minimum speed for visiting websites with graphics. The ***bps*** stands for ***bits per second***. (Eight bits equals one character.)

- **Kbps:** This is the most frequently used measure; _**kilobits per second,**_ or _**Kbps,**_ **are 1 thousand bits per second.** The speed of a modem that is 28,800 bps might be expressed as 28.8 Kbps.
- **Mbps:** Faster means of connection are measured in _**megabits per second,**_ **or _Mbps_—1 million bits per second.**
- **Gbps:** At the extreme are _**gigabits per second, Gbps**_—**1 billion bits per second.**

Why is it important to know these terms? Because the number of bits affects how fast you can upload and download information from a remote computer. _**Download**_ **is the transmission of data from a remote computer to a local computer,** as from a website to your own PC. _**Upload**_ **is the transmission of data from a local computer to a remote computer,** as from your PC to a website you are constructing.

Satellite

Mainframe Individual PC

Download
(reverse the direction of
data transmission to **upload**)

Telephone (Dial-Up) Modem: Low Speed but Inexpensive & Widely Available

The telephone line that you use for voice calls is still the cheapest means of online connection and is available everywhere. Today the majority of home users still use telephone modems to connect their computers to the internet. As we mentioned in Chapter 1, **a _modem_ is a device that sends and receives data over telephone lines to and from computers.** This type of modem uses a _dial-up connection._ These days, the modem is generally installed inside your computer, but there are also external modems. The modem is attached to the telephone wall outlet. _(See_ ● _Panel 2.3.)_ (We discuss modems in more detail in Chapter 6.)

Most standard modems today have a maximum speed of 56 Kbps. That doesn't mean that you'll be sending and receiving data at that rate. The modem in your computer must negotiate with the modems used by your internet service provider (ISP), the organization that connects you to the internet. Your ISP may have modems operating at slower speeds, such as 28.8 Kbps. In addition, lower-quality phone lines or heavy traffic during peak hours—such as 5 p.m. to 11 p.m. in residential areas—can slow down your rate of transmission.

One disadvantage of a telephone modem is that while you're online you can't use that phone line to make voice calls unless you've installed special equipment. In addition, people who try to call you while you're using the modem will get a busy signal. (Call waiting may interrupt an online con-

● PANEL 2.2
Abbreviated history of the internet

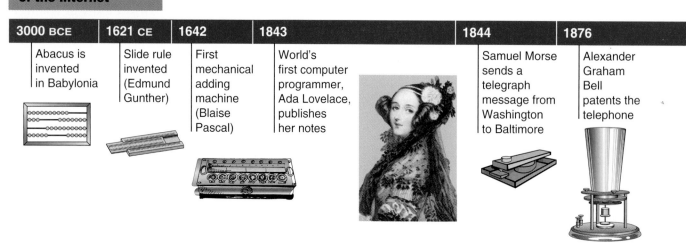

3000 BCE	1621 CE	1642	1843		1844	1876
Abacus is invented in Babylonia	Slide rule invented (Edmund Gunther)	First mechanical adding machine (Blaise Pascal)	World's first computer programmer, Ada Lovelace, publishes her notes		Samuel Morse sends a telegraph message from Washington to Baltimore	Alexander Graham Bell patents the telephone

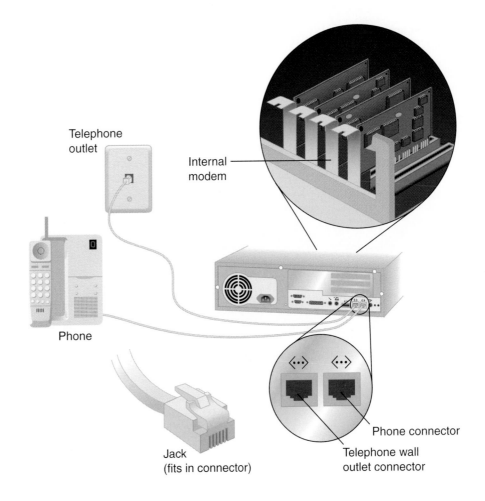

● **PANEL 2.3**

The modem connection
You connect the modem inside your computer from a port (socket) in the back of your computer to a line that is then connected to a wall jack. Your telephone is also connected to your computer so that you can make voice calls.

Telephone outlet

Internal modem

Phone

Jack (fits in connector)

Phone connector

Telephone wall outlet connector

nection, so you need to talk to your phone company about disabling it or purchase a new modem that can handle call waiting. The Windows operating system also has a feature for disabling call waiting.) You generally won't need to pay long-distance phone rates, since most ISPs offer local access numbers. The cost of a dial-up modem connection to the ISP is $10–$50 per month, plus a possible setup charge of $10–$25.

High-Speed Phone Lines: More Expensive but Available in Most Cities

Waiting while your computer's modem takes 25 minutes to transmit a 1-minute low-quality video from a website may have you pummeling the

1890	1895	1907	1927	1930	1944
Electricity used for first time in a data-processing project (punched cards)— Hollerith's automatic census-tabulating machine (used punched cards)	First radio signal transmitted	First regular radio broadcast from New York	First demonstration of television in USA	General theory of computers (MIT)	First electro-mechanical computer (Mark I)

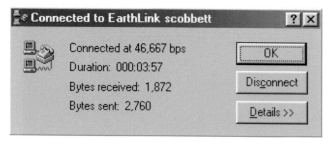

desk in frustration. To get some relief, you could enhance your POTS (for "plain old telephone system") connection with a high-speed adaptation. Among the choices are ISDN, DSL, and T1, available in most major cities, though not in rural and many suburban areas:

- **ISDN line:** ***ISDN (Integrated Services Digital Network)* consists of hardware and software that allow voice, video, and data to be communicated over traditional copper-wire telephone lines.** Capable of transmitting 64 to 128 Kbps, ISDN is able to send digital signals over POTS lines. If you were trying to download an approximately 6-minute-long music video from the World Wide Web, it would take you about 4 hours and 45 minutes with a 28.8-Kbps modem. A 128-Kbps ISDN connection would reduce this to an hour.

    Basically, ISDN is a viable solution for single users of small business networks when other high-speed options are not available. ISDN is not as fast as DSL, cable, or T1 and is expensive.

- **DSL line:** ***DSL (digital subscriber line)* uses regular phone lines, a DSL modem, and special technology to transmit data in megabits per second.** Incoming data is significantly faster than outgoing data. That is, your computer can *receive* data at the rate of 1.5–9 Mbps, but it can *send* data at only 64 Kbps–1.5 Mbps. This arrangement may be fine, however, if you're principally interested in obtaining very large amounts of data (video, music) rather than in sending such data to others. With DSL, you could download that 6-minute music video perhaps in only 11 minutes (compared to an hour with ISDN). A big advantage of DSL is that it is always on (so you don't have to make a dial-up connection) and, unlike cable (discussed shortly), its transmission rate is relatively consistent. Also, one can talk on the phone and send data at the same time.

    There is one big drawback to DSL: You have to live within 3.3 miles of a phone company central switching office, because the access speed and reliability degrade with distance. However, DSL is becoming more popular, and phone companies are building thousands of remote switching facilities to enhance service throughout their regions. Another drawback is that you have to choose from a list of internet service providers that are under contract to the phone company you use, although other DSL providers exist.

1945	1946	1957	1958	1969	1970
John von Neumann introduces the concept of a stored program	First programmable electronic computer in United States (ENIAC)	USSR launches Sputnik satellite; "space race" starts	Eisenhower administration creates the Advanced Research Projects Agency (ARPA) as part of the U.S. Department of Defense	ARPANet established at 4 U.S. universities (4 computers linked by leased lines); led to internet	Microprocessor chips come into use; floppy disk introduced for storing data; 15 ARPA-Net sites established (universities/ research), each with own address

Broadband: Riskier for Security

Unlike dial-up services, broadband services, because they are always switched on, make your computer vulnerable to over-the-internet security breaches. Solution: Install firewall software (Chapter 6).

- **T1 line:** How important is high speed to you? Is it worth $1,500 a month? Then consider getting a **_T1 line_, essentially a traditional trunk line that carries 24 normal telephone circuits and has a transmission rate of 1.5 Mbps.** Generally, T1 lines are leased by corporate, government, and academic sites. Another high-speed line, the T3 line, which transmits at 44 Mbps, costs $10,000 or more a month. Telephone companies and other types of companies are making even faster connections available: An STS-1 connection runs at 51 Mbps, and an STS-48 connection speeds data along at 2.5 Gbps (2.5 billion bits per second).

Cable Modem: Close Competitor to DSL

If DSL's 11 minutes to move a 6-minute video sounds good, 2 minutes sounds even better. That's the rate of transmission for cable modems, which can transmit outgoing data at about 1.4 Mbps and incoming data at up to 50 Mbps. **A _cable modem_ connects a personal computer to a cable-TV system that offers an internet connection.** Like a DSL connection, it is always on; unlike DSL, you don't need to live near a telephone switching station. A disadvantage, however, is that you and your cable-TV-viewing neighbors are sharing the system and consequently, during peak-load times, your service may be slowed to the speed of a regular dial-up modem. Also, using an internet connection that is always on—and that, in the case of cable, you share with other people—invites outside interference with your computer, a risk that we discuss later in the book.

Cable companies may contract you to use their own ISP, but more commonly you may choose your own. (Note that cable modems are for internet connections. They do not take the place of your voice phone system.)

Wireless Systems: Satellite & Other Through-the-Air Connections

You live in a rural area and you're tired of the molasses-like speed of your cranky local phone system. You might consider taking to the air.

- **Satellite:** With a pizza-size satellite dish on your roof, you can receive data at the rate of 256–400 Kbps from a **_communications satellite_, a space station that transmits radio waves called microwaves from earth-based stations.** Satellite internet connections are always on. To surf the internet using this kind of connection, you still need an ISP (that supports two-way satellite transmission), a browser, and email software. (We cover satellites in more detail in Chapter 6.)

1971	1973	1974	1975	1976	1976	1978
Email invented	ARPANet becomes international	TCP (Transmission Control Protocol) specification developed by U.S. Dept. of Defense	First microcomputer (MIT's Altair 8800)	Queen Elizabeth sends the first royal email	Apple I computer (first personal computer sold in assembled form)	TCP/IP developed (released in 1983) as standard internet transmission protocol

Sky connection. Setting up a satellite dish.

- **Other wireless connections:** In urban areas, some businesses are using radio waves transmitted between towers that handle cellular phone calls, which can send data at up to 155 Mbps (but commonly 10 Mbps) and are not only fast and dependable but also always on. The equipment costs from $200 to $2,500, and the operating cost is $159–$1,400 a month, depending on speed.

The table on the next page shows the transmission rates for various connections, as well as their approximate costs (always subject to change, of course) and their pros and cons. *(See ● Panel 2.4.)*

QuickCheck

What are the measures of data transmission speed?

What are some of the differences between these internet connections: dial-up modem, ISDN, DSL, cable modem T1, satellite?

What does *broadband* mean?

2.2 Choosing Your Internet Service Provider (ISP)

KEY QUESTIONS
What is an internet service provider, and what do ISPs provide?

Suppose you have an access device such as a modem and you've signed up for a wired or wireless connection. Next, unless you're already on a college campus network, you'll need to arrange for an **_internet service provider (ISP)_**, **a company that connects you through your communications line to its servers, or central (host) computer, which connect you to the internet via another company's network access points.** *(See ● Panel 2.5, p. 46.)* Some well-known national ISPs, also called *online services*, are America Online (AOL), EarthLink, Microsoft Network (MSN), and AT&T WorldNet. There are also many local, or regional, ISPs. The ISP's local access number for your area is its *point of presence (POP)*.

If you've decided simply to use the regular 56-Kbps dial-up modem in your PC connected to a plain old telephone line, you'll quickly notice the fierce competition between companies vying to become your ISP. For instance, perhaps your new PC comes with a keyboard button labeled "Internet," which, when pressed, begins the steps toward connecting you with a service provider—the provider that has come to a financial arrangement with the computer's manufacturer. You may also receive promotional ISP start-up disks in the mail. In addition, your phone company probably offers an internet service.

Once you have contacted an ISP and paid the required fee (charged to your credit card), the ISP will provide you with information about phone numbers for a local connection. The ISP will also provide you with communications

more info!

For comparison shopping, go online to *www.thelist.com*, which lists ISPs from all over the world and guides you through the process of finding one that's best for you. Which ISPs are available in your area?

1979	1981	1982	1984	1986	1989	1990
First Usenet newsgroups	IBM introduces personal computer	Portable computers	Apple Macintosh; first personal laser printer; William Gibson coins term "cyberspace"	NSFNET (National Science Foundation Network) backbone established	World Wide Web established by Tim Berners-Lee while working at the European Particle Physics Laboratory in Geneva, Switzerland	ARPANet decommissioned; first ISP comes online; Berners-Lee develops first web browser, WorldWideWeb

Service	Cost per Month (Plus Installation, Equipment)	Maximum Speed (Download Only)	Strengths	Weaknesses
Telephone (dial-up) modem	$0–$45	56 Kbps	Inexpensive, available everywhere	Slow; connection supports only a single user
ISDN	$40–$110 (+ $350–$700 installation cost)	64–128 Kbps (1.5 Mbps with special wiring)	Faster than dial-up; uses conventional phone lines	More expensive than dial-up; no longer extensively supported by telephone companies for individuals; used mostly by small businesses
DSL	$50–$300, depending on speed	1.5–9 Mbps	Fast download, on, higher security; uploads faster than cable; users can talk and transmit data at the same time	Needs to be close to phone company switching station; limited choice of service providers; supports only a single user
Cable modem	$40–$60 (+ $5 monthly for leased cable modem)	Up to 50 Mbps (2 Mbps common)	Fast, always on, most popular broadband type of connection; can support many users; downloads faster than DSL; users can talk on phone and transmit cable data at the same time	Slower service during high-traffic times, vulnerability to outside intrusion, limited choice of service providers; not always available to businesses
T1 line	$1,500 (+ $1,000 installation cost)	1.5 Mbps	Can support many users: 24 separate circuits of 64 Kbps each; reliable high speed downloading and uploading; users can talk and transmit data at the same time	Expensive, best for businesses
Satellite	Up to $70 (+ about $600 installation)	256–400 Kbps	Wireless, fast, reliable, always on; goes where DSL and cable can't; users can talk on phone and transmit satellite data at the same time	High set-up and monthly costs

● PANEL 2.4
Methods of going online compared

1992	1993	1994	1995	1996
"Surfing the internet" coined by Jean Armour Polly	Multimedia desktop computers; NAPs replace NSFNET; first graphical web browser, Mosaic, developed by Marc Andreesen	Apple and IBM introduce PCs with full-motion video built in; wireless data transmission for small portable computers; Netscape Navigator released	NSFNET reverts to research project; internet now in commercial hands	Microsoft releases Internet Explorer

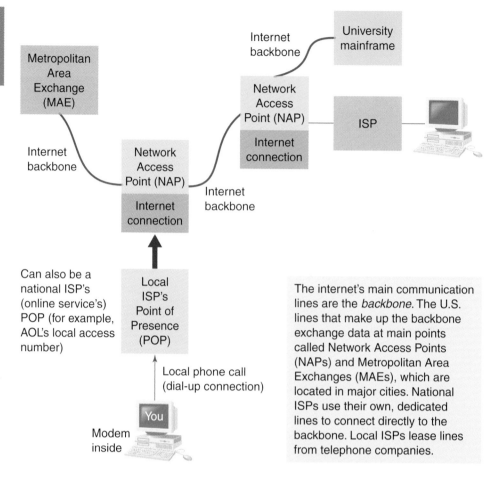

The internet's main communication lines are the *backbone*. The U.S. lines that make up the backbone exchange data at main points called Network Access Points (NAPs) and Metropolitan Area Exchanges (MAEs), which are located in major cities. National ISPs use their own, dedicated lines to connect directly to the backbone. Local ISPs lease lines from telephone companies.

info!
The Internet Traffic Report monitors the flow of data around the world. It displays values between 0 and 100 for many networks. Higher values indicate faster and more reliable connections. Check out your area at www.internettrafficreport.com.

software for setting up your computer and modem to dial into the provider's network of servers. For this you use your user name ("user ID") and your password, a secret word or string of characters that enables you to **_log on_, or make a connection to the remote computer.** The ISP will also help you establish your email address, which must be unique—that is, not the same as anyone else's.

QuickCheck

What is an internet service provider?

Describe the services internet providers offer.

2.3 Sending & Receiving Email

KEY QUESTIONS
What are the options for obtaining email software, what are the components of an email address, and what are netiquette and spam?

Once connected with an ISP, most people want to immediately join the millions of users who send and receive electronic mail. Your incoming email is stored in your mailbox on the ISP's computer, usually a server called a *mail server*. When you use your email software to retrieve your messages, the email is sent from the server to your computer.

Email Software & Carriers

Some people on special networks—such as students on campus networks—may not need to have their own ISP and email software. Otherwise, there are four alternatives for getting and sending email.

Hotmail offers free email services

- **Get an email program as part of other computer software:** As we mentioned, when you buy a new computer, it will probably include email software, perhaps as part of the software (called *browsers*) used to search the World Wide Web, such as Internet Explorer or Netscape Navigator. An example is Microsoft's Outlook Express, which is part of its Explorer.

- **Get email software as part of your ISP package:** Most internet service providers—such as AOL, EarthLink, and AT&T WorldNet—provide email software for their subscribers.

- **Get free email services:** These are available from a variety of sources, ranging from so-called *portals*, or internet gateways, such as Yahoo!, Excite, or Lycos, to cable TV channel CNN's website.

- **Buy email software:** Popular email software programs are Eudora, Outlook Express, and Lotus Notes. Simplified versions of email software may often be downloaded for free from creators' locations on the internet.

Email Addresses

You'll need an email address, of course, a sort of electronic mailbox used to send and receive messages. All such addresses follow the same approach: *user@domain.* (Email addresses are different from website addresses, which do not use the symbol @.) A ___domain___ **is simply a location on the internet.** Consider the following address:

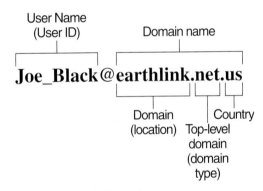

Let's look at the elements of this address.

Joe_Black The first section, the *user name, or user ID,* identifies who is at the address—in this case, *Joe_Black* (note the underscore). (There are many ways that Joe Black's user name might be designated, with and without capital letters: *Joe_Black, joe_black, joe.black, joeblack, jblack, joeb,* and so on.)

@earthlink The second section, the *domain name,* which is located after the @ (called "at") symbol, tells the location and type of address. Domain-name components are separated by periods (called "dots"). The domain portion of the address (such as *Earthlink,* an internet service provider) provides specific information about the location—where the message should be delivered.

.net The *top-level domain* is a three-letter extension that describes the domain type: *.net, .com, .gov, .edu, .org, .mil, .int*—network, commercial, government, educational, nonprofit, military, or international organization. *(See ● Panel 2.6.)*

.us Some domain names also include a two-letter extension for the country—for example, *.us* for United States, *.ca* for Canada, *.mx* for Mexico, *.uk* for United Kingdom, *.jp* for Japan, *.tr* for Turkey.

Sometimes you'll see an address in which people have their own domains—for example,

Some Internet Country Abbreviations

AD	Andorra	IT	Italy
AF	Afghanistan	MX	Mexico
BR	Brazil	NG	Nigeria
CA	Canada	PA	Panama
DE	Germany	PL	Poland
ES	Spain	SG	Singapore
FR	France	UK	United Kingdom
IL	Israel	ZW	Zimbabwe

Domain	Description	Example
.aero	air-transport industry	director@bigwings.aero
.biz	commercial businesses	manager@wearesuccessful.biz
.com		editor@mcgraw-hill.com
.coop	cooperatives	buyer@greatgroceries.coop
.edu	educational and research institutions	professor@stanford.edu
.gov	U.S. government agencies and bureaus	president@whitehouse.gov
.info	research institutions	contact@research.info
.int	international organizations	secretary_general@unitednations.int
.mil	U.S. military organizations	chief_of_staff@pentagon.mil
.museum	museums	curator@modernart.museum
.name	individuals	joe@smith.name
.net	internet network resources	contact@earthlink.net
.org	nonprofit and professional organizations	director@redcross.org

For a list of currently operating registrars, where you can register a top-level domain, go to *www.internic.com*. InterNIC is a registered service mark of the U.S. Department of Commerce. It is licensed to ICANN (Internet Corporation for Assigned Names and Numbers), which operates its website.

info! *more*

What do you think the country abbreviations are for Micronesia? Botswana? Saint Lucia? Go to *www. crayne.com/country.html* or *www.zetnet.co.uk/sigs/ search/country.html* and find out. Are countries listed that you've never heard of? Locate them on an internet map.

Survival Tip

Writing Email: Online or Offline?

You don't have to be online when composing your email messages. Email lets you write messages offline, so you can save them, then go online, and send them all at once.

Survival Tip

Accessing Email While Traveling Abroad

To access your email using a local call while traveling outside North America, get a free email account with Yahoo! (*http://billing.mail. yahoo.com/bm/MailReg?v=8*), MSN Hotmail (*www.hotmail. com*), or Mail.com (*www.mail.com*).

Joe@Black.com. However, you can't simply make up a domain name; it has to be registered. (You can check on whether an address is available, as well, and register it by going to *www.register.com* or *www.internic.net*.)

Incidentally, many people who are unhappy with their ISPs don't change because they don't want to have to notify their friends of a new email address. However, often you can switch ISPs and get a new email address, and then use an email forwarding service from your old address. That way, you can keep one email address no matter how many times you change providers.

Some tips about using email addresses:

- **Type addresses carefully:** You need to type the address *exactly* as it appears (except capitalization), including all underscores and periods. If you type an email address incorrectly (putting in spaces, for example), your message will be returned to you labeled "undeliverable."

- **Use the Reply command:** When responding to an e-message someone has sent you, the easiest way to avoid making address mistakes is to use the Reply command, which will automatically fill in the correct address in the "To" line. (*See* ● *Panel 2.7.*) Be careful not to use the Reply All command unless you want your reply to be sent to *all* the recipients of the original email.

- **Use the address-book feature:** You can store the email addresses of people sending you messages in your program's "address book." This feature also allows you to organize your email addresses according to a nickname or the person's real name so that, for instance, you can look up your friend Joe Black under his real name, instead of under his user name, *bugsme2*, which you might not remember. The address book also allows you to organize addresses into various groups—such as your friends, your relatives, club members—so you can easily send all members of a group the same message with a single command.

- **Deal with each email only once:** When a message comes in, delete it, respond to it, or file it away in a folder. Don't use your inbox for storage.

- **Don't "bloat" your email:** Email messages loaded with fancy type-styles, logos, and background graphics take longer to download. Keep messages simple.

Sending email

PANEL 2.7
Email functions

Address Book: Lists email addresses you use most; can be attached automatically to messages

Send: Command for sending messages

cc: For copying ("carbon/courtesy copy") message to others

bcc: For copying others ("blind carbon copy") without the primary recipient knowing it

Message area

You can conclude every message with a custom "signature"

Subject line: Preview incoming email by reviewing the subject lines to see if you really need to read the messages

Receiving email

Reply, Reply All, Forward, Delete: For helping you handle incoming email

Inbox lists messages waiting in email box. (Unopened envelope icon shows unread mail.)

New message displayed here

Replying to email

Use the **Reply** command icon, and the email program automatically fills in the To, From, and Subject lines in your reply.

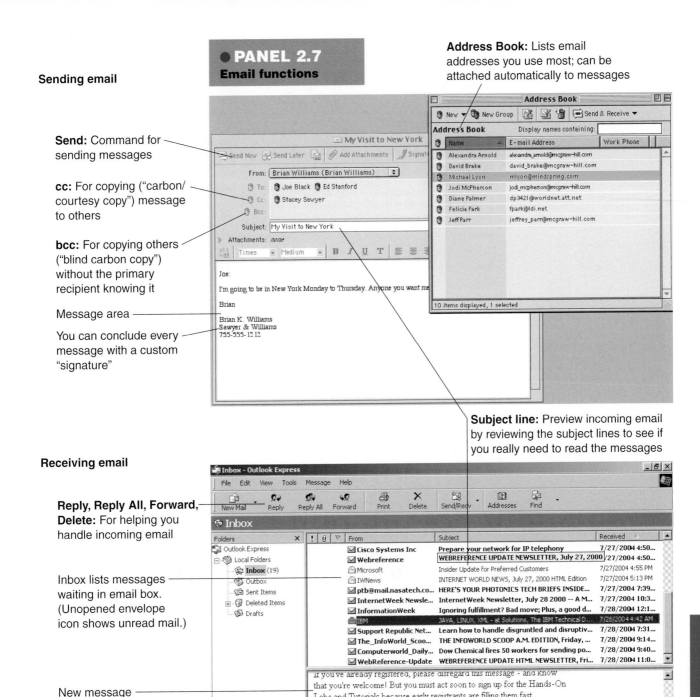

Attachments

You have written a great research paper and you immediately want to show it off to someone. If you were sending it via the Postal Service, you would write a cover note—"Folks, look at this great paper I wrote about globalization! See attached"—then attach it to the paper, and stick it in an envelope. Email has its own version of this. If the file of your paper exists in the computer from which you are sending email, you can write your email message (your cover note) and then use the Attach File command to attach the document. *(See ● Panel 2.8.)* Downloading attachments from the mail server can take a lot of time—so you may want to discourage friends from sending you many attachments. You may also want to use compression software to reduce the size of your attachments. (Compression is covered in Chapter 6.)

While you could also copy your document into the main message and send it that way, some email software loses formatting options such as **bold** or *italic* text or special symbols. And if you're sending song lyrics or poetry, the lines of text may break differently on someone else's display screen than they do on yours. Thus, the benefit of the attachment feature is that it preserves all such formatting, provided the recipient is using the same word processing software that you used. You can also attach pictures, sounds, videos, and other files to your email message.

Note: Many *viruses*—those rogue programs that can seriously damage your PC or programs—ride along with email as attached files. Thus, you should *never open an attached file from an unknown source.* (We describe viruses in Chapter 8.)

Instant Messaging

Some research groups estimate that there are 100 million instant-messaging users worldwide and that in 2004 the total will reach 180 million.[4] Instant messages are like a cross between email and phone, allowing for communication that is far speedier than conventional email. With ___instant messaging (IM)___, **any user on a given email system can send a message and have it pop up instantly on the screen of anyone else logged onto that system.** As soon as you use your computer or portable device to connect to the internet and log on to your IM account, you see a *buddy* list (or *contacts* list), a list you have created that consists of other IM users you want to communicate with. If all parties agree, they can initiate online typed conversations in real time (in a "chat room"). The messages appear on the display screen in a small ___window___—**a rectangular area containing a document or activity**—so that users can exchange messages almost instantaneously while operating other programs.

Examples of present instant-message systems are AOL Instant Messenger, MSN Messenger, ICQ ("I Seek You," also from AOL), AT&T IM Anywhere, and Yahoo! Messenger. Some of these, such as Yahoo!'s, allow voice chats among users, if their PCs have microphones and speakers.

To get instant messaging, which is often free, you download software and register with the service, providing it with a user name and password. When your computer or portable device is connected to the internet, the software checks in with a central server, which verifies your identity and looks to see if any of your "buddies" are also online. You can then start a conversation by sending a message to any buddy currently online.

IM has become a hit with many users. Instant messaging is especially useful in the workplace as a way of reducing long-distance telephone bills when you have to communicate with colleagues who are geographically remote but with whom you must work closely. However, you need to be aware of some drawbacks:

Sending an email attachment

③ Third, use your email software's toolbar buttons or menus to attach the file that contains the attachment.

④ Fourth, click on *Send* to send the email message and attachment.

① First, address the person who will receive the attachment.

② Second, write a "cover letter" email advising the recipient of the attachment.

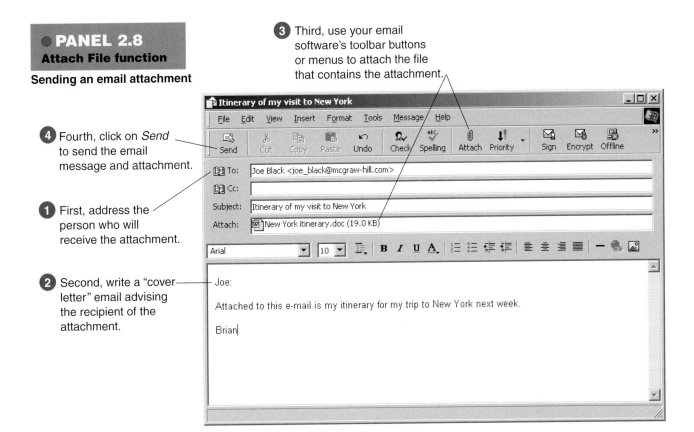

Receiving an email attachment

When you receive a file containing an attachment, you'll see an icon indicating the message contains more than just text. You can click on the icon to see the attachment. If you have the software the attached file was created in, you can open the attachment immediately to read or print, or you can save the attachment in a location of your choice (on your computer). You can also forward the attachment to another person.

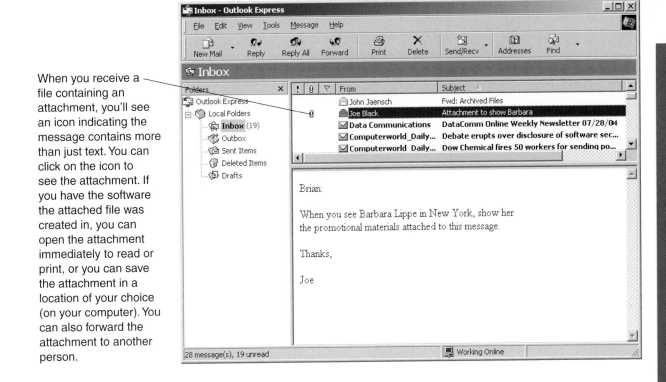

info!

For a list of IM services and products, go to *www.instantmessagingplanet .com*.

- **Lack of privacy:** Most IM services lack the basic privacy that most other forms of communication provide. Efforts are under way to develop IM security software and procedures, but for now IM users should be aware that they have virtually no privacy.

- **Lack of common standards:** Many IM products do not communicate with one another. If you're using AOL's IM, not only can you not communicate with a buddy on Yahoo!—you can't even communicate with a buddy on AOL's ICQ. Perhaps this will have changed by the time you read this. (AT&T IM Anywhere *does* support intrasystem compatibility.)

- **Time wasters when you have to get work done:** An instant message "is the equivalent of a ringing phone because it pops up on the recipient's screen right away," says one writer.[5] Some analysts suggest that, because of its speed, intrusiveness, and ability to show who else is online, IM can destroy workers' concentration in some offices. You can put off acknowledging email, voice mail, or faxes. But instant messaging is "the cyber-equivalent of someone walking into your office and starting up a conversation as if you had nothing better to do," says one critic. "It violates the basic courtesy of not shoving yourself into other people's faces."[6]

  You can turn off your instant messages, but that is like turning off the ringer on your phone; after a while people will wonder why you're never available. Buddy lists or other contact lists can also become very in-groupish. When that happens, people are distracted from their work as they worry about staying current with their circle (or being shut out of one). Some companies have reportedly put an end to instant messaging, sending everyone back to the use of conventional email.

info!

A directory of mailing lists is available at *www.w3org/Mail/ Lists.html* and *www.lsoft .com/catalist.html*. Which ones are you interested in?

Mailing Lists: Email-Based Discussion Groups

Want to receive email from people all over the world who share your interests? You can try finding a mailing list and then "subscribing"—signing up, just as you would for a free newsletter or magazine. **A _listserv_ is an automatic mailing-list server that sends email to subscribers who regularly participate in discussion topics.** Listserv companies include L-Soft's Listserv (*www.lsoft.com*), Majordomo, and Bitnet's Listproc. To subscribe, you send an email to the list-server moderator and ask to become a member, after which you will automatically receive email messages from anyone who responds to the server.

Netiquette: Appropriate Online Behavior

You may think etiquette is about knowing which fork to use at a formal dinner. Basically, though, etiquette has to do with politeness and civility—with rules for getting along so that people don't get upset or suffer hurt feelings.

New internet users, known as "newbies," may accidentally offend other people in a discussion group or in an email simply because they are unaware of **_netiquette_, or "network etiquette"—appropriate online behavior.** In general, netiquette has two basic rules: (a) don't waste people's time, and (b) don't say anything to a person online that you wouldn't say to his or her face.

Some more specific rules of netiquette are as follows:

- **Consult FAQs:** Most online groups post **_FAQs (frequently asked questions)_ that explain expected norms of online behavior for a particular group.** Always read these first—before someone in the group tells you you've made a mistake.

- **Avoid flaming:** A form of speech unique to online communication, _**flaming**_ **is writing an online message that uses derogatory, obscene, or inappropriate language.** Flaming is a form of public humiliation inflicted on people who have failed to read FAQs or have otherwise not observed netiquette (although it can happen just because the sender has poor impulse control and needs a course in anger management). Something that smoothes communication online is the use of _**emoticons**_, **keyboard-produced pictorial representations of expressions.** (See ● _Panel 2.9._)

- **Don't SHOUT:** Use of all-capital letters is considered the equivalent of SHOUTING. Avoid, except when they are required for emphasis of a word or two (as when you can't use italics in your e-messages).

- **Be careful with jokes:** In email, subtleties are often lost, so jokes may be taken as insults or criticism.

- **Avoid sloppiness, but avoid criticizing others' sloppiness:** Avoid spelling and grammatical errors. But don't criticize those same errors in others' messages. (After all, they may not speak English as a native language.) Most email software comes with spell-checking capability, which is easy to use.

- **Don't send huge file attachments, unless requested:** Your cousin living in the country may find it takes many minutes rather than seconds for his or her computer to download a massive file (as of a video that you want to share). This may tie up the system at a time when your relative badly needs to use it. Also, most email programs can be set to refuse emails larger than a designated size—say, 1 megabyte. Better to query in advance before sending large files as attachments. Also, whenever you send an attachment, be sure the recipient has the appropriate software to open your attachment (you both are using Microsoft Word 2000, for example).

- **When replying, quote only the relevant portion:** If you're replying to just a couple of matters in a long email posting, don't send back the entire message. This forces your recipient to wade through lots of text to find the reference. Instead, edit his or her original text down to the relevant paragraph and then put in your response immediately following.

- **Don't "overforward":** Don't automatically forward emails to your friends without checking if the contents are true and appropriate.

Sorting Your Email

On an average day, billions of business and personal emails are sent in North America. If, as many people do, you receive 50–150 emails per day, you'll have to keep them organized, so that you don't lose control.

One way to stay organized is by using instant organizers, also called _filters_, which sort mail on the basis of the name of the sender or the mailing list and put particular emails into one folder. Then you can read emails sent to this folder later when you have time, freeing up your inbox for mail that needs your more immediate attention. Instructions on how to set up such organizers are in your email program's Help section.

Sorting email: Email folders

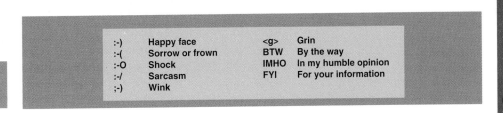

:-)	Happy face	<g>	Grin
:-(	Sorrow or frown	BTW	By the way
:-O	Shock	IMHO	In my humble opinion
:-/	Sarcasm	FYI	For your information
;-)	Wink		

The Internet & the World Wide Web

Spam: Unwanted Junk Email

Several years ago, Monty Python, the British comedy group, did a sketch in which restaurant customers were unable to converse because people in the background (a group of Vikings, actually) kept chanting "Spam, spam, eggs and spam . . ." The term *spam* was picked up by the computer world to describe another kind of "noise" that interferes with communication. Now **_spam_ refers to unsolicited email, or junk mail, in the form of advertising or chain letters.** Usually you won't recognize the sender on your list of incoming mail, and often the subject line will give no hint, stating something such as "The status of your application" or "It's up to you now." The solicitations can range from money-making schemes to online pornography. Spam has become so pestiferous that *Smart Computing* magazine refers to it as a "cockroach infestation."[7] *ZDNet* reports that spam now accounts for 40% of all email.[8] So annoying is spam that the members of the European Union have voted to outlaw bulk email, which includes spam.

Some ways to deal with this nuisance are as follows:

- **Delete without opening the message:** Opening the spam message can actually send a signal to the spammer that someone has looked at the onscreen message and therefore that the email address is valid—which means you'll probably get more spams in the future. If you don't recognize the name on your inbox directory or the topic on the inbox subject line, you can simply delete the message without reading it. Or you can use a preview feature in your email program to look at the message without actually opening it; then delete it. (Hint: Be sure to get rid of all the deleted messages from time to time; otherwise, they will build up in your "trash" area.)

- **Never reply to a spam message:** The following advice needs to be taken seriously: *Never reply in any way to a spam message!* Replying confirms to the spammer that yours is an active email address. Some spam senders will tell you that if you want to be removed from their mailing list, you should type the word *remove* or *unsubscribe* in the subject line and use the Reply command to send the message back. Invariably, however, all this does is confirm to the spammer that your address is valid, setting you up to receive more unsolicited messages.

- **Enlist the help of your ISP or use spam filters:** Your ISP may offer a free spam filter (for example, EarthLink's Spaminator and Hotmail's Brightmail) to stop the stuff before you even see it. If it doesn't, you can sign up for a filtering service, such as ImagiNet (*www.imagin.net*) for a small monthly charge. Or there are do-it-yourself spam-stopping programs. Examples: Choicemail (*www.digportal.com*), Junk Spy (*www.junkspy.com*), and McAffee Spamkiller (*www.mcaffee.com*). More complicated spam-blocker packages exist for businesses.

  Be warned, however: Even so-called spam killers don't always work. "Nothing will work 100%, short of changing your email address," says the operator of an online service called SpamCop. "No matter how well you try to filter a spammer, they're always working to defeat the filter."[9]

- **Fight back:** If you want to get back at spammers—and other internet abusers—check with abuse.net (*www.abuse.net*) or Ed Falk's Spam Tracking Page (*www.rahul.net/falk*). Spamhaus (*www.spamhaus.org*) tracks the internet's worst spammers and works with ISPs and law enforcement agencies to identify and remove persistent spammers from the internet. It also provides a free database of IP addresses of verified spammers. These groups will tell you where to report spammers, the appropriate people to complain to, and other spam-fighting tips.

What About Keeping Email Private?

SECURITY

The single best piece of advice that can be given about sending email is this: *Pretend every electronic message is a postcard that can be read by anyone.* Because the chances are high that it could be. (And this includes email on college campus systems as well.)

Think the boss can't snoop on your email at work? The law allows employers to "intercept" employee communications if one of the parties involved agrees to the "interception." The party "involved" is the employer. And in the workplace, email is typically saved on a server, at least for a while. Indeed, federal laws require that employers keep some email messages for years.

Think you can keep your email address a secret among your friends? You have no control over whether they might send your e-messages on to someone else—who might in turn forward it again. (One thing you can do for them, however, is delete their names and addresses before sending one of their messages on to someone.)

Think your ISP will protect your privacy? Often service providers post your address publicly or even sell their customer lists.

Think spammers can't find you? They will if you post an email to an internet message or bulletin board, making yourself a target for pieces of software (known as "harvester bots") that scour such boards for active email addresses.

And we have not even mentioned your email being intercepted by those knowledgeable individuals known as *hackers* or *crackers*, which we discuss elsewhere.

If you're really concerned about preserving your privacy, you can try certain technical solutions—for instance, installing software that encodes and decodes messages (discussed in Chapter 8). But the simplest solution is the easiest: Don't put any sensitive or embarrassing information in your email. Even deleted email removed from trash can still be traced on your hard disk. Software—for example, Spytech Eradicator and Webroot's Window Washer— is available to completely eliminate deleted files. (Be aware, however: your email may already have been backed up on the company—or campus— server.)

QuickCheck

What are the options for getting and sending email?

What are some features available with email?

What are attachments, and why are they useful?

What is listserv?

What is spam, and what can you do about it?

2.4 The World Wide Web

KEY QUESTIONS
What are websites, web pages, browsers, URLs, and search engines?

After email, visiting sites ("surfing") on the World Wide Web is the most popular use of the internet. Among the forces driving its popularity are entertainment and e-commerce. *Entertainment* offerings range from listening to music to creating your own, from playing online games by yourself to playing with others, from checking out local restaurants to researching overseas travel. *E-commerce* offers online auctions, retail stores, and discount travel services as well as all kinds of "B2B," or business-to-business, connections, as when General Motors buys online from its steel suppliers.

Recall that the internet and the World Wide Web are not the same thing. The internet is a massive network of networks, connecting millions of computers via protocols, hardware, and communications channels. The web is a means of accessing information available on the internet using software called a *browser.*

What makes the web so graphically inviting and easily navigable is that the international collection of servers that support the web (1) stores information in multimedia form and (2) is connected by hypertext links, or hyperlinks:

1. *Multimedia form—what makes the web graphically inviting:* Whereas email messages are generally text, the web provides information in multimedia form—graphics, video, and audio as well as text. You can see color pictures, animation, and full-motion video. You can download music. You can listen to radio broadcasts. You can have telephone conversations with others.

2. *Use of hypertext—what makes the web easily navigable:* Whereas with email you can connect only with specific addresses you know about, with the web you have hypertext. **<u>Hypertext</u> is a system in which documents scattered across many internet sites are directly linked—with *hyperlinks*—so that a word or phrase in one document becomes a connection to a document in a different place.**

The format used on the web is called *hypertext markup language.* (It is not, however, a programming language.) **<u>Hypertext markup language (HTML)</u> is the set of special instructions (called "tags" or "markups") that are used to specify document structure, formatting, and links to other multimedia documents.** *(See ● Panel 2.10.)*

For example, if you were reading this book onscreen, you could use your mouse to click on the word *hypertext*—which would be highlighted—in the preceding paragraph, and that would lead you to another location, where perhaps *hypertext* is defined. Then you could click on a word in that definition, and that would lead you to some related words—or even some pictures.

The result is that one term or phrase will lead to another, and so you can access all kinds of databases and libraries all over the world. Among the droplets in what amounts to a Niagara Falls of information available: *Weather maps and forecasts. Guitar chords. Recipe archives. Sports schedules. Daily newspapers in all kinds of languages. Nielsen television ratings. A ZIP code guide. Works of literature. And on and on.*

The Web & How It Works

If Rip Van Winkle fell asleep in 1989 (the year computer scientist Tim Berners-Lee developed the web software) and awoke today, he would be completely baffled by the new vocabulary that we now encounter on an almost daily basis: *website, home page, www.* Let's see how we would explain to him what these and similar web terms mean.

Web inventor. Tim Berners-Lee.

- **Website—the domain on the computer:** You'll recall we described top-level domains, such as .com, .edu, .org, and .net, in our discussion of email addresses. **A computer with a domain name is called a <u>website</u> (site).** When you decide to buy books online at bookseller Barnes & Noble, you would visit its website *www.barnesandnoble.com;* the website is the location of a web domain name in a computer somewhere on the internet. That computer might be located in Barnes & Noble offices, but it might be located somewhere else entirely. (The website for New Mexico's Carlsbad Caverns is not located underground in the caverns, but the website for your college is probably on the campus.)

In HTML, every command is surrounded by < and >. And in most commands, you need to tell the web browser when to end this command. You do this by putting a back slash (/) in front of the ending command, as shown below. Since HTML isn't case sensitive, <title> is the same as <TITLE>, which is the same as <TiTLe>. Next, you need to decide what you want to put on your page. Text, links, graphics, and text fields are just a few ideas. Following are examples of what to put on your page.

TITLE

The first thing to put on your web page is a title. The title is what will show up in the very top of the window. Let's say that your title is going to be "John Doe's Web Page." Type:

< title>John Doe's Web Page</title>

HEADINGS

HTML has six levels of headings, numbered 1 through 6, with 1 being the largest. Headings are displayed in larger or smaller typestyles, and usually bolder. If you want to type "Hello," this is what you would type for each heading and what the outcome would be.

<H1>Hello</H1>   <H2>Hello</H2>

Hello   ## Hello

<H3>Hello</H3>   <H4>Hello</H4>

Hello   #### Hello

<H5>Hello</H5>   <H6>Hello</H6>

Hello   ###### Hello

PARAGRAPHS

To make a paragraph of "This is a web page. How do you like what I've done? Please email me with any suggestions at a@a.com," type:

<P>This is a web page. How do you like what I've done? Please email me with any suggestions at a@a.com</P>

The outcome is

This is a web page. How do you like what I've done? Please email me with any suggestions at a@a.com

LISTS

There are two types of lists that you can make in HTML, dotted (bulleted) and numbered. To make a dotted list of: red, orange, green, blue, purple, black, and brown, type:

<UL>	The result is	• **red**
<LI>red		• **orange**
<LI>orange		• **green**
<LI>green		• **blue**
<LI>blue		• **purple**
<LI>purple		• **black**
<LI>black		• **brown**
<LI>brown		
</UL>		

To make a numbered list of red, orange, green, blue, purple, black, and brown, type:

<OL>	The result is	1. **red**
<LI>red		2. **orange**
<LI>orange		3. **green**
<LI>green		4. **blue**
<LI>blue		5. **purple**
<LI>purple		6. **black**
<LI>black		7. **brown**
<LI>brown		
</OL>		

CHARACTER FORMATTING

You may want to format some of your text differently than others using text styles. There are several types of styles of text that you can use: **bold**, *italic*, <u>underline</u>, ~~strikeout~~, superscript, subscript, teletype, and blinking text are examples. To do these styles, surround your text with the following commands:

<B>, </B> for **bold**   [,] for superscript

<I>, </I> for *italic*   _, for subscript

<U>, </U> for <u>underlined</u>   <TT>, </TT> for teletype

<STRIKE>, </STRIKE> for ~~strikeout~~

<BLINK>, </BLINK> for blinking text (very annoying)

~~You can also mix styles together like this!~~

LINKING WEB ADDRESSES

When you make a link, you are making colored text or even a graphic. When somebody clicks on this text, it will take them to another web page, or possibly a certain section of a web page. Let's say that you wanted to make a link from your web page to Yahoo!. The web address of Yahoo! is http://www.yahoo.com

Type:

<A HREF="http://www.yahoo.com">Whatever text that you want to be colored goes here</A>

The result:

Whatever text that you want to be colored goes here

Source: www.make-a-web-site.com/making1.html; May 16, 2003.

● PANEL 2.10
How HTML works

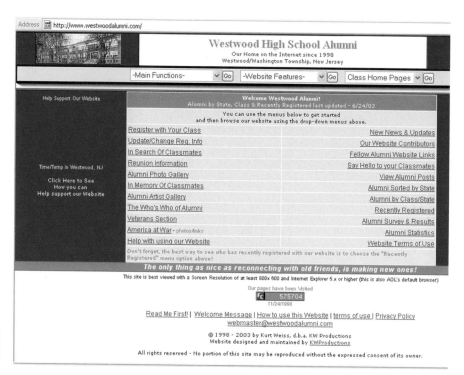

Graphical browser inventor:
In the early 1990s, Marc Andreesen was a student and an assistant at the National Center for Supercomputing Applications at the University of Illinois when the World Wide Web began to take off. His work allowed him to become very familiar with the internet and with the web. The software used to get aound the internet and the web was not user-friendly, so Marc and his friend Eric Bina developed the first graphical browser, called Mosaic, which was released in 1993. Mosaic was the predecessor of Netscape.

- **Web pages—the documents on a website:** A website is composed of a web page or collection of related web pages. **A _web page_ is a document on the World Wide Web that can include text, pictures, sound, and video.** The first page you see at a website is like the title page of a book. This is the **_home page_, or welcome page, which identifies the website and contains links to other pages at the site.** *(See ● Panel 2.11.)* If you have your own personal website, it might consist of just one page—the home page. Large websites have scores or even hundreds of pages. (Note: The contents of home pages often change. Or they may disappear, and so the connecting links to them in other web pages become links to nowhere.)

- **Browsers—software for connecting with websites:** A **_web browser_, or simply _browser_, is software that enables users to locate and view web pages and to jump from one page to another.** It's what you use to get around the web. The two best-known browsers are Microsoft Internet Explorer, more commonly used, and Netscape Navigator, once the leader but now used by fewer people. *(See ● Panel 2.12.)* When you connect to a particular website with your browser, the first thing you will see is the home page. Then, using your mouse, you can move from one page to another by clicking on hypertext links.

- **URLs—addresses for web pages:** Before your browser can connect with a website, it needs to know the site's address, the URL. **The _URL (Uniform Resource Locator)_ is a string of characters that points to a specific piece of information anywhere on the web.** In other words, the URL is the website's unique address. A URL consists of (1) the web *protocol*, (2) the name of the web *server*, (3) the *directory* (or folder) on that server, and (4) the *file* within that directory (perhaps with an *extension* such as *html* or *htm*).

  Consider the following example of a URL for a website offered by the National Park Service for Yosemite National Park:

Netscape/Explorer home pages
These screens show opening pages for
the Netscape browser *(top)* and Microsoft Internet Explorer *(bottom)*.

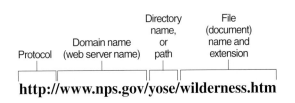

Protocol   Domain name (web server name)   Directory name, or path   File (document) name and extension

http://www.nps.gov/yose/wilderness.htm

Let's look at these elements.

http:// A *protocol* **is a set of communications rules for exchanging information.** It allows web browsers to communicate with web servers. When you see the *http://* at the beginning of some web addresses (as in *http://www.mcgraw-hill.com*), that stands for *Hyper-Text Transfer Protocol (HTTP)*, **the communications rules that allow browsers to connect with web servers.** Note: Most browsers assume that all web addresses begin with *http://*, and so you don't need to type this part; just start with whatever follows, such as *www*.

www.nps.gov/ The *web server* is the particular computer on which this website is located. The *www* stands for "World Wide Web," of course; the *.nps* stands for "National Park Service," and *.gov* is the top-level domain name indicating that this is a government website. The server might be physically located in Yosemite National Park in California; in the Park Service's headquarters in Washington, D.C.; or somewhere else entirely.

yose/ The *directory* name is the name on the server for the direc- tory, or folder, from which your browser needs to pull the file. Here it is *yose* for "Yosemite." For Yellowstone National Park, it is *yell*.

wilderness.htm The *file* is the particular page or document that you are seeking. Here it is *wilderness.htm*, because you have gone to a web page about Yosemite's hiking and camping facilities. The *.htm* is an extension to the file name, and this extension informs the browser that the file is an HTML file.

A URL, you may have observed, is not the same thing as an email address. Some people might type in *president@whitehouse.gov.us* and expect to get a website, but that won't happen. The website for the White House (which includes presidential information, history, a tour, and a guide to federal services) is *www.whitehouse.gov.*

Note: Be careful about information found on the web. To find out who is running a site, go to *www.internic.net* and use the *Registry Whois* link to search the database of registered domain names. Just because information is posted on the web does not mean that it is true.

Using Your Browser to Get Around the Web

The World Wide Web consists of more than 1 billion web pages. Moreover, the web is constantly changing; more sites are created and old ones are retired. Without a browser and various kinds of search tools, there would be no way any of us could begin to make any kind of sense of this enormous amount of data.

As we mentioned, a web page may include *hyperlinks*—words and phrases that appear as underlined or color text—that are references to other web pages. On a home page, for instance, the hyperlinks serve to connect the top page with other pages throughout the website. Other hyperlinks will connect to pages on other websites, whether located on a computer next door or one on the other side of the world.

If you buy a new computer, it will come with a browser already installed. Most browsers have a similar look and feel. Note that the web browser screen has five basic elements: *menu bar, toolbar, URL bar, workspace,* and *status bar.* To execute menu-bar and toolbar commands, you use the mouse to move the pointer over the word, known as a *menu selection,* and click the left button of the mouse. This will result in a *pull-down menu* of other commands for other options. (See ● *Panel 2.13.*)

● **PANEL 2.13**
The commands on a browser screen

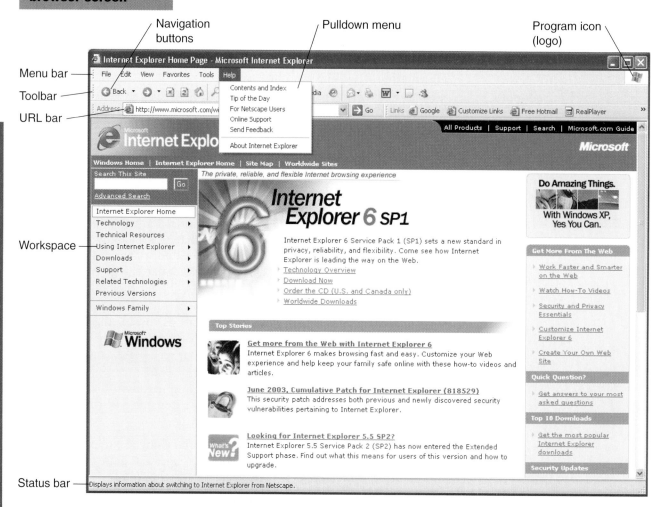

Chapter 2

Survival Tip

Don't Be Traced

In Windows 95 and 98, the graphics and sound files for many websites are stored on your computer, on your hard disk in a folder called *Cache* that's associated with your browser. Don't want other users of your computer to know where you've been on the web? Then put all the cached items in the trash and empty the trash bin. (The Cache folder is inside the browser folder—for example, the Netscape folder—in the Program Files folder.)

After you've been using a mouse for a while, you may find moving the pointer around somewhat time-consuming. As a shortcut, if you click on the right mouse button, you can reach many of the commands on the toolbar (*Back, Forward,* and so on) via a pop-up menu.

- **Starting out from home:** The first page you see when you start up your browser is the *home page* or *start page.* (You can also start up from just a blank page, if you don't want to wait for the time it takes to connect with a home page.) You can choose any page on the web as your start page, but a good start page offers links to sites you want to visit frequently. Often you may find that the ISP with which you arrange your internet connection will provide its own start page. However, you'll no doubt be able to customize it to make it your own personal home page.

- **Personalizing your home page:** Want to see the weather forecast for your college and/or hometown areas when you first log on? Or your horoscope, "message of the day," or the day's news (general, sports, financial, health, and so on)? Or the websites you visit most frequently? Or a reminder page (as for deadlines or people's birthdays)? You can probably personalize your home page following the directions provided with the first start page you encounter. Or if you have an older Microsoft or Netscape browser, you can get a customizing system from either company. A customized start page is also provided by Yahoo!, Google, AltaVista, and similar services.

- **Getting around—Back, Forward, Home, and Search features:** Driving in a foreign city (or even Boston or San Francisco) can be an interesting experience in which street names change, turns lead into unknown neighborhoods, and signs aren't always evident, so that soon you have no idea where you are. That's what the internet is like, although on a far more massive scale. Fortunately, unlike being lost in Rome, here your browser toolbar provides navigational aids. *(See Panel 2.14.) Back* takes you back to the previous page. *Forward* lets you look again at a page you returned from. If you really get lost, you can start over by clicking on *Home,* which returns you to your home page. *Search* lists various other search tools, as we will describe. Other navigational aides are history lists and bookmarks.

● PANEL 2.14
Back, Forward, Home, Search

Menu bar

Back: Moves you to a previous page or site

Forward: Lets you revisit a page you have just returned from

Stop: You can halt any ongoing transfer of page information

Refresh: If page you are loading is garbled or stalled in transmission, this will retrieve it again

Home: To return to your start page

Search: Displays page containing a directory of search engine sites

Favorites: List of sites can be created so you can quickly jump to the ones used frequently (also called bookmarks)

History: Names and descriptions of sites most recently visited

Print: To print a page, click on this button

Logo: Technical support and free copies of the web browser

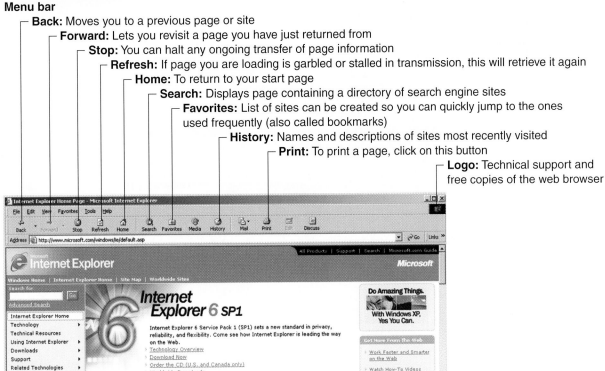

The Internet & the World Wide Web

History List

If you want to return to a previously viewed site and are using Netscape, you click on *Communicator*, then choose *History* from the menu. If you're using Internet Explorer, click on *History*.

History

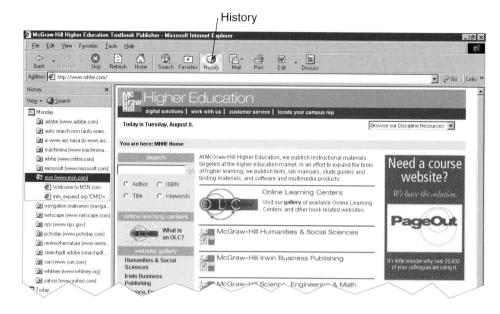

- **History lists:** If you are browsing through many web pages, it can be difficult to keep track of the locations of the pages you've already visited. The *history list* allows you to quickly return to the pages you have recently visited. *(See ● Panel 2.15.)*
- **Bookmarks or favorites:** One great helper for finding your way is the bookmark or favorites system, which lets you store the URLs of web pages you frequently visit so that you don't have to remember and retype your favorite addresses. *(See ● Panel 2.16.)* Say you're visiting a site that you really like and that you know you'd like to come back to. You click on your *Bookmark* or *Favorites* feature, which displays the URL on your screen, and then click on *Add*, which automatically

Adding Bookmarks (Favorites)

If you are at a website you may want to visit again, you click on your *Bookmarks* (in Netscape) or *Favorites* (in Internet Explorer) button and choose *Add Bookmark* or *Add to Favorites.* Later, to revisit the site, you can go to the bookmark menu, and the site will reappear.

Favorites

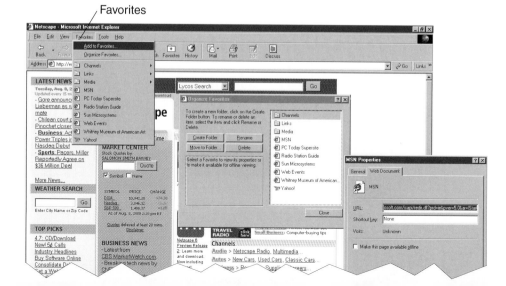

stores the address. Later you can locate the site name on your book-mark menu, click on it, and the site will reappear. (When you want to delete it, you can use the right mouse button and select the Delete command.)

- **Interactivity—hyperlinks, radio buttons, and fill-in text boxes:** For any given web page that you happen to find yourself on, there may be one of three possible ways to interact with it—or sometimes even all three on the same page. *(See ● Panel 2.17.)*

    1. By using your mouse to click on the hyperlinks, which will transfer you to another web page.

● **PANEL 2.17**
Hyperlinks, radio buttons, text box

Hyperlinks
Clicking on underlined or color term transfers you to another web page.

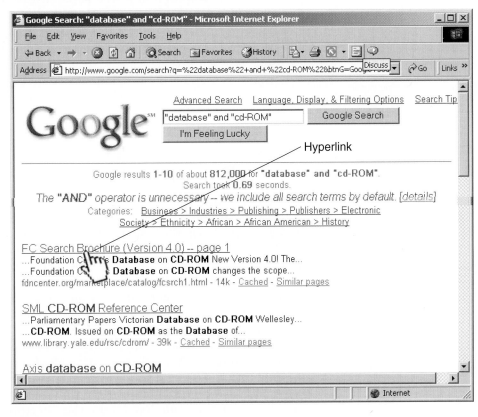

Radio buttons
Act like station selector buttons on a car radio

Text boxes
Require you to type in information

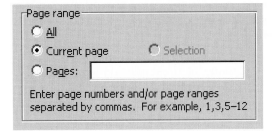

info!

If you refuse cookies? Read the article at *http://computer.howstuffworks.com/cookie.htm.*

2. By using your mouse to click on a *radio button* and then clicking on a *Submit* command or pressing the Enter key. **_Radio buttons_ are little circles located in front of various options; selecting an option with the mouse places a dot in the corresponding circle.**

3. By typing text in a fill-in text box, and then hitting the Enter key or clicking on a *Go* or *Continue* command, which will transfer you to another web page.

- **Scrolling and frames:** To the bottom and side of your screen display, you will note **_scroll arrows_, small up/down and left/right arrows. Clicking on scroll arrows with your mouse pointer moves the screen so that you can see the rest of the web page, a movement known as _scrolling_.** You can also use the arrow keys on your keyboard for scrolling.

  Some web pages are divided into different rectangles known as *frames*, each with its own scroll arrows. **A _frame_ is an independently controllable section of a web page.** A web page designer can divide a page into separate frames, each with different features or options.

- **Looking at two pages simultaneously:** If you want to look at more than one web page at the same time, you can position them side by side on your display screen. Select *New* from your File menu to open more than one browser window.

Web Portals: Starting Points for Finding Information

Using a browser is sort of like exploring an enormous cave with flashlight and string. You point your flashlight at something, go there, and at that location you can see another cave chamber to go to; meanwhile, you're unrolling the ball of string behind you, so that you can find your way back.

But what if you want to visit only the most spectacular rock formations in the cave and skip the rest? For that you need a guidebook. There are many such "guidebooks" for finding information on the web, sort of internet superstations known as *web portals*. **A _web portal_ is a type of gateway website that offers a broad array of resources and services, online shopping malls, email support, current news and weather, stock quotes, travel information, and links to other popular subject categories.** Portals can be customized or personalized to fit your interests. The most popular portals are America Online, Yahoo!, Microsoft Network, Google, Netscape, Lycos, Go Network, Infoseek, Snap, Excite Network, AltaVista, and WebCrawler. *(See* ● *Panel 2.18.)*

When you log on to a portal, you can do three things: (1) check the home page for general information, (2) use the directories to find a topic you want, and (3) use a keyword to search for a topic.

- **Check the home page for general information:** You can treat a portal's home or start page as you would a newspaper—for example, to get news headings, weather forecasts, sports scores, and stock-market prices.

- **Use the directory to find a topic:** Before they acquired their other features, many of these portals began as a type of search tool known as a **_directory_, providing lists of several categories of websites classified by topic,** such as (with Yahoo!) "Business & Economy" or "Recreation & Sports." Such a category is also called a *hypertext index*, and its purpose is to allow you to access information in specific categories by clicking on a hypertext link.

  Many users are increasingly bypassing the better known web portals and going directly to specialty sites or small portals, such as those featuring education, finance, and sports. Examples are Webstart Communications' computer and communications site

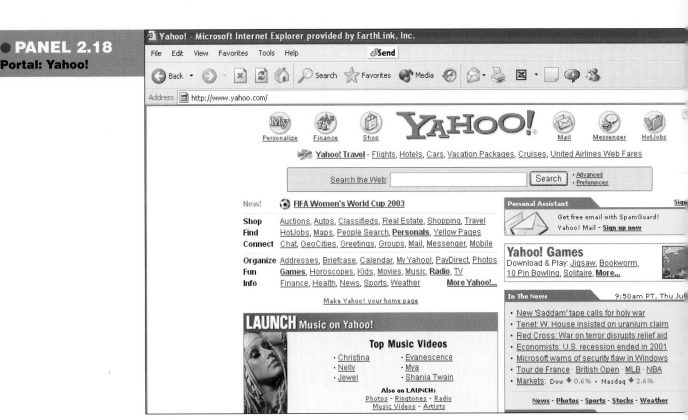

● PANEL 2.18
Portal: Yahoo!

(*www.cmpcmm.com/cc*), Travel.com's travel site (*www.travel.com/ sitemap.htm*), and the *New York Times* home page used by the paper's own newsroom staff to find journalism-related sites (*www.nytimes.com/library/tech/reference/cynavi.html*). Some colleges are also installing portals for their students.

- **Use keywords to search for a topic:** At the top of each portal's home page is a blank space into which you can type a ***keyword*, the subject word or words of the topic you wish to find.** If you want a biography on former San Francisco football quarterback Joe Montana, then *Joe Montana* is the keyword. This way you don't have to plow through menu after menu of subject categories. The results of your keyword search will be displayed in a short summary of documents containing the keyword you typed.

Four Types of Search Engines: Human-Organized, Computer-Created, Hybrid, & Metasearch

When you use a keyword to search for a topic, you are using a piece of software known as a *search engine*. Whereas directories are lists of websites classified by topic (as offered by portals), search engines allow you to find specific documents through keyword searches and menu choices. The type of search engine you use depends on what you're looking for.

There are four types of such search tools: (1) human-organized, (2) computer-created, (3) hybrid, and (4) metasearch:[10]

- **Human-organized search sites:** If you're looking for a biography of Apple Computer founder Steve Jobs, a search engine based on human judgment is probably your best bet. Why? Because, unlike a computer-created search site, the search tool won't throw everything remotely associated with his name at you. More and more, the top search sites on the web are going in the direction of human indexing. Whereas computers can't discriminate in organizing data, humans can judge data for relevance and categorize items in ways that are useful to you. Many of these sites hire people who are subject-area experts (with the idea that, for example, someone interested in gardening would be best able to organize gardening sites). Examples of human-organized search sites are Yahoo! and Open Directory.

- **Computer-created search sites:** If you want to see what things show up next to Steve Jobs's name or every instance in which it appears, a computer-created search site may be best. These are assembled by software "spiders" that crawl all over the web and send back reports to be collected and organized with little human intervention. The downside is that computer-created indexes may deliver you more information than you want. Examples of this type are Google, Excite, and WebCrawler. Google ranks listings by popularity as well as by how well they match the request. Some search engines rank results of a search according to who paid the most money for top billing.

- **Hybrid search sites:** Hybrid sites generally use human organization supplemented by computer-created indexes. The idea is to see that nothing falls through the cracks. Many of the principal sites are now hybrid: AOL Search, AltaVista, Lycos, MSN Search, Ask Jeeves, Teoma, Alltheweb, HotBot, and Snap. Ask Jeeves pioneered the use of natural-language queries (you ask a question as you would to a person: "Where can I find a biography of Steve Jobs?").

- **Metasearch sites:** Metasearch sites send your query to several other different search tools and compile the results so as to present the broadest view. Examples are Copernic, MetaCrawler, and Dogpile. Some search engines of the first three types include metasearching.

more info!

The basic version of Copernic can be downloaded for free at *www.copernic.com.*

Tips for Smart Searching

The phrase "trying to find a needle in a haystack" will come vividly to mind the first time you type a word into a search engine and back comes a response on the order of "63,173 listings found." Clearly, it becomes mandatory that you have a strategy for narrowing your search. The following are some tips.

- **Choose your search terms well, and watch your spelling:** Use the most precise words possible. If you're looking for information about novelist Thomas Wolfe (author of *Look Homeward Angel*, published 1929) rather than novelist/journalist Tom Wolfe (*A Man in Full*, 1998), details are important: *Thomas*, not *Tom*; *Wolfe*, not *Wolf*. Use *poodle* rather than *dog*, *Maui* rather than *Hawaii*, *Martin guitar* rather than *guitar*, or you'll get thousands of responses that have little or nothing to do with what you're looking for. You may need to use several similar words to explore the topic you're investigating: *car racing, auto racing, drag racing, drag-racing, dragracing,* and so on.

- **Use phrases with quotation marks rather than separate words:** If you type *ski resort*, you could get results of (1) everything to do with skis, on the one hand, and (2) everything to do with resorts—winter, summer, mountain, seaside—on the other. Better to put your phrase in quotation marks—*"ski resort"*—to narrow your search.

- **Put unique words first in a phrase:** Better to have *"Tom Wolfe novels"* rather than *"Novels Tom Wolfe."* Or if you're looking for the Hoagy Carmichael song rather than the southern state, indicate *"Georgia on My Mind."*

- **Use operators—AND, OR, NOT, and + and - signs:** Most search sites use symbols called *Boolean operators* to make searching more precise. To illustrate how they are used, suppose you're looking for the song "Strawberry Fields Forever."[11]

AND connects two or more search words and means that all of them must appear in the search results. Example: *Strawberry AND Fields AND Forever.*

OR connects two or more search words and indicates that any of the two may appear in the results. Example: *Strawberry Fields OR Strawberry fields.*

NOT, when inserted before a word, excludes that word from the results. Example: *Strawberry Fields NOT Sally NOT W.C.* (to distinguish from the actress Sally Field and comedian W.C. Fields).

+ (plus sign), like *AND*, precedes a word that must appear: Example: *+ Strawberry + Fields.*

− (minus sign), like *NOT*, excludes the word that follows it. Example: *Strawberry Fields − Sally.*

- **Use wildcards:** If you want as many results as possible on a keyword, use an asterisk (*) to mean "anything/everything." For example, type *dance** and you will get hits for *dance, dances, dancers, dancing, dancewear,* and so on. If you can't remember how to spell something, use the question mark (?). For instance, if you type *Solzhe?* you will get page matches for the Russian author *Solzhenitsyn.*

- **Read the Help or Search Tips section:** All search sites provide a Help section and tips. This could save you time later.

- **Try an alternate general search site or a specific search site:** If you're looking for very specific information, a general type of search site such as Yahoo! may not be the best way to go. Instead, you should turn to a specific search site. Examples: To explore public companies, Hoover's Online *(www.hoovers.com)* or KnowX *(www.knowx.com).* For news stories, try Yahoo! News *(http://dailynews.yahoo.com)* or CNN *(www.cnn.com).* For pay-per-view information from all sorts of articles, journals, and reports, try Dialog Web *(www.dialogweb.com),* Lexis-Nexis *(www.lexis-nexis.com),* and Dow Jones Interactive *(www.factiva.com).*

more info!

What do these terms mean: *glurge gallery, inboxer rebellion, wooden spoons, rumors of war?* Go to *www.snopes.com* and find out. Then check out a category of interest to you and see how much untrue information is circulating about it.

Multimedia on the Web

Many websites (especially those trying to sell you something) employ complicated multimedia effects, using a combination of text, images, sound, video, and animation. While most web browsers can handle basic multimedia elements on a web page, eventually you'll probably want more dramatic capabilities.

- **Plug-ins:** In the 1990s, as the web was evolving from text to multimedia, browsers were unable to handle many kinds of graphic, sound, and video files. To do so, external application files called *plug-ins* had to be loaded into the system. **A *plug-in*—also called a *player* or a *viewer*—is a program that adds a specific feature to a browser, allowing it to play or view certain files.** For example, to view certain documents, you may need to download Adobe Acrobat Reader; to view high-quality video and hear radio, you may need to download RealOne. QuickTime is an audio/video plug-in for the Apple Macintosh. Plug-ins are required by many websites if you want to fully experience their content.

  Recent versions of Microsoft Internet Explorer and Netscape can handle a lot of multimedia. Now if you come across a file for which you need a plug-in, the browser will ask whether you want it, and then tell you how to go about downloading it, usually at no charge.

- **Developing multimedia—applets, Java, and Visual Studio.NET:** How do website developers get all those nifty special multimedia effects? Often web pages contain links to ***applets,*** **small programs that can be**

quickly downloaded and run by most browsers. Applets are written in _**Java**_, **a complex programming language that enables programmers to create animated and interactive web pages.** Java applets enhance web pages by playing music, displaying graphics and animation, and providing interactive games. Java-compatible browsers such as Internet Explorer and Netscape automatically download applets from the website and run them on your computer so that you can experience the multimedia effects. Microsoft recently introduced Visual Studio.NET to compete with Java.

- **Text and images:** You can call up all kinds of text documents on the web, such as newspapers, magazines, famous speeches, and works of literature. You can also view images, such as scenery, famous paintings, and photographs. Most web pages combine both text and images.

- **Animation:** _**Animation**_ **is the rapid sequencing of still images to create the appearance of motion,** as in a Road Runner cartoon. Animation is used in online video games as well as in moving banners displaying sports scores or stock prices.

- **Video:** Video can be transmitted in two ways. (1) A file, such as a movie or video clip, may have to be completely downloaded before you can view it. This may take several minutes in some cases. (2) A file may be displayed as streaming video and viewed while it is still being downloaded to your computer.

**Streaming video** **is the process of transferring data in a continuous flow so that you can begin viewing a file even before the end of the file is sent.** For instance, RealOne (previously RealPlayer) offers live, television-style broadcasts over the internet as streaming video for viewing on your PC screen. You download RealOne's software, install it, and then point your browser to a site featuring RealVideo. That will produce a streaming-video television image in a window a few inches wide.

- **Audio:** Audio, such as sound or music files, may also be transmitted in two ways: (1) downloaded completely before the file can be played or (2) downloaded as _**streaming audio,**_ **allowing you to listen to the file while the data is still being downloaded to your computer.** A popular standard for transmitting audio is RealAudio. Supported by most web browsers, it compresses sound so that it can be played in real time, even though sent over telephone lines. You can, for instance, listen to 24-hour-a-day net radio, which features "vintage rock," or English-language services of 19 shortwave outlets from World Radio Network in London. Many large radio stations outside the United States have net radio, allowing people around the world to listen in.

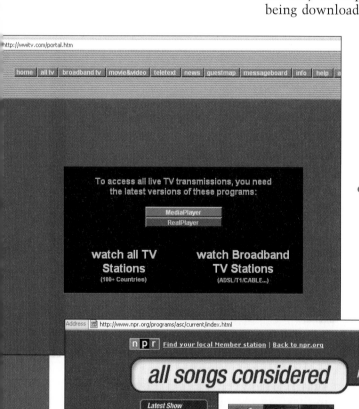

Streaming

(Top) Website for streaming video; _(bottom)_ site for streaming audio.

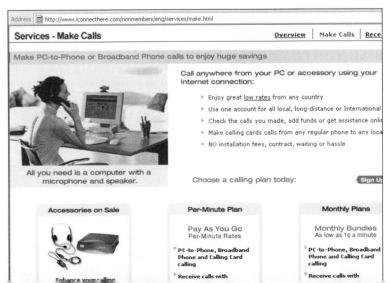

info!

For more information on web radio, check:

www.web-radio.fm

www.shoutcast.com

www.grooveradio.com

For web TV:

www.tv.com/portal.htm

Push Technology & Webcasting

It used to be that you had to do the searching on the web. Now, if you wish, the web will come searching for you. The driving force behind this is **_push technology_, software that automatically downloads information to your computer** (as opposed to "pull" technology, in which you go to a website and pull down the information you want—in other words, the web page isn't delivered until a browser requests it).

One result of push technology is **_webcasting_, in which customized text, video, and audio are sent to you automatically on a regular basis.** You can view or listen to the information immediately or access it later. The idea here is that you choose the categories, or (in Microsoft Internet Explorer) the channels, of websites that will automatically send you updated information. Thus, webcasting saves you time because you don't have to go out searching for the information. Webcasting companies are also called *subscription services*, because they are sell-on-demand services.

Several services offer personalized news and information, based on a profile that you define when you register with them. For example, Latimes.com, the website of the *Los Angeles Times*, has NewsDirect (*http://newsdirect. latimes.com*), a personalized subscription service that delivers news alerts, full-text articles, and other information directly to subscribers.

The Internet Telephone & Videophone

The internet breaks up conversations (as it does any other transmitted data) into "information packets" that can be sent over separate lines and then regrouped at the destination, whereas conventional voice phone lines carry a conversation over a single path. Thus, the internet can move a lot more traffic over a network than the traditional telephone link can.

With **_internet telephony_—using the net to make phone calls, either one to one or for audioconferencing**—you can make long-distance phone calls that are surprisingly inexpensive. Indeed, it's theoretically possible to do this without owning a computer, simply by picking up your standard telephone and dialing a number that will "packetize" your conversation. However, it's a more common practice to use a PC with a sound card and a microphone, a modem linked to a standard internet service provider, and internet telephone software such as Netscape Conference (part of Netscape's browser) or Microsoft NetMeeting (part of Microsoft Internet Explorer). Companies such as CrystalVoice and Peoplecall have websites where users can set up telephone voice connections.

Besides carrying voice signals, internet telephone software also allows videoconferencing, in which participants are linked by a videophone that will transmit their pictures, thanks to a video camera attached to their PCs.

Internet telephony site

Designing Web Pages

If you want to advertise a business online or just have your own personal website, you will need to design a web page, determine any hyperlinks, and hire 24-hour-a-day space on a web server or buy one of your own. Professional web page designers can produce a website for you, or you can do it yourself using a menu-driven program included with your web browser or a web-page design software package such as Microsoft FrontPage or Macromedia Dreamweaver. After you have designed your web page, you can put it on your ISP's server. (We provide more information about web-page design in Chapter 8.)

QuickCheck

Describe how the World Wide Web works. How does it differ from the internet?

What is a browser, and how do you use it to get around the web?

What is a website? Web page? URL?

Describe the types of search engines, and give some tips for searching.

What are plug-ins used for?

What is webcasting?

2.5 The Online Gold Mine: More Internet Resources

KEY QUESTIONS

What are FTP, Telnet, newsgroups, real-time chat, blogs, distance learning, and e-commerce?

The opportunities offered by the net seem inexhaustible. Here we'll examine several internet resources other than email and the web:

- **FTP—for copying all the free files you want:** Many net users enjoy "FTPing"—cruising the system and checking into some of the tens of thousands of FTP sites, which predate the web and offer interesting free or inexpensive files to download. *FTP (File Transfer Protocol)* **is a method whereby you can connect to a remote computer called an** *FTP site* **and transfer files to your own microcomputer's hard disk via the internet.** Free files offered cover nearly anything that can be stored on a computer: software, games, photos, maps, art, music, books, statistics. *(See ● Panel 2.19.)*

  Some FTP files are open to the public (at *anonymous FTP sites*); some are not. For instance, a university might maintain an FTP site with private files (such as lecture transcripts) available only to professors and students with assigned user names and passwords. It might also have public FTP files open to anyone with an email address. You can download FTP files using either your web browser or special software (called an *FTP client program*), such as Fetch, Cute, and FTP pro.

- **Telnet—to connect to remote computers:** *Telnet* **is a protocol that allows you to connect to remote computers on the internet by using a user name and a password and to run programs on those computers.** This feature, which allows microcomputers to communicate successfully with mainframes, enables you to tap into internet computers and access public files as though you were connected directly instead of, for example, through your ISP site. *(See ● Panel 2.20.)*

Survival Tip

Learning Telnet

To learn how to use Telnet, go to *www.telnet.org*. Try a connection.

The Telnet feature is especially useful for perusing large databases at universities, government agencies, or libraries. As an electronic version of a library card catalog, Telnet can be used to search most major public and university library catalogs. (See, for example, Internet Public Library, *www.ipl.org*, and Library Spot, *www.libraryspot. com*.) To use Telnet, you may have to open Telnet accounts for the computers you want to connect with. (Telnet software is included in recent browser versions.)

- **Newsgroups—for online typed discussions on specific topics: A _newsgroup_ (or _forum_) is a giant electronic bulletin board on which users conduct written discussions about a specific subject.** There are thousands of internet newsgroups—which charge no fee—and they cover an amazing array of topics. In addition, for a small fee, services such as Meganetnews.com and Corenews.com will get you access to more than 100,000 newsgroups all over the world. Newsgroups take place on a special network of computers called _Usenet_, **a worldwide public network of servers that can be accessed through the internet** (*www.usenet.com*). To participate, you need a _newsreader_, **a program included with most browsers that allows you to access a newsgroup and read or type messages.** (Messages, incidentally, are known as *articles*.)

  One way to find a newsgroup of interest to you is to use a portal such as Yahoo!, Excite, or Lycos to search for specific topics. Or you can use Google's Groups (*http://groups.google.com*), which will present the newsgroups matching the topic you specify. About a dozen major topics, identified by abbreviations ranging from *alt* (alternative topics) to *talk* (opinion and discussion), are divided into hierarchies of subtopics.

- **Real-time chat—typed discussions among online participants:** With newsgroups (and mailing lists, which we described under email), participants may contribute to a discussion, go away, and return hours or days later to catch up on others' typed contributions. With _real-time chat (RTC)_, **participants have a typed discussion ("chat") while online at the same time,** just like a telephone conversation except that messages are typed rather than spoken. Otherwise the format is much like a newsgroup, with a message board to which participants may send ("post") their contributions. To start a chat, you use a service available on your browser such as IRC (Internet Relay Chat) that will connect you to a chat server.

  Unlike instant messaging (discussed under email), which tends to involve one-on-one conversation, real-time chat usually involves several participants. As a result, RTC is often like being at a party, with many people and many threads of conversation occurring at once.

- **Blogs:** Many users of the internet have fun **keeping journals, or *web logs*—called _blogs_ for short—accessible to other users.** Blogs are often updated daily and reflect the personality and views of the blogger. Blog sites—for example, blogging network (*www.bloggingnetwork. com*) and Pyra Labs (*www.blogger.com*)—provide information about how you can create and maintain your own web log for a small fee.

- **Relationships—online matchmaking:** It's like walking into "a football stadium full of single people of the gender of your choice," says Trish McDermott, an expert for Match.com, a San Francisco online dating service. People who connect online before meeting in the real world, she points out, have the chance to base their relationship on personality, intelligence, and sense of humor rather than purely physical attributes. "Online dating allows people to take some risks in an anonymous capacity," she adds. "When older people look back at their lives, it's the risks that they didn't take that they most regret."[12] (Still, serious risks exist in trying to establish intimacy through online means because people may pretend to be quite different from who they really are.)

People can also use search sites such as Infospace.com and Switch-board.com to try to track down old friends and relatives.[13] Others find common bonds by joining online communities such as The WELL *(www.well.com)*, the women's site Ivillage.com *(www.ivillage. com)*, the older people's site Third Age *(www.thirdage.com)*, and the gardening site GardenWeb *(www.gardenweb.com)*.

- **Education—the rise of distance learning:** Sally Wells of Oregon has four children, a full-time job, and 14 cows to milk. She'd like to get a master's degree, but with no time to drive an hour to campus she takes four marketing courses online.[14] Adult learners—defined by educators as those over age 24—aren't the only ones involved in ***distance learning*, the name given to online education programs.** Younger college students also like it because they don't have to spend time commuting, the scheduling is flexible, and they often have a greater selection of course offerings. Although for instructors an online class is more labor-intensive than a regular chalk-and-talk class, they often find there is better interaction with students.[15]

- **Health—patient self-education:** Health is one of the most popular subject areas of research on the web, although it can be difficult to get accurate information. (Many sites are trying to sell you something.) Among the sites offering reputable advice are Intelihealth *(www.intelihealth.com)*, Mayo Clinic Health Oasis *(www. mayohealth.org)*, Cyber Diet *(www.cyberdiet.com)*, the American College of Physicians *(www.acponline.org)*, and Medline *(www.nlm.nih.gov/medlineplus)*.

- **Entertainment—amusing yourself:** Some groups estimate that two-thirds of all internet users in the United States seek out entertainment on the web. No wonder so many major media companies have created websites to try to help promote or sell movies, music, TV shows, and the like. Of course, there are many other types of entertainment sites, devoted to games, hobbies, jokes, and so on.

- **E-commerce:** The explosion in ***e-commerce (electronic commerce)— conducting business activities online***—is not only widening consumers' choice of products and services but also creating new businesses and compelling established businesses to develop internet strategies. Many so-called brick-and-mortar retailers—those operating out of physical buildings—have been surprised at the success of such online companies as Amazon.com, seller of books, CDs, and other products. As a result, traditional retailers from giant Wal-Mart to very small one-person businesses now offer their products online.

  Retail goods can be classified into two categories—hard and soft. *Hard goods* are those that can be viewed and priced online, such as computers, clothes, groceries, and furniture, but are then sent to buyers by mail or truck. *Soft goods* are those that can be downloaded directly from the retailer's site, such as music, software, travel tickets, and greeting cards.

- **Auctions—linking individual buyers and sellers:** Today millions of buyers and sellers are linking up at online auctions, where everything is available from comic books to wines. The internet is also changing the tradition-bound art and antiques business (dominated by such venerable names as Sotheby's, Christie's, and Butterfield & Butterfield). There are generally two types of auction sites: (1) person-to-person auctions, such as eBay *(www.ebay.com)*, that connect buyers and sellers for a listing fee and a commission on sold items, and (2) vendor-based auctions, such as OnSale *(www.onsale.com)*, that buy

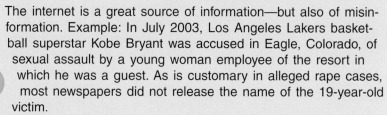

merchandise and sell it at discount. Some auctions are specialized, such as Priceline *(www.priceline.com)*, an auction site for airline tickets and other items.

- **Online finance—trading, banking, and e-money:** The internet has changed the nature of stock trading. Anyone with a computer, a connection to the global network, and the information, tools, and access to transaction systems required to play the stock market can do so online. Companies such as E*Trade and Ameritrade are building one-stop financial supermarkets offering a variety of money-related services, including home mortgage loans and insurance. More than 1,000 banks have websites, offering services that include account access, funds transfer, bill payment, loan and credit card applications, and investments.

- **Online job hunting:** There are more than 2,000 websites that promise to match job hunters with an employer. Some are specialty "boutique" sites looking for, say, scientists or executives. Some are general sites, the leaders being Monster.com, CareerPath.com, USAJOBS (U.S. government/federal jobs; *www.usajobs.opm.gov*), and CareerBuilder.com. Job sites can help you keep track of job openings and applications by downloading them to your own computer. Résumé sites such as Employment911.com help you prepare professional-quality résumés.

- **B2B commerce:** Of course, every kind of commerce has taken to the web, ranging from travel bookings to real estate. One of the most important variations is ***B2B (business-to-business) commerce*, the electronic sales or exchange of goods and services directly between companies, cutting out traditional intermediaries.** Expected to grow even more rapidly than other forms of e-commerce, B2B commerce covers an extremely broad range of activities, such as supplier-to-buyer display of inventories, provision of wholesale price lists, and sales of closed-out items and used materials—usually without agents, brokers, or other third parties.

Describe FTP, Telnet, newsgroups, and real-time chat.

What are blogs?

What are some ways the internet can be of personal use and of e-commerce use?

The Jhai computer: Pedal-powered networking for remote villages.
Laos is one of the poorest countries in the world. The U.S.-based Jhai Foundation (Jhai means "hearts and minds working together") has developed this low-wattage computer that can be powered by a car battery drawing electricity from a bicycle-powered generator. The computer is linked to a high-bandwidth wireless network, which gives support for small businesses in remote Laotian villages that have no telephone lines or electricity. Farmers can now grow surpluses of rice and other crops and can use the system's email to find out if the crop price is high enough to warrant the 30-kilometer walk into town to sell it. The radio signal will also go to a microwave tower and then to a server in Vientiane, the capital, which will connect the villages to the internet. Weavers in the villages hope to use the internet for help in selling their natural-dyed weavings for export.

PRACTICAL ACTION BOX
Web Research, Term Papers, & Plagiarism

No matter how much students may be able to rationalize cheating in college—for example, trying to pass off someone else's term paper as their own (plagiarism)—ignorance of the consequences is not an excuse. Most instructors announce the penalties for cheating at the beginning of the course—usually a failing grade in the course and possible suspension or expulsion from school.

Even so, probably every student becomes aware before long that the World Wide Web contains sites that offer term papers, either for free or for a price. Some dishonest students may download papers and just change the author's name to their own. Others are more likely just to use the papers for ideas. Perhaps, suggests one article, "the fear of getting caught makes the online papers more a diversion than an invitation to wide-scale plagiarism."[16]

How the Web Can Lead to Plagiarism

Two types of term-paper websites are as follows:

- *Sites offering papers for free:* Such a site requires that users fill out a membership form and then provides at least one free student term paper. (Good quality is not guaranteed, since free-paper mills often subsist on the submissions of poor students, whose contributions may be subliterate.)

- *Sites offering papers for sale:* Commercial sites may charge $6–$10 a page, which users may charge to their credit card. (Expense is no guarantee of quality. Moreover, the term-paper factory may turn around and make your $350 custom paper available to others—even fellow classmates working on the same assignment—for half the price.)

How Instructors Catch Cheaters

How do instructors detect and defend against student plagiarism? Professors are unlikely to be fooled if they tailor term-paper assignments to work done in class, monitor students' progress—from outline to completion—and are alert to papers that seem radically different from a student's past work.[17]

Eugene Dwyer, a professor of art history at Kenyon College, requires that papers in his classes be submitted electronically, along with a list of World Wide Web site references. "This way I can click along as I read the paper. This format is more efficient than running around the college library, checking each footnote."[18]

Just as the internet is the source of cheating, it is also a tool for detecting cheaters. Search programs make it possible for instructors to locate texts containing identified strings of words from the millions of pages found on the web. Thus, a professor can input passages from a student's paper into a search program that scans the web for identical blocks of text. Indeed, some websites favored by instructors build a database of papers over time so that students can't recycle work previously handed in by others. One system can lock on to a stolen phrase as short as eight words. It can also identify copied material even if it has been changed slightly from the original. (More than 1,000 educational institutions have turned to Oakland, California-based Turnitin.com—*www.turnitin.com*—a service that searches documents for unoriginality.)[19]

How the Web Can Lead to Low-Quality Papers

William Rukeyser, coordinator for Learning in the Real World, a nonprofit information clearinghouse, points out another problem: The web enables students "to cut and paste together reports or presentations that appear to have taken hours or days to write but have really been assembled in minutes with no actual mastery or understanding by the student."[20]

Philosophy professor David Rothenberg, of New Jersey Institute of Technology, reports that as a result of students' doing more of their research on the web, he has seen "a disturbing decline in both the quality of the writing and the originality of the thoughts expressed."[21] How does an instructor spot a term paper based primarily on web research? Rothenberg offers four clues:

- *No books cited:* The student's bibliography cites no books, just articles or references to websites. Sadly, says Rothenberg, "one finds few references to careful, in-depth commentaries on the subject of the paper, the kind of analysis that requires a book, rather than an article, for its full development."

- *Outdated material:* A lot of the material in the bibliography is strangely out of date, says Rothenberg. "A lot of stuff on the web that is advertised as timely is actually at least a few years old."

- *Unrelated pictures and graphs:* Students may intersperse the text with a lot of impressive-looking pictures and graphs that actually bear little relation to the precise subject of the paper. "Cut and pasted from the vast realm of what's out there for the taking, they masquerade as original work."

- *Superficial references:* "Too much of what passes for information [online] these days is simply advertising for information," points out Rothenberg. "Screen after screen shows you where you can find out more, how you can connect to this place or that." Other kinds of information are detailed but often superficial: "pages and pages of federal documents, corporate propaganda, snippets of commentary by people whose credibility is difficult to assess."

Summary

animation (p. 68, KQ 2.4) The rapid sequencing of still images to create the appearance of motion, as in a cartoon. Why it's important: Animation is a component of multimedia; it is used in online video games as well as in moving banners displaying sports scores or stock prices.

applets (p. 67, KQ 2.4) Small programs that can be quickly downloaded and run by most browsers. Why it's important: Web pages contain links to applets, which add multimedia capabilities.

B2B (business-to-business) commerce (p. 74, KQ 2.5) Electronic sale or exchange of goods and services directly between companies, cutting out traditional intermediaries. Why it's important: Expected to grow even more rapidly than other forms of e-commerce, B2B commerce covers an extremely broad range of activities, such as supplier-to-buyer display of inventories, provision of wholesale price lists, and sales of closed-out items and used materials—usually without agents, brokers, or other third parties.

bandwidth (p. 38, KQ 2.1) Expression of how much data—text, voice, video, and so on—can be sent through a communications channel in a given amount of time. Why it's important: Different communications systems use different bandwidths for different purposes. The wider the bandwidth, the faster data can be transmitted.

blog (p. 72, KQ 2.5) Web log, an internet journal. Blogs are usually updated daily; they reflect the personality and views of the blogger. Why it's important: Blogs are becoming important sources of current information.

bps (p. 39, KQ 2.1) Bits per second. Why it's important: Data transfer speeds are measured in bits per second.

broadband (p. 38, KQ 2.1) Very high speed connection. Why it's important: Access to information is much faster than with traditional phone lines.

cable modem (p. 43, KQ 2.1) Device connecting a personal computer to a cable-TV system that offers an Internet connection. Why it's important: Cable modems transmit data faster than standard modems.

communications satellite (p. 43, KQ 2.1) Space station that transmits radio waves called microwaves from earth-based stations. Why it's important: An orbiting satellite contains many communications channels and receives signals from ground microwave stations anywhere on earth.

directory (p. 64, KQ 2.4) Search tool that provides lists of several categories of websites classified by topic, such as "Business & Economy" or "Recreation & Sports." Such a category is also called a *hypertext index*, and its purpose is to allow you to access information in specific categories by clicking on a hypertext link. Why it's important: Directories are useful for browsing—looking at web pages in a general category and finding items of interest. Search engines may be more useful for hunting specific information.

distance learning (p. 73, KQ 2.5) Online education programs. Why it's important: Distance learning provides educational opportunities for people who are not able to get to a campus; also, distance-learning students don't have to spend time commuting, the scheduling is flexible, and they often have a greater selection of course offerings.

domain (p. 47, KQ 2.3) A location on the internet. Why it's important: A domain name is necessary for sending and receiving email and for many other internet activities.

cable modem

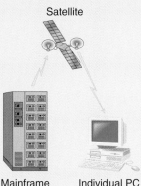

Satellite

Mainframe   Individual PC

Download
(reverse the direction of
data transmission to **upload**)

download (p. 40, KQ 2.1) To transmit data from a remote computer to a local computer. Why it's important: Downloading enables users to save files on their own computers for later use, which reduces the time spent online and the corresponding charges.

DSL (digital subscriber line) (p. 42, KQ 2.1) A hardware and software technology that uses regular phone lines to transmit data in megabits per second. Why it's important: DSL connections are much faster than regular modem connections.

e-commerce (electronic commerce) (p. 73, KQ 2.5) Conducting business activities online. Why it's important: E-commerce not only is widening consumers' choice of products and services but is also creating new businesses and compelling established businesses to develop internet strategies.

emoticons (p. 53, KQ 2.3) Keyboard-produced pictorial representations of expressions. Why it's important: Emoticons can smooth online communication.

:-)	Happy face	<g>	Grin
:-(	Sorrow or frown	BTW	By the way
:-O	Shock	IMHO	In my humble opinion
:-/	Sarcasm	FYI	For your information
;-)	Wink		

FAQs (frequently asked questions) (p. 52, KQ 2.3) Guides that explain expected norms of online behavior for a particular group. Why it's important: Users should read a group's/site's FAQs to know how to proceed properly.

flaming (p. 53, KQ 2.3) Writing an online message that uses derogatory, obscene, or inappropriate language. Why it's important: Flaming should be avoided. It is a form of public humiliation inflicted on people who have failed to read FAQs or have otherwise not observed netiquette (although it can happen just because the sender has poor impulse control and needs a course in anger management).

frame (p. 64, KQ 2.4) An independently controllable section of a web page. Why it's important: A web page designer can divide a page into separate frames, each with different features or options.

FTP (File Transfer Protocol) (p. 70, KQ 2.5) Method whereby you can connect to a remote computer called an *FTP site* and transfer publicly available files to your own microcomputer's hard disk via the internet. Why it's important: The free files offered cover nearly anything that can be stored on a computer: software, games, photos, maps, art, music, books, statistics.

gigabits per second (Gbps) (p. 40, KQ 2.1) 1 billion bits per second. Why it's important: Gbps is a common measure of data transmission speed.

home page (p. 58, KQ 2.4) Also called *welcome page;* web page that, somewhat like the title page of a book, identifies the website and contains links to other pages at the site. Why it's important: The first page you see at a website is the home page.

hypertext (p. 56, KQ 2.4) System in which documents scattered across many internet sites are directly linked, so that a word or phrase in one document becomes a connection to a document in a different place. Why it's important: Hypertext links many documents by topics, allowing users to find information on topics they are interested in.

hypertext markup language (HTML) (p. 56, KQ 2.4) Set of special instructions (called "tags" or "markups") used to specify web document structure, formatting, and links to other documents. Why it's important: HTML enables the creation of web pages.

Hypertext markup language
(HTML)

Hello   # Hello

<H3>Hello</H3>   <H4>Hello</H4>

Hello   **Hello**

<H5>Hello</H5>   <H6>Hello</H6>

Hello   Hello

PARAGRAPHS

To make a paragraph of "This is a web page. How do you like what I've done? Please email me with any suggestions at a@a.com," type:

<P>This is a web page. How do you like what I've done? Please email me with any suggestions at a@a.com</P>

CHARACTER FORMATTI
You may want to format so
others using text styles. The
of text that you can use: **bo**
superscript, subscript, teletype
examples. To do these style
following commands:

<B>, </B> for **bold**

<I>, </I> for *italic*

<U>, </U> for <u>underlined</u>

<STRIKE>, </STRIKE> for

<BLINK>, </BLINK> for blin

~~*You can also mix styles t*~~

HyperText Transfer Protocol (HTTP) (p. 59, KQ 2.4) Communications rules that allow browsers to connect with web servers. Why it's important: Without HTTP, files could not be transferred over the web.

instant messaging (IM) (p. 50, KQ 2.3) Service that enables any user on a given email system to send a message and have it pop up instantly on the screen of anyone else logged onto that system. Why it's important: People can initiate online typed conversations in real time. As they are typed, the messages appear on the display screen in a small window.

internet service provider (ISP) (p. 44, KQ 2.2) Company that connects you through your communications line to its servers, or central computer, which connects you to the internet via another company's network access points. Why it's important: Unless they subscribe to an online information service (such as AOL) or have a direct network connection (such as a T1 line), microcomputer users need an ISP to connect to the internet.

internet telephony (p. 69, KQ 2.4) Using the internet to make phone calls, either one to one or for audioconferencing. Why it's important: Long-distance phone calls by this means are surprisingly inexpensive.

ISDN (Integrated Services Digital Network) (p. 42, KQ 2.1) Hardware and software that allow voice, video, and data to be communicated over traditional copper-wire telephone lines (POTS). Why it's important: ISDN provides faster data transfer speeds than do regular modem connections.

Java (p. 68, KQ 2.4) Complex programming language that enables programmers to create animated and interactive web pages using applets. Why it's important: Java applets enhance web pages by playing music, displaying graphics and animation, and providing interactive games.

type the keyword here

keyword (p. 65, KQ 2.4) The subject word or words of the topic you wish to find in a web search. Why it's important: The results of your keyword search will be displayed in a short summary of documents containing the keyword you typed.

kilobits per second (Kbps) (p. 40, KQ 2.1) 1,000 bits per second. Why it's important: Kbps is a common measure of data transfer speed. The speed of a modem that is 28,800 bps might be expressed as 28.8 Kbps.

listserv (p. 52, KQ 2.3) Automatic mailing list server that sends email to subscribers who regularly participate in discussion topics. To subscribe, the user sends an email to the list-serve moderator and asks to become a member, after which he or she automatically receives email messages from anyone who responds to the server. Why it's important: Anyone connected to the internet can subscribe to listserv services. Subscribers receive information on particular subjects and can post email to other subscribers.

log on (p. 46, KQ 2.2) To make a connection to a remote computer. Why it's important: Users must be familiar with log-on procedures to go online.

megabits per second (Mbps) (p. 40, KQ 2.1) 1 million bits per second. Why it's important: Mbps is a common measure of data transmission speed.

modem (p. 40, KQ 2.1) Device that sends and receives data over telephone lines to and from computers. Why it's important: The modem provides a means for computers to communicate with one another using the standard copper-wire telephone network, an analog system that was built to transmit the human voice but not computer signals.

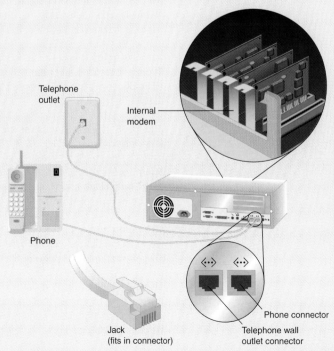

Telephone outlet

Internal modem

Phone

Jack (fits in connector)

Phone connector

Telephone wall outlet connector

netiquette (p. 52, KQ 2.3) "Network etiquette," or appropriate online behavior. Why it's important: In general, netiquette has two basic rules: (a) Don't waste people's time, and (b) don't say anything to a person online that you wouldn't say to his or her face.

newsgroup (p. 72, KQ 2.5) Also called *forum;* Giant electronic bulletin board on which users conduct written discussions about a specific subject. Why it's important: There are thousands of newsgroup forums—which charge no fee—and they cover an amazing array of topics.

newsreader (p. 72, KQ 2.5) Program included with most browsers that allows users to access a newsgroup and read or type messages. Why it's important: Users need a newsreader to participate in a newsgroup.

plug-in (p. 67, KQ 2.4) Also called *player* or *viewer;* program that adds a specific feature to a browser, allowing it to play or view certain files. Why it's important: To fully experience the contents of many web pages, you need to use plug-ins.

protocol (p. 59, KQ 2.4) Set of communications rules for exchanging information. Why it's important: Protocols enable all computers to use data transmitted on the internet. HyperText Transfer Protocol (HTTP) provides the communications rules that allow browsers to connect with web servers.

push technology (p. 69, KQ 2.4) Software that automatically downloads information to your computer, as opposed to "pull" technology, in which you go to a website and pull down the information you want. Why it's important: With little effort, users can obtain information that is important to them.

radio buttons (p. 64, KQ 2.4). An interactive tool displayed as little circles in front of options; selecting an option with the mouse places a dot in the corresponding circle. Why it's important: Radio buttons are one way of interacting with a web page.

real-time chat (RTC) (p. 72, KQ 2.5) Typed discussion ("chat") among participants who are online at the same time; it is just like a telephone conversation, except that messages are typed rather than spoken. Why it's important: RTC provides a means of immediate electronic communication.

scroll arrows (p. 64, KQ 2.4) Small up/down and left/right arrows located to the bottom and side of your screen display. Why it's important: Clicking on scroll arrows with your mouse pointer moves the screen so that you can see the rest of the web page, or the content displayed on the screen.

scrolling (p. 64, KQ 2.4) Moving quickly upward or downward through text or other screen display, using the mouse and scroll arrows (or the arrow keys on the keyboard). Why it's important: Normally a computer screen displays only part of, for example, a web page. Scrolling enables users to view an entire document, no matter how long.

scroll arrows

search engine (p. 65, KQ 2.4) Search tool that allows you to find specific documents through keyword searches and menu choices, in contrast to directories, which are lists of websites classified by topic. Why it's important: Search engines enable users to find websites of specific interest or use to them.

site (p. 56, KQ 2.4) Computer with a domain name. Why it's important: Sites provide internet and web content.

spam (p. 54, KQ 2.3) Unsolicited email in the form of advertising or chain letters. Why it's important: Spam filters are available that can spare users the annoyance of receiving junk mail, ads, and other unwanted email.

streaming audio (p. 68, KQ 2.4) Process of downloading audio in which you can listen to the file while the data is still being downloaded to your computer. Why it's important: Users don't have to wait until the entire audio is downloaded to hard disk before listening to it.

streaming video (p. 68, KQ 2.4) Process of downloading video in which the data is transferred in a continuous flow so that you can begin viewing a file even before the end of the file is sent. Why it's important: Users don't have to wait until the entire video is downloaded to the hard disk before watching it.

T1 line (p. 43, KQ 2.1) Traditional trunk line that carries 24 normal telephone circuits and has a transmission rate of 1.5 Mbps. Why it's important: High-capacity T1 lines are used at many corporate, government, and academic sites; these lines provide greater data transmission speeds than do regular modem connections.

Telnet (p. 70, KQ 2.5) Program or command that allows you to connect to remote computers on the internet and to run programs on those computers. Why it's important: This feature, which allows microcomputers to communicate successfully with mainframes, enables users to tap into internet computers and access public files as though they were connected directly instead of, for example, through an ISP site.

upload (p. 40, KQ 2.1) To transmit data from a local computer to a remote computer. Why it's important: Uploading allows users to easily exchange files over networks.

URL (Universal Resource Locator) (p. 58, KQ 2.4) String of characters that points to a specific piece of information anywhere on the web. A URL consists of (1) the web protocol, (2) the name of the web server, (3) the directory (or folder) on that server, and (4) the file within that directory (perhaps with an extension such as *html* or *htm*). Why it's important: URLs are necessary to distinguish among websites.

Usenet (p. 72, KQ 2.5) Worldwide network of servers that can be accessed through the internet. Why it's important: Newsgroups take place on Usenet.

web browser (browser) (p. 58, KQ 2.4) Software that enables users to locate and view web pages and to jump from one page to another. Why it's important: Users can't surf the web without a browser. The two most well-known browsers are Microsoft Internet Explorer and Netscape Communicator.

webcasting (p. 69, KQ 2.4) Service, based on push technology, in which customized text, video, and audio are sent to the user automatically on a regular basis. Why it's important: Users choose the categories, or the channels, of websites that will automatically send updated information. Thus, webcasting saves time because users don't have to go out searching for the information.

web page (p. 58, KQ 2.4) Document on the World Wide Web that can include text, pictures, sound, and video. Why it's important: A website's content is provided on web pages. The starting page is the home page.

web portal (p. 64, KQ 2.4) Website that groups together popular features such as search tools, email, electronic commerce, and discussion groups. The most popular portals are America Online, Yahoo!, Microsoft Network, Google Netscape, Lycos, Go Network, Infoseek, Snap, Excite Network, AltaVista, and WebCrawler. Why it's important: Web portals provide an easy way to access the web.

website (p. 56, KQ 2.4) Location of a web domain name in a computer somewhere on the internet. Why it's important: Websites provide multimedia content to users.

http://www.iconnecthere.com/nonmembers/eng/services/make.html

window (p. 50, KQ 2.3) Rectangular area containing a document or activity. Why it's important: This feature enables different outputs to be displayed at the same time on the screen. For example, users can exchange messages almost instantaneously while operating other programs.

Chapter Review

"I can recognize and recall information."

Self-Test Questions

1. Today's data transmission speeds are measured in _____, _____, _____, and _____.

2. A(n) _____ connects a personal computer to a cable-TV system that offers an internet connection.

3. A space station that transmits data as microwaves is a _____.

4. A company that connects you through your communications line to its server, which connects you to the internet, is a(n) _____.

5. A small rectangular area on the computer screen that contains a document or displays an activity is called a(n) _____.

6. _____ is writing an online message that uses derogatory, obscene, or inappropriate language.

7. A(n) _____ is software that enables users to view web pages and to jump from one page to another.

8. A computer with a domain name is called a(n) _____.

9. _____ comprises the communications rules that allow browsers to connect with web servers.

10. A(n) _____ is a program that adds a specific feature to a browser, allowing it to play or view certain files.

11. Unsolicited email in the form of advertising or chain letters is known as _____.

12. The expression of how much data—text, voice, video, and so on—can be sent through a communications channel in a given amount of time is known as _____.

Multiple-Choice Questions

1. Kbps means _____ bits per second.
   a. 1 billion
   b. 1 thousand
   c. 1 million
   d. 1 hundred
   e. 1 trillion

2. A location on the internet is called a(n):
   a. network
   b. user ID
   c. domain
   d. browser
   e. web

3. In the email address *Kim_Lee@earthlink.net.us,* Kim_Lee is the:
   a. domain
   b. URL
   c. site
   d. user ID
   e. location

4. Which of the following is *not* one of the four components of a URL?
   a. web protocol
   b. name of the web server
   c. name of the browser
   d. name of the directory on the web server
   e. name of the file within the directory

5. Which of the following is the fastest method of data transmission?
   a. ISDN
   b. DSL
   c. modem
   d. T1 line
   e. cable modem

6. Which of the following is *not* a netiquette rule?
   a. Consult FAQs.
   b. Flame only when necessary.
   c. Don't shout.
   d. Avoid huge file attachments.
   e. Avoid sloppiness and errors.

True or False

T F 1. Bookmarks (Favorites) let you store the URLs of web pages you frequently visit.

T F 2. A dial-up modem is an ISP (internet service provider).

T F 3. Search engines do not allow you to use keywords to initiate information searches.

T F 4. Replying to spam email messages with the statement "remove" will always get spammers to stop sending you unsolicited email.

T F 5. All computer communications use the same bandwidth.

"I can recall information in my own terms and explain them to a friend."

Short-Answer Questions

1. Name three methods of data transmission that are faster than a regular modem connection.

2. What does *log on* mean?

3. What is netiquette, and why is it important?

4. Briefly define *bandwidth.*

5. Many web documents are "linked." What does that mean?

6. Compare and contrast a cable modem service to a DSL service.

7. Briefly explain what TCP/IP does.

 **LEARNING** **APPLYING, ANALYZING, SYNTHESIZING, EVALUATING**

"I can apply what I've learned, relate these ideas to other concepts, build on other knowledge, and use all these thinking skills to form a judgment."

Knowledge in Action

1. Distance learning uses electronic links to extend college campuses to people who otherwise would not be able to take college courses. Is your school or someone you know involved in distance learning? If so, research the system's components and uses. What hardware and software do students need in order to communicate with the instructor and classmates? What courses are offered? Prepare a short report on this topic.

2. It's difficult to conceive how much information is available on the internet and the web. One method you can use to find information among the millions of documents is to use a search engine, which helps you find web pages based on typed keywords or phrases. Use your browser to visit the following search sites: *www.yahoo.com* and *www.goto.com.* Click in the Search box and then type the phrase *"personal computers";* then hit *Go, Find it!* or the Enter key. When you locate a topic that interests you, print it out by choosing *File, Print* from the menu bar or by clicking the *Print* button on the toolbar. Report on your findings.

3. As more and more homes get high-speed broadband internet connections, the flow of data will become exponentially faster and will open up many new possibilities for sharing large files such as video. What types of interactive services can you envision for the future?

4. How do the latest cellphones incorporate the internet into their functions? What functions could be improved? Have any of these extra functions affected your daily life?

6. How has the internet affected your life? Start keeping a list.

7. Why is it possible for people to have voice chats over the internet for surprisingly low rates or for free?

Web Exercises

1. Some websites go overboard with multimedia effects, while others don't include enough. Locate a website that you think makes effective use of multimedia. What is the purpose of the site? Why is the site's use of multimedia effective? Take notes, and repeat the exercise for a site with too much multimedia and one with too little.

2. Visit the following job-hunting websites:

   www.monster.com
   www.careerbuilders.com
   www.careerpath.com

   Investigate job offerings in a field you are interested in. Which is the easiest site to use? Why? What recommendations would you make for improving the site? How does each site warn people who want to post their résumés about improper use of their personal information?

3. If you have never done a search before, try this: Find out how much car dealers pay for cars, what they charge consumers, and what you should know about buying a new car. A company called Edmund publishes a magazine with all that information, but you can get the same information on its website for free.

   Click on the Yahoo! search engine. Search for *"automobile buyer's guide."* The search engine may treat this as a request to find references that match the word *automobile* or *buyer's* or *guide.* If this is not what you want, see if you can find a place on the search engine site that will "find" matches for you that contain all three words. In Yahoo!, click on *Options*—it takes you to a page that allows you to select matches that include all the words in your requested phrase.

   Read some of the entries that the search returns. If any of them aims you at Edmund's website, then go there. If not, then experiment with changing your request; for example, try searching on *"Edmund's automobile buyer's guide."* If that fails, then just go to *www.edmunds.com.*

   Explore the Edmunds site and see if you get any useful information on car prices.

4. Ever wanted your own dot-com in your name? Visit these sites to see if your name is still available:

   www.register.com
   www.namezero.com
   www.domainname.com

The Internet & the World Wide Web

5. Interested in PC-to-phone calls through your internet connection? Visit these sites and check out their services:

www.dialpad.com
www.phonefree.com
www.net2phonedirect.com

6. HTTP (HyperText Transfer Protocol) on the World Wide Web isn't the only method of browsing and transferring data. FTP is the original method and is still a useful internet function. To use FTP, you'll need an FTP client software program, just as you need a web browser to surf the web. Download one of these shareware clients and visit its default sites, which come preloaded:

CuteFtp   *www.cuteftp.com*

WS_FTP   *www.ipswitch.com*

FTP Voyager   *www.ftpvoyager.com*

You will need an FTP client program to upload files to a server if you ever decide to build a website. Some online website builders have browser uploaders, but the conventional method has always been FTP. After you download an FTP client, visit *www.oth.net* to search for FTP servers that house files you would like to download.

7. The videophone isn't an invention of the future. It exists now and is extremely affordable. You can get a PC camera for about $30–$80 and free software to contact friends. If you and the other party have a high-speed connection, you can have a close to full-motion videoconference for free, even if it's long distance. Here are some sites that have videoconferencing software available for download:

http://netconference.miningco.com
www.webattack.com/shareware/
   comm/swvoice.shtml

8. Next time you are going to attach a file to an email and send it to multiple users, try posting the file to a web server (an email hosting service) and give the URL out instead. This method will ease tension on bandwidth and storage of data and is a more efficient method of sharing data. Your friends will also be happier because they won't have a large file stored in their account. The following sites provide this service; check out how they work.

www.ssimail.com/Interchange.htm
www.swishmail.com
www.intermedia.net
www.esmtp.net

9. Make a simple website using HTML. If you're using Windows, open up Notepad and type the following:

A very simple demonstration of how to use HTML.

Hey look at me. I made a web page.

After you've typed that in, choose *File, Save As* and *Save As File Type;* switch from text document to *All Files,* and type for the filename *lookatme.html.* Then double click the file you just created to see how easily a website can be created. After you are done, visit these websites to learn more about creating websites with HTML:

www.make-a-web-site.com
www.lissaexplains.com
http://packages.homestead.com
www.htmltutorials.com

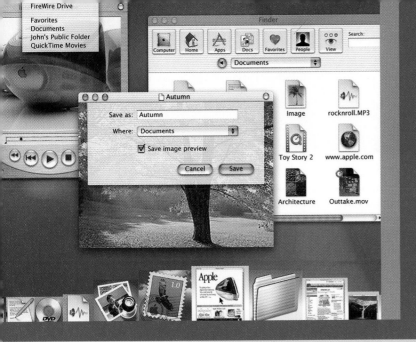

Software

For Productivity & Creativity

Chapter Topics & Key Questions

3.1   **System Software** What are three components of system software; what does the operating system (OS) do; what is an OS interface; and what are some common desktop, network, and portable OSs?

3.2   **Application Software: Getting Started** What are five ways of obtaining application software, tools available to help you learn to use software, three common types of files, and the types of software?

3.3   **Word Processing** What can you do with word processing software that you can't do with pencil and paper?

3.4   **Spreadsheets** What can you do with an electronic spreadsheet that you can't do with pencil and paper and a standard calculator?

3.5   **Database Software** What is database software, and what is personal information management software?

3.6   **Specialty Software** What are the principal uses of specialty software such as presentation graphics, financial, desktop publishing, drawing and painting, video/audio editing, project management, computer-aided design, and web page design software?

W

"hat we need is a science called *practology*, a way of thinking about machines that focuses on how things will actually be used."

So says Alan Robbins, a professor of visual communications, on the subject of *machine interfaces*—the parts of a machine that people actually manipulate.[1] An *interface* is a machine's "control panel," ranging from the volume and tuner knobs on an old radio to all the switches and dials on the flight deck of a jetliner. You may have found, as Robbins thinks, that on too many of today's machines—digital watches, VCRs, even stoves—the interface is often designed to accommodate the machine or some engineering ideas rather than the people actually using it. Good interfaces are intuitive—that is, based on prior knowledge and experience—like the twin knobs on a 1950s radio, immediately usable by both novices and sophisticates. Bad interfaces, such as a software program with a bewildering array of menus and icons, force us to relearn the required behaviors every time. Of course, you can prevail over a bad interface if you repeat the procedures often enough.

So how well are computer hardware and software makers doing at giving us useful, helpful interfaces? The answer is, getting better all the time. In time, as interfaces are refined, computers may become no more difficult to use than a car. Until then, however, for smoother computing you need to know something about how system software works. Today people communicate one way, computers another. People speak words and phrases; computers process bits and bytes. For us to communicate with these machines, we need an intermediary, an interpreter. This is the function of system software. We interact mainly with the application software, which interacts with the system software, which controls the hardware.

3.1 System Software

Software, or *programs,* consist of the instructions that tell the computer how to perform a task. As we've said, software is of two types. *Application software* is software that can perform useful work on general-purpose tasks, such as word processing or spreadsheet calculations, or that is used for entertainment. Hundreds of application software packages are available for personal computers. *System software,* which you will find already installed if you buy a new computer, enables the application software to interact with the computer and helps the computer manage its internal and external resources. There are only a few system software packages for personal computers.

There are three basic components of system software that you need to know about. *(See ● Panel 3.1.)*

- **Operating systems:** An operating system is the principal component of system software in any computing system.
- **Device drivers:** Device drivers help the computer control peripheral devices.
- **Utility programs:** Utility programs are generally used to support, enhance, or expand existing programs in a computer system.

A fourth type of system software, *language translators,* is described in the appendix.

● PANEL 3.1

Three components of system software

System software is the interface between the user and the application software and the computer hardware.

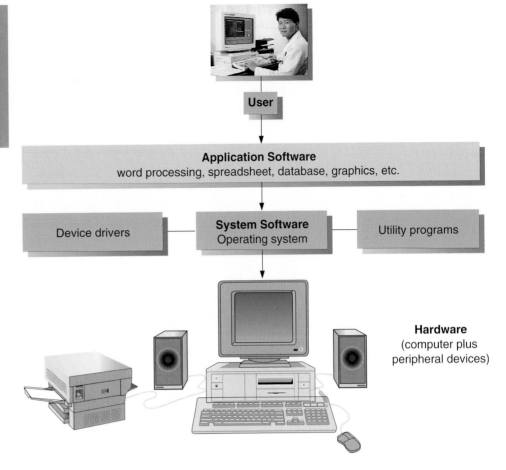

User

Application Software
word processing, spreadsheet, database, graphics, etc.

Device drivers

System Software
Operating system

Utility programs

Hardware
(computer plus peripheral devices)

The Operating System: What It Does

The operating system (OS), **also called the** *software platform*, **consists of the low-level, master system of programs that manage the basic operations of the computer.** These programs provide resource management services of many kinds. In particular, they handle the control and use of hardware resources, including disk space, memory, CPU time allocation, and peripheral devices. Every general-purpose computer must have an operating system to run other programs. The operating system allows you to concentrate on your own tasks or applications rather than on the complexities of managing the computer. Each application program is written to run on top of a particular operating system.

Some important functions of the operating system are as follows:

- **Booting:** The work of the operating system begins as soon as you turn on, or "boot," the computer. ***Booting*** **is the process of loading an operating system into a computer's main memory.** This loading is accomplished by programs stored permanently in the computer's electronic circuitry (called *read-only memory*, or *ROM*, covered in the next chapter). When you turn on the machine, programs called *diagnostic routines* test the main memory, the central processing unit, and other parts of the system to make sure they are running properly. Next, BIOS (for "basic input/output system") programs are copied to main memory and help the computer interpret keyboard characters or transmit characters to the display screen or to a diskette. Then the boot program obtains the operating system, usually from hard disk, and loads it into the computer's main memory, where it remains until you turn the computer off.

- **CPU management:** The central component of the operating system is the supervisor. Like a police officer directing traffic, the ***supervisor***, **or** *kernel*, **manages the CPU. It remains in main memory while the** computer is running and directs other "nonresident" programs (programs that are not in main memory) to perform tasks that support application programs. The operating system also manages memory—it keeps track of the locations within main memory where the programs and data are stored.

- **File management:** A *file* is a named collection of related information stored on a storage device (p. 12, Chapter 1). A file can be a program, such as a word processing program. Or it can be a data file, such as a word processing document, a spreadsheet, images, songs, and the like. (We cover files in more detail later on in the chapter.)

    Files containing programs and data are located in many places on your hard disk and other secondary storage devices. The operating system records the storage location of all files. If you move, rename, or delete a file, the operating system manages such changes and helps you locate and gain access to it. For example, you can *copy*, or duplicate, files and programs from one disk to another. You can *back up*, or make a duplicate copy of, the contents of a disk. You can *erase*, or remove, from a disk any files or programs that are no longer useful. You can *rename*, or give new file names to, the files on a disk.

- **Task management:** A computer is required to perform many different tasks at once. In word processing, for example, it accepts input data, stores the data on a disk, and prints out a document—seemingly simultaneously. Some computers' operating systems can also handle more than one program at the same time—word processing, spreadsheet, database searcher. Each program is displayed in a separate window on the screen. Other operating systems can accommodate the needs of several different users at the same time. All these examples illustrate *task management*. A *task* is an operation such as storing, printing, or calculating.

    Multitasking is the execution of two or more programs by one user at the same time on the same computer with one central processor. You may be writing a report on your computer with one program while another program plays a music CD. How does the computer handle both programs at once?

    The answer is that the operating system directs the processor to spend a predetermined amount of time executing the instructions for each program, one at a time. Thus, a small part of the first program is processed, and then the processor moves to the remaining programs, one at a time, processing small parts of each. The cycle is repeated until processing is complete. Because the processor is usually very fast, it may appear that all the programs are being executed at the same time. However, the processor is still executing only one instruction at a time.

- **Formatting:** **Formatting, or initializing, a disk is the process of preparing that disk so that it can store data files and program files.** Today it is easier to buy preformatted diskettes, which bear the label "Formatted PC" or "Formatted IBM" for floppies designed to run on PCs or "Formatted Macintosh." However, it's useful to know how to format a blank floppy disk or reformat a floppy disk that wasn't intended for your machine. *(See ● Panel 3.2.)*

How to Format a Floppy Disk on the PC

1. Insert unformatted (blank) disk in the floppy disk drive.

2. In My Computer, click once on the icon for the disk you want to format (the floppy disk).

3. On the File menu, click Format.

Notes:

- Be aware that when you format a disk, it *removes all information already on the disk*, such as files previously stored there.

- You can't format a disk if files are already open on that disk.

● **PANEL 3.2**
Formatting

QuickCheck

Describe the three components of system software.

Explain the important features of the OS.

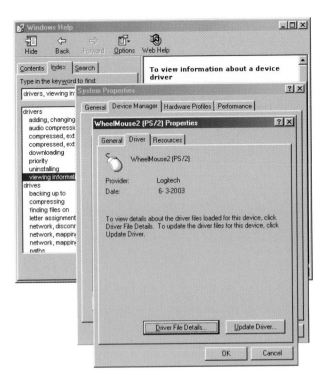

Device Drivers: Running Peripheral Hardware

Device drivers are specialized software programs that allow input and output devices to communicate with the rest of the computer system. Each device's brand and model are supported by a different driver that works with only one operating system. Many basic device drivers come with system software when you buy a computer, and the system software will guide you through choosing and installing the necessary drivers. If, however, you buy a new peripheral device, such as a mouse, scanner, or printer, the package will include a device driver (probably on a CD or floppy disk).

Newer operating systems recognize much new hardware on their own and automatically install the driver. If your OS does not recognize your new hardware, it will display a message and ask you to install the driver from the CD or floppy that came with your hardware.

Utilities: Service Programs

Utility programs, also known as _service programs_, perform tasks related to the control and allocation of computer resources. They enhance existing functions or provide services not supplied by other system software programs. Most computers come with built-in utilities as part of the system software. However, they may also be bought separately as external utility programs (such as Norton SystemWorks and McAfee utilities).

Among the tasks performed by utilities are backing up data, recovering lost data, and identifying hardware problems.

QuickCheck

What are device drivers?

What are utility programs?

Describe tasks performed by utilities.

The Operating System's User Interface: Your Computer's Dashboard

When you power up your computer and it goes through the boot process, it displays a starting screen. From that screen you choose the application programs you want to run or the files of data you want to open. This part of the operating system is called the **_user interface_—the user-controllable display screen that allows you to communicate, or interact, with the computer.** Like the dashboard on a car, the user interface has gauges that show you what's going on and switches and buttons for controlling what you want to do.

You can interact with this display screen using the keys on your keyboard, but you will frequently use the mouse. The mouse allows you to direct an on-screen pointer to perform any number of activities. **The _pointer_ usually appears as an arrow, although it changes shape depending on the application. The mouse is used to move the pointer to a particular place on the display**

screen or to point to little symbols, or icons. You can activate the function corresponding to the symbol by pressing ("clicking") buttons on the mouse. Using the mouse, you can pick up and slide ("drag") an image from one side of the screen to the other or change its size. *(See ● Panel 3.2.)*

In the beginning, personal computers had *command-driven interfaces,* which required that you type in complicated-looking instructions (such as *copy a:\filename c:* to copy a file from a floppy disk to a hard disk). In the next version, they also had *menu-driven interfaces,* in which you could use the arrow keys on your keyboard (or a mouse) to choose a command from a menu, or list of activities. Today the computer's "dashboard" is usually a **_graphical user interface (GUI)_ (pronounced "gooey"), which allows you to use a mouse or keystrokes to select icons (little symbols) and commands**

Resting your hand on the mouse, use your thumb and outside two fingers to move the mouse on your desk or mouse pad. Use your first two fingers to press the mouse buttons.

Mouse pad provides smooth surface.

Left button. Click once on an item on screen to select it. Click twice to perform an action.

Right button. Click on an object to display a shortcut list of options.

Term	Action	Purpose
Point 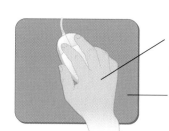	Move mouse across desk to guide pointer to desired spot on screen. The pointer assumes different shapes, such as arrow, hand, or I-beam, depending on the task you're performing.	To execute commands, move objects, insert data, or similar actions on screen
Click Click	Press and quickly release left mouse button.	To select an item on the screen
Double-click Click Click	Quickly press and release left mouse button twice.	To open a document or start a program
Drag and drop 	Position pointer over item on screen, press and hold down left mouse button while moving pointer to location in which you want to place item, then release.	To move an item on the screen
Right-click Click	Press and release right mouse button.	To display a shortcut list of commands, such as a pop-up menu of options

from menus (lists of activities). The GUIs on the PC and on the Apple Macintosh (which was the first easy-to-use personal computer available on a wide scale) are somewhat similar. Once you learn one version, it's fairly easy to learn the other. However, the best-known GUI is that of Microsoft Windows system software. *(See ● Panel 3.3.)*

Outlook Express: Part of Microsoft's browser, Internet Explorer, that enables you to use email.

Microsoft Network: Click here to connect to Microsoft Network (MSN), the company's online service.

My Documents: Where your documents are stored unless you specify otherwise.

Network Neighborhood: If your PC is linked to a network, click here to get a glimpse of everything on the network.

My Computer: Gives you a quick overview of all the files and programs on your PC.

Documents: Multitasking capabilities allow users to smoothly run more than one program at once.

Menu bar   Title bar   Minimize Maximize Close

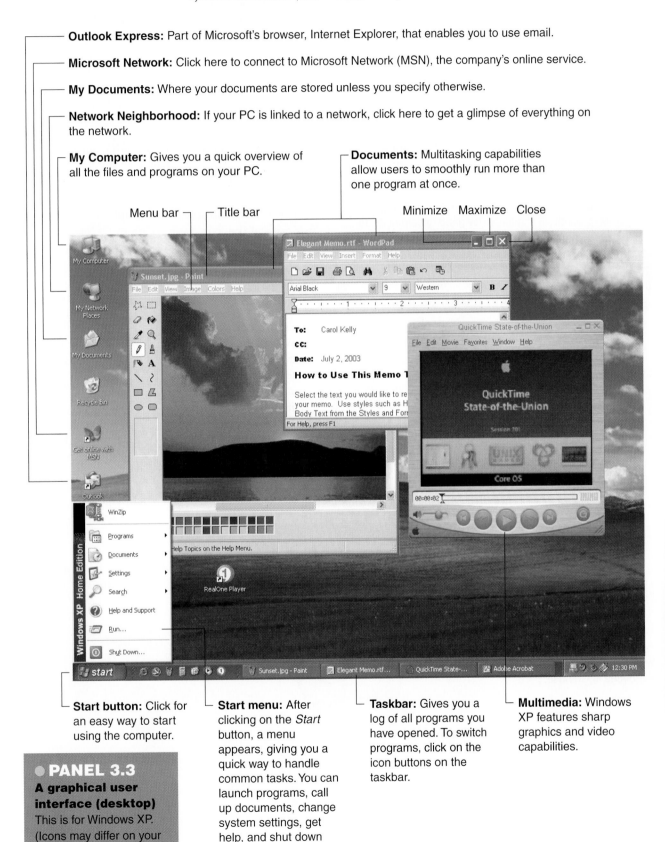

Start button: Click for an easy way to start using the computer.

Start menu: After clicking on the *Start* button, a menu appears, giving you a quick way to handle common tasks. You can launch programs, call up documents, change system settings, get help, and shut down your PC.

Taskbar: Gives you a log of all programs you have opened. To switch programs, click on the icon buttons on the taskbar.

Multimedia: Windows XP features sharp graphics and video capabilities.

● PANEL 3.3
A graphical user interface (desktop)
This is for Windows XP. (Icons may differ on your PC.)

Software

Three features of a GUI are the *desktop, icons,* and *menus.*

Folder icons

To-do list

Class schedules

Term paper

Finances

Letters

Icon: Symbol representing a program, data file, or procedure. Icons are designed to communicate their function, such as a floppy disk for saving.

Rollover: When you roll your mouse pointer over an icon or graphic (in this case, the "Save" icon), a small box with text appears that briefly explains its function.

- **Desktop:** After you turn on the computer, the first screen you will encounter is the *desktop,* a term that embodies the idea of folders of work (memos, schedules, to-do lists) on a businessperson's desk. **The <u>desktop</u>, which is the system's main interface screen, displays pictures (icons) that provide quick access to programs and information.**

- **Icons and rollovers:** <u>*Icons*</u> **are small pictorial figures that represent programs, data files, or procedures.** For example, a trash can represents a place to dispose of a file you no longer want. If you click your mouse pointer on a little picture of a printer, you can print out a document. One of the most important icons is the *folder,* a representation of a manila folder; folders hold the files in which you store your documents and other data.

  Of course, you can't always be expected to know what an icon or graphic means. **A <u>*rollover*</u> feature, a small text box explaining the icon's function, appears when you roll the mouse pointer over the icon. A rollover may also produce an animated graphic.**

- **Menus:** Like a restaurant menu, a <u>**menu**</u> **offers you a list of options to choose from**—in this case, a list of commands for manipulating data, such as Print or Edit. Menus are of several types. Resembling a pull-down window shade, a <u>**pull-down menu**</u>, **also called a *drop-down menu*, is a list of options that pulls down from the menu bar at the top of the screen.** *(See ● Panel 3.4.)* For example, if you use the mouse to "click on" (activate) a command (for example, File) on the menu bar, you will see a pull-down menu offering further commands. Choosing one of these options may produce further menus called <u>**cascading menus**</u>, **menus that seem to fly back to the left or explode out to the right,** wherever there is space.

  A <u>*pull-up menu*</u> is a list of options that pulls up from the menu bar at the bottom of the screen. In Windows XP, a pull-up menu appears in the lower left-hand corner when you click on the Start button.

  A <u>*pop-up menu*</u> is a list of command options that can "pop up" anywhere on the screen when you click the right mouse button. In contrast to pull-down or pull-up menus, pop-up menus are not connected to a menu bar.

A German company, Siemens AG, was one of the first to work with designing user interfaces in Chinese.

Pull-down menu: When you click the mouse on the menu bar, a list of options appears or pulls down like a shade.

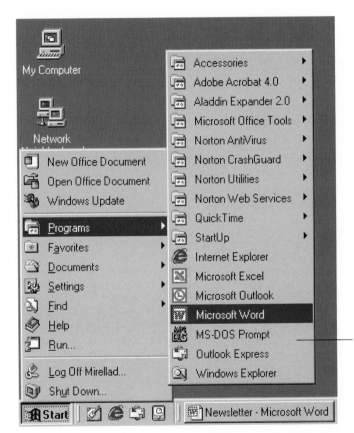

Cascading menu: Moving the mouse pointer to an option on the pull-up menu produces a flyout menu with more options.

Pull-up menu: When you click the mouse pointer on the *Start* button, it produces a pull-up menu offering access to programs and documents.

Suppose you want to go to a document—say, a term paper you've been working on. There are two ways to begin working from a typical Microsoft Windows GUI desktop: (1) You can click on the *Start* button at lower left and then make a selection from the pull-up menu that appears. Or (2) you can click on one of the icons on the desktop, probably the most important of which is the *My Computer* icon, and pursue the choices offered there. Either way, the result is the same: The document will be displayed in the window. *(See ● Panel 3.5.)*

Once past the desktop—the GUI's opening screen—if you click on the *My Computer* icon, you will encounter various "bars" and window functions. *(See ● Panel 3.6.)*

- **Title bar, menu bar, toolbar, taskbar: The *title bar* runs across the very top of the display window and shows the name of the folder you are in**—for example, "My Computer." Below the title bar is the ***menu bar*, which shows the names of the various pull-down menus available.** Examples of menus are File, Edit, View, Favorites, Tools, and Help. **The *toolbar*, below the menu bar, displays menus and icons representing frequently used options or commands.** An example of an

● PANEL 3.5
Two ways to go to a document in Windows XP

From Start menu

Click on *Start* button to produce Start menu, then go to *Documents* option, then to *My Documents*.

From My Computer icon

Click on C, which opens a window that provides access to information stored on your hard disk.

Click on *My Documents* icon, which opens a window providing access to document files and folders.

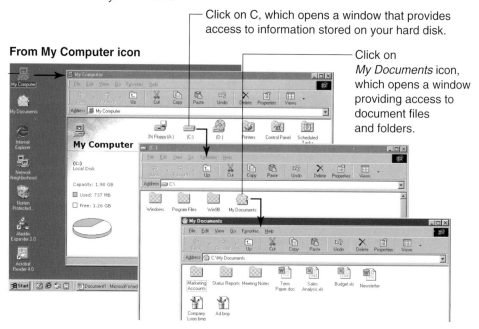

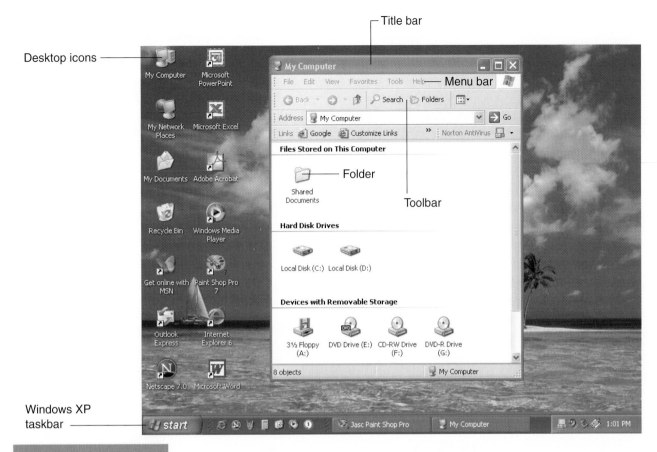

Title bar

Desktop icons

Menu bar

Folder

Toolbar

Windows XP taskbar

Minimize

Maximize/ Restore

Close

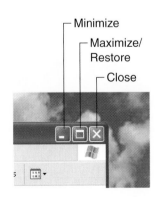

icon is the picture of two pages in an open folder with a superimposed arrow, which issues a *Copy to* command. In Windows, the **_taskbar_ is the bar across the bottom of the desktop screen that contains the Start button and that appears by default.** Small boxes appear here that show the names of open files. You can switch among the files by clicking on the boxes.

- **Windows:** When spelled with a capital "W," Windows is the name of Microsoft's system software (Windows 95, 98, Me, XP, and so on). When spelled with a lowercase "w," a **_window_ is a rectangular frame on the computer display screen. Through this frame you can view a file of data—such as a document, spreadsheet, or database—or an application program.**

    In the right-hand corner of the Windows title bar are some window controls—three icons that represent *Minimize, Maximize and Restore,* and *Close.* By clicking on these icons, you can *minimize* the window (shrink it down to an icon at the bottom of the screen), *maximize* it (enlarge it), or *close* it (exit the file and make the window disappear). You can also use the mouse to move the window around the desktop, by clicking on and dragging the title bar.

    Finally, you can create *multiple windows* to show programs running concurrently. For example, one window might show the text of a paper you're working on, another might show the reference section for the paper, and a third might show something you're downloading from the internet. If you have more than one window open, click on the *Maximize* button of the window you want to be the main window to *restore* it.

- **The Help command:** Don't understand how to do something? Forgotten a command? Accidentally pressed some keys that messed up your screen layout and you want to undo it? Most toolbars contain a **_Help command_—a command generating a table of contents, an index, and**

On Windows computers, you can find the Help area by pressing the *F1* key. Or use the mouse to click on *Start* in the lower left screen; then click on *Help*. On the Macintosh, Help is located under the main menu bar.

a search feature that can help you locate answers. In addition, many applications have *context-sensitive help*, which leads you to information about the task you're performing. *(See ● Panel 3.7.)*

QuickCheck

Describe the features of the GUI: desktop, icons, and the various kinds of menus and bars.

What does the mouse do?

What do toolbars and windows enable you to do?

What is the Help command?

Now that we've described the three components of system software—the operating system, device drivers, and utility programs—let's take a more detailed look at specific operating systems.

Common Desktop & Notebook Operating Systems: DOS, Macintosh, & Windows

The _platform_ is the particular processor model and operating system on which a computer system is based. For example, there are "Mac platforms" (Apple Macintosh) and "Windows platforms" or "PC platforms" (for personal computers such as Dell, Compaq, Gateway, Hewlett-Packard, or IBM that run Microsoft Windows). Sometimes the latter are called *Wintel platforms,* for "Windows + Intel," because they often combine the Windows operating system with the Intel processor chip. (We discuss processors in Chapter 4.)

● **PANEL 3.7**
Help features
The Help command yields a pull-down menu.

The *Help* menu provides a list of help options.

Index: Lets you look up Help topics in alphabetical order

Search: Lets you hunt for Help topics that contain particular words or phrases

Question mark icon: Double-click to see Help screens.

This window displays the selected Help topic.

Let us quickly describe the principal platforms used on desktop computers: DOS, the Macintosh OS, and the Windows series—3.X, 95, 98, Millennium (Me), and XP. Desktop operating systems are used mainly on single-user computers (both desktops and laptops) rather than on mainframes or servers. We discuss operating systems for servers and for portable information appliances shortly.

- **DOS—the old-timer:** ___DOS___ (rhymes with "boss")—for ___Disk Operating___ ___System___—**was the original operating system produced by Microsoft and had a hard-to-use command-driven user interface.** Its initial 1982 version was designed to run on the IBM PC as PC-DOS. Later Microsoft licensed the same system to other computer makers as MS-DOS. With the growing popularity of cheaper PCs produced by these companies, MS-DOS came to dominate the industry. Two years before the advent of Windows 95, which eventually grew out of DOS, there were reportedly more than 100 million users of DOS, which at that time made it the most popular software ever adopted—of any sort.

- **The Macintosh operating system—for the love of Mac:** The ___Macintosh___ ___operating system (Mac OS),___ **which runs only on Apple Macintosh computers, set the standard for icon-oriented, easy-to-use graphical user interfaces.** The software generated a strong legion of fans shortly after its launch in 1984 and inspired rival Microsoft to upgrade DOS to the more user-friendly Windows operating systems. Much later, in 1998, Apple introduced its iMac computer (the "i" stands for "internet"), which added capabilities such as small-scale networking.

  The newest version of the operating system, Mac OS X (called "ten"), broke with 15 years of Mac software to use Unix (discussed shortly) to offer a dramatic new look and feel. *(See ● Panel 3.8.)* The new user interface, *Aqua*, has Hollywood-like tricks (thanks to Apple chairman Steve Jobs's experience running Pixar Animation Studios, makers of such animated films as *Toy Story* and *A Bug's Life*). "Jelly-colored onscreen buttons pulse as if alive," says one description. "Menu borders are translucent, allowing you to see the documents under them. Sliders glow luminously."[2] In addition, many Apple users claim that OS X won't allow software conflicts, a frequent headache with Microsoft's Windows operating systems. For example, you might

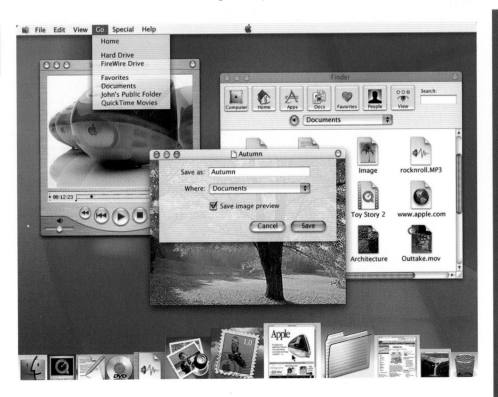

● **PANEL 3.8**
Mac OS X

Don't Trash Those Icons

Don't delete unwanted software programs by using the mouse to drag their icons to the recycle bin, because this might leave behind system files that cause problems. Best to use an "uninstall" utility. (In Windows, go to *Start, Settings, Control Panel;* double-click *Add/Remove Programs.* Find the program you want to delete, and click the *Add/Remove* button.)

install a game and find that it interferes with the device driver for a sound card. Then, when you uninstall the game, the problem persists. With Mac OS X, when you try to install an application program that conflicts with any other program, the Mac simply won't allow you to run it.

Mac OS X also offers free universal email services, improved graphics and printing, CD burning capability, DVD player, easier ways to find files (using *Dock*), and support for building and storing web pages. There are still more System 9-compatible applications available than there are for Mac OS X, but the situation is improving rapidly.

- **Microsoft Windows 3.X, 95, and 98:** In the 1980s, taking its cue from the popularity of Mac's easy-to-use GUI, Microsoft began working on Windows—to make DOS more user-friendly. Early attempts (Windows 1.0, 2.0, 3.0) did not catch on. However, in 1992, Windows 3.X emerged as the preferred system among PC users. (Technically, Windows 3.X wasn't a full operating system; it was simply a layer or shell over DOS.) Later, this version evolved into the Windows 95 operating system, which was succeeded by Windows 98.

  Microsoft Windows 95/98 **is still a popular operating system for desktop and portable microcomputers, supporting the most hardware and the most application software.** Among other improvements over their predecessors, Windows 95 and 98 adhere to a standard called Universal Plug and Play, which is supposed to let a variety of electronics seamlessly network with each other.

  Microsoft Windows Millennium Edition, or *Windows Me* **(the *Me* stands for "Millennium Edition"), is the successor for home users to Windows 95 and 98, designed to support desktop and portable computers.** It provided improved support of multimedia features—still pictures, digital video, and audio files.

Bill Gates. The founder of Microsoft has been identified with every PC operating system since the 1980 DOS.

Network Operating Systems: NetWare, Windows NT/2000/2003/XP, Microsoft .NET, Unix, & Linux

The operating systems described so far were principally designed for use with stand-alone desktop machines. Now let's consider the important operating systems designed to work with networks—NetWare, Windows NT/2000/2003/XP, Microsoft .NET, Unix/Solaris, and Linux:

- **Novell's NetWare—PC networking software:** *NetWare* **has long been a popular network operating system for coordinating microcomputer-based local area networks (LANs) throughout a company or a campus.** LANs allow PCs to share programs, data files, and printers and other devices. Novell, the maker of NetWare, thrived as corporate data managers realized that networks of PCs could exchange information more cheaply than the previous generation of mainframes and midrange computers. The biggest challenge to NetWare has been Windows NT, Windows 2000/2003, and Windows XP. However, Novell is continuing to improve its networking OS with its new version, 6.5.

- **Windows NT and 2000/2003—the challenge from Microsoft:** Windows desktop operating systems (95/98/Me/XP) can be used to link PCs in small networks in homes and offices. However, something more powerful was needed to run the huge networks linking a variety of computers—PCs, workstations, mainframes—used by many companies, universities, and other organizations, which previously were served principally by Unix and NetWare operating systems. *Microsoft Windows NT* **(the *NT* stands for "New Technology"), later upgraded to**

Windows 2000, is the company's multitasking operating system designed to run on network servers in businesses of all sizes. It allows multiple users to share resources such as data, programs, and printers and to build web applications and connect to the internet.

When it first appeared, in 1993, the system came in two versions. The *Windows NT Workstation* version enabled graphic artists, engineers, and others using stand-alone workstations to do intensive computing at their desks. The *Windows NT Server* version was designed to benefit multiple users tied together in networks. In early 2000, Microsoft rolled out its updated version, *Windows 2000*, to replace Windows NT version 4.0.

The choice of the name Windows 2000 is somewhat confusing. This is not the successor to Windows 95 and 98 for home and non-network use. If you're interested in arcade-style games, for instance, 2000 won't work, since it was specifically designed for businesses. (Windows Millennium was designed for home users.)

Windows 2000 includes the Windows 2000 server family, for various levels of network servers: Windows 2000 Professional, Windows 2000 Server, Windows 2000 Advanced Server, and Windows 2000 Datacenter Server. In 2003, Microsoft introduced a new version of Windows 2000 called the *Windows Server 2003* family. This version enhances security, reliability, and manageability, among other things, and includes the Microsoft .NET Framework, a means for building, distributing, and maintaining web services and applications.

- **Microsoft Windows XP: *Windows XP* is the company's current OS, introduced in 2001; it combines elements of Windows networking software and Windows Me with a new GUI.** It has improved stability and increased driver and hardware support. It also has features such as built-in instant messaging, centralized shopping managers to help you keep track of your favorite online stores and products, and music, video, and photography managers. Windows XP Home Edition is for typical home users. Windows XP Professional Edition is for businesses of all sizes and for home users who need to do more than get email, browse the internet, and do word processing. Windows XP Tablet PC Edition is for business notebook computers that support data entry via a special pen used to write on the display screen.

  In late 2002, Microsoft updated XP to a "second edition" by supplying a downloadable service pack called *Windows XP Service Pack 1.*

- **Microsoft .NET: *Microsoft .NET* (pronounced "Microsoft dot-net") is a set of Microsoft software technologies for connecting information, people, and systems through the use of special building-block web service programs.** These programs are complicated to explain, but basically they let applications share data, even across networks, and enable applications to run cross-platform and cross-network regardless of how they were built, what operating system or platform they run on, and what devices are used to access them.

As of late 2003, employment of .NET was just getting going.

Defining the Basic Elements of .NET
January 24, 2003

Microsoft® .NET is a set of Microsoft software technologies for connecting information, people, systems, and devices. It enables a high level of software integration through the use of Web services—small, discrete, building-block applications that connect to each other as well as to other, larger applications over the Internet.

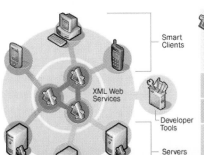

Smart Clients

Web services are small, reusable applications written in XML, a universal language for data exchange. They allow data to be communicated across the Internet (or internal intranet) between otherwise unconnected sources that are enabled to host or act on them, for example:

Client-to-client: "Smart" clients or devices can host and apply XML Web services that allow data to be shared anywhere, any time.

XML Web Services

Client-to-server: XML Web services can share data from a server application to a desktop or mobile computing device via the Internet.

Developer Tools

Server-to-server: XML Web services provide a common interface between existing applications within an environment of independent servers.

Servers

- **Unix, Solaris, and BSD—first to exploit the internet:** Unix (pronounced "*you*-nicks") was developed at AT&T's Bell Laboratories in 1969 as an operating system for minicomputers. By the 1980s, AT&T entered into partnership with Sun Microsystems to develop a standardized version of Unix for sale to industry. Today **Unix is a proprietary multitasking operating system for multiple users that has built-in networking capability and versions that can run on all kinds of computers.** It is used mostly on mainframes, workstations, and servers, rather than on PCs. Government agencies, universities, research institutions, large corporations, and banks all use Unix for everything from designing airplane parts to currency trading. Unix is also used for website management and runs the backbone of the internet. The developers of the internet built their communications system around Unix because it has the ability to keep large systems (with hundreds of processors) churning out transactions day in and day out for years without fail.

  Sun Microsystems' *Solaris* is a version of Unix that is popular for handling large e-commerce servers and large websites. Another interesting variant is *BSD*, free software derived from Unix. BSD began in the 1970s in the computer science department of the University of California, Berkeley, when students and staff began to develop their own derivative of Unix, known as the Berkeley Software Distribution, or BSD. There are now three variations, which are distributed online and on CD.

- **Linux—software built by a community:** It began in 1991 when programmer Linus Torvalds, a graduate student in Finland, posted his free Linux operating system on the internet. Linux (pronounced "*linn*-uks") is the rising star of network software. **Linux is a free (nonpro-**

Linus Torvalds

prietary) version of Unix, and its continual improvements result from the efforts of tens of thousands of volunteer programmers. Whereas Windows is Microsoft's proprietary product, Linux is _**open-source software**_—meaning any programmer can download it from the internet for free and modify it with suggested improvements. The only qualification is that changes can't be copyrighted; they must be made available to all and remain in the public domain. From these beginnings, Linux has attained cult-like status. "What makes Linux different is that it's part of the internet culture," says an IBM general manager. "It's essentially being built by a community."[3] (The People's Republic of China announced in 2000 that it was adopting Linux as a national standard for operating systems because it feared being dominated by the OS of a company of a foreign power—namely, Microsoft.)

If Linux belongs to everyone, how do companies like Red Hat Software—a company that bases its business on Linux—make money? Their strategy is to give away the software but then sell services and support. Red Hat, for example, makes available an inexpensive application software package that offers

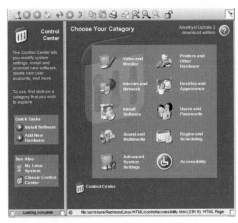

Linux screens. Modifying system settings and adding hardware.

word processing, spreadsheets, email support, and the like for users of its PC OS version. It also offers more powerful versions of its Linux OS for small and medium-size businesses, along with applications, networking capabilities, and support services. Wal-Mart now offers packaged Linux operating systems and applications from Lycoris and Lindows, two companies that produce slightly different versions of Linux that both look similar to Windows, although they are still more difficult to use.

Because it was originally built for use on the internet, Linux is more reliable than Windows for online applications. Hence, it is better suited to run websites and e-commerce software. Its real growth, however, may come as it reaches outward to other applications and, possibly, replaces Windows in many situations.

Operating Systems for Handhelds: Palm OS & Windows CE/Pocket PC/Windows CE .NET

Microsoft Windows for handhelds

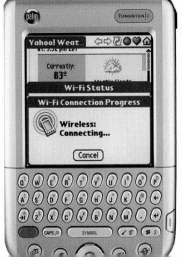

Maybe you're not one of the millions of owners of a handheld computer or personal digital assistant (PDA). But no doubt you've seen people poking through calendars and address books, beeping through games, or checking email or the web on these palm-size devices. Handhelds have gained headway in the corporate world and on college campuses. Because of their small size, they rely on specialized operating systems, including the Palm OS and Windows CE/Pocket PC/Windows CE .NET.

info!

Do you think Linux will overtake Windows? Will more users switch to Mac OS X? To research Linux, go to *www.kernel.org*, *www.lwn.net*, or *www.wired.com/news/linux/ 0,1411,47888,00.html.* For Mac OS, go to *www.macosrumors.com*, *www.spymac.com*, or *www.thinksecret.com.* For Windows, go to *www.winsupersite.com*, *www.neowin.net*, or *www.winbeta.org.* For general OS matters, go to *www.betanews.com*, *www.osnews.com*, *www.cpumag.com/cpufeb03/ marketbattle*, *http://dir.yahoo .com/Computers_and_ Internet/Software/Operating/ Systems.*

- Palm OS—the dominant OS for handhelds: **The _Palm OS_, produced by Palmsource, is the dominant operating system for handhelds.** In 1994, Jeff Hawkins took blocks of mahogany and plywood into his garage and emerged with a prototype for the PalmPilot. Two years later, Hawkins and business brain Donna Dubinsky pulled one of the most successful new-product launches in history. Today the company, Palm Computing, sells the popular Palm Tungsten T, Palm !705, Palm m515, Palm m500, and so on. Hawkins and Dubinsky left to form another company, Handspring, whose products, Visor and Treo, act like a Palm but cost less. Acer, AlphaSmart, Garmin, Samsung, and Sony PDAs and smartphones also use Palm OS.

- Windows CE/Pocket PC/CE .NET—Microsoft Windows for handhelds: In 1996, Microsoft released **_Microsoft Windows CE_, now known as _Microsoft Pocket PC_—or, in its newest form,** *Windows CE .NET.* **This OS is a slimmed-down version of Windows** for handhelds such as those made by Casio, Compaq, and Hewlett-Packard. Windows CE had some of the familiar Windows look and feel and included mobile versions of word processing, spreadsheet, email, web browsing, and other software.

QuickCheck

What are the principal desktop operating systems and some of their features?

What are the common network operating systems and some of their features?

What is the leading operating system for handhelds?

3.2 Application Software: Getting Started

KEY QUESTIONS

What are five ways of obtaining application software, tools available to help you learn to use software, three common types of files, and the types of software?

As we have stated, **_application software_ is software that has been developed to solve a particular problem for users—to perform useful work on specific tasks or to provide entertainment.** New microcomputers are usually equipped not only with system software but also with some application software.

Application Software: For Sale, for Free, or for Rent?

At one time, just about everyone paid for microcomputer application software. You bought it as part of the computer or in a software store, or you downloaded it online with a credit card charge. Now, other ways exist to obtain software. *(See ● Panel 3.9.)* We also discuss *pirated software* and *abandonware.*

- Commercial software: *Commercial software*, also called *proprietary software* or *packaged software*, is software that's offered for sale, such as Microsoft Word, Microsoft Office XP, or Adobe PhotoShop. Although such software may not show up on the bill of sale when you buy a new PC, you've paid for some of it as part of the purchase. And, most likely, whenever you order a new game or other commercial program, you'll have to pay for it. This software is copyrighted. **A _copyright_ is the exclusive legal right that prohibits copying of intellectual property without the permission of the copyright holder.**

Software manufacturers don't sell you their software; rather, they sell you a license to become an authorized user of it. What's the difference? In paying for a **_software license_, you sign a contract in**

Types	Definition
Commercial software	Copyrighted. If you don't pay for it, you can be prosecuted.
Public-domain software	Not copyrighted. You can copy it for free without fear of prosecution.
Shareware	Copyrighted. Available free, but you should pay to continue using it.
Freeware	Copyrighted. Available free.
Rentalware	Copyrighted. Lease for a fee.

which you agree not to make copies of the software to give away or resell. That is, you have bought only the company's permission to use the software and not the software itself. This legal nicety allows the company to retain its rights to the program and limits the way its customers can use it. The small print in the licensing agreement usually allows you to make one copy *(backup copy* or *archival copy)* for your own use. (Each software company has a different license; there is no industry standard.)

Every year or so, software developers find ways to enhance their products and put forth new versions or new releases. A *version* is a major upgrade in a software product, traditionally indicated by numbers such as 1.0, 2.0, 3.0. More recently, other notations have been used. After 1995, for a while Microsoft labeled its Windows and Office software versions by year instead of by number, as in Microsoft's Office 97, Office 2000, and so forth. However, its latest software version is Office XP. A *release*, which now may be called an "add" or "addition," is a minor upgrade. Often this is indicated by a change in number after the decimal point. (For instance, 3.0 may become 3.1, 3.11, 3.2, and so on.) Some releases are now also indicated by the year in which they are marketed. And, unfortunately, some releases are not clearly indicated at all. (These are "patches," which may be downloaded from the software maker's website, as can version updates.)

info! SECURITY

Security
Check out these links to public-domain and commercial security software:
www.alw.nih.gov/Security/security-prog.html
www.wiretapped.net/
www.symantec.com

info!

What kinds of shareware and freeware are available? To find out, go to *http://shareware.cnet.com/.* *www.downloadalot.com,* and *www.sharewareking.com.*

- **Public-domain software:** ***Public-domain software* is not protected by copyright and thus may be duplicated by anyone at will.** Public-domain programs—sometimes developed at taxpayer expense by government agencies—have been donated to the public by their creators. They are often available through sites on the internet. You can download and duplicate public domain software without fear of legal prosecution.

- **Shareware:** ***Shareware* is copyrighted software that is distributed free of charge but requires that users make a monetary contribution, or pay a registration fee, to continue using it** Shareware is distributed primarily through the internet, but because it is copyrighted, you cannot use it to develop your own program that would compete with the original product.

- **Freeware:** ***Freeware* is copyrighted software that is distributed free of charge,** today most often over the internet. Why would any software creator let his or her product go for free? Sometimes developers want to see how users respond, so that they can make improvements in a later version. Sometimes they want to further some scholarly or humanitarian purpose—for instance, to create a standard for software on which people are apt to agree. In its most recent form, freeware is made available by companies trying to make money some other way—actually, by attracting viewers to their advertising. (The web-browsers Internet Explorer and Netscape Navigator are of this type.)

Software

Freeware developers generally retain all rights to their programs; technically, you are not supposed to duplicate and redistribute the programs.

- **Rentalware:** **_Rentalware_ is software that users lease for a fee and download whenever they want it.** This is the concept behind *application services providers (ASPs)*, firms that lease software, usually over the internet.

- **Pirated software:** **_Pirated software_ is software obtained illegally,** as when you get a floppy disk from a friend who has made an illicit copy of, say, a commercial video game. Sometimes pirated software can be downloaded off the internet. Sometimes it is sold in retail outlets in foreign countries. If you buy such software, not only do the original copyright owners not get paid for their creative work but you risk getting inferior goods and, worse, picking up a *virus*, a deviant program that can corrupt or destroy your computer's programs or data. (We discuss viruses in Chapter 8.)

- **Abandonware:** "Abandonware" does not refer to a way to obtain software. It refers to software that is no longer being sold or supported by its publisher. U.S. copyright laws state that copyrights owned by corporations are valid for up to 95 years from the date the software was first published. Copyrights are not considered abandoned even if the software is no longer being produced. Therefore, abandoned software does not enter the public domain just because it is no longer supported. Don't copy it.

Occasionally, companies or individuals need software written specifically for them, to meet unique needs. This software is called *custom software*, and it's created by software engineers and programmers. (See the appendix for more information on programming.)

Tutorials & Documentation

How are you going to learn a given software program? Most commercial packages come with tutorials and documentation.

- **Tutorials:** **A _tutorial_ is an instruction book or program that helps you learn to use the product by taking you through a prescribed series of steps.** For instance, our publisher offers several how-to books, known as the Advantage Series, that enable you to learn different kinds of software. Tutorials may also form part of the software package.

- **Documentation:** **_Documentation_ is all information that describes a product to users, including a user guide or reference manual that provides a narrative and graphical description of a program.** While documentation may be print-based, today it is usually available on CD, as well as via the internet. Documentation may be instructional, but features and functions are usually grouped by category for reference purposes. For example, in word processing documentation, all features related to printing are grouped together so that you can easily look them up.

A Few Facts About Files—& the Usefulness of Importing & Exporting

There is only one reason for having application software: to take raw data and manipulate it into useful files of information. **A _file_ is (1) a named collection of data or (2) a program that exists in a computer's secondary storage** (Chapter 1, p. 12), such as floppy disk, hard disk, or CD/DVD.

Three well-known types of data files are as follows:

- **Document files:** Document files are created by word processing programs and consist of documents such as reports, letters, memos, and term papers.
- **Worksheet files:** Worksheet files are created by electronic spreadsheets and usually consist of collections of numerical data such as budgets, sales forecasts, and schedules.
- **Database files:** Database files are created by database management programs and consist of organized data that can be analyzed and displayed in various useful ways. Examples are student names and addresses that can be displayed according to age, grade-point average, or home state.

Other common types of files (such as graphics, audio, and video files) are discussed in Chapter 7.

It's useful to know that often files can be exchanged—that is, *imported* and *exported*—between programs.

- **Importing:** **_Importing_ is defined as getting data from another source and then converting it into a format compatible with the program in which you are currently working.** For example, you might write a letter in your word processing program and include in it—that is, import—a column of numbers from your spreadsheet program.
- **Exporting:** **_Exporting_ is defined as transforming data into a format that can be used in another program and then transmitting it.** For example, you might work up a list of names and addresses in your database program and then send it—export it—to a document you wrote in your word processing program.

QuickCheck

Distinguish among the following kinds of software: commercial, public-domain, shareware, freeware, rentalware, and pirated software.

Describe tutorials and documentation.

What are three types of data files?

Distinguish importing from exporting.

The Types of Software

Application software can be classified in many ways—for entertainment, personal, education/reference, productivity, and specialized uses. *(See ● Panel 3.10 on the next page.)*

In the rest of this chapter we will discuss types of **_productivity software_— such as word processing programs, spreadsheets, and database managers— whose purpose is to make users more productive at particular tasks.** Some productivity software comes in the form of an *office suite*, which bundles several applications together into a single large package. Microsoft Office, for example, includes (among other things) Word, Excel, and Access—word processing, spreadsheet, and database programs, respectively. Corel offers similar programs. Other productivity software, such as Lotus Notes, is sold as *groupware*—online software that allows several people to collaborate on the same project and share some resources.

We now consider the three most important types of productivity software: word processing, spreadsheet, and database software (including personal information managers). We then discuss more specialized software: presentation graphics, financial, desktop-publishing, drawing and painting, video/audio editing software, project management, computer-aided design, and web page design.

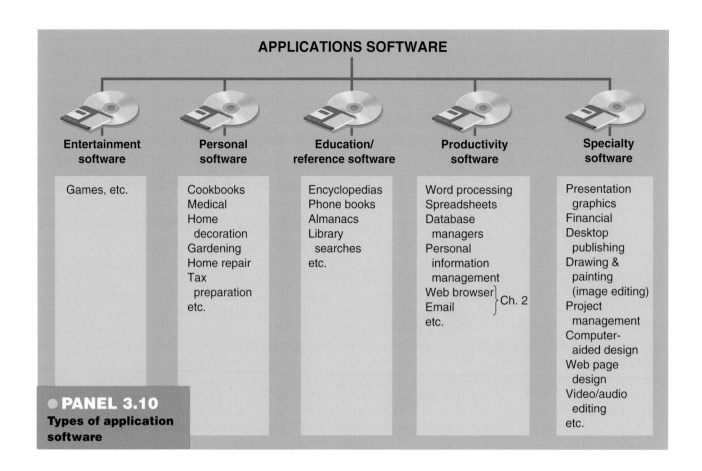

APPLICATIONS SOFTWARE

Entertainment software	Personal software	Education/ reference software	Productivity software	Specialty software
Games, etc.	Cookbooks Medical Home decoration Gardening Home repair Tax preparation etc.	Encyclopedias Phone books Almanacs Library searches etc.	Word processing Spreadsheets Database managers Personal information management Web browser} Ch. 2 Email etc.	Presentation graphics Financial Desktop publishing Drawing & painting (image editing) Project management Computer- aided design Web page design Video/audio editing etc.

● PANEL 3.10
Types of application software

● PANEL 3.11
Keyboard functions

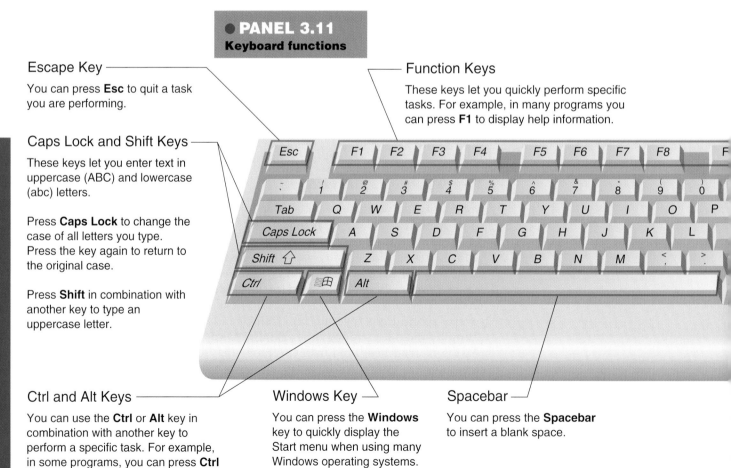

Escape Key
You can press **Esc** to quit a task you are performing.

Function Keys
These keys let you quickly perform specific tasks. For example, in many programs you can press **F1** to display help information.

Caps Lock and Shift Keys
These keys let you enter text in uppercase (ABC) and lowercase (abc) letters.

Press **Caps Lock** to change the case of all letters you type. Press the key again to return to the original case.

Press **Shift** in combination with another key to type an uppercase letter.

Ctrl and Alt Keys
You can use the **Ctrl** or **Alt** key in combination with another key to perform a specific task. For example, in some programs, you can press **Ctrl** and **S** to save a document.

Windows Key
You can press the **Windows** key to quickly display the Start menu when using many Windows operating systems.

Spacebar
You can press the **Spacebar** to insert a blank space.

After a long and productive life, the typewriter has gone to its reward. Indeed, it is practically as difficult today to get a manual typewriter repaired as to find a blacksmith. Word processing software offers a much-improved way of dealing with documents.

**Word processing software** **allows you to use computers to create, edit, format, print, and store text material,** among other things. Word processing is the most common software application. The best-known word processing program is probably Microsoft Word, but there are others such as Corel Word-Perfect and the word processing components of Lotus Smart Suite and Sun Microsystems' StarOffice. Word processing software allows users to work through a document and *delete, insert,* and *replace* text, the principal edit/correction activities. It also offers such additional features as *creating, formatting, printing,* and *saving.*

Features of the Keyboard

Besides the mouse, the principal tool of word processing is the keyboard. As well as letter, number, and punctuation keys and often a calculator-style numeric keypad, computer keyboards have special-purpose and function keys. *(See* ● *Panel 3.11, below.)* Sometimes, for the sake of convenience, strings of keystrokes are used in combinations called *macros.*

- **Special-purpose keys:** _**Special-purpose keys**_ **are used to enter, delete, and edit data and to execute commands.** An example is the *Esc* (for "Escape") key, which tells the computer to cancel an operation or leave ("escape from") the current mode of operation. The Enter, or

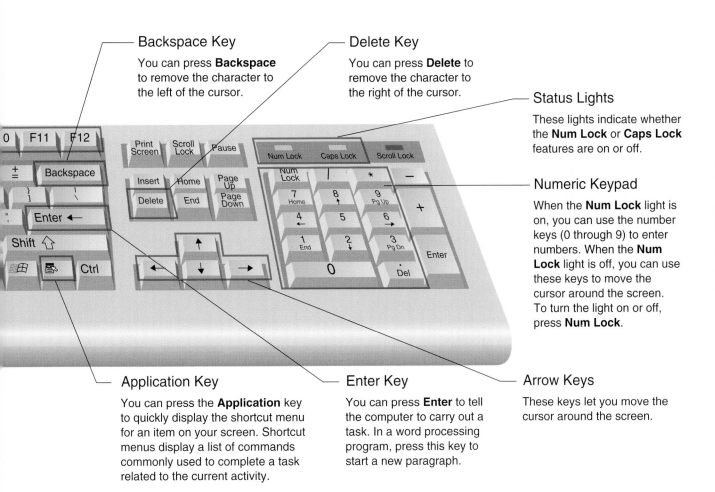

Backspace Key

You can press **Backspace** to remove the character to the left of the cursor.

Delete Key

You can press **Delete** to remove the character to the right of the cursor.

Status Lights

These lights indicate whether the **Num Lock** or **Caps Lock** features are on or off.

Numeric Keypad

When the **Num Lock** light is on, you can use the number keys (0 through 9) to enter numbers. When the **Num Lock** light is off, you can use these keys to move the cursor around the screen. To turn the light on or off, press **Num Lock**.

Application Key

You can press the **Application** key to quickly display the shortcut menu for an item on your screen. Shortcut menus display a list of commands commonly used to complete a task related to the current activity.

Enter Key

You can press **Enter** to tell the computer to carry out a task. In a word processing program, press this key to start a new paragraph.

Arrow Keys

These keys let you move the cursor around the screen.

You don't always need to use the mouse to pull down menus to perform functions. These menus provide information about which shortcut keys serve the same mouse-click function. For instance, pull down the Edit menu and look for "select-all" (select all the text in the document)—you will see to the right of that selection "ctrl-A," the shortcut. So, if you press *Ctrl+A*, you select all the text in your document, just as if you used the mouse to click on that item in the pull-down menu. Most commands have a shortcut key, and common functions usually have the same shortcut command in different programs.

Return, key, which you will use often, tells the computer to execute certain commands and to start new paragraphs in a document. *Commands* are instructions that cause the software to perform specific actions.

Special-purpose keys are generally used the same way regardless of the application software package being used. Most keyboards include the following special-purpose keys: *Esc, Ctrl, Alt, Del, Ins, Home, End, PgUp, PgDn, Num Lock*, and a few others. (*Ctrl* means "Control," *Del* means "Delete," *Ins* means "Insert," for example.)

- **Function keys:** *Function keys*, **labeled "F1," "F2," and so on, are positioned along the top or left side of the keyboard. They are used to execute commands specific to the software being used.** For example, one application software package may use F6 to exit a file, whereas another may use F6 to underline a word.

- **Macros:** Sometimes you may wish to reduce the number of keystrokes required to execute a command. To do this, you use a macro. **A** *macro*, **also called a** *keyboard shortcut*, **is a single keystroke or command—or a series of keystrokes or commands—used to automatically issue a longer, predetermined series of keystrokes or commands.** Thus, you can consolidate several activities into only one or two keystrokes. The user names the macro and stores the corresponding command sequence; once this is done, the macro can be used repeatedly. (To set up a macro, pull down the Help menu and type in *macro*.)

Although many people have no need for macros, individuals who find themselves continually repeating complicated patterns of keystrokes say they are quite useful.

Creating Documents

Creating a document means entering text using the keyboard or the dictation function associated with speech-recognition software. Word processing software has three features that affect this process—the *cursor, scrolling*, and *word wrap*:

To clean your printer, first open the top by pressing the button on the left side near the top. Swing the lid

Cursor

- **Cursor: The** *cursor* **is the movable symbol on the display screen that shows you where you may next enter data or commands.** The symbol is often a blinking rectangle or an I-beam. You can move the cursor on the screen using the keyboard's directional arrow keys or a mouse. The point where the cursor is located is called the *insertion point*.

- **Scrolling:** *Scrolling* **means moving quickly upward, downward, or sideways through the text or other screen display.** A standard computer screen displays only 20–22 lines of standard-size text. Of course, most documents are longer than that. Using the directional arrow keys, or the mouse and a scroll bar located at the side of the screen, you can move ("scroll") through the display screen and into the text above and below it.

- **Word wrap:** *Word wrap* **automatically continues text to the next line when you reach the right margin.** That is, the text "wraps around" to the next line. You don't have to hit a "carriage-return" key or Enter key, as was necessary with a typewriter.

Scrolling

To help you organize term papers and reports, the *Outline View* feature puts tags on various headings to show the hierarchy of heads—for example, main head, subhead, and sub-subhead. Word processing software also allows you to insert footnotes that are automatically numbered and renumbered when changes are made. The basics of word processing are shown in the accompanying illustration. (*See* ● *Panel 3.12.*)

Toolbar:
Allows quick access to frequently used commands

Menu bar:
Allows access to all commands

Title bar:
Shows name of document you're working on

Spelling and Grammar button:
Click on to check for misspelled words and incorrect grammar.

Text alignment buttons:
Click on to align text to be left, center, right, or full justified.

Style button:
Click on to access variety of format styles.

Ruler:
Shows tabs and margins

Insertion point:
Blinking symbol shows where the next character you type will appear

Status bar:
Shows details about the document you're working on

Window controls:
Let you enlarge a window, restore its previous position, or hide it from view

Mouse pointer:
Use the mouse to move the insertion point, to click on icons, or to select text for editing.

Scroll bars:
Let you scroll the document to reveal hidden portions

Taskbar

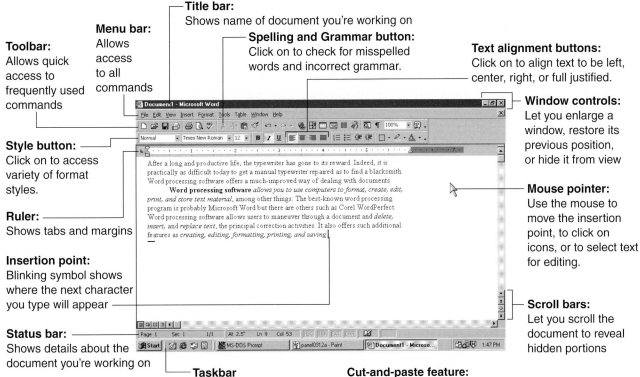

Outline feature:
Enables you to view headings in your document

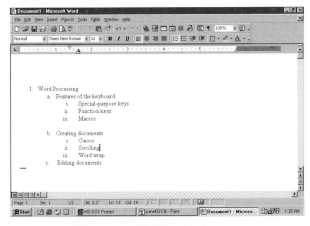

Cut-and-paste feature:
Enables you to move blocks of text. First highlight the text. On Edit menu, select Cut option. Then, on Edit menu, select Paste option. (You can also use the icons in the toolbar.)

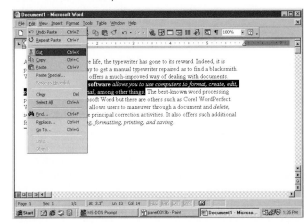

Font button   **Font size button**

To format text, first highlight it.   Then select formatting

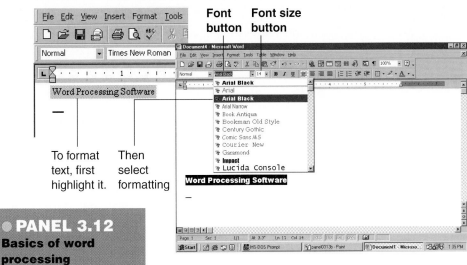

Formatting feature:
Enables you to change type font and size. First highlight the text. Then click next to Font button for pull-down menu of fonts. Click next to Font Size button for menu of type sizes.

● **PANEL 3.12**
Basics of word processing

Software

PRACTICAL ACTION BOX
Installing & Reinstalling Software

Crashes, freezes, slowdowns, glitches, error messages, grey-outs, screen darkness. And frustration and apoplexy. Hell hath no fury greater than a Windows user whose PC for no apparent reason abruptly quits working. The problem may be the fault of the operating system, although it is more likely caused by application programs or device drivers (p. 154; the programs that allow the OS to communicate with specific hardware). Often crashes occur when you've upgraded your operating system (from Windows Me to Windows XP, say), for which your application programs are no longer as workable.

What to do?

The Restore Disk

Maybe your PC didn't come with Windows backed up on a disk (the result of a licensing agreement between the PC's manufacturer and the software maker), but it should have come with a Restore disk, usually a CD. Put it in your CD drive, follow the on-screen instructions, and your operating system will be restored. Unfortunately, any application programs you installed since buying the PC will have to be reinstalled.

The Windows Service Pack

A *service pack* is a collection of files for various updates, software bug fixes, and security improvements. Windows XP Service Pack 1 (SP 1) includes around 300 fixes and is designed to bolster the operating system's security and software and hardware stability. You can also use SP1 to remove features that have been mandatory parts of Windows (such as Internet Explorer and Windows Media Player). For information, go to *www.microsoft.com/windowsxp* (you can download SP1, but the size of the file is so huge you may wish to order it on a CD for a "nominal fee"). In addition, Windows XP constantly offers pop-up update alerts at the bottom of the screen, which invite users to download automatic "patches" or software fixes.

Installing & Reinstalling

Here's how to approach installing or reinstalling software, especially application programs. You will need the *Readme* instructions, the *disk* containing the program, and perhaps the *serial number* of either the software or your computer.

1. **Read *Readme*.** Most software comes with an instruction manual or documentation (long and wordy). Set this aside. Instead, look for a piece of paper that came with your software or a file on the software CD or floppy disk that says "Readme" or "Read Me." Read or at least skim it.

2. **Put the Install disk in the drive.** Most software comes with an Installation or Setup disk. These days it's probably a CD, although it could be one or a series of floppy disks. Insert the disk into the CD drive (or floppy drive, if appropriate). Most will start automatically. If yours doesn't, click on the Windows *Start* menu (bottom left of screen), then click on *Control Panel,* then click on the *Add or Remove Programs* icon, then click on *Change or Remove Programs.*

3. **Follow the instructions.** You should delete the old program and insert the new one from the disk. Follow the instructions for doing so. If the screen asks for your name, program serial number, and the like, type that in. (The serial number will be in the box of software, on the system cabinet, or inside the manual.)

4. **Keep going until done.** You may be asked to choose among various options. It's best to choose *default,* which will reinstate the conditions that were standard with the program as you purchased it. If you're installing from several floppy disks, just keep inserting and removing and inserting them one after the other (disk 1, then disk 2, and so on) until finished.

5. **Reboot, if necessary.** After you've finished installing, you may be directed to shut off the computer and then turn it on again—that is, reboot it.

Your software will probably work now. If it doesn't, call tech support.

Editing Documents

Editing is the act of altering your document. Some Edit features are *insert* and *delete, undelete, find and replace, cut/copy and paste, spelling checker, grammar checker,* and *thesaurus.* Some of these commands are in the Edit pull-down menu and icons on the toolbar.

- **Insert and delete:** *Inserting* is the act of adding to the document. Simply place the cursor wherever you want to add text and start typing; the existing characters will be pushed along. If you want to write over (replace) text as you write, press the *Insert* key before typing. When you're finished typing, press the *Insert* key again to exit Insert mode.

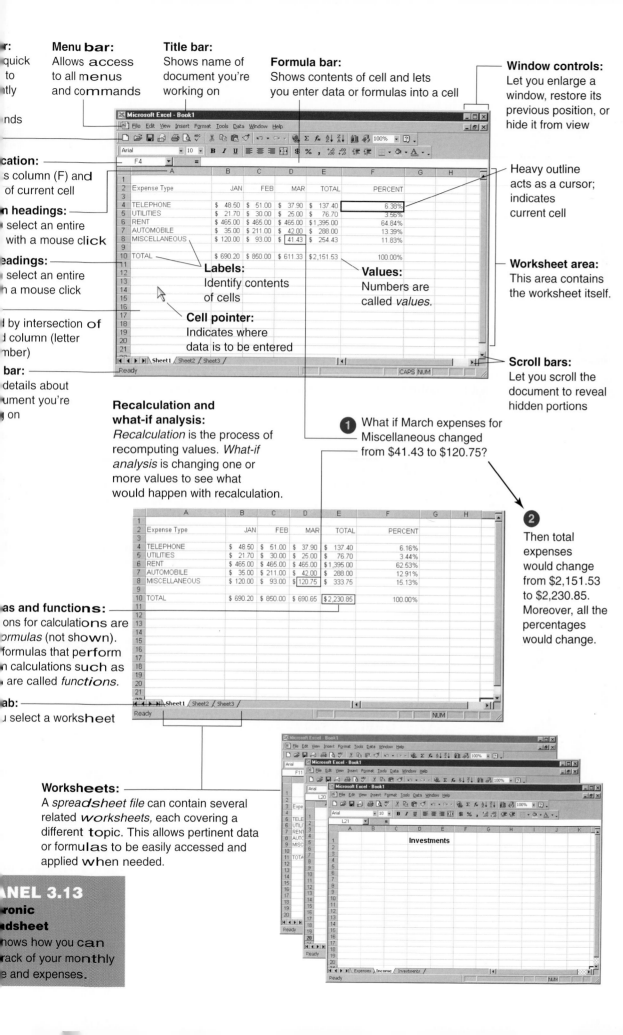

Menu bar: Allows access to all menus and commands

Title bar: Shows name of document you're working on

Formula bar: Shows contents of cell and lets you enter data or formulas into a cell

Window controls: Let you enlarge a window, restore its previous position, or hide it from view

Heavy outline acts as a cursor; indicates current cell

Worksheet area: This area contains the worksheet itself.

Labels: Identify contents of cells

Values: Numbers are called *values*.

Cell pointer: Indicates where data is to be entered

Scroll bars: Let you scroll the document to reveal hidden portions

Recalculation and what-if analysis: *Recalculation* is the process of recomputing values. *What-if analysis* is changing one or more values to see what would happen with recalculation.

1 What if March expenses for Miscellaneous changed from $41.43 to $120.75?

2 Then total expenses would change from $2,151.53 to $2,230.85. Moreover, all the percentages would change.

...as and functions: ...ons for calculations are ...ormulas (not shown). ...formulas that perform ...n calculations such as ...are called *functions*.

...ab: ...u select a worksheet

Worksheets: A *spreadsheet file* can contain several related *worksheets*, each covering a different topic. This allows pertinent data or formulas to be easily accessed and applied when needed.

...ation: ...s column (F) and ...of current cell

...n headings: ...select an entire ...with a mouse click

...eadings: ...select an entire ...h a mouse click

...by intersection of ...column (letter ...mber)

...bar: ...details about ...ument you're ...g on

...ANEL 3.13
...ronic
...dsheet
...nows how you can
...rack of your monthly
...e and expenses.

Deleting is the act of removing text, usually using the *Delete* or *Backspace* key.

The *Undo command* allows you to change your mind and restore text that you have deleted. Some word processing programs offer as many as 100 layers of "undo," so that users who delete several paragraphs of text, but then change their minds, can reinstate the material.

- **Find and replace:** The *Find*, or *Search, command* allows you to find any word, phrase, or number that exists in your document. The *Replace command* allows you to automatically replace it with something else.

- **Cut/copy and paste:** Typewriter users who wanted to move a paragraph or block of text from one place to another in a manuscript used scissors and glue to "cut and paste." With word processing, moving text takes only a few keystrokes. You select (highlight) the portion of text you want to copy or move. Then you use the *Copy* or *Cut command* to move it to the *clipboard*, a special holding area in the computer's memory. From there, you use *Paste* to transfer the material to any point (indicated with the cursor) in the existing document or in a new document. The clipboard retains its material, so repeated pastes of the same item will work without your having to recopy each time.

- **Spelling checker:** Most word processors have a **_spelling checker_**, **which tests for incorrectly spelled words.** As you type, the spelling checker indicates (perhaps with a squiggly line) words that aren't in its dictionary and thus may be misspelled. Special add-on dictionaries are available for medical, engineering, and legal terms. In addition, programs such as Microsoft Word have an Auto Correct function that automatically fixes such common mistakes as transposed letters— replacing "teh" with "the," for instance.

- **Grammar checker:** **A _grammar checker_ highlights poor grammar, wordiness, incomplete sentences, and awkward phrases.** The grammar checker won't fix things automatically, but it will flag (perhaps with a different-color squiggly line) possible incorrect word usage and sentence structure.

- **Thesaurus:** If you find yourself stuck for the right word while you're writing, you can call up an on-screen **_thesaurus_, which will present you with the appropriate word or alternative words.**

Formatting Documents with the Help of Templates & Wizards

In the context of word processing, **_formatting_ means determining the appearance of a document.** To this end, word processing programs provide two helpful devices—templates and wizards. **A _template_ is a preformatted document that provides basic tools for shaping a final document**—the text, layout, and style for a letter, for example. **A _wizard_ answers your questions and uses the answers to lay out and format a document** (or perform other actions). In Word, you can use the Memo wizard to create professional-looking memos or the Résumé wizard to create a résumé.

Among the many aspects of formatting are the following: You can decide what **_font_—typeface and type size—**you wish to use. You can choose whether you want the lines to be *single-spaced* or *double-spaced* (or something else). You can specify whether you want text to be *one column* (like this page), *two columns* (like many magazines and books), or *several columns* (like newspapers). You can indicate the dimensions of the margins—left, right, top, and bottom—around the text. You can specify the text *justification*—how the letters and words are spaced in each line. To *justify* means to align text

Some different fonts

10 point
Times Roman

**14 point
Arial Black**

`16 point
Courier`

60

(60 point Arial)

evenly between left and right margins, as in most newspaper columns and this paragraph. To *left-justify* means to align text evenly on the left. (Left-justified text has a "ragged-right" margin, as do many business letters.) *Centering* centers each text line in the available white space between the left and right margins.

You can also indicate headers or footers and include page numbers. *A header* is common text (such as a date or document name) printed at the top of every page. A *footer* is the same thing printed at the bottom of every page. If you want page numbers, you can determine what number to start with, among other things.

You can specify *borders* or other decorative lines, *shading, tables,* and *footnotes.* You can even import *graphics* or drawings from files in other software programs, including *clip art*—collections of ready-made pictures and illustrations available online or on CDs/DVDs.

It's worth noting that word processing programs (and indeed most forms of application software) come from the manufacturer with default settings. **Default settings are the settings automatically used by a program unless the user specifies otherwise, thereby overriding them.** Thus, for example, a word processing program may automatically prepare a document single-spaced, left-justified, with 1-inch right and left margins, unless you alter these default settings.

Left-justified

Justified

Centered

Right-justified

Printing, Faxing, or Emailing Documents

Most word processing software gives you several options for printing. For example, you can print *several copies* of a document. You can print *individual pages* or a *range of pages.* You can even preview a document before printing it out. *Previewing (print previewing)* means viewing a document on-screen to see what it will look like in printed form before it's printed. Whole pages are displayed in reduced size.

You can also send your document off to someone else by fax or email attachment if your computer has the appropriate communications link.

Saving Documents

Saving means storing, or preserving, a document as an electronic file permanently—on floppy disk, hard disk, or CD, for example. Saving is a feature of nearly all application software. Having the document stored in electronic form spares you the tiresome chore of retyping it from scratch whenever you want to make changes. You need only retrieve it from the storage medium and make the changes you want. Then you can print it out again. (Save your documents often while you are working; don't wait until the document is finished.)

Tracking Changes & Inserting Comments

What if you have written an important document and have asked other people to edit it? Word processing software allows editing changes to be tracked by highlighting them, underlining additions, and crossing out deletions. Each person working on the document can choose a different color so that you can tell who's done what. And anyone can insert hidden questions or comments that become visible when you pass the mouse pointer over yellow-highlighted words or punctuation. An edited document can be printed out showing all the changes, as well as a list of comments keyed to the text by numbers. Or it can be printed out "clean," showing the edited text in its new form, without the changes.

When Several Word Documents Are Open

You can write with several Word documents open simultaneously. To go ("toggle") back and forth, hold down *Ctrl* and press *F6.* To go backward, press *Ctrl, Shift,* and press *F6.* To display several documents at once, go to the *Window* menu and select *Arrange All.* You can cut and paste text from one document to another.

Web Document Creation

Most word processing programs allow you to automa uments into HTML (see Chapter 2, p. 64) so that th web.

QuickCheck

What are the important features of the keyboard?

Describe the role of the cursor, scrolling, and word documents.

What word processing features are available to help

What assistance is available to help you format doc aspects of formatting should be of concern to you

3.4 Spreadsheets

KEY QUESTION

What can you do with an electronic spreadsheet that you can't do with pencil and paper and a standard calculator?

What is a spreadsheet? Traditionally, it was simpl columns, printed on special light-green paper, that was cial projections and reports. A person making up a s days and weekends at the office penciling tiny numbe rectangles. When one figure changed, all other numb had to be recomputed. Ultimately, there might be wa soned worksheets.

In 1978, Daniel Bricklin was a student at the Har One day he was staring at columns of numbers on a bl the idea for computerizing the spreadsheet. He creat *spreadsheet,* now called simply a *spreadsheet.* **The sp to create tables and financial schedules by entering d rows and columns arranged as a grid on a display sc** electronic spreadsheet was the most popular small bus tunately for Bricklin, his version (called VisiCalc) was others. Today the principal spreadsheets are Microsoft Pro, and Lotus 1-2-3. Spreadsheets are used for main books, tracking investments, creating and tracking bud payments, estimating project costs, and creating oth reports.

The Basics: How Spreadsheets Work

A spreadsheet is arranged as follows. *(See ● Panel 3.13*

- **How a spreadsheet is organized—column headings labels:** A spreadsheet's arrangement of columns, r called a *worksheet.* In the worksheet's frame area *column headings* appear across the top ("A" is the column, "B" the second, and so on). Numbered *ro* down the left side ("1" is the name of the first ro and so forth). **Labels are any descriptive text that** such as APRIL, RENT, or GROSS SALES. You use keyboard to type in the various headings and label has 256 columns and 65,536 rows, and each spread to 255 related worksheets.

Toolb
Allows
acces
freque
used
comm

Cell l
Displa
row (

Colu
Let yo
colum

Row
Let yo
row w

Cell:
Form
row a
and r

Statu
Show
the d
worki

For
Instr
calle
Built
com
add

She
Lets

B
s
T
k
i

Deleting is the act of removing text, usually using the *Delete* or *Backspace* key.

The *Undo command* allows you to change your mind and restore text that you have deleted. Some word processing programs offer as many as 100 layers of "undo," so that users who delete several paragraphs of text, but then change their minds, can reinstate the material.

- **Find and replace:** The *Find*, or *Search*, *command* allows you to find any word, phrase, or number that exists in your document. The *Replace command* allows you to automatically replace it with something else.

- **Cut/copy and paste:** Typewriter users who wanted to move a paragraph or block of text from one place to another in a manuscript used scissors and glue to "cut and paste." With word processing, moving text takes only a few keystrokes. You select (highlight) the portion of text you want to copy or move. Then you use the *Copy* or *Cut command* to move it to the *clipboard*, a special holding area in the computer's memory. From there, you use *Paste* to transfer the material to any point (indicated with the cursor) in the existing document or in a new document. The clipboard retains its material, so repeated pastes of the same item will work without your having to recopy each time.

- **Spelling checker:** Most word processors have a **_spelling checker_, which tests for incorrectly spelled words.** As you type, the spelling checker indicates (perhaps with a squiggly line) words that aren't in its dictionary and thus may be misspelled. Special add-on dictionaries are available for medical, engineering, and legal terms. In addition, programs such as Microsoft Word have an Auto Correct function that automatically fixes such common mistakes as transposed letters—replacing "teh" with "the," for instance.

- **Grammar checker:** A **_grammar checker_ highlights poor grammar, wordiness, incomplete sentences, and awkward phrases.** The grammar checker won't fix things automatically, but it will flag (perhaps with a different-color squiggly line) possible incorrect word usage and sentence structure.

- **Thesaurus:** If you find yourself stuck for the right word while you're writing, you can call up an on-screen **_thesaurus_, which will present you with the appropriate word or alternative words.**

Formatting Documents with the Help of Templates & Wizards

In the context of word processing, **_formatting_ means determining the appearance of a document.** To this end, word processing programs provide two helpful devices—templates and wizards. **A _template_ is a preformatted document that provides basic tools for shaping a final document**—the text, layout, and style for a letter, for example. **A _wizard_ answers your questions and uses the answers to lay out and format a document** (or perform other actions). In Word, you can use the Memo wizard to create professional-looking memos or the Résumé wizard to create a résumé.

Among the many aspects of formatting are the following: You can decide what **_font_—typeface and type size**—you wish to use. You can choose whether you want the lines to be *single-spaced* or *double-spaced* (or something else). You can specify whether you want text to be *one column* (like this page), *two columns* (like many magazines and books), or *several columns* (like newspapers). You can indicate the dimensions of the margins—left, right, top, and bottom—around the text. You can specify the text *justification*—how the letters and words are spaced in each line. To *justify* means to align text

Some different fonts

10 point
Times Roman

**14 point
Arial Black**

16 point
Courier

60

(60 point Arial)

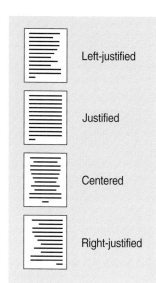

Left-justified

Justified

Centered

Right-justified

~~Four score and~~ <u>Eighty</u>-seven years ago, our fathers <u>and mothers</u> brought forth on this continent a new nation

evenly between left and right margins, as in most newspaper columns and this paragraph. To *left-justify* means to align text evenly on the left. (Left-justified text has a "ragged-right" margin, as do many business letters.) *Centering* centers each text line in the available white space between the left and right margins.

You can also indicate headers or footers and include page numbers. *A header* is common text (such as a date or document name) printed at the top of every page. A *footer* is the same thing printed at the bottom of every page. If you want page numbers, you can determine what number to start with, among other things.

You can specify *borders* or other decorative lines, *shading, tables,* and *footnotes.* You can even import *graphics* or drawings from files in other software programs, including *clip art*—collections of ready-made pictures and illustrations available online or on CDs/DVDs.

It's worth noting that word processing programs (and indeed most forms of application software) come from the manufacturer with default settings. ***Default settings* are the settings automatically used by a program unless the user specifies otherwise, thereby overriding them.** Thus, for example, a word processing program may automatically prepare a document single-spaced, left-justified, with 1-inch right and left margins, unless you alter these default settings.

Printing, Faxing, or Emailing Documents

Most word processing software gives you several options for printing. For example, you can print *several copies* of a document. You can print *individual pages* or a *range of pages.* You can even preview a document before printing it out. *Previewing (print previewing)* means viewing a document on-screen to see what it will look like in printed form before it's printed. Whole pages are displayed in reduced size.

You can also send your document off to someone else by fax or email attachment if your computer has the appropriate communications link.

Saving Documents

***Saving* means storing, or preserving, a document as an electronic file permanently**—on floppy disk, hard disk, or CD, for example. Saving is a feature of nearly all application software. Having the document stored in electronic form spares you the tiresome chore of retyping it from scratch whenever you want to make changes. You need only retrieve it from the storage medium and make the changes you want. Then you can print it out again. (Save your documents often while you are working; don't wait until the document is finished.)

Tracking Changes & Inserting Comments

What if you have written an important document and have asked other people to edit it? Word processing software allows editing changes to be tracked by highlighting them, underlining additions, and crossing out deletions. Each person working on the document can choose a different color so that you can tell who's done what. And anyone can insert hidden questions or comments that become visible when you pass the mouse pointer over yellow-highlighted words or punctuation. An edited document can be printed out showing all the changes, as well as a list of comments keyed to the text by numbers. Or it can be printed out "clean," showing the edited text in its new form, without the changes.

Web Document Creation

Most word processing programs allow you to automatically format your documents into HTML (see Chapter 2, p. 64) so that they can be used on the web.

QuickCheck

What are the important features of the keyboard?

Describe the role of the cursor, scrolling, and word wrap in creating documents.

What word processing features are available to help edit documents?

What assistance is available to help you format documents, and what aspects of formatting should be of concern to you

3.4 Spreadsheets

KEY QUESTION

What can you do with an electronic spreadsheet that you can't do with pencil and paper and a standard calculator?

What is a spreadsheet? Traditionally, it was simply a grid of rows and columns, printed on special light-green paper, that was used to produce financial projections and reports. A person making up a spreadsheet spent long days and weekends at the office penciling tiny numbers into countless tiny rectangles. When one figure changed, all other numbers on the spreadsheet had to be recomputed. Ultimately, there might be wastebaskets full of jettisoned worksheets.

In 1978, Daniel Bricklin was a student at the Harvard Business School. One day he was staring at columns of numbers on a blackboard when he got the idea for computerizing the spreadsheet. He created the first *electronic spreadsheet,* now called simply a *spreadsheet.* **The _spreadsheet_ allows users to create tables and financial schedules by entering data and formulas into rows and columns arranged as a grid on a display screen.** Before long, the electronic spreadsheet was the most popular small business program. Unfortunately for Bricklin, his version (called VisiCalc) was quickly surpassed by others. Today the principal spreadsheets are Microsoft Excel, Corel Quattro Pro, and Lotus 1-2-3. Spreadsheets are used for maintaining student grade books, tracking investments, creating and tracking budgets, calculating loan payments, estimating project costs, and creating other types of financial reports.

The Basics: How Spreadsheets Work

A spreadsheet is arranged as follows. *(See ● Panel 3.13, next page.)*

- **How a spreadsheet is organized—column headings, row headings, and labels:** A spreadsheet's arrangement of columns, rows, and labels is called a *worksheet.* In the worksheet's frame area (work area), lettered *column headings* appear across the top ("A" is the name of the first column, "B" the second, and so on). Numbered *row headings* appear down the left side ("1" is the name of the first row, "2" the second, and so forth). **_Labels_ are any descriptive text that identifies categories,** such as APRIL, RENT, or GROSS SALES. You use your computer's keyboard to type in the various headings and labels. Each worksheet has 256 columns and 65,536 rows, and each spreadsheet file holds up to 255 related worksheets.

Toolbar:
Allows quick access to frequently used commands

Menu bar:
Allows access to all menus and commands

Title bar:
Shows name of document you're working on

Formula bar:
Shows contents of cell and lets you enter data or formulas into a cell

Window controls:
Let you enlarge a window, restore its previous position, or hide it from view

Cell location:
Displays column (F) and row (4) of current cell

Column headings:
Let you select an entire column with a mouse click

Row headings:
Let you select an entire row with a mouse click

Cell:
Formed by intersection of row and column (letter and number)

Status bar:
Shows details about the document you're working on

Heavy outline acts as a cursor; indicates current cell

Worksheet area:
This area contains the worksheet itself.

Labels:
Identify contents of cells

Values:
Numbers are called *values.*

Cell pointer:
Indicates where data is to be entered

Scroll bars:
Let you scroll the document to reveal hidden portions

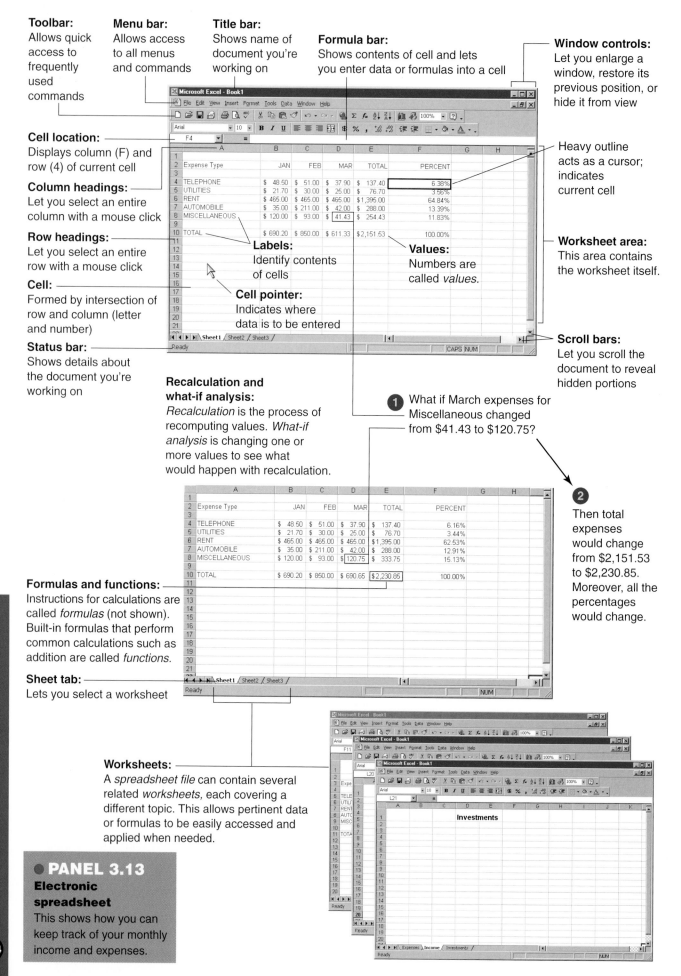

Recalculation and what-if analysis:
Recalculation is the process of recomputing values. *What-if analysis* is changing one or more values to see what would happen with recalculation.

1 What if March expenses for Miscellaneous changed from $41.43 to $120.75?

2 Then total expenses would change from $2,151.53 to $2,230.85. Moreover, all the percentages would change.

Formulas and functions:
Instructions for calculations are called *formulas* (not shown). Built-in formulas that perform common calculations such as addition are called *functions.*

Sheet tab:
Lets you select a worksheet

Worksheets:
A *spreadsheet file* can contain several related *worksheets,* each covering a different topic. This allows pertinent data or formulas to be easily accessed and applied when needed.

● PANEL 3.13
Electronic spreadsheet
This shows how you can keep track of your monthly income and expenses.

Databases are a lot more interesting than they used to be. Once they included only text. Now they can also include pictures, sound, and animation. It's likely, for instance, that your personnel record in a future company database will include a picture of you and perhaps even a clip of your voice. If you go looking for a house to buy, you will be able to view a real estate agent's database of video clips of homes and properties without leaving the realtor's office.

Today the principal microcomputer database programs are Microsoft Access, Corel Paradox, and Lotus Approach. (In larger systems, Oracle is a major player.)

The Basics: How Databases Work

Let's consider some basic features of databases:

info!

Do a keyword search on *databases.* What kinds of databases and database services are available? Did you find any databases that could be useful to you?

- **How a relational database is organized—tables, records, and fields:** The most widely used form of database, especially on PCs, is the **_relational database_, in which data is organized into related tables.** Each table contains rows and columns; the rows are called *records*, and the columns are called *fields*. An example of a record is a person's address—name, street address, city, and so on. An example of a field is that person's last name; another field would be that person's first name; a third field would be that person's street address; and so on. *(See ● Panel 3.15 on the next page.)*

  Just as a spreadsheet file may include several worksheets, so a relational database might include a database with several tables. For instance, if you're running a small company, you might have one database headed *Employees*, containing three tables—*Addresses*, *Payroll*, and *Benefits*. You might have another database headed *Customers*, with *Addresses*, *Orders*, and *Invoices* tables.

- **How various records can be linked—the key:** In relational databases a **_key_—also called *key field*, *sort key*, *index*, or *keyword*—is a field used to sort data.** For example, if you sort records by age, then the age field is a key. Most database management systems allow you to have more than one key so that you can sort records in different ways. One of the keys is designated the *primary key* and must hold a unique value for each record. A key field that identifies records in different tables is called a *foreign key*. Foreign keys are used to cross-reference data among relational tables. The most frequent key field used in the United States is the Social Security number, but any unique identifier, such as employee number or student number, can be used.

- **Finding what you want—querying and displaying records:** The beauty of database software is that you can locate records quickly. For example, several offices at your college may need access to your records, but for different reasons: registrar, financial aid, student housing, and so on. Any of these offices can *query records—locate and display records—*by calling them up on a computer screen for viewing and updating. Thus, if you move, your address field will need to be corrected for all relevant offices of the college. A person making a search might make the query, *"Display the address of [your name]."* Once a record is displayed, the address field can be changed. Thereafter, any office calling up your file will see the new address.

- **Sorting and analyzing records and applying formulas:** With database software you can easily find and change the order of records in a table—in other words, they can be *sorted* in different ways—arranged alphabetically, numerically, geographically, or in some other order. For example, they can be rearranged by state, by age, or by Social Security number.

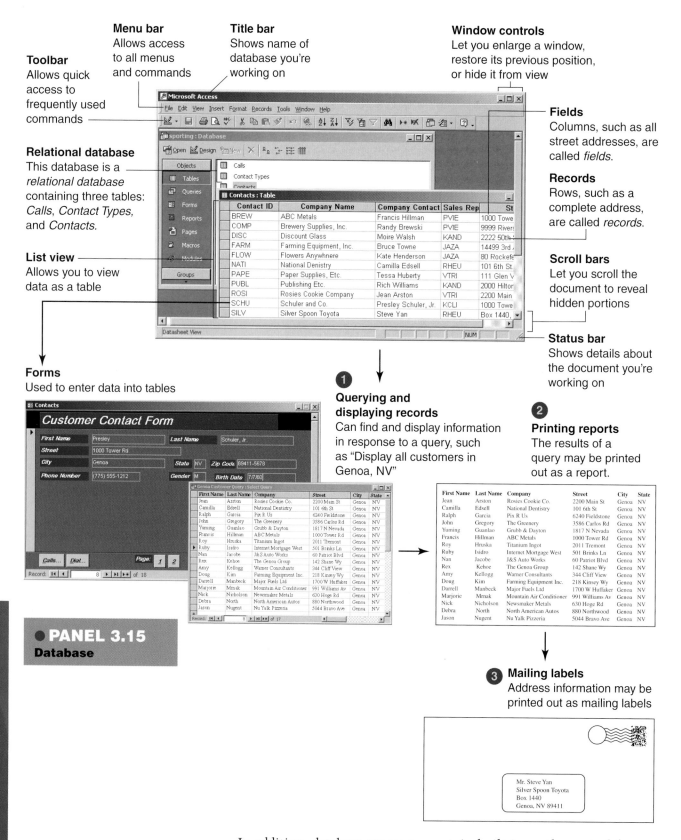

Toolbar
Allows quick access to frequently used commands

Menu bar
Allows access to all menus and commands

Title bar
Shows name of database you're working on

Window controls
Let you enlarge a window, restore its previous position, or hide it from view

Relational database
This database is a *relational database* containing three tables: *Calls*, *Contact Types*, and *Contacts*.

List view
Allows you to view data as a table

Fields
Columns, such as all street addresses, are called *fields*.

Records
Rows, such as a complete address, are called *records*.

Scroll bars
Let you scroll the document to reveal hidden portions

Status bar
Shows details about the document you're working on

Forms
Used to enter data into tables

1 Querying and displaying records
Can find and display information in response to a query, such as "Display all customers in Genoa, NV"

2 Printing reports
The results of a query may be printed out as a report.

3 Mailing labels
Address information may be printed out as mailing labels

● **PANEL 3.15**
Database

In addition, database programs contain built-in mathematical formulas so that you can analyze data. This feature can be used, for example, to find the grade-point averages for students in different majors or in different classes.

- **Putting search results to use—saving, formatting, printing, copying, or transmitting:** Once you've queried, sorted, and analyzed the records and fields, you can simply save them to your hard disk, floppy disk, or CD. You can format them in different ways, altering headings and typestyles. You can print them out on paper as reports, such as an employee list with up-to-date addresses and phone numbers. A common use is to print out the results as names and addresses on *mailing labels*—adhesive-backed stickers that can be run through your printer, and then stuck on envelopes. You can use the copy command to copy your search results and then paste them into a paper produced on your word processor. You can also cut and paste data into an email message or make the data an attachment file to an email, so that it can be transmitted to someone else.

Personal Information Managers

Pretend you are sitting at a desk in an old-fashioned office. You have a calendar, a Rolodex-type address file, and a notepad. Similar items could also be found on a student's desk. How would a computer and software improve on this arrangement?

Many people find ready uses for specialized types of database software known as personal information managers. **A *personal information manager (PIM)* is software that helps you keep track of and manage information you use on a daily basis, such as addresses, telephone numbers, appointments, to-do lists, and miscellaneous notes.** Some programs feature phone dialers, outliners (for roughing out ideas in outline form), and ticklers (or reminders). With a PIM, you can key in notes in any way you like and then retrieve them later based on any of the words you typed.

Popular PIMs are Microsoft Outlook, Lotus SmartSuite Organizer, and Act. Microsoft Outlook, for example, has sections such as Inbox, Calendar, Contacts, Tasks (to-do list), Journal (to record interactions with people), Notes (scratchpad), and Files. *(See ● Panel 3.16.)* Other PIM programs are Day-Timer and !SBiSTER International Time & Chaos.

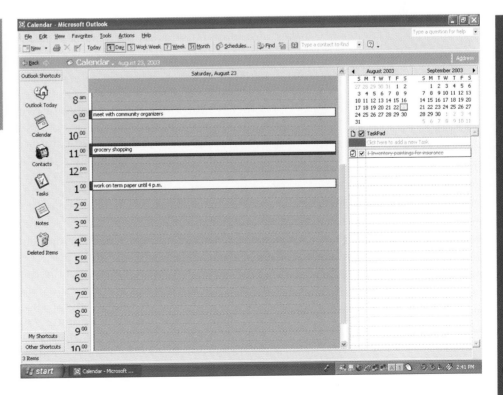

● **PANEL 3.16**
Personal information manager
This shows the calendar available with Microsoft Outlook.

3.6 Specialty Software

KEY QUESTIONS

What are the principal uses of specialty software such as presentation graphics, financial, desktop publishing, drawing and painting, video/audio editing, project management, computer-aided design, and web page design software?

After learning some of the productivity software just described, you may wish to become familiar with more specialized programs. For example, you might first learn word processing and then move on to desktop publishing, or first learn spreadsheets and then learn personal-finance software. We will consider the following kinds of software, although they are but a handful of the thousands of specialized programs available: *presentation graphics, financial, desktop-publishing, drawing and painting, video/audio editing, project management, computer-aided design,* and *web page design software.*

Presentation Graphics Software

You may already be accustomed to seeing presentation graphics because many college instructors now use such software to accompany their lectures. **_Presentation graphics software_ uses graphics, animation, sound, and data or information to make visual presentations.** Well-known presentation graphics packages include Microsoft PowerPoint, Corel Presentations, Innovus Multimedia Presentations, Design Intelligence i publish, and Lotus Freelance Graphics. *(See ● Panel 3.17.)*

Visual presentations are commonly called *slide shows,* although they can consist not only of 35-mm slides but also of paper copies, overhead transparencies, video, animation, and sound. Presentation graphics packages often come with slide sorters, which group together a dozen or so slides in miniature. The person making the presentation can use a mouse or keyboard to bring the slides up for viewing or even start a self-running electronic slide show. You can also use a projection system from the computer itself.

Let's examine the process of using presentation software:

- **Using templates to get started:** Just as word processing programs offer templates for faxes, business letters, and the like, presentation graphics programs offer templates to help you organize your presentation, whether it's for a roomful of people or over the internet. Templates are of two types: design and content. *Design templates* offer formats, layouts, background patterns, and color schemes that can apply to general forms of content material. *Content templates* offer formats for specific subjects; for instance, PowerPoint offers templates for "Selling Your Ideas," "Facilitating a Meeting," and "Motivating a Team." The software offers wizards that walk you through the process of filling in the template.

- **Getting assistance on content development and organization:** To provide assistance as you're building your presentation, PowerPoint displays three windows on your screen at the same time—*Outline View, Slide View,* and *Notes Page View.* This enables you to add new slides, create and edit the text on the slides, and create notes (to use as lecture or speech notes) while developing your presentation.

    Outline View helps you organize the content of your material in standard outline form. The text you enter into the outline is automatically formatted into slides according to the template you selected. If

1 **Outline View**
This view helps you organize the content of your material in standard outline form.

2 **Dressing up your presentation**
PowerPoint offers professional design templates of text format, background, and borders. You place your text for each slide into one of these templates. You can also import a graphic from the clip art that comes with the program.

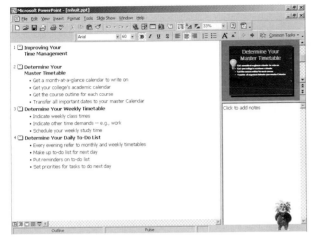

3 **Slide View**
This view allows you to see what a single slide will look like. You can use this view to edit the content and looks of each slide.

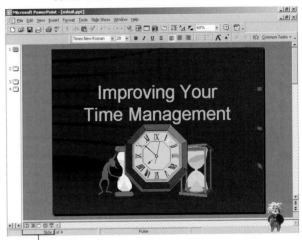

4 **Notes Page View**
This view displays a small version of the slide plus the notes you will be using as speaker notes.

View icons
Clicking on these offers different views: *Slide, Outline, Slide Sorter, Notes Page,* and *Slide Show*

5 **Slide Sorter View**
This view displays miniatures of each slide, enabling you to adjust the order of your presentation.

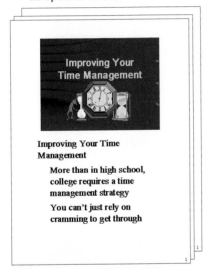

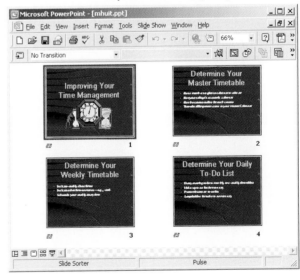

● **PANEL 3.17**
Presentation graphics
Microsoft PowerPoint helps you prepare and make visual presentations.

you wish, you can pull in (import) your outline from a word processing document. *Slide View* helps you see what a single slide will look like. The outline text appears as slide titles and subtitles in subordinate order. *Notes Page View* displays the notes you will be using as speaker notes. It includes a small version of the slide.

Two other views are helpful in organizing and practicing. *Slide Sorter View* allows you to view a number of slides (4 to 12 or more) at once, so you can see how to order and reorder them. *Slide Show View* presents the slides in the order in which your audience will view them, so you can practice your presentation.

- **Dressing up your presentation:** Presentation software makes it easy to dress up each visual page ("slide") with artwork by pulling in clip art from other sources. Although presentations may make use of some basic analytical graphics—bar, line, and pie charts—they usually look much more sophisticated. For instance, they may utilize different texture (speckled, solid, cross-hatched), color, and three-dimensionality. In addition, you can add audio clips, special visual effects (such as blinking text), animation, and video clips.

QuickCheck

What are the benefits of presentation graphics software?

What kind of help is available with a presentation graphics package?

Financial Software

Financial software is a growing category that ranges from personal-finance managers to entry-level accounting programs to business financial-management packages.

Consider the first of these, which you may find particularly useful. **_Personal-finance managers_ let you keep track of income and expenses, write checks, do online banking, and plan financial goals.** Such programs don't promise to make you rich, but they can help you manage your money. They may even get you out of trouble. *(See ● Panel 3.18.)* Many personal-finance programs, such as Quicken and Microsoft Money, include a calendar and a calculator, but the principal features are the following:

- **Tracking of income and expenses:** The programs allow you to set up various account categories for recording income and expenses, including credit card expenses.
- **Checkbook management:** All programs feature checkbook management, with an on-screen check writing form and check register that

● PANEL 3.18
Financial software
Microsoft Money can be used for all sorts of money-related management. It includes guidance tips for setting up your accounts.

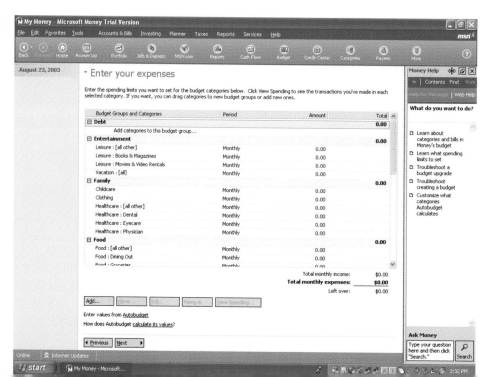

look like the ones in your checkbook. Checks can be purchased to use with your computer printer.

- **Reporting:** All programs compare your actual expenses with your budgeted expenses. Some will compare this year's expenses to last year's.
- **Income tax:** All programs offer tax categories, for indicating types of income and expenses that are important when you're filing your tax return.
- **Other:** Some of the more versatile personal-finance programs also offer financial-planning and portfolio-management features.

Besides personal-finance managers, financial software includes small business accounting and tax software programs, which provide virtually all the forms you need for filing income taxes. Tax programs such as TaxCut and TurboTax make complex calculations, check for mistakes, and even unearth deductions you didn't know existed. Tax programs can be linked to personal-finance software to form an integrated tool.

Many financial software programs may be used in all kinds of enterprises. For instance, accounting software automates bookkeeping tasks, while payroll software keeps records of employee hours and produces reports for tax purposes.

Some programs go beyond financial management and tax and accounting management. For example, Business Plan Pro, Management Pro, and Performance Now can help you set up your own business from scratch.

Finally, there are investment software packages, such as StreetSmart Pro from Charles Schwab and Online Xpress from Fidelity, as well as various retirement-planning programs.

QuickCheck

What is financial software?

What functions does financial software perform?

Desktop Publishing

Not everyone can be successful at desktop publishing, because many complex layouts require experience, skill, and knowledge of graphic design. Indeed, use of these programs by nonprofessional users can lead to rather unprofessional-looking results. Nevertheless, the availability of microcomputers and reasonably inexpensive software has opened up a career area formerly reserved for professional typographers and printers.

***Desktop publishing (DTP)* involves mixing text and graphics to produce high-quality output for commercial printing, using a microcomputer and mouse, scanner, laser or ink-jet printer, and DTP software.** Often the printer is used primarily to get an advance look before the completed job is sent to a typesetter service bureau for even higher-quality output. Service bureaus have special machines that convert the DTP files to film, which can then be used to make plates for offset printing. Offset printing produces higher-quality documents, especially if color is used, but is generally more expensive than laser printing.

Professional DTP programs are QuarkXPress, Adobe InDesign, and Adobe PageMaker. Microsoft Publisher is a "low-end," consumer-oriented DTP package. Some word processing programs, such as Word and WordPerfect, also have many DTP features, although still not at the sophisticated level of the specialized DTP packages. DTP packages, for example, give you more control over typographical characteristics, such as kerning, and provide more support for full-color output.

Desktop publishing has the following characteristics:

- **Mix of text with graphics:** Desktop-publishing software allows you to precisely manage and merge text with graphics. As you lay out a page on-screen, you can make the text "flow," liquid-like, around graphics such as photographs. You can resize art, silhouette it, change the colors, change the texture, flip it upside down, and make it look like a photo negative.

- **Varied type and layout styles:** As do word processing programs, DTP programs provide a variety of fonts, or typestyles, from readable Times Roman to staid Tribune to wild Jester and Scribble. Additional fonts can be purchased on disk or downloaded online. You can also create all kinds of rules, borders, columns, and page-numbering styles.

- **Use of files from other programs:** It's usually not efficient to do word processing, drawing, and painting with the DTP software. As a rule, text is composed on a word processor, artwork is created with drawing and painting software, and photographs are input using a scanner and then modified and stored using image editing software. Prefabricated art to illustrate DTP documents may be obtained from disks containing clip art, or "canned" images. The DTP program is used to integrate all these files. You can look at your work on the display screen as one page or as two facing pages (in reduced size). Then you can see it again after it has been printed out. *(See ● Panel 3.19.)*

Drawing & Painting Programs

It may be no surprise to learn that commercial artists and fine artists have begun to abandon the paintbox and pen and ink for software versions of palettes, brushes, and pens. The surprise, however, is that an artist can use mouse and pen-like stylus to create computer-generated art as good as that achievable with conventional artist's tools. More surprising, even nonartists can produce good-looking work with these programs.

There are two types of computer art programs, also called *illustration software:* drawing and painting:

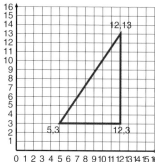

Vector image

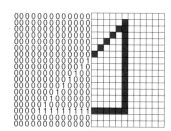

Bit-mapped image

- **Drawing programs:** A **_drawing program_ is graphics software that allows users to design and illustrate objects and products.** Some drawing programs are CorelDRAW, Adobe Illustrator, Macromedia Freehand, and Sketcher.

  Drawing programs create *vector images*—images created from geometrical formulas. Almost all sophisticated graphics programs use vector graphics.

- **Painting programs:** **_Painting programs_ are graphics programs that allow users to simulate painting on screen.** A mouse or a tablet stylus is used to simulate a paintbrush. The program allows you to select "brush" sizes as well as colors from a color palette. Examples of painting programs are MetaCreations' Painter 3D, Adobe PhotoShop, Corel PhotoPaint, and JASC's PaintShop Pro.

  Painting programs produce *bit-mapped images,* or *raster images,* made up of little dots.

  Painting software is also called *image-editing software* because it allows you to retouch photographs, adjust the contrast and the colors, and add special effects, such as shadows.

Video/Audio Editing Software

The popularity of digital camcorders ("camera recorders") has caused an increase in sales of video editing software. This software allows you to

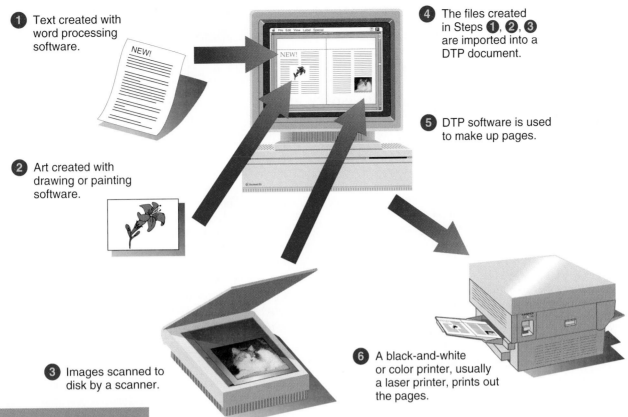

① Text created with word processing software.

② Art created with drawing or painting software.

③ Images scanned to disk by a scanner.

④ The files created in Steps ①, ②, ③ are imported into a DTP document.

⑤ DTP software is used to make up pages.

⑥ A black-and-white or color printer, usually a laser printer, prints out the pages.

PANEL 3.19
How desktop publishing uses other files

import video footage to your PC and edit it—for example, deleting parts you don't want, reordering sequences, and adding special effects. Popular video editing software packages include Adobe Premiere, Pinnacle Studio DV, and Unlead VideoStudio.

Audio editing software provides similar capabilities for working with sound tracks, and you can also clean up background noise (called *artifacts*) and emphasize certain sound qualities. Sound editing software includes Audacity, GoldWave, FASoft, Ace of WAV, Cakewalk Home Studio, Cool Edit Pro, Cubase SX, and WaveLab.

QuickCheck

What can you do with desktop-publishing software?

What are some characteristics of DTP software?

What are some features of drawing programs? Of painting programs?

What can you do with video/audio editing software?

Project Management Software

As we have seen, a personal information manager (PIM) can help you schedule your appointments and do some planning. That is, it can help you manage your own life. But what if you need to manage the lives of others in order to accomplish a full-blown project, such as steering a political campaign or handling a nationwide road tour for a band? Strictly defined, a *project* is a one-time operation involving several tasks and multiple resources that must be organized toward completing a specific goal within a given period of time. The project can be small, such as an advertising campaign for an in-house advertising department, or large, such as construction of an office tower or a jetliner.

PRACTICAL ACTION BOX
How to Buy Software

Whatever type of software you're interested in, you need to be clear on a few things before you buy:

- *Do you know your needs?* You should understand what you want your computer to do for you. Are you mainly writing research papers? Projecting sales figures? Building a mailing list? Creating artwork?

- *Do you know what software you want?* The safest course is to pick software packages used successfully by people you know or packages given high ratings in computer magazines. If you have a particular brand and type in mind, make sure it's the most recent version and release. (If a new version will be released soon, you may want to hold off buying until it's available.)

- *Will the salespeople speak your language?* Some sales people know their wares but talk down to newcomers to try to impress them with their knowledge. Others have only the barest familiarity with their products, although they may be patient with novices' questions. You hope, of course, you'll get someone who is both knowledgeable and helpful.

The types of software sellers are as follows:

- *Computer retail stores:* Small retail stores may offer you a well-informed, knowledgeable staff. Such stores may be those in dealer chains, such as MicroAge Computer Centers, or they may be home-grown independents. Computer superstores, such as ComputerLand, may offer computers for trying out software and classes for learning particular software packages. Retailers also have technical departments for installing software and readying and repairing hardware.

- *Electronics, office, department, and warehouse stores:* Electronics stores (Radio Shack, Circuit City, Best Buy), large office-supply stores (Staples, Office Depot), department stores (Sears, Macys), and certain discount warehouse stores (Costco, Target) all may sell software at steeply discounted prices. The drawbacks are that these stores may not have repair services, customer support, or salespeople with deep product knowledge.

- *Online sellers:* Amazon.com *(www.amazon.com)*, BuyCheapSoftware *(www.buycheapsoftware.com)*, MicroWarehouse *(www.warehouse.com/pm)*, and TigerDirect *(www.tigerdirect.com)* are all online sellers with toll-free numbers or websites from which you may order software. You charge the order to your credit card, and the product is delivered to you by UPS, FedEx, or Priority Mail.

Project management software **is a program used to plan and schedule the people, costs, and resources required to complete a project on time.** For instance, the associate producer on a feature film might use such software to keep track of the locations, cast and crew, materials, dollars, and schedules needed to complete the picture on time and within budget. The software would show the scheduled beginning and ending dates for a particular task—such as shooting all scenes on a certain set—and then the date that task was actually completed. Examples of project management software are Mindjet MindManager, Harvard Project Manager, Microsoft Project, and Suretrack Project Manager.

Computer-Aided Design

Computers have long been used in engineering design. ***Computer-aided design (CAD)*** **programs are intended for the design of products, structures, civil engineering drawings, and maps.** CAD programs, which are available for microcomputers, help architects design buildings and workspaces and help engineers design cars, planes, electronic devices, roadways, bridges, and subdivisions. CAD and drawing programs are similar. However, CAD programs provide precise dimensioning and positioning of the elements being drawn, so that they can be transferred later to computer-aided manufacturing (CAM) programs. Also, CAD programs lack the special effects for illustrations that

■more info!

The Ultimate CAD Directory has information about all sorts of CAD products to suit every type of need: *www.tenlinks.com/CAD*

come with drawing programs. One advantage of CAD software is that the product can be drawn in three dimensions and then rotated on the screen so the designer can see all sides. *(See ● Panel 3.20.)* Examples of CAD programs for beginners are Autosketch, Turbocad, and CorelCAD.

Computer-aided design/computer-aided manufacturing (CAD/CAM) software allows products designed with CAD to be input into an automated manufacturing system that makes the products. For example, CAD/CAM systems brought a whirlwind of enhanced creativity and efficiency to the fashion industry. Some CAD systems, says one writer, "allow designers to electronically drape digital-generated mannequins in flowing gowns or tailored suits that don't exist, or twist imaginary threads into yarns, yarns into weaves, weaves into sweaters without once touching needle to garment."[4] The designs and specifications are then input into CAM systems that enable robot pattern-cutters to automatically cut thousands of patterns from fabric with only minimal waste. Whereas previously the fashion industry worked about a year in advance of delivery, CAD/CAM has cut that time to 8 months—a competitive edge for a field that feeds on fads.

QuickCheck

Describe what project management software can do.

What is the purpose of CAD software? CAD/CAM software?

Survival Tip

Want to Learn How to Use Flash?

www.macromedia.com/ support/training
www.fmctraining.com
www.learnit.com

Web Page Design/Authoring Software

As we mentioned in Chapter 2, web page design software is used to create web pages with sophisticated multimedia features. A few of these packages are easy enough for even beginners to use. Among the best-known are Macromedia Dreamweaver, Macromedia Flash, Adobe GoLive, and Microsoft FrontPage.

Chapter 6 includes a box on how to design your own web page.

● PANEL 3.20
CAD
CAD software is used for nearly all three-dimensional designing.

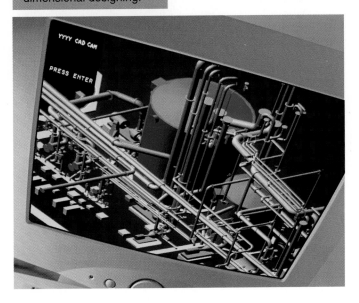

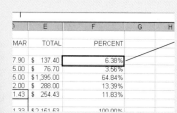

Summary

analytical graphics (p. 115, KQ 3.4) Also called *business graphics;* graphical forms that make numeric data easier to analyze than when it is organized as rows and columns of numbers. The principal examples of analytical graphics are bar charts, line graphs, and pie charts. Why it's important: Whether viewed on a monitor or printed out, analytical graphics help make sales figures, economic trends, and the like easier to comprehend and analyze.

application software (p. 102, KQ 3.2) Software that has been developed to solve a particular problem for users—to perform useful work on specific tasks or to provide entertainment. Why it's important: Application software consists of most of the software you are familiar with and use on a daily basis

booting (p. 87, KQ 3.1) Loading an operating system into a computer's main memory. Why it's important: Without booting, computers could not operate. The programs responsible for booting are stored permanently in the computer's electronic circuitry. When you turn on the machine, programs called *diagnostic routines* test the main memory, the central processing unit, and other parts of the system to make sure they are running properly. Next, BIOS (basic input/output system) programs are copied to main memory and help the computer interpret keyboard characters or transmit characters to the display screen or to a diskette. Then the boot program obtains the operating system, usually from hard disk, and loads it into the computer's main memory, where it remains until you turn the computer off.

cascading menu (p. 92, KQ 3.1) Menu that seems to fly back to the left or explode out to the right. Why it's important: Menus make software easier to use.

cell (p. 115, KQ 3.4) Place where a row and a column intersect in a spreadsheet worksheet; its position is called a *cell address.* Why it's important: The cell is the smallest working unit in a spreadsheet. Data and formulas are entered into cells. Cell addresses provide location references for spreadsheet users.

cell pointer (p.115, KQ 3.4) Also called *spreadsheet cursor,* indicates where data is to be entered. Why it's important: The cell pointer can be moved around like a cursor in a word processing program, and it shows you where the user is in the worksheet.

computer-aided design (CAD) programs (p. 126, KQ 3.6) Programs intended for the design of products, structures, civil engineering drawings, and maps. Why it's important: CAD programs, which are available for microcomputers, help architects design buildings and workspaces and help engineers design cars, planes, electronic devices, roadways, bridges, and subdivisions. While similar to drawing programs, CAD programs provide precise dimensioning and positioning of the elements being drawn, so that they can be transferred later to computer-aided manufacturing programs; in addition, they lack special effects for illustrations. One advantage of CAD software is that three-dimensional drawings can be rotated on screen, so the designer can see all sides of the product.

computer-aided design/computer-aided manufacturing (CAD/CAM) software (p. 127, KQ 3.6) Programs allowing products designed with CAD to be input into an automated manufacturing system that makes the products. Why it's important: CAM systems have greatly enhanced efficiency in many industries.

copyright (p. 102, KQ 3.2) Exclusive legal right that prohibits copying of intellectual property without the permission of the copyright holder. Why it's important: Copyright law aims to prevent people from taking credit for and profiting from other people's work.

To clean your printer, first open the top by pressing the button on the left side near the top. Swing the lid

Cursor

cursor (p. 108, KQ 3.3) Movable symbol on the display screen that shows where the user may next enter data or commands. The symbol is often a blinking rectangle or an I-beam. You can move the cursor on the screen using the keyboard's directional arrow keys or a mouse. The point where the cursor is located is called the insertion point. Why it's important: All application software packages use cursors to show the current work location on the screen.

database (p. 116, KQ 3.5) Collection of interrelated files in a computer system. These computer-based files are organized according to their common elements, so that they can be retrieved easily. Why it's important: Businesses and organizations build databases to help them keep track of and manage their affairs. In addition, online database services put enormous resources at the user's disposal.

database software (p. 116, KQ 3.5) Also called *database manager* or *database management system (DBMS);* application software that sets up and controls the structure of a database and access to the data. Why it's important: Database software allows users to organize and manage huge amounts of data.

default settings (p. 112, KQ 3.3) Settings automatically used by a program unless the user specifies otherwise, thereby overriding them. Why it's important: Users need to know how to change default settings in order to customize documents.

desktop (p. 92, KQ 3.1) The operating system's main interface screen. Why it's important: The desktop displays pictures (icons) that provide quick access to programs and information.

desktop publishing (DTP) (p. 123, KQ 3.6) Application software and hardware system that involves mixing text and graphics to produce high-quality output for commercial printing, using a microcomputer and mouse, scanner, laser or ink-jet printer, and DTP software (such as QuarkXPress and PageMaker or, at a more consumer-oriented level, Microsoft Publisher). Often the printer is used primarily to get an advance look before the completed job is sent to a typesetter for even higher-quality output. Some word processing programs, such as Word and WordPerfect, have rudimentary DTP features. Why it's important: Desktop publishing has reduced the number of steps, the time, and the money required to produce professional-looking printed projects.

device drivers (p. 89, KQ 3.1) Specialized software programs—usually components of system software—that allow input and output devices to communicate with the rest of the computer system. Why it's important: Drivers are needed so that the computer's operating system can recognize and run peripheral hardware.

documentation (p. 104, KQ 3.2) All information that describes a product to users, including a user guide or reference manual that provides a narrative and graphical description of a program. While documentation may be print-based, today it is usually available on CD-ROM, as well as via the internet. Why it's important: Documentation helps users learn software commands and use of function keys, solve problems, and find information about system specifications.

DOS (Disk Operating System) (p. 97, KQ 3.1) Original operating system produced by Microsoft, with a hard-to-use command-driven user interface. Its initial 1982 version was designed to run on the IBM PC as PC-DOS. Later Microsoft licensed the same system to other computer makers as MS-DOS. Why it's important: DOS used to be the most common microcomputer operating system, and it is still used on many microcomputers. Today the most popular operating systems use GUIs.

drawing program (p. 124, KQ 3.6) Graphics software that allows users to design and illustrate objects and products. Why it's important: Drawing programs are vector-based and are best used for straightforward illustrations based on geometric shapes.

exporting (p. 105, KQ 3.2) Transforming data into a format that can be used in another program and then transmitting it. Why it's important: Users need to know how to export many types of files.

Software

Hor

Har

Fire

Fav

Doc

Joh

Qui

file (p. 104, KQ 3.2) A named collection of data or a program that exists in a computer's secondary storage, such as on a floppy disk, hard disk, or CD-ROM disk. Why it's important: Dealing with files is an inescapable part of working with computers. Users need to be familiar with the different types of files.

financial software (p. 122, KQ 3.6) Application software that ranges from personal-finance managers to entry-level accounting programs to business financial-management packages. Why it's important: Financial software provides users with powerful management tools (personal-finance managers) as well as small business programs. Moreover, tax programs provide virtually all the forms needed for filing income taxes, make complex calculations, check for mistakes, and even unearth deductions you didn't know existed. Tax programs can also be integrated with personal finance software to form an integrated tool. Accounting software automates bookkeeping tasks, while payroll software keeps records of employee hours and produces reports for tax purposes. Some programs allow users to set up a business from scratch. Financial software also includes investment software packages and various retirement planning programs.

fonts

10 point
Times Roman

**14 point
Arial Black**

16 point
Courier

60

(60 point Arial)

font (p. 111, KQ 3.3) A particular typeface and type size. Why it's important: Fonts influence the appearance and effectiveness of documents, brochures, and other publications.

formatting (p. 88, KQ 3.1) Also called *initializing;* the process of preparing a floppy disk so that it can store data or programs. Why it's important: Different computers take disks with different formats; thus, you can't run a "Formatted IBM" disk on a Macintosh or a "Formatted Macintosh" disk on an IBM-compatible PC. In word processing (p. 111, KQ 3.3) and desktop publishing, determining the appearance of a document. Why it's important: The document format should match its users' needs. Ways to format a document include using different fonts, boldface, italics, variable spacing, columns, and margins.

formulas (p. 115, KQ 3.4) In a spreadsheet, instructions for calculations entered into designated cells. Why it's important: When spreadsheet users change data in one cell, all the cells linked to it by formulas automatically recalculate their values.

freeware (p. 103, KQ 3.2) Copyrighted software that is distributed free of charge, today most often over the internet. Why it's important: Freeware saves users money.

F1

function key

function keys (p. 108, KQ 3.3) Keys labeled "F1," "F2," and so on, positioned along the top or left side of the keyboard. Why it's important: They are used to execute commands specific to the software being used.

functions (p. 115, KQ 3.4) In a spreadsheet, built-in formulas that perform common calculations. Why it's important: After the values have been entered into the worksheet, formulas and functions can be used to calculate outcomes.

grammar checker (p. 111, KQ 3.3) Word processing feature that highlights poor grammar, wordiness, incomplete sentences, and awkward phrases. The grammar checker won't fix things automatically, but it will flag (perhaps with a color squiggly line) possible incorrect word usage and sentence structure. Why it's important: Grammar checkers help users produce better-written documents.

graphical user interface (GUI) (p. 90, KQ 3.1) User interface in which icons and commands from menus may be selected by means of a mouse or keystrokes. Why it's important: GUIs are easier to use than command-driven interfaces.

Help command (p. 95, KQ 3.1) Command generating a table of contents, an index, and a search feature that can help users locate answers to questions about the software. Why it's important: Help features provide a built-in electronic instruction manual.

icons

icons (p. 92, KQ 3.1) Small pictorial figures that represent programs, data files, or procedures. Why it's important: Icons have simplified the use of software. The feature represented by the icon can be activated by clicking on the icon.

importing (p. 105, KQ 3.2) Getting data from another source and then converting it into a format compatible with the program in which the user is currently working. Why it's important: Users will often have to import files.

key (p. 117, KQ 3.5) Also called *key field*, *sort key*, *index,* or *key word;* field used to sort data in a database. For example, if users sort records by age, then the age field is a key. Why it's important: Key fields are needed to identify and retrieve specific items in a database. Most database management systems allow you to have more than one key so that you can sort records in different ways. The most frequent key field used in the United States is the Social Security number, but any unique identifier, such as employee number or student number, can be used.

label (p. 113, KQ 3.4) Any descriptive text that identifies a category, such as RENT, LOANS, INCOME, etc. Why it's important: Various headings and labels in spreadsheets give meaning to the data.

Linux (p. 100, KQ 3.1) Free version of Unix, supported by efforts of thousands of volunteer programmers. Why it's important: Linux is an inexpensive, open-source operating system useful for online applications and to PC users who have to maintain a web server or a network server.

Macintosh operating system (Mac OS) (p. 97, KQ 3.1) System software that runs only on Apple Macintosh computers. Why it's important: Although Macs are not as common as PCs, many people believe they are easier to use. Macs are often used for graphics and desktop publishing.

macro (p. 108, KQ 3.3) Also called *keyboard shortcut;* a single keystroke or command—or a series of keystrokes or commands—used to automatically issue a longer, predetermined series of keystrokes or commands. Why it's important: Users can consolidate several activities into only one or two keystrokes. The user names the macro and stores the corresponding command sequence; once this is done, the macro can be used repeatedly.

menu (p. 92, KQ 3.1) Displayed list of options—such as commands—to choose from. Why it's important: Menus are a feature of GUIs that make software easier to use.

menu bar (p. 94, KQ 3.1) Bar across the top of the display window, below the title bar. Why it's important: It shows the names of the various pull-down menus available.

Microsoft .NET (p. 99, KQ 3.1) Pronounced "Microsoft dot-net"; set of Microsoft software technologies for connecting information, people, and systems through the use of special building-block web service programs. These programs basically let applications share data, even across networks, and enable applications to run cross-platform and cross-network regardless of how they were built, what operating system or platform they run on, and what devices are used to access them. Why it's important: .NET is Microsoft's platform for an operating system for the entire internet. Designed to link unrelated websites so that people can organize all the information in their lives using PCs and smaller devices, such as cellphones, handheld computers, and set-top boxes. It will incorporate new technology being explored by Microsoft, including speech recognition, handwriting recognition, real-time video, and intelligent browsers. The purpose of .NET is to make the internet easier and more useful.

Microsoft Pocket PC (p. 102, KQ 3.1) Operating system for handhelds that is simpler and less cluttered than CE and looks and feels a lot less like desktop Windows. Its newest form is called *Windows CE .NET.* Why it's important: Pocket PC offers pocket versions of Word and Excel that let users read standard word processing and spreadsheet files sent as email attachments from their PCs.

Microsoft Windows CE (p. 102, KQ 3.1) Greatly slimmed-down version of Windows 95 for handheld computing devices, such as those made by Casio, Compaq, and Hewlett-Packard. Windows CE had some of the familiar Windows look and feel and included rudimentary word processing, spreadsheet, email, web browsing, and other software. Why it's important: Windows CE was Microsoft's first attempt to modify its Windows desktop operating system for use with handhelds. It has been succeeded by the Pocket PC system.

Microsoft Windows Millennium Edition (Windows Me) (p. 98, KQ 3.1) Successor to Windows 95 and 98, operating system designed to support desktop and portable computers. Why it's important: Windows Me is considered a boon to multimedia users because of its ability to handle still pictures, digital video, and audio files. Also, Microsoft claims the system has reduced the problem of frequent "crashes."

Hor
Har
Fire
Fav
Doc
Joh
Qui

Microsoft Windows 95/98 (p. 98, KQ 3.1) Operating system for desktop and portable micro-computers that supports the most hardware and the most application software. Why it's important: Windows has become the most common system software used on microcomputers.

Microsoft Windows NT/2000/2003 (p. 98, KQ 3.1) Multitasking operating system designed to run on network servers. Why it's important: It allows multiple users to share resources such as data, programs, and printers and to build web applications and connect to the internet.

Microsoft Windows XP (p. 99, KQ 3.1) Microsoft's newest OS; it combines elements of Windows networking software and Windows Me and has a new GUI. Why it's important: With this new version, Microsoft is finally giving up the last of the Windows software carried forward from the aging DOS programming technology.

multitasking (p. 88, KQ 3.1) Feature of OS software that allows the execution of two or more programs by one user at the same time on the same computer with one CPU. For instance, you might write a report on your computer with one program while another plays a music CD. Why it's important: Multitasking allows the computer to switch rapidly back and forth among different tasks. The user is generally unaware of the switching process.

NetWare (p. 98, KQ 3.1) Long-popular network operating system for coordinating microcom-puter-based local area networks (LANs) throughout an organization. Why it's important: LANs allow PCs to share programs, data files, and printers and other devices.

open-source software (p. 101, KQ 3.1) Software that any programmer can download from the internet free and modify with suggested improvements. The only qualification is that changes can't be copyrighted; they must be made available to all and remain in the public domain. Why it's important: Because this software is not proprietary, any programmer can make improvements, which can result in better-quality software.

operating system (OS) (p. 87, KQ 3.1) Also called *software platform;* low-level master system of programs that manage the basic operations of the computer. Why it's important: These programs provide resource management services of many kinds. In particular, they handle the control and use of hardware resources, including disk space, memory, CPU time allocation, and peripheral devices. The operating system allows users to concentrate on their own tasks or applications rather than on the complexities of managing the computer.

painting program (p. 124, KQ 3.6) Graphics program that allows users to simulate painting on-screen. A mouse or a tablet stylus is used to simulate a paintbrush. The program allows you to select "brush" sizes, as well as colors from a color palette. Why it's important: Painting programs, which produce raster images made up of little dots, are good for creating art with soft edges and many colors.

Palm OS (p. 102, KQ 3.1) Operating system for the Palm and Visor; the dominant operating system for handhelds. Why it's important: Because it is not a Windows derivative but was specifically designed for handhelds, Palm OS is a smoother-running operating system.

personal-finance manager (p. 122, KQ 3.6) Application software that lets users keep track of income and expenses, write checks, do online banking, and plan financial goals. Why it's important: Personal-finance software can help people manage their money more effectively.

personal information manager (PIM) (p. 119, KQ 3.5) Software that helps users keep track of and manage information they use on a daily basis, such as addresses, telephone numbers, appointments, to-do lists, and miscellaneous notes. Some programs feature phone dialers, outliners (for roughing out ideas in outline form), and ticklers (or reminders). Why it's important: PIMs can help users better organize and manage daily business activities.

pirated software (p. 104, KQ 3.2) Software that is obtained illegally. Why it's important: If you buy such software, not only do the original copyright owners not get paid for their creative work but you risk getting inferior goods and, worse, picking up a virus. To discourage software piracy, many software manufacturers require that users register their software when they install it on their computers. If the software is not registered, it will not work properly.

platform (p. 96, KQ 3.1) Particular processor model and operating system on which a computer system is based. Why it's important: Generally, software written for one platform will not run on any other. Users should be aware that there are Mac platforms (Apple Macintosh) and Windows platforms, or "PC platforms" (for personal computers such as Dell, Compaq, Gateway, Hewlett-Packard, or IBM that run Microsoft Windows). Sometimes the latter are called *Wintel platforms,* for "Windows + Intel," because they often combine the Windows operating system with the Intel processor chip.

pointer (p. 89, KQ 3.1) Indicator that usually appears as an arrow, although it changes shape depending on the application. The mouse is used to move the pointer to a particular place on the display screen or to point to little symbols, or icons. Why it's important: It is often easier to manipulate the pointer on the screen by means of the mouse than to type commands on a keyboard.

pop-up menu (p. 92, KQ 3.1) List of command options that can "pop up" anywhere on the screen when you click the right mouse button. In contrast to pull-down or pull-up menus, pop-up menus are not connected to a toolbar. Why it's important: Pop-up menus make programs easier to use.

presentation graphics software (p. 120, KQ 3.6) Software that uses graphics, animation, sound, and data or information to make visual presentations. Why it's important: Presentation graphics software provides a means of producing sophisticated graphics.

productivity software (p. 105, KQ 3.2) Application software such as word processing programs, spreadsheets, and database managers. Why it's important: Productivity software makes users more productive at particular tasks.

project management software (p. 126, KQ 3.6) Program used to plan and schedule the people, costs, and resources required to complete a project on time. Why it's important: Project management software increases the ease and speed of planning and managing complex projects.

public-domain software (p. 103, KQ 3.2) Software, often available on the internet, that is not protected by copyright and thus may be duplicated by anyone at will. Why it's important: Public-domain software offers lots of software options to users who may not be able to afford much commercial software. Users may download such software from the internet free and make as many copies as they wish.

pull-down menu (p. 92, KQ 3.1) Also called *drop-down menu;* list of options that pulls down from the menu bar at the top of the screen. Why it's important: Like other menu-based and GUI features, pull-down menus make software easier to use.

pull-up menu (p. 92, KQ 3.1) List of options that pulls up from the menu bar at the bottom of the screen. Why it's important: *See* pull-down menu.

range (p. 115, KQ 3.4) A group of adjacent cells in a spreadsheet—for example, A1 to A5. Why it's important: Ranges help sort data for calculation or reports.

recalculation (p. 115, KQ 3.4) The process of recomputing values in a spreadsheet, either as an ongoing process as data is entered or afterward, with the press of a key. Why it's important: With this simple feature, the hours of mind-numbing work required to manually rework paper spreadsheets became a thing of the past.

relational database (p. 117, KQ 3.5) Database in which data is organized into related tables. Each table contains rows and columns; the rows are called *records*, and the columns are called *fields.* An example of a record is a person's address—name, street address, city, and so on. An example of a field is that person's last name; another field would be that person's first name; a third field would be that person's street address; and so on. Why it's important: The relational database is a common type of database.

rentalware (p. 104, KQ 3.2) Software that users lease for a fee and download whenever they want it. Why it's important: This is the concept behind application services providers (ASPs).

rollover (p. 92, KQ 3.1) Icon feature in which a small text box explaining the icon's function appears when you roll the mouse pointer over the icon. A rollover may also produce an animated graphic. Why it's important: The rollover gives the user an immediate explanation of an icon's meaning.

Hon
Har
Fire

Fav
Doc
Joh
Qui

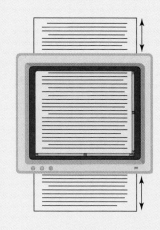

special-purpose keys

saving (p. 112, KQ 3.3) Storing, or preserving, a document as an electronic file permanently—on diskette, hard disk, or CD-ROM, for example. Why it's important: Saving is a feature of nearly all application software. Having the document stored in electronic form spares users the tiresome chore of retyping it from scratch whenever they want to make changes. Users need only retrieve it from the storage medium and make the changes, then resave it and print it out again.

scrolling (p. 108, KQ 3.3) Moving quickly upward, downward, or sideways through the text or other screen display. Why it's important: A standard computer screen displays only 20–22 lines of standard-size text; however, most documents are longer than that. Using the directional arrow keys, or the mouse and a scroll bar located at the side of the screen, users can move ("scroll") through the display screen and into the text above and below it.

shareware (p. 103, KQ 3.2) Copyrighted software that is distributed free of charge but requires that users make a monetary contribution in order to continue using it. Shareware is distributed primarily through the internet. Because it is copyrighted, you cannot use it to develop your own program that would compete with the original product. Why it's important: Like public-domain software and freeware, shareware offers an inexpensive way to obtain new software.

software license (p. 102, KQ 3.2) Contract by which users agree not to make copies of software to give away or resell. Why it's important: Software manufacturers don't sell people software; they sell them licenses to become authorized users of the software.

special-purpose keys (p. 107, KQ 3.3) Keys used to enter, delete, and edit data and to execute commands. For example, the *Esc* (for "Escape") key tells the computer to cancel an operation or leave (" escape from") the current mode of operation. The Enter, or Return, key tells the computer to execute certain commands and to start new paragraphs in a document. Why it's important: Special-purpose keys are essential to the use of software.

spelling checker (p. 111, KQ 3.3) Word processing feature that tests for incorrectly spelled words. As the user types, the spelling checker indicates (perhaps with a squiggly line) words that aren't in its dictionary and thus may be misspelled. Special add-on dictionaries are available for medical, engineering, and legal terms. Why it's important: Spelling checkers help users prepare accurate documents.

spreadsheet (p. 113, KQ 3.4) Application software that allows users to create tables and financial schedules by entering data and formulas into rows and columns arranged as a grid on a display screen. Why it's important: When data is changed in one cell, values in other cells in the spreadsheet are automatically recalculated.

supervisor (p. 87, KQ 3.1) Also called *kernel;* the central component of the operating system that manages the CPU. Why it's important: The supervisor remains in main memory while the computer is running. As well as managing the CPU, it directs other nonresident programs to perform tasks that support application programs.

taskbar (p. 95, KQ 3.1) Graphic toolbar that appears at the bottom of the Windows screen. Why it's important: The taskbar presents the applications that are running.

template (p. 111, KQ 3.3) In word processing, a preformatted document that provides basic tools for shaping a final document—the text, layout, and style for a letter, for example. Why it's important: Templates make it very easy for users to prepare professional-looking documents, because most of the preparatory formatting is done.

thesaurus (p. 111, KQ 3.3) Word processing feature that will present the user with the appropriate word or alternative words. Why it's important: The thesaurus feature helps users prepare well-written documents.

title bar (p. 94, KQ 3.1) Bar across the very top of the display window. Why it's important: It shows the name of the folder the user is in.

toolbar (p. 94, KQ 3.1) Bar across the top of the display window below the menu bar. It displays menus and icons representing frequently used options or commands. Why it's important: Toolbars make it easier to identify and execute commands.

tutorial (p. 104, KQ 3.2) Instruction book or program that helps users learn to use the product by taking them through a prescribed series of steps. Why it's important: Tutorials enable users to practice using new software in a graduated fashion and learn the software in an effective manner.

Unix (p. 100, KQ 3.1) Multitasking operating system for multiple users that has built-in networking capability and versions that can run on all kinds of computers. Why it's important: Government agencies, universities, research institutions, large corporations, and banks all use Unix for everything from designing airplane parts to currency trading. Unix is also used for website management. The developers of the internet built their communication system around Unix because it has the ability to keep large systems (with hundreds of processors) churning out transactions day in and day out for years without fail.

user interface (p. 89, KQ 3.1) User-controllable display screen that allows the user to communicate, or interact, with his or her computer. Why it's important: The interface determines the ease of use of hardware and software. The most common user interface is the graphical user interface (GUI).

utility programs (p. 89, KQ 3.1) Also known as *service programs*; system software component that performs tasks related to the control and allocation of computer resources. Why it's important: Utility programs enhance existing functions or provide services not supplied by other system software programs. Most computers come with built-in utilities as part of the system software.

value (p. 115, KQ 3.4) A number or date entered in a spreadsheet cell. Why it's important: Values are the actual numbers used in the spreadsheet—dollars, percentages, grade points, temperatures, or whatever.

what-if analysis (p. 115, KQ 3.4) Spreadsheet feature that employs the recalculation feature to investigate how changing one or more numbers changes the outcome of the calculation. Why it's important: Users can create a worksheet, putting in formulas and numbers, and then ask, "What would happen if we change that detail? "—and immediately see the effect.

window (p. 95, KQ 3.1) Rectangular frame on the computer display screen. Through this frame users can view a file of data—such as a document, spreadsheet, or database—or an application program. Why it's important: Using windows, users can display at the same time portions of several documents and/or programs on the screen.

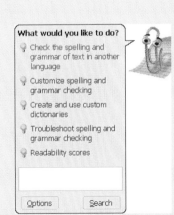

wizard (p. 111, KQ 3.3) Word processing software feature that answers your questions and uses the answers to lay out and format a document or perform other actions. Why it's important: Wizards make it easy to prepare professional-looking memos, faxes, résumés, and other documents.

word processing software (p. 107, KQ 3.3) Application software that allows users to use computers to format, create, edit, print, and store text material, among other things. Why it's important: Word processing software allows users to maneuver through a document and delete, insert, and replace text, the principal correction activities. It also offers such additional features as creating, editing, formatting, printing, and saving.

word wrap (p. 108, KQ 3.3) Special feature that automatically continues text to the next line by "wrapping around" when the user reaches the right margin. Why it's important: You don't have to hit a "carriage-return" key or Enter key to move to the next line.

Chapter Review

"I can recognize and recall information."

Self-Test Questions

1. _____ enables the computer to perform essential operating tasks.

2. _____ is the activity in which a computer works on more than one process at a time.

3. _____ is the term for programs designed to perform specific tasks for the user.

4. _____ is the activity of moving upward or downward through the text or other screen display.

5. Name four editing features offered by word processing programs: _____, _____, _____, _____.

6. In a spreadsheet, the place where a row and a column intersect is called a _____.

7. _____ is the scattering of portions of files about the disk in nonadjacent areas, thus greatly slowing access to the files.

8. A(n) _____ is a keyboard shortcut used to automatically issue a longer, predetermined series of keystrokes or commands.

9. When you buy software, you pay for a _____, a contract by which you agree not to make copies of the software to give away or resell.

10. Records in a database are sorted according to a _____.

11. The _____ is the movable symbol on the display screen that shows you where you may next enter data or commands.

12. _____ involves mixing text and graphics to produce high-quality output for commercial printing.

13. Windows and Mac OS are generally used on _____ computers.

14. _____ is the process of loading an operating system into a computer's main memory.

15. A(n) _____ is a utility that will find all the scattered files on your hard disk and reorganize them as contiguous files.

16. The _____ is the component of system software that comprises the master system of programs that manage the basic operations of the computer.

17. The _____ is the user-controllable display screen that allows you to communicate, or interact, with your computer.

Multiple-Choice Questions

1. Which of the following are functions of the operating system?
   a. file management
   b. CPU management
   c. task management
   d. booting
   e. all the above

2. Which of the following is *not* an advantage of using database software?
   a. integrated data
   b. improved data integrity
   c. lack of structure
   d. elimination of data redundancy

3. Which of the following is (are) *not* a type of menu?
   a. cascading menu
   b. pop-in menu
   c. pop-out menu
   d. pull-down menu
   e. pull-out menu

4. Which of the following is *not* a feature of word processing software?
   a. spelling checker
   b. cell address
   c. formatting
   d. cut and paste
   e. find and replace

True/False Questions

T F 1. Spreadsheet software enables you to perform what-if calculations.

T F 2. *Font* refers to a preformatted document that provides basic tools for shaping the final document.

T F 3. Rentalware is software that users lease for a fee.

T F 4. Public-domain software is protected by copyright and so is offered for sale by license only.

T F 5. The records within the various tables in a database are linked by a key field.

"I can recall information in my own terms and explain them to a friend."

Short-Answer Questions

1. Briefly define *booting*.
2. What is the difference between a command-driven interface and a graphical user interface (GUI)?
3. Why can't you run your computer without system software?
4. Why is multitasking useful?
5. What is a device driver?
6. What is a utility program?
7. What is a platform?
8. What are the three components of system software? What is the basic function of each?
9. What is importing? Exporting?

"I can apply what I've learned, relate these ideas to other concepts, build on other knowledge, and use all these thinking skills to form a judgment."

Knowledge in Action

1. Here's a Windows exercise in defragmenting your hard-disk drive. Defragmenting is a housekeeping procedure that will speed up your system and often free up hard-disk space.

   Double-click on *My Computer* on your Windows desktop (opening screen). Now use your right mouse button to click on *C drive*, then right-click on *Properties,* then left-click on the *Tools* tab. You will see the status of your system (error checking, backup, and defragmenting) and the last time the task was performed on the system. To clear out any errors, click the *Check Now* button; this will run a scan.

   Once the scan is complete, return to the Tools window and click the *Defragment Now* button. Click on *Show Details*. This will visually display on the screen the process of your files being reorganized into a contiguous order.

   Many times when your PC isn't performing well, such as when it's sluggish, running both ScanDisk (Disk Cleanup) and Defragment will solve the problem.

2. Several websites include libraries of shareware programs. Visit the *www.download.cnet.com* site, click on the Windows shareware icon, and identify three shareware programs that interest you. State the name of each program, the operating system it runs on, and its capabilities. Also, describe the contribution you must make to receive technical support.

3. What is your favorite application software program of all? Why?

Web Exercises

1. Some people are fascinated by the error message commonly referred to as the "Blue Screen of Death" (or "Doom") (BSOD). If you run a search on the internet, you can find websites that sell T-shirts with the BSOD image on it, photo galleries of public terminals displaying the BSOD, fictional stories of BSOD attacks, and various other forms of entertainment based on the infamous error message.

To prevent a BSOD attack, keep an eye on how your system is using resources:

a. On Windows 9x: Right-click on the *My Computer* icon on the Windows desktop, click *Properties,* and then choose the *Performance* tab. Next to "system resources" you will see the amount of free resources available as a percentage. Try to keep that value above 18%. If your resources dip below that level, save all your work and reboot.

b. You can also view this information from the System Information file by using the Start menu in this sequence: *Start, Programs, Accessories, System Tools, System Information.*

c. You can also view your system resources constantly in the bottom right-hand corner of the screen, next to the clock. If you have Microsoft Plus! installed, you can use the program entitled "System Resource Meter." This is found by using the same sequence as finding the System Information file, but instead choose *System Resource Meter*, which displays the resource usage.

d. On Windows 2000 or Windows XP, click *Ctrl+ Alt+ Del* and select the *Performance* tab.

   Do a search on the web to find users' hypotheses of why the BSOD occurs, and find more methods to avoid it. Following are some humorous BSOD sites:

   http://zem.squidly.org/bsod/
   www.bbspot.com/News/2002/10/bsod_ads.html
   http://bsod.org
   http://pla-netx.com/linebackn/news/bsod.html

   And a site that explains some of the BSOD errors:

   www.ntbrad.com/bsod.htm

2. Many productivity programs designed after 1997 have features built into them for converting files into web pages. If you have Microsoft Word 97 or later, or Microsoft PowerPoint 97 or later, try saving a document as a website. Under the File menu, select *Save As HTML* or *Save As Webpage* and then view the file in your web browser. What possibilities does this open up for you?

3. Did your computer come with a Windows Startup disk, and have you misplaced it? If your computer crashes, you'll need this disk to reinstall the operating system. This exercise shows you how to create your own Startup disk. Insert a blank disk in your floppy-disk drive. From your Windows desktop, click on *Start, Settings,* and then *Control Panel.* Now click on *Add/Remove.* Click on the tab *Startup Disk,* then click on the *Create Disk* button.

   After the disk is created, label it "Startup Disk for Windows" and write the date on the disk. Also note the version of Windows you are using. Store the disk somewhere safe. You'll never know when you might need it.

   To learn the benefits of having a Startup disk, visit *www.microsoft.com.* Type *startup* in the "search for" box; then click on the link *How to create a Windows 98 startup disk.*

4. Visit the manufacturer's website for your computer (Gateway, Dell, Compaq, Toshiba, etc.). Locate the hyperlink named *Driver* or *Driver downloads.* If you ever call Customer Tech Support, they may ask you to get an updated driver from their website. Familiarize yourself with the location of this essential link, so that you'll know where to go when that time comes. Sometimes there are driver updates that provide extended functionality or fix errors for a device (such as a printer or a scanner), so you should check for driver updates from time to time.

5. Is it more economical to purchase an entire office suite or just the stand-alone programs that you need? Search online for different versions of Microsoft Office and compare the price of the entire suite with what it would cost to purchase each program separately. Then compare the prices of the different suite versions: Small Business, Premium, Professional, Standard, Developer. Which bundled offer is the best purchase for you?

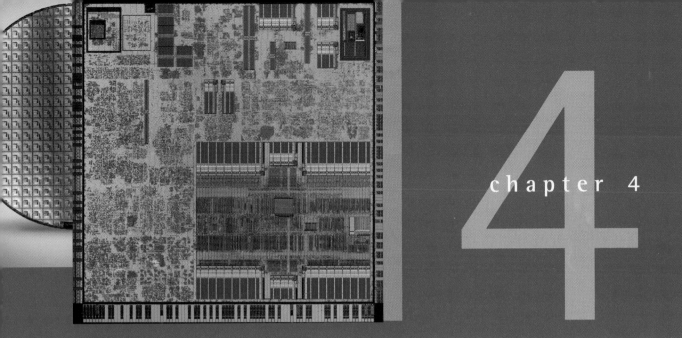

Hardware: The CPU & Storage

How to Buy a Multimedia Computer System

Chapter Topics & Key Questions

4.1   **Microchips, Miniaturization, & Mobility** What are the differences between transistors, integrated circuits, chips, and microprocessors?

4.2   **The System Unit** How is data represented in a computer; what are the components of the system cabinet; what are processing speeds; how do the processor and memory work; and what are some important ports, buses, and cards?

4.3   **Secondary Storage** What are the features of floppy disks, hard disks, optical disks, magnetic tape, smart cards, and online secondary storage?

he microprocessor "is the most important invention of the 20th century," says Michael Malone, author of *The Microprocessor: A Biography.*[1]

Quite a bold claim, considering the incredible products that have issued forth during those 100 years. More important than the airplane? More than television? More than atomic energy?

According to Malone, the case for the exalted status of this thumbnail-size information-processing device is demonstrated, first, by its pervasiveness in the important machines in our lives, from computers to transportation. Second, "The microprocessor is, intrinsically, something special," he says. "Just as [the human being] is an animal, yet transcends that state, so too the microprocessor is a silicon chip, but more." Why? Because it can be programmed to recognize and respond to patterns in the environment, as humans do. Malone writes:

> Implant [a microprocessor] into a traditional machine—say an automobile engine or refrigerator—and suddenly that machine for the first time can learn, it can adapt to its environment, respond to changing conditions, become more efficient, more responsive to the unique needs of its user.[2]

4.1 Microchips, Miniaturization, & Mobility

KEY QUESTION

What are the differences between transistors, integrated circuits, chips, and microprocessors?

The microprocessor has presented us with gifts that we may only barely appreciate—*portability* and *mobility* in electronic devices.

In 1955, for instance, portability was exemplified by the ads showing a young woman holding a Zenith television set over the caption: IT DOESN'T TAKE A MUSCLE MAN TO MOVE THIS LIGHTWEIGHT TV. That "lightweight" TV weighed a hefty 45 pounds. Today, by contrast, there is a handheld Casio 2.3-inch color TV weighing a mere 7 ounces.

Had the transistor not arrived, as it did in 1947, the Age of Portability and consequent mobility would never have happened. To us a "portable" telephone might have meant the 40-pound backpack radio-phones carried by some American GIs during World War II, rather than the 6-ounce shirt-pocket cellular models available today.

From Vacuum Tubes to Transistors to Microchips

Old-time radios used vacuum tubes—small lightbulb-size electronic tubes with glowing filaments. One computer to use these tubes, the ENIAC, which was switched on in 1946 at the University of Pennsylvania, employed about 18,000 of them. Unfortunately, a tube failure occurred on average once every 7 minutes. Since it took more than 15 minutes to find and replace the faulty tube, it was difficult to get any useful computing work done. Moreover, the ENIAC was enormous, occupying 1,800 square feet and weighing more than 30 tons.

The transistor changed all that. **A _transistor_ is essentially a tiny electrically operated switch, or gate, that can alternate between "on" and "off" many millions of times per second.** The transistor was developed by Bell Labs in 1947. The first transistors were one-hundredth the size of a vacuum tube, needed no warm-up time, consumed less energy, and were faster and more reliable. *(See ● Panel 4.1.)* Moreover, they marked the beginning of a process of miniaturization that has not ended yet. In 1960 one transistor fit into an area about a half-centimeter square. This was sufficient to permit Zenith, for instance, to market a transistor radio weighing about 1 pound (convenient, the company advertised, for "pocket or purse"). Today more than 3 million transistors can be squeezed into a half centimeter, and a Sony headset radio, for example, weighs only 6.2 ounces.

In the old days, transistors were made individually and then formed into an electronic circuit with the use of wires and solder. Today transistors are part of an ***integrated circuit***—**an entire electronic circuit, including wires, formed on a single "chip," or piece, of special material, usually silicon,** as part of a single manufacturing process.

An integrated circuit embodies what is called solid-state technology. **In a *solid-state device*, the electrons travel through solid material**—in this case, silicon. They do not travel through a vacuum, as was the case with the old radio vacuum tubes.

What is silicon, and why use it? ***Silicon* is an element that is widely found in clay and sand. It is used not only because its abundance makes it cheap but also because it is a semiconductor. A *semiconductor* is material whose electrical properties are intermediate between a good conductor of electricity and a nonconductor of electricity.** (An example of a good conductor of electricity is the copper in household wiring; an example of a nonconductor is the plastic sheath around that wiring.) Because it is only a semiconductor, silicon has partial resistance to electricity. As a result, highly conducting materials can be overlaid on the silicon to create the electronic circuitry of the integrated circuit. *(See ● Panel 4.2 on the next page.)*

A *chip*, or *microchip*, is a tiny piece of silicon that contains millions of microminiature electronic circuits. Chip manufacture requires very clean environments, which is why chip manufacturing workers appear to be dressed for a surgical operation. Such workers must also be highly skilled, which is why chip makers are not found everywhere in the world.

Miniaturization Miracles: Microchips, Microprocessors, & Micromachines

Microchips—"industrial rice," as the Japanese call them—are responsible for the miniaturization that has revolutionized consumer electronics, computers, and communications. They store and process data in all the electronic gadgetry we've become accustomed to—from microwave ovens to video game controllers to music synthesizers to cameras to automobile fuel-injection systems to pagers to satellites.

There are different kinds of microchips—for example, microprocessor, memory, logic, communications, graphics, and math coprocessor chips. Perhaps the most important is the microprocessor chip. **A *microprocessor* ("microscopic processor" or "processor on a chip") is the miniaturized circuitry of a computer processor—the CPU, the part that processes, or manipulates, data into information** (p. 12). When modified for use in machines other than computers, microprocessors are called *microcontrollers*, or *embedded computers* (p. 10).

Mobility

Smallness in TVs, phones, radios, camcorders, CD players, and computers is now largely taken for granted. In the 1980s portability, or mobility, meant trading off computing power and convenience in return for smaller size and less weight. Today, however, we are getting close to the point where we don't have to give up anything. As a result, experts have predicted that small, powerful, wireless personal electronic devices will

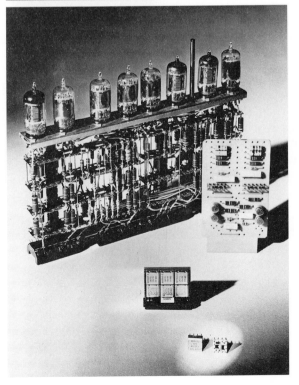

● PANEL 4.2

Making of a chip
How microscopic circuitry
is put onto silicon.

1. A large drawing of the electrical circuitry is made; it looks something like the map of a train yard. The drawing is photo-graphically reduced hundreds of times, to microscopic size.

2. That reduced photograph is then dupli-cated many times so that, like a sheet of postage stamps, there are multiple copies of the same image or circuit.

3. That sheet of multiple copies of the circuit is then printed (in a printing process called *photolithography*) and etched onto a round slice of silicon called a *wafer*. Wafers have gone from 4 inches in diameter to 6 inches to 8 inches, and now are moving toward 12 inches; this allows semiconductor manufacturers to produce more chips at lower cost.

4. Subsequent printings of layer after layer of additional circuits produce multilayered and interconnected electronic circuitry built above and below the original silicon surface.

5. Later an automated die-cutting machine cuts the wafer into separate *chips,* which are usually less than 1 centimeter square and about half a millimeter thick. A *chip,* or microchip, is a tiny piece of silicon that contains millions of microminiature electronic circuit components, mainly transistors. An 8-inch silicon wafer will have a grid of nearly 300 chips, each with as many as 5.5 million transistors.

6. After testing, each chip is mounted in a protective frame with protruding metallic pins that provide electrical connections through wires to a computer or other electronic device.

Chip designers checking out an enlarged drawing of chip circuits

(above) Pentium 4 microprocessor chip mounted in protective frame with pins that can be connected to an electronic device such as a microcomputer.

A wafer imprinted with many microprocessors.

Modern chip with etched transistors. This chip would be about 1/2 inch by 1/2 inch and be several layers deep, with transistors etched on each level.

transform our lives far more than the personal computer has done so far. "The new generation of machines will be truly personal computers, designed for our mobile lives," wrote one reporter in 1992. "We will read office memos between strokes on the golf course, and answer messages from our children in the middle of business meetings."[3] Today such activities are becoming commonplace.

QuickCheck

Describe the evolution of the processor.

How has the invention of the microprocessor been important?

Buying an Inexpensive Personal Computer: Understanding Computer Ads

You're in the market for a new PC and are studying the ads. What does "256 MB DDR SDRAM" mean? How about "40 GB Ultra ATA Hard Drive"? Let's see how to interpret a typical computer ad. *(See ● Panel 4.3.)*

These days a desktop computer is usually a *multimedia computer*, with sound and graphics capability. As we explained in Chapter 1, the word *multimedia* means "combination of media"—the combination of pictures, video, animation, and sound in addition to text. A multimedia computer features such equipment as a fast processor, DVD drive, sound card, graphics card, and speakers, and you may wish to have headphones and a microphone. You may also want to add a scanner, sound recorder, and digital camera.

Let us now go through the parts of a computer system so that you can understand what you're doing when you buy a new computer. First we look at how the system processes data. In the remainder of this chapter, we will consider the *system unit* and *storage devices.* In Chapter 5, we look at *input devices* and *output devices.*

4.2 The System Unit

KEY QUESTIONS

How is data represented in a computer; what are the components of the system cabinet; what are processing speeds; how do the processor and memory work; and what are some important ports, buses, and cards?

Computers run on electricity. What is the most fundamental thing you can say about electricity? Electricity is either *on* or *off*. This two-state situation allows computers to use the binary system to represent data and programs.

The Binary System: Using On/Off Electrical States to Represent Data & Instructions

The decimal system that we are accustomed to has 10 digits (0, 1, 2, 3, 4, 5, 6, 7, 8, 9). By contrast, the **<u>binary system</u> has only two digits: 0 and 1.** Thus, in the computer, the 0 can be represented by the electrical current being off

● **PANEL 4.3**

Advertisement for a PC

The terminology in microcomputer ads does not change as quickly as the numbers; users will continue to need most of these components for a while, but the speeds and capacities change quickly, as do methods of connection.

Great PC Buy!

- 7-Bay Mid-Tower Case
- Intel Pentium 4 Processor 2 GHz
- 128 MB 266 MHz DDR SDRAM
- 512KB L2 Cache
- 2 USB Ports
- 56 Kbps Internal Modem
- 3D AGP Graphics Card (64 MB)
- Sound Blaster Digital Sound Card
- 3.5" Floppy Drive
- Iomega 250 MB Zip Drive
- 80 GB Ultra ATA 7200 RPM Hard Drive
- 4X DVD-RW
- 104-Key Keyboard
- Microsoft IntelliMouse
- 17", .27dp Monitor (16" Display)
- HP DeskJet 970Cse Printer

Details of this ad are explained throughout this chapter. See the little magnifying glass: 🔍

Hardware: The CPU & Storage

● **PANEL 4.4**

Binary data representation

How the letters "G-R-O-W" are represented in one type of on/off, 1/0 binary code.

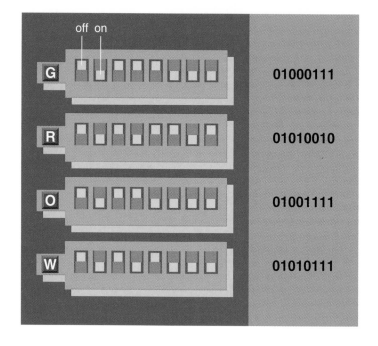

off on

G 01000111

R 01010010

O 01001111

W 01010111

and the 1 by the current being on. Although the use of binary systems is not restricted to computers, *all data and program instructions that go into the computer are represented in terms of these binary numbers.* (See ● *Panel 4.4.*)

For example, the letter "G" is a translation of the electronic signal 01000111, or off-on-off-off-off-on-on-on. When you press the key for "G on the computer keyboard, the character is automatically converted into the series of electronic impulses that the computer can recognize. Inside the computer, the character "G" is represented by a combination of eight *transistors* (as we will describe). Some are off, or closed (representing the 0s), and some are on, or open (representing the 1s).

How many representations of 0s and 1s can be held in a computer or a storage device such as a hard disk? Capacity is denoted by *bits* and *bytes* and multiples thereof:

- **Bit:** In the binary system, **each 0 or 1 is called a *bit*, which is short for "binary digit."**

- **Byte:** To represent letters, numbers, or special characters (such as ! or *), bits are combined into groups. **A group of 8 bits is called a *byte*, and a byte represents one character, digit, or other value.** (As we mentioned, in one scheme, 01000111 represents the letter "G.") The capacity of a computer's memory or of a floppy disk is expressed in numbers of bytes or multiples such as kilobytes and megabytes. (There are 256 combinations of 8 bits available: $2^8 = 256$.)

- **Kilobyte:** A **_kilobyte (K, KB)_** **is about 1,000 bytes.** (Actually, it's precisely 1,024 bytes, but the figure is commonly rounded.) The kilobyte was a common unit of measure for memory or secondary storage capacity on older computers. 1 KB equals about one-half page of text.

- **Megabyte:** A **_megabyte (M, MB)_** **is about 1 million bytes** (1,048,576 bytes). Measures of microcomputer primary-storage capacity today are expressed in megabytes. 1 MB equals about 500 pages of text.

- **Gigabyte:** A **_gigabyte (G, GB)_** **is about 1 billion bytes** (1,073,741,824 bytes). This measure was formerly used mainly with "big iron" (mainframe) computers, but is typical of the secondary storage (hard-disk) capacity of today's microcomputers. 1 GB equals about 500,000 pages of text.

- **Terabyte:** A _terabyte (T, TB)_ represents about 1 trillion bytes (1,009,511,627,776 bytes). 1 TB equals about 500,000,000 pages of text.
- **Petabyte:** A _petabyte (P, PB)_ represents about 1 quadrillion bytes (1,048,576 gigabytes).

Letters, numbers, and special characters are represented within a computer system by means of binary coding schemes. _(See ● Panel 4.5.)_ That is, the off/on 0s and 1s are arranged in such a way that they can be made to represent characters, digits, or other values.

- **ASCII:** Pronounced _"ask-ee,"_ **_ASCII (American Standard Code for Information Interchange)_ is the binary code most widely used with microcomputers.** Besides having the more conventional characters, a version known as Extended ASCII includes such characters as math symbols and Greek letters.
- **EBCDIC:** Pronounced _"eb-see-dick,"_ **_EBCDIC (Extended Binary Coded Decimal Interchange Code)_** is a binary code used with large computers, such as mainframes.
- **Unicode:** Unlike ASCII, **_Unicode_ uses two bytes (16 bits) for each character, rather than one byte (8 bits).** Instead of having the 256 character combinations of ASCII, Unicode can handle 65,536 character combinations. Thus, it allows almost all the written languages of the world to be represented using a single character set.

Machine Language

Why won't word processing software that runs on an Apple Macintosh run (without special arrangements) on an IBM or Dell microcomputer? It's because each computer has its own machine language. **_Machine language_ is a binary-type programming language built into the CPU that the computer can run directly.** To most people, an instruction written in machine language, consisting only of 0s and 1s, is incomprehensible. To the computer, however, the 0s and 1s represent precise storage locations and operations.

<table>
<tr><td>● PANEL 4.5
Binary coding schemes: ASCII and EBCDIC</td><td colspan="6"></td></tr>
<tr><td>Character</td><td>EBCDIC</td><td>ASCII-8</td><td>Character</td><td>EBCDIC</td><td>ASCII-8</td></tr>
<tr><td>A</td><td>1100 0001</td><td>0100 0001</td><td>N</td><td>1101 0101</td><td>0100 1110</td></tr>
<tr><td>B</td><td>1100 0010</td><td>0100 0010</td><td>O</td><td>1101 0110</td><td>0100 1111</td></tr>
<tr><td>C</td><td>1100 0011</td><td>0100 0011</td><td>P</td><td>1101 0111</td><td>0101 0000</td></tr>
<tr><td>D</td><td>1100 0100</td><td>0100 0100</td><td>Q</td><td>1101 1000</td><td>0101 0001</td></tr>
<tr><td>E</td><td>1100 0101</td><td>0100 0101</td><td>R</td><td>1101 1001</td><td>0101 0010</td></tr>
<tr><td>F</td><td>1100 0110</td><td>0100 0110</td><td>S</td><td>1110 0010</td><td>0101 0011</td></tr>
<tr><td>G</td><td>1100 0111</td><td>0100 0111</td><td>T</td><td>1110 0011</td><td>0101 0100</td></tr>
<tr><td>H</td><td>1100 1000</td><td>0100 1000</td><td>U</td><td>1110 0100</td><td>0101 0101</td></tr>
<tr><td>I</td><td>1100 1001</td><td>0100 1001</td><td>V</td><td>1110 0101</td><td>0101 0110</td></tr>
<tr><td>J</td><td>1101 0001</td><td>0100 1010</td><td>W</td><td>1110 0110</td><td>0101 0111</td></tr>
<tr><td>K</td><td>1101 0010</td><td>0100 1011</td><td>X</td><td>1110 0111</td><td>0101 1000</td></tr>
<tr><td>L</td><td>1101 0011</td><td>0100 1100</td><td>Y</td><td>1110 1000</td><td>0101 1001</td></tr>
<tr><td>M</td><td>1101 0100</td><td>0100 1101</td><td>Z</td><td>1110 1001</td><td>0101 1010</td></tr>
<tr><td></td><td></td><td></td><td></td><td></td><td></td></tr>
<tr><td>0</td><td>1111 0000</td><td>0011 0000</td><td>5</td><td>1111 0101</td><td>0011 0101</td></tr>
<tr><td>1</td><td>1111 0001</td><td>0011 0001</td><td>6</td><td>1111 0110</td><td>0011 0110</td></tr>
<tr><td>2</td><td>1111 0010</td><td>0011 0010</td><td>7</td><td>1111 0111</td><td>0011 0111</td></tr>
<tr><td>3</td><td>1111 0011</td><td>0011 0011</td><td>8</td><td>1111 1000</td><td>0011 1000</td></tr>
<tr><td>4</td><td>1111 0100</td><td>0011 0100</td><td>9</td><td>1111 1001</td><td>0011 1001</td></tr>
<tr><td>!</td><td>0101 1010</td><td>0010 0001</td><td>;</td><td>0101 1110</td><td>0011 1011</td></tr>
</table>

How do people-comprehensible program instructions become computer-comprehensible machine language? Special systems programs called *language translators* rapidly convert the instructions into machine language. This translating occurs virtually instantaneously, so you are not aware it is happening. Machine language is discussed in more detail in Appendix A.

Because the type of computer you will most likely be working with is the microcomputer, we'll now take a look at what's inside the microcomputer's system unit.

QuickCheck

What is the binary system?

Define *bits, bytes, kilobytes, megabytes, gigabytes, terabytes,* and *petabytes.*

Distinguish among ASCII, EBCDIC, and Unicode.

Survival Tip

Bay Access

Drive bays are the openings in your computer's case into which drives are installed. If the bay is "accessible," it's open to the outside of the PC (tape, floppy, CD/DVD drives). If it's "hidden," it's closed inside the PC case (hard drive).

A line from the PC ad on page 143

7-Bay Mid-Tower Case

The Computer Case: Bays, Buttons, & Boards

The *system unit* houses the motherboard (including the processor chip and memory chips), the power supply, and storage devices. *(See ● Panel 4.6.)* In computer ads, the part of the system unit that is the empty box with just the power supply is called the *case* or *system cabinet*.

For today's desktop PC, the system unit may be advertised as something like a "4-bay micro-tower case" or a "7-bay mid-tower case." **A _bay_ is a shelf or opening used for the installation of electronic equipment,** generally storage devices such as a hard drive or DVD drive. A computer may come equipped with four or seven bays. Empty bays are covered by a panel.

A *tower* is a cabinet that is tall, narrow, and deep (so that it can sit on the floor beside or under a table) rather than short, wide, and deep. Originally a tower was considered to be 24 inches high. Micro- and mid-towers may be less than half that size.

The number of buttons on the outside of the computer case will vary, but the on/off power switch will appear somewhere, either front or back. There may also be a "sleep" switch; this allows you to suspend operations without terminating them, so that you can conserve electrical power without the need for subsequently "rebooting," or restarting, the computer.

Inside the case—not visible unless you remove the cabinet—are various electrical circuit boards, chief of which is the motherboard, as we'll discuss.

Power Supply

The electricity available from a standard wall outlet is alternating current (AC), but a microcomputer runs on direct current (DC). **The _power supply_ is a device that converts AC to DC to run the computer.** The on/off switch in your computer turns on or shuts off the electricity to the power supply. Because electricity can generate a lot of heat, a fan inside the computer keeps the power supply and other components from becoming too hot.

The Motherboard & the Microprocessor Chip

The *motherboard*, or *system board*, is the main circuit board in the system unit. The motherboard consists of a flat board that fills one side of the case. It contains both soldered, nonremovable components and sockets or slots for

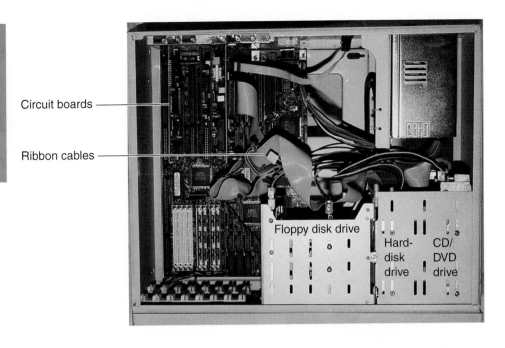

Circuit boards

Ribbon cables

Floppy disk drive

Hard-disk drive

CD/DVD drive

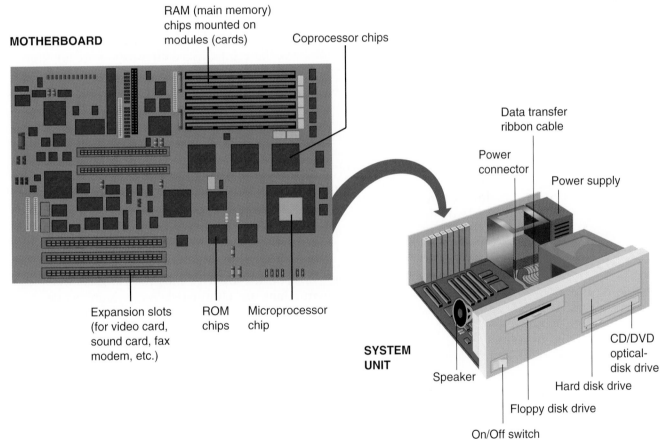

MOTHERBOARD

RAM (main memory) chips mounted on modules (cards)

Coprocessor chips

Data transfer ribbon cable

Power connector

Power supply

Expansion slots (for video card, sound card, fax modem, etc.)

ROM chips

Microprocessor chip

SYSTEM UNIT

Speaker

CD/DVD optical-disk drive

Hard disk drive

Floppy disk drive

On/Off switch

components that can be removed—microprocessor chip, RAM chips, and various expansion cards, as we explain later. *(See ● Panel 4.7 on the next page.)* Making some components removable allows you to expand or upgrade your system. **_Expansion_ is a way of increasing a computer's capabilities by adding hardware to perform tasks that are beyond the scope of the basic system.** For example, you might want to add video and sound cards. **_Upgrading_ means changing to newer, usually more powerful or sophisticated versions,** such as a more powerful microprocessor or more memory chips.

RAM (main memory) chips mounted on modules (cards)

Microprocessor chip (with CPU)

The most fundamental part of the motherboard is the microprocessor chip. As mentioned, a *microprocessor* is the miniaturized circuitry of a computer processor. It stores program instructions that process, or manipulate, data into information. The key parts of the microprocessor are transistors. *Transistors*, as we stated, are tiny electronic devices that act as on/off switches, which process the on/off (1/0) bits used to represent data. According to *Moore's law*, named for legendary Intel cofounder Gordon Moore, the number of transistors that can be packed onto a chip doubles about every 18 months, while the price stays the same. In 1961 a chip had only 4 transistors; in 1971 it had 2,300; in 1979 it had 30,000; and in 1997 it had 7.5 million. Current chips have 42–95 million transistors.

Two principal "architectures" or designs for microprocessors are CISC and RISC. ___CISC (complex instruction set computing) chips___, **which are used mostly in PCs and in conventional mainframes, can support a large number of instructions,** but at relatively low processing speeds. In ___RISC (reduced instruction set computing) chips___, **which are used mostly in workstations, a great many seldom-used instructions are eliminated.** As a result, workstations can work up to 10 times faster than most PCs. RISC chips have been used in many Macintosh computers since 1993.

Most personal computers today use microprocessors of two kinds—those based on the model made by Intel and those based on the model made by Motorola.

- **Intel-type chips—for PCs:** About 90% of microcomputers use Intel-type microprocessors. Indeed, the Microsoft Windows operating system is designed to run on Intel chips. As a result, people in the computer industry tend to refer to the Windows/Intel joint powerhouse as *Wintel.*

  ___Intel-type chips___ **for PCs are made principally by Intel Corp. and Advanced Micro Devices (AMD), but also by Cyrix, DEC, and others.** They are used by manufacturers such as Compaq, Dell, Gateway, Hewlett-Packard, and IBM. Since 1993, Intel has marketed its chips under the names "Pentium," "Pentium Pro," "Pentium MMX," "Pentium II," "Pentium III," "Celeron," "Pentium 4" (P4), and "Centrino" (for mobile computers). Currently, the most commonly used PC Intel chip is the P4, with 42 million

(intel inside)

Intel Pentium 4
Processor 2 GHz

more info!

Which is the better Intel processor, Pentium or Celeron, for basic word processing and web surfing versus video games and complex applications? Find out by doing a web search.

transistors. Many ads for PCs contain the logo "Intel inside" to show that the systems run an Intel microprocessor.

- **Motorola-type chips—for Macintoshes:** **_Motorola-type chips_ are made by Motorola for Apple Macintosh computers.** Since 1993, Motorola has joined forces with IBM and Apple to produce the PowerPC family of chips. With certain hardware or software configurations, a PowerPC can run PC as well as Mac applications software.

Processing Speeds: From Megahertz to Picoseconds

Often a PC ad will carry a line that says something like "Intel Celeron processor 1.80 Ghz," "Intel Pentium 4 processor 3.06 GHz," or "AMD Athlon XP processor 2.16 GHz." *GHz* stands for "gigahertz." These figures indicate how fast the microprocessor can process data and execute program instructions.

Every microprocessor contains a **_system clock_, which controls how fast all the operations within a computer take place.** The system clock uses fixed vibrations from a quartz crystal to deliver a steady stream of digital pulses or "ticks" to the CPU. These ticks are called *cycles*. Faster clock speeds will result in faster processing of data and execution of program instructions, as long as the computer's internal circuits can handle the increased speed.

There are four main ways in which processing speeds are measured:

- **For microcomputers—megahertz and gigahertz:** Older microcomputer microprocessor speeds are expressed in **_megahertz (MHz)_, a measure of frequency equivalent to 1 million cycles (ticks of the system clock) per second.** The original IBM PC had a clock speed of 4.77 MHz, which equaled 4.77 million cycles per second. The latest-generation processors (from AMD and Intel) operate in **_gigahertz (GHz)_—a billion cycles per second.** Intel's latest chip, the Pentium 4, operates at up to 3.06 gigahertz, or 3.06 billion cycles per second. The AMD 64-bit chip, the Athlon 64 FX-SI, runs at 2.2 GHz. Some experts predict that advances in microprocessor technology will produce a 50 GHz CPU by 2010. This kind of power will be necessary to support such functions as true speech interfaces and real-time speech translation.

  At the time of this writing, the new Intel mobile processor—for notebooks—is the Pentium 4M (Centrino), which runs at 1.6–2.4 GHz. The AMD Athlon XP mobile processor runs at about 2.2 GHz. The newest Pentium 4 runs at 3.2 GHz.

  Since a new high-speed processor can cost many hundred dollars more than a previous-generation chip, experts often recommend that buyers fret less about the speed of the processor (since the work most people do on their PCs doesn't even tax the limits of the current hardware) and more about spending money on extra memory. (However, game playing *does* tax the system. Thus, if you're an avid computer game player, you may want to purchase the fastest processor.)

- **For workstations, midrange computers, and mainframes—MIPS:** Processing speed can also be measured according to the number of instructions per second that a computer can process. **_MIPS_ stands for "millions of instructions per second."**

- **For supercomputers—flops:** The abbreviation **_flops_ stands for "floating-point operations per second."** A *floating-point operation* is a special kind of mathematical calculation. This measure, used mainly with supercomputers, is expressed as *megaflops* (mflops, or millions of floating-point operations per second), *gigaflops* (gflops, or billions), and *teraflops* (tflops, or trillions). The Cray Inc. X1 System supercomputer cranks out 52.4 teraflops. (To put this in perspective, a person able to complete one arithmetic calculation every second would take about 1.2 million years to do what X1 does in a single second.) New super-computer speeds will be measured in petaflops (1 quadrillion operations per second).

- **For all computers—fractions of a second:** Another way to measure cycle times is in fractions of a second. A microcomputer operates in microseconds, a supercomputer in nanoseconds or picoseconds—thousands or millions of times faster. A *millisecond* is one-thousandth of a second. A *microsecond* is one-millionth of a second. A *nanosecond* is one-billionth of a second. A *picosecond* is one-trillionth of a second.

QuickCheck

Distinguish expansion from upgrading.

Discuss the most fundamental part of the motherboard, its features, its two principal architectures, and the two principal kinds of processors used in personal computers.

What is the system clock, and what is the common unit of processing speed for microcomputers?

How the Processor or CPU Works: Control Unit, ALU, & Registers

Once upon a time, the processor in a computer was measured in feet. A processing unit in the 1946 ENIAC (which had 20 such processors) was about 2 feet wide and 8 feet high. Today, computers are based on *microprocessors*, less than 1 centimeter square. It may be difficult to visualize components so tiny. Yet it is necessary to understand how microprocessors work if you are to grasp what PC advertisers mean when they throw out terms such as "256 MB DDR-SDRAM" or "512 K Level 2 Advanced Transfer Cache."

Computer professionals often discuss a computer's word size. **__Word size__ is the number of bits that the processor may process at any one time.** The more bits in a word, the faster the computer. A 32-bit computer—that is, one with a 32-bit-word processor—will transfer data within each microprocessor chip in 32-bit chunks or 4 bytes at a time. (Recall there are 8 bits in a byte.) A 64-bit-word computer, such as Apple's PowerPC G5, is faster; it transfers data in 64-bit chunks or 8 bytes at a time.

A processor is also called the *CPU* (p. 12), and it works hand in hand with other circuits known as *main memory* to carry out processing. **The __CPU (central processing unit)__ is the "brain" of the computer; it follows the instructions of the software (program) to manipulate data into information. The CPU consists of two parts—(1) the control unit and (2) the arithmetic/logic unit (ALU), both of which contain registers, or high-speed storage areas** (as we discuss shortly). All are linked by a kind of electronic "roadway" called a *bus*. (See ● *Panel 4.8.*)

- **The control unit—for directing electronic signals:** The __control unit__ **deciphers each instruction stored in the CPU and then carries out the instruction.** It directs the movement of electronic signals between main memory and the arithmetic/logic unit. It also directs these electronic signals between main memory and the input and output devices.

    For every instruction, the control unit carries out four basic operations, known as the *machine cycle*. In the **__machine cycle__, the CPU (1) fetches an instruction, (2) decodes the instruction, (3) executes the instruction, and (4) stores the result.**

● PANEL 4.8
The CPU and main memory

The two main CPU components on a microprocessor are the control unit and the ALU, which contain working storage areas called *registers* and are linked by a kind of electronic roadway called a *bus*.

- **The arithmetic/logic unit—for arithmetic and logical operations: The <u>*arithmetic/logic unit (ALU)*</u> performs arithmetic operations and logical operations and controls the speed of those operations.**

  As you might guess, *arithmetic operations* are the fundamental math operations: addition, subtraction, multiplication, and division.

  Logical operations are comparisons. That is, the ALU compares two pieces of data to see whether one is equal to (=), greater than (>), greater than or equal to (>=), less than (<), less than or equal to (<=), or not equal to (≠) the other.

- **Registers—special high-speed storage areas:** The control unit and the ALU also use registers, special CPU areas that enhance the computer's performance. <u>**Registers**</u> **are high-speed storage areas that temporarily store data during processing.** They may store a program instruction while it is being decoded, store data while it is being processed by the ALU, or store the results of a calculation.

- **Buses—data roadways: <u>Buses</u>, or *bus lines*, are electrical data roadways through which bits are transmitted within the CPU and between the CPU and other components of the motherboard.** A bus resembles a multilane highway: The more lanes it has, the faster the bits can be transferred. The old-fashioned 8-bit-word bus of early microprocessors had only eight pathways. Data is transmitted four times faster in a computer with a 32-bit bus, which has 32 pathways, than in a computer with an 8-bit bus. Intel's Pentium chip is a 64-bit processor as are the Macintosh G5 processors (some models have two processors). Some supercomputers have 128-bit processors. Today there are several principal expansion bus standards, or "architectures," for microcomputers.

  We return to a discussion of buses in a few pages.

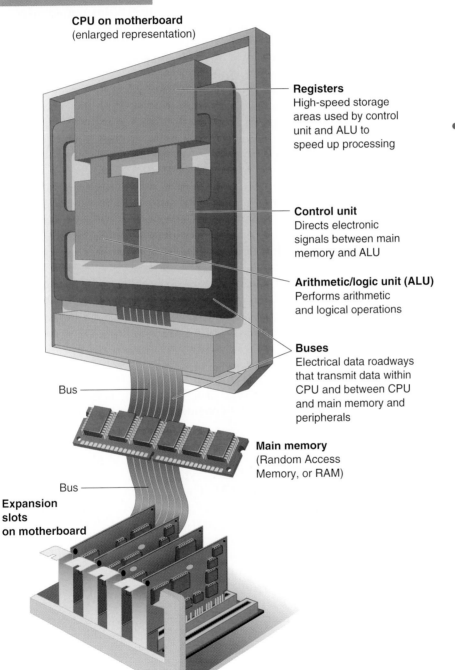

CPU on motherboard
(enlarged representation)

Registers
High-speed storage areas used by control unit and ALU to speed up processing

Control unit
Directs electronic signals between main memory and ALU

Arithmetic/logic unit (ALU)
Performs arithmetic and logical operations

Buses
Electrical data roadways that transmit data within CPU and between CPU and main memory and peripherals

Bus

Main memory
(Random Access Memory, or RAM)

Bus

Expansion slots on motherboard

128 MB 266 MHz
DDR SDRAM

How Memory Works: RAM, ROM, CMOS, & Flash

So far we have described only the kinds of chips known as microprocessors. But other silicon chips called *memory chips* are attached to the motherboard. The four principal types of memory chips are *RAM, ROM, CMOS,* and *flash*.

- **RAM chips—to temporarily store program instructions and data:** Recall from Chapter 1 that there are two types of storage, primary and secondary. Primary storage is temporary or working storage and is often called *memory* or *main memory*; secondary storage, usually called just *storage*, is relatively permanent storage. *Memory* refers to storage media in the form of chips, and *storage* refers to media such as disks and tape. **RAM (random access memory) chips temporarily hold (1) software instructions and (2) data before and after it is processed by the CPU.** Because its contents are temporary, RAM is said to be **volatile—the contents are lost when the power goes off or is turned off.** This is why you should *frequently*—every 5 minutes, say—transfer (save) your work to a secondary storage medium such as your hard disk, in case the electricity goes off while you're working. (However, there is one kind of RAM, called *flash RAM*, that is not temporary, as we'll discuss shortly.)

Several types of RAM chips are used in personal computers—*DRAM, SDRAM, SRAM, RDRAM,* and *DDR-SDRAM:*

—The first type (pronounced "dee-ram"), *DRAM* (dynamic RAM), must be constantly refreshed by the CPU or it will lose its contents.

—The second type of dynamic RAM, used in most PCs today, is *SDRAM (synchronous dynamic RAM),* which is synchronized by the system clock and is much faster than DRAM. Often in computer ads, the speed of SDRAM is expressed in megahertz.

—The third type, *static RAM,* or *SRAM* (pronounced "ess-ram"), is faster than DRAM and retains its contents without having to be refreshed by the CPU.

—The fourth type, *rambus dynamic RAM,* or *RDRAM,* is faster and more expensive than SDRAM and is the type of memory used with Intel's P4 chip.

—The fifth type, *DDR-SDRAM (double-data rate synchronous dynamic RAM)* is the newest type of RAM chip; it is becoming popular in notebook computers and is considered to be the main competitor to RDRAM.

Microcomputers come with different amounts of RAM, which is usually measured in megabytes. An ad may list "128 MB SDRAM," but you can also get 256 or 512 megabytes of RAM. The Macintosh G5 can provide up to 8 GB of RAM. The more RAM you have, the more efficiently the computer operates and the better your software performs. *Having enough RAM is a critical matter.* Before you buy a software package, look at the outside of the box or check the manufacturer's website to see how much RAM is required. Microsoft Office XP, for instance, states that a minimum of 24–64 megabytes of RAM is required, depending on the operating system, plus 8 MB of RAM for each application the user plans to run simultaneously.

If you're short on memory capacity, you can usually add more RAM chips by plugging a RAM *memory module* into the motherboard. A memory module is a small fiberglass circuit board that can be plugged into an expansion slot on the motherboard. There are two types of such modules: SIMMs and the newer DIMMS. A *SIMM (single inline memory module)* has RAM chips on only one side. A *DIMM (dual inline memory module)* has RAM chips on both sides.

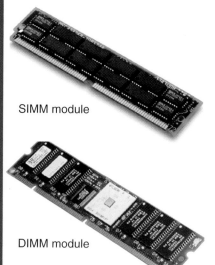

SIMM module

DIMM module

Need Info on RAM?

If your system is giving you low-system-resources messages, you may need more memory. Go to these websites for detailed information on your system:
www.crucial.com
www.kingston.com
www.tomshardware.com

- **ROM chips—to store fixed start-up instructions:** Unlike RAM, to which data is constantly being added and removed, ___ROM (read-only memory)___ **cannot be written on or erased by the computer user without special equipment. ROM chips contain fixed start-up instructions.** That is, ROM chips are loaded, at the factory, with programs containing special instructions for basic computer operations, such as those that start the computer or put characters on the screen. These chips are nonvolatile; their contents are not lost when power to the computer is turned off.

    In computer terminology, ___read___ **means to transfer data from an input source into the computer's memory or CPU. The opposite is** ___write___**—to transfer data from the computer's CPU or memory to an output device.** Thus, with a ROM chip, *read-only* means that the CPU can retrieve programs from the ROM chip but cannot modify or add to those programs. A variation is *PROM (programmable read-only memory)*, which is a ROM chip that allows you, the user, to load read-only programs and data. However, this can be done only once.

- **CMOS chips—to store flexible start-up instructions:** Pronounced "*see-moss*," ___CMOS (complementary metal-oxide semiconductor) chips___ **are powered by a battery and thus don't lose their contents when the power is turned off.** CMOS chips contain flexible start-up instructions—such as time, date, and calendar—that must be kept current even when the computer is turned off. Unlike ROM chips, CMOS chips can be reprogrammed, as when you need to change the time for daylight savings time. (Your system software may prompt you to do this; newer systems do it automatically.)

- **Flash memory chips—to store flexible programs:** Also a nonvolatile form of memory, ___flash memory chips___ **can be erased and reprogrammed more than once** (unlike PROM chips, which can be programmed only once). Flash memory, which doesn't require a battery and which can range from 32 to 128 megabytes in capacity, is used to store programs not only in personal computers but also in pagers, cellphones, MP3 players, Palm organizers, printers, and digital cameras.

512K L2 Cache

How Cache Works: Level 1 (Internal) & Level 2 (External)

Because the CPU runs so much faster than the main system RAM, it ends up waiting for information, which is inefficient. To reduce this effect, we have cache. Pronounced "cash," ___cache___ **temporarily stores instructions and data that the processor is likely to use frequently. Thus, cache speeds up processing.**

There are two kinds of cache—Level 1 and Level 2:

- **Level 1 (L1) cache—part of the microprocessor chip:** *Level 1 (L1) cache*, also called *internal cache*, is built into the processor chip. Ranging from 8 to 256 kilobytes, its capacity is less than that of Level 2 cache, although it operates faster.

- **Level 2 (L2) cache—not part of the microprocessor chip:** This is the kind of cache usually referred to in computer ads. *Level 2 (L2) cache*, also called *external cache*, resides outside the processor chip and consists of SRAM chips. Capacities range from 64 kilobytes to 2 megabytes. (In Intel ads, L2 is called *Advanced Transfer Cache*.) L2 cache is generally quite a bit larger than L1 cache (most new systems have at least 512 kilobytes of L2 cache) and is the most commonly cited type of cache when measuring PC performance.

Cache is not upgradable; it is set by the type of processor purchased with the system.

In addition, most current computer operating systems allow for the use of _virtual memory_—**that is, some free hard-disk space is used to extend the capacity of RAM.** The processor searches for data or program instructions in the following order: (1) first L1, (2) then L2, (3) then RAM, (4) then hard disk (or CD). In this progression, each kind of memory or storage is slower than its predecessor.

QuickCheck

Describe the following: word size, CPU, the control unit and the machine cycle, the ALU and arithmetic and logical operations, registers, and buses.

What is RAM, and what are some variants?

What is ROM?

Discuss CMOS chips and flash memory chips.

How does L1 cache differ from L2 cache?

Ports & Cables

A _port_ is a connecting socket or jack on the outside of the system unit into which are plugged different kinds of cables. *(See ● Panel 4.9.)* A port allows you to plug in a cable to connect a peripheral device, such as a monitor, printer, or modem, so that it can communicate with the computer system.

Ports are of several types. Following are the common ones.

- Serial ports—for transmitting slow data over long distances: **A line connected to a _serial port_ will send bits one at a time, one after another,** like cars on a one-lane highway. Because individual bits must follow each other, a serial port is usually used to connect devices that do not require fast transmission of data, such as keyboard, mouse, monitors, and modems. It is also useful for sending data over a long distance. The standard for PC serial ports is the 9-pin or 25-pin RS-232C connector.

- Parallel ports—for transmitting fast data over short distances: **A line connected to a _parallel port_ allows 8 bits (1 byte) to be transmitted simultaneously,** like cars on an eight-lane highway. Parallel lines move information faster than serial lines do, but they can transmit information efficiently only up to 15 feet. Thus, parallel ports are used principally for connecting printers or external disk or magnetic-tape backup storage devices.

- SCSI ports—for transmitting fast data to up to seven devices in a daisy chain: Pronounced "scuzzy," a _SCSI (small computer system interface) port_ allows data to be transmitted in a "daisy chain" to up to seven devices at speeds (32 bits at a time) higher than those possible with serial and parallel ports. Among the devices that may be connected are external hard-disk drives, CD drives, scanners, and magnetic-tape backup units. The term *daisy chain* means that several devices are connected in series to each other, so that data for the seventh device, for example, has to go through the other six devices first. Sometimes the equipment on the chain is inside the computer, an internal daisy chain; sometimes it is outside the computer, an external daisy chain.

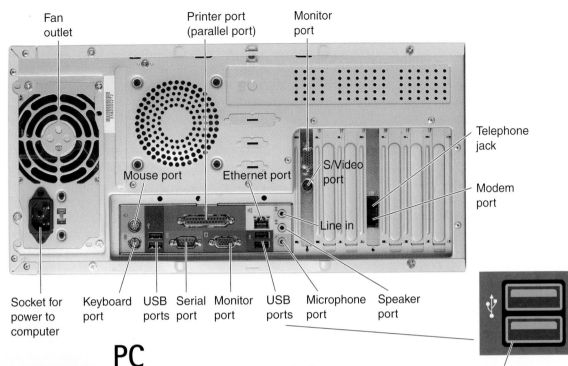

Fan outlet | Printer port (parallel port) | Monitor port

Mouse port | Ethernet port | S/Video port | Telephone jack | Modem port | Line in

Socket for power to computer | Keyboard port | USB ports | Serial port | Monitor port | USB ports | Microphone port | Speaker port

USB ports

PC

● **PANEL 4.9**

Ports

The backs of a PC and a Macintosh.

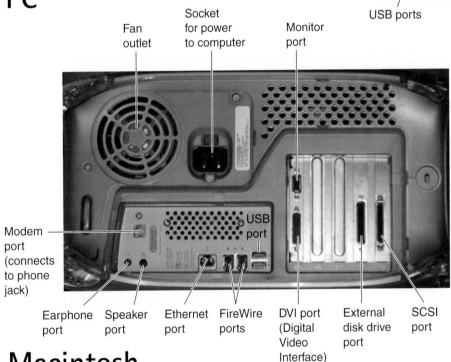

Fan outlet | Socket for power to computer | Monitor port

Modem port (connects to phone jack) | USB port

Earphone port | Speaker port | Ethernet port | FireWire ports | DVI port (Digital Video Interface) | External disk drive port | SCSI port

2 USB Ports

S u r v i v a l   T i p

Are Your PC's USB ports 1.1 or 2.0?

Find the USB port by looking for the ⊷ icon. If there's a tiny + (plus sign) next to the icon, you have USB 2.0.

Macintosh

- **USB ports—for transmitting data to up to 127 devices in a daisy chain: A _USB (universal serial bus) port_ can theoretically connect up to 127 peripheral devices daisy-chained to one general-purpose port.** USB ports are useful for all kinds of peripherals. USB is "hot swappable," or "hot pluggable"—it allows USB devices to be connected or disconnected even while the PC is running.

    In addition, USB permits **_plug and play_, which allows peripheral devices and expansion cards to be automatically configured while they are being installed.** This avoids the hassle of setting switches and creating special files, which plagued earlier users.

    Common USB standards are USB 1.1 and USB 2.0. Nearly all new PCs have USB 2.0 ports. Users with an older PC with USB 1.1 ports will have to buy a 2.0 add-in upgrade card to be able to hook up 2.0

Hardware: The CPU & Storage

155

peripherals. (USB 2.0 data "throughput"—the speed at which data passes through the cable—is 2–13 times faster than USB 1.1.) Windows 95 and Windows NT do not support USB.

Can you really connect up to 127 devices on a single chain? An Intel engineer did set a world record at an industry trade show before a live audience by connecting 111 peripheral devices to a single USB port on a PC. But many USB peripherals do not support such long daisy chains. Thus, though many PCs contain only two USB ports, it's worth shopping around to find a model with extra USB connectors.

USB hub

You can also hook up a *USB hub* to one of the USB ports. A hub typically has four USB ports. You plug the hub into your computer, and then plug your devices (or other hubs) into the hub. By chaining hubs together, you can build up dozens of available USB ports on a single computer.

Individual USB cables can run as long as 5 meters (about 5.4 yards); with hubs, devices can be up to 30 meters (about 32.8 yards) away. Each USB cable has an A connector, which plugs into the computer, and a B connector, which plugs into the peripheral USB device.

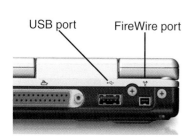

USB port   FireWire port

- **FireWire ports—for camcorders, DVD players, and TVs:** Most new peripherals are available with USB link or FireWire links to your PC. **Following a standard created by Apple Computer and the Institute of Electrical and Electronics Engineers (IEEE), *FireWire* was developed to improve PC/peripheral connections and to compete with USB.** Unlike USB, FireWire is used not with simple peripherals like mice and keyboards but rather with camcorders, DVD players, digital audio equipment, TVs, and gaming consoles. FireWire doesn't always require the use of a PC; you can connect a FireWire camcorder directly to a digital TV, for example, without a PC in the middle. Like USB devices, FireWire devices can be powered or unpowered, and they are also hot pluggable.

  In the PC market, USB is still more popular than FireWire, because it is less expensive. FireWire requires a special card in the PC. Some 400 million devices were shipped with USB in 2002 versus 60 million with FireWire.[4] A few new peripherals can support both standards if used with PCs also equipped for both.

- **Dedicated ports—for keyboard, mouse, phone, and so on:** So far, we have been considering general-purpose ports, but the back of a computer also has other, *dedicated ports*—ports for special purposes. Among these are the round ports for connecting the keyboard and the mouse (if they're not USB). There are also jacks for speakers and microphones and modem-to-telephone jacks. Finally, there is one connector that is not a port at all—the power plug socket, into which you insert the power cord that brings electricity from a wall plug.

Infrared port

- **Infrared ports—for cableless connections over a few feet:** When you use a handheld remote unit to change channels on a TV set, you're using invisible radio waves of the type known as infrared waves. **An *infrared port* allows a computer to make a cableless connection with infrared-capable devices,** such as some printers. This type of connection requires an unobstructed line of sight between transmitting and receiving ports, and they can be only a few feet apart. Other wireless connection modes are available; we discuss wireless networking in Chapter 6.

Expandability: Buses & Cards

Today many new microcomputer systems can be expanded. As mentioned earlier, *expansion* is a way of increasing a computer's capabilities by adding hardware to perform tasks that are not part of the basic system. *Upgrading* means changing to a newer, usually more powerful or sophisticated version. (Computer ads often make no distinction between expansion and upgrading. Their main interest is simply to sell you more hardware or software.)

Whether a computer can be expanded depends on its "architecture"—closed or open. *Closed architecture* means a computer has no expansion slots; *open architecture* means it does have expansion slots. (An alternative definition is that closed architecture is a computer design whose specifications are not made freely available by the manufacturer. Thus, other companies cannot create ancillary devices to work with it. With open architecture, the manufacturer shares specifications with outsiders.) **_Expansion slots_ are sockets on the motherboard into which you can plug expansion cards. _Expansion cards_—also known as _expansion boards, adapter cards, interface cards, plug-in boards, controller cards, add-ins,_ or _add-ons_—are circuit boards that provide more memory or that control peripheral devices.** *(See* ● *Panel 4.10.)*

Common expansion cards connect to the monitor (graphics card), speakers and microphones (sound card), and network (network card), as we'll discuss. Most computers have four to eight expansion slots, some of which may already contain expansion cards included in your initial PC purchase.

Expansion cards are made to connect with different types of buses on the motherboard. As we mentioned, *buses* are electrical data roadways through which bits are transmitted The bus that connects the CPU within itself and to main memory is the *local bus* (also called the *memory bus* or the *frontside bus—FSB*). The buses that connect the CPU with expansion slots on the motherboard and thus with peripheral devices are *expansion buses*. We already alluded to the universal serial bus (USB), whose purpose, in fact, is to *eliminate* the need for expansion slots and expansion cards, since you can just connect USB devices in a daisy chain outside the system unit. Three expansion buses to be aware of are *ISA*, *PCI*, and *AGP*:

Expansion card   Expansion slot

● **PANEL 4.10**
Expandability
(Above) How an expansion card fits into an expansion slot. *(Right)* Types of cards

Type of Card (Board)	What It Does
Accelerator board	Speeds up processing; also known as turbo board or upgrade board
Cache card	Improves disk performance
Coprocessor board	Contains specialized processor chips that increase processing speed of computer system
Disk controller card	Allows certain type of disk drive to be connected to computer system
Emulator board	Permits microcomputer to be used as a terminal for a larger computer system
Fax modem board	Enables computer to transmit and receive fax messages and data over telephone lines
Graphics (Video) adapter board	Permits computer to have a particular graphics standard
Memory expansion board	Enables additional RAM to be added to computer system
Sound board	Enables certain types of systems to produce sound output

- **ISA bus—for ordinary low-speed uses:** The _ISA (industry standard architecture) bus_ **used to be the most widely used expansion bus.** Pronounced "_eye_-sa," ISA is the oldest expansion bus and, at 8 or 16 bits, the slowest at transmitting data, though it is still used for mice, modem cards, and low-speed network cards.

- **PCI bus—for higher-speed uses:** The _PCI (peripheral component interconnect) bus_ **is a higher-speed bus, and at 32 or 64 bits wide it is over four times faster than ISA buses.** PCI is widely used to connect PC graphics cards, sound cards, modems, and high-speed network cards. Many current PCs have both an ISA bus and a PCI bus.

- **AGP bus—for even higher speeds and 3D graphics:** The _AGP (accelerated graphics port) bus_ **transmits data at even higher speeds and was designed to support video and three-dimensional (3D) graphics.** An AGP bus is twice as fast as a PCI bus.

Among the types of expansion cards are graphics, sound, modem, and network interface cards. A special kind of card is the PC card.

3D AGP Graphics Card (64 MB)

- **Graphics cards—for monitors:** Graphics cards are included in all PCs. **Also called a** _video card_ **or** _video adapter_**, a** _graphics card_ **converts signals from the computer into video signals that can be displayed as images on a monitor.** Each graphics card has its own memory chips, a graphics BIOS ROM chip, and a dedicated processor. The processor is designed specifically to handle the intense computational requirements of displaying graphics. Graphics cards are usually connected to an AGP slot on the motherboard.

Sound Blaster Digital Sound Card

- **Sound cards—for speakers and audio output:** A _sound card_ **is used to convert and transmit digital sounds through analog speakers, microphones, and headsets.** Sound cards come installed on most new PCs. Cards such as PCI wavetable sound cards are used to add music and sound effects to computer video games. _Wavetable synthesis_ is a method of creating music based on a wave table, which is a collection of digitized sound samples taken from recordings of actual instruments. The sound samples are then stored on a sound card and are edited and mixed together to produce music. Wavetable synthesis produces higher-quality audio output than other sound techniques.

- **Modem cards—for remote communication via phone lines:** Occasionally you may still see a modem that is outside the computer. Most new PCs, however, come with internal modems—modems installed inside as circuit cards. The modem not only sends and receives digital data over telephone lines to and from other computers but can also transmit voice and fax signals. (Modems are discussed in more detail in Chapter 6.)

- **Network interface cards—for remote communication via cable:** A _network interface card (NIC)_ **allows the transmission of data over a cable network,** which connects various computers and other devices such as printers. (Various types of networks are covered in Chapter 6.)

- **PC cards—for laptop computers:** Originally called _PCMCIA cards_ (for the Personal Computer Memory Card International Association), _PC cards_ **are thin, credit-card-size (2.1 by 3.4 inches) devices used principally on notebook computers to expand capabilities.** _(See_ ● _Panel 4.11.)_ Examples are extra memory (flash RAM), sound cards, modem, hard disks, and even pagers and cellular communicators. At present there are three sizes for PC cards—I (thin), II (thick), and III (thickest). Type I is used primarily for flash memory cards. Type II, the kind you'll find most often, is used for fax modems and network interface cards. Type III is for rotating disk devices, such as hard-disk drives, and for wireless communication devices.

QuickCheck

Distinguish among the following ports: serial, parallel, SCSI, USB, FireWire, dedicated, and infrared.

Distinguish closed architecture from open architecture.

Define the following three expansion buses: ISA, PCI, AGP.

What is the difference between a frontside bus and a backside bus?

Why would you need the following cards: graphics, sound, modem, network interface, and PC?

4.3 Secondary Storage

KEY QUESTION
What are the features of floppy disks, hard disks, optical disks, magnetic tape, smart cards, and online secondary storage?

You're on a trip with your notebook, or maybe just a cellphone or a personal digital assistant, and you don't have a crucial file of data. Or maybe you need to look up a phone number that you can't get through the phone company's directory assistance. Fortunately, you backed up your data online, using any one of several storage services (Driveway, *www.driveway.com*; FreeDesk.com, *www.aspstreet*.com; MagicalDesk.com, *www.webwizards. net.useful/wbfs*; or X:Drive, *www.xdrive.com*, for example) and are able to access it through your modem.

Here is yet another example of how the World Wide Web is offering alternatives to traditional computer functions that once resided within stand-alone machines. We are not, however, fully into the all-online era just yet. Let us consider more traditional forms of ***secondary storage hardware***, **devices that permanently hold data and information as well as programs.** We will look at the following types of secondary storage devices:

- Floppy disks
- Hard disks
- Optical disks
- Magnetic tape
- Smart cards
- Flash memory cards

Finally, we will return to online secondary storage, and look at how it actually works.

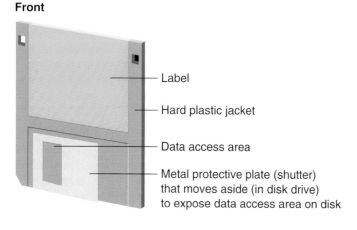

3.5" Floppy Drive

Floppy Disks

A *floppy disk*, **often called a** *diskette* **or simply a** *disk*, **is a removable flat piece of mylar plastic packaged in a 3.5-inch plastic case.** Data and programs are stored on the disk's coating by means of magnetized spots, following standard on/off patterns of data representation (such as ASCII). The plastic case protects the mylar disk from being touched by human hands. Originally, when most disks were larger (5.25 inches) and covered in paper, the disks actually were "floppy"; now only the disk inside the rigid plastic case is flexible, or floppy.

Floppy disks are inserted into a floppy-disk drive, a device that holds, spins, reads data from, and writes data to a floppy disk. *Read* means that the data in secondary storage is converted to electronic signals and a copy of that data is transmitted to the computer's memory (RAM). *Write* means that a copy of the electronic information processed by the computer is transferred to secondary storage. Floppy disks have a **write-protect notch, which allows you to prevent a diskette from being written to.** In other words, it allows you to protect the data already on the disk. To write-protect, use your thumbnail or the tip of a pen to move the small sliding tab on the lower right side of the disk (viewed from the back), thereby uncovering the square hole. (*See* ● *Panel 4.12.*)

On the diskette, **data is recorded in concentric recording bands called** *tracks*. Unlike on a vinyl phonograph record, these tracks are neither visible grooves nor a single spiral. Rather, they are closed concentric rings; each track forms a full circle on the disk. **When a disk is formatted, the disk's storage locations are divided into wedge-shaped sections, which break the tracks into small arcs called** *sectors*. When you save data from your computer to a diskette, the data is distributed by tracks and sectors on the disk. That is, the system software uses the point at which a sector intersects a track to reference the data location.

When you insert a floppy disk into the system-unit slot (the *drive gate* or *drive door*) in the front of the disk drive, the disk is fixed in place over the spindle of the drive mechanism. **The** *read/write head* **transfers data between the computer and the disk.** When the disk spins inside its case, the read/write head moves back and forth over the *data access area* on the disk. When the disk is not in the drive, a metal or plastic shutter covers this access area. An access light goes on when the disk is in use. After using the disk, you can retrieve it by pressing an eject button beside the drive. (*See* ● *Panel 4.13.*)

The regular 3.5-inch floppy disk cannot match the storage capacity of *floppy-disk cartridges*, **or higher-capacity removable disks,** such as Zip disks.

● **PANEL 4.12**
The parts of a 3.5-inch floppy disk

Front

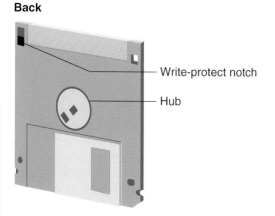

Label

Hard plastic jacket

Data access area

Metal protective plate (shutter) that moves aside (in disk drive) to expose data access area on disk

Back

Write-protect notch

Hub

Tracks and sectors

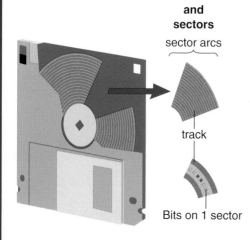

sector arcs

track

Bits on 1 sector

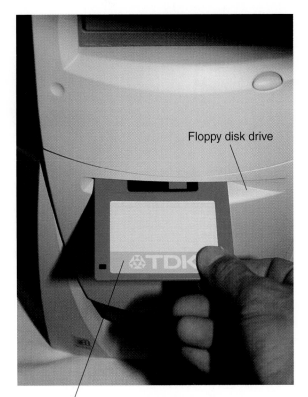

Floppy disk drive

Floppy disk

Zip disk drive

Zip disk

- **3.5-inch floppy disks—1.44 megabytes:** Today's standard for floppy disks is 1.44 megabytes, the equivalent of 400 typewritten pages. Today's floppy carries the label "2HD," in which *2* stands for "double-sided" (it holds data on both sides) and *HD* stands for "high density" (which means it stores more data than the previous standard—*DD*, for "double density").

  When you buy a box of floppies, be sure to check whether they are "IBM formatted" or "PC formatted" (for PCs only) or "Macintosh formatted" (for Apple machines). You can also buy "unformatted" disks, which means you have to *format* or *initialize* them yourself—that is, prepare the disks for use so that the operating system can write information on them. Your system software will lead you through the formatting process. (New Macintoshes will accept PC-formatted disks.)

- **Zip disks—100, 250, or 750 megabytes:** Produced by Iomega Corp., **_Zip disks_ are disks with a special high-quality magnetic coating that have a capacity of 100, 250, or 750 megabytes.** Even at 100 megabytes, this is nearly 70 times the storage capacity of the standard floppy. Among their other uses, Zip disks are used to store large spreadsheet files, database files, image files, multimedia presentation files, and websites. Zip disks require their own Zip-disk drives, which may come installed on new computers, although external Zip drives are also available.

  Both floppy-disk drives and Zip drives are usually built into the computer case, but they are also available in external versions—for parallel, SCSI, or USB ports. Note that Zip cartridges cost $12.50–$15 each, whereas CDs cost $.50–$1 each. CD and DVD drives are quickly taking over as file backup methods. We cover them shortly.

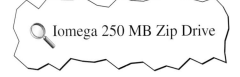

Iomega 250 MB Zip Drive

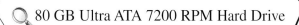

🔍 80 GB Ultra ATA 7200 RPM Hard Drive

Hard Disks

Floppy disks use flexible plastic, but hard disks are rigid. <u>**Hard disks**</u> **are thin but rigid metal, glass, or ceramic platters covered with a substance that allows data to be held in the form of magnetized spots.** Most hard-disk drives have at least two platters; the greater the number of platters, the larger the capacity of the drive. The platters in the drive are separated by spaces and are clamped to a rotating spindle that turns all the platters in unison. Hard disks are tightly sealed within an enclosed hard-disk-drive unit to prevent any foreign matter from getting inside. Data may be recorded on both sides of the disk platters. *(See* ● *Panel 4.14.)*

Hard disks are quite sensitive devices. The read/write head does not actually touch the disk but rather rides on a cushion of air about 0.000001 inch thick. *(See* ● *Panel 4.15.)* The disk is sealed from impurities within a container, and the whole apparatus is manufactured under sterile conditions. Otherwise, all it would take is a human hair, a dust particle, a fingerprint smudge, or a smoke particle to cause what is called a *head crash*. **A** <u>*head crash*</u> **happens when the surface of the read/write head or particles on its surface come into contact with the surface of the hard-disk platter, causing the loss of some or all of the data on the disk.** A head crash can also happen when you bump a computer too hard or drop something heavy on the system cabinet. An incident of this sort could, of course, be a disaster if the data has not been backed up. There are firms that specialize in trying to retrieve data from crashed hard disks (for a hefty price), though this cannot always be done.

There are two types of hard disks—nonremovable and removable:

● **Nonremovable hard disks: An internal** <u>*nonremovable hard disk*</u>**, also known as a** *fixed disk***, is housed in the microcomputer system unit and is used to store nearly all programs and most data files.** Usually it consists of four 3.5-inch metallic platters sealed inside a drive case the size of a small sandwich, which contains disk platters on a drive spindle, read/write heads mounted on an access arm that moves back and forth, and power connections and circuitry. *(See* ● *Panel 4.16.)* Operation is much the same as for a floppy-disk drive: The read/write heads locate specific instructions or data files according to track or sector.

Fixed-disk units can also be *external* and portable. For example, Maxtor makes 80-gigabyte external hard disk drives for both PCs and Macs that are USB 1.1- and 2.0-compatible.

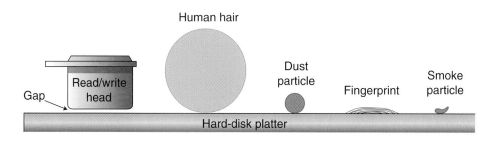

Human hair

Gap | Read/write head

Dust particle

Fingerprint

Smoke particle

Hard-disk platter

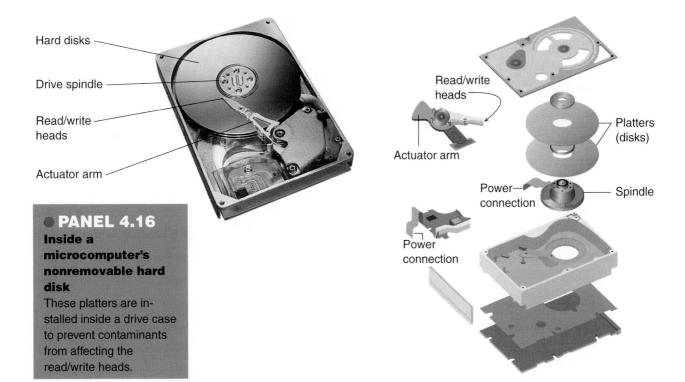

Hard disks

Drive spindle

Read/write heads

Actuator arm

Read/write heads

Actuator arm

Platters (disks)

Power connection

Spindle

Power connection

Bits on disk. Magnetic bits on a disk surface, caught by a magnetic force microscope. The dark stripes are 0 bits; the bright stripes are 1 bits.

Microcomputer hard drives with capacities measured in tens of gigabytes—up to 120 gigabytes or more (500 gigabytes in the Mac G5), according to current ads—are becoming essential because today's programs are so huge. You can fit about 20,000 pages of regular text per gigabyte of storage space; video and sound files take up much more room. As for speed, hard disks allow faster access to data than floppy disks do, because a hard disk spins many times faster. Computer ads frequently specify speeds in revolutions per minute. A floppy-disk drive rotates at only 360 rpm; a 7,200-rpm hard drive is going about 300 miles per hour.

In addition, ads may specify the type of ***hard-disk controller***, **a special-purpose circuit board that positions the disk and read/write heads and manages the flow of data and instructions to and from the disk.** Popular hard-disk controllers are Ultra ATA (or EIDE) and SCSI. Commonly found on new PCs, *Ultra ATA (advanced technology attachment)* allows fast data transfer and high storage capacity; it is also known as *EIDE (enhanced integrated drive electronics).* Ultra ATA can support only one or two hard disks. By contrast, *SCSI (small computer system interface),* pronounced "scuzzy," supports several disk drives as well as other peripheral devices by linking them in a daisy chain of up to seven devices. SCSI controllers are faster and have more storage capacity than EIDE controllers; they are typically found in servers and workstations.

● **Removable hard disks:** ***Removable hard disks,* or *hard-disk cartridges,* consist of one or two platters enclosed along with read/write heads in a hard plastic case, which is inserted into a microcomputer's cartridge drive.** Typical capacity is 1.5 gigabytes. These cartridges are frequently used to back up data and to transport huge files, such as large spreadsheets and desktop-publishing files with color and graphics. One popular system is SyQuest's SparQ, which comes in several models (PC parallel port external, PC/Mac SCSI external, EIDE PC internal). Western Digital and Iomega also make portable hard-disk drives, which hold 40–120 gigabytes.

Optical Disks: CDs & DVDs

Everyone who has ever played an audio CD is familiar with optical disks. **An _optical disk_ is a removable disk, usually 4.75 inches in diameter and less than one-twentieth of an inch thick, on which data is written and read through the use of laser beams.** An audio CD holds up to 74 minutes (2 billion bits' worth) of high-fidelity stereo sound. Some optical disks are used strictly for digital data storage, but many are used to distribute multimedia programs that combine text, visuals, and sound.

With an optical disk, there is no mechanical arm, as with floppy disks and hard disks. Instead, a high-power laser beam is used to write data by burning tiny pits or indentations into the surface of a hard plastic disk. To read the data, a low-power laser light scans the disk surface: Pitted areas are not reflected and are interpreted as 0 bits; smooth areas are reflected and are interpreted as 1 bits. *(See ● Panel 4.17.)* Because the pits are so tiny, a great deal more data can be represented than is possible in the same amount of space on a diskette and many hard disks. An optical disk can hold over 4.7 gigabytes of data, the equivalent of 1 million typewritten pages.

Nearly every PC marketed today contains a CD or DVD drive, which can also read audio CDs. These, along with their recordable and rewritable variations, are the two principal types of optical-disk technology used with computers. *(See ● Panel 4.18.)*

- **CD-ROM—for reading only:** The first kind of optical disk for microcomputers was the CD-ROM. **_CD-ROM (compact disk read-only memory)_ is an optical-disk format that is used to hold prerecorded text, graphics, and sound.** Like music CDs, a CD-ROM is a read-only disk. *Read-only* means the disk's content is recorded at the time of

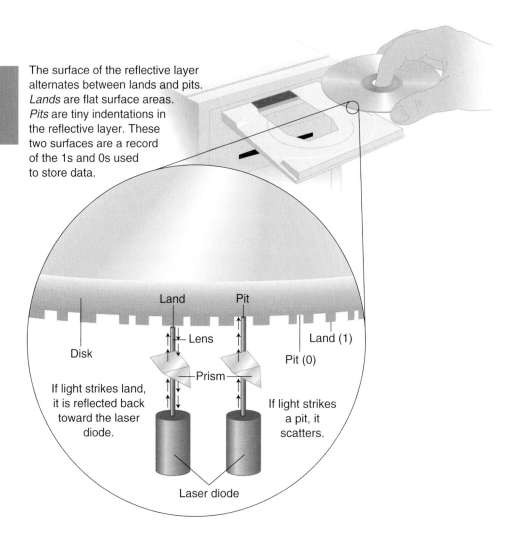

● PANEL 4.17
How a laser reads data on an optical disk

The surface of the reflective layer alternates between lands and pits. *Lands* are flat surface areas. *Pits* are tiny indentations in the reflective layer. These two surfaces are a record of the 1s and 0s used to store data.

Land   Pit

Lens

Disk

Land (1)

Pit (0)

Prism

If light strikes land, it is reflected back toward the laser diode.

If light strikes a pit, it scatters.

Laser diode

CD/DVD, label side up

Slide-out tray for DVD/CD disk drive

manufacture and cannot be written on or erased by the user. As the user, you have access only to the data imprinted by the disk's manufacturer. A CD-ROM disk can hold up to 650 megabytes of data, equal to over 300,000 pages of text.

A CD-ROM drive's speed is important because with slower drives, images and sounds may appear choppy. In computer ads, drive speeds are indicated by the symbol "X," as in "56X," which is a high speed. *X* denotes the original data transfer rate of 150 kilobytes per second. The data transfer rate is the time the drive takes to transmit data to another device. A 56X drive runs at 56 times 150, or 8,400 kilobytes (8.4 megabytes) per second. If an ad carries the word *Max*, as in "56X Max," this indicates the device's maximum speed. Drives range in speed from 16X to 75X; the faster ones are more expensive.

● **CD-R—for recording on once:** <u>***CD-R (compact disk–recordable) disks***</u> **can be written to only once but can be read many times.** This allows users to make their own CD disks. Once recorded, the information cannot be erased. A CD-R can read and write audio CDs and standard CD-ROMs with read speeds of up to 24X and write speeds of up to 8X. CD-R is often used by companies for archiving—that is, to store vast amounts of information. A variant is the Photo CD, an optical disk developed by Kodak that can digitally store photographs taken with an ordinary 35-millimeter camera. Once you've shot a roll of color photographs, you take it for processing to a photo shop, which produces a disk containing your images. You can view the disk on any personal computer with a CD-ROM drive and the right software. Many new computers come equipped with CD-R drives.

● **CD-RW—for rewriting many times:** A <u>***CD-RW (compact disk–rewritable) disk***</u>**, also known as an *erasable optical disk*, allows users to record and erase data, so the disk can be used over and over again.** CD-RW drives are becoming more common on microcomputers. CD-RW disks are useful for archiving and backing up large amounts of data or work in multimedia production or desktop publishing. The read speed of CD-RW drives is up to 44X, the write speed is up to 44X, and the rewrite speed is up to 24X. CD-RW disks cannot be read by CD-ROM drives. CD-RW disks have a capacity of 650–700 megabytes.

● **DVD-ROM—the versatile video disk:** A <u>***DVD-ROM (digital versatile disk or digital video disk, with read-only memory)***</u> **is a CD-style disk with extremely high capacity, able to store 4.7 or more gigabytes.** How is this done? Like a CD or CD-ROM, the surface of a DVD contains microscopic pits, which represent the 0s and 1s of digital code that can be read by a laser. The pits on the DVD, however, are much smaller and grouped more closely together than those on a CD, allowing far more information to be represented. Also, the laser beam used focuses on pits roughly half the size of those on current audio CDs. In addition, the DVD format allows for two layers of data-defining

info!

"'Rip' a DVD movie to your hard drive if you can when you are using a laptop. This will save battery power." What does this mean? Visit the following links:
www.dvdrhelp.com/dvdripping
www.vcdhelp.com

4X DVD-RW

info!

What's a DVD Easter Egg? DVDs often contain hidden features, called "Easter eggs," such as previews for movies, software, or music. For some great examples, go to *www.dvdreview.com*.

Survival Tip

Zip vs. Tape

The first time you back up your hard disk, it will take a while. Subsequent backups will take less time, because the backup software will archive only the new files. You must be present to back up using Zip disks, because you will have to swap disks. If you plan to back up your computer often, consider tape, which is cheaper than Zip cartridges and which can be set to run automatically, even if you are not there.

pits, not just one. Finally, engineers have succeeded in squeezing more data into fewer pits, principally through data compression.

Many new computer systems now come with a DVD drive as standard equipment. A great advantage is that these drives can also take standard CD-ROM disks, so now you can watch DVD movies and play CD-ROMs using just one drive. DVDs have enormous potential to replace CDs for archival storage, mass distribution of software, and entertainment. They not only store far more data but are different in quality from CDs. As one writer points out, "DVDs encompass much more: multiple dialogue tracks and screen formats, and best of all, smashing sound and video."[5] The theater-quality video and sound, of course, are what make DVD a challenger to videotape as a vehicle for movie rentals.

Like CDs, DVDs have their recordable and rewritable variants. **_DVD-R (DVD–recordable) disks_ allow one-time recording by the user.** Three types of reusable disks are *DVD-RW* (*DVD-rewritable*), *DVD-RAM* (*DVD-random access memory*), and *DVD+RW* (*DVD+rewritable*), all of which can be recorded on and erased many times. DVD-R disks have a capacity of 4.7 (single-sided)–9.6 (double-sided) gigabytes. DVD read speed is usually 16X.

Not all the optical-disk drives and different types of optical media (read-only, rewritable, and so on) are mutually compatible. Check product information before you buy to make sure you get what you want.

As a way to maximize movie revenues, the film industry decided to split the world up into eight DVD zones. This is to prevent the DVD version of a movie made in one country from being sold in another country in which the theater version has not yet opened. DVD disks with a particular region code will play only on DVD players with that region code. However, some of the newest DVD players are code-free—they are not "region locked." (Thus, if you plan to travel and use a DVD player for movies, check out the compatibility restrictions.)

Magnetic Tape

Similar to the tape used on an audio tape recorder (but of higher density), **_magnetic tape_ is thin plastic tape coated with a substance that can be magnetized. Data is represented by magnetized spots (representing 1s) or nonmagnetized spots (representing 0s).** Today, "mag tape" is used mainly for backup and archiving—that is, for maintaining historical records—where there is no need for quick access.

On large computers, tapes are used on magnetic-tape units or reels and in special cartridges. These tapes store up to 160 gigabytes each. On microcomputers, tape is used in the form of **_tape cartridges_, modules resembling audiocassettes that contain tape in rectangular, plastic housings.** The two most common types of tape drives are DAT and Traven TR-5. (*See* ● *Panel 4.19.*) An internal or external tape drive is required to use tape media.

Tape fell out of favor for a while, supplanted by such products as Iomega's Jaz (since discontinued) and Zip-disk cartridge drives. However, as hard drives swelled to multigigabyte size, using Zip disks for backup became less convenient. Since a single tape cassette can hold up to 40 gigabytes, tape is still an alternative. However, as we mentioned, CD-R and DVD-R are quickly becoming the most popular backup methods.

Smart Cards

Today in the United States, most credit cards are old-fashioned magnetic-

strip cards. A *magnetic-strip card* has a strip of magnetically encoded data on its back and holds about 0.2–0.9 kilobytes of data. The encoded data might include your name, account number, and PIN (personal identification number). The strip contains information needed to use the card, but the strip also has drawbacks. First, it can degrade over time, making the data unreadable. Second, the magnetic strip doesn't hold much information. Third, such data as the magnetic strip does contain is easy to access and duplicate, raising the risk of fraud.

Two other kinds of cards, smart cards and optical cards, which hold far more information, are already popular in Europe. Manufacturers are betting they will become more popular in the United States.

Smart card

ActivCard®

- **Smart cards: A _smart card_ looks like a credit card but has a microprocessor embedded in it.** Smart cards hold more information than standard credit cards—about 8–40 megabytes of data. Some can be reloaded for reuse.

  Smart cards are well suited for prepaid, disposable applications such as cash cards or telephone debit cards. For example, when you're using a phone card, which is programmed to contain a set number of available minutes, you insert the card into a slot in the phone, wait for a tone, and dial the number. The length of your call is automatically calculated on the card, and the corresponding charge is deducted from the balance. Other uses of smart cards are as student cards, building-entrance cards, bridge-toll cards, and (as in Germany) national-health-care cards.

- **Optical cards:** The conventional magnetic-strip credit card holds the equivalent of a half page of data. The smart card with a microprocessor and memory chip holds the equivalent of 250 pages. The optical card presently holds about 2,000 pages of data. Optical cards use the same type of technology as music compact disks but look like silvery credit cards. **_Optical cards_ are plastic, laser-recordable, wallet-type cards used with an optical-card reader.**

  Because they can cram so much data into so little space, they may become popular in the future. For instance, a health card based on an optical card would have room not only for the individual's medical history and health-insurance information but also for digital images, such as electrocardiograms. The U.S. Immigration and Naturalization Service recently selected the LaserCard, an optical card, for use as new Permanent Resident and Border Crossing cards because of its highly secure, counterfeit-resistant features. LaserCards containing shipping manifest data are attached to shipping containers and sea vans, speeding up receipt processing considerably. VISX Corporation uses a LaserCard to operate the STAR Excimer Laser System for each of its eye surgery patients. The high-capacity card stores parameter settings and patient data for each surgery performed. Honda dealers in the Philippines use the LaserCard as a comprehensive vehicle record/database that Honda car owners keep. The cards are also used to obtain discounts at participating retail stores and restaurants.

SECURITY

Flash Memory Cards, Sticks, & Keychains

Disk drives, whether for diskettes, hard disks, or CD-ROMs, all involve moving parts—and moving parts can break. Flash memory cards, by contrast, are variations on conventional computer memory chips, which have no moving parts. **_Flash memory cards_, or _flash RAM cards_, consist of circuitry on credit-card-size PC cards that can be inserted into slots connecting to the motherboard on notebook computers.**

The Sony Memory Stick uses flash memory and holds 128 megabytes. Memory sticks are smaller than a stick of chewing gum and are used in digital cameras and camcorders. Other versions of flash memory, such as CompactFlash (192 megabytes) and SmartMedia (2–128 megabytes), are also used in pocket PCs, in PDAs, and as electronic "film" in digital cameras. Mushkin sells a 256-megabyte USB 1.1 external flash drive for the PC.

More a "pod" than a card, _keychain memory_, also called _flash drive_, consists of finger-size modules of flash memory that plug into the USB ports of nearly any PC or Macintosh. Examples are M-Systems' DiskOnKey, Sony's Micro Vault, Lexar's Jump Drive, and SanDisk's Cruzer. They generally have 64–128 megabytes of storage, which is less than a CD but equivalent to about 45–90 floppy disks, making the device extremely useful if you're traveling from home to office, say, and don't want to carry a laptop. The 128-megabyte size can also hold the equivalent of 200 high-resolution images or 20–25 songs. When you plug the device into your USB port, it shows up as an external drive on the computer.[6]

Flash memory sticks and cards are not infallible. Their circuits wear out after repeated use, limiting their life span. Still, unlike conventional computer memory (RAM, or primary storage), flash memory is _nonvolatile_. That is, it retains data even when the power is turned off.

Keychain memory

Online Secondary Storage

Online storage services, mentioned at the start of this section (p. 159), allow you to use the internet to back up your data. Examples are @Backup _(www.atbackup.com)_ and Connected Online Backup _(www.connected.com)_. Some services are free; others charge a small fee. When you sign up, you obtain software that lets you upload whatever files you wish to the company's server. For security, you are given a password, and the files are supposedly encrypted to guard against unwanted access.

SECURITY

From a practical standpoint, online backup should be used only for vital files. Tape, removable hard-disk (Zip) cartridges, tape, CDs/DVDs, and/or flash memory cards are the best media for backing up entire hard disks, including files and programs.

QuickCheck

What are two types of floppy disks, and what are their features?

What are characteristics of hard disks, both nonremovable and removable?

Explain the various types of optical disks—CD-ROM, CD-R, CD-RW, and DVD-ROM.

How is magnetic tape used?

Describe smart cards and optical cards.

What are flash memory cards, sticks, and keychains?

PRACTICAL ACTION BOX
How to Buy a Notebook

"Selecting a notebook computer is much more complicated than buying a desktop PC," observes *Wall Street Journal* technology writer Walter Mossberg.[7] The reason: Notebooks can vary a lot more than the desktop "generic boxes," which tend to be similar, at least within a price class.[8] Trying to choose among the many Windows-based notebooks is a particularly brow-wrinkling experience. (Macintosh notebooks tend to be more straightforward since there are only two models.)

Nevertheless, here are some suggestions:[9]

Purpose. What are you going to use your notebook for? You can get a notebook that's essentially a desktop replacement and won't be moved much. If you expect to use the machine a lot in class, in libraries, or on airplanes, however, weight and battery life are important.

Budget & Weight. Notebooks range from $1,000 to $4,000, with high-end brands aimed mainly at business people.

In the $2,000 range are the light machines, 3–4 pounds. Designed for mobility, they tend to lack internal disk drives and all the standard ports. The heavy machines (7 pounds and up), in the $3,000-plus range, generally include all the features, such as DVD drives and big screens.

Batteries: The Life-Weight Trade-Off. A rechargeable lithium ion battery lasts longer than the nickel–metal hydride battery. Even so, a battery in the less expensive machines will usually run continuously for only about $2\frac{1}{4}$ hours. (DVD players are particularly voracious consumers of battery power, so it's the rare notebook that will allow you to finish watching a 2-hour movie.)

The trade-off is that heavier machines usually have longer battery life. The lightweight machines tend to get less than 2 hours, and toting extra batteries offsets the weight savings. (A battery can weigh a pound or so.)

Software. Many notebooks come with less software than you would get with a typical desktop, though what you get will probably be adequate for most student purposes. On notebook PCs, count on getting Microsoft Works rather than the more powerful Microsoft Office to handle word processing, spreadsheets, databases, and the like.

Keyboards & Pointing Devices. The keys on a notebook keyboard are usually the same size as those on a desktop machine, although they can be smaller. However, the up-and-down action feels different, and the keys may feel wobbly. In addition, some keys may be omitted altogether, or keys may do double duty or appear in unaccustomed arrangements.

Most notebooks have a small touch-sensitive pad in lieu of a mouse—you drag your finger across the touchpad to move the cursor. Others use a pencil-eraser-size pointing stick in the middle of the keyboard.

Screens. If you're not going to carry the notebook around much, go for a big, bright screen. Most people find they are comfortable with a 12- to 14-inch display, measured diagonally, though screens can be as small as 10.4 inches and as large as 15 inches.

The best screens are active-matrix display (TFT). However, some low-priced models have the cheaper passive-matrix screens (HPA, STN, or DSTN), which are harder to read, though you may find you can live with them. XGA screens (1,024 × 768 pixels) have a higher resolution than SVGA screens (800 × 600 pixels), but fine detail may not be important to you.

Memory, Speed, & Storage Capacity. If you're buying a notebook to complement your desktop, you may be able to get along with reduced memory, slow processor, small hard disk, and no CD-ROM. Otherwise, all these matters become important.

Memory (RAM) is the most important factor in computer performance, even though processor speed is more heavily hyped. Most notebooks have at least 128 megabytes (MB) of memory, but 256 MB is better. A microprocessor running 350–500 megahertz (MHz) or higher is adequate, and more recent models are faster than this.

Sometimes notebooks are referred to as "three-spindle" or "two-spindle" machines. In a three-spindle machine, a hard drive, a floppy-disk drive, and a CD/DVD drive all reside internally (not as external peripherals). A two-spindle machine has a hard drive and space for either a floppy-disk drive or a CD/DVD drive (or a second battery). A hard drive of 6 gigabytes or more is sufficient for most people.

For more information about buying computers, go to *http://reviews-zdnet.com/com* and *http://micro.uoregon.edu/buyersguide.*

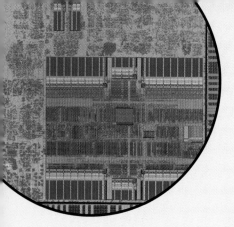

Summary

AGP (accelerated graphics port) bus (p. 158, KQ 4.2) Bus that transmits data at very high speeds; designed to support video and three-dimensional (3D) graphics. *Why it's important:* An AGP bus is twice as fast as a PCI bus.

arithmetic/logic unit (ALU) (p. 151, KQ 4.2) Part of the CPU that performs arithmetic operations and logical operations and controls the speed of those operations. *Why it's important:* Arithmetic operations are the fundamental math operations: addition, subtraction, multiplication, and division. Logical operations are comparisons such as "equal to," "greater than," or "less than."

ASCII (American Standard Code for Information Interchange) (p. 145, KQ 4.2) Binary code used with microcomputers. Besides having the more conventional characters, the Extended ASCII version includes such characters as math symbols and Greek letters. *Why it's important:* ASCII is the binary code most widely used in microcomputers.

bay (p. 146, KQ 4.2) Shelf or opening in the computer case used for the installation of electronic equipment, generally storage devices such as a hard drive or DVD drive. *Why it's important:* Bays permit the expansion of system capabilities. A computer may come equipped with four or seven bays.

Character	EBCDIC	ASCII-8
A	1100 0001	0100 0001
B	1100 0010	0100 0010
C	1100 0011	0100 0011
D	1100 0100	0100 0100
E	1100 0101	0100 0101
F	1100 0110	0100 0110
G	1100 0111	0100 0111
H	1100 1000	0100 1000
I	1100 1001	0100 1001
J	1101 0001	0100 1010
K	1101 0010	0100 1011
L	1101 0011	0100 1100
M	1101 0100	0100 1101
0	1111 0000	0011 0000
1	1111 0001	0011 0001
2	1111 0010	0011 0010
3	1111 0011	0011 0011
4	1111 0100	0011 0100
!	0101 1010	0010 0001

binary system (p. 143, KQ 4.2) A two-state system used for data representation in computers; has only two digits—0 and 1. *Why it's important:* In the computer, 0 can be represented by electrical current being off and 1 by the current being on. All data and program instructions that go into the computer are represented in terms of these binary numbers.

bit (p. 144, KQ 4.2) Short for "binary digit," which is either a 0 or a 1 in the binary system of data representation in computer systems. *Why it's important:* The bit is the fundamental element of all data and information processed and stored in a computer system.

bus (p. 151, KQ 4.2) Also called *bus line;* electrical data roadway through which bits are transmitted within the CPU and between the CPU and other components of the motherboard. *Why it's important:* A bus resembles a multilane highway: The more lanes it has, the faster the bits can be transferred.

byte (p. 144, KQ 4.2) Group of 8 bits. *Why it's important:* A byte represents one character, digit, or other value. It is the basic unit used to measure the storage capacity of main memory and secondary storage devices (kilobytes and megabytes).

cache (p. 153, KQ 4.2) Special high-speed memory area on a chip that the CPU can access quickly. It temporarily stores instructions and data that the processor is likely to use frequently. *Why it's important:* Cache speeds up processing.

CD-R (compact disk-recordable) disk (p. 165, KQ 4.3) Optical-disk form of secondary storage that can be written to only once but can be read many times. *Why it's important:* This format allows consumers to make their own CD disks, though it's a slow process. Once recorded, the information cannot be erased. CD-R is often used by companies for archiving—that is, to store vast amounts of information. A variant is the Photo CD, an optical disk developed by Kodak that can digitally store photographs taken with an ordinary 35-millimeter camera.

CD-ROM (compact disk read-only memory) (p. 164, KQ 4.3) Optical-disk form of secondary storage that is used to hold prerecorded text, graphics, and sound. *Why it's important:* Like music CDs, a CD-ROM is a read-only disk. Read-only means the disk's content is recorded at the time of manufacture and cannot be written on or erased by the user. A CD-ROM disk can hold up to 650 megabytes of data, equal to over 300,000 pages of text.

CD/DVD, label side up

CD-RW (compact disk–rewritable) disk (p. 165, KQ 4.3) Also known as *erasable optical disk;* optical-disk form of secondary storage that allows users to record and erase data, so the disk can be used over and over again. Special CD-RW drives and software are required. Why it's important: CD-RW disks are useful for archiving and backing up large amounts of data or work in multimedia production or desktop publishing; however, they are relatively slow.

chip (p. 141, KQ 4.1) Also called a *microchip,* or *integrated circuit;* consists of millions of micro-miniature electronic circuits printed on a tiny piece of silicon. Silicon is an element widely found in sand that has desirable electrical (or "semiconducting") properties. Why it's important: Chips have made possible the development of small computers.

CISC (complex instruction set computing) chips (p. 148, KQ 4.2) Design that allows a microprocessor to support a large number of instructions. Why it's important: CISC chips are used mostly in PCs and in conventional mainframes. CISC chips are generally slower than RISC chips.

CMOS (complementary metal-oxide semiconductor) chips (p. 153, KQ 4.2) Battery-powered chips that don't lose their contents when the power is turned off. Why it's important: CMOS chips contain flexible start-up instructions, such as time, date, and calendar, that must be kept current even when the computer is turned off. Unlike ROM chips, CMOS chips can be reprogrammed—for example, when you need to change the time for daylight savings time.

control unit (p. 150, KQ 4.2) Part of the CPU that deciphers each instruction stored in it and then carries out the instruction. Why it's important: The control unit directs the movement of electronic signals between main memory and the arithmetic/logic unit. It also directs these electronic signals between main memory and the input and output devices.

CPU (central processing unit) (p. 150, KQ 4.2) The processor; it follows the instructions of the software (program) to manipulate data into information. The CPU consists of two parts—(1) the control unit and (2) the arithmetic/logic unit (ALU), which both contain registers, or high-speed storage areas. All are linked by a kind of electronic "roadway" called a bus. Why it's important: The CPU is the "brain" of the computer.

DVD-R (DVD-recordable) disks (p. 166, KQ 4.3) DVD disks that allow one-time recording by the user. Three types of reusable disks are DVD-RW (DVD-rewritable), DVD-RAM (DVD random access memory), and DVD+rewritable, all of which can be recorded on and erased more than once. Why it's important: Recordable DVDs offer the user yet another option for storing large amounts of data.

DVD-ROM (digital versatile disk or digital video disk, with read-only memory) (p. 165, KQ 4.3) CD-type disk with extremely high capacity, able to store 4.7 or more gigabytes. Why it's important: It is a powerful and versatile secondary storage medium.

EBCDIC (Extended Binary Coded Decimal Interchange Code) (p. 145, KQ 4.2) Binary code used with large computers. Why it's important: EBCDIC is commonly used in mainframes.

expansion (p. 147, KQ 4.2) Way of increasing a computer's capabilities by adding hardware to perform tasks that are beyond the scope of the basic system. Why it's important: Expansion allows users to customize and/or upgrade their computer systems.

expansion card (p. 157, KQ 4.2) Also known as *expansion board, adapter card, interface card, plug-in board, controller card, add-in,* or *add-on;* circuit board that provides more memory or that controls peripheral devices. Why it's important: Common expansion cards connect to the monitor (graphics card), speakers and microphones (sound card), and network (network card). Most computers have four to eight expansion slots, some of which may already contain expansion cards included in your initial PC purchase.

expansion slot (p. 157, KQ 4.2) Socket on the motherboard into which the user can plug an expansion card. Why it's important: *See* expansion card.

FireWire (p. 156, KQ 4.2) Following a standard created by Apple Computer and the Institute of Electrical and Electronics Engineers (IEEE), FireWire was developed to improve PC/peripheral connections and to compete with USB. Why it's important: Unlike USB, FireWire is used not with simple peripherals like mice and keyboards but rather with camcorders, DVD players, digital audio equipment, TVs, and gaming consoles. FireWire doesn't always require the use of a PC; you can connect a FireWire camcorder directly to a digital TV, for example, without a PC in the middle.

flash memory cards (p. 168, KQ 4.3) Also known as *flash RAM cards;* form of secondary storage consisting of circuitry on credit-card-size cards that can be inserted into slots connecting to the motherboard on notebook computers. Why it's important: Flash memory is nonvolatile, so it retains data even when the power is turned off.

flash memory chips (p. 153, KQ 4.2) Chips that can be erased and reprogrammed more than once (unlike PROM chips, which can be programmed only once). Why it's important: Flash memory, which can range from 1 to 64 megabytes in capacity, is used to store programs not only in personal computers but also in pagers, cellphones, printers, and digital cameras. Unlike standard RAM chips, flash memory is nonvolatile—data is retained when the power is turned off.

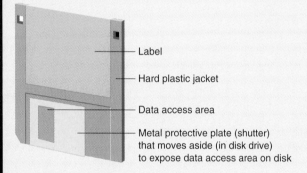

Front

— Label

— Hard plastic jacket

— Data access area

— Metal protective plate (shutter) that moves aside (in disk drive) to expose data access area on disk

Back

— Write-protect notch

— Hub

floppy disk (p. 160, KQ 4.3) Often called *diskette* or simply *disk;* removable flat piece of mylar plastic packaged in a 3.5-inch plastic case. Data and programs are stored on the disk's coating by means of magnetized spots, following standard on/off patterns of data representation (such as ASCII). The plastic case protects the mylar disk from being touched by human hands. Why it's important: Floppy disks are used on all microcomputers.

floppy-disk cartridges (p. 160, KQ 4.3) High-capacity removable 3.5-inch disks, such as Zip disks. Why it's important: These cartridges store more data than regular floppy disks and are just as portable.

flops (p. 149, KQ 4.2) Stands for "floating-point operations per second." A *floating-point operation* is a special kind of mathematical calculation. This measure, used mainly with supercomputers, is expressed as *megaflops* (mflops, or millions of floating-point operations per second), *gigaflops* (gflops, or billions), and *teraflops* (tflops, or trillions). Why it's important: The measure is used to express the processing speed of supercomputers.

gigabyte (G, GB) (p. 144, KQ 4.2) Approximately 1 billion bytes (1,073,741,824 bytes); a measure of storage capacity. Why it's important: This measure was formerly used mainly with "big iron" (mainframe) computers but is typical of the secondary storage (hard-disk) capacity of today's microcomputers.

gigahertz (GHz) (p. 149, KQ 4.2) Measure of speed used for the latest generation of processors: 1 billion cycles per second. Why it's important: Since a new high-speed processor can cost many hundred dollars more than the previous generation of chip, experts often recommend that buyers fret less about the speed of the processor (since the work most people do on their PCs doesn't even tax the limits of the current hardware) and more about spending money on extra memory.

graphics card (p. 158, KQ 4.2) Also called a *video card* or *video adapter;* expansion card that converts signals from the computer into video signals that can be displayed as images on a monitor. Why it's important: The power of a graphics card, often expressed in megabytes, as in 8, 16, or 32 MB, determines the clarity of the images on the monitor.

hard disk (p. 162, KQ 4.3) Secondary storage medium; thin but rigid metal, glass, or ceramic platter covered with a substance that allows data to be stored in the form of magnetized spots. Hard disks are tightly sealed within an enclosed hard-disk-drive unit to prevent any foreign matter from getting inside. Data may be recorded on both sides of the disk platters. Why it's important: Hard disks hold much more data than do floppy disks. All microcomputers use hard disks as their principal storage medium.

hard-disk controller (p. 163, KQ 4.3) Special-purpose circuit board that positions the disk and read/write heads and manages the flow of data and instructions to and from the disk. Why it's important: Common PC hard-disk controllers are Ultra ATA (or EIDE) and SCSI.

head crash (p. 162, KQ 4.3) Occurrence in which the surface of the read/write head or particles on its surface come into contact with the surface of the hard-disk platter, causing the loss of some or all of the data on the disk. Why it's important: Because head crashes are always a possibility, users should always back up data from their hard disks on another storage medium, such as floppy disks.

infrared port (p. 156, KQ 4.2) Port that allows a computer to make a cableless connection with infrared-capable devices, such as some printers. Why it's important: Infrared ports eliminate the need for cabling.

integrated circuit (p. 141, KQ 4.1). An entire electronic circuit, including wires, formed on a single "chip," or piece, of special material, usually silicon. Why it's important: In the old days, transistors were made individually and then formed into an electronic circuit with the use of wires and solder. An integrated circuit is formed as part of a single manufacturing process.

Intel-type chip (p. 148, KQ 4.2) Processor chip for PCs; made principally by Intel Corp. and Advanced Micro Devices (AMD), but also by Cyrix, DEC, and others. Why it's important: These chips are used by manufacturers such as Compaq, Dell, Gateway 2000, Hewlett-Packard, and IBM. Since 1993, Intel has marketed its chips under the names "Pentium," "Pentium Pro," "Pentium MMX," "Pentium II," "Pentium III," "Pentium 4," and "Celeron." Many ads for PCs contain the logo "Intel inside" to show that the systems run an Intel microprocessor.

ISA (industry standard architecture) bus (p. 158, KQ 4.2) Low-speed bus that used to be the most widely used expansion bus. Why it's important: ISA is the oldest expansion bus and, at 8 or 16 bits, the slowest at transmitting data, though it is still used for mice, modem cards, and low-speed network cards.

kilobyte (K, KB) (p. 144, KQ 4.2) Approximately 1,000 bytes (1,024 bytes); a measure of storage capacity. Why it's important: The kilobyte was a common unit of measure for memory or secondary storage capacity on older computers.

machine cycle (p. 150, KQ 4.2) Series of operations performed by the control unit to execute a single program instruction. It (1) fetches an instruction, (2) decodes the instruction, (3) executes the instruction, and (4) stores the result. Why it's important: The machine cycle is the essence of computer-based processing.

machine language (p. 145, KQ 4.2) Binary code (language) that the computer uses directly. The 0s and 1s represent precise storage locations and operations. Why it's important: For a program to run, it must be in the machine language of the computer that is executing it.

magnetic tape (p. 166, KQ 4.3) Thin plastic tape coated with a substance that can be magnetized. Data is represented by magnetized spots (representing 1s) or nonmagnetized spots (representing 0s). Why it's important: Today, "mag tape" is used mainly for backup and archiving—that is, for maintaining historical records—where there is no need for quick access.

megabyte (M, MB) (p. 144, KQ 4.2) Approximately 1 million bytes (1,048,576 bytes); measure of storage capacity. Why it's important: Microcomputer primary storage capacity is expressed in megabytes.

megahertz (MHz) (p. 149, KQ 4.2) Measure of microcomputer processing speed, controlled by the system clock. Why it's important: Generally, the higher the megahertz rate, the faster the computer can process data. A 550-MHz Pentium III–based microcomputer, for example, processes 550 million cycles per second.

microprocessor (p. 141, KQ 4.1) Miniaturized circuitry of a computer processor. It stores program instructions that process, or manipulate, data into information. The key parts of the microprocessor are transistors. Why it's important: Microprocessors enabled the development of microcomputers.

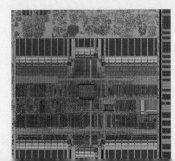

MIPS (p. 149, KQ 4.2) Stands for "millions of instructions per second"; a measure of processing speed. Why it's important: MIPS is used to measure processing speeds of mainframes, midrange computers, and workstations.

Motorola-type chips (p. 149, KQ 4.2) Microprocessors made by Motorola for Apple Macintosh computers. Why it's important: Since 1993, Motorola has provided an alternative to the Intel-style chips made for PC microcomputers.

network interface card (NIC) (p. 158, KQ 4.2) Expansion card that allows the transmission of data over a cable network. Why it's important: Installation of a network interface card in the computer enables the user to connect with various computers and other devices such as printers.

nonremovable hard disk (p. 162, KQ 4.3) Also known as *fixed disk;* hard disk housed in a microcomputer system unit and used to store nearly all programs and most data files. Usually it consists of four 3.5-inch metallic platters sealed inside a drive case the size of a small sandwich, which contains disk platters on a drive spindle, read/write heads mounted on an access arm that moves back and forth, and power connections and circuitry. Operation is much the same as for a diskette drive: The read/write heads locate specific instructions or data files according to track or sector. Hard disks can also come in removable cartridges. Why it's important: *See* hard disk.

optical card (p. 167, KQ 4.3) Plastic, laser-recordable, wallet-type card used with an optical-card reader. Why it's important: Because they can cram so much data (6.6 megabytes) into so little space, they may become popular in the future. For instance, a health card based on an optical card would have room not only for the individual's medical history and health-insurance information but also for digital images, such as electrocardiograms.

optical disk (p. 164, KQ 4.3) Removable disk, usually 4.75 inches in diameter and less than one-twentieth of an inch thick, on which data is written and read through the use of laser beams. Why it's important: An audio CD holds up to 74 minutes (2 billion bits' worth) of high-fidelity stereo sound. Some optical disks are used strictly for digital data storage, but many are used to distribute multimedia programs that combine text, visuals, and sound.

parallel port (p. 154, KQ 4.2) A connector for a line that allows 8 bits (1 byte) to be transmitted simultaneously, like cars on an eight-lane highway. Why it's important: Parallel lines move information faster than serial lines do. However, because they can transmit information efficiently only up to 15 feet, they are used principally for connecting printers or external disk or magnetic-tape backup storage devices.

PC card (p. 158, KQ 4.2) Thin, credit-card-size (2.1 by 3.4 inches) hardware device. Why it's important: PC cards are used principally on notebook computers to expand capabilities.

PCI (peripheral component interconnect) bus (p. 158, KQ 4.2) High-speed bus; at 32 or 64 bits wide, it is more than four times faster than ISA buses. Why it's important: PCI is widely used in microcomputers to connect graphics cards, sound cards, modems, and high-speed network cards.

petabyte (P, PB) (p. 145, KQ 4.2) Approximately 1 quadrillion bytes (1,048,576 gigabytes); measure of storage capacity. Why it's important: The huge storage capacities of modern databases are now expressed in petabytes.

plug and play (p. 155, KQ 4.2) USB peripheral connection standard that allows peripheral devices and expansion cards to be automatically configured while they are being installed. Why it's important: Plug and Play avoids the hassle of setting switching and creating special files that plagued earlier users.

port (p. 154, KQ 4.2) A connecting socket or jack on the outside of the system unit into which are plugged different kinds of cables. Why it's important: A port allows the user to plug in a cable to connect a peripheral device, such as a monitor, printer, or modem, so that it can communicate with the computer system.

power supply (p. 146, KQ 4.2) Device that converts AC to DC to run the computer. Why it's important: The electricity available from a standard wall outlet is alternating current (AC), but a microcomputer runs on direct current (DC).

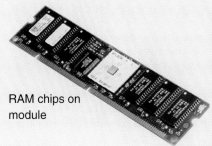

RAM chips on module

RAM (random access memory) chips (p. 152, KQ 4.2) Also called *primary storage* and *main memory;* chips that temporarily hold software instructions and data before and after it is processed by the CPU. RAM is a volatile form of storage. Why it's important: RAM is the working memory of the computer. Having enough RAM is critical to users' ability to run many software programs.

read (p. 153, KQ 4.2) To transfer data from an input source into the computer's memory or CPU. Why it's important: Reading, along with writing, is an essential computer activity.

read/write head (p. 160, KQ 4.3) Mechanism used to transfer data between the computer and the disk. When the disk spins inside its case, the read/write head moves back and forth over the data access area on the disk. Why it's important: The read/write head enables the essential activities of reading and writing data.

Hard disks

Drive spindle

Read/write heads

Actuator arm

registers (p. 151, KQ 4.2) High-speed storage areas that temporarily store data during processing. Why it's important: Registers may store a program instruction while it is being decoded, store data while it is being processed by the ALU, or store the results of a calculation.

removable hard disk (p. 163, KQ 4.3) Also called *hard-disk cartridge;* one or two platters enclosed along with read/write heads in a hard plastic case, which is inserted into a microcomputer's cartridge drive. Typical capacity is 2 gigabytes. Two popular systems are Iomega's Jaz and SyQuest's SparQ. Why it's important: These cartridges offer users greater storage capacity than do floppy disks but with the same portability.

RISC (reduced instruction set computing) chips (p. 148, KQ 4.2) Type of chip in which the complexity of the microprocessor is reduced by eliminating many seldom-used instructions, thereby increasing the processing speed. Why it's important: RISC chips are used mostly in workstations. As a result, workstations can work up to 10 times faster than most PCs. RISC chips have been used in many Macintosh computers since 1993.

ROM (read-only memory) (p. 153, KQ 4.2) Memory chip that cannot be written on or erased by the computer user without special equipment. Why it's important: ROM chips contain fixed start-up instructions. They are loaded, at the factory, with programs containing special instructions for basic computer operations, such as starting the computer or putting characters on the screen. These chips are nonvolatile; their contents are not lost when power to the computer is turned off.

SCSI (small computer system interface) port (p. 154, KQ 4.2) Pronounced "scuzzy," a connector that allows data to be transmitted in a "daisy chain" to up to seven devices at speeds (32 bits at a time) higher than those possible with serial and parallel ports. The term *daisy chain* means that several devices are connected in series to each other, so that data for the seventh device, for example, has to go through the other six devices first. Why it's important: A SCSI enables users to connect external hard-disk drives, CD-ROM drives, scanners, and magnetic-tape backup units.

secondary storage hardware (p. 159, KQ 4.3) Devices that permanently hold data and information as well as programs. Why it's important: Secondary storage—as opposed to primary storage—is nonvolatile; that is, saved data and programs are permanent, or remain intact, when the power is turned off.

Tracks and sectors

sector arcs

sectors (p. 160, KQ 4.3) The small arcs created in tracks when a disk's storage locations are divided into wedge-shaped sections. Why it's important: The system software uses the point at which a sector intersects a track to reference the data location.

semiconductor (p. 141, KQ 5.1) Material, such as silicon (in combination with other elements), whose electrical properties are intermediate between a good conductor and a nonconductor of electricity. When highly conducting materials are laid on the semiconducting material, an electronic circuit can be created. Why it's important: Semiconductors are the materials from which integrated circuits (chips) are made.

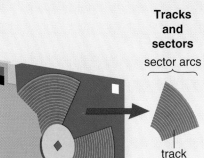

track

Bits on 1 sector

serial port (p. 154, KQ 4.2) A connector for a line that sends bits one after another, like cars on a one-lane highway. The standard for PC serial ports is the 9-pin or 25-pin RS-232C connector. Why it's important: Because individual bits must follow each other, a serial port is usually used to connect devices that do not require fast transmission of data, such as keyboard, mouse, monitors, and modems. It is also useful for sending data over a long distance.

silicon (p. 141, KQ 4.1) An element that is widely found in clay and sand and is used in the making of solid-state integrated circuits. Why it's important: It is used not only because its abundance makes it cheap but also because it is a good semiconductor. As a result, highly conducting materials can be overlaid on the silicon to create the electronic circuitry of the integrated circuit.

Smart card

smart card (p. 167, KQ 4.3) Wallet-type card that looks like a credit card but has a microprocessor embedded in it. When inserted into a reader, it transfers data to and from a central computer. Why it's important: Unlike conventional credit cards, smart cards can hold a fair amount of data and can store some basic financial records. Thus, they are used as telephone debit cards, health cards, and student cards.

solid-state device (p. 141, KQ 4.1) Electronic component made of solid materials with no moving parts, such as an integrated circuit. Why it's important: Solid-state integrated circuits are far more reliable, smaller, and less expensive than electronic circuits made from several components.

sound card (p. 158, KQ 4.2) Expansion card used to convert and transmit digital sounds through analog speakers, microphones, and headsets. Why it's important: Cards such as PCI wavetable sound cards are used to add music and sound effects to computer video games.

system clock (p. 149, KQ 4.2) Internal timing device that uses fixed vibrations from a quartz crystal to deliver a steady stream of digital pulses or "ticks" to the CPU. These ticks are called *cycles*. Why it's important: Faster clock speeds will result in faster processing of data and execution of program instructions, as long as the computer's internal circuits can handle the increased speed.

tape cartridge (p. 166, KQ 4.3) Module resembling an audiocassette that contains tape in a rectangular plastic housing. The two most common types of tape drives are DAT and Traven TR-5. Why it's important: Tape cartridges are used for secondary storage on microcomputers and also on some large computers. Tape is used mainly for archiving purposes and backup.

terabyte (T, TB) (p. 145, KQ 4.2) Approximately 1 trillion bytes (1,009,511,627,776 bytes); measure of storage capacity. Why it's important: The storage capacities of some mainframes and supercomputers are expressed in terabytes.

tracks (p. 160, KQ 4.3) The rings on a diskette along which data is recorded. Why it's important: See sectors.

Tape cartridge in external tape drive

transistor (p. 140, KQ 4.1) Tiny electronic device that acts as an on/off switch, switching between "on" and "off" millions of times per second. Why it's important: Transistors are part of the microprocessor.

Unicode (p. 145, KQ 4.2) Binary coding scheme that uses 2 bytes (16 bits) for each character, rather than 1 byte (8 bits). Why it's important: Instead of the 256 character combinations of ASCII, Unicode can handle 65,536 character combinations. Thus, it allows almost all the written languages of the world to be represented using a single character set.

upgrading (p. 147, KQ 4.2) Changing to newer, usually more powerful or sophisticated versions, such as a more powerful microprocessor or more memory chips. Why it's important: Through upgrading, users can improve their computer systems without buying completely new ones.

USB connector

USB (universal serial bus) port (p. 155, KQ 4.2) Port that can theoretically connect up to 127 peripheral devices daisy-chained to one general-purpose port. Why it's important: USB ports are useful for peripherals such as digital cameras, digital speakers, scanners, high-speed modems, and joysticks. The so-called USB hot plug or hot swappable allows such devices to be connected or disconnected even while the PC is running.

virtual memory (p. 154, KQ 4.2) Type of hard-disk space that mimics primary storage (RAM). Why it's important: When RAM space is limited, virtual memory allows users to run more software at once, provided the computer's CPU and operating system are equipped to use it. The system allocates some free disk space as an extension of RAM; that is, the computer swaps parts of the software program between the hard disk and RAM as needed.

volatile (p. 152, KQ 4.2) Temporary; the contents of volatile storage media, such as RAM, are lost when the power is turned off. Why it's important: To avoid data loss, save your work to a secondary storage medium, such as a hard disk, in case the electricity goes off while you're working.

word size (p. 150, KQ 4.2) Number of bits that the processor may process at any one time. Why it's important: The more bits in a word, the faster the computer. A 32-bit computer—that is, one with a 32-bit-word processor—will transfer data within each microprocessor chip in 32-bit chunks, or 4 bytes at a time. A 64-bit computer transfers data in 64-bit chunks, or 8 bytes at a time.

write (p. 153, KQ 4.2) To transfer data from the computer's CPU or memory to an output device. Why it's important: *See* read.

write-protect notch (p. 160, KQ 4.3) Floppy-disk feature that prevents a diskette from being written to. Why it's important: This feature allows the user to protect the data already on the disk. To write-protect, use your thumbnail or the tip of a pen to move the small sliding tab on the lower right side of the disk (viewed from the back), thereby uncovering the square hole.

Zip disk (p. 161, KQ 4.3) Floppy-disk cartridge with a capacity of 100, 250, or 750 megabytes. At 100 megabytes, this is nearly 70 times the storage capacity of the standard floppy. Why it's important: Among other uses, Zip disks are used to store large spreadsheet files, database files, image files, multimedia presentation files, and websites. Zip disks require their own Zip-disk drives, which may come installed on new computers, although external Zip drives are also available. *See also* floppy-disk cartridges.

Chapter Review

"I can recognize and recall information."

Self-Test Questions

1. A(n) _____ is about 1,000 bytes; a(n) _____ is about 1 million bytes; a(n) _____ is about 1 billion bytes.

2. The _____ is the part of the microprocessor that tells the rest of the computer how to carry out a program's instructions.

3. The process of retrieving data from a storage device is referred to as _____; the process of copying data to a storage device is called _____.

4. To avoid losing data, users should always _____ their files.

5. Formatted disks have _____ and _____ that the system software uses to reference data locations.

6. The _____ is often referred to as the "brain" of a computer.

7. The electrical data roadways through which bits are transmitted are called _____.

8. A cable connected to a _____ port sends bits one at a time, one after the other; a cable connected to a _____ port sends 8 bits simultaneously.

9. Part of the disk-drive mechanism, the _____ transfers data between the computer and the disk.

10. _____ is the most important factor in computer performance.

11. _____ operations are the fundamental math operations: addition, subtraction, multiplication, and division. _____ operations are comparisons such as "equal to," "greater than," or "less than."

12. A group of 8 bits is a _____.

13. A tiny electronic device that acts as an on/off switch, switching between "on" and "off" millions of times per second, is called a _____.

Multiple-Choice Questions

1. Which of the following is another term for primary storage?
   a. ROM
   b. ALU
   c. CPU
   d. RAM
   e. CD-R

2. Which of the following is *not* included on a computer's motherboard?
   a. RAM chips
   b. ROM chips
   c. keyboard
   d. microprocessor
   e. expansion slots

3. Which of the following is used to hold data and instructions that will be used shortly by the CPU?
   a. ROM chips
   b. peripheral devices
   c. RAM chips
   d. CD-R
   e. hard disk

4. Which of the following coding schemes is widely used on microcomputers?
   a. EBCDIC
   b. Unicode
   c. ASCII
   d. Microcode
   e. Unix

5. Which of the following is used to measure processing speed in microcomputers?
   a. MIPS
   b. flops
   c. picoseconds
   d. megahertz
   e. millihertz

6. Which expansion bus transmits data at 8 or 16 bits?
   a. PCI
   b. ISA
   c. CMOS
   d. AGP
   e. AMR

7. Which instruction design allows a microprocessor to support a large number of instructions?
   a. Binary
   b. EBCDIC
   c. RISC
   d. CISC
   e. ASCII

8. Which company is the main manufacturer of microprocessors for Apple Macintosh computers?

    a. Intel

    b. AMD

    c. Motorola

    d. Pentium

    e. Cyrix

9. Which element is commonly used in the making of solid-state integrated circuits?

    a. pentium

    b. lithium

    c. copper

    d. iron

    e. silicon

True/False Questions

T F   1. A bus connects a computer's control unit and ALU.

T F   2. The machine cycle comprises the instruction cycle and the execution cycle.

T F   3. Magnetic tape is the most common secondary storage medium used with microcomputers.

T F   4. Main memory is nonvolatile.

T F   5. Today's laptop computers can perform more calculations per second than the ENIAC, an enormous machine occupying more than 1,800 square feet and weighing more than 30 tons.

T F   6. USB can theoretically connect up to 127 peripheral devices.

T F   7. A petabyte is approximately 1 quadrillion bytes.

stage **LEARNING**   COMPREHENSION

"I can recall information in my own terms and explain them to a friend."

Short-Answer Questions

1. What is ASCII, and what do the letters stand for?

2. Why should measures of capacity matter to computer users?

3. What's the difference between RAM and ROM?

4. What is the significance of the term *megahertz*?

5. What is a motherboard? Name at least four components of a motherboard.

6. What advantage does a floppy-disk cartridge have over a regular floppy disk?

7. Why is it important for your computer to be expandable?

8. What would you use a Zip disk for?

9. Explain the binary system.

10. What are UNICODE and ASCII?

11. Why is silicon such a popular element used in the manufacture of microprocessors?

stage **LEARNING**   APPLYING, ANALYZING, SYNTHESIZING, EVALUATING

"I can apply what I've learned, relate these ideas to other concepts, build on other knowledge, and use all these thinking skills to form a judgment."

Knowledge in Action

1. If you're using Windows 98, you can easily determine what microprocessor is in your computer and how much RAM it has. To begin, click the *Start* button in the Windows desktop pull-up menu bar and then choose *Settings, Control Panel.* Then locate the System icon in the Control Panel window and double-click on the icon.

    The System Properties dialog box will open. It contains four tabs: General, Device Manager, Hardware Profiles, and Performance. The name of your computer's microprocessor will display on the General tab. To see how much RAM is in your computer, click the *Performance* tab.

2. Visit a local computer store and note the system requirements listed on five software packages. What are the requirements for processor? RAM? Operating system? Available hard-disk space? CD/DVD speed? Audio/video cards? Are there any output hardware requirements?

3. Develop a binary system of your own. Use any two objects, states, or conditions, and encode the following statement: "I am a rocket scientist."

4. The floppy drive no longer comes with a standard Dell PC (other companies will probably follow suit). What do you think will be the next "legacy" device to be abandoned?

6. Storing humans: If the human genome is 800 million bytes (according to Raymond Kurzweil**),** how many humans could you fit on a 120-GB hard drive?

Chapter 5

Web Exercises

1. The objective of this project is to introduce you to an online encyclopedia that's dedicated to computer technology. The *www.webopaedia* website is a good resource for deciphering computer ads and clearing up difficult concepts. For practice, visit the site and type *main memory* into the Search text box and then press the *Enter key.* Print out the page that displays. Then locate information on other topics of interest to you.

2. You can customize your own PC through a brand-name company such as Dell or Gateway, or you can create your own personal model by choosing each component on your own. Decide which method is best for you. Go to the following sites and customize your ideal PC:

   www.dell.com
   www.gateway.com
   www.compaq.com
   www.ibm.com
   www.hpshopping.com

   Then go to

   www.pricewatch.com
   www.computerwarehouse.com

   and see if you could save money by putting your own PC together piece by piece. (This includes purchasing each component separately and verifying compatibility of all components.)

3. DVD Formats. DVD+R, DVD-R, DVD+RW, DVD-RW, so many formats! Are they all the same? Visit these websites to get current information on the issues surrounding recordable DVD media:

   www.dvddemystified.com/dvdfaq.html#4.3
   www.plextor.com/english/support/faqs/G00015.htm
   www.idvd.ca/dvd-format-guide.htm
   www.dvd-r-media.com/Different-Formats.html

4. What is a qubit? You've learned about binary digits in this chapter; now learn about the qubit, the basic unit of information in a quantum computer. Beware: When you step into the realm of quantum theory, things become bizarre.

   http://whatis.techtarget.com/definition/
   *   0,sid9_gci341232,00.html*
   www.qubit.org/

5. What is an exabyte?

6. DNA computing—Visit the following websites to learn more about DNA software and computing:

   www.nature.com/nsu/nsu_pf/011122/011122-11.html
   www.arstechnica.com/reviews/2q00/dna/dna-1.html
   www.cis.udel.edu/~dna3/DNA/dnacomp.html
   www.liacs.nl/home/pier/webPagesDNA/
   http://dna2z.com/dnacpu/dna.html
   www.hypography.com/topics/dnacomputers.cfm
   http://corninfo.chem.wisc.edu/writings/
   *   DNAcomputing.html*

7. You mean the Matrix was real? Visit this website for analysis of real-world applications of concepts from the movie *Matrix:*

   www.kurzweilai.net/

SECURITY

7. Security issue—Credit card fraud: When buying parts or making any kind of purchase over the internet, always make sure that the web address says HTTPS to let you know it is an encrypted SSL (Secured Socket Layer) website. Visit the site below for safety tips when using your credit card online.

   www.credit-land.com/online.php

8. Files that have been moved to the Recycle Bin (Windows) or the Trash Can (Macs) stay in those folders until the user empties the Recycle Bin or the Trash Can. After the files have been removed, however, they are still on the hard drive; they have not been erased. What has been erased is the information that points to the files' locations on the hard drive. The operating system uses this information to build the directory tree structure (p. 150). When the address pointers have been erased, the files still exist on the hard drive; they just become invisible to the OS. The right software can retrieve them.

   The only way to completely erase a file with no trace is to overwrite it. The OS will eventually overwrite files that have no address pointer information in the directory tree structure, but this may take some time. File-erasing software products are available to automatically and permanently erase files as soon as they have been emptied from the Trash Can or the Recycle Bin. Examples are Advanced File Shredder

   (*www.ashkon.com/shredder.html*)

   and Window Washer

   (*www.webroot.com/wb/index.php*).

Hardware: Input & Output

Taking Charge of Computing & Communications

Chapter Topics & Key Questions

5.1 **Input & Output** How is input and output hardware used by a computer system?

5.2 **Input Hardware** What are the three categories of input hardware, what devices do they include, and what are their features?

5.3 **Output Hardware** What are the two categories of output hardware, what devices do they include, and what are their features?

Automated teller machines have become so common, it now seems there are almost as many places to get cash as to spend it," says one account.[1]

Not only are automated teller machines (ATMs), or cash machines, showing up in office buildings, convenience stores, nightclubs, and even the lobbies of some big apartment buildings; they are also becoming something quite different from devices for people who need fast cash: They are migrating into different kinds of *kiosks* (pronounced "*key*-osks"), computerized booths or small standing structures providing any number of services, from electronic banking options to corporate job benefits, from tourism advice to garage-sale permits. *(See ● Panel 5.1.)*

In New York City, kiosks can be used by citizens to pay parking tickets and check for building-code violations. In San Antonio, they provide information on animals available for adoption. In Seattle, commuters at car-ferry terminals view images of traffic conditions on major highways. Many colleges and universities use kiosks to provide students with information about classes, schedules, activity locations, maps, and so on.

Kiosks also sell stamps, print out checks, and issue movie and plane tickets. Alamo car rental offices have kiosks on which travelers can print out directions, get descriptions of hotel services, and obtain restaurant menus and reviews—in four languages. At Main Stay Suites, guests may not even find front-desk clerks; kiosks have replaced them at many locations. Many kiosks have been transformed into full-blown multimedia centers, offering publicized corporate and governmental activities, job listings, and benefits, as well as ads, coupons, and movie previews. One company has even experimented with launching an 18-foot-wide vending machine described as looking like "a 7-Eleven in a box," to dispense everything from olive oil and milk to towels and pantyhose.[2]

The kiosk presents the two faces of the computer that are important to humans: It allows them to input data and to output information. For example, many kiosks use touch screens (and sometimes also keyboards) for input and thermal printers for output. In this chapter, we discuss what the principal input and output devices are and how you can make use of them.

● **PANEL 5.1**
Kiosks
(Left) The Bell Atlantic public internet access kiosk at T. F. Green airport in Warwick, Rhode Island; *(right)* a check-cashing kiosk at a 7-Eleven store in Dallas, Texas.

5.1 Input & Output

KEY QUESTION

How is input and output hardware used by a computer system?

Recall from Chapter 1 that *input* refers to data entered into a computer for processing—for example, from a keyboard or from a file stored on disk. Input includes program instructions that the CPU receives after commands are issued by the user. Commands can be issued by typing keywords or by pressing certain keyboard keys defined by the application program. Commands can also be issued by choosing menu options or clicking on icons. Finally, input includes user responses—for example, when you reply to a question posed by the application or the operating system, such as "Are you sure you want to put this file in the Recycle Bin?" *Output* refers to the results of processing—that is, information sent to the screen or the printer or to be stored on disk or sent to another computer in a network. Some devices combine both input and output functions, examples being not only ATMs and kiosks, as we just mentioned, but also combination scanner-printer devices.

In this chapter we focus on the common input and output devices used with a computer. *(See ● Panel 5.2.)* **<u>Input hardware</u> consists of devices that translate data into a form the computer can process.** The people-readable form of the data may be words like those on this page, but the computer-readable form consists of binary 0s and 1s, or off and on electrical signals. **<u>Output hardware</u> consists of devices that translate information processed by the computer into a form that humans can understand.** The computer-processed information consists of 0s and 1s, which need to be translated into words, numbers, sounds, and pictures.

● **PANEL 5.2**
Common input and output devices

INPUT   **OUTPUT**

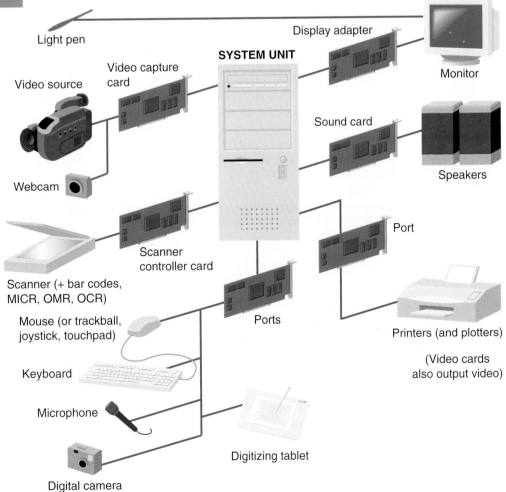

Input hardware devices are categorized as three types: *keyboards, pointing devices*, and *source data-entry devices. (See ● Panel 5.3.)* Quite often a computer system will combine all three.

Keyboards

A _keyboard_ is a device that converts letters, numbers, and other characters into electrical signals that can be read by the computer's processor. The keyboard may look like a typewriter keyboard to which some special keys have been added. Alternatively, it may look like the keys on a bank ATM or the keypad of a pocket computer. It may even be a Touch-Tone phone or cable-TV set-top box.

Let's look at *traditional computer keyboards* and various kinds of *specialty keyboards and terminals.*

- **Traditional computer keyboards:** Picking up where we left off with the PC ad presented in Chapter 4 *(Panel 4.3 on p. 143)*, we see that the seller lists a "104-Key Keyboard." Conventional computer keyboards have all the keys on typewriter keyboards, plus other keys unique to computers. This totals 104–108 keys for desktop computers and 85 keys for notebooks. Newer keyboards include extra keys for special activities such as instant web access, CD/DVD controls, and Windows shortcut keys. Wired keyboards connect a cable to the computer via a serial port or a USB port. Wireless keyboards are also available. In notebook computers the keyboard is built in.

    The keyboard illustration in Chapter 3 shows keyboard functions. *(Refer to Panel 3.11, p. 106.)*

- **Specialty keyboards and terminals:** Specialty keyboards range from Touch-Tone telephone keypads to keyboards featuring pictures of food for use in fast-food restaurants. Here we will consider dumb terminals, intelligent terminals, and internet terminals.

    A _dumb terminal_, **also called a** *video display terminal (VDT)*, **has a display screen and a keyboard and can input and output but cannot process data.** Usually the output is text only. For instance, airline reservations clerks use these terminals to access a mainframe computer containing flight information. Dumb terminals cannot perform functions independent of the mainframe to which they are linked.

● PANEL 5.3
Three types of input devices

Keyboards	Pointing Devices	Source Data-Entry Devices
Traditional computer keyboards	Mice, trackballs, pointing sticks, touchpads	Scanner devices: imaging systems, bar-code readers, mark- and character-recognition devices (MICR, OMR, OCR), fax machines
Specialty keyboards and terminals: dumb terminals, intelligent terminals (ATMs, POS terminals), internet terminals	Touch screens	Audio-input devices
	Pen-based computer systems, light pens, digitizers (digitizing tablets)	Webcams and video-input devices
		Digital cameras
		Speech-recognition systems
		Sensors
		Radio-frequency identification
		Human-biology input devices

(Left) A dumb terminal at an airline check-in counter. *(Right)* A point-of-sale (POS) terminal at a retail store. It records purchases and processes the buyer's credit card.

■more info!

What kinds of terminals are most common? Go to *http://computer.howstuffworks .com* for more information on terminals; then follow the web links. Have you used terminals you didn't even know were terminals at the time?

An *intelligent terminal* has its own memory and processor, as well as a display screen and keyboard. Such a terminal can perform some functions independent of any mainframe to which it is linked. One example is the familiar *automated teller machine (ATM),* the self-service banking machine that is connected through a telephone network to a central computer. Another example is the *point-of-sale (POS) terminal,* used to record purchases at a store's checkout counter.

An *internet terminal* provides access to the internet. There are several variants: (1) the *set-top box* or *web terminal,* which displays web pages on a TV set; (2) the *network computer,* a cheap, stripped-down computer that connects people to networks; (3) the *online game player,* which not only lets the user play games but also connects to the internet; (4) the full-blown *PC/TV* (or *TV/PC),* which merges the personal computer with the television set; and (5) the *wireless pocket PC* or *personal digital assistant (PDA),* a handheld computer with a tiny keyboard that can do two-way wireless messaging.

Pointing Devices

One of the most natural of all human gestures, the act of pointing, is incorporated in several kinds of input devices. **_Pointing devices_ control the position of the cursor or pointer on the screen and allow the user to select options displayed on the screen.** Pointing devices include the *mouse* and its variants, the *touch screen,* and various forms of *pen input.* We also describe recent innovations in *handwriting input.*

Microsoft IntelliMouse

- **The mouse and its variants—trackball, pointing stick, and touchpad:** The principal pointing tool used with microcomputers is the **_mouse_, a device that is rolled about on a desktop mouse pad and directs a pointer on the computer's display screen.**

  When the mouse is moved, a ball inside the mouse touches the desktop surface and rolls with the mouse. A mouse pad—a rectangular rubber/foam pad—provides traction for the traditional mouse, often called a *mechanical mouse* or a *wheeled mouse.* Newer mice, such as the Microsoft IntelliMouse, are *optical;* that is, they use laser beams and special chips to encode data for the computer. Optical

Mouse on a mouse pad—the cord looks a bit like a mouse tail.

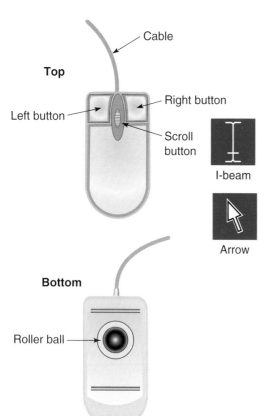

Top

Cable

Left button

Right button

Scroll button

Bottom

Roller ball

I-beam

Arrow

mice have no moving parts, have a smoother response, and don't require a mouse pad. The *mouse pointer*—an arrow, a rectangle, a pointing finger—is the symbol that indicates the position of the mouse on the display screen or that activates icons. When the mouse pointer changes to the shape of an I-beam, it shows the place where text may be inserted or selected for special treatment.

On the top side of the mouse are one to five buttons. The first button is used for common functions, such as clicking and dragging. The functions of the other buttons are determined by the software you're using. Some mice have a scroll wheel on top to make it easier for you to scroll down the screen.

There are three main variations on the mouse:

—The **_trackball_ is a movable ball, mounted on top of a stationary device, that can be rotated using your fingers or palm.** In fact, the trackball looks like the mouse turned upside down. Instead of moving the mouse around on the desktop, you move the trackball with the tips of your fingers. A trackball is not as accurate as a mouse, and it requires more frequent cleaning, but it's a good alternative when desktop space is limited. Trackballs come in wired and wireless versions, and newer optical trackballs use laser technology.

Trackball

—A **_pointing stick_ looks like a pencil eraser protruding from the keyboard between the G, H, and B keys. When you move the pointing stick with your finger, the screen pointer moves accordingly.** IBM developed the pointing stick for use with its notebook computers. (A forerunner of the pointing stick is the joystick, which consists of a vertical handle like a gearshift lever mounted on a base with one or two buttons.)

—A **_touchpad_ is a small, flat surface over which you slide your finger, using the same movements as you would with a mouse.** The cursor follows the movement of your finger. You "click" by tapping your finger on the pad's surface or by pressing buttons positioned close by the pad. Touchpads are most often found on notebook computers, but free-standing touchpads are available for use with PCs.

Pointing stick

Touchpad

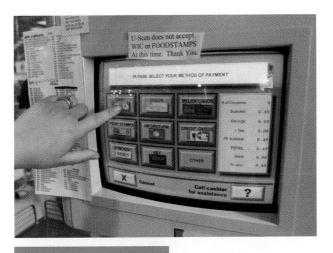
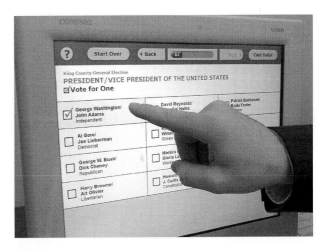

● **PANEL 5.4**

Touch-screen menus
(Left) Touch-screen menu on a self-scanning checkout system; *(right)* touch-screen voting menu.

- **Touch screen:** A *__touch screen__* **is a video display screen that has been sensitized to receive input from the touch of a finger.** The specially coated screen layers are covered with a plastic layer. Depending on the type of touch screen, the pressure of the user's finger creates a connection of electrical current between the glass layers, decreases the electrical charge at the touched point, or otherwise disturbs the electrical field. The change in electrical current creates a signal that is sent to the computer. You can input requests for information by pressing on displayed buttons or menus. *(See* ● *Panel 5.4.)* The answers to your requests are then output as displayed words or pictures on the screen. (There may also be sound.) You can find touch screens in kiosks, ATMs, airport tourist directories, hotel TV screens (for guest checkout), department store bridal registries, and campus information kiosks making available everything from lists of coming events to (with proper ID and personal code) student financial-aid records and grades.

- **Pen input:** Some input devices use variations on an electronic pen. Examples are *pen-based systems, light pens,* and *digitizers:*

  __Pen-based computer systems__ **allow users to enter handwriting and marks onto a computer screen by means of a penlike stylus rather than by typing on a keyboard.** Pen computers use handwriting-recognition software that translates handwritten characters made by the pen, or stylus, into data that is usable by the computer. Pen input has long been a feature of Palms and other stylus-based personal digital assistants. Several computer makers offer notetop computers with screens that double as electronic notepads, the most famous being the Microsoft Tablet PC. *(See* ● *Panel 5.5.)* The Tablet PC presents you with a screen that looks like lined paper on which you write with a stylus. You can save your notes in handwritten format and then search for terms, email the notes, or transfer them to a non-Tablet PC. You are supposedly also able to save your notes as computer text, although critics say this function works only moderately well.[3]

● **PANEL 5.5**

Pen-based computer systems
Handheld Tablet PC.

  The *__light pen__* **is a light-sensitive penlike device that uses a wired connection to a computer terminal.** The user brings the pen to a desired point on the display screen and presses the pen button, which identifies that screen location to the computer. Light pens are used by engineers, graphic designers, and illustrators. They also are used in the health, food service, and chemical fields in situations in which users' hands need to be covered. *(See* ● *Panel 5.6 on the next page.)*

PANEL 5.6
Light pen
This person is using a light pen to input to the computer.

A *digitizer* uses an electronic pen or a mouselike copying device called a *puck* that can convert drawings and photos to digital data. One form of digitizer is **the *digitizing tablet*, used in engineering and architecture applications, in which a specific location on an electronic plastic board corresponds to a location on the screen.** *(See ● Panel 5.7.)* Recently several electronic pens have come to market that capture handwritten notes as digital data.[4] *(See ● Panel 5.8.)*

Scanning & Reading Devices

In old-fashioned grocery stores, checkout clerks read the price on every can and box, and then enter those prices on the keyboard—a wasteful, duplicated effort. In newer stores, of course, the clerks merely wave the products over a scanner, which automatically enters the price (from the bar code) in digital form. This is the difference between keyboard entry and source data entry.

Source data-input devices do not require keystrokes (or require only a few keystrokes) to input data to the computer. In most cases, data is entered directly from the source, without human intervention. **_Source data-entry devices_ create machine-readable data on magnetic media or paper or feed it directly into the computer's processor.** One type of source data-entry device includes scanning and reading devices—scanners, bar-code readers, mark- and character-recognition devices, and fax machines:

PANEL 5.8
Handwritten notes via electronic pen
Seiko's Ink Link System instantly captures handwriting and drawings directly to your handheld, notebook, or desktop PC.

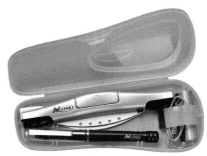

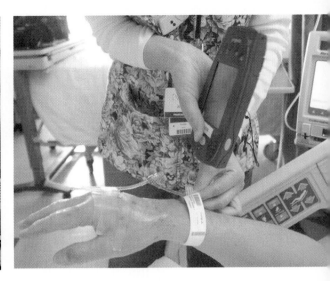

S u r v i v a l   T i p

Can Your PC Connect Your New Scanner?

No USB ports on your PC? Then no USB scanner. Connections must be compatible.

info!

What is TWAIN? (Maybe "Technology Without An Interesting Name"?) It's a driver that's a go-between for a scanner and the applications on the computer. Do a web search for *TWAIN*. What's its origin; how does it work?

● **Scanners:** *Scanners*, **or** *optical scanners*, **use light-sensing (optical) equipment to translate images of text, drawings, photos, and the like into digital form.** *(See* ● *Panel 5.9.)* The images can then be processed by a computer, displayed on a monitor, stored on a storage device, or transmitted to another computer. Scanners are similar to photocopy machines except they create electronic files of scanned items instead of paper copies. The system scans each image—color or black and white—with light and breaks the image into rows and columns of light and dark dots or color dots, which are then converted to digital code, called a *bitmap*. A *dot* is the smallest identifiable part of an image. The more bits in each dot, the more shades of gray and the more colors that can be represented.

Scanners vary in resolution. *Resolution* refers to the clarity and sharpness of an image and is measured in dots per inch (dpi)—the number of columns and rows of dots per inch. The higher the number of dots, the clearer and sharper the image. Popular color desktop scanners currently have the following dpi: 300×200, 600×600, $600 \times 1,200$, $1,200 \times 1,200$, or $2,400 \times 2,400$. Commercial scanners range up to 8,000 dpi. (Resolution also applies to monitors and printers, which we cover shortly.) The quality of the scanner's optical equipment also affects the quality of the scanned images. PC users can get a decent scanner with good software for less than $200 or a fantastic one for about $1,000.

One of the most popular types of scanners is the *flatbed scanner*, **or** *desktop scanner*, **which works much like a photocopier—the image being scanned is placed on a glass surface, where it remains stationary, and the scanning beam moves across it.** Three other types of scanners are *sheet-fed, handheld,* and *drum.*

Scanning technology has led to a whole new art or industry called *electronic imaging,* the software-controlled integration of separate images, using scanners, digital cameras, and advanced graphic computers. This technology has become an important part of multimedia.

● **Bar-code readers:** *Bar codes* **are the vertical, zebra-striped marks you see on most manufactured retail products**—everything from candy to cosmetics to comic books. *(See* ● *Panel 5.10 on the next page.)* In North America, supermarkets, food manufacturers, and others have agreed to use a bar-code system called the *Universal Product Code (UPC),* established by the Uniform Code Council (UCC). Other kinds of bar-code systems are used on everything from FedEx and Postal Service packages to railroad cars, video-store videos, and the jerseys of long-distance runners.

Bar codes and bar-code reader
This bar-code scanner is being used to scan prices of items in a supermarket. The prices and other item information are stored in the supermarket's database, which is connected to the checkout stations.

info!

Bar-code readers **are photoelectric (optical) scanners that translate the symbols in the bar code into digital code.** In this system, the price of a particular item is set within the store's computer. Once the bar code has been scanned, the corresponding price appears on the salesclerk's point-of-sale terminal and on your receipt. Records of sales from the bar-code readers are input to the store's computer and used for accounting, restocking store inventory, and weeding out products that don't sell well.

Self-scanning is becoming increasingly available in stores throughout the United States. *(See ● Panel 5.11.)* Self-scanning checkout is an automated process that enables shoppers to scan, bag, and pay for their purchases without human assistance. The self-scanning checkout lane looks like a traditional checkout lane except that the shopper interacts with a computer's user interface instead of a store employee.

- **Mark-recognition and character-recognition devices:** There are three types of scanning devices that sense marks or characters. They are usually referred to by their abbreviations—MICR, OMR, and OCR:

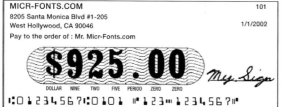

Magnetic ink character recognition (MICR) **is a character recognition system that uses magnetizable ink and special characters.** When an MICR document needs to be read, it passes through a special scanner that magnetizes the special ink and then translates the magnetic information into characters. MICR technology is used by banks.

Optical mark recognition (OMR) **uses a special scanner that reads "bubble" marks and converts them into computer-usable form.** The best-known example is the OMR technology used to read students' answers to the College Board Scholastic Aptitude Test (SAT) and the

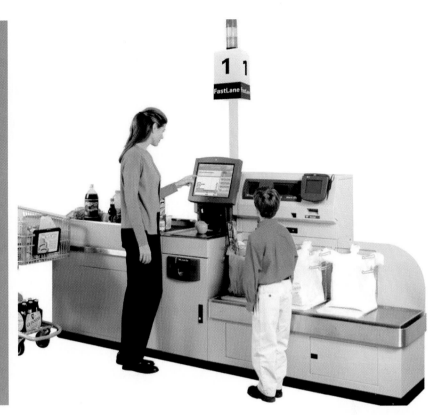

The NCR FastLane self-service scanning system allows consumers to check themselves out of the supermarket. The shopper begins the process by touching the computer's welcome screen. Then the computer's voice output provides the shopper with instructions about how to scan the items and where to place them once they've been scanned. When the shopper scans in an item, the item's bar-code provides the computer with the information it needs to determine what item is being scanned, its weight, and its price. The system also deactivates any security tags on the items. The items are placed in shopping bags placed on security scales, so the system can check that heavy iitems were not substituted for light ones.

Graduate Record Examination (GRE). In these cases, the scanner reads pencil marks that fill in circles, or bubbles, on specially designed documents. OMR is also used in forms and surveys.

These days almost all scanners come with OCR software. _**Optical character-recognition (OCR)**_ **software converts scanned text from images (pictures of the text) to an editable text format (usually ASCII) that can be imported into a word processing application and manipulated.** Special OCR characters appear on utility bills and price tags on department-store merchandise. The wand reader is a common OCR scanning device. _(See_ ● _Panel 5.12.)_

- **Fax machines:** A _**fax machine**_—or _facsimile transmission machine_— scans an image and sends it as electronic signals over telephone lines to a receiving fax machine, which prints out the image on paper.

● **PANEL 5.12**

Optical character recognition

OCR is often used in stores to encode and read price tags. A handheld wand is used as a reading device.

OCR-A	
NUMERIC	0123456789
ALPHA	ABCDEFGHIJ
SYMBOLS	KLMNOPQRST
	UVWXYZ
	>$/-+-#"

OCR-B	
NUMERIC	00123456789
ALPHA	ACENPSTVX
SYMBOLS	<+>-¥

Dedicated fax machine

Fax modem circuit board, which plugs into an expansion slot inside the computer

PC modem card. This plugs into the USB port on a notebook computer.

There are two types of fax machines—dedicated fax machines and fax modems. _**Dedicated fax machines**_ **are specialized devices that do nothing except send and receive fax documents.** These are what we usually think of as fax machines. They are found not only in offices and homes but also alongside regular phones in public places such as airports.

A _**fax modem**_ **is installed as a circuit board inside the computer's system cabinet. It is a modem with fax capability that enables you to send signals directly from your computer to someone else's fax machine or computer fax modem.** With this device, you don't have to print out the material from your printer and then turn around and run it through the scanner on a fax machine. The fax modem allows you to send information more quickly than if you had to feed it page by page into a machine.

The fax modem is another feature of mobile computing; it's especially powerful as a receiving device. Fax modems are installed inside portable computers, including pocket PCs and PDAs. If you link up a cellular phone to a fax modem in your portable computer, you can send and receive wireless fax messages no matter where you are in the world.

Audio-Input Devices

An _**audio-input device**_ **records analog sound and translates it for digital storage and processing.** An analog sound signal is a continuously variable wave within a certain frequency range. For the computer to process them, these variable waves must be converted to digital 0s and 1s. The principal use of audio-input devices is to produce digital input for multimedia computers.

An audio signal can be digitized in two ways—by a _sound board_ or a _MIDI board_. Analog sound from a cassette player or a microphone goes through a special circuit board called a _sound board_. **A _sound board_ is an add-on circuit board in a computer that converts analog sound to digital sound and stores it for further processing and/or plays it back, providing output directly to speakers or an external amplifier. A _MIDI board_**—_MIDI_, pronounced "middie," stands for "Musical Instrument Digital Interface"—**uses a standard for the interchange of musical information between musical instruments, synthesizers, and computers.**

Webcams & Video-Input Cards

Are you the type who likes to show off for the camera? Maybe, then, you'd like to a acquire a _**webcam**_, **a video camera attached to a computer to record live moving images that can then be posted on a website in real time.** _(See Panel 5.13.)_ You could join the thousands of other web-camera users out there who are hosting such riveting material as a 24-hour view of the aquarium of a turtle named Pixel. Or you could show your living quarters or messy desk for all to see. Webcam connections require special software, usually included with the camera, and a USB or video cable or a wireless radio-frequency connection.

● **PANEL 5.13**
Webcam in use
The camera is mounted on the top left of the screen.

info!
The first webcam was the "Trojan room coffee pot cam." What was this? Search the web to find out.

Digital Cameras

Digital still cameras are particularly interesting because they are changing the entire industry of photography. Instead of using traditional (chemical) film, **a _digital camera_ uses a light-sensitive processor chip to capture photographic images in digital form and store them on a small diskette inserted into the camera or on flash-memory cards** (p. 168.) The bits of digital information can then be copied right into a computer's hard disk for manipulation, emailing, posting on websites, and printing out.

Of course, in case you haven't heard, digital-camera technology has migrated to cellphones (which can also be used for web surfing, playing games, and downloading music), enabling you to visually share your vacation experiences in real time. You compose the shot on your phone's color LCD screen, point and shoot, then wait a minute or so for the picture to "develop," and then send it.

HP Photosmart digital camera connected to a computer to download pictures.

Sony Ericsson camera phone.

S u r v i v a l   T i p

Digital Camera Resource

For more information on digital cameras, go to _www.dcresource.com._

Speech-Recognition Systems

Can your computer tell whether you want it to "recognize speech" or "wreck a nice beach"? **A _speech-recognition system_, using a microphone (or a telephone) as an input device, converts a person's speech into digital signals by comparing the electrical patterns produced by the speaker's voice with a set of prerecorded patterns stored in the computer.** _(See Panel 5.14.)_ Most of today's speech-recognition packages come with a database of about 200,000 words from which they try to match the words you say. These programs let you accomplish two tasks: turn spoken dictation into typed text, and issue oral commands (such as "Print file" or "Change font") to control your computer.

Speech-recognition systems have had to overcome many difficulties, such as different voices, pronunciations, and accents. Recently, however, the systems have measurably improved. Two major recognition systems are IBM's Via Voice and Dragon Naturally Speaking. Windows XP has some basic built-in speech-recognition features. Some special software is available for specific professions, such as law, medicine, and public safety.

PANEL 5.14

Speech recognition

Speech-recognition systems are finding many uses. Warehouse workers are able to speed inventory taking by recording inventory counts verbally. Traders on stock exchanges can communicate their trades by speaking to computers. Radiologists can dictate their interpretations of X-rays directly into transcription machines. Nurses can fill out patient charts by talking to a computer. Drivers can talk to their car radios to change stations. Indeed, for many individuals with disabilities, a computer isn't so much a luxury or a productivity tool as a necessity. It provides freedom of expression, independence, and empowerment.

Sensors

A _sensor_ **is an input device that collects specific data directly from the environment and transmits it to a computer.** Although you are unlikely to see such input devices connected to a PC in an office, they exist all around us, often in nearly invisible form and as part of some larger electronic system. Sensors can be used to detect all kinds of things: speed, movement, weight, pressure, temperature, humidity, wind, current, fog, gas, smoke, light, shapes, images, and so on.

Sensors are used to detect the speed and volume of traffic and adjust traffic lights. They are used on mountain highways in wintertime in the Sierra Nevada as weather-sensing devices to tell workers when to roll out snowplows. In California, sensors have been planted along major earthquake fault lines in an experiment to see whether scientists can predict major earth movements. (See ● Panel 5.15.) In aviation, sensors are used to detect ice buildup on airplane wings or to alert pilots to sudden changes in wind direction. Building security systems use sensors to detect movement.

● **PANEL 5.15**
Earthquake sensor

Radio-Frequency Identification Tags

Radio-frequency identification (RFID) **tags are based on an identifying tag bearing a microchip that contains specific code numbers. These code numbers are read by the radio waves of a scanner linked to a database.** Drivers with RFID tags can breeze through the tollbooths without having to even roll down their windows; the toll is automatically charged to their accounts. Radio-wave-readable ID tags are also used by the Postal Service to monitor the flow of mail, by stores for inventory control and warehousing, and in the railroad industry to keep track of rail cars. They are even injected into dogs and cats, so that veterinarians with the right scanning equipment can identify them if they become separated from their owners.

Drivers can buy RFID tags to drive through tollbooths without having to stop; the tolls are automatically charged to their accounts.

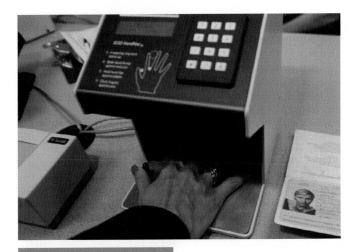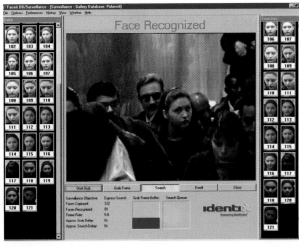

● **PANEL 5.16**

Some types of biometric devices
(Left) Palmprint recognition; (right) a screen from a face recogniton system.

SECURITY

Human-Biology-Input Devices

Security concerns following the terrorist attacks of September 11, 2001, on the New York World Trade Center and the Pentagon have made more people aware of **_biometrics_, the science of measuring individual body characteristics.** Biometric security devices identify a person through a fingerprint; hand, eye, or facial characteristics; voice intonation; or some other biological trait. *(See ● Panel 5.16.)*

QuickCheck

Describe the various types of keyboards.

Discuss the mouse and its variants.

Identify the other types of pointing devices.

What is source-data entry?

Name and characterize the various types of scanning devices.

Describe all the other types of source-data-entry devices.

5.3 Output Hardware

KEY QUESTIONS

What are the two categories of output hardware, what devices do they include, and what are their features?

Are we back to old-time radio? Almost. Except that you can call up local programs by downloading them from the internet. The sound quality isn't even as good as that of AM radio, but no doubt that will improve eventually. Computer output is taking more and more innovative forms and getting better and better.

As mentioned, output hardware consists of devices that convert machine-readable information, obtained as the result of processing, into people-readable form. The principal kinds of output are softcopy and hardcopy. *(See ● Panel 5.17 on the next page.)*

- **Softcopy: _Softcopy_ is data that is shown on a display screen or is in audio or voice form; it exists only electronically.** This kind of output is not tangible; it cannot be touched. It's like music: You can see musical scores and touch CDs and tapes, but the music itself is intangible. Similarly, you can touch floppy disks on which programs are stored, but the software itself is intangible.

Softcopy Devices	Hardcopy Devices	Other Devices
CRT display screens	Impact printers: dot-matrix printer	Sound output
Flat-panel display screen (e.g., liquid-crystal display)	Nonimpact printers: laser, ink-jet, thermal	Voice output
		Video output

Reading hardcopy *(top)* and softcopy *(bottom)*.

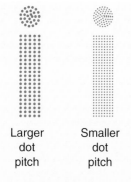

Larger dot pitch   Smaller dot pitch

The Letter " i "

● **Hardcopy:** <u>*Hardcopy*</u> **is printed output.** The principal examples are printouts, whether text or graphics, from printers. Film, including microfilm and microfiche, is also considered hardcopy output.

There are several types of softcopy and hardcopy output devices. In the following three sections we discuss, first, traditional *softcopy* output—*display screens*; second, traditional *hardcopy* output—*printers*; and, third, *mixed* output—including *sound, voice,* and *video.*

Traditional Softcopy Output: Display Screens

<u>*Display screens*</u>—**also variously called** *monitors, CRTs,* **or simply** *screens*—**are output devices that show programming instructions and data as they are being input and information after it is processed** for showing the results of computing.

As with TV screens, the size of a computer screen is measured diagonally from corner to corner in inches. For desktop microcomputers, the most common sizes are 13, 15, 17, 19, 21, and 24 inches. For notebook computers, they are 12.1, 13.3, 14.1, and 15.1 inches. Increasingly, computer ads state the actual display area, called the *viewable image size (vis),* which may be an inch or so less. A 15-inch monitor may have about a 14-inch vis; a 17-inch monitor may have a 16-inch vis.

monitor screen size	viewable image size
15 inches	14 inches
17 inches	16 inches
21 inches	20 inches

In deciding which display screen to buy, you will need to consider issues of screen clarity (dot pitch, resolution, color depth, and refresh rate), type of display technology (CRT versus flat panel, active-matrix flat panel versus passive-matrix flat panel), and color and resolution standards (SVGA and XGA).

● **Screen clarity—dot pitch, resolution, color depth, and refresh rate:** Among the factors affecting screen clarity (often mentioned in ads) are *dot pitch, resolution, color depth,* and *refresh rate.* These relate to the individual dots on the screen known as *pixels,* which represent the images on the screen. **A** <u>*pixel*</u>**, for "picture** *el***ement," is the smallest unit on the screen that can be turned on and off or made different shades.** Pixels are tiny squares, not circles.

<u>*Dot pitch (dp)*</u> **is the amount of space between the centers of adjacent pixels; the closer the pixels, the crisper the image.** For a .25-dp monitor, for instance, the dots (pixels) are 25/100ths of a millimeter apart. Generally, a dot pitch of .25 dp will provide clear images.

Here, <u>*resolution*</u> refers to the image sharpness of the display screen; the more pixels, or dots, there are per

🔍 17", .27dp Monitor (16" Display)

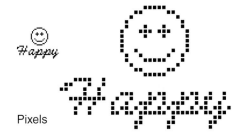

Pixels

Standard monitor resolutions, in pixels

640 × 480

800 × 600

1,024 × 768

1,280 × 1,024

1,600 × 1,200

1,920 × 1,400

Standard bit depths for color

4-bit—16 colors

8-bit—256 colors

16-bit—65,536 colors

24-bit—10 million colors

●**PANEL 5.18**
CRT *(left)* and flat-panel display *(right)*

S u r v i v a l   T i p

Buying a Flat Panel

Defective transistors stuck on or off can cause dead or bright pixels. A couple may not bother you, but check a new screen carefully.

square inch, the finer the level of detail. As with scanners, resolution is expressed in *dots per inch (dpi)*, the number of columns and rows of dots per inch. The higher the number of dots, the clearer and sharper the image. Resolution clarity is measured by the formula *horizontal-row pixels × vertical-row pixels*. For example, a 640 × 480 screen displays 640 pixels on each of 480 lines, for a total of 307,200 pixels. On color monitors, each pixel is assigned some red, some green, some blue, or particular shades of gray.

<u>*Color depth*</u>, **or** *bit depth*, **is the amount of information, expressed in bits, that is stored in a dot.** The more bits in a dot or pixel, the more shades of gray and colors can be represented. With 24-bit color depth, for example, 8 bits are dedicated to each primary color—red, green, and blue. Eight-bit color is standard for most of computing; 24-bit, called *true color*, requires more resources, such as video memory.

<u>*Refresh rate*</u> **is the number of times per second that the pixels are recharged so that their glow remains bright.** That is, refresh rate refers to the number of times that the image on the screen is redrawn each second. The higher the refresh rate, the more solid the image looks on the screen—that is, the less it flickers. In general, displays are refreshed 56–120 times per second, or *hertz (Hz)*, with speeds of 70–87 hertz being common. A high-quality monitor has a refresh rate of 90 hertz—the screen is redrawn 90 times per second. A low-quality monitor will be under 72 hertz, which will cause noticeable flicker and lead to headaches and eyestrain.

● **Two types of monitors—CRT and flat-panel:** Display screens are of two types: CRT and flat-panel. *(See* ● *Panel 5.18.)*

A <u>*CRT (cathode-ray tube)*</u> **is a vacuum tube used as a display screen in a computer or video display terminal.** The same kind of technology is found not only in the screens of desktop computers but also in television sets and flight-information monitors in airports. *Note:* Advertisements for desktop computers often *do not* include a monitor as part of the system. You need to be prepared to spend a few hundred dollars extra for the monitor.

Compared to CRTs, flat-panel displays are much thinner, weigh less, and consume less power, which is why they are used in portable computers. <u>*Flat-panel displays*</u> **are made up of two plates of glass separated by a layer of a substance in which light is manipulated. One flat-panel technology is** <u>*liquid crystal display (LCD)*</u>**, in which molecules of liquid crystal line up in a way that alters their optical properties, creating images on the screen by transmitting or blocking out light.**

Flat-panel monitors are available for desktop computers as well, and because they are smaller than CRTs, they fit more easily onto a crowded desk. CRTs are still cheaper, but flat-panel prices are coming down: The average price for a 17-inch CRT in 2003 was $155, but 15-inch flat panels averaged $297.

● **Active-matrix versus passive-matrix flat-panel displays:** Flat-panel screens are either active-matrix or passive-matrix displays, according to where their transistors are located.

In an <u>*active-matrix display*</u>, **also known as a** *TFT (thin-film transistor) display*, **each pixel on the flat-panel screen is controlled by its own transistor.** Active-matrix screens are much brighter and sharper than passive-matrix screens, but they are more complicated and thus more expensive. They also require more power, affecting the battery life in notebook computers. A newer type of TFT, called *organic TFT*, or *organic light-emitting diode (OLED)*, uses films of organic molecules sandwiched between two charged electrodes to produce even brighter and more readable displays than traditional TFT displays.

Buying a New Monitor?

Be sure it can work with your computer and video card and has enough video RAM to support what you want to do.

Your Choice: More Colors or More Resolution?

You can't have the best of both. A video card may let you have 16.8 million colors at 800 × 600 resolution or 65,536 colors at 1,600 × 1,200 resolution.

In a **_passive-matrix display_, a transistor controls a whole row or column of pixels on the flat-screen display.** Passive matrix provides a sharp image for one-color (monochrome) screens but is more subdued for color. The advantage is that passive-matrix displays are less expensive and use less power than active-matrix displays, but they aren't as clear and bright and can leave "ghosts" when the display changes quickly. Passive-matrix displays go by the abbreviations _HPA, STN,_ or _DSTN._

- **Color and resolution standards for monitors—SVGA and XGA:** As mentioned earlier, PCs come with _graphics cards_ (also known as _video cards_ or _video adapters_) that convert signals from the computer into video signals that can be displayed as images on a monitor. The monitor then separates the video signal into three colors: red, green, and blue signals. Inside the monitor, these three colors combine to make up each individual pixel. Video cards have their own memory, video RAM, or VRAM, which stores the information about each pixel. The more VRAM you have, which can range from 2 to 64 megabytes, the higher the resolution you can use. Video gamers and desktop publishers (Photoshop users) will want a video card with lots of VRAM.

  The common color and resolution standards for monitors are _SVGA, XGA, SXGA, UXGA,_ and, most recently, _QXGA._ (See ● _Panel 5.19.)_

  SVGA (super video graphics array) supports a resolution of 800 × 600 pixels, or variations, producing up to 16 million possible simultaneous colors (depending on the amount of VRAM). SVGA is the most common standard used today with 15-inch monitors. This standard is best for simpler applications: word processing, email, and so on.

  XGA (extended graphics array) has a resolution of up to 1,024 × 768 pixels, with 65,536 possible colors. It is used mainly for 17-, 19-, and 21-inch monitors. It's useful for simple applications plus spreadsheets and graphics software.

  SXGA (super extended graphics array) has a resolution of up to 1,280 × 1,024 pixels. It is often used with 19- and 21-inch monitors by graphic designers, engineers, and programmers.

  UXGA (ultra extended graphics array) has a resolution of up to 1,600 × 1,200 pixels and supports up to 16.8 million colors. Common applications for it include CAD (computer-aided design, p. 132) and business presentations, such as trade show displays.

● **PANEL 5.19**
Video graphics standards compared for pixels

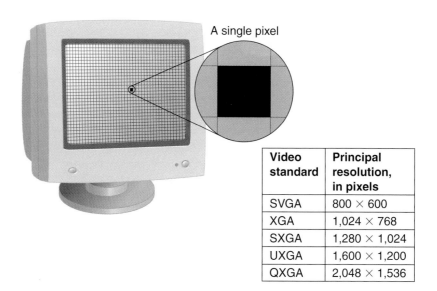

A single pixel

Video standard	Principal resolution, in pixels
SVGA	800 × 600
XGA	1,024 × 768
SXGA	1,280 × 1,024
UXGA	1,600 × 1,200
QXGA	2,048 × 1,536

QXGA (quantum extended graphics array) **is a new display standard with a resolution of up to 2,048 x 1,536 pixels.** Presently costing as much as $10,000, QXGA is being used for large LCD screens for computer users needing to view extreme detail, for businesspeople needing to enlarge images that will still be crisp in big-screen presentations, for high-density television (to be discussed), and for special applications involving viewing multiple images on a single screen.

Traditional Hardcopy Output: Printers

HP DeskJet 970Cse Printer

The prices in ads for computer systems often do not include a printer. Thus, you will need to budget an additional $100 to $1,000 or more for a printer. **A _printer_ is an output device that prints characters, symbols, and perhaps graphics on paper or another hardcopy medium. The resolution, or quality of sharpness, of the printed image is indicated by _dpi (dots per inch)_, which is a measure of the number of rows and columns of dots that are printed in a square inch.** For microcomputer printers, the resolution is in the range of 60–1,500 dpi.

Printers can be separated into two categories, according to whether or not the image produced is formed by physical contact of the print mechanism with the paper. *Impact printers* do have contact with paper; *nonimpact printers* do not. We will also consider plotters and multifunction printers.

- **Impact printers: An _impact printer_ forms characters or images by striking a mechanism such as a print hammer or wheel against an inked ribbon, leaving an image on paper.** A *dot-matrix printer* contains a print head of small pins that strike an inked ribbon against paper, to form characters or images. Print heads are available with 9, 18, or 24 pins; the 24-pin head offers the best quality. Dot-matrix printers can print *draft quality*, a coarser-looking 72 dpi, or *near-letter-quality (NLQ)*, a crisper-looking 144 dpi. The machines print 40–300 characters per second and can handle graphics as well as text. A disadvantage is the noise they produce, because of the print head striking the paper. Nowadays impact printers are more commonly used with mainframes than with personal computers. Note that dot-matrix printers are the only desktop printers that can use multilayered forms to print "carbon copies."

- **Nonimpact printers:** Nonimpact printers are faster and quieter than impact printers because no print head strikes paper. **_Nonimpact printers_ form characters and images without direct physical contact between the printing mechanism and paper.** Two types of nonimpact printers often used with microcomputers are *laser printers* and *ink-jet printers*. A third kind, the *thermal printer*, is seen less frequently.

Like a dot-matrix printer, a **_laser printer_ creates images with dots. However, as in a photocopying machine, these images are produced on a drum, treated with a magnetically charged ink-like toner (powder), and then transferred from drum to paper.** *(See ● Panel 5.20, next page.)* (Laser printers are also called *page printers*, because they print one page at a time.)

Laser printers run with software called a _page description language (PDL)_. This software tells the printer how to lay out the printed page, and it supports various fonts. A laser printer comes with one of two types of PDL: PostScript (developed by Adobe) or PCL (Printer Control Language, developed by Hewlett-Packard).

There are good reasons that laser printers are among the most common types of nonimpact printer. They produce sharp, crisp images of both text and graphics. They are quiet and fast—able to print 11–32 text-only pages per minute for individual microcomputers and up to

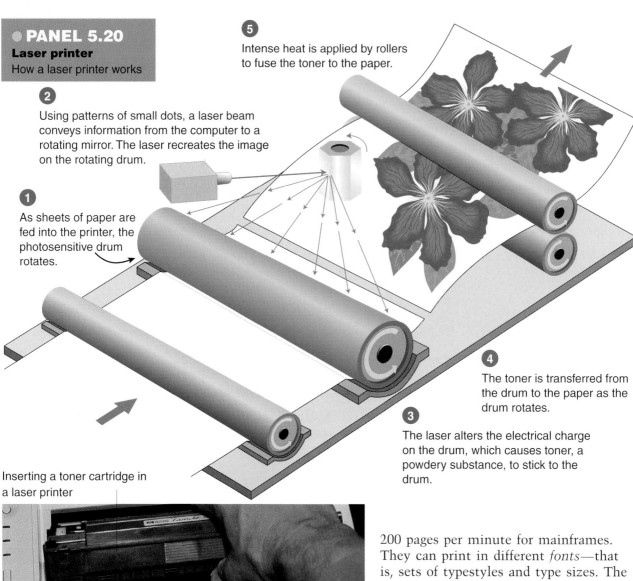

⑤ Intense heat is applied by rollers to fuse the toner to the paper.

② Using patterns of small dots, a laser beam conveys information from the computer to a rotating mirror. The laser recreates the image on the rotating drum.

① As sheets of paper are fed into the printer, the photosensitive drum rotates.

④ The toner is transferred from the drum to the paper as the drum rotates.

③ The laser alters the electrical charge on the drum, which causes toner, a powdery substance, to stick to the drum.

Inserting a toner cartridge in a laser printer

Ink-jet printer

200 pages per minute for mainframes. They can print in different *fonts*—that is, sets of typestyles and type sizes. The more expensive models can print in different colors. Laser printers have a dpi of 600–1,200.

Ink-jet printers spray onto paper small, electrically charged droplets of ink from four nozzles through holes in a matrix at high speed. Like laser and dot-matrix printers, ink-jet printers form images with little dots. Ink-jet printers have a dpi of 300–2,400 and spray ink onto the page a line at a time, in both high-quality black-and-white text and high-quality color graphics.

The advantages of ink-jet printers are that they can print in color, are quiet, and are much less expensive than color laser printers. The disadvantages are that they print a bit less precisely than laser printers do and they are slower. Ink-jet printing a document with high-resolution color graphics may take 10 minutes or more for a single page. Also, ink-jet cartridges are more expensive than laser toner. Moreover, a freshly printed page is apt to smear unless handled carefully. Still, a color ink-jet printer's cost is considerably less than the cost of color laser printers.

● **PANEL 5.21**

Multifunction device

This machine combines four functions in one— printer, copier, fax machine, and scanner.

Thermal printers **use colored waxes and heat elements to produce images by burning dots onto special paper.** The colored wax sheets are not required for black-and-white output. However, thermal printers are expensive, and they require expensive paper. For people who want the highest-quality color printing available with a desktop printer, thermal printers are the answer.

- Multifunction printers—printers that do more than print: ***Multifunction printers*** **combine several capabilities, such as printing, scanning, copying, and faxing.** *(See* ● *Panel 5.21.)* Xerox and Hewlett-Packard make machines that combine a photocopier, fax machine, scanner, and laser printer. Multifunction printers take up less space and cost less than the four separate office machines that they replace. The drawback is that if one component breaks, nothing works.

Specialty printers also exist for such purposes as printing photos and labels, and printing text in Braille. The accompanying box gives some questions to consider when you're buying a printer. *(See* ● *Panel 5.22.)*

Mixed Output: Sound, Voice, & Video

Most PCs are now multimedia computers, capable of displaying and printing not only traditional softcopy and hardcopy text and graphics but also sound, voice, and video, as we consider next.

- Sound output: ***Sound-output devices*** **produce digitized sounds, ranging from beeps and chirps to music.** To use sound output, you need appropriate software and a sound card. The sound card could be

● **PANEL 5.22**

Buying a printer

Do I need color, or will black-only do? Are you mainly printing text or will you need to produce color charts and illustrations (and, if so, how often)? If you print lots of black text, consider getting a laser printer. If you might occasionally print color, get an ink-jet that will accept cartridges for both black and color. Unless you are in the publishing or design business, you will probably not need an expensive color laser printer.

Do I have other special output requirements? Do you need to print envelopes or labels? special fonts (type styles)? multiple copies? transparencies or on heavy stock? unusual paper size? Find out if the printer comes with envelope feeders, sheet feeders holding at least 100 sheets, or whatever will meet your requirements.

Is the printer easy to set up? Can you easily put the unit together, plug in the hardware, and adjust the software (the "driver" programs) to make the printer work with your computer?

Is the printer easy to operate? Can you add paper, replace ink/toner cartridges or ribbons, and otherwise operate the printer without much difficulty?

Does the printer provide the speed and quality I want? A regular laser printer prints 4–30 pages per minute (ppm); a color ink-jet printer prints 1–12 ppm. Colors and graphics take longer to print. Are the blacks dark enough and the colors vivid enough?

Will I get a reasonable cost per page? Special paper, ink or toner cartridges (especially color), and ribbons are all ongoing costs. Ink-jet color cartridges, for example, may last 100–500 pages and cost $25–$30 new. Laser toner cartridges can cost up to $100 each but last much longer. Ribbons for dot-matrix printers are inexpensive. Ask the seller what the cost per page works out to.

Does the manufacturer offer a good warranty and good telephone technical support? Find out if the warranty lasts at least 2 years. See if the printer's manufacturer offers telephone support in case you have technical problems. The best support systems offer toll-free numbers and operate evenings and weekends as well as weekdays.

In Windows, open the Control Panel and the Sounds section. Once there you can change all the sounds Windows outputs. Click on the event you want to alter the sound for, click the *Browse* button, and then select a new sound file from the folders. Don't assign long sound sequences to common events; they'll become annoying. Many websites offer "themes" for your computer—you can download sound bites from your favorite movies and TV shows.

Sound Blaster or, since that brand has become a de facto standard, one that is "Sound Blaster-compatible." Well-known brands include Creative Labs, Diamond, and Turtle Beach. The sound card plugs into an expansion slot in your computer; on newer computers, it is integrated with the motherboard. Most computers have simple internal speakers. Many users hook up external speakers for high-quality sound.

- **Voice output: _Voice-output devices_ convert digital data into speech-like sounds.** You hear such forms of voice output on telephones ("Please hang up and dial your call again"), in soft-drink machines, in cars, in toys and games, and recently in mapping software for vehicle-navigation devices. Voice portals read news and other information to users on the go.

  One form of voice output that is becoming popular is *text-to-speech (TTS) systems*, which convert computer text into audible speech. TTS benefits not only the visually impaired but also anyone with a computer system sound card and speakers who wants to reduce reading chores (and eyestrain) and do other tasks at the same time. Windows XP offers a TTS program called Narrator. Others are CoolSpeech, CrazyTalk, and Digalo (which can read computer text in eight languages).

- **Video output: _Video_ consists of photographic images, which are played at 15–29 frames per second to give the appearance of full motion.** Video is input into a multimedia system using a video camera or VCR and, after editing, is output on a computer's display screen. Because video files can require a great deal of storage—a 3-minute video may require 1 gigabyte of storage—video is often compressed (a topic we discuss in Chapter 6). Good video output requires a powerful processor as well as a video card.

  Another form of video output is _videoconferencing_, in which people in different geographic locations can have a meeting—can see and hear one another—using computers and communications. Videoconferencing systems range from videophones to group conference rooms with cameras and multimedia equipment to desktop systems with small video cameras, microphones, and speakers.

QuickCheck

What is the difference between softcopy and hardcopy output?

What are the different characteristics of display screens?

What is the difference between impact and nonimpact printers?

Identify the characteristics of dot-matrix, laser, ink-jet, thermal, and multifunction printers.

Distinguish among sound, voice, and video output.

PRACTICAL ACTION BOX
Good Habits: Protecting Your Computer System, Your Data, & Your Health

Whether you set up a desktop computer and never move it or tote a portable PC from place to place, you need to be concerned about protecting not only your computer but yourself. You don't want your computer to get stolen or zapped by a power surge. You don't want to lose your data. And you certainly don't want to lose your health for computer-related reasons. Here are some tips for taking care of these vital areas.

Guarding Against Hardware Theft & Loss

Portable computers are easy targets for thieves. Obviously, anything conveniently small enough to be slipped into your briefcase or backpack can be slipped into someone else's. Never leave a notebook computer unattended in a public place.

It's also possible to simply lose a portable, as in forgetting it's in the overhead-luggage bin in an airplane. To help in its return, use a wide piece of clear tape to tape a card with your name and address to the outside of the machine. You should tape a similar card to the inside also. In addition, scatter a few such cards in the pockets of the carrying case.

Desktop computers are also easily stolen. However, for under $25, you can buy a cable and lock, like those used for bicycles, and secure the computer, monitor, and printer to a work area. If your hardware does get stolen, its recovery may be helped if you have inscribed your driver's license number or home address on each piece. Some campus and city police departments lend inscribing tools for such purposes. Finally, insurance to cover computer theft or damage is surprisingly cheap. Look for advertisements in computer magazines. (If you have standard tenants' or homeowners' insurance, it may not cover your computer. Ask your insurance agent.)

Guarding Against Heat, Cold, Spills, & Drops

"We dropped 'em, baked 'em, we even froze 'em," proclaimed the *PC Computing* cover, ballyhooing a story about its notebook "torture test."[a]

The magazine put eight notebook computers through durability trials. One approximated putting these machines in a car trunk in the desert heat; another, leaving them outdoors in a Buffalo, New York, winter. A third test simulated sloshing coffee on a keyboard, and a fourth dropped computers from desktop height to a carpeted floor. All passed the bake test, but one failed the freeze test. Three completely flunked the coffee-spill test, one other revived, and the rest passed. One that was dropped lost the right side of its display; the others were unharmed. Of the eight, half passed all tests unscathed. In a more recent torture test, nine notebooks survived the heat, cold, and spill tests, but three failed the drop test.

This gives you an idea of how durable computers are. Designed for portability, notebooks may be hardier than desktop machines. Even so, you really don't want to tempt fate by dropping your computer, which could cause your hard-disk drive to fail.

Guarding Against Damage to Software

Systems software and applications software generally come on CD-ROM disks or flexible diskettes. The unbreakable rule is simply this: Copy the original disk, either onto your hard-disk drive or onto another diskette. Then store the original disk in a safe place. If your computer gets stolen or your software destroyed, you can retrieve the original and make another copy.

Protecting Your Data

Computer hardware and commercial software are nearly always replaceable, although perhaps with some expense and difficulty. Data, however, may be major trouble to replace or even be irreplaceable. If your hard-disk drive crashes, do you have the same data on a backup disk? Almost every microcomputer user sooner or later has the experience of accidentally wiping out or losing material and having no copy. This is what makes people true believers in backing up their data—making a duplicate in some form. If you're working on a research paper, for example, it's fairly easy to copy your work onto a floppy disk at the end of your work session. Then store the copy in a safe place.

Floppy disks can be harmed by any number of enemies. These include spills, dirt, heat, moisture, weights, and magnetic fields and magnetized objects. Here are some diskette maintenance tips:

- Insert the floppy disk carefully into the disk drive.
- Don't manipulate the metal shutter on the floppy; it protects the surface of the magnetic material inside.
- Do not place heavy objects on the diskette.
- Do not expose the floppy to excessive heat or light.
- Do not use or place the diskette near a magnetic field, such as a telephone or paper clips stored in magnetic holders. Data can be lost if exposed.
- Do not use alcohol, thinners, or freon to clean the diskette.

Protecting Your Health

More important than any computer system and (probably) any data is your health. What adverse effects might computers cause? The most serious are painful hand and wrist injuries, eyestrain and headache, and back and neck pains.

Many people set up their computers in the same way as they would a typewriter. However, the two machines are ergonomically different for various reasons. (*Ergonomics* is the study of the physical relationships between people and their work environment.) With a computer, it's important to sit with both feet on the floor, thighs at right angles to your body. The chair should be adjustable and support your lower back. Your forearms should be parallel to the floor. You should look down slightly at the screen. *(See ● Panel 6.33.)* This setup is particularly important if you are going to be sitting at a computer for hours at a stretch.

To avoid wrist and forearm injuries, you should keep your wrists straight and hands relaxed as you type. Instead of putting the keyboard on top of a desk, therefore, you should put it on a low table or in a keyboard drawer under the desk. Otherwise the nerves in your wrists will rub against the sheaths surrounding them, possibly leading to RSI (Repetitive Stress Injury) pains. Some experts also suggest using a padded, adjustable wrist rest, attached to the keyboard, or a $10 hand brace. Or try setting an hourly alarm on your watch or on an alarm clock; when the alarm goes off, take a short break and rotate your wrist and hand a bit.

Eyestrain and headaches usually arise because of improper lighting, screen glare, and long shifts staring at the screen. Make sure that your windows and lights don't throw a glare on the screen and that your computer is not framed by an uncovered window. Headaches may also result from too much noise, such as listening for hours to an impact printer printing out.

Back and neck pains occur because furniture is not adjusted correctly or because of heavy computer use. Adjustable furniture and frequent breaks should provide relief here.

Some people worry about emissions of electromagnetic waves and whether they could cause problems in pregnancy or even cause cancer. The best approach is to simply work at an arm's length from computers with CRT-type monitors.

HEAD Directly over shoulders, without straining forward or backward, about an arm's length from screen.

NECK Elongated and relaxed.

SHOULDERS Kept down, with the chest open and wide.

BACK Upright or inclined slightly forward from the hips. Maintain the slight natural curve of the lower back.

ELBOWS Relaxed, at about a right angle, try to keep forearms parallel to floor.

WRISTS Relaxed, and in a neutral position, without flexing up or down.

KNEES Slightly lower than the hips.

CHAIR Sloped slightly forward to facilitate proper knee position.

LIGHT SOURCE Should come from behind the head.

SCREEN At eye level or slightly lower. Use an anti-glare screen.

FINGERS Gently curved.

KEYBOARD Best when kept flat (for proper wrist positioning) and at or just below elbow level. Computer keys that are far away should be reached by moving the entire arm, starting from the shoulders, rather than by twisting the wrists or straining the fingers. Take frequent rest breaks.

FEET Firmly planted on the floor. Shorter people may need a footrest.

● PANEL 5.23
How to set up your computer work area

Summary

active-matrix display (p. 197, KQ 5.3) Also known as *TFT (thin-film transistor) display;* flat-panel display in which each pixel on the screen is controlled by its own transistor. Why it's important: Active-matrix screens are much brighter and sharper than passive-matrix screens, but they are more complicated and thus more expensive. They also require more power, affecting the battery life in laptop computers.

audio-input device (p. 192, KQ 5.2) Hardware that records analog sound and translates it for digital storage and processing. Why it's important: Analog sound signals are continuous variable waves within a certain frequency range. For the computer to process them, these variable waves must be converted to digital 0s and 1s. The principal use of audio-input devices is to produce digital input for multimedia computers. An audio signal can be digitized in two ways—by an audio board or a MIDI board.

bar-code reader (p. 190, KQ 5.2) Photoelectric (optical) scanner that translates bar codes into digital codes. Why it's important: With bar-code readers and the appropriate software system, store clerks can total purchases and produce invoices with increased speed and accuracy and stores and other businesses can monitor inventory and services with increased efficiency.

bar codes (p. 189, KQ 5.2) Vertical, zebra-striped marks imprinted on most manufactured retail products. Why it's important: Bar codes provide a convenient means of identifying and tracking items. In North America, supermarkets, food manufacturers, and others have agreed to use a bar-code system called the *Universal Product Code (UPC).* Other kinds of bar-code systems are used on everything from FedEx packages to railroad cars to the jerseys of long-distance runners.

biometrics (p. 195, KQ 5.2) Science of measuring individual body characteristics. Why it's important: Biometric security devices identify a person through a fingerprint, voice intonation, or some other biological characteristic. For example, retinal-identification devices use a ray of light to identify the distinctive network of blood vessels at the back of the eyeball.

color depth (p. 197, KQ 5.3) Also called *bit depth;* the amount of information, expressed in bits, that is stored in a dot. Why it's important: The more bits in a dot or pixel, the more shades of gray and colors can be represented. With 24-bit color depth, for example, 8 bits are dedicated to each primary color—red, green, and blue. Eight-bit color is standard for most of computing; 24-bit, called *true color*, requires more resources, such as video memory.

CRT

CRT (cathode-ray tube) (p. 197, KQ 5.3) Vacuum tube used as a display screen in a computer or video display terminal. Why it's important: This technology is found not only in the screens of desktop computers but also in television sets and flight-information monitors in airports.

dedicated fax machine (p. 192, KQ 5.2) Specialized device that does nothing except send and receive fax documents. Why it's important: Fax machines permit the transmission of text and graphic data over telephone lines quickly and inexpensively. They are found not only in offices and homes but also alongside regular phones in public places such as airports. *See also* fax modem.

digital camera (p. 193, KQ 5.2) Electronic camera that uses a light-sensitive processor chip to capture photographic images in digital form and store them on a small diskette inserted into the camera or on flash-memory chips (cards). Why it's important: The bits of digital information—the snapshots you have taken, say—can be copied right onto a computer's hard disk for manipulation and printing out. The environmentally undesirable stage of chemical development required for conventional film is completely eliminated.

digitizer (p. 188, KQ 5.2) Input unit based on an electronic pen or a mouselike copying device called a *puck* that converts drawings and photos to digital data. Why it's important: *See* digitizing tablet.

digitizing tablet (p. 188, KQ 5.2) One form of digitizer; an electronic plastic board on which each specific location corresponds to a location on the screen. When the user uses a puck, the tablet converts his or her movements into digital signals that are input to the computer. Why it's important: Digitizing tablets are often used to make maps and engineering drawings, as well as to trace drawings.

display screen (p. 196, KQ 5.3) Also called *monitor, CRT,* or simply *screen;* output device that shows programming instructions and data as they are being input and information after it is processed. Why it's important: Screens are needed to display softcopy output.

dot pitch (dp) (p. 196, KQ 5.3) Amount of space between the centers of adjacent pixels; the closer the pixels (dots), the crisper the image. Why it's important: Dot pitch is one of the measures of display-screen crispness. For a .25dp monitor, for instance, the dots are 25/100ths of a millimeter apart. Generally, a dot pitch of .25dp will provide clear images.

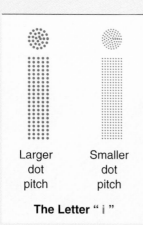

Larger dot pitch   Smaller dot pitch

The Letter " i "

dpi (dots per inch) (p. 199, KQ 5.2) Measure of the number of columns and rows of dots per inch. For microcomputer printers, resolution is in the range 60–1,500 dpi. Why it's important: The higher the dpi, the better the resolution. (*See also* resolution.)

dumb terminal (p. 184, KQ 5.2) Also called *video display terminal (VDT);* display screen and a keyboard hooked up to a computer system. It can input and output but not process data. Why it's important: Dumb terminals are used, for example, by airline reservations clerks to access a mainframe computer containing flight information.

fax machine (p. 191, KQ 5.2). Also called a *facsimile transmission machine;* input device that scans an image and sends it as electronic signals over telephone lines to a receiving fax machine, which prints the image on paper. Why it's important: *See* dedicated fax machine *and* fax modem.

fax modem (p. 192, KQ 5.2) Input device installed as a circuit board inside the computer's system cabinet; a modem with fax capability that enables the user to send signals directly from her or his computer to someone else's fax machine or computer fax modem. Why it's important: With this device, users don't have to print out the material via a printer and then turn around and run it through the scanner on a fax machine. The fax modem allows users to send information more quickly than if they had to feed it page by page into a machine. Fax modems are installed inside portable computers, including pocket PCs and PDAs. If you can link up a cellphone to a fax modem in your portable computer, you can send and receive wireless fax messages no matter where you are in the world.

Flatbed scanner

flatbed scanner (p. 189, KQ 5.2) Also called *desktop scanner;* the image being scanned is placed on a glass surface, where it remains stationary, and the scanning beam moves across it. Three other types of scanners are *sheet-fed, handheld,* and *drum.* Why it's important: Flatbed scanners are one of the most popular types of scanner.

flat-panel display (p. 197, KQ 5.3) Display screen that is much thinner, weighs less, and consumes less power than a CRT. Flat-panel displays are made up of two plates of glass separated by a layer of a substance in which light is manipulated. Why it's important: Flat-panel displays are essential to portable computers, although they are available for desktop computers as well.

hardcopy (p. 196, KQ 5.3) Printed output. The principal examples are printouts, whether text or graphics, from printers. Film, including microfilm and microfiche, is also considered hardcopy output. Why it's important: Hardcopy is an essential form of computer output.

impact printer (p. 199, KQ 5.3) Printer that forms characters or images by striking a mechanism such as a print hammer or wheel against an inked ribbon, leaving an image on paper. Why it's important: Nonimpact printers are more commonly used than impact printers, but dot-matrix printers are still used in some businesses.

ink-jet printer (p. 200, KQ 5.3) Printer that sprays onto paper small, electrically charged droplets of ink from four nozzles through holes in a matrix at high speed. Like laser and dot-matrix printers, ink-jet printers form images with little dots. Why it's important: Because they produce high-quality images on special paper, ink-jet printers are often used in graphic design and desktop publishing. However, ink-jet printers are slower than laser printers and print at a lower resolution on regular paper.

input hardware (p. 183, KQ 5.1) Devices that translate data into a form the computer can process. Why it's important: Without input hardware, computers could not function. The computer-readable form consists of 0s and 1s, represented as off and on electrical signals. Input hardware devices are categorized as three types: keyboards, pointing devices, and source data-entry devices.

intelligent terminal (p. 185, KQ 5.2) Hardware unit with its own memory and processor, as well as a display screen and keyboard, hooked up to a larger computer system. Why it's important: Such a terminal can perform some functions independent of any mainframe to which it is linked. Examples include the automated teller machine (ATM), a self-service banking machine connected through a telephone network to a central computer, and the point-of-sale (POS) terminal, used to record purchases at a store's customer checkout counter. Recently, many intelligent terminals have been replaced by personal computers.

internet terminal (p. 185, KQ 5.2) Terminal that provides access to the internet. There are several variants of internet terminal: (1) the set-top box or web terminal, which displays web pages on a TV set; (2) the network computer, a cheap, stripped-down computer that connects people to networks; (3) the online game player, which not only lets you play games but also connects to the internet; (4) the full-blown PC/TV (or TV/PC), which merges the personal computer with the television set; and (5) the wireless pocket PC or personal digital assistant (PDA), a handheld computer with a tiny keyboard that can do two-way wireless messaging. Why it's important: In the near future, most likely, internet terminals will be everywhere.

keyboard (p. 184, KQ 5.2) Input device that converts letters, numbers, and other characters into electrical signals that can be read by the computer's processor. Why it's important: Keyboards are the most popular kind of input device.

laser printer (p. 199, KQ 5.3) Nonimpact printer that creates images with dots. As in a photocopying machine, images are produced on a drum, treated with a magnetically charged ink-like toner (powder), and then transferred from drum to paper. Why it's important: Laser printers produce much better image quality than do dot-matrix printers and can print in many more colors; they are also quieter. Laser printers, along with page description languages, enabled the development of desktop publishing.

light pen (p. 187, KQ 5.2) Light-sensitive penlike device connected by a wire to the computer terminal. The user brings the pen to a desired point on the display screen and presses the pen button, which identifies that screen location to the computer. Why it's important: Light pens are used by engineers, graphic designers, and illustrators.

liquid crystal display (LCD) (p. 197, KQ 5.3) Flat-panel display in which molecules of liquid crystal line up in a way that alters their optical properties, creating images on the screen by transmitting or blocking out light. Why it's important: LCD is useful not only for portable computers but also as a display for various electronic devices, such as watches and radios.

magnetic ink character recognition (MICR) (p. 190, KQ 5.2) Scanning technology that reads magnetized-ink characters printed at the bottom of checks and converts them to digital form. Why it's important: MICR technology is used by banks to sort checks.

MIDI board (p. 192, KQ 5.2) MIDI, pronounced "middie," stands for "Musical Instrument Digital Interface." MIDI sound boards use this standard. Why it's important: MIDI provides a standard for the interchange of musical information between musical instruments, synthesizers, and computers.

mouse (p. 185, KQ 5.2) A pointing device that is rolled about on a desktop mouse pad and directs a pointer on the computer's display screen. The name is derived from the device's shape, which is a bit like a mouse, with the cord to the computer being the tail. Why it's important: The mouse is the principal pointing tool used with microcomputers.

multifunction printer (p. 201, KQ 5.3) Hardware device that combines several capabilities, such as printing, scanning, copying, and faxing. Why it's important: Multifunction printers take up less space and cost less than the four separate office machines that they replace. The downside, however, is that if one component breaks, nothing works.

nonimpact printer (p. 199, KQ 5.3) Printer that forms characters and images without direct physical contact between the printing mechanism and paper. Two types of nonimpact printers often used with microcomputers are laser printers and ink-jet printers. A third kind, the thermal printer, is seen less frequently. Why it's important: Nonimpact printers are faster and quieter than impact printers.

optical character-recognition (OCR) (p. 191, KQ 5.2) Software technology that converts scanned text from images (pictures of the text) to an editable text format (usually ASCII) that can be imported into a word processing application and manipulated. Why it's important: Special OCR characters appear on utility bills and price tags on department-store merchandise. The wand reader is a common OCR scanning device. These days almost all scanners come with OCR software.

optical mark recognition (OMR) (p. 190, KQ 5.2) Scanning technology that reads "bubble" marks and converts them into computer-usable form. Why it's important: OMR technology is used to read the College Board Scholastic Aptitude Test (SAT) and the Graduate Record Examination (GRE).

output hardware (p. 183, KQ 5.1) Hardware devices that convert machine-readable information, obtained as the result of processing, into people-readable form. The principal kinds of output are softcopy and hardcopy. Why it's important: Without output devices, people would have no access to processed data and information.

page description language (p. 199, KQ 5.3) Software that describes the shape and position of characters and graphics to the printer. PostScript and PCL are common page description languages. Why it's important: Page description languages are essential to desktop publishing.

passive-matrix display (p. 198, KQ 5.3) Flat-panel display in which a transistor controls a whole row or column of pixels. Passive matrix provides a sharp image for one-color (monochrome) screens but is more subdued for color. Why it's important: Passive-matrix displays are less expensive and use less power than active-matrix displays, but they aren't as clear and bright and can leave "ghosts" when the display changes quickly. Passive-matrix displays go by the abbreviations *HPA, STN,* or *DSTN.*

pen-based computer system (p. 187, KQ 5.2) Input system that allows users to enter handwriting and marks onto a computer screen by means of a penlike stylus rather than by typing on a keyboard. Pen computers use handwriting recognition software that translates handwritten characters made by the stylus into data that is usable by the computer. Why it's important: Many handheld computers and PDAs have pen input, as do digital notebooks.

pixel (p. 196, KQ 5.3) Short for "picture element"; the smallest unit on the screen that can be turned on and off or made different shades. Why it's important: Pixels are the building blocks that allow text and graphical images to be displayed on a screen.

pointing device (p. 185, KQ 5.2) Hardware that controls the position of the cursor or pointer on the screen. It includes the mouse and its variants, the touch screen, and various forms of pen input. Why it's important: In many contexts, pointing devices permit quick and convenient data input.

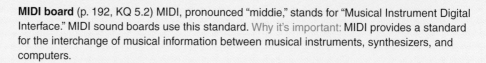

pointing stick (p. 186, KQ 5.2) Pointing device that looks like a pencil eraser protruding from the keyboard between the G, H, and B keys. The user moves the pointing stick with a forefinger. Why it's important: Pointing sticks are used principally in video games, in computer-aided design systems, and in robots.

printer (p. 199, KQ 5.3) Output device that prints characters, symbols, and perhaps graphics on paper or another hardcopy medium. Why it's important: Printers provide one of the principal forms of computer output.

QXGA (quantum extended graphics array) (p. 199, KQ 5.3) New, expensive display standard with a resolution of up to 2,048–1,536 pixels. Why it's important: QXGA is used for large LCD screens for computer users needing to view extreme detail, for businesspeople needing to enlarge images that will still be crisp in big-screen presentations, for high-density television, and for special applications involving viewing multiple images on a single screen.

radio-frequency identification (RFID) tags (p. 194, KQ 5.2) Source data-entry technology based on an identifying tag bearing a microchip that contains specific code numbers. These code numbers are read by the radio waves of a scanner linked to a database. Why it's important: Drivers with RFID tags can breeze through tollbooths without having to even roll down their windows; the toll is automatically charged to their accounts. Radio-wave-readable ID tags are also used by the Postal Service to monitor the flow of mail, by stores for inventory control and warehousing, and in the railroad industry to keep track of rail cars.

refresh rate (p. 197, KQ 5.3) Number of times per second that screen pixels are recharged so that their glow remains bright. In general, displays are refreshed 45–100 times per second. Why it's important: The higher the refresh rate, the more solid the image looks on the screen—that is, the less it flickers.

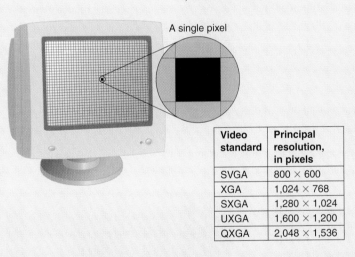

A single pixel

Video standard	Principal resolution, in pixels
SVGA	800 × 600
XGA	1,024 × 768
SXGA	1,280 × 1,024
UXGA	1,600 × 1,200
QXGA	2,048 × 1,536

resolution (p. 196, KQ 5.3) Clarity or sharpness of display-screen/scanned/printed images; the more pixels (dots) there are per square inch, the finer the level of detail attained. Resolution is expressed in terms of the formula horizontal pixels × vertical pixels. Each pixel can be assigned a color or a particular shade of gray. Standard screen resolutions are 640 × 480, 800 × 600, 1,024 × 768, 1,280 × 1,024, and 1,600 × 1,200 pixels. Scanner resolutions are 300 × 200, 600 × 600, 600 × 1,200, 1,200 × 1,200, and 1,200 × 2,400. Why it's important: Users need to know what resolution is appropriate for their purposes.

scanner (p. 189, KQ 5.2) Source-data-input device that uses light-sensing (optical) equipment to translate images of text, drawings, photos, and the like into digital form. Why it's important: Scanners simplify the input of complex data. The images can be processed by a computer, displayed on a monitor, stored on a storage device, or communicated to another computer.

sensor (p. 194, KQ 5.2) Input device that collects specific data directly from the environment and transmits it to a computer. Why it's important: Although you are unlikely to see such input devices connected to a PC in an office, they exist all around us, often in nearly invisible form. Sensors can be used to detect all kinds of things: speed, movement, weight, pressure, temperature, humidity, wind, current, fog, gas, smoke, light, shapes, images, and so on. In aviation, for example, sensors are used to detect ice buildup on airplane wings and to alert pilots to sudden changes in wind direction.

softcopy (p. 195, KQ 5.3) Data on a display screen or in audio or voice form. This kind of output is not tangible; it cannot be touched. Why it's important: This term is used to distinguish non-printed output from printed (hardcopy) output.

sound board (p. 192, KQ 5.2) An add-on circuit board in a computer that converts analog sound to digital sound and stores it for further processing and/or plays it back, providing output directly to speakers or an external amplifier. Why it's important: The sound board enables users to work with audible sound.

sound-output device (p. 201, KQ 5.3) Hardware that produces digitized sounds, ranging from beeps and chirps to music. Why it's important: To use sound output, the user needs appropriate software and a sound card. Such devices are used to produce the sound effects when the user plays a CD-ROM, for example.

source data-entry devices (p. 188, KQ 5.2) Data-entry devices that create machine-readable data on magnetic media or paper or feed it directly into the computer's processor, without the use of a keyboard. Categories include scanning devices (imaging systems, bar-code readers, mark- and character-recognition devices, and fax machines), audio-input devices, video input, photographic input (digital cameras), voice-recognition systems, sensors, radio-frequency identification devices, and human-biology-input devices. Why it's important: Source-data-entry devices lessen reliance on keyboards for data entry and can make data entry more accurate.

speech-recognition system (p. 193, KQ 5.2) Input system that uses a microphone (or a telephone) as an input device and converts a person's speech into digital signals by comparing the electrical patterns produced by the speaker's voice with a set of prerecorded patterns stored in the computer. Why it's important: Voice-recognition technology is useful in situations where people are unable to use their hands to input data or need their hands free for other purposes.

SVGA (super video graphics array) (p. 198, KQ 5.3) Graphics board standard that supports a resolution of 800 × 600 pixels, or variations, producing 16 million possible simultaneous colors. Why it's important: SVGA is the most common standard used today with 15-inch monitors.

SXGA (super extended graphics array) (p. 198, KQ 5.3) Graphics board standard that supports a resolution of 1,280 × 1,024 pixels. Why it's important: SXGA is often used with 19- and 21-inch monitors.

thermal printer (p. 201, KQ 5.3) Printer that uses colored waxes and heat to produce images by burning dots onto special paper. The colored wax sheets are not required for black-and-white output. Thermal printers are expensive, and they require expensive paper. Why it's important: For people who want the highest-quality color printing available with a desktop printer, thermal printers are the answer.

touchpad (p. 186, KQ 5.2) Input device; a small, flat surface over which the user slides a finger, using the same movements as those used with a mouse. The cursor follows the movement of the finger. The user "clicks" by tapping a finger on the pad's surface or by pressing buttons positioned close by the pad. Why it's important: Touchpads let users control the cursor/pointer with a finger, and they require very little space to use. Most laptops have touchpads.

touch screen (p. 187, KQ 5.2) Video display screen that has been sensitized to receive input from the touch of a finger. The screen is covered with a plastic layer, behind which are invisible beams of infrared light. Why it's important: Users can input requests for information by pressing on buttons or menus displayed. The answers to requests are displayed as output in words or pictures on the screen. (There may also be sound.) Touch screens are found in kiosks, ATMs, airport tourist directories, hotel TV screens (for guest checkout), and campus information kiosks making available everything from lists of coming events to (with proper ID and personal code) student financial-aid records and grades.

trackball (p. 186, KQ 5.2) Movable ball, mounted on top of a stationary device, that can be rotated by the user's fingers or palm. It looks like the mouse turned upside down. Instead of moving the mouse around on the desktop, you move the trackball with the tips of your fingers. Why it's important: Trackballs require less space to use than does a mouse.

UXGA (ultra extended graphics array) (p. 198, KQ 5.3) Graphics board standard that supports a resolution of 1,600 x 1,200 pixels, producing up to 16.8 million colors. Why it's important: UXGA is popular with graphic artists, engineering designers, and others using 21-inch monitors.

video (p. 202, KQ 5.3) Output consisting of photographic images played at 15–29 frames per second to give the appearance of full motion. Why it's important: Video is input into a multimedia system using a video camera or VCR and, after editing, is output on a computer's display screen. Because video files can require a great deal of storage—a 3-minute video may require 1 gigabyte of storage—video is often compressed. Digital video has revolutionized the movie industry, as in the use of special effects.

videoconferencing (p. 202, KQ 5.3) Form of video output in which people in different geographic locations can have a meeting—can see and hear one another—using computers and communications. Why it's important: Many organizations use videoconferencing to take the place of face-to-face meetings. Videoconferencing systems range from videophones to group conference rooms with cameras and multimedia equipment to desktop systems with small video cameras, microphones, and speakers.

voice-output device (p. 202, KQ 5.3) Hardware that converts digital data into speech-like sounds. Why it's important: We hear such voice output on telephones ("Please hang up and dial your call again"), in soft-drink machines, in cars, in toys and games, and recently in mapping software for vehicle-navigation devices. For people with physical challenges, computers with voice output help to level the playing field.

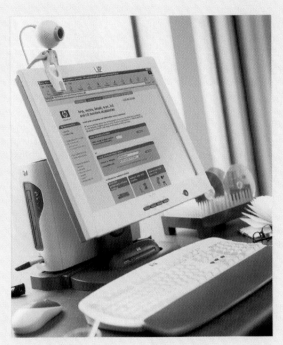

webcam (p. 192, KQ 5.2) A video camera attached to a computer to record live moving images that can then be posted on a website in real time. Why it's important: The webcam is an affordable tool that enables users to have videoconferencing capabilities and may change the future of communications.

XGA (extended graphics array) (p. 198, KQ 5.3) Graphics board display standard with a resolution of up to 1,024 × 768 pixels, corresponding to 65,536 possible colors. Why it's important: XGA is used mainly for simple applications plus spreadsheets and graphics software.

Chapter Review

"I can recognize and recall information."

Self-Test Questions

1. A(n) _____ terminal is entirely dependent for all its processing activities on the computer system to which it is connected.

2. _____ is the study of the physical relationships between people and their work environment.

3. A(n) _____ is an input device that is rolled about on a desktop and directs a pointer on the computer's display screen.

4. _____ consists of devices that translate information processed by the computer into a form that humans can understand.

5. _____ is the science of measuring individual body characteristics and how they interact with machines.

6. CRT is short for _____.

7. LCD is short for _____.

8. A _____ is software that describes the shape and position of characters and graphics to the printer.

9. When people in different geographic locations can have a meeting using computers and communications, it is called _____.

10. _____-matrix screens are much brighter and sharper than _____-matrix screens, but they are more complicated and thus more expensive.

11. The measure of the number of rows and columns of dots that are printed in a square inch is called _____ or _____ _____ _____.

12. A printer that forms characters or images by striking a mechanism such as a print hammer of wheel against an inked ribbon, leaving images on a paper, is called a(n) _____ printer.

Multiple-Choice Questions

1. Which of the following is *not* a pointing device?
   a. mouse
   b. touchpad
   c. keyboard
   d. joystick

2. Which of the following is not a source data-entry device?
   a. bar-code reader
   b. sensor
   c. digital camera
   d. scanner
   e. mouse

3. Which of the following display standards has the highest screen resolution?
   a. XGA
   b. UXGA
   c. VGA
   d. SVGA
   e. QXGA

4. Which of the following *isn't* considered hardcopy output?
   a. microfilm
   b. microfiche
   c. fax report
   d. Word document file
   e. printed invoice

True/False Questions

T F 1. On a computer screen, the more pixels that appear per square inch, the higher the resolution.

T F 2. Photos taken with a digital camera can be downloaded to a computer's hard disk.

T F 3. Resolution concerns the amount of space between the centers of adjacent pixels; the more pixels per square inch, the higher the resolution.

T F 4. The abbreviation *dpi* stands for "dense pixel intervals."

T F 5. Pointing devices control the position of the cursor on the screen.

T F 6. Output hardware consists of devices that translate information processed by the computer into a form that humans can understand.

T F 7. Optical character-recognition software reads "bubble" marks and converts them into computer-usable form.

T F 8. The lower the refresh rate, the more solid the image looks on the screen.

T F 9. CRTs consume more power than flat-panel displays.

"I can recall information in my own terms and explain them to a friend."

Short-Answer Questions

1. What determines how a keyboard's function keys work?

2. What characteristics determine the clarity of a computer screen?

3. Describe two situations in which scanning is useful.

4. What is source data entry?

5. Why is it important for your computer to be expandable?

6. What is *pixel* short for? What is a pixel?

7. What is a font?

8. Discuss the different types of printers and their features.

9. Explain the differences between CRT monitors and LCD monitors.

10. What can OCR be used for?

"I can apply what I've learned, relate these ideas to other concepts, build on other knowledge, and use all these thinking skills to form a judgment."

Knowledge in Action

1. Cut out an advertisement from a newspaper or a magazine that features a new microcomputer system. Circle all the terms that are familiar to you now that you have read the first six chapters of this text. Define these terms on a separate sheet of paper. Is this computer expandable? How much does it cost? Is the monitor included in the price? A printer?

2. *Paperless office* is a term that has been around for some time. However, the paperless office has not yet been achieved. Do you think the paperless office is a good idea? Do you think it's possible? Why do you think it has not yet been fully achieved?

3. Many PC warranties do not cover protection against lightning damage, which is thought to be an "act of God." Does your PC warranty provide coverage for "acts of God"? Read it to find out.

4. Compare and contrast the pros and cons of different types of monitors. Decide which one is best for you and explain why. Do some research on how each monitor type creates displayed images.

5. Do you have access to a computer with (a) speech-recognition software and (b) word processing software that determines writing level (such as eighth grade, ninth grade, and so on)? Dictate a few sentences about your day into the microphone. After your speech is encoded into text, use the word processing software to determine the grade level of your everyday speech.

Web Exercises

1. Visit an online shopping site such as *www.yahoo.com*. Click on *Computers & Internet*; then click on *Hardware*, then on *Printers*. Investigate five different types of printers. Note (a) the type of printer, (b) its price, (c) its resolution, and (d) whether the printer is PC- or Mac-compatible. Which page description language does it use? Which printer would you choose? Why?

2. Concerned about electromagnetic radiation? For a question-and-answer session on electromagnetic frequencies, go to *http://vitatech.net/q_a.html*.

3. Do you see any ethical problems involved with self-scanning checkout? Can people cheat the system? Are store jobs being lost to automation? Are people without credit cards and/or computer experience being excluded? Do a keyword search for *self-scanning* and *self-checkout* and other terms related to these issues. Do you think self-scanning is a good idea?

4. Applied Digital Solutions impressed world markets with its implantable microchip called the VERICHIP. The company also created other controversial products such as the Digital Angel and Thermo Life. Visit some websites to learn more about this company and its plans for its products:

   www.adsx.com/ — company website
   www.digitalangel.net/
   *www.techtv.com/news/culture/story/
   0,24195,3372523,00.html* — famous story of family getting "chipped"
   *http://abcnews.go.com/sections/scitech/TechTV/
   techtv_chipfamily020510.html*
   www.techtv.com/news/print/0,23102,3384927,00.html
   www.newsfactor.com/perl/story/17127.html

5. The Human Cyborg: Visit Professor Kevin Warwick's website to learn about the implant microchips he has been creating and surgically implanting in his body to allow it to communicate with a computer. Investigate the many applications he has been working on. After visiting his site, run a search on *"Kevin Warwick"* to read what others have to say about him and his ideas.

   www.kevinwarwick.com/
   www.kevinwarwick.org.uk/
   www.cyber.rdg.ac.uk/people/K.Warwick.htm
   www.wired.com/wired/archive/8.02/warwick.html

SECURITY

6. Security Issue—Biometric Security Solutions: Visit the following website for an in-depth article about the emergence of biometric technology since the September 11 attacks. How does biometrics improve security? What does the technology still lack?

   www.informit.com/isapi/product_id~%7BC3A2803B 7E73-4341-AB9F-BC91D275E970%7D/content/ index.asp

Networks & Communications

The "New Story" in Computing

Chapter Topics & Key Questions

6.1 **From the Analog to the Digital Age** How do digital data and analog data differ, and what does a modem do?

6.2 **The Practical Uses of Communications** What are some uses of new telecommunications technology?

6.3 **Communications Media & Transfer Rates** What are types of wired and wireless communications media, and what affects data transmission efficiency and speed?

6.4 **Networks** What are the benefits of networks, and what are their types, components, and variations?

6.5 **Cyberethics: Controversial Material & Censorship** What are some concerns regarding censorship of internet information?

The essence of all revolution, stated philosopher Hannah Arendt, is the start of a *new story* in human experience.

Before the 1950s, computing devices processed data into information, and communications devices communicated information over distances. The two streams of technology developed pretty much independently, like rails on a railroad track that never merge. Now we have a new story, a revolution.

For us, the new story has been *digital convergence*—the gradual merger of computing and communications into a new information environment, in which the *same information is exchanged among many kinds of equipment, using the language of computers. (See • Panel 6.1.)* At the same time, there has been a convergence of several important industries—computers, telecommunications, consumer electronics, entertainment, mass media—producing new electronic products that perform multiple functions.

6.1 From the Analog to the Digital Age

KEY QUESTIONS
How do digital data and analog data differ, and what does a modem do?

Why have the worlds of computers and of telecommunications been so long in coming together? Because *computers are digital, but most of the world has been analog.*

● PANEL 6.1
Timeline: Developments in computers and communications

Computer Technology

1621 CE	1642	1833	1843	1890
Slide rule invented (Edmund Gunther)	First mechanical adding machine (Blaise Pascal)	Babbage's difference engine (automatic calculator)	World's first computer programmer, Ada Lovelace, publishes her notes	Electricity used for first time in a data-processing project (punched cards); Hollerith's automatic census-tabulating machine (used punched cards)

Communications Technology

1562	1594	1639	1827	1835	1846	1857	1876	1888	1894
First monthly newspaper (Italy)	First magazine (Germany)	First printing press in North America	Photographs on metal plates	Telegraph (first long-distance digital communication system)	High-speed printing	Trans-atlantic telegraph cable laid	Telephone invented	Radio waves identified	Edison makes a movie

The Digital Basis of Computers: Electrical Signals as Discontinuous Bursts

Computers may seem like incredibly complicated devices but, as we saw in Chapter 4, their underlying principle is simple. Because they are based on on/off electrical states, they use the *binary system*, which consists of only two digits—0 and 1 (p. 143). In general, *digital* means "computer-based." Specifically, <u>**digital**</u> **describes any system based on discontinuous data or events; in the case of computers, it refers to communications signals or information represented in a two-state (binary) way using electronic or electromagnetic signals. Each 0 and 1 signal represents a *bit*.**

The Analog Basis of Life: Electrical Signals as Continuous Waves

"The shades of a sunset, the flight of a bird, or the voice of a singer would seem to defy the black or white simplicity of binary representation," points out one writer.[1] Indeed, these and most other phenomena of the world are <u>**analog**</u>, **continuously varying in strength and/or quality—fluctuating, evolving, or continually changing.** Sound, light, temperature, and pressure values, for instance, can be anywhere on a continuum or range. The highs, lows, and in-between states have historically been represented with analog devices rather than in digital form. Examples of analog devices are a speedometer, a thermometer, and a tire-pressure gauge, all of which can measure continuous fluctuations. The electrical signals on a telephone line, for instance, have been analog-data representations of the original voices, transmitted in the shape of a wave (called a *carrier wave*).

Why bother to change analog signals into digital ones, especially since the digital representations are only *approximations* of analog events? The reason is that digital signals are easier to store and manipulate electronically.[2]

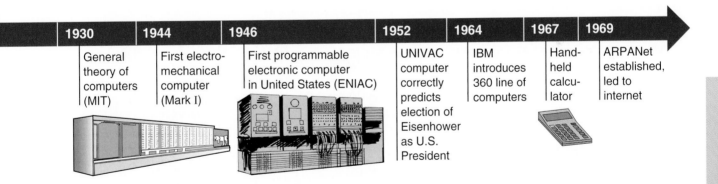

1930	1944	1946	1952	1964	1967	1969
General theory of computers (MIT)	First electro-mechanical computer (Mark I)	First programmable electronic computer in United States (ENIAC)	UNIVAC computer correctly predicts election of Eisenhower as U.S. President	IBM introduces 360 line of computers	Hand-held calculator	ARPANet established, led to internet

1895	1907	1912	1915	1928	1939	1946	1947	1948	1950
Marconi develops radio; motion-picture camera invented	First regular radio broadcast from New York	Motion pictures become a big business	AT&T long-distance service reaches San Francisco	First TV demonstrated; first sound movie	Commercial TV broadcasting	Color TV demonstrated	Transistor invented	Reel-to-reel tape recorder	Cable TV

Purpose of the Modem: Converting Digital Signals to Analog Signals & Back

To understand the differences between digital and analog transmission, consider a graphic representation of an on/off digital signal emitted from a computer. Like a regular light switch, this signal has only two states—on and off. Compare this with a graphic representation of a wavy analog signal emitted as a signal. The changes in this signal are gradual, as in a dimmer switch, which gradually increases or decreases brightness.

Because telephone lines have traditionally been analog, you need to have a modem if your computer is to send communications signals over a telephone line. The modem translates the computer's digital signals into the telephone line's analog signals. The receiving computer also needs a modem to translate the analog signals back into digital signals. *(See ● Panel 6.2.)*

How, in fact, does a modem convert the continuous analog wave to a discontinuous digital pulse that can represent 0s and 1s? The modem can make adjustments to the frequency—the number of cycles per second, or the number of times a wave repeats during a specific time interval (the fastness/slowness). Or it can make adjustments to the analog signal's amplitude—the height of the wave (the loudness/softness). Thus, in frequency, a slow wave might represent a 0 and a quick wave might represent a 1. In amplitude, a low wave might represent a 0 and a high wave might represent a 1. *(See ● Panel 6.3 on page 220.)*

Modem is short for "_mo_dulate/_dem_odulate"; a sending modem modulates digital signals into analog signals for transmission over phone lines. A receiving modem demodulates the analog signals back into digital signals. The modem provides a means for computers to communicate with one another using the standard copper-wire telephone network, an analog system that was built to transmit the human voice but not computer signals.

1970	1971	1973	1975	1976	1978	1981	1982	1984
Micro-processor chips come into use; floppy disk introduced for storing data	First pocket calculator	FTP is developed	First micro-computer (MITs Altair 8800)	Apple I computer (first personal computer sold in assembled form); has 512 KB RAM	5¼" floppy disk; Atari home videogame	IBM introduces personal computer	Portable computers; TCP/IP is established as an internet standard; *internet* is coined	Apple Macintosh; first personal laser printer; desktop publishing takes hold; Domain Name System (DNS) is introduced

Fusing of computer and communications lines of development

1952	1957	1961	1961–1968	1968	1975	1976	1977	1979	1982
Direct-distance dialing (no need to go through operator); transistor radio introduced	First satellite launched (Russia's Sputnik)	Push-button telephones	Packet-switching networks developed	Portable video recorders; video cassettes	Flat-screen TV	First wide-scale marketing of TV computer games (Atari)	First inter-active cable TV	3-D TV demonstrated	Compact disks; European consortium launches multiple communications satellites

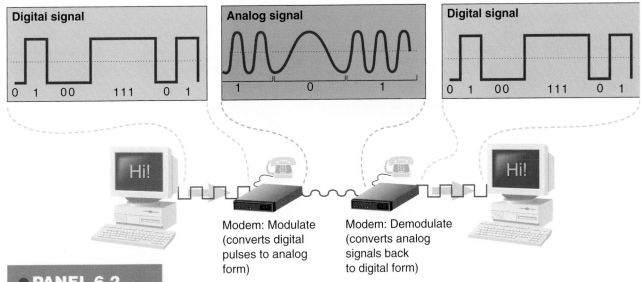

Digital signal

0 1   00   111   0   1

Analog signal

1   0   1

Digital signal

0 1   00   111   0   1

Hi!

Hi!

Modem: Modulate (converts digital pulses to analog form)

Modem: Demodulate (converts analog signals back to digital form)

● PANEL 6.2
Analog versus digital signals, and the modem

Note that an analog signal represents a continuous electrical signal in the form of a wave. A digital signal is discontinuous, expressed as discrete bursts in on/off electrical pulses.

Our concern, however, goes far beyond telephone transmission. How can the analog realities of the world be expressed in digital form? How can light, sounds, colors, temperatures, and other dynamic values be represented so that they can be manipulated by a computer? Let us consider this.

Converting Reality to Digital Form

Suppose you are using an analog tape recorder to record a singer during a performance. The analog wave from the microphone, which is recorded onto the

Computer Technology

1993	1994	1997	1998	2000	2001	2003	2047?
Multimedia desktop computers; personal digital assistants	Apple and IBM introduce PCs with full-motion video built in; wireless data transmission for small portable computers; Web browser Mosaic invented	Network computers; Pathfinder robot lands on Mars	Digital HDTV broad-casts begin	Microsoft .NET announced	Windows XP Mac OS X	Mac G5	By this date, some experts predict, all electronically encodable information will be in cyberspace

Communications Technology

1985	1990	1991	1994	1996	1997	1998	2000	2001
Cellular phone; Nintendo	IRS accepts electronically filed tax returns	CD-ROM games (Sega)	FCC selects HDTV standard	WebTV	Internet telephone-to-telephone service	Video stores begin shift from tape to DVDs	Napster popular; 3.8% of music sales online	2.5 G wireless services

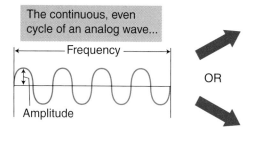

The continuous, even cycle of an analog wave...

← Frequency →

Amplitude

OR

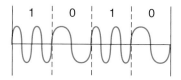

... is converted to digital form through *frequency modulation*—the frequency of the cycle increases to represent a 1 and stays the same to represent a 0.

1 0 1 0

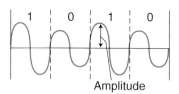

... or is converted to digital form through *amplitude modulation*—the height of the wave is increased to represent a 1 and stays the same to represent a 0.

1 0 1 0

Amplitude

tape as an analog wave as well, will produce a near duplicate of the sounds—including distortions, such as buzzings and clicks, or electronic hums if an amplified guitar is used.

The digital recording process is different. The way that music is captured for digital audio CDs, for example, does not provide a duplicate of a musical performance. Rather, the digital process uses a device (called an *analog-to-digital converter*) to record *representative selections*, or *samples*, of the sounds and convert the analog waves into a stream of numbers that the computer then uses to express the sounds. To play back the music, the stream of numbers is converted (by a *digital-to-analog converter*) back into an analog wave. The samples of sounds are taken at regular intervals—nearly 44,100 times a second—and the copy obtained is virtually exact and free from distortion and noise. The sampling rate of 44,100 times per second and the high precision fool our ears into hearing a smooth, continuous sound.

Digital photography also uses sampling: A computer takes samples of values such as brightness and color. The same is true of digitizing other aspects of real-life experience, such as pressure, temperature, and motion.

Does digital sampling cheat us out of our experience of "reality" by allowing computers to sample sounds, images, and so on? Actually, people willingly made this compromise years ago, before computers were invented. Movies, for instance, carve up reality into 24 frames a second. Television pictures are drawn at 30 frames per second. These processes happen so quickly that our eyes and brains easily jump the visual gaps. Digital processing of analog experience is just one more way of expressing or translating reality.

Turning analog reality into digital form provides tremendous opportunities. One of the most important is that all kinds of multimedia can now be changed into digital form and transmitted as data to all kinds of devices.

Now let us examine the digital world of telecommunications.

QuickCheck

Distinguish between digital and analog signals.

Explain what a modem does.

What is sampling?

KEY QUESTION

What are some uses of new telecommunications technology?

They're called the "Always On" generation. "Seventy-four percent of teens use instant messaging," says high-tech magazine editor Tony Perkins. "No matter what numbers you look at, the Always On generation is in full swing. They communicate through the computer."[3]

But it's not just teens and young adults anymore. Broadband use has tripled in three years. The use of wireless-networking hardware has exploded. Traveling businesspeople like Daniel Mintz, who is on the road for weeks at a time and misses his family a lot, particularly his 17-month-old daughter, Noa, uses "whatever new and clever technology I can, including digital photographs sent via email and birthday notes faxed from airplanes," to stay connected.[4]

Such is the power of communications connections, or connectivity, which give us all instant, around-the-clock information from all over the globe. Let's consider some of the forms this connectivity takes:

- Videoconferencing and videophones
- Workgroup computing and groupware
- Telecommuting and virtual offices
- Home networks
- Smart television

Videoconferencing & Videophones: Video/Voice Communication

Videoconferencing, also called _teleconferencing_, is the use of television video and sound technology as well as computer networks (including the internet) to enable people in different locations to see, hear, and talk with one another.
Two types of videoconferencing are *point-to-point* and *multipoint*.

- **Point-to-point:** A *point-to-point* videoconferencing system is a two-person system. Each participant has a video camera, a microphone, and a computer with speakers and monitor. While they talk to each other, their voices are delivered over the speakers and their images appear on each other's monitor.
- **Multipoint:** *Multipoint* videoconferencing allows three or more participants in different locations, each equipped with a videophone or with a large monitor along with video camera, microphone, and speakers, to interact with one another.

Increasingly, videoconferencing is taking the place of face-to-face meetings.

Almost anyone with a properly configured PC and a connection to the internet can do videoconferencing. It's easy to acquire a microcomputer equipped with a video camera, called a *PC camera* or *webcam* (p. 192), and network interface card (p. 158), which allows you to see the people you're communicating with on the internet. Principal software programs for videoconferencing are CUSeeMe and Click to Meet Express.

The main difficulty with videoconferencing and videophones is that POTS ("plain old telephone service," p. 44) equipment based on standard copper wire cannot transmit or receive images very rapidly. Thus, unless you can afford expensive high-speed communications lines, present-day screens will convey a series of jerky, stop-action images of the participants' faces.

Workgroup Computing & Groupware

When microcomputers were first brought into the workplace, they were used simply as another personal-productivity tool, like typewriters or calculators. Gradually, however, companies began to link microcomputers together on a network, usually to share an expensive piece of hardware, such as a laser printer. Then employees found that networks allowed them to share files and databases. Networking using common software also allowed users to buy equipment from different manufacturers—a mix of computers from both Sun Microsystems and Hewlett-Packard, for example. Sharing resources has led to workgroup computing.

In **_workgroup computing_, also called *collaborative computing*, teams of co-workers, often at different sites, use networks of microcomputers to share information and to cooperate on projects.** Workgroup computing is made possible not only by networks and microcomputers but also by *groupware*, software that allows two or more people on a network to work on the same information at the same time.

In general, groupware, such as Lotus Notes and MS NetMeeting (which now also supports videoconferencing), permits office workers to collaborate with colleagues and to tap into company information through computer networks. It also enables them to link up with crucial contacts outside their organization.

Telecommuting & Virtual Offices

Computers and communications tools have led to telecommuting and virtual offices.

Telecommuter. An at-home worker stays connected to his office.

- **Telecommuting: Working at home or on the road while in telecommunication with the office is called _telecommuting_, or *telework*.** In the United States, telecommuting has been on the rise for several years.

    Telecommunication can have many benefits. The advantages to society are reduced traffic congestion, energy consumption, and air pollution. The advantages to employers, it's argued, are increased productivity, because telecommuters may experience fewer distractions at home than in the office and can work flexible hours. Absenteeism may be reduced, teamwork improved, and the labor pool expanded because hard-to-get employees don't have to uproot themselves from where they want to live. Costs for office space, parking, insurance, and other overhead are reduced.

    Despite the advantages, however, telecommuting has some drawbacks. Employees sometimes feel isolated, even deserted, or they are afraid that working outside the office will hinder their career advancement. They also find the arrangements blur the line between office and home, straining family life. Employers may feel telecommuting causes resentments among office-bound employees, and they may find it difficult to measure employees' productivity. In addition, with teamwork now more a workplace requirement, managers may worry that telecommuters cannot keep up with the pace of change. Finally, some employers worry that telecommuters create more opportunities for security breeches by hackers or equipment thieves.[5]

- **Virtual offices: The _virtual office_ is an often nonpermanent and mobile office run with computer and communications technology.** Employees work from their homes, cars, and other new work sites. They use pocket pagers, portable computers, fax machines, and various phone and network services to conduct business. Such an office exists more in virtual space than physical space.

The rise in telecommuting and virtual offices is only part of a larger trend. "Powerful economic forces are turning the whole labor force into an army of freelancers—temps, contingents, and independent contractors and consultants," says business strategy consultant David Kline. The result, he believes, is that "computers, the net, and telecommuting systems will become as central to the conduct of 21st-century business as the automobile, freeways, and corporate parking lots were to the conduct of mid-20th-century business."[6] The transformation will really gather momentum, some observers believe, when more homes have broadband internet access.

Home Networks

info!

Curious about networked homes? For starters, try www.hometoys.com/howto/index.htm.

As we shall see, computers linked by telephone lines, cable, or wireless systems are an established component of information technology. Today, however, many new buildings and even homes are built as "network enabled." The new superconnected home or small office is equipped with a _local area network (LAN),_ which allows all the personal computers under the same roof to share peripherals (such as a printer or a fax machine) and a single modem and internet service. The next development is supposed to be the networking of home appliances, linking stereos, lights, heating systems, phones, and TV sets. Once that has been accomplished, you could walk into your house and give a voice command to turn on the lights or bring up music, for example. Even kitchen appliances would be linked, so that your refrigerator, for instance, could alert a grocery store that you need more milk.

Smart Television: DTV, HDTV, & SDTV

Today experts differentiate between interactive TV, personalized TV, and internet TV.

Interactive TV, which is popular in Europe, lets you interact with the show you're watching, so that you can request information about a product or play along with a game show.

Personalized TV consists of hard-drive-equipped personal video recorders (PVRs), such as TiVo and ReplayTV, that let you not only record shows but also pause, rewind, and replay live TV programs.

Internet TV, such as the MSN TV Service, lets you read internet text and web pages on your television set.

In the future, interactive, personal, and internet TV will probably come together in a single box that goes under the umbrella name of "digital television."

- **Digital television (DTV):** When most of us tune in our TV sets, we get analog television, a system of varying signal amplitude and frequency that represents picture and sound elements. In 1996, however, broadcasters and their government regulator, the Federal Communications Commission (FCC), adopted a standard called _**digital television**_

(DTV), which uses a digital signal, or series of 0s and 1s. DTV is much clearer and less prone to interference than analog TV. You see digital satellite TV systems and digital cable TV systems widely advertised, but they are not digital TV. These systems take normal analog broadcast signals, convert them to digital signals for transmission purposes, and then convert them back (using a set-top box) to analog signals for your TV viewing. Real digital TV, by contrast, is completely digital: It uses digital cameras, digital transmission, and digital receivers.

- High-definition television (HDTV): A form of real digital TV, **_high-definition television (HDTV)_ works with digital broadcasting signals and has a wider screen and higher resolution than standard television.**

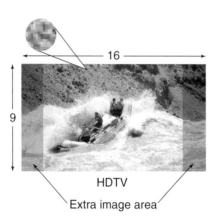

Standard TV

HDTV

Extra image area

Whereas standard analog TV has a width-to-height ratio, or *aspect ratio*, of 4 to 3, HDTV has an aspect ratio of 16 to 9, which is similar to the wide-screen approach used in movies. In addition, compared to analog display screens, an HDTV display has 10 times more pixels on a screen—1,920 × 1,080 pixels or more. Thus, HDTV could have 1,080 lines on a screen, compared with 525-line resolution for analog TV.

Why don't more people have HDTV sets? In the past, the biggest reason was expense.

- Standard-definition television (SDTV): HDTV takes a lot of bandwidth that broadcasters could use instead for *standard-definition television (SDTV)*, which has a lower resolution, a minimum of 480 vertical lines, and a picture quality similar to that required to watch DVD movies. What's important about the SDTV standard is that it enables broadcasters to transmit more information within the HDTV bandwidth. That is, broadcasters can *multicast* their products, transmitting up to five SDTV programs simultaneously—and getting perhaps five times the revenue—instead of just one HDTV program. (Analog broadcasts only one program at a time.)

more info!

Curious about the latest HDTV developments? Go to the government's website: *www.fcc.gov.*

Can your PC handle accessDTV? To find out, go to *http://entertainment. howstuffworks.com/ accessdtv.htm*

QuickCheck

Explain videoconferencing, workgroup computing, telecommuting, virtual offices, and home networks.

What is DTV? What is the difference between HDTV and SDTV?

6.3 Communications Media & Transfer Rates

KEY QUESTIONS

What are types of wired and wireless communications media, and what affects data transmission efficiency and speed?

It used to be that two-way individual communications were accomplished mainly in two ways. They were carried by the medium of (1) a telephone wire or (2) a wireless method such as shortwave radio. Today there are many kinds of communications media, although they are still wired or wireless. **_Communications media_ carry signals over a *communications path*, the route between two or more communications media devices.** The speed, or data transfer rate, at which transmission occurs—and how much data can be carried by a signal—depends on the media and the type of signal.

In this section we will first look at wired communications media. Then we will look at the electromagnetic spectrum and wireless communications media and signals. Finally we'll discuss other modes and characteristics that affect communications, including data compression.

Wired Communications Media: Transmitting Data by Wires & Cables

Three types of wired communications media are *twisted-pair wire* (conventional telephone lines), *coaxial cable*, and *fiber-optic cable.*

Twisted-pair wire

- **Twisted-pair wire:** The telephone line that runs from your house to the pole outside, or underground, is probably twisted-pair wire. **_Twisted-pair wire_ consists of two strands of insulated copper wire, twisted around each other. This twisted-pair configuration (compared to straight wire) somewhat reduces interference (called "crosstalk") from electrical fields.** Twisted-pair is relatively slow. Moreover, it does not protect well against electrical interference. However, because so much of the world is already served by twisted-pair wire, it will no doubt be used for years to come, both for voice messages and for modem-transmitted computer data.

    The prevalence of twisted-pair wire gives rise to what experts call the "last-mile problem." That is, it is relatively easy for telecommunications companies to upgrade the physical connections between cities and even between neighborhoods. But it is expensive for them to replace the "last mile" of twisted-pair wire that connects to individual houses.

- **Coaxial cable:** **_Coaxial cable_, commonly called "co-ax," consists of insulated copper wire wrapped in a solid or braided metal shield and then in an external plastic cover.** Co-ax is widely used for cable television and cable internet connections. Thanks to the extra insulation, coaxial cable is much better than twisted-pair wiring at resisting noise. Moreover, it can carry voice and data at a faster rate (up to 200 megabits per second). Often many coaxial cables are bundled together.

Coaxial cable

- **Fiber-optic cable:** A **_fiber-optic cable_ consists of dozens or hundreds of thin strands of glass or plastic that transmit pulsating beams of light rather than electricity.** These strands, each as thin as a human hair, can transmit up to about 2 billion pulses per second (2 gigabits); each "on" pulse represents 1 bit. When bundled together, fiber-optic strands in a cable 0.12 inch thick can support a quarter- to a half-million voice conversations at the same time. Moreover, unlike electrical signals, light pulses are not affected by random electromagnetic interference in the environment. In addition, fiber-optic cable is lighter and more durable than twisted-pair wire and co-ax cable. A final advantage is that it cannot easily be wiretapped, so transmissions are more secure.

The various kinds of wired internet connections discussed in Chapter 2—dial-up modem, DSL, ISDN, cable modem, T1 lines—are created by using these wired communications media.

Fiber-optic strands

Fiber-optic cable

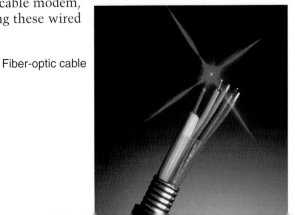

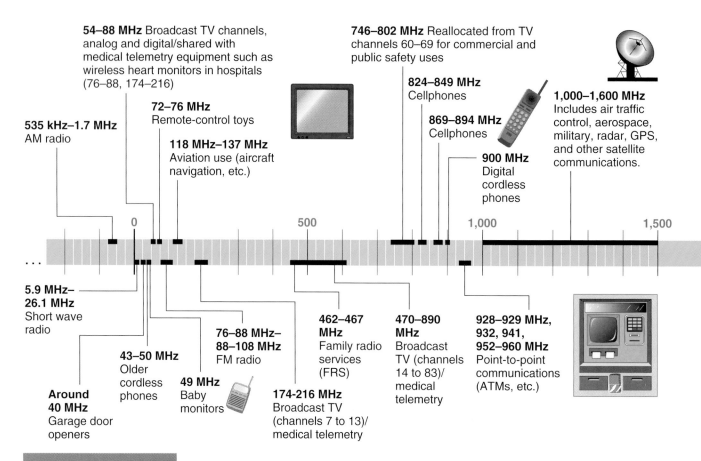

54–88 MHz Broadcast TV channels, analog and digital/shared with medical telemetry equipment such as wireless heart monitors in hospitals (76–88, 174–216)

746–802 MHz Reallocated from TV channels 60–69 for commercial and public safety uses

72–76 MHz Remote-control toys

824–849 MHz Cellphones

1,000–1,600 MHz Includes air traffic control, aerospace, military, radar, GPS, and other satellite communications.

535 kHz–1.7 MHz AM radio

118 MHz–137 MHz Aviation use (aircraft navigation, etc.)

869–894 MHz Cellphones

900 MHz Digital cordless phones

0   500   1,000   1,500

5.9 MHz– 26.1 MHz Short wave radio

43–50 MHz Older cordless phones

76–88 MHz– 88–108 MHz FM radio

462–467 MHz Family radio services (FRS)

470–890 MHz Broadcast TV (channels 14 to 83)/ medical telemetry

928–929 MHz, 932, 941, 952–960 MHz Point-to-point communications (ATMs, etc.)

Around 40 MHz Garage door openers

49 MHz Baby monitors

174-216 MHz Broadcast TV (channels 7 to 13)/ medical telemetry

---

PANEL 6.4

The radio-frequency spectrum

The radio-frequency spectrum, which carries most communications signals, appears as part of the electromagnetic spectrum.

The Radio-Frequency Spectrum, & Bandwidth

Telephone signals, radar waves, microwaves, and the invisible commands from a garage-door opener all represent different waves on what is called the *electromagnetic spectrum of radiation*. Part of the electromagnetic spectrum is the ***radio-frequency (RF) spectrum*, fields of electrical energy and magnetic energy that carry most communications signals.** (See • Panel 6.4.)

Electromagnetic waves vary according to *frequency*—the number of times a wave repeats, or makes a cycle, in a second. The radio-frequency spectrum ranges from low-frequency waves, such as those used for garage-door openers, through the medium frequencies for certain cellphones and air-traffic control monitors (960–1,215 megahertz), to deep-space radio communications.

The *bandwidth* is the range, or *band*, of frequencies that a transmission medium can carry in a given period of time. For analog signals, bandwidth is expressed in *hertz (Hz)*, or *cycles per second* (p. 194). For example, certain cellphones operate within the range 824–849 megahertz—that is, their bandwidth is 25 megahertz. *The wider a medium's bandwidth, the more frequencies it can use to transmit data and thus the faster the transmission.* ***Broadband connections* are characterized by very high speed.** For digital signals, bandwidth can be expressed in hertz but also in *bits per second (bps)* (p. 41). For instance, the connections that carry the newest types of digital cellphone signals range from 144 kilobits (14,400 bits) per second to 2 megabits (2 million bits) per second.

Wireless Communications Media: Transmitting Data Through the Air

Four types of wireless media are *infrared transmission, broadcast radio, microwave radio,* and *communications satellite.*

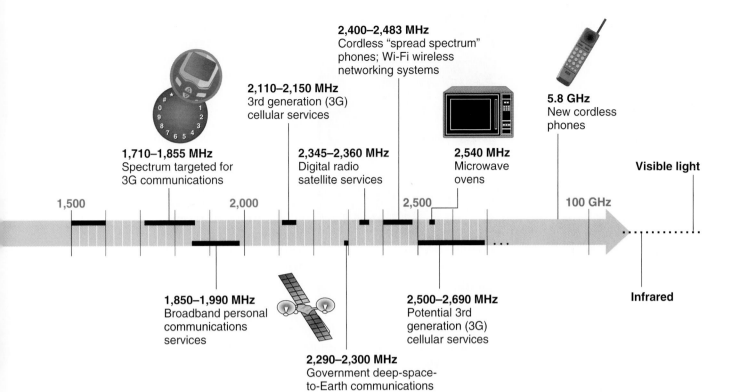

2,400–2,483 MHz
Cordless "spread spectrum" phones; Wi-Fi wireless networking systems

2,110–2,150 MHz
3rd generation (3G) cellular services

5.8 GHz
New cordless phones

1,710–1,855 MHz
Spectrum targeted for 3G communications

2,345–2,360 MHz
Digital radio satellite services

2,540 MHz
Microwave ovens

Visible light

1,500   2,000   2,500   100 GHz

Infrared

1,850–1,990 MHz
Broadband personal communications services

2,500–2,690 MHz
Potential 3rd generation (3G) cellular services

2,290–2,300 MHz
Government deep-space-to-Earth communications

- Infrared transmission: <u>*Infrared wireless transmission*</u> **sends data signals using infrared-light waves at a frequency too low (1–4 megabits per second) for human eyes to receive and interpret.** Infrared ports can be found on some laptop computers, digital cameras, and printers, as well as wireless mice. TV remote-control units use infrared transmission. The drawbacks are that *line-of-sight* communication is required—there must be an unobstructed view between transmitter and receiver—and transmission is confined to short range.

- Broadcast radio: When you tune in to an AM or FM radio station, you are using <u>*broadcast radio*</u>, **a wireless transmission medium that sends data over long distances at up to 2 megabits per second—between regions, states, or countries.** A transmitter is required to send messages and a receiver to receive them; sometimes both sending and receiving functions are combined in a *transceiver.*

  In the lower frequencies of the radio spectrum, several broadcast radio bands are reserved not only for conventional AM/FM radio but also for broadcast television, CB (citizens band) radio, ham (amateur) radio, cellphones, and private radio-band mobile services (such as police, fire, and taxi dispatch). Some organizations use specific radio frequencies and networks to support wireless communications. For example, UPC (Universal Product Code) bar-code readers (p. 189) are used by grocery-store clerks restocking store shelves to communicate with a main computer so that the store can control inventory levels.

- Microwave radio: <u>*Microwave radio*</u> **transmits voice and data at 45 megabits per second through the atmosphere as superhigh-frequency radio waves called *microwaves*, which vibrate at 1 gigahertz (1 billion hertz) per second or higher.** These frequencies are used not only to operate microwave ovens but also to transmit messages between ground-based stations and satellite communications systems.

Microwave radio. These dishes are on Midway Island, 1,100 miles from Hawaii.

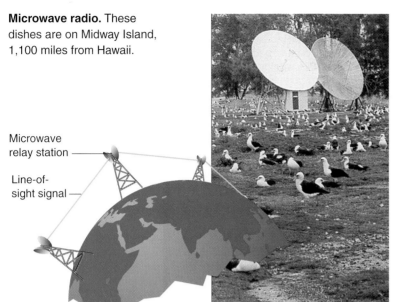

Microwave relay station ——
Line-of-sight signal ——

Microwave tower on mountaintop.

Microwave towers on buildings in Shanghai.

Nowadays dish- or horn-shaped microwave reflective dishes, which contain transceivers and antennas, are nearly everywhere—on towers, buildings, and hilltops.

Why, you might wonder, do we have to interfere with nature by putting a microwave dish on top of a mountain? As with infrared waves, microwaves are line-of-sight; they cannot bend around corners or around the earth's curvature, so there must be an unobstructed view between transmitter and receiver. Thus, microwave stations need to be placed within 25–30 miles of each other, with no obstructions in between. The size of the dish varies with the distance (perhaps 2–4 feet in diameter for short distances, 10 feet or more for long distances). In a string of microwave relay stations, each station will receive incoming messages, boost the signal strength, and relay the signal to the next station.

More than half of today's telephone systems uses dish microwave transmission. However, the airwaves are becoming so saturated with microwave signals that future needs will have to be satisfied by other channels, such as satellite systems.

● **Communications satellites:** To avoid some of the limitations of microwave earth stations, communications companies have added microwave "sky stations"—communications satellites. **_Communications satellites_ are microwave relay stations in orbit around the earth.** Transmitting a signal from a ground station to a satellite is called *uplinking*; the reverse is called *downlinking*. The delivery process will be slowed if, as is often the case, more than one satellite is required to get the message delivered.

Satellite systems may occupy one of three zones in space: *GEO, MEO,* and *LEO. (See ● Panel 6.5.)*

The highest level, known as *geostationary earth orbit (GEO)*, is 22,300 miles and up and is always directly above the equator. Because the satellites in this orbit travel at the same speed as the earth, they appear to an observer on the ground to be stationary in space—that is, they are geostationary. Consequently, microwave earth stations are always able to beam signals to a fixed location above. The orbiting satellite has solar-powered transceivers to receive the signals, amplify them, and retransmit them to another earth station. At this high orbit, fewer satellites are required for global coverage; however, their quarter-second delay makes two-way conversations difficult.

The *medium-earth orbit (MEO)* is 5,000–10,000 miles up. It requires more satellites for global coverage than does GEO.

The *low-earth orbit (LEO)* is 200–1,000 miles up and has no signal delay. LEO satellites may be smaller and are cheaper to launch.

Satellites cost from $300 million to $700 million each. A satellite launch costs between $50 million and $400 million.

Types of Long-Distance Wireless Communications

There are essentially two ways to move information through the air long distance on radio frequencies. The first is via *one-way communications*, as

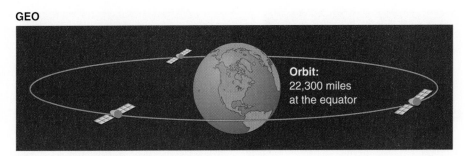

Orbit:
22,300 miles
at the equator

MEO

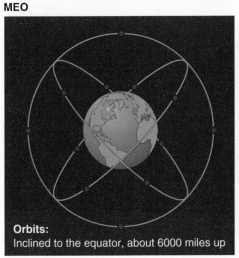

Orbits:
Inclined to the equator, about 6000 miles up

LEO

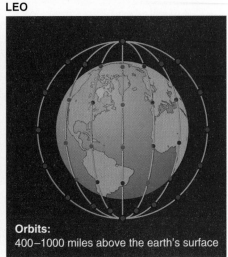

Orbits:
400–1000 miles above the earth's surface

● **PANEL 6.5**
Satellites
Communications satellite *(above)* and orbits *(right)*, which carries most communications signals, appears as part of the electromagnetic spectrum.

typified by the satellite navigation system known as the Global Positioning System, and by most pagers. The second is via *two-way communications*: (1) two-way pagers, (2) analog cellphones, (3) 2G digital wireless, and (4) 3G digital wireless. (Other wireless methods operate at short distances.)

- **One-way communications—the Global Positioning System:** A $10 billion infrastructure developed by the military in the mid-1980s, the ***Global Positioning System (GPS)*** **consists of earth-orbiting satellites continuously transmitting timed radio signals that can be used to identify earth locations.** A GPS receiver—handheld or mounted in a vehicle, plane, or boat—can pick up transmissions from any four satellites, interpret the information from each, and pinpoint the receiver's longitude, latitude, and altitude. *(See ● Panel 6.6 on the next page.)* Some GPS receivers include map software for finding your way around, as with the navigation systems available with some rental cars.

  The system, accurate within 3–50 feet, with 10 feet being the norm, is used to tell military units carrying special receivers where they are. GPS is used for such civilian activities as tracking trucks and taxis, locating stolen cars, orienting hikers, and aiding in surveying. Some public transportation systems have installed GPS receivers on buses, where they can tell drivers when they fall behind schedule. GPS has been used by scientists to keep a satellite watch over a Hawaiian volcano, Mauna Loa, and to capture infinitesimal movements that may be used to predict eruptions.[7] It is used by surveyors, wildlife managers, forestry managers, search-and-rescue teams, archaeologists, and many others.

  Cellular carriers are now required to have E-911 (for "Enhanced 911") capability. This enables them to locate, through tiny GPS receivers embedded in users' digital cellphones, the position of every person making an emergency 911 call.

GPS

The Global Positioning System uses 24 satellites, developed for military use, to pinpoint a location on the earth's surface.

(Top) A GPS unit with a Braille keyboard and voice output guides a blind user. *(Bottom left)* Brian Sniatkowski is holding a GPS unit in the Kekeout Reservoir Forest while geocaching, a high-tech treasure hunt for GPS users. Participants set up caches all over the world and share the locations via the internet. GPS users can then use the location coordinates to find the caches. Each cache may provide the finder with a variety of rewards; each finder is asked to put something new in the cache. *(Bottom right)* Many cars now come with GPS units to guide users to their destinations.

Space

There are 24 satellites orbiting the Earth at an altitude of 11,000 nautical miles. Each is equipped with an atomic clock that keeps time to three-billionths of a second. The satellites send time-stamped radio signals to Earth at the speed of light. The signals include information about each satellite's exact position.

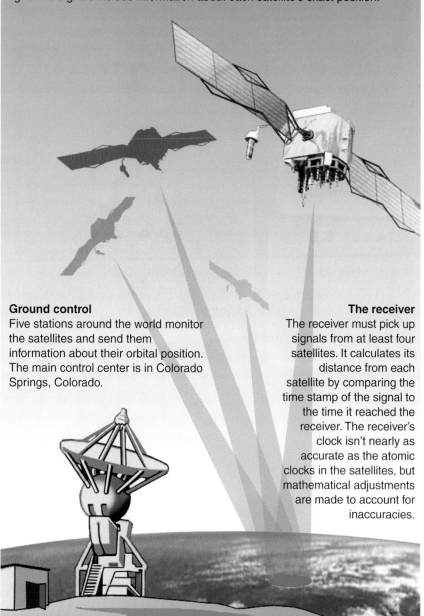

Ground control

Five stations around the world monitor the satellites and send them information about their orbital position. The main control center is in Colorado Springs, Colorado.

The receiver

The receiver must pick up signals from at least four satellites. It calculates its distance from each satellite by comparing the time stamp of the signal to the time it reached the receiver. The receiver's clock isn't nearly as accurate as the atomic clocks in the satellites, but mathematical adjustments are made to account for inaccuracies.

Pager

Blackberry

- **One-way communications—pagers:** Commonly known as *beepers*, for the sound they make when activated, ***pagers* are simple radio receivers that receive data sent from a special radio transmitter.** The radio transmitter broadcasts signals over a specific frequency. All of the pagers for that particular network have a built-in receiver that is tuned to the same frequency broadcast from the transmitter. The pagers listen to the signal from the transmitter constantly as long as the pager is turned on.

  Often the pager has its own telephone number. When the number is dialed from a phone, the call goes by way of the transmitter straight to the designated pager. Pagers are very efficient for transmitting one-way information—emergency messages, news, prices, stock quotations, delivery-route assignments, even sports news and scores—at low cost to single or multiple receivers.

  Some pagers do more than beep or vibrate, transmitting full-blown alphanumeric text (such as four-line, 80-character messages) and other data. Newer ones are mini-answering machines, capable of relaying digitized voice messages.

- **Two-way communications—pagers:** Recent advances have given us *two-way paging,* or *enhanced paging.* Service is provided by carriers like SkyTel, and you can use paging gadgets such as the BlackBerry RIM 950. For instance, in one version, users can send a pre-programmed message or acknowledgment that they have received a message. Another version allows consumers to compose and send email to anyone on the internet and to other pagers. Typing a message on a tiny keyboard no larger than those on pocket calculators can pose a challenge, however. Perhaps the most popular of two-way pagers, BlackBerry is used by delivery services and other users (including members of the U.S. Congress) who want to get simple messages to people spread over a wide geographic area.

- **Two-way communications—first-generation (1G) analog cellular service:** Cellphones are essentially two-way radios that operate using either analog or digital signals. ***Analog cellphones* are designed primarily for communicating by voice through a system of ground-area cells. Each cell is hexagonal in shape, usually 8 miles or less in diameter, and is served by a transmitter-receiving tower.** Communications are handled in the bandwidth of 824–894 megahertz. Calls are directed between cells by a mobile-telephone switching office (MTSO). Movement between cells requires that calls be "handed off" by this switching office. *(See ● Panel 6.7 on the next page.)* This technology is known as *1G,* for "first generation."

  Handing off voice calls between cells poses only minimal problems. However, handing off data transmission (where every bit counts), with the inevitable gaps and pauses on moving from one cell to another, is much more difficult.

- **Two-way communications—second-generation (2G) digital wireless services:** ***Digital wireless services*—which support digital cellphones and personal digital assistants—use a network of cell towers to send voice communications and data over the airwaves in digital form.** Known as *2G,* for "second-generation," technology, digital cellphones began replacing analog cellphones during the 1990s as telecommunications companies added digital transceivers to their cell towers. 2G technology not only dramatically increased voice clarity; it also allowed the telecoms to cram many more voice calls into the same slice of bandwidth.

  Cellphone ads from Sprint, Verizon, and Voicestream often feature the abbreviation "PCS." A set of 2G digital technologies operating in the 1,900-frequency range, PCS stands for "Personal Communications

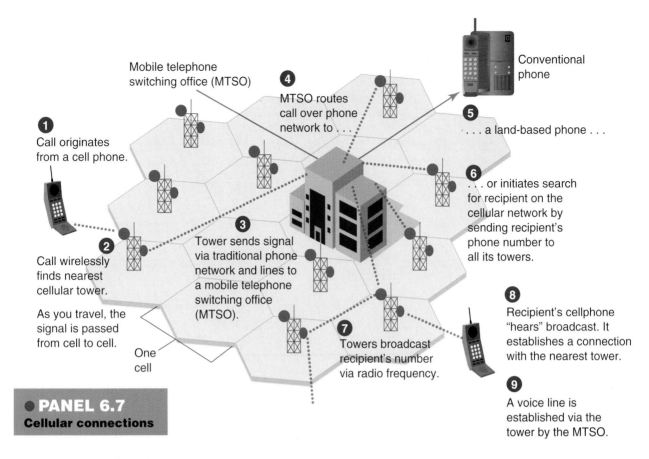

1 Call originates from a cell phone.

2 Call wirelessly finds nearest cellular tower.

As you travel, the signal is passed from cell to cell.

One cell

Mobile telephone switching office (MTSO)

3 Tower sends signal via traditional phone network and lines to a mobile telephone switching office (MTSO).

4 MTSO routes call over phone network to . . .

Conventional phone

5 . . . a land-based phone . . .

6 . . . or initiates search for recipient on the cellular network by sending recipient's phone number to all its towers.

7 Towers broadcast recipient's number via radio frequency.

8 Recipient's cellphone "hears" broadcast. It establishes a connection with the nearest tower.

9 A voice line is established via the tower by the MTSO.

● **PANEL 6.7**
Cellular connections

Cellphone towers

info!

What's the ideal cellphone and service for your area? Go to *www.cellmania.com* or *www.epinions.com* to compare plans.

Services" and covers several services that can be bundled together in one device and paid for with just one bill: voice communications, voice mail, text and numeric messaging, and other features.

Other countries adhere to a single standard for wireless, but in the United States there are four incompatible digital technologies operating at different frequencies in the electromagnetic spectrum: Time Division Multiple Access (TDMA), Global System for Mobile Communications (GSM), Code Division Multiple Access (CDMA), and Frequency Division Multiple Access (FDMA). Thus, there is no true national coverage. In the future, however, it appears that GSM and CDMA will prevail in the United States. GSM has become the standard not only in Western Europe but in many other countries, especially in the Middle East and Asia. Unfortunately, in the United States, GSM is on a different frequency from the GSM phones in the rest of the world, which limits use of an American GSM cellphone in other countries. (There are a few phones on the market that include both U.S. and European-based GSM frequencies.)

● **Two-way communications—third-generation (3G) broadband wireless digital services:** <u>**Broadband wireless digital services**</u>**, usually referred to as *third-generation (3G) technology*, are based on the U.S. GSM standard and support devices that (like cable modems) are "always on," carry data at high speeds (144 kilobits per second up to about 2 megabits per second), accept emails with attachments, provide internet and web access, are able to display color video and still pictures, and play music.** 3G cellphones look more like PDAs. The leaders in 3G cellphone technology are Japan and Europe.

Short-Range Wireless Communication: Bluetooth & WiFi

We have discussed the standards for high-powered wireless digital communications in the 800–1,900 megahertz part of the radio-frequency spectrum, which are considered long-range waves. Now let us consider low-powered wireless communications in the 2.4-gigahertz part of the radio spectrum, which are short-range and effective only within several feet of a wireless access point. The 2.4-gigahertz band is available globally for unlicensed, low-power uses and is set aside as an innovation zone where new devices can be tested without the need for a government license; it's also used for industrial, scientific, and medical devices.

There are two common short-distance wireless standards—Bluetooth and WiFi.

Bluetooth PC card for notebook

- **Bluetooth—up to 30 feet: _Bluetooth_ is a short-range wireless digital standard aimed at linking cellphones, PDAs, computers, and peripherals up to distances of 30 feet.** Transmitting in the range of 57.6 kilobits to 1 megabit per second, Bluetooth is designed to replace cables connecting PCs to printers and PDAs or wireless phones and to overcome line-of-sight problems with infrared transmission. When Bluetooth-capable devices come within range of one another, an automatic electronic "conversation" takes place to determine whether they have data to share, and then they form a mini-network (called a _personal-area network_ or _piconet_) to exchange that data.

  Bluetooth is being promoted as a technology of convenience rather than as a substitute for local high-speed connections such as USB. Bluetooth capabilities are built into newer smart cellphones, PDAs, and notebook computers featuring Intel Centrino chips.

WiFi symbol on WiFi-enabled notebook

- **WiFi—up to 300 feet:** Known formally as an _802.11 network_ (for the wireless technical standard specified by the Institute of Electrical and Electronics Engineers, **_WiFi_—short for "wireless _fidelity_"—is a short-range wireless digital standard aimed at helping portable computers and handheld wireless devices to communicate at high speeds and share internet connections at distances up to 300 feet. It connects through access points to a kind of local area network known as the _Ethernet_.** You can find WiFi connections, which operate at 2.5–5 gigahertz, inside offices, airports, and internet cafés, and some enthusiasts have set up transmitters on rooftops, distributing wireless connections throughout their neighborhoods.

  The Ethernet standard for wiring computers into local networks has been popular for over two decades because it is an "open" standard—no single company controls it. Because of this openness and because it is cheaper than Bluetooth, WiFi is becoming the more popular standard. It is also 10 times faster than Bluetooth and has about 10 times the range. WiFi is supported by Windows XP and is a standard in most new computers.

  Wireless devices such as WiFi machines use the _Wireless Application Protocol (WAP)_, the main set of communications conventions, or "protocols," for connecting wireless users to the World Wide Web.

A display promotes WiFi at a train station in Paris, France.

Compression & Decompression: Putting More Data in Less Space

The vast streams of text, audio, and visual information threaten to overwhelm us. The file of a 2-hour movie, for instance, contains so much sound and visual information that, if stored without modification on standard CDs, it would require 360 disk changes during a single showing. A broadcast of _Oprah_ that presently fits into one conventional, or analog, television channel would require 45 channels if sent in digital language.

To fit more data into less space and increase the speed of data transmission, we use the mathematical process called *compression*. __Compression__, or __*digital-data compression*, is a method of removing repetitive elements from a file so that the file requires less storage space and therefore less time to transmit.__ Before we use the data, it is decompressed—the repeated patterns are restored. These methods are sometimes referred to as *codec* (for "compression/*de*compression") techniques.

- **Lossless versus lossy compression:** There are two principal methods of compressing data—lossless and lossy. In any situation, which of these two techniques is more appropriate will depend on whether data quality or storage space is more critical.

  Lossless compression uses mathematical techniques to replace repetitive patterns of bits with a kind of coded summary. During decompression, the coded summaries are replaced with the original patterns of bits. In this method, the data that comes out is exactly the same as what went in; it has merely been repackaged for purposes of storage or transmission. Lossless techniques are used when it's important that nothing be lost—for instance, for computer data, database records, spreadsheets, and word processing files.

  Lossy compression techniques permanently discard some data during compression. Lossy data compression involves a certain loss of accuracy in exchange for a high degree of compression (to as little as 5% of the original file size). This method of compression is often used for graphics files and sound files. Thus, a lossy codec might discard subtle shades of color or sounds outside the range of human hearing. Most users wouldn't notice the absence of these details.

- **Compression standards—JPEG and MPEG:** Several standards exist for compression, particularly of visual data. Data recorded and compressed in one standard cannot be played back in another. The main reason for the lack of agreement is that different industries have different priorities. What will satisfy the users of still photographs, for instance, will not work for the users of movies.

  As we have seen, lossless compression schemes are used for text and numeric data files, whereas lossy compression schemes are used with graphics and video files. The principal lossy compression schemes are *JPEG* and *MPEG*.

  The leading compression standard for still images is __JPEG__ (pronounced "*jay*-peg"), which stands for the "Joint Photographic Experts Group" of the International Standards Organization. The file extension that identifies graphic image files in the JPEG format is *.jpeg* or *.jpg*. In storing and transmitting still photographs, the data must remain of high quality. The JPEG codec looks for a way to squeeze a single image, mainly by eliminating repetitive pixels (picture-element dots) within the image. Higher or lower degrees of JPEG compression may be chosen; greater compression corresponds to greater image loss.

  The leading compression standard for moving images is __MPEG__ ("*em*-peg"), for "Motion Picture Experts Group." The file extension that identifies video (and sound) files compressed in this format is *.mpeg* or *.mpg*. People who work with videos are mainly interested in storing or transmitting an enormous amount of visual information in economical form; preserving details is a secondary consideration. The Motion Picture Experts Group sets standards for weeding out redundancies between neighboring images in a stream of video. Three MPEG standards have been developed for compressing visual information—MPEG-1, MPEG-2, and MPEG-4.

Three MPEG Standards

MPEG-1: For microcomputers and consumer gadgets. Provides full-screen video (VHS-like quality) of images similar to those on videocassette.

MPEG-2: For broadcast and cable television. Provides digital-TV-quality video for use with cable networks, satellite dishes, and new types of CD-ROMs. (MPEG-3 was incorporated into MPEG-4.)

MPEG-4: For wireless videoconferencing.

QuickCheck

What is the radio-frequency (RF) spectrum?

What does *bandwidth* refer to? What does it have to do with data transfer rate?

What are wired communications media? Wireless media?

What is Bluetooth? WiFi?

What are JPEG and MPEG used for?

6.4 Networks

KEY QUESTIONS

What are the benefits of networks, and what are their types, components, and variations?

More and more people are now designing their homes to accommodate networks. For instance, when Lisa Guernsey and her husband, Rob Krupicka, were planning their new house, they wanted modern conveniences without the modern-day headaches. "We didn't want to face another nest of tangled cables or to see speaker wires snaking beneath the rugs," Guernsey said. "What Rob and I wanted was . . . a so-called networked home with 'digital plumbing' for internet and television connections hidden behind walls, and just enough equipment to make tapping into video and audio as easy as filling a glass of water."[8]

Whether wired, wireless, or both, all the communications media we've described can be used singly or in mix-and-match fashion to form networks. **A _network_, or *communications network*, is a system of interconnected computers, telephones, or other communications devices that can communicate with one another and share applications and data.** The tying together of so many communications devices in so many ways is changing the world we live in.

The Benefits of Networks

People and organizations use networks for the following reasons, the most important of which is the sharing of resources.

- **Sharing of peripheral devices:** Peripheral devices such as laser printers, big disk drives, and scanners can be expensive. Consequently, to justify their purchase, management wants to maximize their use. Usually the best way to do this is to connect the peripheral to a network serving several computer users.

- **Sharing of programs and data:** In most organizations, people use the same software and need access to the same information. It is less expensive for a company to buy one word processing program that serves many employees than to buy a separate word processing program for each employee.

  Moreover, if all employees have access to the same data on a shared storage device, the organization can save money and avoid serious problems. If each employee has a separate machine, some employees may update customer

Networked computers monitor the national voting results in Pretoria, South Africa.

addresses, while others remain ignorant of the changes. Updating information on a shared server is much easier than updating every user's individual system.

Finally, network-linked employees can more easily work together online on shared projects.

- **Better communications:** One of the greatest features of networks is electronic mail. With email, everyone on a network can easily keep others posted about important information.

- **Security of information:** Before networks became commonplace, an individual employee might be the only one with a particular piece of information, which was stored in his or her desktop computer. If the employee was dismissed—or if a fire or flood demolished the office—the company would lose that information. Today such data would be backed up or duplicated on a networked storage device shared by others.

- **Access to databases:** Networks enable users to tap into numerous databases, whether private company databases or public databases available online through the internet.

Types of Networks: WANs, MANs, & LANs

Networks, which consist of various combinations of computers, storage devices, and communications devices, may be divided into three main categories, differing primarily in their geographic range.

- **Wide area network: A _wide area network (WAN)_ is a communications network that covers a wide geographic area, such as a country or the world.** Most long-distance and regional Bell telephone companies are WANs. A WAN may use a combination of satellites, fiber-optic cable, microwave, and copper wire connections and link a variety of computers, from mainframes to terminals. *(See ● Panel 6.8.)*

- **Metropolitan area network: A _metropolitan area network (MAN)_ is a communications network covering a city or a suburb.** The purpose of a MAN is often to bypass local telephone companies when accessing long-distance services. Many cellphone systems are MANs.

● PANEL 6.8
Wide area network

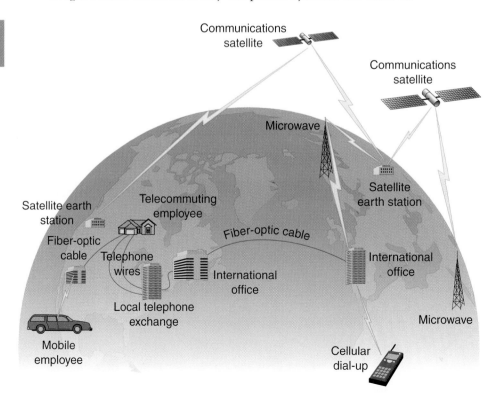

- **Local area network:** A _**local area network (LAN)**_ **connects computers and devices in a limited geographic area, such as one office, one building, or a group of buildings close together** (for instance, a college campus). A small LAN in a modest office, or even in a home, might link a file server with a few terminals or PCs and a printer or two. Such small LANs are sometimes called _PANs,_ for "personal area networks."

Most large computer networks have at least one _host computer,_ a mainframe or midsize central computer that controls the network. The other devices within the network are called nodes. A _node_ is any device that is attached to a network—for example, a microcomputer, terminal, storage device, or printer.

Networks may be connected together—LANs to MANs and MANs to WANs. _**Backbones**_ **are high-speed networks that connect LANs and MANs to the internet.**

A LAN for internet users at a McDonalds restaurant north of San Jose, Costa Rica.

Types of LANs: Client/Server & Peer to Peer

Local area networks consist of two principal types: _client/server_ and _peer to peer._ _(See ● Panel 6.9.)_

- **Client/server LANs:** A _**client/server LAN**_ **consists of _clients_, which are microcomputers that request data, and _servers_, which are computers used to supply data.** The server is a powerful microcomputer that manages shared devices, such as laser printers. It runs server software for applications such as email and web browsing.

Client/server LAN
In a client/server LAN, individual microcomputer users, or "clients," share the services of a centralized computer called a "server." In this case, the server is a file server, allowing users to share files of data and some programs.

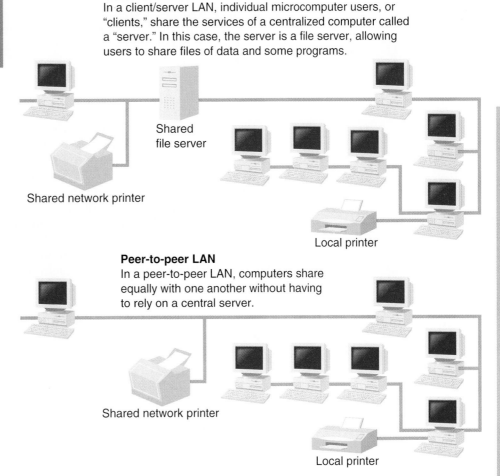

Shared file server

Shared network printer

Local printer

Peer-to-peer LAN
In a peer-to-peer LAN, computers share equally with one another without having to rely on a central server.

Shared network printer

Local printer

Networks & Communications

Different servers may be used to manage different tasks. A *file server* is a computer that acts like a disk drive, storing the programs and data files shared by users on a LAN. A *database server* is a computer in a LAN that stores data but doesn't store programs. A *print server* controls one or more printers and stores the print-image output from all the microcomputers on the system. *Web servers* contain web pages that can be viewed using a browser. *Mail servers* manage email.

- **Peer-to-peer LANs:** The word *peer* denotes one who is equal in standing with another (as in the phrases "peer pressure" and "jury of one's peers"). **In a _peer-to-peer LAN_, all microcomputers on the network communicate directly with one another without relying on a server.** Every computer can share files and peripherals with all other computers on the network, given that all are granted access privileges. Peer-to-peer networks are less expensive than client/server networks and work effectively for up to 25 computers. Beyond that, they slow down under heavy use. They are appropriate for small networks.

Many LANs mix elements from both client/server and peer-to-peer models.

Components of a LAN

Local area networks are made up of several standard components.

- **Connection or cabling system:** LANs may use a wired or wireless connection system. Wired connections may be twisted-pair wiring, coaxial cable, or fiber-optic cable. Wireless connections may be infrared, radio-wave transmission, Bluetooth, or WiFi.

- **Microcomputers with network interface cards:** Two or more microcomputers are required, along with network interface cards. As we mentioned in Chapter 4 (p. 158), a *network interface card (NIC)* enables the computer to send and receive messages over a cable network. The network card can be inserted into an expansion slot in a PC. Alternatively, a network card in a stand-alone box may serve a number of devices. Many new computers come with network cards already installed.

- **Network operating system:** The *network operating system (NOS)* is the system software that manages the activity of a network. The NOS supports access by multiple users and provides for recognition of users based on passwords and terminal identifications. Depending on whether the LAN is client/server or peer-to-peer, the operating system may be stored on the file server, on each microcomputer on the network, or on a combination of both.

  Examples of popular NOS software are Novell NetWare, Microsoft Windows NT/2000, Unix, and Linux. Peer-to-peer networking can also be accomplished with Microsoft Windows 95/98/Me/XP and Microsoft Windows for Workgroups. Apple Macintoshes come preconfigured for peer-to-peer networking.

- **Other shared devices:** Printers, scanners, storage devices, and other peripherals may be added to the network as necessary and shared by all users.

- **Routers, bridges, gateways, and hubs:** In principle, a LAN may stand alone. Today, however, it invariably connects to other networks, especially the internet. Network designers determine the types of hardware and software necessary as interfaces to make these connections. Routers, bridges, gateways, and hubs are used for this purpose. *(See ● Panel 6.10.)*

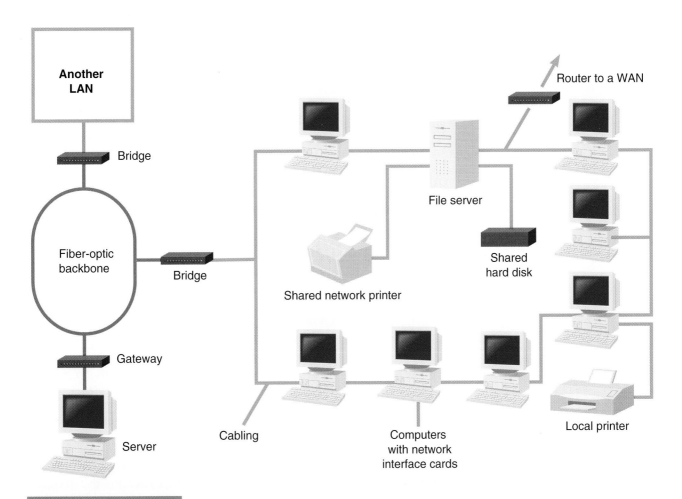

Another LAN

Bridge

Fiber-optic backbone

Bridge

Gateway

Server

Router to a WAN

File server

Shared hard disk

Shared network printer

Cabling

Computers with network interface cards

Local printer

● **PANEL 6.10**
Components of a typical LAN

A **_router_ is a special computer that directs communicating messages when several networks are connected together.** High-speed routers can serve as part of the internet backbone, or transmission path, handling the major data traffic.

A **_bridge_ is an interface used to connect the same types of networks.** Similar networks (local area networks) can be joined together to create larger area networks.

A **_gateway_ is an interface permitting communication between dissimilar networks**—for instance, between a LAN and a WAN or between two LANs based on different network operating systems or different layouts.

In general, a hub is the central part of a wheel where the spokes come together. In computer terminology, a **_hub_ is a common connection point for devices in a network—a place of convergence where data arrives from one or more directions and is forwarded out in one or more other directions.** Hubs are commonly used to connect segments of a LAN. A hub contains multiple ports. When a packet arrives at one port, it is copied to the other ports so that all segments of the LAN can see all packets.

There are three types of hubs. A _passive hub_ serves simply as a conduit for the data, enabling it to go from one device (or segment) to another. _Intelligent hubs_ include additional features that enable an administrator to monitor the traffic passing through the hub and to configure each port in the hub. A third type of hub, called a _switching hub_, reads the destination address of each packet and then forwards the packet to the correct port.

Intranets, Extranets, & Firewalls: Private Internet Networks

Early in the Online Age, businesses discovered the benefits of using the World Wide Web to get information to customers, suppliers, or investors. For example, in the mid-1990s, FedEx found it could save millions by allowing customers to click through web pages to trace their parcels, instead of having FedEx customer-service agents do it. From there, it was a short step to the application of the same technology inside companies—in internal internet networks called *intranets*.

- **Intranets—for internal use only:** An *__intranet__* **is an organization's internal private network that uses the infrastructure and standards of the internet and the web.** When a corporation develops a public website, it is making selected information available to consumers and other interested parties. When it creates an intranet, it enables employees to have quicker access to internal information and to share knowledge so that they can do their jobs better. Information exchanged on intranets may include employee email addresses and telephone numbers, product information, sales data, employee benefit information, and lists of jobs available within the organization.

- **Extranets—for certain outsiders:** Taking intranet technology a few steps further, extranets offer security and controlled access. As we have seen, intranets are internal systems, designed to connect the members of a specific group or a single company. By contrast, *__extranets__* **are private intranets that connect not only internal personnel but also selected suppliers and other strategic parties.** Extranets have become popular for standard transactions such as purchasing. Ford Motor Company, for instance, has an extranet that connects more than 15,000 Ford dealers worldwide. Called FocalPt, the extranet supports sales and servicing of cars, with the aim of improving service to Ford customers.

- **Firewalls—to keep out unauthorized users:** Security is essential to an intranet (or even an extranet). Sensitive company data, such as payroll information, must be kept private, by means of a firewall. **A *__firewall__* is a system of hardware and software that blocks unauthorized users inside and outside the organization from entering the intranet.** The firewall software monitors all internet and other network activity, looking for suspicious data and preventing unauthorized access. Always-on internet connections such as cable modem and DSL, as well as WiFi devices, are particularly susceptible to unauthorized intrusion, so users are advised to install a firewall.

    A firewall consists of two parts, a choke and a gate. The *choke* forces all data packets flowing between the internet and the intranet to pass through a gate. The *gate* regulates the flow between the two networks. It identifies authorized users, searches for viruses, and implements other security measures. Thus, intranet users can gain access to the internet (including key sites connected by hyperlinks), but outside internet users cannot enter the intranet.

Firewall software

PRACTICAL ACTION BOX
How to Create Your Own Simple Website, Easily & for Free

"The full power of the Web will only be unleashed," says technology writer Stephen Wildstrom, "when it's as easy to post information online as it is to write a memo."[a]

We're getting closer. The World Wide Web is a great way to get information about yourself and your work to co-workers or to potential customers. To do so, however, you need to create a web page and put it online. Fortunately, providers offer some free, easy-to-use web-authoring tools for building simple websites. They help you create web pages using icons and menus to automate the process; you don't need to know hypertext markup language (HTML, p. 56) to get the job done. These automated tools let you select a prepared, template web page design, type a few words, add a picture or two—and you're done.[b] To save the pages and make them accessible on the internet, the provider grants you a certain amount of space on its web servers.

Yahoo! calls its web page building tools and templates "PageWizards." It also offers a service called PageBuilder for advanced users. With this service, you can add music to your web pages and add components that track how many people visit your site. Yahoo! offers 15 megabytes of storage for your PageWizard or PageBuilder pages in its GeoCities area (*http://geocities.yahoo.com*). Advertising banners will appear on your pages unless you pay $4.95 per month not to have them.

Lycos (*www.lycos.com*) also offers free space—20 megabytes in its Tripod area. Lycos offers templates and tools, but it also offers tutorials to help you get started if you want to build your own pages from scratch. Again, you will have advertising on your pages unless you pay $4.95 per month to get rid of them.

For its subscribers, America Online (AOL) offers more than 100 templates, 5,000 free images, and 2 megabytes per screen name.

Local and national ISPs offer tools and space also. Contact your ISP for information.

Netscape's Navigator comes with a web-building program, as does Microsoft Explorer.

Microsoft also offers Internet Assistant, which can be used with Word, its word processing program. You can create a web page from a template, from an existing Word document by choosing *Save as web page,* or by using the Web Page Wizard.

If you've taken up desktop publishing, you should know that Adobe PageMaker and Microsoft Publisher come with simple web page editors. Macromedia's web-authoring software, Dreamweaver, and Microsoft's FrontPage allow you to create complicated web pages from scratch—but these tools are not for the novice. You will need to learn some HTML to use these packages; Lycos's Webmonkey (*http://hotwired. lycos.com/webmonkey/*) has useful HTML tutorials as well as a tutorial on page design. Yale University also has a good page design site: *http://info.med.yale.edu/calm/manual/ contents.html.* Other sites include *www.davesite.com/ Webstation/html* and *www.htmlgoodies.com/toolbox/.* Once you've created your website, you'll need to "publish" it—upload it to a web server for viewing on the internet. You can get upload instructions from your online service or internet service provider (ISP). Some ISPs will give you free space on their servers; some will charge you for the server space.

QuickCheck

What are the benefits of networks?

Characterize WANs, MANs, and LANs.

What is the main difference between a client/server LAN and a peer-to-peer LAN?

What are the components of a LAN?

What functions do intranets, extranets, and firewalls fulfill?

6.5 Cyberethics: Controversial Material & Censorship

KEY QUESTION

What are some concerns regarding censorship of internet information?

◀ethics▶

Communications technology gives us more choices of nearly every sort. It provides us with different ways of working, thinking, and playing. It also presents us with some different moral choices—determining right actions in the digital and online universe. Let's consider one important aspect of "cyberethics"—controversial material and censorship.

Since computers are simply another way of communicating, there should be no surprise that many people use them to communicate about sex. Yahoo! says that the word *sex* is the most popular search word on the net.[9] All kinds of online X-rated message boards, chat rooms, and Usenet newsgroups exist. These raise serious issues for parents. Do we want children to have access to sexual conversations, to download hard-core pictures, or to encounter criminals who might try to meet them offline? "Parents should never use [a computer] as an electronic baby sitter," computer columnist Lawrence Magid says. People online are not always what they seem to be, he points out, and a message seemingly from a 12-year-old girl could really be from a 30-year-old man. "Children should be warned never to give out personal information," says Magid, "and to tell their parents if they encounter mail or messages that make them uncomfortable."[10]

What can be done about X-rated materials? Some possibilities:

- **Blocking software:** Some software developers have discovered a golden opportunity in making programs like SurfWatch, Net Nanny, and CYBERsitter. These "blocking" programs screen out objectionable material, typically by identifying certain unapproved keywords in a user's request or comparing the user's request for information against a list of prohibited sites.

- **Browsers with ratings:** Another proposal in the works is browser software that contains built-in ratings for internet, Usenet, and World Wide Web files. Parents could, for example, choose a browser that has been endorsed by the local school board or the online service provider.

- **The V-chip:** The 1996 Telecommunications Law officially launched the era of the *V-chip*, a device that is to be required equipment in most new television sets. The V-chip allows parents to automatically block out programs that have been labeled as high in violence, sex, or other objectionable material.

However, any attempts at restricting the flow of information are hindered by the basic design of the internet itself, with its strategy of offering different roads to the same place. "If access to information on a computer is blocked by one route," writes the *New York Times*'s Peter Lewis, "a moderately skilled computer user can simply tap into another computer by an alternative route." Lewis cites an internet axiom attributed to an engineer named John Gilmore: "The internet interprets censorship as damage and routes around it."[11]

Summary

analog (p. 217, KQ 6.1) Continuous and varying in strength and/or quality. An analog signal is a continuous electrical signal with such variation. Why it's important: Sound, light, temperature, and pressure values, for instance, can fall anywhere on a continuum or range. The highs, lows, and in-between states have historically been represented with analog devices rather than in digital form. Examples of analog devices are a speedometer, a thermometer, and a tire-pressure gauge, all of which can measure continuous fluctuations. The electrical signals on a telephone line have traditionally been analog-data representations of the original voices. Telephone, radio, television, and cable-TV technologies have long been based on analog data.

analog cellphone (p. 231, KQ 6.3) Mobile telephone designed primarily for communicating by voice through a system of ground-area cells. Calls are directed to cells by a mobile-telephone switching office (MTSO). Moving between cells requires that calls be "handed off" by the MTSO. Why it's important: Cellphone systems allow callers mobility.

backbones (p. 237, KQ 6.4) High-speed networks that connect LANs and MANs to the internet. Why it's important: Without backbones, there would be no internet.

bandwidth (p. 226, KQ 6.3) Also called *band;* range of frequencies that a transmission medium can carry in a given period of time and thus a measure of the amount of information that can be delivered. The bandwidth is the difference between the lowest and the highest frequencies transmitted. For analog signals, bandwidth is expressed in hertz (Hz), or cycles per second. For digital signals, bandwidth is expressed in bits per second (bps). In the United States, certain bands are assigned by the Federal Communications Commission (FCC) for certain purposes. Why it's important: The wider the bandwidth, the faster the data can be transmitted. The narrower the band, the greater the loss of transmission power. This loss of power must be overcome by using relays or repeaters that rebroadcast the original signal.

Bluetooth (p. 233, KQ 6.3) Short-range wireless digital standard aimed at linking cellphones, PDAs, computers, and peripherals. Why it's important: Bluetooth technology can replace cables between PCs and printers and can connect PCs to PDAs and wireless phones.

bridge (p. 239, KQ 6.4) Interface used to connect the same types of networks. Why it's important: Similar networks (local area networks) can be joined together to create larger area networks.

broadband connection (p. 226, KQ 6.3) Connection characterized by very high speed. For digital signals, bandwidth can be expressed in hertz but also in *bits per second (bps)*. For instance, the connections that carry the newest types of digital cellphone signals range from 144 kilobits (14,400 bits) per second to 2 megabits (2 million bits) per second. Digital signals carry much more information than analog signals do. Why it's important: The wider a medium's bandwidth, the more frequencies it can use to transmit data and thus the faster the transmission.

broadband wireless digital services (p. 232, KQ 6.3) Two-way, third-generation (3G) wireless digital services based on an "always-on" standard. Why it's important: 3G technology is faster than 2G technology; it can send pictures and data clearly and quickly.

broadcast radio (p. 227, KQ 6.3) Wireless transmission medium that sends data over long distances—between regions, states, or countries. A transmitter is required to send messages and a receiver to receive them; sometimes both sending and receiving functions are combined in a transceiver. Why it's important: In the lower frequencies of the radio spectrum, several broadcast radio bands are reserved not only for conventional AM/FM radio but also for broadcast television, CB (citizens band) radio, ham (amateur) radio, cellphones, and private radio-band mobile services (such as police, fire, and taxi dispatch). Some organizations use specific radio frequencies and networks to support wireless communications.

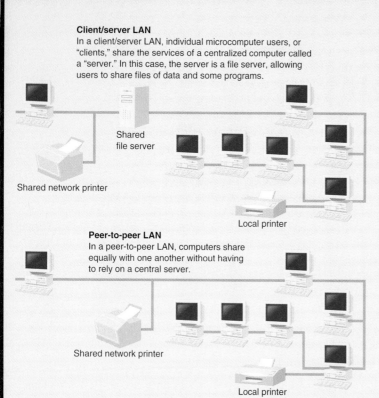

Client/server LAN
In a client/server LAN, individual microcomputer users, or "clients," share the services of a centralized computer called a "server." In this case, the server is a file server, allowing users to share files of data and some programs.

Shared file server

Shared network printer

Local printer

Peer-to-peer LAN
In a peer-to-peer LAN, computers share equally with one another without having to rely on a central server.

Shared network printer

Local printer

client/server LAN (p. 237, KQ 6.4) Local area network that consists of *clients,* which are microcomputers that request data, and *servers,* which are computers used to supply data. Why it's important: Client/server LANs are part of the domain infrastructure of networks.

coaxial cable (p. 225, KQ 6.3) Commonly called "coax"; insulated copper wire wrapped in a solid or braided metal shield and then in an external plastic cover. Why it's important: Co-ax is widely used for cable television. Because of the extra insulation, coaxial cable is much better than twisted-pair wiring at resisting noise. Moreover, it can carry voice and data at a faster rate.

communications media (p. 224, KQ 6.3) Any medium that carries signals over a communications path, the route between two or more communications media devices. Why it's important: Media may be wired or wireless. Three types of wired channels are twisted-pair wire (conventional telephone lines), coaxial cable, and fiber-optic cable.

communications satellite (p. 228, KQ 6.3) Microwave relay station in orbit around the earth. Why it's important: Transmitting a signal from a ground station to a satellite is called *uplinking;* the reverse is called *downlinking.* The delivery process will be slowed if, as is often the case, more than one satellite is required to get the message delivered.

compression (p. 234, KQ 6.3) Also called *digital-data compression;* method of removing repetitive elements from a file so that the file requires less storage space and therefore less time to transmit. Before we use the data, it is decompressed—the repeated patterns are restored. These methods are sometimes referred to as codec (for "*co*mpression/*dec*ompression") techniques. Why it's important: Many of today's files, with graphics, sound, and video, require huge amounts of storage space; data compression makes the storage and transmission of these files more feasible.

digital (p. 217, KQ 6.1) Communications signals or information represented in a two-state (binary) way using electronic or electromagnetic signals. Why it's important: Digital signals are the basis of computer-based communications. *Digital* is usually synonymous with *computer-based.*

digital television (DTV) (p. 223, KQ 6.2) A television standard that uses a digital signal, or series of 0s and 1s, rather than the customary analog standard, a system of varying signal amplitude and frequency that represents picture and sound elements. DTV was adopted as a standard in 1996 by television broadcasters and the Federal Communications Commission. Why it's important: DTV is much clearer and less prone to interference than analog TV and is better suited to handling computer and internet data.

digital wireless services (p. 231, KQ 6.3) Two-way, second-generation (2G) wireless services that support digital cellphones and PDAs. They use a network of cell towers to send voice communications and data over the airwaves in digital form. Why it's important: This technology is a dramatic improvement over analog cellphones. Voice clarity is better, and more calls can be squeezed into the same bandwidth.

extranet (p. 240, KQ 6.4) Private intranet that connects not only internal personnel but also selected suppliers and other strategic parties. Why it's important: Extranets have become popular for standard transactions such as purchasing.

fiber-optic cable (p. 225, KQ 6.3) Cable that consists of dozens or hundreds of thin strands of glass or plastic that transmit pulsating beams of light rather than electricity. Why it's important: These strands, each as thin as a human hair, can transmit up to 2 billion pulses per second (2 Gbps); each "on" pulse represents 1 bit. When bundled together, fiber-optic strands in a cable 0.12 inch thick can support a quarter-million to a half-million voice conversations at the same time. Moreover, unlike electrical signals, light pulses are not affected by random electromagnetic interference in the environment. Thus, they have much lower error rates than normal telephone wire and cable. In addition, fiber-optic cable is lighter and more durable than twisted-pair wire and co-ax cable. A final advantage is that it cannot easily be wiretapped, so transmissions are more secure.

firewall (p. 240, KQ 6.4) System of hardware and software that blocks unauthorized users inside and outside the organization from entering the intranet. Why it's important: Security is essential to an intranet. A firewall consists of two parts, a choke and a gate. The choke forces all data packets flowing between the internet and the intranet to pass through a gate. The gate regulates the flow between the two networks. It identifies authorized users, searches for viruses, and implements other security measures. Thus, intranet users can gain access to the internet (including key sites connected by hyperlinks), but outside internet users cannot enter the intranet.

gateway (p. 239, KQ 6.4) Interface permitting communication between dissimilar networks. Why it's important: Gateways permit communication between a LAN and a WAN or between two LANs based on different network operating systems or different layouts.

Global Positioning System (GPS) (p. 229, KQ 6.3) A series of earth-orbiting satellites continuously transmitting timed radio signals that can be used to identify earth locations. Why it's important: A GPS receiver—handheld or mounted in a vehicle, plane, or boat—can pick up transmissions from any four satellites, interpret the information from each, and calculate to within a few hundred feet or less the receiver's longitude, latitude, and altitude. Some GPS receivers include map software for finding one's way around, as with the Guidestar system available with some rental cars.

high-definition television (HDTV) (p. 224, KQ 6.2) A high-resolution type of digital television (DTV), with a display resolution from 1,280 × 720 pixels to 1,920 × 1,080 pixels and higher and an aspect ratio (the width-to-height ratio of the screen) of 16:9, for a viewing experience similar to watching a movie in a theater. Why it's important: The Federal Communications Commission expects that eventually HDTV will supplant analog TV as the dominant digital standard.

hub (p. 239, KQ 6.4) A common connection point for devices in a network—a place of convergence where data arrives from one or more directions and is forwarded out in one or more other directions. Why it's important: Hubs are commonly used to connect segments of a LAN.

infrared wireless transmission (p. 227, KQ 6.3) Transmission of data signals using infrared-light waves. Why it's important: Infrared ports can be found on some laptop computers and printers, as well as wireless mouses. The advantage is that no physical connection is required among devices. The drawbacks are that line-of-sight communication is required—there must be an unobstructed view between transmitter and receiver—and transmission is confined to short range.

intranet (p. 240, KQ 6.4) An organization's internal private network that uses the infrastructure and standards of the internet and the web. Why it's important: When an organization creates an intranet, it enables employees to have quicker access to internal information and to share knowledge so that they can do their jobs better. Information exchanged on intranets may include employee email addresses and telephone numbers, product information, sales data, employee benefit information, and lists of jobs available within the organization.

JPEG (p. 234, KQ 6.3) Stands for "Joint Photographic Experts Group" of the International Standards Organization; the leading compression standard for still images. The file extension that identifies graphic image files in the JPEG format is *.jpeg* or *.jpg*. Why it's important: JPEG compression is commonly used to store and transmit still graphic images. Higher or lower degrees of JPEG compression may be chosen; greater compression corresponds to greater image loss.

local area network (LAN) (p. 237, KQ 6.4) Communications network that connects computers and devices in a limited geographical area, such as one office, one building, or a group of buildings close together (for instance, a college campus). Why it's important: LANs have replaced large computers for many functions and are considerably less expensive.

metropolitan area network (MAN) (p. 236, KQ 6.4) Communications network covering a city or a suburb. Why it's important: The purpose of a MAN is often to bypass local telephone companies when accessing long-distance services. Many cellphone systems are MANs.

microwave radio (p. 227, KQ 6.3) Transmission of voice and data through the atmosphere as superhigh-frequency radio waves called *microwaves*. These frequencies are used to transmit messages between ground-based stations and satellite communications systems. Why it's important: Microwaves are line-of-sight; they cannot bend around corners or around the earth's curvature, so there must be an unobstructed view between transmitter and receiver. Thus, microwave stations need to be placed within 25–30 miles of each other, with no obstructions in between. In a string of microwave relay stations, each station receives incoming messages, boosts the signal strength, and relays the signal to the next station. Nowadays dish- or horn-shaped microwave reflective dishes, which contain transceivers and antennas, are nearly everywhere.

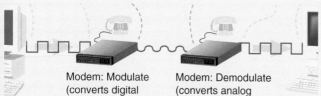

Modem: Modulate (converts digital pulses to analog form)

Modem: Demodulate (converts analog signals back to digital form)

modem (p. 218, KQ 6.1) Short for "modulate/demodulate"; device that converts digital signals into a representation of analog form (modulation) to send over phone lines. A receiving modem then converts the analog signal back to a digital signal (demodulation). Why it's important: The modem provides a means for computers to communicate with one another using the standard copper-wire telephone network, an analog system that was built to transmit the human voice but not computer signals.

MPEG (p. 234, KQ 6.3) Stands for "Motion Picture Experts Group"; the leading compression standard for video images. The file extension that identifies video (and sound) files compressed in this format is *.mpeg* or *.mpg.* Why it's important: People who work with videos are mainly interested in storing or transmitting an enormous amount of visual information in economical form; preserving details is a secondary consideration. The Motion Picture Experts Group sets standards for weeding out redundancies between neighboring images in a stream of video. Three MPEG standards have been developed for compressing visual information—MPEG-1, MPEG-2, and MPEG-4.

network (p. 235, KQ 6.4) Also called *communications network;* system of interconnected computers, telephones, or other communications devices that can communicate with one another and share applications and data. Why it's important: The tying together of so many communications devices in so many ways is changing the world we live in.

pager (p. 231, KQ 6.3) Commonly known as *beeper;* simple radio receiver that receives data sent from a special radio transmitter. The pager number is dialed from a phone and travels via the transmitter to the pager. Why it's important: Pagers have become a common way of receiving notification of phone calls so that the user can return the calls immediately; some pagers can also display messages of up to 80 characters and send preprogrammed messages.

peer-to-peer LAN (p. 238, KQ 6.4) Type of local area network in which all microcomputers on the network communicate directly with one another without relying on a server. Why it's important: Peer-to-peer networks are less expensive than client/server networks and work effectively for up to 25 computers. Beyond that, they slow down under heavy use. They are appropriate for small networks.

radio-frequency (RF) spectrum (p. 226, KQ 6.3) The part of the electromagnetic spectrum that carries most communications signals. Why it's important: The radio spectrum ranges from low-frequency waves, such as those used for aeronautical and marine navigation equipment, through the medium frequencies for CB radios, cordless phones, and baby monitors, to ultra-high-frequency bands for cellphones and also microwave bands for communications satellites.

router (p. 239, KQ 6.4) Special computer that directs communicating messages when several networks are connected together. Why it's important: High-speed routers can serve as part of the internet backbone, or transmission path, handling the major data traffic.

telecommuting (p. 222, KQ 6.2) Also called *telework;* working at home or on the road while in telecommunication with the office. Why it's important: Telecommuting has many benefits. Examples are reduced traffic congestion, energy consumption, and air pollution; increased productivity; and improved teamwork. A disadvantage is that people may feel isolated.

twisted-pair wire (p. 225, KQ 6.3) Two strands of insulated copper wire, twisted around each other. Why it's important: Twisted-pair wire has been the most common channel or medium used for telephone systems. However, it is relatively slow and does not protect well against electrical interference.

videoconferencing (p. 221, KQ 6.2) Also called *teleconferencing;* use of television video and sound technology as well as computer networks (including the internet) to enable people in different locations to see, hear, and talk with one another. Why it's important: Videoconferencing may eliminate the need for some travel for the purpose of meetings and allow people who cannot travel to visit face to face.

virtual office (p. 223, KQ 6.2) Nonpermanent and mobile office run with computer and communications technology. Why it's important: Employees work from their homes, cars, and other new work sites, using pagers, portable computers, and cellphones to conduct business. This reduces the office expenses of their employer.

wide area network (WAN) (p. 236, KQ 6.4) Communications network that covers a wide geographic area, such as a country or the world. Why it's important: Most long-distance and regional Bell telephone companies are WANs. A WAN may use a combination of satellites, fiber-optic cable, microwave, and copper wire connections and link a variety of computers, from mainframes to terminals.

WiFi (p. 233, KQ 6.3) Short for "*wireless fidelity*"; short-range wireless digital standard aimed at helping machines inside offices to communicate at high speeds and share internet connections at distances up to 300 feet. It connects to Ethernet LANs. Why it's important: WiFi is a standard in most new computers.

workgroup computing (p. 222, KQ 6.2) Also called *collaborative computing;* technology by which teams of co-workers, often at different sites, can use networks of microcomputers to share information and to cooperate on projects. Workgroup computing is made possible not only by networks and microcomputers but also by groupware. Why it's important: Workgroup computing allows co-workers to collaborate with colleagues, suppliers, and customers and to tap into company information through computer networks.

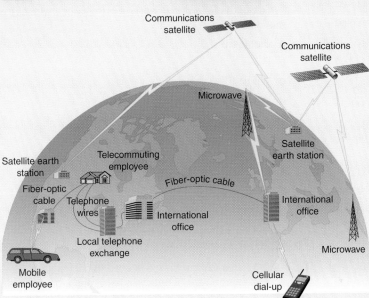

Chapter Review

"I can recognize and recall information."

Self-Test Questions

1. A(n) _____ converts digital signals into analog signals for transmission over phone lines.

2. A(n) _____ network covers a wide geographic area, such as a state or a country.

3. _____ cable transmits data as pulses of light rather than as electricity.

4. _____ refers to waves continuously varying in strength and/or quality; _____ refers to communications signals or information in a binary form.

5. _____ is a method of removing repetitive elements from a file so that the file requires less storage space.

6. A(n) _____ is a computer that acts as a disk drive, storing programs and data files shared by users on a LAN.

7. The _____ is the system software that manages the activities of a network.

8. *Modem* is short for _____.

9. The leading compression standard for still images is _____.

10. _____ programs can screen out objectionable material on the internet.

Multiple-Choice Questions

1. Which of the following best describes the telephone line that is used in most homes today?
   a. coaxial cable
   b. modem cable
   c. twisted-pair wire
   d. fiber-optic cable
   e. LAN

2. Which of the following do local area networks enable?
   a. sharing of peripheral devices
   b. sharing of programs and data
   c. better communications
   d. access to databases
   e. all of the above

3. Which of the following is *not* a data compression standard/method?
   a. lossless
   b. JPEG
   c. MPEG
   d. lossy
   e. NOS

4. Which of the following is *not* a short-distance wireless standard?
   a. Bluetooth
   b. PDA
   c. WiFi
   d. WAP

5. How do fiber-optic cables transmit data?
   a. via copper wire
   b. via infrared
   c. via AC electric current
   d. via radio waves
   e. via pulsating beams of light

True/False Questions

T F 1. In a LAN, a bridge is used to connect the same type of networks, whereas a gateway is used to enable dissimilar networks to communicate.

T F 2. Frequency and amplitude are two characteristics of analog carrier waves.

T F 3. *Bandwidth* refers to the range of frequencies that a transmission medium can carry in a given period of time.

T F 4. Twisted-pair wire commonly connects residences to external telephone systems.

T F 5. Lossless compression permanently discards some data during compression; lossy compression doesn't lose information but repackages repetitive patterns of bits.

T F 6. Photonics is the science of sending data bits by means of light pulses carried on hair-thin glass fibers.

T F 7. WiFi signals can travel up to 300 feet.

"I can recall information in my own terms and explain them to a friend."

Short-Answer Questions

1. What is the difference between an intranet and an extranet?
2. What is workgroup computing?
3. What is the difference between a LAN and a WAN?
4. Why is bandwidth a factor in data transmission?
5. What is a firewall?
6. What do 2G and 3G mean?
7. What are the differences between DTV, HDTV, and SDTV?

stage 3 LEARNING APPLYING, ANALYZING, SYNTHESIZING, EVALUATING

"I can apply what I've learned, relate these ideas to other concepts, build on other knowledge, and use all these thinking skills to form a judgment."

Knowledge in Action

1. Are the computers at your school connected to a network? If so, what kind of network(s)? What types of computers are connected? What hardware and software allows the network to function? What department(s) did you contact to find the information you needed to answer these questions?

2. Using current articles, publications, and/or the web, research cable modems. Where are they being used? What does a residential user need to hook up to a cable modem system? Do you think you will use a cable modem in the near future?

3. Research the role of the Federal Communications Commission in regulating the communications industry. How are new frequencies opened up for new communications services? How are the frequencies determined? Who gets to use new frequencies?

4. Would you like to have a job for which you telecommute instead of "going in to work"? Why or why not?

5. From your experience with cellphones, do you think it is wise to continue also paying for a "land-line" POTS phone line, or is cellphone service reliable enough to use as your sole means of telephony? As cell service advances, how do you think the POTS infrastructure will be used?

Web Exercises

1. Compare digital cable and satellite TV in your area. Which offers more channels? Which offers more features? How much do the services cost? Does either allow internet connectivity? Does either use a telephone line to download the programming listings?

2. Wondering what those astronauts are doing on the International Space Station? NASA has a TV station via the internet dedicated to providing real-time coverage of what is going on in, and out of, this world. Visit the following website to get the programming schedule: *www.nasa.gov/multimedia/nasatv /index.html.*

3. Calculate the amount of airborne data transmission that travels through your body. To do this, research the amount of radio and television station broadcast signals in your area, as well as the estimated number of mobile-phone users. Imagine what the world would look like if you could see all the radio-wave signals the way you can see the waves in the ocean.

4. On the web, go to *www.trimble.com* and work through some of the tutorial on "About GPS Technology." Then write a short report on the applications of a GPS system.

5. Microchips are implanted in animals to track them with GPS technology. Humans can now be tracked when they use their cellphones. Visit the following websites for more details:

   www.wired.com/news/business/0,1367,21781,00.html
   http://europe.cnn.com/2001/TECH/ptech/04/20/ location.services.idg
   www.pcworld.com/news/article/0,aid,55986,00.asp

6. What is wardriving? Visit these sites to see what is being done to fix this security hole.

   www.wardriving.com/
   www.netstumbler.com/
   http://online.securityfocus.com/news/192
   www.pasadena.net/vacation/

7. TDMA, GSM, and CDMA. What do these terms mean? The following websites do a good job of explaining these technologies and other cellphone-related issues.

   http://w3.iarc.org/~ronen/cellular.html
   www.arcx.com/sites/CDMAvsTDMA.htm

8. Why AM radio during the day is different from AM radio at night: Read the information at the following websites to learn more about the propagation of AM radio signals and how AM is governed by the FCC.

   www.wmox.net/power.htm
   www.grc.nasa.gov/WWW/MAEL/ag/agprop4.htm
   http://musicradio.computer.net/transm.html

9. Security Issue—WiFi Security Issues: As WiFi becomes more widespread, how will users protect their networks? WiFi is hacked almost as a harmless hobby to detect its vulnerabilities. Visit the following websites to learn about some issues of the WiFi future.

www.netstumbler.com/
www.wardriving.com/
www.acsac.org/2002/case/wed-c-330-Miller.pdf
www.webmasterworld.com/forum45/127.htm
www.cio.com/research/communications/security.html

chapter 7

Files, Databases, & E-Commerce

Digital Engines for the New Economy

Chapter Topics & Key Questions

7.1   Managing Files: Basic Concepts What are the data storage hierarchy, the key field, types of files, and some methods of data access and storage?

7.2   Database Management Systems What are two types of database access?

7.3   Database Models What are four types of database models?

7.4   Databases & the New Economy: E-Commerce, Data Mining, & B2B Systems How are e-commerce, data mining, and business-to-business systems using databases?

7.5   The Ethics of Using Databases: Concerns About Accuracy & Privacy What are some ethical concerns about the uses of databases?

Marketing research firm IDC predicts that by 2007 internet users worldwide will access, download, and share information equivalent to the entire Library of Congress more than 64,000 times over—*every day*. This represents a doubling every year from the internet traffic of 2002, rising from 180 petabits to 5,175 petabits per day.[1] How will all this information be organized and made accessible? The answer has to do with databases.

7.1 Managing Files: Basic Concepts

An electronic database is not just the computer-based version of what used to go into manila folders and filing cabinets. A *database* **is a logically organized collection of related data designed and built for a specific purpose,** a technology for pulling together facts that allows the slicing and dicing and mixing and matching of data in all kinds of ways. The data in a database has some inherent meaning. In other words, a random assortment of data cannot correctly be called a *database*.[2]

How Data Is Organized: The Data Storage Hierarchy

Data in a database can be grouped into a hierarchy of categories, each increasingly more complex. **The *data storage hierarchy* consists of the levels of data stored in a computer database: bits, characters (bytes), fields, records, and files.** *(See ● Panel 7.1.)*

- **Bits:** Computers, as we have said, are based on the principle that electricity may be on or off (p. 143). Thus, **the *bit* is the smallest unit of data the computer can store in a database—represented by 0 for off or 1 for on.**

- **Characters:** A *character* **(byte) is a letter, number, or special character.** *A, B, C, 1, 2, 3, #, $, %* are all examples of single characters. A combination of bits represents a character.

Bits and bytes are the building blocks for representing data, whether it is being processed, telecommunicated, or stored in a database. The computer deals with the bits and bytes; you, however, will need to deal mostly with fields, records, and files.

- **Field:** A *field* **is a unit of data consisting of one or more characters (bytes).** It is the smallest unit of meaningful information in the database. Each field has a *field name* that describes the kind of data that should be entered into the field. An example of a field is your first name, your street address, *or* your Social Security Number.

- **Record:** A *record* **is a collection of related fields.** Each record stores data about only one entity, which can be a person, a place, a thing, an occurrence, or a phenomenon. An example of a record would be your name *and* address *and* Social Security Number.

- **File:** A *file* **is a collection of related records.** An example of such a file is data collected on everyone employed in the same department of a company, including all names, addresses, and Social Security

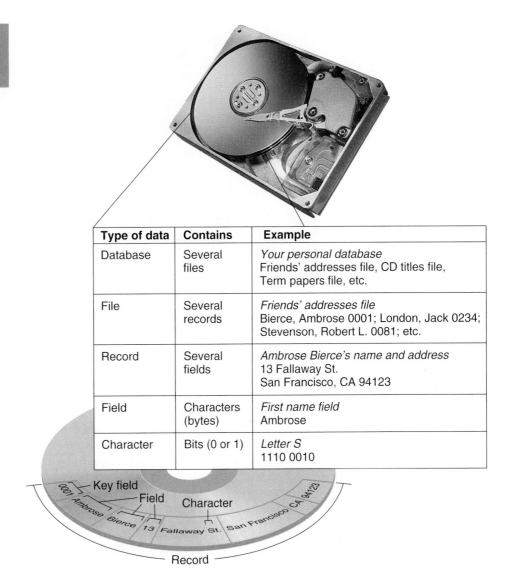

Type of data	Contains	Example
Database	Several files	*Your personal database* Friends' addresses file, CD titles file, Term papers file, etc.
File	Several records	*Friends' addresses file* Bierce, Ambrose 0001; London, Jack 0234; Stevenson, Robert L. 0081; etc.
Record	Several fields	*Ambrose Bierce's name and address* 13 Fallaway St. San Francisco, CA 94123
Field	Characters (bytes)	*First name field* Ambrose
Character	Bits (0 or 1)	*Letter S* 1110 0010

Numbers. You use files a lot because the file is the collection of data or information that is treated as a unit by the computer.

The file is at the top of the data hierarchy. A collection of related files forms the database. A company database might include files on all past and current employees in all departments. There would be various files for each employee: payroll, retirement benefits, sales quotas and achievements (if in sales), and so on.

The Key Field

An important concept in data organization is that of the key field, also called *key, sort key, index,* or *keyword.* **A *key field* (p. 117) is a field that is chosen to uniquely identify a record so that it can be easily retrieved and processed.** The key field is often an identification number, Social Security number, customer account number, or the like or a combination of letters and numbers set up as a meaningful code. The primary characteristic of the key field is that it is *unique.* Thus, numbers are clearly preferable to names as key fields because there are many people with common names like James Johnson, Susan Williams, Ann Wong, or Roberto Sanchez, whose records might be confused. Student records are often identified by student ID numbers used as key fields.

At the Genoscope project in Evry, France, an employee analyzes genetic information from a database of various types of organisms.

Types of Files: Program Files, Data Files, & Others

As we said, the *file* is the collection of data or information that is treated as a unit by the computer. **Files are given names—_filenames_.** If you're using a word processing program to write a psychology term paper, you might name it "Psychreport." In a database, a filename might be "AccountingPersonnel."

Filenames also have *extension names*. These extensions of usually three letters are added after a period following the filename—for example, the *.doc* in *Psychreport.doc* is recognized by Microsoft Word as a "document." Extensions are usually inserted automatically by the application software.

When you look up the filenames listed on your hard drive, you will notice a number of extensions, such as *.doc*, *.exe*, and *.com*. There are many kinds of files, but two principal ones are *program files* and *data files*.

- **Program files: _Program files_ are files containing software instructions.** Examples are word processing or spreadsheet programs, which are made up of several different program files. The two most important are source program files and executable files.

    Source program files contain high-level computer instructions in the original form written by the programmer. Some source program files have the extension of the language in which they are written, such as *.bas* for BASIC, *.pas* for Pascal, or *.jav* for Java. (The appendix has information about programming languages.)

    For the processor to use source program instructions, they must be translated into an *executable file*, which contains the instructions that tell the computer how to perform a particular task. You can identify an executable file by its extension, *.exe*. You use an executable file by running it—as when you select Microsoft Excel from your on-screen menu and run it. (There are some executable files that you cannot run—other computer programs called *runtime libraries* cause them to execute. These are identified by such extensions as *.dll*, *.drv*, *ocx*, *.sys*, and *.vbx*.)

- **Data files: _Data files_ are files that contain data**—words, numbers, pictures, sounds, and so on. These are the files used in databases. Unlike program files, data files don't instruct the computer to do anything. Rather, data files are there to be acted on by program files. Examples of common extensions in data files are *.txt* (text) and *.xls* (Excel worksheets). Certain proprietary software programs apply their own extensions, such as *.ppt* for PowerPoint and *.mdb* for Access.

Other common types of files are shown in the accompanying box. *(See Panel 7.2.)*

Other Common Types of Files

- *ASCII files:* ASCII is a common binary coding scheme used to represent data in a computer. *ASCII files* are text-only files that contain no graphics and no formatting, such as boldface or italics. This format is used to transfer documents between incompatible computers, such as PC and Macintosh. Such files may use the *.txt* extension.

- *Image (graphic) files:* If ASCII files are for text, *image files* are for digitized graphics, such as art or photographs. They are indicated by such extensions as *.bmp* (bitmap), *.gif* (graphics interchange format), *.jpg*, *.png* (portable network graphics), *.tif* (tagged image file format), and *.wmf.*

- *Audio files: Audio files* contain digitized sound and are used for conveying sound in CD multimedia and over the internet. They have extensions such as *.wav, ,mid,* and *.au.*

- *Animation/video files:* Video files, used for such purposes as conveying moving images over the internet, contain digitized video images. Common extensions are *.avi, .flc, .fli,* and .mpg.

- *Web files: Web files* are files carried over the World Wide Web. Their extensions include *.html, .htm,* and *.xml,* and *.asp* (active server page).

- *Desktop publishing:* File formats that include PostScript commands, which tell a PostScript printer how to print a file and use *.eps* (encapsulated PostScript).

- *Drivers:* Software drivers often have the extension *.drv.*

- *Windows operating system files:* Files such as *Autoexec.bat* and *Config.sys* relate to the operating system setup.

Two Types of Data Files: Master File & Transaction File

Among the several types of data files, two are commonly used to update data in a database: a *master file* and a *transaction file.*

- Master file: The *master file* is a data file containing relatively permanent records that are generally updated periodically. An example of a master file is the address-label file for all students currently enrolled at your college.

- Transaction file: The *transaction file* is a temporary holding file that holds all changes to be made to the master file: additions, deletions, revisions. For example, in the case of the address labels for your college, a transaction file would hold new names and addresses to be added (because over time new students enroll) and names and addresses to be deleted (because students leave). It would also hold revised names and addresses (because students change their names or move). Each month or so, the master file would be updated with the changes called for in the transaction file.

Data Access Methods: Sequential versus Direct Access

The way that a secondary storage device allows access to the data stored on it affects its speed and its usefulness for certain applications. The two main types of data access are *sequential* and *direct.*

- Sequential storage: *Sequential storage* means that data is stored and retrieved in sequence, such as alphabetically. Tape storage falls in the category of sequential storage. Thus, if you are looking for employee number 8888 on a tape, the computer will have to start with 0001, then go past 0002, 0003, and so on, until it finally comes to 8888. This data access method is less expensive than other methods because it uses magnetic tape, which is cheaper than disks. The disadvantage of sequential file organization is that searching for data is slow.

- Direct access storage: *Direct access storage* means that the computer can go directly to the information you want—just as a CD player can go directly to a particular track on a music CD. The data is retrieved (accessed) according to the *key field*. Direct access also uses a *file allocation table (FAT)*, a hidden on-disk table that records exactly where the parts of a given file are stored.

This method of file organization is used with hard disks and other types of disks. It is ideal for applications where there is no fixed pattern to the requests for data—for example, in airline reservation systems or computer-based telephone directory-assistance operations.

If you need to find specific data, direct file access is much faster than sequential access. However, direct file access is also more expensive, for two reasons: (1) the complexity involved in maintaining a file allocation table and (2) the need to use hard-disk technology rather than cheaper, magnetic-tape technology.

Offline versus Online Storage

Whether it's on magnetic tape or on some form of disk, data may be stored either *offline* or *online*.

- Offline: **_Offline storage_ means that data is not directly accessible for processing until the tape or disk it is stored on has been loaded onto an input device.** That is, the storage is not under the direct, immediate control of the central processing unit. The data is gathered and processed in batches at periodic intervals, such as at the end of every day or once a week; this is called *batch processing.*

- Online: **_Online storage_ means that stored data is randomly (directly) accessible for processing.** That is, storage is under the direct, immediate control of the central processing unit. You need not wait for a tape or disk to be loaded onto an input device. *Real-time* processing is done with data on online storage devices.

For processing to be online, the storage must be online and fast. This nearly always means storage on disk (direct access storage) rather than magnetic tape (sequential storage).

QuickCheck

Describe the data storage hierarchy and the concept of a key field.

Distinguish program files from data files.

List other types of files. What are their extension names?

Distinguish sequential from direct access.

How are offline and online storage different?

7.2 Database Management Systems

KEY QUESTION

What are the two types of database access?

As we said earlier, a *database* is an organized collection of related (integrated) files. A database may be small, contained entirely within your own personal computer, or it may be massive, available through online connections. Such massive databases are of particular interest because they offer phenomenal resources that until recently were unavailable to most ordinary computer users.

In the 1950s, when commercial use of computers was just beginning, a large organization would have different files for different purposes. For example, a university might have one file for course grades, another for student

Feline phrasing. The toy maker Takara of Japan has marketed a "cat's words translator," which uses a database of cat voices to output cat "phrases." Humans can use these translators to supposedly communicate with their cats.

records, another for tuition billing, and so on. In a corporation, people in the accounting, order-entry, and customer-service departments all had their own separate files. Thus, if an address had to be changed, for example, each file would have to be updated separately. The database files were stored on magnetic tape and had to be accessed in sequence in what was called a *file-processing system*. Later, magnetic-disk technology came along, allowing any file to be accessed randomly. This permitted the development of new technology and new software: the database management system. **A _database management system (DBMS)_, or *database manager*, refers to software written specifically to control the structure of a database and access to the data.** In a DBMS, an address change need be entered only once, and the updated information is then available in any relevant file.

Two Main Types of Database Access

Databases can be set up to serve people in different ways.

- **Individual databases:** _Individual databases_, **or *single-user databases*, are collections of integrated files used by one person.** As we discussed in Chapter 3, microcomputer users can set up their own individual databases using popular database management software; the information is stored on the hard drives of their personal computers. Today the principal database programs are Microsoft Access, Corel Paradox, Elibrium's MyDatabase, and FileMaker Pro. Such so-called low-end database programs are used, for example, by graduate students to conduct research, by salespeople to keep track of clients, by purchasing agents to monitor orders, by coaches to keep watch on other teams and players, and by home microcomputer users to maintain holiday card lists, hobby collection inventories, and inventories of valuables.

  Personal information managers (PIMs) (p. 119) are small individual databases: They can help you keep track of and manage information you use on a daily basis, such as addresses, telephone numbers, appointments, to-do lists, and miscellaneous notes. Popular PIMs are Microsoft Outlook, Lotus Organizer, and askSam.

  Spreadsheet programs such as Excel also provide some simple data-management functions.

- **Multiuser databases:** **A _shared database_, or *centralized database*, is a client/server network** (p. 237) **shared by many users in one company or organization in one location.** The organization owns the database, which may be stored on a server such as a mainframe (p. 9). Users on computers with client software are linked to the database via a client/server arrangement on a local area network (LAN) or wide area network (WAN) (p. 236).

A *distributed database*, or *peer-to-peer (P2P) network* (p. 238), **is shared by many users but is stored on different computers operating as equals in different locations.** The internet Domain Name System (p. 54) is an example of a distributed database. If you spend any time on the internet sending email or visiting the web, you use domain-name servers. Every time you use a domain name, you use the internet's DNS database servers to translate the human-readable domain name into the machine-readable IP address (p. 51). Without the DNS distributed database, the internet would shut down.

Both of these types of databases are much larger and more heavily used than individual databases. They use high-end DBMS software such as IBM's DB2, Microsoft SQL Server, Oracle 9*i* Database, or Sybase Adaptive Server Enterprise, which are designed to handle up to billions of records and as many as hundreds of transactions each second. Some of these databases are available only to organization members, and some are open to the public, for free or for a subscription fee. For example, subscribers to Factiva may use the Dow Jones Publishing website to access the company's database and research its publications. Certain fee-based public databases are specialized, such as Lexis, which gives lawyers access to local, state, and federal laws, or Nexis, which gives journalists access to published articles in a range of newspapers. The U.S. government provides a great deal of free information, such as economic figures from the Bureau of Labor Statistics.

7.3 Database Models

KEY QUESTION
What are four types of database models?

Just as files can be organized in different ways, so databases can be organized in ways that best fit their use. Older, arrangements are the *hierarchical* and the *network* models, introduced in the 1960s. New models include *relational* and *object-oriented*.

Hierarchical Database

In a *hierarchical database*, **fields or records are arranged in related groups resembling a family tree, with child (lower-level) records subordinate to parent (higher-level) records.** The parent record at the top of the database is called the *root record. (See ● Panel 7.3.)*

The hierarchical database is the oldest and simplest of the four models. It lent itself well to the tape storage systems used by mainframes in the 1970s. It is still used in some types of passenger reservation systems. In hierarchical databases, accessing or updating data is very fast, because the relationships have been predefined. However, because the structure must be defined in advance, it is quite rigid. There can be only one parent per child, and no relationships among the child records are possible. Moreover, adding new fields to database records requires that the entire database be redefined. A new database model was needed to address the problems of data redundancy and complex data relationships.

Network Database

The network database was in part developed to solve some of the problems of the hierarchical database model. **A *network database* is similar to a hierarchical database, but each child record can have more than one parent record.** *(See ● Panel 7.4.)* Thus, a child record, which in network database

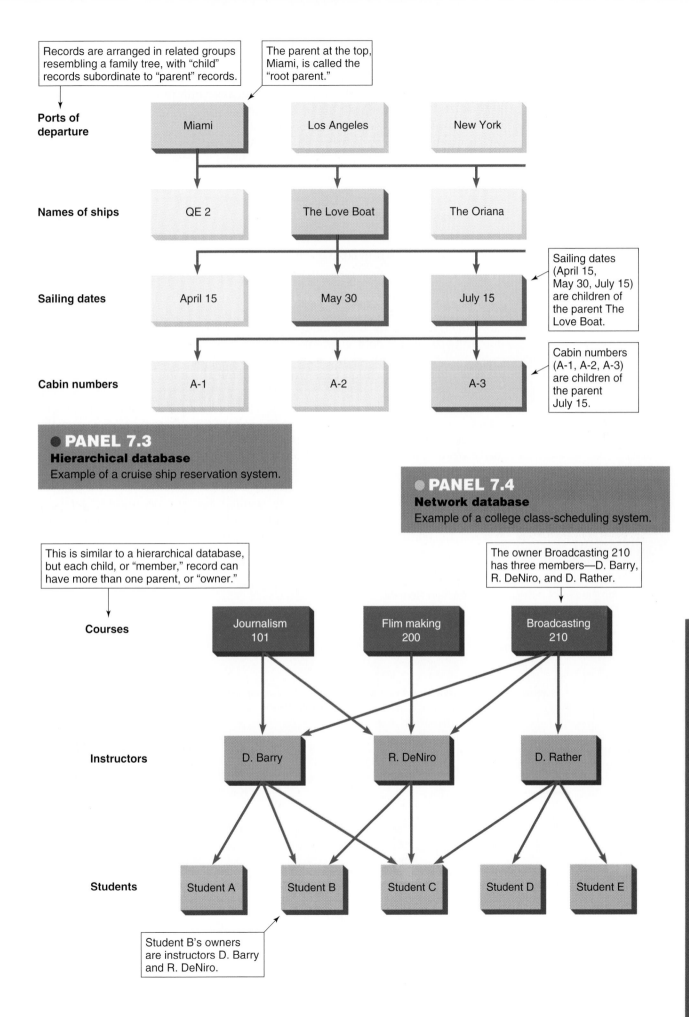

Records are arranged in related groups resembling a family tree, with "child" records subordinate to "parent" records.

The parent at the top, Miami, is called the "root parent."

Ports of departure

Miami   Los Angeles   New York

Names of ships

QE 2   The Love Boat   The Oriana

Sailing dates

April 15   May 30   July 15

Sailing dates (April 15, May 30, July 15) are children of the parent The Love Boat.

Cabin numbers

A-1   A-2   A-3

Cabin numbers (A-1, A-2, A-3) are children of the parent July 15.

● **PANEL 7.3**
Hierarchical database
Example of a cruise ship reservation system.

● **PANEL 7.4**
Network database
Example of a college class-scheduling system.

This is similar to a hierarchical database, but each child, or "member," record can have more than one parent, or "owner."

The owner Broadcasting 210 has three members—D. Barry, R. DeNiro, and D. Rather.

Courses

Journalism 101   Flim making 200   Broadcasting 210

Instructors

D. Barry   R. DeNiro   D. Rather

Students

Student A   Student B   Student C   Student D   Student E

Student B's owners are instructors D. Barry and R. DeNiro.

Files, Databases, & E-Commerce

259

terminology is called a *member*, may be reached through more than one parent, which is called an *owner*.

Also used principally with mainframes, the network database is more flexible than the hierarchical arrangement, because different relationships may be established between different branches of data. However, it still requires that the structure be defined in advance, and, as with the hierarchical model, the user must be very familiar with the structure of the database. Moreover, there are limits to the number of possible links among records. Although the network database was an improvement over the hierarchical database, some people in the database community believed there must be a better way to manage large amounts of data.[3]

Relational Database

More flexible than hierarchical and network database models, the **_relational_** **_database_** **relates, or connects, data in different files through the use of a key, or common data element** (p. 112). *(See ● Panel 7.5.)* In this arrangement—developed in 1970 by E. F. Codd—there are no access paths down through a hierarchy. Instead, data elements are stored in different tables made up of rows and columns. In database terminology, the tables are called *relations* (files), the rows are called *tuples* (records), and the columns are called *attributes* (fields). The physical order of the records or fields in a table is completely immaterial. Each record in the table is identified by a field—the primary key—that contains a unique value. These two characteristics allow the data in a relational database to exist independently of the way it is physically stored on the computer. Thus a user is not required to know the physical location of a record in order to retrieve its data—as is the case with hierarchical and network databases.[4]

The relational model has become popular for microcomputer database management programs, such as Paradox and Access. Oracle, Informix, and Sybase are relational models used on larger systems.

info!

Who was E. F. Codd? To find out about him and other people who have influenced the development of database technology, go to *www.scsite.com/dc2003/people.htm.*

● **PANEL 7.5**
Relational database
Example of a state department of motor vehicles database.

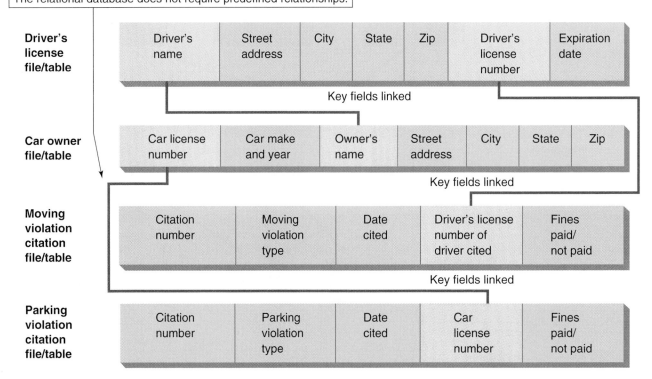

This kind of database relates, or connects, data in different files through the use of a key, or common data element. The relational database does not require predefined relationships.

Driver's license file/table

Driver's name	Street address	City	State	Zip	Driver's license number	Expiration date

Key fields linked

Car owner file/table

Car license number	Car make and year	Owner's name	Street address	City	State	Zip

Key fields linked

Moving violation citation file/table

Citation number	Moving violation type	Date cited	Driver's license number of driver cited	Fines paid/ not paid

Key fields linked

Parking violation citation file/table

Citation number	Parking violation type	Date cited	Car license number	Fines paid/ not paid

Object-Oriented Database

Traditional database models, including the relational model, have worked well in traditional business situations. However, they fall short in areas such as engineering design and manufacturing, scientific experiments, telecommunications, geographic information systems, and multimedia.[5] The object-oriented database model was developed to meet the needs of these applications. **An _object-oriented database_ uses "objects," software written in small, reusable chunks, as elements within database files.** An *object* consists of (1) data in any form, including graphics, audio, and video, and (2) instructions on the action to be taken on the data.

An object-oriented database is a multimedia database; it can store more types of data than a relational database can. For example, an object-oriented student database might contain each student's photograph, a "sound bite" of his or her voice, and even a short piece of video, in addition to grades and personal data. Moreover, the object would store operations, called *methods*, the programs that objects use to process themselves. For example, these programs might indicate how to calculate the student's grade-point average or how to display or print the student's record. Examples of object-oriented databases are FastObjects, eXcelon, Objectware, Jeevan, GemStone, and KE Texpress.

QuickCheck

Distinguish between the two main types of database access.

Describe the four basic models of database organization.

7.4 Databases & the New Economy: E-Commerce, Data Mining, & B2B Systems

KEY QUESTION

How are e-commerce, data mining, and business-to-business systems using databases?

At one time there was a difference between the Old Economy and the New Economy. The first consisted of traditional companies—car makers, pharmaceuticals, retailers, publishers. The second consisted of computer, telecommunications, and internet companies (AOL, Amazon, eBay, and a raft of "dot-com" firms). Now, however, Old Economy companies have largely absorbed the new internet-driven technologies, and the differences between the two sectors have dwindled.

One sign of growth is that the number of internet host computers has been almost doubling every year. But the mushrooming of computer networks and the booming popularity of the World Wide Web are only the most obvious signs of the digital economy. Behind them lies something equally important: the growth of vast stores of information in databases.

How are databases underpinning the New Economy? Let us consider three aspects: *e-commerce, data mining*, and *business-to-business (B2B) systems*.

E-Commerce

The internet might have remained a text-based realm, the province of academicians and researchers, had it not been for the creative contributions of Tim Berners-Lee. He was the computer scientist who came up with the coding system (hypertext markup language, p. 64), linkages, and addressing scheme (URLs) that debuted in 1991 as the graphics-laden and multimedia World Wide Web. "It's hard to overstate the impact of the global system he created," states *Time* technology writer Joshua Quittner. "He took a powerful communications system [the internet] that only the elite could use, and turned it into a mass medium."[6]

E-caskets. There seem to be no limits on the uses of e-commerce.

The arrival of the web quickly led to ***e-commerce*, or *electronic commerce*, the buying and selling of products and services through computer networks.** By 2004, worldwide e-commerce revenues were expected to total $2.7 trillion, according to one marketing firm.[7] Indeed, online shopping is growing even faster than the increase in computer use, which has been fueled by the falling price of personal computers. Among the best-known e-firms are bookseller Amazon.com; auction network eBay; and Priceline.com, which lets you name the price you're willing to pay for airline tickets and hotel rooms.

Probably the foremost example of e-commerce is Amazon.com.[8] In 1994, seeing the potential for electronic retailing on the World Wide Web, Jeffrey Bezos left a successful career on Wall Street to launch an online bookstore called Amazon.com. Why the name "Amazon"?

"Earth's biggest river, Earth's biggest bookstore," said Bezos in a 1996 interview. "The Amazon River is ten times as large as the next largest river, which is the Mississippi, in terms of volume of water. Twenty percent of the world's fresh water is in the Amazon River Basin, and we have six times as many titles as the world's largest physical bookstore."[9] A more hardheaded reason is that, according to consumer tests, words starting with "A" show up on search-engine lists first.

Still, Bezos realized that no bookstore with four walls could possibly stock the more than 2.5 million titles that are now active and in print. Moreover, he saw that an online bookstore wouldn't have to make the same investment in retail clerks, store real estate, or warehouse space (in the beginning, Amazon.com ordered books from the publisher *after* it took the book buyer's order), so it could pass savings along to customers in the form of discounts. In addition, he appreciated that there would be opportunities to obtain demographic information about customers in order to offer personalized services. For example, Amazon could let customers know of books that might be of interest to them. Such personalized attention is difficult for traditional large bookstores. Finally, Bezos saw that there could be a good deal of online interaction: Customers could post reviews of books they read and could reach authors by email to provide feedback. All this was made possible on the web by the recording of information on giant databases.

Amazon.com sold its first book in July 1995, and by the end of 2002 had revenues of $3.93 billion.[10] What began as Earth's biggest bookstore also has rapidly become Earth's biggest anything store, offering CDs, DVDs, videos, electronics, toys, tools, home furnishings, clothing, prescription drugs, and film-processing services. For a long time the company put market share ahead of profits, but now it's focusing on profits. The lasting impact of Amazon's trail blazing is clear from the surge of Old Economy "brick-and-mortar" companies into the online sector.

Data Mining

A personal database, such as the address list of friends you have on your microcomputer, is generally small. But some databases are almost unimaginably vast, involving records for millions of households and trillions of bytes of data. Some record-keeping activities require the use of so-called massively parallel database computers that cost $1 million or more. "These machines gang together scores or even hundreds of the fastest microprocessors around," says one description, "giving them the oomph to respond in minutes to complex database queries."[11]

These large-scale efforts go under the name "data mining." ***Data mining (DM)* is the computer-assisted process of sifting through and analyzing vast amounts of data in order to extract meaning and discover new knowledge.** The purpose of DM is to describe past trends and predict future trends. Thus, data-mining tools might sift through a company's immense collections of customer, marketing, production, and financial data and identify what's worth noting and what's not.

Some applications of data mining:[12]

- **Marketing:** Marketers use DM tools to mine point-of-sale databases of retail stores, which contain facts (such as prices, quantities sold, dates of sale) for thousands of products in hundreds of geographic areas. By understanding customer preferences and buying patterns, marketers hope to target consumers' individual needs.

- **Health:** A coach in the U.S. Gymnastics Federation used a DM system (called *IDIS*) to discover what long-term factors contributed to athletes' performance, so as to know what problems to treat early on. A Los Angeles hospital used the same tool to see what subtle factors affect success and failure in back surgery. Another system helps health care organizations pinpoint groups whose costs are likely to increase in the near future, so that medical interventions can be made.

- **Science:** DM techniques are being employed to find new patterns in genetic data, molecular structures, global climate changes, and more. For instance, one DM tool (called *SKICAT*, for "SKy Image CATaloging") is being used to catalog more than 50 million galaxies, which will be reduced to a 3-terabyte galaxy catalog.

Clearly, short-term payoffs can be dramatic. One telephone company, for instance, mined its existing billing data to identify 10,000 supposedly "residential" customers who spent more than $1,000 a month on their phone bills. When it looked more closely, the company found that these customers were really small businesses trying to avoid paying the more expensive business rates for their telephone service.[13] However, the payoffs in the long term could be truly astonishing. Sifting medical-research data or subatomic-particle information may reveal new treatments for diseases or new insights into the nature of the universe.[14]

Business-to-Business (B2B) Systems

In a **_business-to-business (B2B) system_, a business sells to other businesses, using the internet or a private network to cut transaction costs and increase efficiencies.** In 2001, according to U.S. government figures, 93% of e-commerce was B2B, the rest was B2C (business-to-consumer).[15]

One of the most famous examples of B2B is the auto industry online exchange developed by the big three U.S. automakers—General Motors, Ford, and DaimlerChrysler. The companies have been putting their entire system of purchasing, involving more than $250 billion in parts and materials and 60,000 suppliers, on the internet. Already so-called reverse auctions, in which suppliers bid to provide the lowest price, have driven down the cost of parts such as tires and window sealers. This system replaces the old-fashioned bureaucratic procurement process built on phone calls and fax machines and provides substantial cost savings.[16]

Online B2B exchanges have been developed to serve a variety of businesses, from manufacturers of steel and airplanes to convenience stores to olive oil producers.[17] B2B exchanges are expected to help business by moving beyond pricing mechanisms and encompassing product quality, customer support, credit terms, and shipping reliability, which often count for more than price. The name given to this system is the *business web*, or *b-web*, in which suppliers, distributors, customers, and e-commerce service providers use the internet for communications and transactions. In addition, b-webs are expected to provide extra revenue from ancillary services, such as financing and logistics.[18] *(See ● Panel 7.6 on the next page.)*

None of these innovations is possible without databases and the communications lines connecting them.

Databases for marketing.
Harrah's casino empire uses data mining to identify gambling patron preferences for marketing and special promotions.

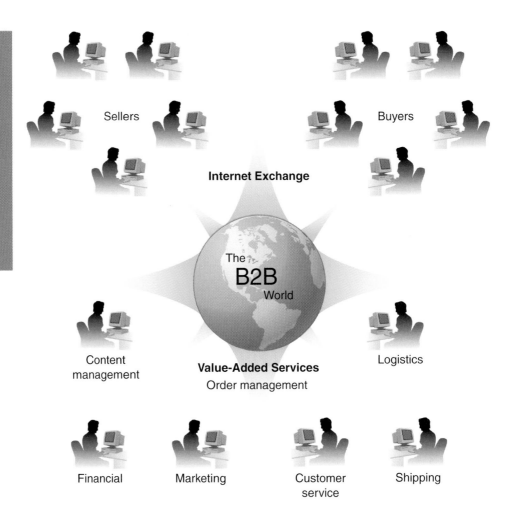

PANEL 7.6

B2B Exchanges

B2B exchanges, which draw on data from various databases, act as centralized online markets for buyers and sellers in specific fields, such as car parts or olive oil. Exchanges are expected to evolve into "b-webs," or business webs, encompassing other factors besides price.

Sellers

Buyers

Internet Exchange

The **B2B** World

Content management

Value-Added Services
Order management

Logistics

Financial   Marketing   Customer service   Shipping

QuickCheck

What is data mining, and how is it used?

Describe e-commerce.

What is a B2B system?

7.5 The Ethics of Using Databases: Concerns About Accuracy & Privacy

KEY QUESTION
What are some ethical concerns about the uses of databases?

The enormous capacities of today's storage devices have given photographers, graphics professionals, and others a new tool—the ability to manipulate images at the pixel level. For example, photographers can easily do *morphing*—transforming one image into another. In morphing, a film or video image is displayed on a computer screen and altered pixel by pixel, or dot by dot. As a result, the image metamorphoses into something else—a pair of lips morphs into the front of a Toyota, for example, or an owl into a baby.

The ability to manipulate digitized output—images and sounds—has brought a wonderful new tool to art. However, it has created some big new problems in the area of credibility, especially for journalism. How can we know that what we're seeing or hearing is the truth? Consider the following issues.

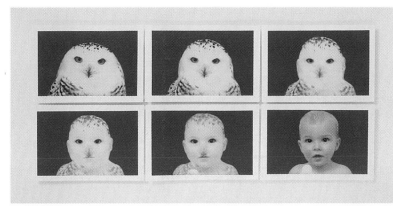

Morphing

Manipulation of Sound

Frank Sinatra's 1994 album *Duets* paired him through technological tricks with singers like Barbra Streisand, Liza Minnelli, and Bono of U2. Sinatra recorded solos in a recording studio. His singing partners, while listening to his taped performance on earphones, dubbed in their own voices. These second voices were recorded not only at different times but often, through distortion-free phone lines, from different places. The illusion in the final recording is that the two singers are standing shoulder to shoulder.

Newspaper columnist William Safire called *Duets* "a series of artistic frauds." Said Safire, "The question raised is this: When a performer's voice and image can not only be edited, echoed, refined, spliced, corrected, and enhanced—but can be transported and combined with others not physically present—what is performance? . . . Enough of additives, plasticity, virtual venality; give me organic entertainment."[19] Some listeners feel that the technology changes the character of a performance for the better. Others, however, think the practice of assembling bits and pieces in a studio drains the music of its essential flow and unity.

Whatever the problems of misrepresentation in art, however, they pale beside those in journalism. What if, for example, a radio station were to edit a stream of digitized sound so as to misrepresent what actually happened?

Manipulation of Photos

When O. J. Simpson was arrested in 1994 on suspicion of murder, two of the principal American newsmagazines both ran pictures of him on their covers.[20] *Newsweek* ran the mug shot unmodified, as taken by the Los Angeles Police Department. At *Time,* an artist working with a computer modified the shot with special effects as a "photo-illustration." Simpson's image was darkened so that it still looked like a photo but, some critics said, with a more sinister cast to it.

Should a magazine that reports the news be taking such artistic license? Should *National Geographic* in 1982 have photographically moved two Egyptian pyramids closer together so that they would fit on a vertical cover? Was it even right for *TV Guide* in 1989 to run a cover showing Oprah Winfrey's head placed on Ann-Margret's body? In another case, to show what can be done, a photographer digitally manipulated the famous 1945 photo showing the meeting of the leaders of the wartime Allied powers at Yalta. Joining Stalin, Churchill, and Roosevelt are some startling newcomers: Sylvester Stallone and Groucho Marx. The additions are so seamless that it is impossible to tell the photo has been altered. *(See ● Panel 7.7 on the next page.)*

The potential for abuse is clear. "For 150 years, the photographic image has been viewed as more persuasive than written accounts as a form of 'evidence,'" says one writer. "Now this authenticity is breaking down under the assault of technology."[21] Asks a former photo editor of the *New York Times Magazine,* "What would happen if the photograph appeared to be a straightforward recording of physical reality, but could no longer be relied upon to depict actual people and events?"[22]

Many editors try to distinguish between photos used for commercialism (advertising) versus for journalism, or for feature stories versus for news stories. However, this distinction implies that the integrity of photos is only important for some narrow category of news. In the end, it can be argued, altered photographs pollute the credibility of all of journalism.

Files, Databases, & E-Commerce

● PANEL 7.7
Photo manipulation
A cat or a cat-erpillar? A dog with a million-dollar smile. And in a 1945 photo, World War II leaders Joseph Stalin, Winston Churchhill, and Franklin Roosevelt are shown from left to right. Digital manipulation has added Sylvester Stallone standing behind Roosevelt and Groucho Marx seated at right.

Manipulation of Video & Television

◄ethics►

The technique of morphing, used in still photos, takes a massive jump when used in movies, videos, and television commercials. Digital image manipulation has had a tremendous impact on filmmaking. Director and digital pioneer Robert Zemeckis *(Death Becomes Her)* compares the new technology to the advent of sound in Hollywood.[23] It can be used to erase jet contrails from the sky in a western and to make digital planes do impossible stunts. It can even be used to add and erase actors.

Films and videotapes are widely thought to accurately represent real scenes (as evidenced by the reaction to the amateur videotape of the 1992 Rodney King beating by police in Los Angeles). Thus, the possibility of digital alterations raises some real problems. Videotapes supposed to represent actual events could easily be doctored. Another concern is for film archives: Because digital videotapes suffer no loss in resolution when copied, there are no "generations." Thus, it will be impossible for historians and archivists to tell whether the videotape they're viewing is the real thing or not.[24]

Indeed, it is possible to create virtual images during live television events. These images—such as a Coca-Cola logo in the center of a soccer field—don't exist in reality but millions of viewers see them on their TV screens.[25]

Virtual advertising. The oil company 76's logo doesn't really appear on this wall, but on TV it looks as though it does.

Accuracy & Completeness

Databases—including public data banks such as Nexis/Lexis—can provide you with more facts and faster facts but not always better facts. Penny Williams, professor of broadcast journalism at Buffalo State College in New York and formerly a television anchor and reporter, suggests five limitations to bear in mind when using databases for research:[26]

- **You can't get the whole story:** For some purposes, databases are only a foot in the door. There may be many facts or facets of the topic that are not in a database. Reporters, for instance, find a database is a starting point. It may take intensive investigation to get the rest of the story.

- **It's not the gospel:** Just because you see something on a computer screen doesn't mean it's accurate. Numbers, names, and facts must be verified in other ways.

- **Know the boundaries:** One database service doesn't have it all. For example, you can find full text articles from the *New York Times* on Lexis/Nexis, from the *Wall Street Journal* on Factiva, and from the *San Jose Mercury News* on America Online, but no service carries all three.

- **Find the right words:** You have to know which keywords (search words) to use when searching a database for a topic. As Lynn Davis, a professional researcher with ABC News, points out, if you're searching for stories on guns, the keyword "can be guns, it can be firearms, it can be handguns, it can be pistols, it can be assault weapons. If you don't cover your bases, you might miss something."[27]

- **History is limited:** Most public databases, Davis says, have information going back to 1980, and a few into the 1970s, but this poses problems if you're trying to research something that happened or was written about earlier.

Matters of Privacy

ethics

***Privacy* is the right of people not to reveal information about themselves.** Who you vote for in a voting booth and what you say in a letter sent through the U.S. mail are private matters. However, the ease of pulling together information from databases and disseminating it over the internet has put privacy under extreme pressure.

As you've no doubt discovered, it's no trick at all to get your name on all kinds of mailing lists. Theo Theoklitas, for instance, received applications for credit cards, invitations to join video clubs, and notification of his finalist status in Ed McMahon's $10 million sweepstakes. Theo is a black cat who's been getting mail ever since his owner sent in an application for a rebate on cat food. Once you're in one database, clearly, your name seems to migrate to others. Retired language-school owner Paul Kameny, 64, of San Francisco, along with his wife and two grown children, received 217 credit card solicitations in 2002, or about four a week, worth somewhere between $2.7 million and $8.5 million in credit. "This is criminal," said Kameny. "Banks are doing everything they can to saddle people with debt."[28]

Over the years, concerns about privacy have led to the enactment of a number of laws to protect individuals from invasions of privacy. *(See ● Panel 7.8 on the next page.)*

info!

The following websites offer ways to guard your privacy:
www.epic.org
www.privacyfoundation.org
www.eff.org
www.ncinet.org/essentials/ privacy.html
www.ftc.gov/privacy/ index.html
www.junkbusters.com
www.kidsprivacy.org
www.spamfree.org

Important Federal Privacy Laws

Freedom of Information Act (1970): Gives you the right to look at data concerning you that is stored by the federal government. A drawback is that sometimes a lawsuit is necessary to pry it loose.

Fair Credit Reporting Act (1970): Bars credit agencies from sharing credit information with anyone but authorized customers. Gives you the right to review and correct your records and to be notified of credit investigations for insurance or employment. A drawback is that credit agencies may share information with anyone they reasonably believe has a "legitimate business need." Legitimate is not defined.

Privacy Act (1974): Prohibits federal information collected about you for one purpose from being used for a different purpose. Allows you the right to inspect and correct records. Federal agencies share information anyway.

Family Educational Rights and Privacy Act (1974): Gives students and their parents the right to review, and to challenge and correct, students' school and college records; limits sharing of information in these records.

Right to Financial Privacy Act (1978): Sets strict procedures that federal agencies must follow when seeking to examine customer records in banks; regulates financial industry's use of personal financial records. A drawback is that the law does not cover state and local governments.

Privacy Protection Act (1980): Prohibits agents of federal government from making unannounced searches of press offices if no one there is suspected of a crime.

Cable Communications Policy Act (1984): Restricts cable companies in the collection and sharing of information about their customers.

Computer Fraud and Abuse Act (1984): Allows prosecution for unauthorized access to computers and databases. A drawback is that people with legitimate access can still get into computer systems and create mischief without penalty.

Electronic Communications Privacy Act (1986): Makes eavesdropping on private conversations illegal without a court order.

Computer Security Act (1987): Makes actions that affect the security of computer files and telecommunications illegal.

Computer Matching and Privacy Protection Act (1988): Regulates computer matching of federal data; allows individuals a chance to respond before government takes adverse actions against them. A drawback is that many possible computer matches are not affected, such as those done for law enforcement or tax reasons.

Video Privacy Protection Act (1988): Prevents retailers from disclosing video-rental records without the customer's consent or a court order.

Telephone Consumer Protection Act (1991): Restricts the activities of telemarketing salespeople.

Cable Act (1992): Extends to cellphone and wireless services the privacy protections of the Cable Communications Policy Act of 1984.

Computer Abuse Amendments Act (1994): Outlaws transmission of harmful computer codes such as worms and viruses.

National Information Infrastructure Protection Act (1996): Provides penalties for trespassing of computer systems, threats made to networks, and theft of information across state lines.

No Electronic Theft (NET) Act (1997): Eliminates legal loophole that enabled people to give away copyrighted material.

Child Online Protection Act (COPA) (1998): Penalties for commercial firms that knowingly distribute materials harmful to minors.

Identity Theft and Assumption Deterrence Act (1998): Makes identity theft a Federal crime with penalties up to 15 years' imprisonment and a maximum fine of $250,000.

Children's Online Privacy Protection Act (COPPA) (2000): Requires online sites that attract young children to get permission from parents before asking for names, locations, and other details.

Health Insurance Portability and Accountability Act (2003): Requires patients' consent before doctors, hospitals, health plans, and others disclose patient data to employers, marketers, or life-insurance firms.

● PANEL 7.8
Privacy laws
Important federal privacy laws

PRACTICAL ACTION BOX
Preventing Your Identity from Getting Stolen

One day, Kathryn Rambo, 28, of Los Gatos, California, learned that she had a new $35,000 sports utility vehicle listed in her name, along with five credit cards, a $3,000 loan, and even an apartment—none of which she'd asked for. "I cannot imagine what would be weirder, or would make you angrier, than having someone pretend to be you, steal all this money, and then leave you to clean up all their mess later," said Rambo, a special-events planner.[a] Added to this was the eerie matter of constantly having to prove that she was, in fact, herself: "I was going around saying, 'I am who I am!'"[b]

Identity Theft: Stealing Your Good Name—and More

Theft of identity (TOI) is a crime in which thieves hijack your very name and identity and use your good credit rating to get cash or to buy things. To begin, all they need is your full name and Social Security number. Using these, they tap into internet databases and come up with other information—your address, phone number, employer, driver's license number, mother's maiden name, and so on. Then they're off to the races, applying for credit everywhere.

In Rambo's case, someone had used information lifted from her employee-benefits form. The spending spree went on for months, unbeknownst to her. The reason it took so long to discover the theft was that Rambo never saw any bills. They went to the address listed by the impersonator, a woman, who made a few payments to keep creditors at bay while she ran up even more bills. For Rambo, straightening out the mess required months of frustrating phone calls, time off from work, court appearances, and legal expenses.

How Does Identity Theft Start?

Identity theft typically starts in one of several ways:[c]

- *Wallet or purse theft:* There was a time when a thief would steal a wallet or purse, take the cash, and toss everything else. No more. Everything from keys to credit cards can be parlayed into further thefts.

- *Mail theft:* Thieves also consider mailboxes fair game. The mail will yield them bank statements, credit-card statements, new checks, tax forms, and other personal information.

- *Mining the trash:* You might think nothing of throwing away credit-card offers, portions of utility bills, or old canceled checks. But "dumpster diving" can produce gold for thieves. Credit-card offers, for instance, may have limits of $5,000 or so.

- *Telephone solicitation:* Prospective thieves may call you up and pretend to represent a bank, credit-card company, government agency, or the like in an attempt to pry loose essential data about you.

- *Insider access to databases:* You never know who has, or could have, access to databases containing your personnel records, credit records, car-loan applications, bank documents, and so on. This is one of the harder TOI methods to guard against.

What to Do Once Theft Happens

If you're the victim of a physical theft (or even loss), as when your wallet is snatched, you should immediately contact—first by phone, and then in writing—all your credit-card companies, other financial institutions, the Department of Motor Vehicles, and any other organization whose cards you use that are now compromised. Be sure to call utility companies—telephone, electricity, and gas; identity thieves can run up enormous phone bills. Also call the local police and your insurance company to report the loss.

It's important to notify financial institutions within two days of learning of your loss because then you are legally responsible for only the first $50 of any theft. If you become aware of fraudulent transactions, immediately contact the fraud units of the three major credit bureaus. *(See ● Panel 7.9.)*

If your Social Security number has been fraudulently used, alert the Social Security Administration (800-772-1213). It's possible, as a last resort, to have your Social Security Number changed.

If you have a check guarantee card that was stolen, if your checks have been lost, or if a new checking account has been opened in your name, there are two organizations to notify so that payment on any fraudulent checks will be denied. They are Telecheck (800-366-2424) and National Processing Company (800-526-5380).

If your mail has been used for fraudulent purposes or if an identity thief filed a change of address form, look in the phone directory under U.S. Government Postal Service for the local postal inspector's office.

● PANEL 7.9
The three major credit bureaus

Equifax	Experian	TransUnion
To check your credit report: 800-685-1111	To check your credit report: 800-397-3742	To check your credit report: 800-888-4213
www.equifax.com	*www.experian.com*	*www.tuc.com*

How to Prevent Identity Theft

One of the best ways to keep your finger on the pulse of your financial life is, on a regular basis—once a year, say—to get a copy of your credit report from one or all three of the main credit bureaus. This will show you whether there is any unauthorized activity. Reports cost $8.

In addition, there are some specific measures you can take to guard against personal information getting into the public realm.

- *Check your credit-card billing statements:* If you see some fraudulent charges, report them immediately. If you don't receive your statement, call the creditor first. Then call the post office to see if a change of address has been filed under your name.

- *Treat credit cards and other important papers with respect:* Make a list of your credit cards and other important documents and a list of numbers to call if you need to report them lost. (You can photocopy the cards front and back, but make sure the numbers are legible.)

  Carry only one or two credit cards at a time. Carry your Social Security card, passport, or birth certificate only when needed.

  Don't dispose of credit-card receipts in a public place.

Don't give out your credit-card numbers or Social Security number over the phone, unless you have some sort of trusted relationship with the party on the other end.

Tear up credit-card offers before you throw them away.

Keep tax records and other financial documents in a safe place.

- *Treat passwords with respect:* Memorize passwords and PINs. Don't use your birth date, mother's maiden name, or similar common identifiers, which thieves may be able to guess.

- *Treat checks with respect:* Pick up new checks at the bank. Shred canceled checks before throwing them away. Don't let merchants write your credit-card number on the check.

- *Watch out for "shoulder surfers" when using phones and ATMs:* When using PINs and passwords at public telephones and automated teller machines, shield your hand so that anyone watching through binoculars or using a video camera—"shoulder surfers"—can't read them.

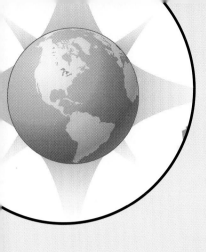

Summary

bit (p. 252, KQ 7.1) In the binary system, short for "binary digit." Why it's important: The bit is the smallest unit of data the computer can store in a database—represented by 0 for off or 1 for on.

business-to-business (B2B) system (p. 263, KQ 7.4) Direct sales between businesses that involve using the internet or a private network to cut transaction costs and increase efficiencies. Why it's important: Business-to-business activity is expected to balloon to a $2.8 trillion industry by 2004.

character (p. 252, KQ 7.1) Also called *byte;* a single letter, number, or special character. Why it's important: Characters—such as A, B, C, 1, 2, 3, #, $, %—are part of the data storage hierarchy.

Type of data	Contains	Example
Database	Several files	*Your personal database* Friends' addresses file, CD titles file, Term papers file, etc.
File	Several records	*Friends' addresses file* Bierce, Ambrose 0001; London, Jack 0234; Stevenson, Robert L. 0081; etc.
Record	Several fields	*Ambrose Bierce's name and address* 13 Fallaway St. San Francisco, CA 94123
Field	Characters (bytes)	*First name field* Ambrose
Character	Bits (0 or 1)	*Letter S* 1110 0010

database (p. 252, KQ 7.1) Logically organized collection of related data designed and built for a specific purpose, a technology for pulling together facts that allows the slicing and dicing and mixing and matching of data. Why it's important: Businesses and organizations build databases to help them keep track of and manage their affairs. In addition, online database services put enormous research resources at the user's disposal.

database management system (DBMS) (p. 257, KQ 7.2) Also called *database manager;* software that controls the structure of a database and access to the data. It allows users to manipulate more than one file at a time. Why it's important: This software enables sharing of data (same information is available to different users); economy of files (several departments can use one file instead of each individually maintaining its own files, thus reducing data redundancy, which in turn reduces the expense of storage media and hardware); data integrity (changes made in the files in one department are automatically made in the files in other departments); and security (access to specific information can be limited to selected users).

data files (p. 254, KQ 7.1) Files that contain data—words, numbers, pictures, sounds, and so on. Why it's important: Unlike program files, data files don't instruct the computer to do anything. Rather, data files are there to be acted on by program files. Examples of common extensions in data files are *.txt* (text) and *.xls* (spreadsheets). Certain proprietary software programs have their own extensions, such as *.ppt* for PowerPoint and *.mdb* for Access.

data mining (DM) (p. 262, KQ 7.4) Computer-assisted process of sifting through and analyzing vast amounts of data in order to extract meaning and discover new knowledge. Why it's important: The purpose of DM is to describe past trends and predict future trends. Thus, data-mining tools might sift through a company's immense collections of customer, marketing, production, and financial data and identify what's worth noting and what's not.

data storage hierarchy (p. 252, KQ 7.1) The levels of data stored in a computer database: bits, bytes (characters), fields, records, and files. Why it's important: Understanding the data storage hierarchy is necessary to understand how to use a database.

direct access storage (p. 255, KQ 7.1) Storage system that allows the computer to go directly to the desired information. The data is retrieved (accessed) according to a unique data identifier called a *key field*. The system also uses a file allocation table (FAT), a hidden on-disk table that records exactly where the parts of a given file are stored. Why it's important: This method of file organization, used with hard disks and other types of disks, is ideal for applications where there is no fixed pattern to the requests for data—for example, in airline reservation systems or computer-based directory-assistance operations. Direct access storage is much faster than sequential access storage.

distributed database (p. 258, KQ 7.2) Database that is stored on different computers operating as equals in different locations connected by a peer-to-peer (P2P) network. Why it's important: Data need not be centralized in one location. The internet Domain Name System uses a distributed system.

e-commerce (p. 262, KQ 7.4) Electronic commerce; the buying and selling of products and services through computer networks. Why it's important: U.S. e-commerce and online shopping are growing even faster than the increase in computer use.

field (p. 252, KQ 7.1) Unit of data consisting of one or more characters (bytes). Examples of fields are your first name, your street address, or your Social Security number. Why it's important: A collection of fields makes up a record. Also *see* key field.

file (p. 252, KQ 7.1) Collection of related records. An example of a file is data collected on everyone employed in the same department of a company, including all names, addresses, and Social Security numbers. Why it's important: A file is the collection of data or information that is treated as a unit by the computer; a collection of related files makes up a database.

filename (p. 254, KQ 7.1) The name given to a file. Why it's important: Files are given names so that they can be differentiated. Filenames also have extension names. These extensions of up to three or four letters are added after a period following the filename—for example, the *.doc* in *Psychreport.doc* is recognized by Microsoft Word as the extension for "document"; *.html* stands for "hypertext markup language." Extensions are usually inserted automatically by the application software.

hierarchical database (p. 258, KQ 7.3) Database in which fields or records are arranged in related groups resembling a family tree, with child (lower-level) records subordinate to parent (higher-level) records. The parent record at the top of the database is called the root record. Why it's important: The hierarchical database is one of the common database structures.

individual database (p. 257, KQ 7.2) Collection of integrated files used by one person. Why it's important: Microcomputer users can set up their own individual databases using popular database management software; the information is stored on the hard drives of their personal computers. Today the principal database programs are Microsoft Access, Corel Paradox, and Lotus Approach. In addition, types of individual databases known as *personal information managers (PIMs)* can help users keep track of and manage information used on a daily basis, such as addresses, telephone numbers, appointments, to-do lists, and miscellaneous notes. Popular PIMs are Microsoft Outlook, Lotus Organizer, and Act.

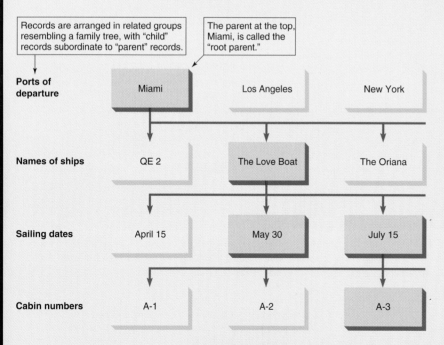

key field (p. 253, KQ 7.1) Also called *key*, *sort key*, *index*, or *keyword*; field that is chosen to uniquely identify a record so that it can be easily retrieved and processed. Why it's important: The primary characteristic of the key field is that it is unique and thus can be used to identify one specific record. For example, if you sort records by age, then the age field is a key. Most database management systems allow you to have more than one key so that you can sort records in different ways. One of the keys is designated the *primary key* and must hold a unique value for each record. The most frequent key field used in the United States is the Social Security Number, but any unique identifier, such as employee number or student number, can be used.

master file (p. 255, KQ 7.1) Data file containing records that are generally updated periodically. Why it's important: Master files contain relatively permanent information used for reference purposes. They are updated through the use of transaction files.

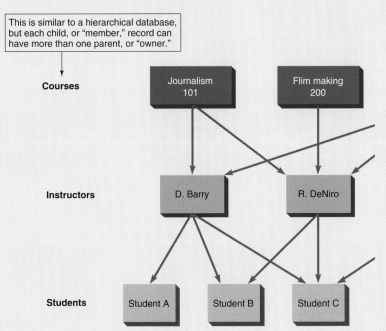

This is similar to a hierarchical database, but each child, or "member," record can have more than one parent, or "owner."

Courses — Journalism 101, Flim making 200

Instructors — D. Barry, R. DeNiro

Students — Student A, Student B, Student C

network database (p. 258, KQ 7.3) Database similar in structure to a hierarchical database; however, each child record can have more than one parent record. Thus, a child record, which in network database terminology is called a *member,* may be reached through more than one parent, which is called an owner. Why it's important: The network database is one of the common database structures.

object-oriented database (p. 261, KQ 7.3) Database that uses "objects," software written in small, reusable chunks, as elements within database files. An object consists of (1) data in any form, including graphics, audio, and video, and (2) instructions on the action to be taken on the data. Why it's important: A hierarchical or network database might contain only numeric and text data. By contrast, an object-oriented database might also contain photographs, sound bites, and video clips. Moreover, the object would store operations, called *methods,* the programs that objects use to process themselves.

offline storage (p. 256, KQ 7.1) System in which stored data is not directly accessible for processing until the tape or disk it's on has been loaded onto an input device. Why it's important: The storage medium and data are not under the direct, immediate control of the central processing unit.

online storage (p. 256, KQ 7.1) System in which stored data is randomly (directly) accessible for processing. Why it's important: The storage medium and data are under the direct, immediate control of the central processing unit. There's no need to wait for a tape or disk to be loaded onto an input device.

privacy (p. 267, KQ 7.5) Right of people not to reveal information about themselves. Why it's important: The ease of pulling together and disseminating information via databases and communications lines has put the basic democratic right of privacy under extreme pressure.

program files (p. 254, KQ 7.1) Files containing software instructions. Why it's important: *Contrast* data files.

record (p. 252, KQ 7.1) Collection of related fields. An example of a record is your name and address and Social Security number. Why it's important: Related records make up a file.

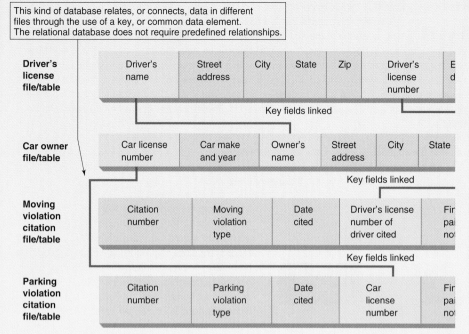

This kind of database relates, or connects, data in different files through the use of a key, or common data element. The relational database does not require predefined relationships.

Driver's license file/table

| Driver's name | Street address | City | State | Zip | Driver's license number | E d |

Key fields linked

Car owner file/table

| Car license number | Car make and year | Owner's name | Street address | City | State |

Key fields linked

Moving violation citation file/table

| Citation number | Moving violation type | Date cited | Driver's license number of driver cited | Fir pai not |

Key fields linked

Parking violation citation file/table

| Citation number | Parking violation type | Date cited | Car license number | Fir pai not |

relational database (p. 260, KQ 7.3) Database structure that relates, or connects, data in different files through the use of a key or common data element. In this arrangement there are no access paths down through a hierarchy. Instead, data elements are stored in different tables made up of rows and columns. In database terminology, the tables are called *relations* (files), the rows are called *tuples* (records), and the columns are called *attributes* (fields). All related tables must have a key that uniquely identifies each row; that is, the key must be in all tables. Why it's important: The relational database is one of the common database structures; it is more flexible than hierarchical and network database models.

sequential storage (p. 255, KQ 7.1) Storage system whereby data is stored and retrieved in sequence, such as alphabetically. Why it's important: An inexpensive form of storage, sequential storage is the only type of storage provided by tape, which is used mostly for archiving and backup. The disadvantage of sequential file organization is that searching for data is slow. *Compare* direct access storage.

shared database (p. 257, KQ 7.2) Also called a *centralized database;* client/server networked database shared by users in one company or organization in one location. The organization owns the database, which may be stored on a server such as a mainframe. Users are linked to the database via a local area or wide area network; the users access the network through terminals or microcomputers using client software. Why it's important: Shared databases, such as those you find when surfing the web, are the foundation for a great deal of electronic commerce, particularly B2B commerce.

transaction file (p. 255, KQ 7.1) Temporary holding file that holds all changes to be made to the master file: additions, deletions, revisions. Why it's important: The transaction file is used to periodically update the master file.

Chapter Review

"I can recognize and recall information."

Self-Test Questions

1. According to the data storage hierarchy, databases are composed of _____, _____, _____, _____, and _____.

2. An individual piece of data within a record is called a _____.

3. _____ is the right of people not to reveal information about themselves.

4. The buying and selling of products and services through computer networks is called _____.

5. _____ files contain software instructions; _____ files contain data.

6. _____ storage means that the computer can go directly to the information you want.

7. A _____ is a collection of related fields.

Multiple-Choice Questions

1. What are .wav, .gif, .txt, .and .asp examples of?
   a. programming languages
   b. file extensions
   c. databases
   d. data files
   e. master files

2. Which of the following database models relates, or connects, data in different files through the use of relations, tuples, and attributes?
   a. hierarchical
   b. network
   c. object-oriented
   d. relational
   e. offline

True/False Questions

T F 1. The use of key fields makes it easier to locate a record in a database.

T F 2. A transaction file contains permanent records that are periodically updated.

T F 3. A database is an organized collection of integrated files.

T F 4. A shared database is stored on different computers in different locations connected by a client/server network.

T F 5. A directory (folder) is a storage place for files in one of your drives.

"I can recall information in my own terms and explain them to a friend."

Short-Answer Questions

1. What is the difference between master files and transaction files?

2. What is data mining?

3. What is the difference between offline and online storage?

4. What is an ASCii file?

5. Explain e-commerce.

"I can apply what I've learned, relate these ideas to other concepts, build on other knowledge, and use all these thinking skills to form a judgment."

Knowledge in Action

1. Interview someone who works with or manages an organization's database. What types of records make up the database? Which departments use it? What database structure is used? What are the types and sizes of storage devices? Are servers used? Was the database software custom-written?

2. Are you comfortable with giving away some of your privacy for increased security? Why or why not? How far would you let the government go in examining people's private lives?

3. Which do you prefer: shopping in a "brick-and-mortar" store or browsing a website via the internet? What could be done to make the physical-store experience better? What could be done to make the internet experience better?

Web Exercises

1. Visit these online stock-trading websites and compare their services:

   www.etrade.com
   www.datek.com
   www.ameritrade.com
   www.schwab.com
   www.fidelity.com
   www.daytrade.com
   www.stocks.com
   www.daytradingstocks.com
   www.nettradedirect.com

2. Visit the following websites to read about the petabyte.

   http://content.techweb.com/wire/story/
       TWB20010226S0026
   www.jamesshuggins.com/h/tek1/how_big.htm
   www.sdsc.edu/GatherScatter/GSfall95/1petabyte.html
   http://siliconvalley.internet.com/news/
       article/0,2198,3531_534901,00.html

3. Visit *www.cisco.com* to learn more about the company that uses its worldwide intranet to connect its distributive databases.

4. Visit these sites about data mining and the search for meaningfulness in large quantities of data.

   www.almaden.ibm.com/software/quest
   www.dmbenchmarking.com
   www.dmg.org
   www.spss.com/datamine

   What do you think the next technology will be for handling and analyzing massive amounts of data?

5. How much information about you is out there? Run various search strings about yourself to see just how private your life is.

6. Call up the tech support phone number for your computer's manufacturer. The first thing they will ask you for is your serial number. This is the key field required to bring up all of your information in their customer database. With that serial number, they should be able to bring up information and troubleshooting issues for each and every part of your PC. They will know everything that came with your PC down to the exact version of the system restore disk.

7. An extensive database featuring photographs and detailed information of each inmate of the Florida Department of Corrections can be found at the following website: *www.dc.state.fl.us/inmateinfo/inmateinfomenu.asp*

   Run several searches of common last names like "smith" to see how this database works. Is it efficient? How would you improve it?

8. DNA Databases: What is a DNA database? Visit the following websites to learn more.

   www.beyond2000.com/news/Mar_03/story_1429.html
   www.ebi.ac.uk/embl/
   www.usnews.com/usnews/nycu/tech/
       articles/021202/2dnabanks.htm
   http://ndbserver.rutgers.edu/
   www.msnbc.com/news/710648.asp?cp1=1

SECURITY

9. Homeland Security Database: Read the following articles regarding the Homeland Security Database.

   www.foxnews.com/story/0,2933,70992,00.html
   www.mrsdutoit.com/2002-11/200211-29.htm
   www.dbta.com/pancha/
   http://ppri.tamu.edu/homeland_security/prepare.htm

S u r v i v a l   T i p

What's an .asp Page?

When it appears in a web page address, *.asp* stands for "active server page." This page is created anew each time, often with fresh data requested by the user or automatically refreshed by the site.

chapter 8

Society & the Digital Age

Challenges & Promises

Chapter Topics & Key Questions

8.1   The Digital Environment: Is There a Grand Design? What are the Internet 2, the 1996 Telecommunications Act, and ICANN?

8.2   Security Issues: Threats to Computers & Communications Systems What are some characteristics of the key security issues for information technology?

8.3   Security: Safeguarding Computers & Communications What are the characteristics of the four components of security?

8.4   Quality-of-Life Issues: The Environment, Mental Health, & the Workplace How does information technology create environmental, mental-health, and workplace problems?

8.5   Economic Issues: Employment & the Haves/Have-Nots How may technology affect the unemployment rate and the gap between rich and poor?

8.6   Artificial Intelligence What are the main areas of artificial intelligence?

8.7   The Promised Benefits of the Digital Age What are some benefits of the digital age?

SECURITY

omputers have invaluable uses for specialized work," says San Francisco historian and commentator Harold Gilliam, "but we need to question the assumption that whatever ails modern society can be cured by more information."[1]

Indeed, he goes on, many users "are hypnotized by the computer's power to summon endless arrays of facts—information without context, data without values, knowledge without perspective."

Such matters take on more urgency since the beginning of the War on Terrorism that started on September 11, 2001, when terrorist-hijacked planes destroyed the World Trade Center Twin Towers in New York City and part of the Pentagon in Washington, D.C. Will the resulting tougher security rules imposed everywhere (including on use of information technology) be beneficial? How can we evaluate the effect of more names in more databases, for instance, on lost privacy and even lost liberty? What kind of context or perspective will help us? One possible tool used by advocates at both ends of the political spectrum is that of *cost-benefit analysis*—to analyze the trade-offs of heightened security on privacy, convenience, and ease of movement. Even if we can't always assign precise dollar amounts, it's important to weigh issues in a way that will prevent security goals from overtaking common sense.[2]

College students continually face issues of information technology about which benefits need to be balanced against costs. For instance, should there be tighter government scrutiny of foreign students, even though this may result in their going to Canada, Australia, and Europe instead of to the United States?[3] Should your Social Security number be used as a key identifier in campus records if there's a chance low-paid clerks might steal it to apply for bogus credit cards?[4] Should laptops and wireless technology be allowed in classrooms if students will mainly use them to web surf instead of attending to the lecture?[5] Should online instructor rating systems be allowed if prospective employers can also access them to see whether you mainly took easy courses?[6]

Such are the examples of the many infotech challenges that confront us. Elsewhere in the book we have considered ergonomics (Chapter 5) and privacy (Chapter 7). In this chapter, we consider some other major issues:

- Is there a grand design for the digital environment?
- Security issues—accidents, natural hazards, terrorist hazards, crime, viruses—and security safeguards
- Quality-of-life issues—environment, mental health, the workplace
- Economic issues—employment and the haves/have-nots

8.1 The Digital Environment: Is There a Grand Design?

KEY QUESTION

What are Internet2, the 1996 Telecommunications Act, and ICANN?

The former buzzword "information superhighway" has lost its luster in favor of other coinages such as the "digital environment." The presumed goal of this worldwide system of computers and telecommunications is to give us lightning-fast (high-bandwidth) voice and data exchange, multimedia, interactivity, and near-universal, low-cost access—and to do so reliably and securely. Whether you're a Russian astronaut aloft in a spacecraft, a Bedouin tribesman in the desert with a PDA/cellphone, or a Canadian work-at-home mother with her office in a spare bedroom, you'll be able, it is hoped, to connect with nearly anything or anybody anywhere. You'll be able to participate in telephony, teleconferencing, telecommuting, teleshopping, telemedicine, tele-education, televoting, and even telepsychotherapy (already available), to name a few possibilities.

What shape will this digital environment take? We consider Internet2, the 1996 Telecommunications Act, and ICANN.

Internet2: The New Internet

Internet2 is a cooperative university/business education and research project that enables high-end users to quickly and reliably move huge amounts of data over high-speed networks. In effect, Internet2 adds "toll lanes" to the older internet to speed things up. The purpose is to advance videoconferencing, research, and academic collaboration—to enable a kind of "virtual university." Presently Internet2 links more than 200 research universities. Requiring state-of-the-art infrastructure, Internet2 runs on Abilene, an internet backbone network.[7]

The 1996 Telecommunications Act

After years of legislative attempts to overhaul the 1934 Communications Act, in February 1996 President Bill Clinton signed into law the Telecommunications Act of 1996, undoing 60 years of federal and state communications regulations. The act is designed to let phone, cable, and TV businesses compete and combine more freely. The purpose of the law was to cultivate greater competition between local and long-distance telephone companies, as well as between the telephone and cable industries. Under this legislation, different carriers can offer the same services—for example, cable companies can offer telephone services, phone companies can offer cable.

Is the law successful? Although its goal was lower prices, better quality, and greater consumer choices in telephone and cable services, until recently business customers were apparently the main beneficiaries. In February 2003, in its most important ruling since 1996, the Federal Communications Commission failed to deregulate broadband competition among long-distance carriers but it also failed to deregulate the local phone market, increasing the uncertainty of the future of a competitive broadband industry. Still, local phone services will try to compete for customer loyalty, resulting in lower rates and combination of wireless and traditional phone service under one phone number. And competition from wireless and cable networks may force local telephone companies to invest in their networks, resulting in faster home internet access.[8]

ICANN: The Internet Corporation for Assigned Names & Numbers

As we described in Chapter 2, _ICANN (Internet Corporation for Assigned Names and Numbers)_ is a private corporation that regulates internet domain names, those addresses that end in .com, .org, .net, and so on, that identify a website. ICANN is not a government body and has no statutory authority; it imposes policies through contracts with its world members.

ICANN got off to a rocky start, but it was hoped that it could evolve into the preeminent regulatory body on the internet, with power extending far beyond the arena of domain names. Nevertheless, the organization has been criticized almost from its 1998 inception for inefficiency. As a result, in March 2003, it outlined what it called ICANN 2.0—a more responsive and agile agency. One of the future improvements includes the creation of top-level domains in other languages, such as Chinese and Arabic. Another is the improvement of the ICANN _Whosis database_, which returns the name and address of any domain name entered (p. 54) (entering _microsoft.com_, for instance, returns the name and address of Microsoft Corp.). A third would be more consultation with the world internet community about the adoption of standards.[9]

8.2 Security Issues: Threats to Computers & Communications Systems

KEY QUESTION
What are some characteristics of the key security issues for information technology?

SECURITY

Security issues go right to the heart of the workability of computer and communications systems. Here we discuss several threats to computers and communications systems.

Errors & Accidents

In general, errors and accidents in computer systems may be classified as *human errors, procedural errors, software errors, electromechanical problems,* and *"dirty data" problems.*

- **Human errors:** Which would you trust—human or computer? If you were a pilot and your plane's collision-avoidance computer tells you to ascend but a human air-traffic controller tells you to descend, which order would you follow? In 2001, a Russian pilot near the Swiss-German border ignored his computer (against mandatory regulations) and complied with erroneous human orders, resulting in a collision with another plane.[10]

  Human errors can be of several types. Quite often, when experts speak of the "unintended effects of technology," what they are referring to are the unexpected things people do with it. Among the ways in which people can complicate the workings of a system are the following:[11]

  (1) Humans often are not good at assessing their own information needs. For example, many users will acquire a computer and communications system that either is not sophisticated enough or is far more complex than they need.

  (2) Human emotions affect performance. For example, one frustrating experience with a computer is enough to make some people abandon the whole system. But throwing your computer out the window isn't going to get you any closer to learning how to use it better.

  (3) Humans act on their perceptions, which in modern information environments are often too slow to keep up with the equipment. Decisions influenced by information overload, for example, may be just as faulty as those based on too little information.

- **Procedural errors:** Some spectacular computer failures have occurred because someone didn't follow procedures. In 1999, the $125 million Mars Climate Orbiter was fed data expressed in pounds, the English unit of force, instead of newtons, the metric unit (about 22% of a pound). As a result, the spacecraft flew too close to the surface of Mars and broke apart.[12]

- **Software errors:** We are forever hearing about "software glitches" or "software bugs." A *software bug* is an error in a program that causes it not to work properly. In 2001, the nonprofit American Medical College Application Service launched a new web-based application service that was supposed to make medical-school applications for 115 medical schools easier and more efficient than the old paper version. Instead, it was plagued by seemingly endless software bugs. One applicant, Yale University student Amit Sachdeva, found himself spending night after night logging on again and again. His routine: Stay awake until 2 a.m. when internet traffic slowed down, plod through a few pages until an error message appeared, then watch as the system froze and crashed. Time for completion: an estimated 24–36 hours, instead of the 5–8 hours the process was supposed to take. "It was incredibly frustrating," said Sachdeva.[13]

- **Electromechanical problems:** Mechanical systems, such as printers, and electrical systems, such as circuit boards, don't always work. They may be faultily constructed, get dirty or overheated, wear out, or become damaged in some other way. Power failures (brownouts and blackouts) can shut a system down. Power surges can also burn out equipment.

- **"Dirty data" problems:** When keyboarding a research paper, you undoubtedly make a few typing errors (which, hopefully, you clean up). So do all the data-entry people around the world who feed a continual stream of raw data into computer systems. A lot of problems are caused by this kind of "dirty data." *Dirty data* is incomplete, outdated, or otherwise inaccurate data.

Natural & Other Hazards

Some disasters do not merely lead to temporary system downtime; they can wreck the entire system. Examples are natural hazards and civil unrest and terrorism.

Natural disaster. Tornados not only are destructive to people; they can also cause total disruption to computer systems.

- **Natural hazards:** Whatever is harmful to property (and people) is harmful to computers and communications systems. This certainly includes natural disasters: fires, floods, earthquakes, tornadoes, hurricanes, blizzards, and the like. If they inflict damage over a wide area, as have ice storms in eastern Canada or hurricanes in Florida, natural hazards can disable all the electronic systems we take for granted. Without power and communications connections, automated teller machines, credit-card verifiers, and bank computers are useless.

- **Civil unrest and terrorism:** Even before September 11, 2001, the United States was not immune to civil unrest, as evidenced by the 2000 riot in Los Angeles after the hometown Lakers won the National Basketball Association championship. Nor were we immune to terrorism, as was seen in the first (1993) bombing of New York's World Trade Center and the 1995 bombing of the Murrah Federal Building in Oklahoma City. But what really focused Americans' attention on terrorism, of course, was the 2001 hijacked-plane crashes into the World Trade Center and the Pentagon.

The Pentagon alone has 650,000 terminals and workstations, 100 WANs, and 10,000 LANs, although the September 11, 2001, terrorist attack damaged only a few of them. More serious was the destruction to companies occupying the top floors of the Twin Towers of the World Trade Center, such as Cantor Fitzgerald, which lost 658 of its approximately 1,000 employees there as well as its main data center.

Terrorism. The results of a bomb blast at the U.S. embassy in Nairobi.

Crimes Against Computers & Communications

A _computer crime_ can be of two types. (1) It can be an illegal act perpetrated against computers or telecommunications, or (2) it can be the use of computers or telecommunications to accomplish an illegal act.

Crimes against information technology include theft—of hardware, of software, of computer time, of cable or telephone services, or of information. Other illegal acts are crimes of malice and destruction. Some examples are as follows:

Laptop on a car seat.
Computers left in cars are temptations for smash-and-grab thieves.

Survival Tip

Reporting Software Pirates

Software pirates can be reported to: _www.siia.net/ piracy/default.asp;_ _www.idsa.com/piracy.html;_ and _www.elspa.com/piracy/ index.asp._

- **Theft of hardware:** Hardware theft can range from shoplifting an accessory in a computer store to removing a laptop or cellular phone from someone's car. Professional criminals may steal shipments of microprocessor chips off a loading dock or even pry cash machines out of shopping-center walls.

- **Theft of software and data—including downloaded music files:** Generally, software theft involves illegal copying of programs, rather than physically taking someone's floppy disks. College students, for example, were quick to discover the internet music service Napster, which in the beginning allowed millions of people to exchange songs for free. (It is now a for-pay service.)

  As illegal file swapping has shifted from client/server services like the old Napster to peer-to-peer services like KaZaA, music companies—which saw music-CD sales shrink by 8.8% in 2002—have decided to go after downloaders by getting their names and addresses from internet service providers or by deploying electronic "robots" to monitor traffic on file-swapping networks and seek out offenders. In early 2003, the Recording Industry Association of America filed suit against four college students accused of trading copyrighted songs.[14]

  Another type of software theft is the copying or counterfeiting of well-known software programs. Such pirates often operate in China, Taiwan, Mexico, Russia, and various parts of Asia and Latin America. In some countries, most of the U.S. microcomputer software in use is thought to be illegally copied.

- **Theft of time and services:** The theft of computer time is more common than you might think. Probably the biggest instance is people using their employer's computer time to play games, do online shopping or stock trading, or dip into web pornography. Some people even operate sideline businesses.

  For years "phone phreaks" have bedeviled the telephone companies. For example, they have found ways to get into company voice-mail systems and then use an extension to make long-distance calls at the company's expense. They have also found ways to tap into cellular phone networks and dial for free. Satellite-TV piracy has also grown at an alarming rate, and firms such as DirecTV and EchoStar have reported soaring losses.[15]

- **Theft of information:** "Information thieves" have infiltrated the files of the Social Security Administration, stolen confidential personal records, and sold the information. On college campuses, thieves have snooped on or stolen private information such as grades. Thieves have also broken into computers of the major credit bureaus and stolen credit information. They have then used the information to charge purchases or have resold it to other people.

- **Crimes of malice and destruction:** Sometimes criminals are more interested in abusing or vandalizing computers and telecommunications systems than in profiting from them. For example, a student at a Wisconsin campus deliberately and repeatedly shut down a university computer system, destroying final projects for dozens of students. A judge sentenced him to a year's probation, and he left the campus.

Crimes Using Computers & Communications

During the 2003 Iraq war, the day after the enormous statue of Saddam Hussein was toppled in downtown Baghdad, war souvenirs were already being offered on eBay, the online auction house. One ad posted was for a full-sized statue of the deposed Iraqi leader, although any buyer was supposed to have to pay to have it shipped to the United States on a B-52. The fraudulent listing was pulled from eBay in about an hour.[16]

Just as a car can be used to perpetrate or assist in a crime, so can information technology. One persistent scam is the so-called *Nigerian letter scam*, the cause of 16,000 complaints in 2002 with the Internet Fraud Complaint Center *(www1.ifccfbi.gov/index.asp)*, which is run by the FBI and the National White Collar Crime Center. Most Nigerian-letter perpetrators claim to have discovered inactive or delinquent accounts that hold vast amounts of money ready to be claimed. Victims are given a chance to receive nonexistent government money, often from the "Government of Nigeria," as long as they pay a fee to help transfer the money to an overseas account.[17]

The most common complaints to the Internet Fraud Complaint Center in 2002 were auction fraud (46% of complaints, although the average amount lost was just $320), nondelivery of promised merchandise, credit-card fraud, and fake investments.[18]

Worms & Viruses

● **PANEL 8.1**
Types of worms and viruses

Worms and viruses are forms of high-tech maliciousness. There are about 57,000 known worms and viruses. *(See ● Panel 8.1.)* And researchers say they typically discover between 500 and 800 new ones every month.[19]

- **Boot-sector virus:** The boot sector is that part of the system software containing most of the instructions for booting, or powering up, the system. The boot sector virus replaces these boot instructions with some of its own. Once the system is turned on, the virus is loaded into main memory before the operating system. From there it is in a position to infect other files. Any diskette that is used in the drive of the computer then becomes infected. When that diskette is moved to another computer, the contagion continues. Examples of boot-sector viruses: AntCMOS, AntiEXE, Form.A, NYB (New York Boot), Ripper, Stoned.Empire.Monkey.

- **File virus:** File viruses attach themselves to executable files—those that actually begin a program. (In DOS these files have the extensions .com and .exe.) When the program is run, the virus starts working, trying to get into main memory and infecting other files.

- **Multipartite virus:** A hybrid of the file and boot-sector types, the multipartite virus infects both files and boot sectors, which makes it better at spreading and more difficult to detect. Examples of multipartite viruses are Junkie and Parity Boot.

    A type of multipartite virus is the *polymorphic virus*, which can mutate and change form just as human viruses can. Such viruses are especially troublesome because they can change their profile, making existing antiviral technology ineffective.

    A particularly sneaky multipartite virus is the *stealth virus*, which can temporarily remove itself from memory to elude capture. An example of a multipartite, polymorphic stealth virus is One Half.

- **Macro virus:** Macro viruses take advantage of a procedure in which miniature programs, known as macros, are embedded inside common data files, such as those created by email or spreadsheets, which are sent over computer networks. Until recently, such documents have typically been ignored by antivirus software. Examples of macro viruses are Concept, which attaches to Word documents and email attachments, and Laroux, which attaches to Excel spreadsheet files. Fortunately, the latest versions of Word and Excel come with built-in macro virus protection.

- **Logic bomb:** Logic bombs, or simply bombs, differ from other viruses in that they are set to go off at a certain date and time. A disgruntled programmer for a defense contractor created a bomb in a program that was supposed to go off two months after he left. Designed to erase an inventory tracking system, the bomb was discovered only by chance.

- **Trojan horse:** The Trojan horse covertly places illegal, destructive instructions in the middle of a legitimate program, such as a computer game. Once you run the program, the Trojan horse goes to work, doing its damage while you are blissfully unaware. An example of a Trojan horse is FormatC.

Survival Tip

Keep Antivirus Software Updated

The antivirus software that comes with your computer won't protect you forever. To guard against new worms and viruses, visit the antivirus software maker's website frequently.

A *worm* **is a program that copies itself repeatedly into a computer's memory or onto a disk drive.** Sometimes it will copy itself so often it will cause a computer to crash. Among some famous worms are Code Red, Nimda, Klez, and SQL Slammer. The 2002 worm Klez, dubbed the most common virus ever, spread its damage through Microsoft products by being inside email attachments or part of email messages themselves, so that merely opening an infected message could infect a computer running Outlook or Outlook Express.[20] The 2003 worm called *SQL Slammer* (or *Slammer, SQ hell*, or *Sapphire*), which resembled Code Red, did not affect most home users. However, it did infect computers running Microsoft's database software SQL Server 2000, preventing customers from making withdrawals from ATM machines and interfering with email delivery and web browsing.[21]

A *virus* **is a "deviant" program, stored on a computer floppy drive, hard drive, or CD, that can cause unexpected and often undesirable effects, such as destroying or corrupting data.** The famous email Love Bug (its subject line was I LOVE YOU), which originated in the Philippines in May 2000 and did perhaps as much as $10 billion in damage worldwide, was both a worm and a virus, spreading faster and causing more damage than any other bug before it.[22]

Worms and viruses are passed in two ways:

- **By floppy disk:** The first way is via an infected diskette, perhaps obtained from a friend or a repair person.

- **By the internet or some other network:** The second way is via a network such as the internet, as from email or a downloaded file. This is why, when taking advantage of all the freebie games and other software available online, you should use virus-scanning software to check downloaded files.

The virus usually attaches itself to your hard disk. It might then display annoying messages ("Your PC is stoned—legalize marijuana") or cause Ping-Pong balls to bounce around your screen and knock away text. More seriously, it might add garbage to your files and then erase or destroy your system software. It may evade your detection and spread its havoc elsewhere, since an infected hard disk may well infect every floppy disk used by the system.

If you look in the utility section of any software store, you'll see a variety of virus-fighting programs. *Antivirus software* **scans a computer's hard disk, floppy disks, and main memory to detect viruses and, sometimes, to destroy them.** Such virus watchdogs operate in two ways. First, they scan disk drives for "signatures," characteristic strings of 1s and 0s in the virus that uniquely identify it. Second, they look for suspicious virus-like behavior, such as attempts to erase or change areas on your disks. Examples of antivirus programs are Symantec's Norton AntiVirus, McAfee VirusScan, Panda Antivirus Platinum, and Computer Associates' eTrust EZ Antivirus for Windows, and Virex for Macs.

Computer Criminals

What kind of people are perpetrators of information technology crime? More than 80% may be employees; the rest are outside users, hackers and crackers, and professional criminals.

- **Employees:** Says Michigan State University criminal justice professor David Carter, who surveyed companies about computer crime, "Seventy-five to 80% of everything happens from inside."[23] Most common frauds, Carter found, involved credit cards, telecommunications, employees' personal use of computers, unauthorized access to confidential files, and unlawful copying of copyrighted or licensed software.

Workers may use information technology for personal profit or steal hardware or information to sell. They may also use it to seek revenge for real or imagined wrongs, such as being passed over for promotion. Sometimes they may use the technology simply to demonstrate to themselves they have power over people.

- **Outside users:** Suppliers and clients may also gain access to a company's information technology and use it to commit crimes. This becomes more likely as electronic connections such as intranets and extranets become more commonplace.

- Hackers and crackers: *Hacker* is so overused it has come to be applied to anyone who breaks into a computer system. Some people think it means almost any computer lover. In reality, there is a difference between hackers and crackers, although the term *cracker* has never caught on with the general public.

    The popular press uses the word *hackers* to refer to people who break into computer systems and steal or corrupt data. However, <u>**hackers**</u> **are, in the positive meaning, computer enthusiasts, people who enjoy learning programming languages and computer systems. In the negative meaning, they are people who gain unauthorized access to computer or telecommunications systems, often just for the challenge of it.** Some hackers even believe they are performing a service by exposing security flaws. Whatever the motivation, network system administrators view any kind of unauthorized access as a threat, and they usually try to pursue offenders vigorously. The most flagrant cases of hacking are met with federal prosecution. Former computer science student Ikenna Iffih, who studied at Northeastern University in Boston, could have been sentenced to 20 years in prison for hacking against private and government targets, but under a plea bargain was allowed to serve no more than six months. As a Nigerian national, he also faced deportation.[24]

    <u>*Crackers*</u> **are people who illegally break into computers for malicious purposes—to obtain information for financial gain, shut down hardware, pirate software, or alter or destroy data.** Sometimes you hear of "white-hat" hackers (who aren't malicious) versus "black-hat" hackers (who are). The Federal Bureau of Investigation estimates that cybercrime costs Americans more than $20 billion a year—and that more than 60% of such computer crime goes unreported.

- **Professional criminals:** Members of organized crime rings don't just steal information technology. They also use it the way that legal businesses do—as a business tool, but for illegal purposes. For instance, databases can be used to keep track of illegal gambling debts and stolen goods. Not surprisingly, the old-fashioned illegal booking operation has gone high-tech, with bookies using computers and fax machines in place of betting slips and paper tally sheets.

As information technology crime has become more sophisticated, so have the people charged with preventing it and disciplining its outlaws. Campus administrators are no longer being quite as easy on offenders and are turning them over to police. Industry organizations such as the Software Publishers Association are going after software pirates large and small. (Commercial software piracy is now a felony, punishable by up to five years in prison and fines of up to $250,000 for anyone convicted of stealing at least 10 copies of a program, or more than $2,500 worth of software.) Police departments as far apart as Medford, Massachusetts, and San Jose, California, now have officers patrolling a "cyber beat." They regularly cruise online bulletin boards and chat rooms looking for pirated software, stolen trade secrets, child molesters, and child pornography.

Fake-buck buster. This electronic device can quickly (0.7 second) detect whether a U.S. bill is counterfeit.

Police officers now have in-car computers to run checks on vehicle licenses and on individuals. The central database can tell the officer if the car or the person has outstanding warrants.

8.3 Security: Safeguarding Computers & Communications

KEY QUESTION

What are the characteristics of the four components of security?

SECURI**TY**

The ongoing dilemma of the Digital Age is balancing convenience against security. **_Security_ is a system of safeguards for protecting information technology against disasters, systems failure, and unauthorized access that can result in damage or loss.** We consider four components of security.

Identification & Access

Are you who you say you are? The computer wants to know.

There are three ways a computer system can verify that you have legitimate right of access. Some security systems use a mix of these techniques. The systems try to authenticate your identity by determining (1) what you have, (2) what you know, or (3) who you are.

- **What you have—cards, keys, signatures, badges:** Credit cards, debit cards, and cash-machine cards all have magnetic strips or built-in computer chips that identify you to the machine. Many require that you display your signature, which may be compared with any future signature you write. Computer rooms are always kept locked, requiring a key. Many people also keep a lock on their personal computers. A computer room may also be guarded by security officers, who may need to see an authorized signature or a badge with your photograph before letting you in.

  Of course, credit cards, keys, and badges can be lost or stolen. Signatures can be forged. Badges can be counterfeited.

- **What you know—PINs, passwords, and digital signatures:** To gain access to your bank account through an automated teller machine (ATM), you key in your PIN. **A _PIN (personal identification number)_ is the security number known only to you that is required to access the system.** Telephone credit cards also use a PIN. If you carry either an ATM or a phone card, never carry the PIN written down elsewhere in your wallet (even disguised).

  A _password_ **is a special word, code, or symbol required to access a computer system.** Passwords are one of the weakest security links, says AT&T security expert Steven Bellovin. Passwords (and PINs, too) can be guessed, forgotten, or stolen. To foil a stranger's guesses, Bellovin recommends never choosing a real word or variations of your name, your birth date, or those of your friends or family. Instead you should mix letters, numbers, and punctuation marks in an oddball sequence of no fewer than eight characters.[25]

- **Who you are—physical traits:** Some forms of identification can't be easily faked—such as your physical traits. **_Biometrics_, the science of measuring individual body characteristics,** tries to use these in security devices. _Biometric devices_ authenticate a person's identity by verifying his or her physical or behavioral characteristics. For

example, before University of Georgia students can use the all-you-can-eat plan at the campus cafeteria, they must have their hands read. As one writer describes the system, "a camera automatically compares the shape of a student's hand with an image of the same hand pulled from the magnetic strip of an ID card. If the patterns match, the cafeteria turnstile automatically clicks open. If not, the would-be moocher eats elsewhere."[26]

Such so-called *hand-geometry systems* are only one device for verifying *biometric identifiers*, physical or behavioral characteristics that can be used to authenticate a person's identity. Other devices are *fingerprint scanners, face-recognition systems, iris-recognition systems, voice-verification systems*, and *signature verification systems. (See* ● *Panel 8.2.)*

Encryption

<u>*Encryption*</u> **is the process of altering readable data into unreadable form to prevent unauthorized access.** Encryption is able to use powerful mathematical concepts to create coded messages that are virtually impossible to break. As one article points out, it is easy "to encrypt a message on a simple PC so that the biggest computer in the world couldn't decipher it without spending far more time on the problem than exists in the lifespan of the entire universe."[27]

Encryption is clearly useful for some organizations, especially those concerned with trade secrets, military matters, and other sensitive data. A very sophisticated form of encryption is used in most personal computers and is available with every late-model web browser to provide for secure communications over the internet. In fact, encryption is what has given people confidence to do online shopping or stock trading.

However, from the standpoint of society, encryption is a two-edged sword. For instance, the 2001 attacks on the World Trade Center and Pentagon raised the possibility that the terrorists might have communicated with each other using unbreakable encryption programs. (There is no evidence they did.) Should the government be allowed to read the coded email of overseas terrorists, drug dealers, and other enemies? What about the email of all American citizens?

Protection of Software & Data

Organizations go to tremendous lengths to protect their programs and data. As might be expected, this includes educating employees about making backup disks, protecting against viruses, and so on. Other security procedures include the following:

- **Control of access:** Access to online files is restricted to those who have a legitimate right to access—because they need them to do their jobs. Many organizations have a system of transaction logs for recording all accesses or attempted accesses to data.

- **Audit controls:** Many networks have audit controls for tracking which programs and servers were used, which files opened, and so on. This creates an audit trail, a record of how a transaction was handled from input through processing and output.

- **People controls:** Because people are the greatest threat to a computer system, security precautions begin with the screening of job applicants. Résumés are checked to see if people did what they said they did. Another control is to separate employee functions, so that people are not allowed to wander freely into areas not essential to their jobs. Manual and automated controls—input controls, processing controls, and output controls—are used to check that data is handled accurately and completely during the processing cycle. Printouts, printer ribbons, disks, and other waste that may contain passwords and trade secrets to outsiders are disposed of through shredders or locked trash barrels.

The destruction of the New York City World Trade Center by terrorists in 2001 caused massive recovery problems for the many businesses that had offices there.

Disaster-Recovery Plans

A _disaster-recovery plan_ **is a method of restoring information-processing operations that have been halted by destruction or accident.** "Among the countless lessons that computer users have absorbed in the hours, days, and weeks after the [1993 New York] World Trade Center bombing," wrote one reporter, "the most enduring may be the need to have a disaster-recovery plan. The second most enduring lesson may be this: Even a well-practiced plan will quickly reveal its flaws."[28] The 2001 attack on the World Trade Center reinforced these lessons in a spectacular way as companies had to scramble for new office space.

Mainframe computer systems are operated in separate departments by professionals, who tend to have disaster plans. Whereas mainframes are usually backed up, many personal computers, and even entire local area networks, are not, with potentially disastrous consequences. It has been reported that, on average, a company loses as much as 3% of its gross sales within eight days of a sustained computer outage. In addition, the average company struck by a computer outage lasting more than 10 days never fully recovers.[29]

A disaster-recovery plan is more than a big fire drill. It includes a list of all business functions and the hardware, software, data, and people that support those functions, as well as arrangements for alternate locations. The disaster-recovery plan also includes ways for backing up and storing programs and data in another location, ways of alerting necessary personnel, and training for those personnel.

QuickCheck

How do computer systems try to authenticate your identity?

Describe encryption.

What security procedures are used to protect software and data?

What is a disaster-recovery plan?

8.4 Quality-of-Life Issues: The Environment, Mental Health, & the Workplace

KEY QUESTION

How does information technology create environmental, mental-health, and workplace problems?

The worrisome effects of technology on intellectual-property rights and truth in art and journalism, on censorship, on health matters and ergonomics, and on privacy were explained earlier in this book. Here are some other quality-of-life issues related to information technology.

Environmental Problems

Environmental challenges involving information technology take different forms—specifically, manufacturing by-products, disposal by-products, environmental blight, and possible risks of nanotechnology.

- **Manufacturing by-products:** Many communities are eager to have computer and chip manufacturers locate there because they perceive them to be "clean" industries. But there have been lawsuits charging that the semiconductor industry has knowingly exposed workers to a variety of hazardous toxins, some of which were linked to miscarriages, and there is speculation that others may be linked to cancer and birth defects.[30]

- **Disposal by-products:** What to do with the "e-waste"—hundreds of millions of obsolete or broken PCs, monitors, printers, cellphones, TVs, and other electronic gadgetry? Ninety-one percent of it is discarded, according to the Environmental Protection Agency; only 9% is recycled. Only a scant 20% of dead PCs are recovered for recycling. Much of the electronic waste that winds up in the nation's 2,200 landfills contains large amounts of lead and other toxins that can leach into groundwater or produce dioxins and other cancer-causing agents when burned.[31] The problem is worsening as new computer models are introduced on faster cycles, and the National Safety Council estimates that there will be nearly 500 million obsolete computers in the United States by 2007.[32]

Recycle your computer components; don't hurt the environment by throwing them in the trash.

  Don't always assume you can get a school or local charity to take your old personal computer; some will, but many are tired of being stuck with junk. Fortunately, the Electronic Industries Alliance Consumer Education Initiative offers a website *(www.eiae.org)* that helps consumers locate donation programs and recycling companies.

- **Environmental blight:** Call it "techno-blight." This is the visual pollution represented by the forest of wireless towers, roof antennas, satellite dishes, and all the utility poles topped with transformers and strung with electric, phone, cable-TV, and other wires leading off in all directions. As the nation's electrical grid becomes more pervasive, so, people worry, will the obtrusive, ugly technology in our physical environment. Environmentalists worry about its impact on vegetation and wildlife, such as the millions of birds and bats that collide with cellular towers. Residents worry about the effect on views and property values, although antennas can be made into "stealth towers"—fake water towers, flagpoles, trees, and the like—to blend in better with the environment. Some people worry that there may be unknown health effects.

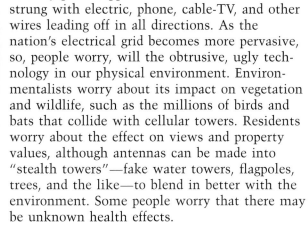

Environmentally friendly cellphone towers disguised as palmtrees and cacti.

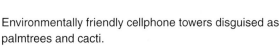

- **Possible risks of nanotechnology:** Although scientists call the fears speculation, some environmentalists worry that the spread of nano-technology—manipulating materials such as carbon, zinc, and gold at the molecular level—could create contaminants whose tiny size makes them ultrahazardous. "If they get in the bloodstream or into the groundwater," says a researcher for ETC Group, an environmental organization, "they could react with other things that are harmful."[33] However, experiments using carbon nanotube molecules, which might replace silicon in ever tinier transistors, have not proved risky in studies of mice and guinea pigs and so probably pose little risk to humans.

Mental-Health Problems

Some of the mental-health problems linked to information technology are the following:

- **Isolation:** A few years ago, a Stanford University survey found that, as people spent more time online, they had less time for real-life rela-tionships with family and friends. "As internet use becomes more widespread," predicted a study coauthor, "it will have an increasingly isolating effect on society."[34] The inclination of heavy internet users to experience isolation, as well as loneliness and depression, was also supported by a 1998 study by Robert Kraut. Three years later, how-ever, the Carnegie Mellon University professor reported the opposite—that the study's subjects experienced *fewer* feelings of lone-liness and isolation. And he found that, for a new group, the more they used computers, the more integrated they were with others, the better their sense of well-being, and the more positive their moods.[35] Indeed, the internet has led to a great many web communities, from cancer survivors to Arab immigrants.

- **Gambling:** Gambling is already widespread in North America, but information technology makes it almost unavoidable. Although gam-bling by wire is illegal in the United States, host computers for inter-net casinos and sports books have been established in Caribbean tax havens. Satellites, decoders, and remote-control devices allow TV viewers to do racetrack wagering from home. In these circumstances, law enforcement is extremely difficult.

- **Stress:** In one survey of 2,802 American PC users, three-quarters of the respondents (ranging in age from children to retirees) said personal computers had increased their job satisfaction and were a key to suc-cess and learning. However, many found PCs stressful: Fifty-nine per-cent admitted getting angry at their PCs within the previous year, and 41% said they thought computers had reduced job opportunities rather than increased them.[36] Another survey found that 83% of cor-porate network administrators reported "abusive and violent behav-ior" by employees toward computers—including smashing monitors, throwing mice, and kicking system units.[37]

Workplace Problems: Impediments to Productivity

First the mainframe computer, then the desktop stand-alone PC, and recently the networked computer were all brought into the workplace for one reason only: to improve productivity. How is it working out? Let's consider three aspects: misuse of technology, fussing with computers, and information over-load.

- **Misuse of technology:** "For all their power," says an economics writer, "computers may be costing U.S. companies tens of billions of dollars a year in downtime, maintenance and training costs, useless game playing, and information overload."[38]

Employees may look busy, as they stare into their computer screens with brows crinkled. But sometimes they're just hard at work playing Quake. Or browsing online malls (forcing corporate mail rooms to cope with a deluge of privately ordered parcels). Or looking at their investments or pornography sites.[39] Indeed, one study found that recreational web surfing accounts for nearly one-third of office workers' time online.[40]

- **Fussing with computers:** Another reason for so much wasted time is all the fussing that employees do with hardware, software, and online connections. One study in the early 1990s estimated microcomputer users wasted 5 billion hours a year waiting for programs to run, checking computer output for accuracy, helping coworkers use their applications, organizing cluttered disk storage, and calling for technical support.[41] And that was before most people had to get involved with making online connections work.

  Comments technology writer Dan Gillmor, "We would never buy a TV that forced us to reboot the set once a month, let alone once a week or every other day."[42] But until recently, this was the current evolutionary stage of the computer age. Windows XP seems to reduce the rebooting frustrations.

- **Information overload:** "It used to be considered a status symbol to carry a laptop computer on a plane," says futurist Paul Saffo. "Now anyone who has one is clearly a working dweeb who can't get the time to relax. Carrying one means you're on someone's electronic leash."[43]

  The new technology is definitely a two-edged sword. Cellphones, pagers, fax machines, and modems may untether employees from the office, but these employees tend to work longer hours under more severe deadline pressure than do their tethered counterparts who stay at the office, according to one study.[44] Moreover, the gadgets that once promised to do away with irksome business travel by ushering in a new era of communications have done the opposite. They have created the office-in-a-bag that allows business travelers to continue to work from airplane seats, hotel desks, and their own kitchen tables.

  To avoid information overload, some people install so-called *Bozo filters*, software for screening out trivial email messages and cellular calls and assigning priorities to the remaining files. But the real change may come as people realize that they need not always be tied to the technological world, that solitude is a scarce resource, and that seeking serenity means streamlining the clutter and reaching for simpler things.

8.5 Economic Issues: Employment & the Haves/Have-Nots

KEY QUESTION

How may technology affect the unemployment rate and the gap between rich and poor?

In recent times, a number of critics have provided a counterpoint to the hype and overselling of information technology to which we have long been exposed. Some critics find that the benefits of information technology are balanced by a real downside. Other critics make the alarming case that technological progress is actually no progress at all—indeed, it is a curse. The two biggest charges (which are related) are, first, that information technology is killing jobs and, second, that it is widening the gap between the rich and the poor.

PRACTICAL ACTION BOX
When the Internet Isn't Productive: Online Addiction & Other Time Wasters

There is a handful of activities that can drain hours of time, putting studying—and therefore college—in serious jeopardy. They include excessive television watching, partying, and working too many hours while going to school. They also include misuse of the computer.

The Great Campus Goof-Off Machine?

"I have friends who have spent whole weekends doing nothing but playing Quake or Warcraft or other interactive computer games," reports Swarthmore College sophomore Nate Stulman, in an article headed "The Great Campus Goof-Off Machine." He goes on: "And many others I know have amassed overwhelming collections of music on their computers. It's the searching and finding they seem to enjoy: some of them have more music files on their computers than they could play in months."[a]

In Stulman's opinion, having a computer in the dorm is more of a distraction than a learning tool for students. "Other than computer science or mathematics majors, few students need more than a word processing program and access to email in their rooms."

Most educators wouldn't banish computers completely from student living quarters. Nevertheless, it's important to be aware that your PC can become a gigantic time sink, if you let it. Reports Rutgers communication professor Robert Kubey: "About 5% to 10% of students, typically males and more frequently first- and second-year students, report staying up late at night using chat lines and email and then feeling tired the next day in class or missing class altogether."[b]

Internet Addiction/Dependency

"A student emails friends, browses the World Wide Web, blows off homework, botches exams, flunks out of school."[c] This is a description of the downward spiral of the "net addict," often a college student—because schools give students no-cost/low-cost linkage to the internet—but it can be anyone. Some become addicted (although until recently some professionals felt *addiction* was too strong a word) to chat groups, some to online pornography, some simply to the escape from real life.[d]

Stella Yu, 21, a college student from Carson, California, was rising at 5 a.m. to get a few hours online before school, logging on to the internet between classes and during her part-time job, and then going home to web surf until 1 a.m. Her grades dropped and her father was irate over her phone bills. "I always make promises I'm going to quit; that I'll just do it for research," she said. "But I don't. I use it for research for 10 minutes, then I spend two hours chatting."[e]

College students are unusually vulnerable to internet addiction, which is defined as "a psychological dependence on the Internet, regardless of type of activity once 'logged on,'" according to psychologist Jonathan Kandell.[f] The American Psychological Association, which officially recognized "pathological internet use" as a disorder in 1997, defines the internet addict as anyone who spends an average of 38 hours a week online.[g] (The average interneter spends $5\frac{1}{2}$ hours on the activity.[h]) More recently, psychologist Keith J. Anderson of Rensselaer Polytechnic Institute found that internet-dependent students, who make up at least 10% of college students, spent an average of 229 minutes a day online for nonacademic reasons, compared with 73 minutes a day for other students. As many as 6% spend an average of more than 400 minutes a day—almost seven hours—using the internet.[i]

What are the consequences of internet addiction disorder? A study of the freshman dropout rate at Alfred University in New York found that nearly half the students who quit the preceding semester had been engaging in marathon, late-night sessions on the internet.[j] The University of California, Berkeley, found some students linked to excessive computer use neglected their course work.[k] A survey by Viktor Brenner of State University of New York at Buffalo found that some internet addicts had "gotten into hot water" with their school for internet-related activities.[l] "Grades decline, mostly because attendance declines," says psychologist Anderson about internet-dependent students. "Sleep patterns go down. And they become socially isolated."

Online Gambling

A particularly risky kind of internet dependence is online gambling. David, a senior at the University of Florida, Gainesville, owed $1,500 on his credit cards as a result of his online gambling habit, made possible by easy access to offshore casinos in cyberspace. He is not alone. A survey of 400 students at Southern Methodist University found that 5% said they gambled frequently via the internet.[m]

Other students do the kind of de facto gambling known as day-trading—buying and selling stocks on the internet. This can be risky, too. "It's a lot like going to a casino," says one finance professor. "You can make or lose money within a few seconds, and there are going to be some people who are addicted to it."[n]

Technology, the Job Killer?

A lights-out factory. The ABA-PGT plastics engineering plant.

Certainly, ATMs do replace bank tellers, E-Z pass electronic systems do replace turnpike-toll takers, and internet travel agents do lure customers away from small travel agencies. Hundreds of companies are replacing service representatives with voice software.[45] In new so-called *lights-out factories*, machines make things—for example, the tiny cutting devices you see mounted on dental-floss containers—even when no one is there; as much as possible is done with no labor.[46] The contribution of technological advances to economic progress is steady, but the contribution to social progress is not purely positive.

But is it true, as technology critic Jeremy Rifkin says, that intelligent machines are replacing humans in countless tasks, "forcing millions of blue-collar and white-collar workers into temporary, contingent, and part-time employment and, worse, unemployment"?[47]

This is too large a question to be fully considered in this book. We can say for sure that the U.S. economy is undergoing powerful structural changes, brought on not only by the widespread diffusion of technology but also by greater competition, increased global trade, the shift from manufacturing to service employment, the weakening of labor unions, more flexible labor markets, more rapid immigration, partial deregulation, and other factors.[48]

A counterargument is that jobs don't disappear, they just change. According to some observers, the jobs that do disappear represent drudgery. "If your job has been replaced by a computer," says Stewart Brand, "that may have been a job that was not worthy of a human."[49]

Gap Between Rich & Poor

"In the long run," says M.I.T. economist Paul Krugman, "improvements in technology are good for almost everyone. . . . Unfortunately, what is true in the long run need not be true over shorter periods."[50] We are now, he believes, living through one of those difficult periods in which technology doesn't produce widely shared economic gains but instead widens the gap between those who have the right skills and those who don't.

More disadvantaged people may have access to computers than ever before, particularly at work, where many computer skills are, in point of fact, not very high tech or demanding. However, it may be a different story at home. According to a Ford Foundation–financed report, "Bringing a Nation Online: The Importance of Federal Leadership," there still exists a so-called *digital divide* "between high and low income households, among different racial groups, between Northern and Southern states, and rural and urban households."[51] For instance, according to the U.S. Commerce Department, about 80% of American households earning more than $75,000 a year use the internet at home, but only 25% of American households earning less than $15,000 annually do so. Only 32% of Latinos and 40% of African Americans had internet access at home in 2001, compared with 60% of whites.[52]

A 2001 report by the General Accounting Office, the investigative arm of Congress, suggests that education and income remain decisive in determining who goes online and in what way. Internet users are more likely to be white, to be well-educated, and to have higher-than-average household incomes. People who use broadband (about 12% of users), which is more expensive than dial-up but also helps make the internet more practical, are apt to be in higher income brackets.[53]

Education—especially college—makes a great difference. Every year of formal schooling after high school adds 5–15% to annual earnings later in life.[54]

Being well educated is only part of it, however; it's essential to be technologically literate. Employees with technology skills "earn roughly 10–15% higher pay," according to the chief economist for the U.S. Labor Department.[55]

> ## QuickCheck
>
> What are some potential environmental consequences of information technology?
>
> Discuss four types of mental-health problems linked to information technology.
>
> Describe some workplace problems associated with computers.
>
> What are some key economic issues related to information technology?

8.6 Artificial Intelligence

KEY QUESTION

What are the main areas of artificial intelligence?

You're having trouble with your new software program. You call the customer "help desk" at the software maker. Do you get a busy signal or get put on hold to listen to music (or, worse, advertising) for several minutes? Technical support lines are often swamped, and waiting is commonplace. Or, to deal with your software difficulty, do you find yourself dealing with . . . other software?

The odds are good that you will. For instance, a software technology has been patented called *automated virtual representatives (vReps)*, which offers computer-generated images (animation or photos of real models) that answer customer questions in real time, using natural language.[56] Programs that can walk you through a problem and help solve it are called *expert systems*. As the name suggests, these are systems imbued with knowledge by a human expert. Expert systems are one of the most useful applications of artificial intelligence.

**Artificial intelligence (AI)** **is a group of related technologies used for developing machines to emulate human qualities, such as learning, reasoning, communicating, seeing, and hearing.** Today the main areas of AI are *robotics, expert systems,* and *natural language processing.*

We will consider these areas and also an area known as *artificial life.*

Robotics

Nearly a half-century ago, in the film *Forbidden Planet*, Robby the Robot could sew, distill bourbon, and speak 187 languages. We haven't caught up with science-fiction movies, but maybe we'll get there yet.

Is this fish for real? This sea bream is about 1$\frac{1}{2}$ feet long, weighs 5$\frac{1}{2}$ pounds, and can swim up to 38 minutes—before recharging. The robot fish, created by Mitsubishi, looks and swims exactly like the real thing.

**Robotics** **is the development and study of machines that can perform work normally done by people.** The machines themselves are called *robots. (See ● Panel 8.3.)* Basically, **a _robot_ is an automatic device that performs functions ordinarily executed by human beings or that operates with what appears to be almost human intelligence.** (The word *robot*, derived from the Czech word for compulsory labor, was first used by Karel Câpek in an early 1920s play.)

ScrubMate—a robot equipped with computerized controls, ultrasonic "eyes," sensors, batteries, three different cleaning and scrubbing tools, and a self-squeezing mop—can clean bathrooms. Rosie the HelpMate delivers special-order meals from the kitchen to nursing stations in hospitals. Robodoc is used in surgery to bore the thighbone so that a hip implant can be attached. A driverless harvester, guided by satellite signals and an artificial vision system, is used to harvest alfalfa and other crops.

Robots are also used for more exotic purposes such as fighting oil-well fires, doing nuclear inspections and cleanups, and checking for mines and booby traps. A six-wheeled robot vehicle called *Sojourner* was used in NASA's 1997 Pathfinder exploration of Mars to sample the planet's atmosphere and soil and to radio data and photos back to Earth. A similar robot has been designed for use on the next Mars expedition.

Expert Systems

An **_expert system_ is an interactive computer program used in solving problems that would otherwise require the assistance of a human expert.** The expert system MYCIN helps diagnose infectious diseases. PROSPECTOR assesses geological data to locate mineral deposits. DENDRAL identifies chemical compounds. MailJail uses more than 600 rules to screen out junk email, or spam. Home-Safe-Home evaluates the residential environment of an elderly person. Business Insight helps businesses find the best strategies for marketing a product. Jnana offers legal advice in narrow, highly regulated areas, such as environmental or securities law. REBES (Residential Burglary Expert System) helps detectives investigate crime scenes. CARES (Computer Assisted Risk Evaluation System) helps social workers assess families for risks of child abuse. Such programs simulate the reasoning process of experts in certain well-defined areas. That is, professionals called *knowledge engineers* interview the expert or experts and determine the rules and knowledge that must go into the system.

Natural Language Processing

Natural languages are ordinary human languages, such as English. (A second definition, discussed in the Appendix, is that they are fifth-generation programming languages.) _Natural language processing_ **is the study of ways for computers to recognize and understand human language,** whether in spoken or written form. Major advances in natural language processing have occurred in _speech recognition,_ in which computers translate spoken speech into text.

Think how challenging it is to make a computer translate English into another language. In one instance, the English sentence "The spirit is willing, but the flesh is weak" came out in Russian as "The wine is agreeable, but the meat is spoiled." The problem with human language is that it is often ambiguous; different listeners may arrive at different interpretations.

Most existing language systems run on large computers, although scaled-down versions are now available for microcomputers. A product called Intellect uses a limited English vocabulary to help users orally query databases on both mainframes and microcomputers. LUNAR, developed to help analyze moon rocks, answers questions about geology on the basis of an extensive database. Verbex, used by the U.S. Postal Service, lets mail sorters read aloud an incomplete address and will reply with the correct ZIP code.

Artificial Life, the Turing Test, & AI Ethics

What is life, and how can we replicate it out of silicon chips, networks, and software? We are dealing now not with artificial intelligence but with artificial life. _Artificial life,_ **or A-life, is the field of study concerned with "creatures"—computer instructions, or pure information—that are created, replicate, evolve, and die as if they were living organisms.** Thus, A-life software (such as LIFE) tries to simulate the responses of a human being.

Of course, "silicon life" does not have two principal attributes associated with true living things—it is not water- and carbon-based. Yet in other respects such creatures mimic life: If they cannot learn or adapt, then they perish.

How can we know when we have reached the point at which computers have achieved human intelligence? How will you know, say, whether you're talking to a human being on the phone or to a computer? Clearly, with the strides made in the fields of artificial intelligence and artificial life, this question is no longer just academic.

Interestingly, Alan Turing, an English mathematician and computer pioneer, addressed this very question in 1950. Turing predicted that by the end of the century computers would be able to mimic human thinking and to conduct conversations indistinguishable from a person's. Out of these observations came the _Turing test,_ **which is intended to determine whether a computer possesses "intelligence" or "self-awareness."**

In the Turing test, a human judge converses by means of a computer terminal with two entities hidden in another location—one a person typing on a keyboard, the other a software program. Following the conversation, the judge must decide which entity is human. In this test, intelligence—the ability to think—is demonstrated by the computer's success in fooling the judge.

Judith Anne Gunther participated as one of eight judges in the third annual Loebner Prize Competition, which is based on Turing's ideas.[57] (There have been other competitions since.) The "conversations"—each limited to 15 minutes—are restricted to predetermined topics, such as baseball, because even today's best programs have neither the databases nor the syntactical ability to handle an unlimited number of subjects.

Gunther found that she wasn't fooled by any of the computer programs. The winning program, for example, relied as much on deflection and wit as it did on responding logically and conversationally. (For example, to a judge trying to discuss a federally funded program, the computer said: "You want

ethics

logic? I'll give you logic: shut up, shut up, shut up, shut up, shut up, now go away! How's that for logic?") However, Gunther *was* fooled by one of the five humans, a real person discussing abortion. "He was so uncommunicative," wrote Gunther, "that I pegged him for a computer."

A new sort of Turing test, one that's simple for humans but that will baffle sophisticated computer programs, has been devised in the form of cognitive puzzles called Captchas, an acronym for Completely Automated Public Turing Test to Tell Computers and Humans Apart.[58]

Behind everything to do with artificial intelligence and artificial life—just as it underlies everything we do—is the whole matter of ethics. In his book *Ethics in Modeling*, William A. Wallace, professor of decision sciences at Rensselaer Polytechnic Institute, points out that computer software, including expert systems, is often subtly shaped by the ethical judgments and assumptions of the people who create it.[59] In one instance, he notes, a bank had to modify its loan-evaluation software on discovering that the software rejected certain applications because it unduly emphasized old age as a negative factor. Another expert system, used by health maintenance organizations (HMOs), tells doctors when they should opt for expensive medical procedures, such as magnetic resonance imaging tests. HMOs like such systems because they help control expenses, but critics are concerned that doctors will have to base decisions not on the best medicine but simply on "satisfactory" medicine combined with cost constraints.[60]

Clearly, there is no such thing as completely "value-free" technology. Human beings build it, use it, and have to live with the results.

QuickCheck

Distinguish among the main areas of AI.

What is artificial life?

8.7 The Promised Benefits of the Digital Age

KEY QUESTION

What are some benefits of the digital age??

We have described the benefits of information technology throghout this book. But there's probably no better way to conclude this subject than to discuss the promises of the future.

Information & Education

Getting the right kind of information is a major challenge. Can everything in the Library of Congress be made available online to citizens and companies? What about government records, patents, contracts, and other legal documents? Or geographic maps photographed from satellites?

As one solution, computer scientists have been developing so-called intelligent agents to find information on computer networks and filter it. **An *intelligent agent* program performs work tasks—such as roaming networks and compiling data—on your behalf.** A software agent is a kind of electronic assistant that filters messages, scans news services, and performs similar secretarial chores. An agent will also travel over communications lines to computer databases, collecting files to add to a personalized database.

With their potential for finding and processing information, computers are pervasive on campus. More than a third of college courses require the use of email, and many have their own dedicated web pages.[61] College students spend an average of 5.6 hours a week on the internet.[62] And as computer prices drop, more and more students have their own PCs. (For the rest, colleges often make public microcomputers available.)

Survival Tip

Libraries Join Forces to Answer Public Queries

The Collaborative Reference Service is a question-and-answer system developed by the Library of Congress to draw on libraries around the world (eventually up to 20 languages). Check out *www.loc.gov/rr/digiref*.

info!

If you can't get the educational offerings you want locally, where do you start your search for the distance-learning equivalent? Try the United States Distance Learning Association *(www.usdla.org),* Distance Learning on the Net *(www.hoyle.com/ distance.htm),* and the Distance Resource Learning Network *(www.dlrn.org).*

Survival Tip

Help in Buying a Car

Checking prices can save you as much as 5% on a new car. See *www.edmunds.com* and *www.kbb.com.* On a used car, you can check its title history at *www.carfax.com* if you have the vehicle identification number.

info!

In the market for a car? Check *www.autobytel.com, www.consumerreports.org, www.edmunds.com, www.autosmsn.com, www.autors.yahoo.com, www.motortrend.com, www.roadandtrack.com, www.caranddriver.com.*

Most students have been exposed to computers since the lower grades. The percentage of elementary schools in the United States with internet access in 2000 was 97%, according to the National Center for Education Statistics. For secondary schools, 100% had Internet access.[63]

One revolution in education—before, during, and after the college years—is the advent of distance learning, or "cyberclasses," along with the explosion of internet resources. The home-schooling movement, for example, has come of age, thanks to internet resources.[64] Many colleges—both individually and in associations such as that of the Western Governors University (backed by 21 states and U.S. flag Pacific islands) and the Community College Distance Learning Network—are offering a variety of internet and/or video-based online courses.[65] Corporations are also offering training classes via the internet or corporate intranet.[66]

Health

For some time, physicians in rural areas lacking local access to radiologists have used "teleradiology" to exchange digital images such as X-rays via telephone-linked networks with expert physicians in metropolitan areas. Now *telemedicine*—medical care delivered via telecommunications—is moving to an exciting new level, as the use of digital cameras and sound, in effect, moves patients to doctors rather than the reverse.[67]

Commerce & Money

Businesses clearly see the internet as a way to enhance productivity and competitiveness. However, as we have already observed, the changes go well beyond this.

The thrust of the original Industrial Revolution was separation—to break work up into its component parts so as to permit mass production. The effect of computer networks in the Digital Revolution, however, is unification—to erase boundaries between company departments, suppliers, and customers.[68] Indeed, the parts of a company can now as easily be scattered around the globe as down the hall from one another. Thus, designs for a new product can be tested and exchanged with factories in remote locations. With information flowing faster, goods can be sent to market faster and inventories reduced. Says an officer of the Internet Society, "Increasingly you have people in a wide variety of professions collaborating in diverse ways in other places. The whole notion of 'the organization' becomes a blurry boundary around a set of people and information systems and enterprises."[69]

Some areas of business that are undergoing rapid change are sales and marketing, retailing, banking, stock trading, and manufacturing.

- **Sales and marketing:** Caradon Everest equips its sales staff with laptops containing software that "configures" customized windows and calculates the prices on the spot, a process that was once handled by the company's technical people and took a week. "The company can also load on product images for multimedia presentations and training programs," says one account. "Using a digital camera, pictures of the customer's house can be loaded into the computer, which can superimpose the company's windows and print out a color preview."[70]

    Other companies are also taking advantage of information technology in marketing. Atlanta company The Mattress Firm, for instance, uses geographic information systems (GIS) software called *MapLinx* that plots drop-off points for a driver's most efficient delivery of mattresses to customers. Moreover, MapLinx depicts sales by neighborhood, showing owner Darin Lewin where his mattresses are selling well and thus where he should spend money to market them. "We can pinpoint our customer," says Lewin.[71]

- **Banking and money:** The world of cybercash has come to banking— not only smart cards but internet banking, electronic deposits, electronic bill paying, online stock and bond trading, and online insurance shopping.

    Some banks are backing an electronic-payment system that will allow internet users to buy tiny online goods and services with "micropayments" of as little as 25 cents from participating merchants. For instance, publishers could charge buyers a quarter to buy an article or listen to a song online, a small transaction that until now has not been practical. "It allows you to buy things by the sip rather than the gulp," says futurist Paul Saffo.[72]

Hong Kong Stock Exchange

- **Stock trading:** Computer technology is unquestionably changing the nature of stock trading. Only a few years ago, hardly anyone had the occupation of "day trader," an investor who relies on quick market fluctuations to turn a profit. Now, points out technology observer Denise Caruso, "anyone with a computer, a connection to the global network, and the requisite ironclad stomach for risk has the information, tools, and access to transaction systems required to play the stock market, a game that was once the purview of an elite few."[73] (Caruso is right that it takes a strong stomach to be a day trader; many have lost their shirts.)

- **Manufacturing:** Computers have been used in manufacturing for some time, most famously, perhaps, in those pictures you see of welding robots on car-assembly lines. But computers, and the internet in particular, are players in other ways. For example, in Benton Harbor, Michigan, Whirlpool, the world's largest maker of dishwashers and other appliances, deploys the internet on three fronts—to deal with customers, manage employees, and buy components from other companies. The last of these— streamlining the way metals, plastics, electronics, and resins come into manufacturing plants—is particularly important for Whirlpool. This business-to-business automation saves space and funds, since the company doesn't have to pay for a part until it arrives (an example of a "just-in-time" system).[74]

Entertainment

Information technology is being used for all kinds of entertainment, ranging from video games to telegambling. It is also being used in the arts, from painting to photography. Let's consider just two examples, music and film.

Not only do websites offer guitar chords and sheet music, but promotional sites feature signed and unsigned artists, both garage bands and established professional musicians.[75] There are legal MP3 sites on the internet but also many illegal ones, which operate in violation of copyright laws protecting ownership of music. Many of these will probably cease to exist now that the recording industry has developed new web technologies that frustrate the pirating of music and instead offer fee-based services.

Now that blockbuster movies routinely meld live action and animation, computer artists are in big demand. *Star Wars: Episode I*, for instance, had fully 1,965 digital shots out of about 2,200 shots. Even when film was used, it was scanned into computers to be tweaked with animated effects, lighting, and the like. Entire beings were created on computers by artists working on designs developed by producer George Lucas and his chief artist.[76]

Computer techniques have even been used to develop digitally created actors—called "synthespians." The late John Wayne was recruited for a Coors beer ad.[77] With the soaring demand for computer-generated imagery—not only for movies but also for TV ads and video games—colleges and trade schools have expanded their digital-animation training programs.

Government & Electronic Democracy

"In general, the internet is being defined not by its civic or political content," says one writer, "but by merchandising and entertainment, much like television."[78] Even so, a Rutgers University study suggests that the internet has great potential for civic betterment because it is free of government intrusion, is fast and cheap for users (once connected), and facilitates communication among citizens better than mass media such as radio and TV.[79]

If we can shop online, could we not vote online for political candidates? This question took on heightened importance following the vote count in Florida for the 2000 presidential election, when punch-card ballots were found to be unreliable.[80] Beyond Florida, flaws in voting technology left perhaps as many as 6 million votes uncounted in that election, according to a study by researchers at Caltech and M.I.T.[81] The study found that optical scanners are the most reliable method of counting votes. (A poor, mostly minority district in Alabama had the lowest rate of disqualified ballots—0.3%, better than any affluent district—because it used optical-scan systems.[82]) Touch-screen voting, however, remains largely unproven. Internet voting is vulnerable because of the potential for fraud and hackers.[83] There is also, surprisingly, the matter of expense: A 2000 experiment by the Pentagon to let overseas soldiers vote by the internet netted just 84 ballots—at a cost of nearly $74,000 per voter.[84] True internet voting, therefore, may still be a decade away. Still, ten states have approved testing of online voting. In 2000, 86,000 citizens in Arizona voted in that state's Democratic presidential primary via the internet.[85]

Survival Tip

Online Government Help

You can gain access to government agencies through the following websites:
www.firstgov.gov
www.govspot.com
www.info.gov

A new way to vote. After you insert your voter ID card, choose your candidates by touching their names on a display screen.

info!

Some government websites of interest: www.senate.gov (U.S. Senate), www.house.gov (House of Representatives), www.whitehouse.gov. The president's email address is president@whitehouse.gov.

QuickCheck

What are some uses of information technology in education and health?

Discuss some uses of information technology in commerce and money.

How are computers being used in entertainment?

Describe some ways computers are being used in the civic realm.

Summary

artificial intelligence (AI) (p. 294, KQ 8.6) Group of related technologies used for developing machines to emulate human qualities, such as learning, reasoning, communicating, seeing, and hearing. Why it's important: Today the main areas of AI are virtual reality, robotics, natural language processing, fuzzy logic, expert systems, neural networks, and genetic algorithms, plus artificial life.

artificial life (p. 296, KQ 8.6) Also called *A-life;* field of study concerned with "creatures"—computer instructions, or pure information—that are created, replicate, evolve, and die as if they were living organisms. Why it's important: A-life software (such as LIFE) tries to simulate the responses of a human being.

antivirus software (p. 284, KQ 8.2) Program that scans a computer's hard disk, floppy disks, and main memory to detect viruses and, sometimes, to destroy them. Why it's important: Computer users must find out what kind of antivirus software to install in their systems—and how to keep it up to date—for protection against damage or shutdown.

biometrics (p. 286, KQ 8.3) Science of measuring individual body characteristics. Why it's important: Biometric technology is used in some computer security systems to restrict user access. Biometric devices, such as those that use fingerprints, eye scans, palm prints, and face recognition, authenticate a person's identity by verifying his or her physical or behavioral characteristics.

computer crime (p. 282, KQ 8.2) Crime of two types: (1) an illegal act perpetrated against computers or telecommunications; (2) the use of computers or telecommunications to accomplish an illegal act. Why it's important: Crimes against information technology include theft—of hardware, of software, of computer time, of cable or telephone services, or of information. Other illegal acts are crimes of malice and destruction.

crackers (p. 285, KQ 8.2) People who illegally break into computers for malicious purposes. Why it's important: Crackers attempt to break into computers to obtain information for financial gain, shut down hardware, pirate software, or alter or destroy data.

disaster-recovery plan (p. 288, KQ 8.3) Method of restoring information processing operations that have been halted by destruction or accident. Why it's important: Such a plan is important if an organization desires to resume computer operations quickly.

encryption (p. 287, KQ 8.3) Process of altering data so that it is not usable unless the changes are undone. Why it's important: Encryption is clearly useful for some organizations, especially those concerned with trade secrets, military matters, and other sensitive data. Some maintain that encryption will determine the future of e-commerce, because transactions cannot flourish over the internet unless they are secure.

expert system (p. 295, KQ 8.6) Interactive computer program that helps solve problems that would otherwise require the assistance of a human expert. Fundamental to an expert system is a knowledge base constructed by experts that can "learn" by adding new knowledge. Why it's important: Expert systems are designed to be users' assistants, not replacements—to help them more easily perform their jobs.

hackers (p. 285, KQ 8.2) People who gain unauthorized access to computer or telecommunications systems, often just for the challenge of it. (In the positive meaning, hackers are computer enthusiasts, people who enjoy learning programming languages and computer systems.) Why it's important: Hackers create problems not only for the institutions that are victims of break-ins but also for ordinary users of the systems.

intelligent agent (p. 297, KQ 8.7) Software with built-in intelligence that monitors work tasks, asks questions, and performs work tasks—such as roaming networks and compiling data—on the user's behalf. Why it's important: A software agent is a kind of electronic assistant that will filter messages, scan news services, and perform similar secretarial chores. An agent will also travel over communications lines to computer databases, collecting files to add to a personalized database.

Internet2 (p. 279, KQ 8.1) Cooperative university/business education and research project that enables high-end users to quickly and reliably move huge amounts of data over high-speed networks. Why it's important: In effect, Internet2 adds "toll lanes" to the older internet to speed things up. The purpose is to advance videoconferencing, research, and academic collaboration—to enable a kind of "virtual university."

natural language processing (p. 296, KQ 8.6) Study of ways for computers to recognize and understand human language, whether in spoken or written form. Why it's important: Natural languages make it easier to work with computers.

password (p. 286, KQ 8.3) Special word, code, or symbol required to access a computer system. Why it's important: Passwords are one of the weakest security links; they can be guessed, forgotten, or stolen.

PIN (personal identification number) (p. 286, KQ 8.3) Security number known only to the user; it is required to access a system. Why it's important: PINs are required to access many computer systems, as well as automated teller machines.

robot (p. 294, KQ 8.6) Automatic device that performs functions ordinarily executed by human beings or that operates with what appears to be almost human intelligence. Why it's important: Robots are performing more and more functions in business and the professions.

robotics (p. 294, KQ 8.6) Development and study of machines that can perform work normally done by people. Why it's important: *See* robot.

security (p. 286, KQ 8.3) System of safeguards for protecting information technology against disasters, systems failure, and unauthorized access that can result in damage or loss. Four components of security are identification and access, encryption, protection of software and data, and disaster-recovery plans. Why it's important: With proper security, organizations and individuals can minimize information technology losses from disasters, system failures, and unauthorized access.

Turing test (p. 296, KQ 8.6) A test for determining whether a computer possesses "intelligence" or "self-awareness." In the Turing test, a human judge converses by means of a computer terminal with two entities hidden in another location. Why it's important: Some experts believe that once a computer has passed the Turing test, it will be judged to have achieved a level of human intelligence.

virus (p. 284, KQ 8.2) Deviant program that can cause unexpected and often undesirable effects, such as destroying or corrupting data. Why it's important: Viruses can cause users to lose data and/or files or can shut down entire computer systems.

worm (p. 284, KQ 8.2) Program that copies itself repeatedly into a computer's memory or onto a disk drive until no space is left. Why it's important: Worms can shut down computers.

Chapter Review

"I can recognize and recall information."

Self-Test Questions

1. The purpose of _____ is to scan a computer's disk devices and memory to detect viruses and, sometimes, to destroy them.

2. So that information-processing operations can be restored after destruction or accident, organizations should adopt a _____.

3. _____ is the altering of data so that it is not usable unless the changes are undone.

4. _____ is incomplete, outdated, or otherwise inaccurate data.

5. An error in a program that causes it not to work properly is called a _____.

6. A(n) _____ is an automatic device that performs functions ordinarily performed by human beings.

Multiple-Choice Questions

1. Which of the following are crimes against computers and communications?
   a. natural hazards
   b. software theft
   c. information theft
   d. software bugs
   e. procedural errors

2. Which of the following are methods or means of safeguarding computer systems?
   a. signatures
   b. keys
   c. physical traits of users
   d. worms
   e. Internet2

True/False Questions

T F   1. Viruses cannot be passed from computer to computer through a network.

T F   2. One of the weakest links in a security system is biometrics.

T F   3. The Turing test determines whether a computer possesses intelligence

T F   4. An intelligent agent performs network work tasks on the user's behalf.

"I can recall information in my own terms and explain them to a friend."

Short-Answer Questions

1. What are intelligent agents used for?
2. What is the difference between a hacker and a cracker?
3. What does a worm do?
4. What was the 1996 U.S. Telecommunications Act intended to do?
5. What does *ICANN* stand for, and what does it do?
6. Name five threats to computers and communications systems.
7. The definition of computer crime distinguishes between two types. What are they?
8. What is the Turing test?

"I can apply what I've learned, relate these ideas to other concepts, build on other knowledge, and use all these thinking skills to form a judgment."

Knowledge in Action

1. If you could design a robot, what kind would you create? What would it do?

2. What, in your opinion, are the most significant disadvantages of using computers? What do you think can be done about these problems?

3. What's your opinion about the issue of free speech on an electronic network? Research some recent legal decisions in various countries, as well as some articles on the topic. Should the contents of messages be censored? If so, under what conditions?

4. Research the problems of stress and isolation experienced by computer users in the United States, Japan, and one other country. Write a brief report on your findings.

5. Should internet-purchased products or services have a sales tax (like items purchased in regular stores)? Why or why not?

Web Exercises

1. For more information about Internet2, visit

   www.internet2.edu

   Identify the three primary goals of Internet2. Also read the Frequently Asked Questions section.

2. The CIH (Chernobyl) virus affected many Windows 95 users. This virus struck intitially on April 26, 1999, and can still strike if your system is still infected. If your PC has Windows 95 installed, or you have had files sent from other users of Windows 95, it may be infected with the virus, and you may not know it's there. Visit this website for an in-depth report about what this virus does, its origins, and how to fix or protect against it:

   www. symantec.com/avcenter/venc/data/cih.html

SECURITY

3. Here's a way to semi-encrypt an email message to a friend. Type out your message; then go to the Edit menu

and choose *Select All.* Next go to the Format menu and select *Font;* then choose a font such as Wingdings that doesn't use letters. When your friend receives your message, he or she need only change the font back to an understandable one (such as Times New Roman) in order to read it. This certainly isn't high-level encryption, but it's a fun activity to try.

4. Internet addiction can be a serious problem. Some games such as Everquest calculate how many days of your life you have spent playing online. These days are calculated as 24-hour days. Most humans do not stay awake for 24 hours. Visit this bulletin board to read about various players and how they can't shake their Everquest habit:

   www.sharkygames.com/forum_frag/2a/5.shtml

   Then visit the following websites, which discuss general internet addiction:

   www.addictions.org/internet.htm
   http://netaddiction.com

   Take the Internet Addiction Survey at:

   www.stresscure.com/hrn/addiction.html

5. If you're spending too much time indoors using a PC or watching TV, you might want to consider going outside. Visit the following website to learn about indoor air versus outdoor air.

   www.who.int/inf-fs/en/fact201.html

   Also, to read more about internet addiction that causes isolation from the real world, visit

   www.sciencenews.org/20000226/fob8.asp

   The following two websites discuss computer health and safety:

   www.ics.uci.edu/~chair/comphealth2.html
   www.stanford.edu/dept/EHS/prod/general/ergo/ computer_ergo.html

Systems & Programming

Development, Programming, & Languages

Key Questions & Concepts

A.1   **Systems Development: The Six Phases of Systems**   What are the six phass of the systems development life cycle?

A.2   **Programming: A Five-Step Procedure**   What is programming, and what are the five steps in accomplishing it?

A.3   **Five Generations of Programming Languages**   What are the five generations of programming languages?

A.4   **Programming Languages Used Today**   What are some third-generation languages, and what are they used for?

A.5   **Object-Oriented & Visual Programming**   How do OOP and visual programming work?

A.6   **Markup & Scripting Languages**   What do markup and scripting languages do?

A.1 Systems Development: The Six Phases of Systems Analysis & Design

Organizations can make mistakes, of course, and big organizations can make really big mistakes.

California's state Department of Motor Vehicles' databases needed to be modernized, and Tandem Computers said it could do it. "The fact that the DMV's database system, designed around an old IBM-based platform, and Tandem's new system were as different as night and day seemed insignificant at the time to the experts involved," said one writer who investigated the project.[1] The massive driver's license database, containing the driving records of more than 30 million people, first had to be "scrubbed" of all information that couldn't be translated into the language used by Tandem computers. One such scrub yielded 600,000 errors. Then the DMV had to translate all its IBM programs into the Tandem language. "Worse, DMV really didn't know how its current IBM applications worked anymore," said the writer, "because they'd been custom-made decades before by long-departed programmers and rewritten many times since." Eventually the project became a staggering $44 million loss to California's taxpayers.

Needless to say, not all mistakes are so huge. Computer foul-ups can range from minor to catastrophic. But this example shows how important planning is, especially when an organization is trying to launch a new kind of system. The best way to avoid such mistakes is to employ systems analysis and design.

But, you may say, you're not going to have to wrestle with problems on the scale of motor-vehicle departments. That's a job for computer professionals. You're mainly interested in using computers and communications to increase your own productivity. Why, then, do you need to know anything about systems analysis and design?

In many types of jobs, you may find that your department or your job is the focus of a study by a systems analyst. Knowing how the procedure works will help you better explain how your job works or what goals your department is supposed to achieve. In progressive companies, management is always interested in suggestions for improving productivity. Systems analysis provides a method for developing such ideas.

The Purpose of a System

A _system_ **is defined as a collection of related components that interact to perform a task in order to accomplish a goal.** A system may not work very well, but it is nevertheless a system. The point of systems analysis and design is to ascertain how a system works and then take steps to make it better.

An organization's computer-based information system consists of hardware, software, people, procedures, and data, as well as communications setups. These compnents work together to provide people with information for running the organization.

Getting the Project Going: How It Starts, Who's Involved

A single individual who believes that something badly needs changing is all it takes to get the project rolling. An employee may influence a supervisor. A customer or supplier may get the attention of someone in higher management. Top management may decide independently to take a look at a system that seems inefficient. A steering committee may be formed to decide which of many possible projects should be worked on.

Participants in the project are of three types:

- **Users:** The system under discussion should *always* be developed in consultation with users, whether floor sweepers, research scientists, or customers. Indeed, if user involvement in analysis and design is inadequate, the system may fail for lack of acceptance.
- **Management:** Managers within the organization should also be consulted about the system.
- **Technical staff:** Members of the company's information systems (IS) department, consisting of systems analysts and programmers, need to be involved. For one thing, they may have to execute the project. Even if they don't, they will have to work with outside IS people contracted to do the job.

Complex projects will require one or several systems analysts. **A _systems analyst_ is an information specialist who performs systems analysis, design, and implementation.** The analyst's job is to study the information and communications needs of an organization and determine what changes are required to deliver better information to the people who need it. "Better" information means information that is summarized in the acronym *CART*— complete, accurate, relevant, and timely. The systems analyst achieves this goal through the problem-solving method of systems analysis and design.

The Six Phases of Systems Analysis & Design

Systems analysis and design is a six-phase problem-solving procedure for examining an information system and improving it. The six phases make up what is called the *systems development life cycle*. **The _systems development life cycle (SDLC)_ is the step-by-step process that many organizations follow during systems analysis and design.**

Whether applied to a Fortune 500 company or a three-person engineering business, the six phases in systems analysis and design are as shown in the illustration. *(See ● Panel A.1.)* Phases often overlap, and a new one may start before the old one is finished. After the first four phases, management must decide whether to proceed to the next phase. User input and review is a critical part of each phase.

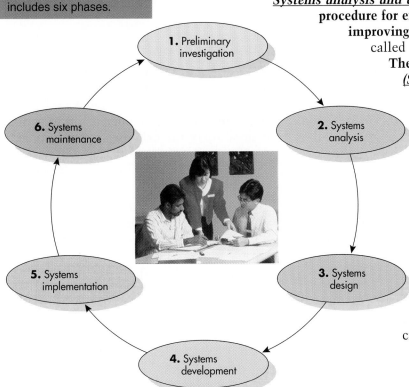

1. Preliminary investigation
2. Systems analysis
3. Systems design
4. Systems development
5. Systems implementation
6. Systems maintenance

The First Phase: Conduct a Preliminary Investigation

The objective of **Phase 1, _preliminary investigation_, is to conduct a preliminary analysis, propose alternative solutions, describe costs and benefits, and submit a preliminary plan with recommendations.**

- **Conduct the preliminary analysis:** In this step, you need to find out what the organization's objectives are and the nature and scope of the problem under study. Even if a problem pertains only to a small segment of the organization, you cannot study it in isolation. You need to find out what the objectives of the organization itself are. Then you need to see how the problem being studied fits in with them.

- **Propose alternative solutions:** In delving into the organization's objectives and the specific problem, you may have already discovered some solutions. Other possible solutions can come from interviewing people inside the organization, clients or customers affected by it, suppliers, and consultants. You can also study what competitors are doing. With this data, you then have three choices. You can leave the system as is, improve it, or develop a new system.

- **Describe the costs and benefits:** Whichever of the three alternatives is chosen, it will have costs and benefits. In this step, you need to indicate what these are. Costs may depend on benefits, which may offer savings. A broad spectrum of benefits may be derived. A process may be speeded up, streamlined through elimination of unnecessary steps, or combined with other processes. Input errors or redundant output may be reduced. Systems and subsystems may be better integrated. Users may be happier with the system. Customers' or suppliers' interactions with the system may be more satisfactory. Security may be improved. Costs may be cut.

- **Submit a preliminary plan:** Now you need to wrap up all your findings in a written report. The readers of this report will be the executives who are in a position to decide in which direction to proceed—make no changes, change a little, or change a lot—and how much money to allow the project. You should describe the potential solutions, costs, and benefits and indicate your recommendations.

The Second Phase: Do an Analysis of the System

The objective of **Phase 2, _systems analysis_, is to gather data, analyze the data, and write a report.** In this second phase of the SDLC, you will follow the course that management has indicated after having read your Phase 1 feasibility report. We are assuming that management has ordered you to perform Phase 2—to do a careful analysis or study of the existing system in order to understand how the new system you proposed would differ. This analysis will also consider how people's positions and tasks will have to change if the new system is put into effect.

- **Gather data:** In gathering data, you will review written documents, interview employees and managers, develop questionnaires, and observe people and processes at work.

- **Analyze the data:** Once the data has been gathered, you need to come to grips with it and analyze it. Many analytical tools, or modeling tools, are available. **_Modeling tools_ enable a systems analyst to present graphic, or pictorial, representations of a system. An example of a modeling tool is a _data flow diagram (DFD)_, which graphically shows the flow of data through a system—that is, the essential processes of a system, along with inputs, outputs, and files.**

CASE tools may also be used during the analysis phase, as well as in most other phases. ___CASE (computer-aided software engineering) tools___ **are programs that automate various activities of the SDLC.** This technology is intended to speed up the process of developing systems and to improve the quality of the resulting systems. Such tools can generate and store diagrams, produce documentation, analyze data relationships, generate computer code, produce graphics, and provide project management functions. (Project management software consists of programs used to plan, schedule, and control the people, costs, and resources required to complete a project on time; p. 125.) Examples of such programs are Analyst Pro, Visible Analyst, Excelerator, Iconix, System Architect, and Powerbuilder.

So-called front-end CASE tools are used during the first three phases—preliminary analysis, systems analysis, systems design—to help with the early analysis and design. So-called back-end CASE tools are used during two later phases—systems development and implementation—to help in coding and testing, for instance.

- **Write a report:** Once you have completed the analysis, you need to document this phase. This report to management should have three parts. First, it should explain how the existing system works. Second, it should explain the problems with the existing system. Finally, it should describe the requirements for the new system and make recommendations on what to do next.

At this point, not a lot of money will have been spent on the systems analysis and design project. If the costs of going forward seem prohibitive, this is a good time for the managers reading the report to call a halt. Otherwise, you will be asked to move to Phase 3.

The Third Phase: Design the System

The objective of **Phase 3,** ___systems design___, **is to do a preliminary design and then a detail design, and write a report.** In this third phase of the SDLC, you will essentially create a "rough draft" and then a "detail draft" of the proposed information system.

- **Do a preliminary design:** A *preliminary design* describes the general functional capabilities of a proposed information system. It reviews the system requirements and then considers major components of the system. Usually several alternative systems (called *candidates*) are considered, and the costs and the benefits of each are evaluated.

  Tools used in the design phase may include CASE tools and project management software.

  Prototyping is often done at this stage. ___Prototyping___ **refers to using workstations, CASE tools, and other software applications to build working models of system components, so that they can be quickly tested and evaluated.** Thus, **a** ___prototype___ **is a limited working system developed to test out design concepts.** A prototype, which may be constructed in just a few days, allows users to find out immediately how a change in the system might benefit them. For example, a systems analyst might develop a menu as a possible screen display, which users could try out. The menu can then be redesigned or fine-tuned, if necessary.

- **Do a detail design:** A *detail design* describes how a proposed information system will deliver the general capabilities described in the preliminary design. The detail design usually considers the following parts of the system in this order: output requirements, input requirements, storage requirements, processing requirements, and system controls and backup.

- **Write a report:** All the work of the preliminary and detail designs will end up in a large, detailed report. When you hand over this report to senior management, you will probably also make some sort of presentation or speech.

The Fourth Phase: Develop the System

In **Phase 4, _systems development_, the systems analyst or others in the organization develop or acquire the software, acquire the hardware, and then test the system.** Depending on the size of the project, this phase will probably involve the organization in spending substantial sums of money. It could also involve spending a lot of time. However, at the end you should have a workable system.

- **Develop or acquire the software:** During the design stage, the systems analyst may have had to address what is called the "make-or-buy" decision, but that decision certainly cannot be avoided now. In the _make-or-buy decision_, you decide whether you have to create a program—have it custom-written—or buy it, meaning simply purchase an existing software package. Sometimes programmers decide they can buy an existing program and modify it rather than write it from scratch.

    If you decide to create a new program, then the question is whether to use the organization's own staff programmers or to hire outside contract programmers (outsource it). Whichever way you go, the task could take many months.

    Programming is an entire subject unto itself, which we discuss in Section A.2; programming languages are discussed in Section A.3.

- **Acquire hardware:** Once the software has been chosen, the hardware to run it must be acquired or upgraded. It's possible your new system will not require any new hardware. It's also possible that the new hardware will cost millions of dollars and involve many items: microcomputers, mainframes, monitors, modems, and many other devices. The organization may find it's better to lease rather than to buy some equipment, especially since, as we mentioned (Moore's law), chip capability has traditionally doubled every 18 months.

- **Test the system:** With the software and hardware acquired, you can now start testing the system. Testing is usually done in two stages: unit testing, then system testing.

    In _unit testing_, the performance of individual parts is examined, using test (made-up, or sample) data. If the program is written as a collaborative effort by multiple programmers, each part of the program is tested separately.

    In _system testing_, the parts are linked together, and test data is used to see if the parts work together. At this point, actual organization data may be used to test the system. The system is also tested with erroneous data and massive amounts of data to see if the system can be made to fail ("crash").

    At the end of this long process, the organization will have a workable information system, one ready for the implementation phase.

The Fifth Phase: Implement the System

Whether the new information system involves a few handheld computers, an elaborate telecommunications network, or expensive mainframes, the fifth phase will involve some close coordination in order to make the system not just workable but successful. **Phase 5, _systems implementation_, con-**

sists of converting the hardware, software, and files to the new system and training the users.

- **Convert to the new system:** Conversion, the process of transition from an old information system to a new one, involves converting hardware, software, and files. There are four strategies for handling conversion: direct, parallel, phased, and pilot.

  Direct implementation means that the user simply stops using the old system and starts using the new one. The risk of this method should be evident: What if the new system doesn't work? If the old system has truly been discontinued, there is nothing to fall back on.

  Parallel implementation means that the old and new systems are operated side by side until the new system has shown it is reliable, at which time the old system is discontinued. Obviously there are benefits in taking this cautious approach. If the new system fails, the organization can switch back to the old one. The difficulty with this method is the expense of paying for the equipment and people to keep two systems going at the same time.

  Phased implementation means that parts of the new system are phased in separately—either at different times (parallel) or all at once in groups (direct).

  Pilot implementation means that the entire system is tried out but only by some users. Once the reliability has been proved, the system is implemented with the rest of the intended users. The pilot approach still has its risks, since all of the users of a particular group are taken off the old system. However, the risks are confined to a small part of the organization.

- **Train the users:** Various tools are available to familiarize users with a new system—from documentation (instruction manuals) to videotapes to live classes to one-on-one, side-by-side teacher-student training. Sometimes training is done by the organization's own staffers; at other times it is contracted out.

The Sixth Phase: Maintain the System

Phase 6, _systems maintenance_, adjusts and improves the system by having system audits and periodic evaluations and by making changes based on new conditions. Even with the conversion accomplished and the users trained, the system won't just run itself. There is a sixth—and continuous—phase in which the information system must be monitored to ensure that it is successful. Maintenance includes not only keeping the machinery running but also updating and upgrading the system to keep pace with new products, services, customers, government regulations, and other requirements.

After some time, maintenance costs will accelerate as attempts continue to keep the system responsive to user needs. At some point, these maintenance costs become excessive, indicating that it may be time to start the entire SDLC again.

A.2 Programming: A Five-Step Procedure

KEY QUESTIONS

What is programming, and what are the five steps in accomplishing it?

To see how programming works, we must understand what constitutes a program. **A _program_ is a list of instructions that the computer must follow in order to process data into information.** The instructions consist of statements used in a programming language, such as BASIC. Examples are programs that do word processing, desktop publishing, or payroll processing.

The decision whether to buy or create a program forms part of Phase 4 in the systems development life cycle. (*See ● Panel A.2 on the next page.*) Once the decision is made to develop a new system, the programmer goes to work.

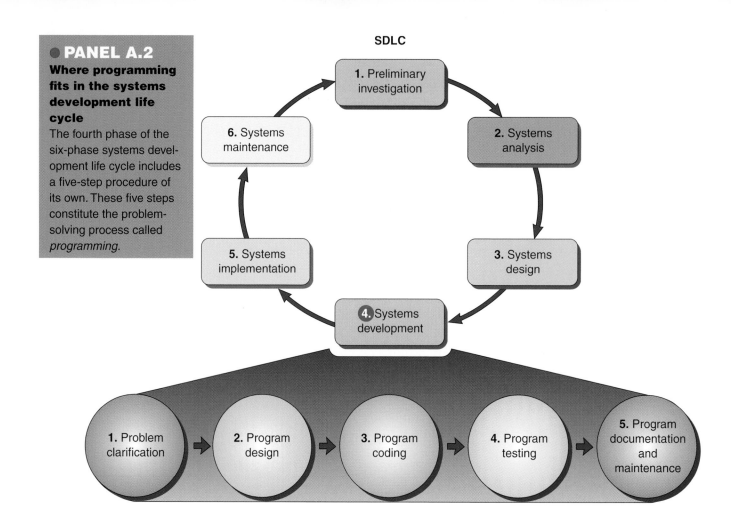

● PANEL A.2
Where programming fits in the systems development life cycle
The fourth phase of the six-phase systems development life cycle includes a five-step procedure of its own. These five steps constitute the problem-solving process called *programming*.

1. Preliminary investigation

2. Systems analysis

3. Systems design

4. Systems development

5. Systems implementation

6. Systems maintenance

1. Problem clarification

2. Program design

3. Program coding

4. Program testing

5. Program documentation and maintenance

info!

Software engineering has many definitions. Go to *wwwsel.iit.nrc.ca/sedefn/ SEdefn.html#Defns* to read more of them.

A program, we said, is a list of instructions for the computer. **_Programming_ is a multistep process for creating that list of instructions.** Programming is sometimes called *software engineering*; however, this term includes in its definition the use of best-practice processes to create and/or maintain software, whether for groups or individuals, in an attempt to get rid of the usual haphazard methods that have plagued the software industry. Software engineering involves the establishment and use of recognized engineering principles to obtain software that is reliable and works efficiently. It requires the application of a systematic, disciplined, quantifiable approach to the development, operation, and maintenance of software.

The five steps in the programming process are as follows:

1. Clarify the problem—include needed output, input, processing requirements.
2. Design a solution—use modeling tools to chart the program.
3. Code the program—use a programming language's syntax, or rules, to write the program.
4. Test the program—get rid of any logic errors, or "bugs," in the program ("debug" it).
5. Document and maintain the program—include written instructions for users, explanation of the program, and operating instructions.

Coding—sitting at the keyboard and typing words into a computer—is how many people view programming. As we see, however, it is only one of the five steps.

The First Step: Clarify the Programming Needs

The **_problem clarification_** step consists of six mini-steps—clarifying program objectives and users, outputs, inputs, and processing tasks; studying the feasibility of the program; and documenting the analysis.

1. *Clarify objectives and users:* You solve problems all the time. A problem might be deciding whether to take a required science course this term or next, or selecting classes that allow you also to fit a job into your schedule. In such cases, you are specifying your objectives. Programming works the same way. You need to write a statement of the objectives you are trying to accomplish—the problem you are trying to solve. If the problem is that your company's systems analysts have designed a new computer-based payroll-processing proposal and brought it to you as the programmer, you need to clarify the programming needs.

    You also need to make sure you know who the users of the program will be. Will they be people inside the company, outside, or both? What kind of skills will they bring?

2. *Clarify desired outputs:* Make sure you understand the outputs— what the system designers want to get out of the system—before you specify the inputs. For example, what kind of hardcopy is wanted? What information should the outputs include? This step may require several meetings with systems designers and users to make sure you're creating what they want.

3. *Clarify desired inputs:* Once you know the kind of outputs required, you can then think about input. What kind of input data is needed? In what form should it appear? What is its source?

4. *Clarify the desired processing:* Here you make sure you understand the processing tasks that must occur in order for input data to be processed into output data.

5. *Double-check the feasibility of implementing the program:* Is the kind of program you're supposed to create feasible within the present budget? Will it require hiring a lot more staff? Will it take too long to accomplish?

    Occasionally programmers suggest to managers that they buy an existing program and modify it rather than having it written from scratch.

6. *Document the analysis:* Throughout program clarification, programmers must document everything they do. This includes writing objective specifications of the entire process being described.

The Second Step: Design the Program

Assuming the decision is to make, or custom-write, the program, you then move on to design the solution specified by the systems analysts. To design the solution, one first needs to create an algorithm. **An _algorithm_ is a formula or set of steps for solving a particular problem.** To be an algorithm, a set of rules must be unambiguous and have a clear stopping point. We use algorithms every day. For example, a recipe for baking bread is an algorithm. Most programs, with the exception of some artificial intelligence applications, consist of algorithms. In computer programming, there are often different algorithms to accomplish any given task, and each algorithm has specific advantages and disadvantages in different situations. Inventing elegant algorithms—algorithms that are simple and require the fewest steps possible—is one of the principal challenges in programming.

Algorithms can be expressed in various ways. **In the _program design step_, the software is designed in two mini-steps. First, the program logic is** determined through a top-down approach and modularization, using a *hierarchy chart*. Then it is designed in detail, either in narrative form, using *pseudocode*, or graphically, using *flowcharts*.

It used to be that programmers took a kind of a seat-of-the-pants approach to programming. Programming was considered an art, not a science. Today, however, most programmers use a design approach called *structured programming*. **Structured programming takes a top-down approach that breaks programs into modular forms.** It also uses standard logic tools called *control structures (sequential, selection, case,* and *iteration).*

The point of structured programming is to make programs more efficient (with fewer lines of code) and better organized (more readable) and to have better notations so that they have clear and correct descriptions.

The two mini-steps of program design are as follows.

1. *Determine the program logic, using a top down approach:* Determining the program logic is like outlining a long term paper before you proceed to write it. **Top-down program design proceeds by identifying the top element, or module, of a program and then breaking it down in hierarchical fashion to the lowest level of detail. The top-down program design is used to identify the program's processing steps, or modules.** After the program is designed, the actual coding proceeds from the bottom up, using the modular approach.

    The concept of modularization is important. Modularization dramatically simplifies program development, because each part can be developed and tested separately.

    A *module* is a processing step of a program. Each module is made up of logically related program statements. (Sometimes a module is called a *subprogram* or *subroutine*.) An example of a module might be a programming instruction that simply says "Open a file, find a record, and show it on the display screen." It is best if each module has only a single function, just as an English paragraph should have a single, complete thought. This rule limits the module's size and complexity.

    Top-down program design can be represented graphically in a hierarchy chart. **A *hierarchy chart*, or structure chart, illustrates the overall purpose of the program, by identifying all the modules needed to achieve that purpose and the relationships among them.** *(See* ● *Panel A.3.)* It works from the general down to the specific, starting with the top-level (high-level) view of what the program is to do. Then each layer refines and expands the previous one until the bottom layer can be made into specific programming modules. The program must move in sequence from one module to the next until all have been processed. There must be three principal modules corresponding to the three principal computing operations—input, processing, and output. (In Panel A.3 they are "Read input," "Calculate pay," and "Generate output.")

2. *Design details, using pseudocode and/or glowcharts:* Once the essential logic of the program has been determined, through the use of top-down programming and hierarchy charts, you can go to work on the details.

    There are two ways to show details—write them or draw them; that is, use *pseudocode* or use *flowcharts*. Most projects use both methods.

    ● **Pseudocode: *Pseudocode* is a method of designing a program using normal human-language statements to describe the logic and processing flow.** *(See* ● *Panel A.4.)* Pseudocode is like an outline or summary form of the program you will write.

    Sometimes pseudocode is used simply to express the purpose of a particular programming module in somewhat general terms. With

This represents a top-down design for a payroll program. Here the modules, or processing steps, are represented from the highest level of the program down to details. The three principal processing operations—input, processing, and output—are represented by the modules in the second layer: "Read input," "Calculate pay," and "Generate output." Before tasks at the top of the chart can be performed, all the ones below must be performed. Each module represents a logical processing step.

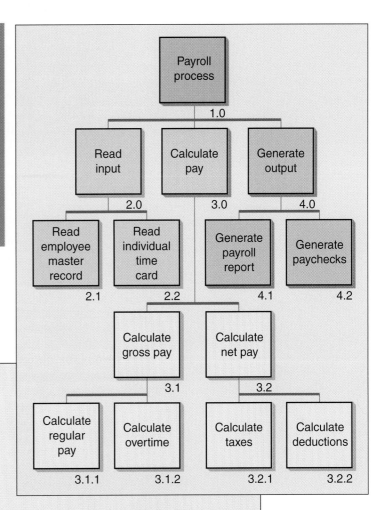

1. Each module must be of manageable size.

2. Each module should be independent and have a single function.

3. The functions of input and output are clearly defined in separate modules.

4. Each module has a single entry point (execution of the program module always starts at the same place) and a single exit point (control always leaves the module at the same place).

5. If one module refers to or transfers control to another module, the latter module returns control to the point from which it was "called" by the first module.

● **PANEL A.4**
Pseudocode

```
START
DO WHILE (so long as) there are records
      Read a customer billing account record
      IF today's date is greater than 30 days from
      date of last customer payment
            Calculate total amount due
            Calculate 5% interest on amount due
            Add interest to total amount due to calculate
            grand total
            Print on invoice overdue amount
      ELSE
            Calculate total amount due
      ENDIF
      Print out invoice
END DO
END
```

the use of such terms as *IF, THEN,* or *ELSE,* however, the pseudocode follows the rules of *control structures,* an important aspect of structured programming, as we shall explain.

- **Program flowcharts:** We described system flowcharts in the previous chapter. Here we consider program flowcharts. **A *program flowchart* is a chart that graphically presents the detailed series of steps (algorithm, or logical flow) needed to solve a programming problem.** The flowchart uses standard symbols—called *ANSI symbols,* after the American National Standards Institute, which developed them. *(See ● Panel A.5.)*

  The symbols at the left of the drawing might seem clear enough. But how do you figure out the logic of a program? How do you reason the program out so that it will really work? The answer is to use control structures, as explained next.

- **Control structures:** When you're trying to determine the logic behind something, you use words like *if* and *then* and *else.* (For example, without using these exact words, you might reason along these lines: "If she comes over, then we'll go out to a movie, else I'll just stay in and watch TV.") Control structures make use of the same words. **A *control structure,* or logic structure, is a structure that controls the logical sequence in which computer program instructions are executed. In structured program design, three control structures are used to form the logic of a program: sequence, selection, and iteration (or loop).** *(See ● Panel A.6, p. A14.)* These are the tools with which you can write structured programs and take a lot of the guesswork out of programming. (Additional variations of these three basic structures are also used.)

The Third Step: Code the Program

Once the design has been developed, the actual writing of the program begins. **Writing the program is called *coding*.** Coding is what many people think of when they think of programming, although it is only one of the five steps. Coding consists of translating the logic requirements from pseudocode or flowcharts into a programming language—the letters, numbers, and symbols that make up the program.

1. *Select the appropriate programming language:* **A *programming language* is a set of rules that tells the computer what operations to do.** Examples of well-known programming languages are C, C++, and Java. These are called "high-level languages," as we explain in a few pages.

   Not all languages are appropriate for all uses. Some, for example, have strengths in mathematical and statistical processing. Others are more appropriate for database management. Thus, in choosing the language, you need to consider what purpose the program is designed to serve and what languages are already being used in your organization or in your field.

2. *Follow the syntax:* For a program to work, you have to follow the **_syntax_, the rules of the programming language.** Programming languages have their own grammar just as human languages do. But computers are probably a lot less forgiving if you use these rules incorrectly.

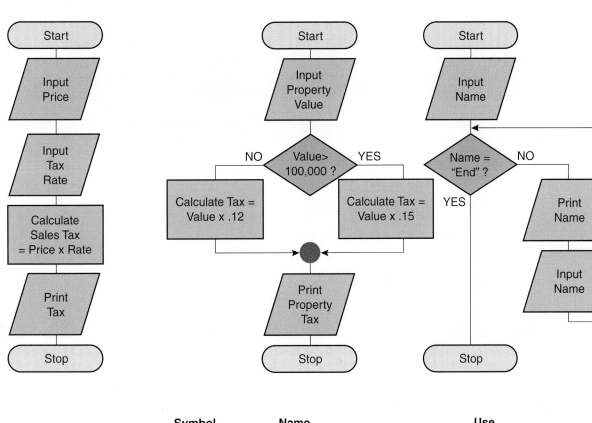

Symbol	Name	Use
	Terminal	Indicates the beginning and end of a program.
	Process	A calculation or assigning of a value to a variable.
	Input/Output (I/O)	Any statement that causes data to be input to a program (INPUT, READ) or output from the program, such as printing on the display screen or printer.
	Decision	Program decisions. Allows alternate courses of action based on a condition. A decision indicates a question that can be answered *yes* or *no* (or *true* or *false*).
	Predefined Process	A group of statements that together accomplish one task. Used extensively when programs are broken into modules.
	Connector	Can be used to eliminate lengthy flowlines. Its use indicates that one symbol is connected to another.
	Flowlines and Arrowheads	Used to connect symbols and indicate the sequence of operations. The flow is assumed to go from top to bottom and from left to right. Arrowheads are only required when the flow violates the standard direction.

● **PANEL A.5**
Example of a program flowchart and explanation of flowchart symbols. This example represents a flowchart for a payroll program.

The three control structures

The three structures used in structured program design to form the logic of a program are sequence, selection, and iteration. Case is an important version of selection.

Sequence control structure
(one program statement follows another in logical order)

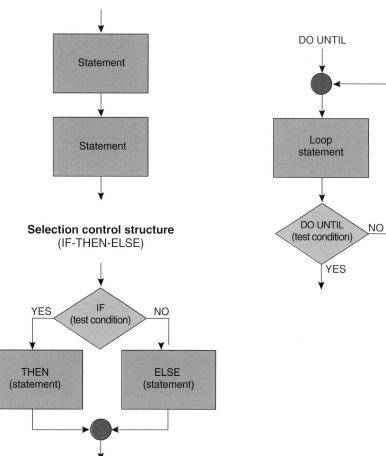

Selection control structure
(IF-THEN-ELSE)

Iteration control structures:
DO UNTIL and DO WHILE

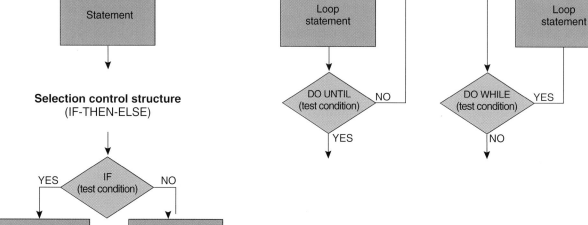

Variation on selection: the case control structure
(more than a single yes-or-no decision)

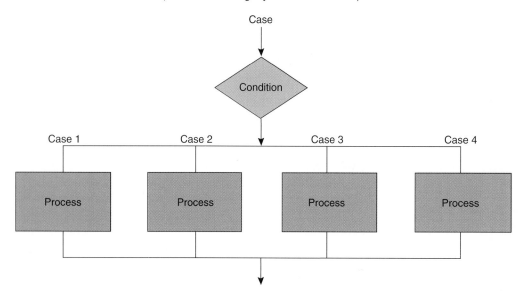

Appendix

The Fourth Step: Test the Program

Program testing involves running various tests and then running real-world data to make sure the program works. Two principal activities are desk-checking and debugging. These steps are called *alpha testing.*

1. *Perform desk-checking:* **_Desk-checking_ is simply reading through, or checking, the program to make sure that it's free of errors and that the logic works.** In other words, desk-checking is like proofreading. This step should be taken before the program is actually run on a computer.

2. *Debug the program:* Once the program has been desk-checked, further errors, or "bugs," will doubtless surface. *(See ● Panel A.7.)* **To _debug_ means to detect, locate, and remove all errors in a computer program.** Mistakes may be syntax errors or logical errors. **_Syntax errors_ are caused by typographical errors and incorrect use of the programming language. _Logic errors_ are caused by incorrect use of control structures.** Programs called *diagnostics* exist to check program syntax and display syntax-error messages. Diagnostic programs thus help identify and solve problems.

3. *Run real-world data:* After desk-checking and debugging, the program may run fine—in the laboratory. However, it needs to be tested with real data; this is called *beta testing.* Indeed, it is even advisable to test the program with bad data—data that is faulty, incomplete, or in overwhelming quantities—to see if you can make the system crash. Many users, after all, may be far more heavy-handed, ignorant, and careless than programmers have anticipated.

   Several trials using different test data may be required before the programming team is satisfied that the program can be released. Even then, some bugs may persist, because there comes a point where the pursuit of errors is uneconomical. This is one reason why many users are nervous about using the first version (version 1.0) of a commercial software package.

The Fifth Step: Document & Maintain the Program

Writing the program documentation is the fifth step in programming. The resulting _documentation_ consists of written descriptions of what a program is and how to use it. Documentation is not just an end-stage process of programming. It has been (or should have been) going on throughout all programming steps. Documentation is needed for people who will be using or be involved with the program in the future.

info!

Go to *www.softwareqatest. com* and read the FAQs about software testing. Would you like to be a software tester? Find job information at *www. softwaretestinginstitute.com/ Profession.html* and *www.betabreakers. com/services_intro. html#automated.*

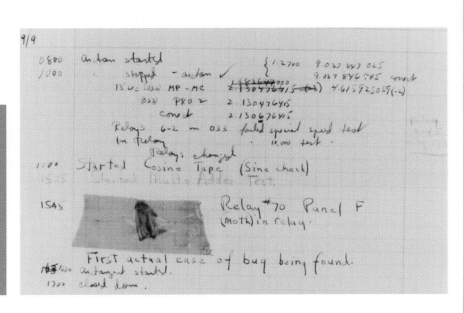

● PANEL A.7
Fourth step: program testing
The fourth step is to test the program and "debug" it of errors so it will work properly. The word "bug" dates from 1945, when a moth was discovered lodged in a relay of the Mark I computer. The moth disrupted the execution of the program.

Documentation should be prepared for several different kinds of readers—users, operators, and programmers.

When you buy a commercial software package, such as a spreadsheet, you normally get a manual with it. This is user documentation. Nowadays manuals are usually on the software CD.

The people who run large computers are called *computer operators.* Because they are not always programmers, they need to be told what to do when the program malfunctions. The *operator documentation* gives them this information.

Long after the original programming team has disbanded, the program may still be in use. If, as is often the case, a fifth of the programming staff leaves every year, after 5 years there could be a whole new bunch of programmers who know nothing about the software. *Program documentation* helps train these newcomers and enables them to maintain the existing system.

A word about maintenance: *Maintenance* includes any activity designed to keep programs in working condition, error-free, and up to date—adjustments, replacements, repairs, measurements, tests, and so on. The rapid changes in modern organizations—in products, marketing strategies, accounting systems, and so on—are bound to be reflected in their computer systems. Thus, maintenance is an important matter, and documentation must be available to help programmers make adjustments in existing systems.

A.3 Five Generations of Programming Languages

KEY QUESTIONS

What are the five generations of programming languages?

As we've said, a programming language is a set of rules that tells the computer what operations to do. Programmers, in fact, use these languages to create other kinds of software. Many programming languages have been written, some with colorful names (SNOBOL, HEARSAY, DOCTOR, ACTORS, EMERALD, JOVIAL). Each is suited to solving particular kinds of problems. What do all these languages have in common? Simply this: Ultimately they must be reduced to digital form—a 1 or 0, electricity on or off—because that is all the computer can work with.

To see how this works, it's important to understand that there are five levels, or generations, of programming languages, ranging from low level to high level. **The *five generations of programming languages* start at the lowest level with (1) machine language. They then range up through (2) assembly language, (3) high-level languages (procedural languages and object-oriented languages), and (4) very high level languages (problem-oriented languages). At the highest level are (5) natural languages.** Programming languages are said to be *lower level* when they are closer to the language that the computer itself uses—the 1s and 0s. They are called *higher level* when they are closer to the language people use—more like English, for example.

Beginning in 1945, the five levels, or generations, have evolved over the years, as programmers gradually adopted the later generations. The births of the generations are as follows. *(See ● Panel A.8.)*

- First generation, 1945—*machine language*
- Second generation, mid-1950s—*assembly language*
- Third generation, mid-1950s to early 1960s—*high-level languages (procedural languages and object-oriented):* Examples are FORTRAN, COBOL, BASIC, C, and C++.
- Fourth generation, early 1970s—*very high level languages (problem-oriented languages):* SQL, Intellect, NOMAD, FOCUS
- Fifth generation, early 1980s—*natural languages*

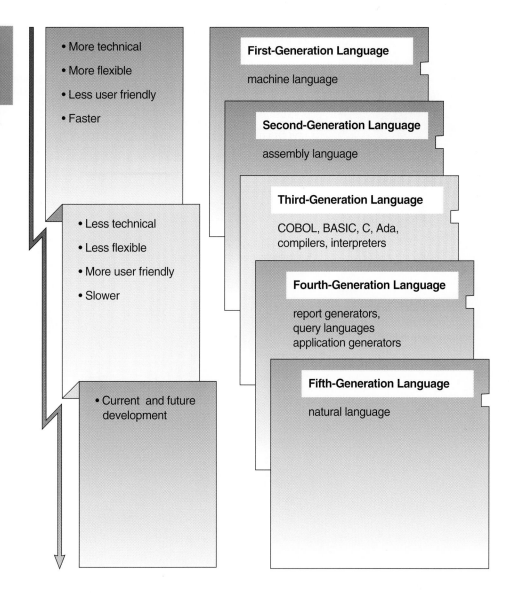

- More technical
- More flexible
- Less user friendly
- Faster

- Less technical
- Less flexible
- More user friendly
- Slower

- Current and future development

First-Generation Language

machine language

Second-Generation Language

assembly language

Third-Generation Language

COBOL, BASIC, C, Ada, compilers, interpreters

Fourth-Generation Language

report generators, query languages application generators

Fifth-Generation Language

natural language

First Generation: Machine Language

__Machine language__ **is the basic language of the computer, representing data as 1s and 0s.** *(See* ● *Panel A.9 on the next page.)* Each CPU model has its own machine language. Machine-language programs vary from computer to computer; that is, they are *machine-dependent*. These binary digits, which correspond to the on and off electrical states of the computer, are clearly not convenient for people to read and use. Believe it or not, though, programmers *did* work with these mind-numbing digits. There must have been great sighs of relief when the next generation of programming languages—assembly language—came along.

Second Generation: Assembly Language

__Assembly language__ **is a low-level programming language that allows a computer user to write a program using abbreviations or more easily remembered words instead of numbers.** For example, the letters "MP" could be used to represent the instruction MULTIPLY and "STO" to represent STORE. As you might expect, a programmer can write instructions in assembly language more quickly than in machine language. Nevertheless, it is still not an easy language to learn, and it is so tedious to use that mistakes are frequent. Moreover, assembly language has the same drawback as machine language: It varies from computer to computer—it is machine-dependent.

● PANEL A.9

Three generations of programming languages

(Top) Machine language is all binary 0s and 1s—difficult for people to work with. *(Middle)* Assembly language uses abbreviations for major instructions (such as MP for MULTIPLY). This is easier for people to use, but still challenging. *(Bottom)* COBOL, a third-generation language, uses English words that people can understand.

First generation
Machine language

```
11110010 01110011 1101 00100010000 0111 00000101011
11110010 01110011 1101 00100011000 0111 00000101111
11111100 01010010 1101 00100010010 1101 00100011101
11110000 01000101 1101 00100010011 0000 00000111110
11110011 01000011 0111 000001010000 1101 00100010100
10010110 11110000 0111 000001010100
```

Second generation
Assembly language

```
PACK  210(8,13),02B(4,7)
PACK  218(8,13),02F(4,7)
MP    212(6,13),21D(3,13)
SRP   213(5,13),03E(0),5
UNPK  050(5,7),214(4,13)
OI    054(7),X'F0'
```

Third generation
COBOL

```
MULTIPLY HOURS-WORKED BY PAY-RATE GIVING GROSS-PAY ROUNDED.
```

We now need to introduce the concept of *language translator*. Because a computer can execute programs only in machine language, a translator or converter is needed if the program is written in any other language. **A _language translator_ is a type of systems software that translates a program written in a second-, third-, or higher-generation language into machine language.**

Language translators are of three types:

- Assemblers
- Compilers
- Interpreters

An _assembler_, or assembler program, is a program that translates the assembly-language program into machine language. We describe compilers and interpreters in the next section.

Third Generation: High-Level or Procedural Languages

A _high-level_, or _procedural/object-oriented_, _language_ resembles some human language such as English; an example is COBOL, which is used for business applications. A procedural language allows users to write in a familiar notation, rather than numbers or abbreviations. Also, unlike machine and assembly languages, most are not machine-dependent—that is, they can be used on more than one kind of computer. Familiar languages of this sort include FORTRAN, COBOL, BASIC, Pascal, and C. (We cover object-oriented languages shortly.)

For a procedural language to work on a computer, it needs a language translator to translate it into machine language. Depending on the procedural language, either of two types of translators may be used—a *compiler* or an *interpreter*.

- **Compiler—execute later: A _compiler_ is a language-translator program that converts the entire program of a high-level language into machine language *before* the computer executes the program.** The programming instructions of a procedural language are called the *source code*. The compiler translates it into machine language, which in this case is called the *object code*. The important point here is that the object code can be saved and thus can be executed later (as many times as desired), rather than run right away. *(See ● Panel A.10.)* These executable files—the output of compilers—have the *.exe* extension.

  Examples of procedural languages using compilers are COBOL, FORTRAN, Pascal, and C.

- **Interpreter—execute immediately: An _interpreter_ is a language-translator program that converts each procedural language statement into machine language and executes it *immediately*, statement by statement.** In contrast to the compiler, no object code is saved. Therefore, interpreted code generally runs more slowly than compiled code. However, code can be tested line by line. BASIC is a procedural language using an interpreter.

Who cares, you might say, whether you can run a program now or later? (After all, "later" could be only a matter of seconds or minutes.) Here's the significance: When a compiler is used, it requires two steps (the source code and the object code) before the program can be executed. The interpreter, on the other hand, requires only *one* step. The advantage of a compiler language is that, once you have obtained the object code, the program executes faster. The advantage of an interpreter language, on the other hand, is that programs are easier to develop. Some language translators—such as those with C++ and Java, covered shortly—can both compile and interpret.

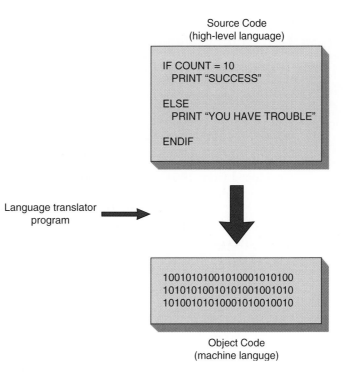

● PANEL A.10
Compiler
This language translator converts the procedural language *(source code)* into machine language *(object code)* before the computer can execute the program.

Source Code
(high-level language)

```
IF COUNT = 10
    PRINT "SUCCESS"

ELSE
    PRINT "YOU HAVE TROUBLE"

ENDIF
```

Language translator program

```
10010101001010001010100
10101010010101001001010
10100101010001010010010
```

Object Code
(machine language)

Some of the most popular procedural languages are Visual BASIC, C, and C++. *(See ● Panel A.11.)*

Fourth Generation: Very High Level or Problem-Oriented Languages

Third-generation languages tell the computer *how* to do something. Fourth-generation languages, in contrast, tell the computer *what* to do. <u>**Very high level**</u>, or <u>**problem-oriented**</u>, <u>**languages**</u>, **also called** <u>**fourth-generation languages (4GLs)**</u>, **are much more user-oriented and allow users to develop programs with fewer commands compared with procedural languages,** although they require more computing power. These languages are called problem-oriented because they are designed to solve specific problems, whereas procedural languages are more general-purpose languages.

Fifth Generation: Natural Languages

<u>*Natural languages*</u> **are of two types. The first comprises ordinary human languages: English, Spanish, and so on. The second type comprises programming languages that use human language to give people a more natural connection with computers.**

With a problem-oriented language, you can type in some rather routine inquiries, such as (in the language known as FOCUS) the following:
SUM SHIPMENTS BY STATE BY DATE.

Natural languages, by contrast, allow questions or commands to be framed in a more conversational way or in alternative forms—for example,
I WANT THE SHIPMENTS OF PERSONAL DIGITAL ASSISTANTS FOR ALABAMA AND MISSISSIPPI BROKEN DOWN BY CITY FOR JANUARY AND FEBRUARY. ALSO, MAY I HAVE JANUARY AND FEBRUARY SHIPMENTS LISTED BY CITIES FOR PERSONAL COMMUNICATORS SHIPPED TO WISCONSIN AND MINNESOTA.

Natural languages are part of the field of study known as artificial intelligence. Artificial intelligence (AI) is a group of related technologies that attempt to develop machines capable of emulating human qualities, such as learning, reasoning, communicating, seeing, and hearing.

A.4 Programming Languages Used Today

Let us now turn back and consider some of the third-generation, or high-level, languages in use today.

FORTRAN: The Language of Mathematics & the First High-Level Language

Developed from 1954 to 1956 by John Backus and others at IBM, *FORTRAN* (for "FORmula TRANslator") was the first high-level language. Originally designed to express mathematical formulas, it is still the most widely used language for mathematical, scientific, and engineering problems. It is also useful for complex business applications, such as forecasting and modeling. However, because it cannot handle a large volume of input/output operations or file processing, it is not used for more typical business problems.

Third-generation languages compared

This shows how five languages handle the same statement. The statement specifies that a customer gets a discount of 7% of the invoice amount if the invoice is greater than $500; if the invoice is lower, there is no discount.

FORTRAN

```
IF (XINVO .GT. 500.00) THEN
    DISCNT = 0.07 * XINVO
ELSE
    DISCNT = 0.0
ENDIF
XINVO = XINVO – DISCNT
```

COBOL

```
OPEN-INVOICE-FILE.
    OPEN I-O INVOICE FILE.

READ-INVOICE-PROCESS.
    PERFORM READ-NEXT-REC THROUGH READ-NEXT-REC-EXIT UNTIL END-OF-FILE.
    STOP RUN.

READ-NEXT-REC.
    READ INVOICE-REC
        INVALID KEY
            DISPLAY 'ERROR READING INVOICE FILE'
            MOVE 'Y' TO EOF-FLAG
            GOTO READ-NEXT-REC-EXIT.
    IF INVOICE-AMT > 500
        COMPUTE INVOICE-AMT = INVOICE-AMT – (INVOICE-AMT * .07)
        REWRITE INVOICE-REC.

READ-NEXT-REC-EXIT.
    EXIT.
```

BASIC

```
10  REM      This Program Calculates a Discount Based on the Invoice Amount
20  REM          If Invoice Amount is Greater Than 500, Discount is 7%
30  REM          Otherwise Discount is 0
40  REM
50  INPUT "What is the Invoice Amount"; INV.AMT
60  IF INV.AMT 500 THEN LET DISCOUNT = .07 ELSE LET DISCOUNT = 0
70  REM          Display results
80  PRINT "Original Amt", "Discount", "Amt after Discount"
90  PRINT INV.AMT, INV.AMT * DISCOUNT, INV.AMT – INV.AMT * DISCOUNT
100 END
```

Pascal

```
if INVOICEAMOUNT > 500.00 then
    DISCOUNT := 0.07 * INVOICEAMOUNT
else
    DISCOUNT := 0.0;
INVOICEAMOUNT := INVOICEAMOUNT – DISCOUNT
```

C

```
if (invoice_amount > 500.00)
    discount = 0.07 * invoice_amount;
else
    discount = 0.00;
invoice_amount = invoice_amount – discount;
```

COBOL: The Language of Business

Developed under the auspices of the U.S. Department of Defense, with Grace Murray Hopper as a major contributor, and formally adopted in 1960, *COBOL* (for "*CO*mmon *B*usiness-*O*riented *L*anguage") is the most frequently used business programming language for large computers. Its most significant attribute is that it is extremely readable. For example, a COBOL line might read:

MULTIPLY HOURLY-RATE BY HOURS-WORKED GIVING GROSS-PAY

Writing a COBOL program resembles writing an outline for a research paper. The program is divided into four divisions—Identification, Environment, Data, and Procedure. The divisions in turn are divided into sections, which are divided into paragraphs, which are further divided into sections. The Identification Division identifies the name of the program and the author (programmer) and perhaps some other helpful comments. The Environment Division describes the computer on which the program will be compiled and executed. The Data Division describes what data will be processed. The Procedure Division describes the actual processing procedures.

Some people believe that COBOL is becoming obsolete. However, others disagree.

BASIC: The Easy Language

BASIC was developed by John Kemeny and Thomas Kurtz in 1964 for use in training their students at Dartmouth College. By the late 1960s, it was widely used in academic settings on all kinds of computers, from mainframes to PCs.

BASIC (*B*eginner's *A*ll-purpose *S*ymbolic *I*nstruction *C*ode) used to be the most popular microcomputer language and is considered the easiest programming language to learn. Although it is available in compiler form, the interpreter form is more popular with first-time and casual users. This is because it is interactive, meaning that user and computer can communicate with each other during the writing and running of the program. Today there is no one version of BASIC. One of the popular current evolutions is Visual BASIC, discussed shortly.

Pascal: The Simple Language

Named after the 17th-century French mathematician Blaise Pascal, *Pascal*—developed in 1970 by Niklaus Wirth—is an alternative to BASIC as a language for teaching purposes and is relatively easy to learn. A difference from BASIC is that Pascal uses structured programming.

C: For Portability & Scientific Use

C is the successor of B, which was the successor of BCPL, which was the successor of CPL (Computer Programming Language), an early programming language that was not implemented. Developed by Dennis Ritchie at Bell Laboratories in the early 1970s, *C* is a general-purpose, compiled language that was developed for minicomputers but that works well for microcomputers and is portable among many computers. It was originally developed for writing system software. The first major program written in C was the Unix operating system, and for many years C was considered to be inextricably linked with Unix. Now, however, C is an important language independent of Unix. Today it is widely used for writing applications, including word processing, spreadsheets, games, robotics, and graphics programs. It is now considered a necessary language for programmers to know.

LISP: For Artificial Intelligence Programs

LISP (LISt Processor) is a third-generation language used principally to construct artificial intelligence programs. Developed at the Massachusetts Institute of Technology in 1958 by mathematician John McCarthy, LISP is used to write expert systems and natural language programs. Expert systems are programs that are imbued with knowledge by a human expert; the programs can walk you through a problem and help solve it.

A.5 Object-Oriented & Visual Programming Languages

KEY QUESTION

How do OOP and visual programming work?

Consider how it was for the computer pioneers, programming in machine language or assembly language. Novices putting together programs in BASIC or C can breathe a collective sigh of relief that they weren't around at the dawn of the Computer Age. Even some of the simpler third-generation languages represent a challenge, because they are procedure-oriented, forcing the programmer to follow a predetermined path.

Fortunately, two developments have made things easier—object-oriented programming and visual programming.

Object-Oriented Programming: Block by Block

Imagine you're programming in a traditional third-generation language, such as BASIC, creating your coded instructions one line at a time. As you work on some segment of the program (such as how to compute overtime pay), you may think, "I'll bet some other programmer has already written something like this. Wish I had it. It would save a lot of time." Fortunately, a kind of recycling technique exists. This is object-oriented programming, an improved version of 3GL languages.

Conventional Programs

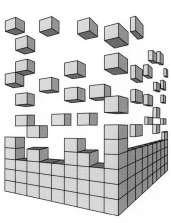

1. *What OOP is:* In ***object-oriented programming*** (**OOP, pronounced "oop"), data and the instructions for processing that data are combined into a self-sufficient "object" that can be used in other programs.** The important thing here is the object.

2. *What an "object" is:* An ***object*** **is a self-contained module consisting of preassembled programming code.** The module contains, or encapsulates, both (1) a chunk of data and (2) the processing instructions that may be performed on that data.

3. *When an object's data is to be processed—sending the "message":* Once the object becomes part of a program, the processing instructions may or may not be activated. A particular set of instructions is activated only when the corresponding "message" is sent. A *message* is an alert sent to the object when an operation involving that object needs to be performed.

Object-Oriented Programs

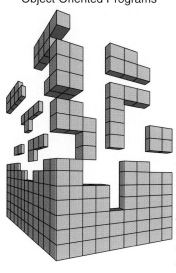

4. *How the object's data is processed—the "methods":* The message need only identify the operation. How it is actually to be performed is embedded within the processing instructions that are part of the object. These processing instructions within the object are called the *methods.*

Once you've written a block of program code (that computes overtime pay, for example), it can be reused in any number of programs. Thus, with OOP, unlike traditional programming, you don't have to start from scratch—that is, reinvent the wheel—each time.

Object-oriented programming takes longer to learn than traditional programming because it means training oneself to a new way of thinking. However, the beauty of OOP is that an object can be used repeatedly in different applications and by different programmers, speeding up development time and lowering costs.

An example of an OOP language is *C++*—the plus signs stand for "more than C"—which combines the traditional C programming language with object-oriented capability. C++ was created by Bjarne Stroustrup. With C++, programmers can write standard code in C without the object-oriented features, use object-oriented features, or do a mixture of both.

Java is also an object-oriented language. A high-level programming language developed by Sun Microsystems in 1995, Java is used to write compact programs that can be downloaded over the internet and immediately executed on many kinds of computers. Java is similar to C++ but is simplified to eliminate language features that cause common programming errors. Java source code files (files with a *.java* extension) are compiled into a format called *bytecode* (files with a *.class* extension), which can then be executed by a Java interpreter. Compiled Java code can run on most computers because Java interpreters and runtime environments, known as *Java Virtual Machines (VMs)*, exist for most operating systems, including Unix, the Macintosh OS, and Windows.

Small Java applications are called Java *applets* and can be downloaded from a web server and run on your computer by a Java-compatible web browser, such as Netscape Navigator or Microsoft Internet Explorer. Java applets make websites more interactive and attractive, adding features such as animation and calculators—but only if a browser is capable of supporting Java. Users also can download free Java applets from various sites on the internet.

Visual Programming: The Example of Visual BASIC

Essentially, visual programming takes OOP to the next level. The goal of visual programming is to make programming easier for programmers and more accessible to nonprogrammers, by borrowing the object orientation of OOP languages but exercising it in a graphical or visual way. Visual programming enables users to think more about the problem solving than about handling the programming language. There is no learning of syntax or actual writing of code

Visual programming **is a method of creating programs in which the programmer makes connections between objects by drawing, pointing, and clicking on diagrams and icons and by interacting with flowcharts.** Thus, the programmer can create programs by clicking on icons that represent common programming routines.

An example of visual programming is *Visual BASIC*, a Windows-based, object-oriented programming language from Microsoft that lets users develop Windows and Office applications by (1) creating command buttons, text boxes, windows, and toolbars, which (2) then may be linked to small BASIC programs that perform certain actions. Visual BASIC is *event-driven*, which means that the program waits for the user to do something (an "event"), such as click on an icon, and then the program responds. At the beginning, for example, the user can use drag-and-drop tools to develop a graphical user interface, which is created automatically by the program. Because of its ease of use, Visual BASIC allows even novice programmers to create impressive Windows-based applications.

Since its launch in 1990, the Visual BASIC approach has become the norm for programming languages. Now there are visual environments for many programming languages, including C, C++, Pascal, and Java. Visual BASIC is sometimes called a *rapid application development (RAD)* system because it enables programmers to quickly build prototype applications.

KEY QUESTION

What do markup and scripting languages do?

A *markup language* **is a kind of coding, or "tags," inserted into text that embeds details about the structure and appearance of the text.** Markup languages have codes for indicating layout and styling (such as boldface, italics, paragraphs, insertion of graphics, and so on) within a text file—for example, HTML (p. 56). The name "markup" is derived from the traditional publishing practice of "marking up" a manuscript, that is, adding printer's instructions in the margins of a paper manuscript.

Some early examples of markup languages available outside the publishing industry could be found in typesetting tools on Unix systems. In these systems, formatting commands were inserted into the document text so that typesetting software could format the text according to the editor's specifications. After a time it was seen that most markup languages had many features in common. This led to the creation of *SGML (Standard Generalized Markup Language)*, which specified a syntax for including the markup in documents, as well as another system (a so-called *metalanguage*) for separately describing what the markup meant. This allowed authors to create and use any markup they wished, selecting tags that made the most sense to them. SGML was developed and standardized by the International Organization for Standards in 1986.

SGML is used widely to manage large documents that are subject to frequent revisions and need to be printed in different formats. Because it is a large and complex system, it is not yet widely used on personal computers. This changed dramatically when Tim Berners-Lee used some of the SGML syntax, without the metalanguage, to create HTML (Hypertext Markup Language). HTML may be the most used document format in the world today.

For some people, the term *script* may conjure up images of actors and actresses on a sound stage practicing lines from a book of text. In web terms, however, a *script* **is a short list of self-executing commands embedded in a web page that perform a specific function or routine.** Scripts are similar to the macros used in Microsoft Word or the batch files used in the early days of DOS, both of which performed functions ranging from generating text to displaying the date and time. Because they are self-executing, scripts can perform their work without user involvement, although some are initiated by an action on the part of the user (such as a mouse click) and others require user input to complete a task.[2]

On web pages, scripting languages are used to perform many duties. For example, they create traffic counters and scrolling text, set cookies so that websites can remember user preferences, and switch out graphics and text when users click buttons or pass their mouse over items. Any time you see something interesting occurring on a website, there is a good chance that a script is involved. Scripting languages are often designed for interactive use.

Following are some popular markup and scripting languages.

info!

Go to *www.webwareindex.com/tutorials* for information and tutorials about many programming and scripting languages.

HTML: For Creating 2-D Web Documents & Links

As we discussed in Chapter 2, *HTML* (Hypertext Markup Language) is a markup language that lets people create onscreen documents for the internet that can easily be linked by words and pictures to other documents. HTML is a type of code that embeds simple commands within standard ASCII text documents to provide an integrated, two-dimensional display of text and graphics. In other words, a document created in any word processor and stored in ASCII format can become a web page with the addition of a few HTML commands.

One of the main features of HTML is the ability to insert hypertext links into a document. *Hypertext links* enable you to display another web document simply by clicking on a link area—usually underlined or highlighted—

info!

For an easy-to-follow tutorial on using HTML, go to *http://computer.howstuffworks.com/web-page.htm*. After you work through the tutorial, create a sample HTML-tagged document for what could become your personal website.

on your current screen. One document may contain links to many other related documents. The related documents may be on the same server as the first document, or they may be on a computer halfway around the world. A link may be a word, a group of words, or a picture.

VRML: For Creating 3-D Web Pages

Mark Pesce and Tony Parisi created VRML at Silicon Graphics in 1994. VRML rhymes with "thermal." **_VRML (Virtual Reality Modeling Language)_ is a type of programming language used to create three-dimensional web pages including interactive animation.** Even though VRML's designers wanted to let nonprogrammers create their own virtual spaces quickly and painlessly, it's not as simple to describe a three-dimensional scene as it is to describe a page in HTML. However, many existing modeling and computer-aided design tools now offer VRML support, and new VRML-centered software tools are arriving. An example of a VRML scene might be a virtual room where the viewer can use controls to move around inside the room (or move the room itself) as though she or he were walking through it in real space.

To view VRML files, users need a special VRML browser (in addition to an internet connection and a web browser). The VRML browser is what interprets VRML commands and lets the user interact with the virtual world. VRML browsers typically work as plug-ins for traditional web browsers, but newer browsers may already have the appropriate VRML browser plug-in installed. There are several VRML browsers available for Windows users, and some, such as Cosmo Software's Cosmo Player _(www.cai.com/cosmo)_, are free to download.

XML: For Making the Web Work Better

The chief characteristics of HTML are its simplicity and its ease in combining plain text and pictures. But, in the words of journalist Michael Krantz, "HTML simply lacks the software muscle to handle the business world's endless and complex transactions."[3] Another, newer markup language is _XML (eXtensible Markup Language)_, a standard maintained by the World Wide Web Consortium for creating special-purpose markup languages. XML's primary purpose is to facilitate the sharing of structured text and information across the internet.

Unlike HTML, which uses a set of "known" tags, XML allows you to create any tags you wish (thus it's extensible) and then describe those tags in a metalanguage known as the _DTD (Document Type Definition)_. XML is similar to the concept of SGML, and in fact XML is a subset of SGML in general terms. The main purpose of XML (as opposed to SGML) is to keep the system simpler by focusing on a particular problem—documents on the internet.

Whereas HTML makes it easy for humans to read websites, XML makes it easy for machines to read websites by enabling web developers to add more "tags" to a web page. At present, when you use your browser to locate a website, search engines can turn up too much, so that it's difficult to find the specific site you want—say, one with a recipe for a low-calorie chicken dish for 12. According to Krantz, "XML makes websites smart enough to tell other machines whether they're looking at a recipe, an airline ticket, or a pair of easy-fit blue jeans with a 34-inch waist." XML lets website developers put "tags" on their web pages that describe information in, for example, a food recipe as "ingredients," "calories," "cooking time," and "number of portions." Thus, your browser no longer has to search the entire web for a low-calorie poultry recipe for 12.

JavaScript: For Dynamic Web Pages

JavaScript (also known as *ECMAScript*) is an object-oriented scripting language originally developed by Netscape Communications under the name "LiveScript" but then renamed to "JavaScript" and given a syntax closer to that of Sun Microsystems' Java language. The change of name happened at about the same time Netscape was including support for Java technology in its Netscape Navigator browser. Consequently, the change proved a source of much confusion. There is no real relation between Java and JavaScript; their only similarities are some syntax and the fact that both languages are used extensively on the World Wide Web.

Many website designers use JavaScript technology to create powerful dynamic web applications. One major use of JavaScript is to write little functions that are embedded in HTML pages and interact with the browser to perform certain tasks not possible in static HTML alone, such as opening a new window and changing images as the mouse cursor moves over them.

ActiveX: For Creating Interactive Web Pages

ActiveX was developed by Microsoft as an alternative to Java for creating interactivity on web pages. Indeed, Java and ActiveX are the two major contenders in the web war for transforming the World Wide Web into a complete interactive environment.

ActiveX is a set of controls, or reusable components, that enable programs or content of almost any type to be embedded within a web page. Whereas Java requires that you download an applet each time you visit a website, with ActiveX the component is downloaded only once (to a windows-based computer) and then stored on your hard drive for later and repeated use.

Thus, the chief characteristic of ActiveX is that it features reusable components—small modules of software code that perform specific tasks (such as a spelling checker), which may be plugged seamlessly into other applications. With ActiveX, you can obtain from your hard disk any file that is suitable for the web—such as a Java applet, animation, or pop-up menu—and insert it directly into an HTML document.

Programmers can create ActiveX controls or components in a variety of programming languages, including C, C++, Visual BASIC, and Java. Thousands of ready-made ActiveX components are now commercially available from numerous software development companies.

Perl: For CGI Scripts

info!

Visit the Perl language page at *www.perl.com/perl/index.html*.

info!

What is genetic programming? Do a keyword search and find out.

Perl (Practical Extraction and Report Language) is the dominant scripting language used to develop CGI scripts in the context of web developent. *CGI (Common Gateway Interface)* is standard for passing information between a server and an application as part of the World Wide Web's HTTP protocol (p. 58). For example, when a user views a web page and inputs information into a form, a CGI program gathers that data and provides a response. Almost any time users are asked to input information on a website, a CGI script is at work. (CGI scripts can also be created using C, Java, and Visual BASIC.)

Notes

Chapter 1

1. Kevin Maney, "Net's Next Phase Will Weave Through Your Life," *USA Today*, March 2, 2001, pp. 1B, 2B.
2. Don Clark, "Managing the Mountain," *Wall Street Journal*, June 21, 1999, p. R4; "Does America Have ADD?" *U.S. News & World Report*, March 26, 2001, p. 14; and Jon Swartz, "Email Overload Taxes Workers and Companies," *USA Today*, June 26, 2001, p. 1A.
3. Dave Wilson, "Some Are Losing It, Bit by Bit," *Los Angeles Times*, July 17, 2001, pp. A1, A8.
4. Howard Rheingold, *Smart Mobs: The Next Social Revolution* (New York: Perseus, 2002).
5. "World Cell Phone Users to Hit 1.25 Bln in 05—JEITA," Reuters, December 6, 2000, *www.kagan.com/archive/reuters/2000/12/06*; B. Chaney, "Stupid Things About Smart Phone," *Fortune*, Summer 2001, p. 26.
6. Michael Specter, "Your Mail Has Vanished," *New Yorker*, December 6, 1999, pp. 96–103.
7. Data from International Data Corp., in "Like It or Not, You've Got Mail," *Business Week*, October 4, 1999, pp. 178–184.
8. IDC, Nua Internet Surveys, March 2003; *www.nua.com/surveys*.
9. "Like It or Not, You've Got Mail," 1999.
10. Robert Rossney, "E-Mail's Best Asset—Time to Think," *San Francisco Chronicle*, October 5, 1995, p. E7.
11. Adam Gopnik, "The Return of the Word," *New Yorker*, December 6, 1999, pp. 49–50.
12. Peter H. Lewis, "The Good, the Bad, and the Truly Ugly Faces of Electronic Mail," *New York Times*, September 6, 1994, p. B7.
13. Gopnik, 1999.
14. David A. Whittler, quoted in "Living Online," *The Futurist*, July–August 1997, p. 54.
15. IDC, March 2003.
16. Kevin Maney, "The Net Effect: Evolution or Revolution?" *USA Today*, August 9, 1999, pp. 1B, 2B.
17. December 10–13, 1999, survey by The Strategis Group, reported in Dru Sefton, "The Big Online Picture: Daily Web Surfing Now the Norm," *USA Today*, March 22, 2000, p. 3D.
18. Kevin Murphy, Gartner Group, quoted in Timothy J. Mullaney, "Death to E-Words Everywhere," *Business Week*, November 15, 1999, p. 10.
19. Roger Highfield, "Imagine a Trillion Laptops in Every Drop of Water—The Next Generation of Computers," *The Daily Telegraph*, December 5, 2001; *http://ptg.djnr.com/ccroot/asp/publib/story_clean_cpy.asp?articles=900273'TW . . .*, Dow Jones Interactive.
20. David M Ewalt, "The Next (not so) Big Thing," *InformationWeek*, May 13, 2002.
21. David Einstein, "Custom Computers," *San Francisco Chronicle*, April 15, 1999, pp. B1, B3.
22. Einstein, 1999.
23. Laurence Hooper, "No Compromises," *Wall Street Journal*, November 16, 1992, p. R8.
24. Tom Forester and Perry Morrison, *Computer Ethics: Cautionary Tales and Ethical Dilemmas in Computing* (Cambridge, MA: MIT Press, 1990), pp. 1–2.
25. Jane Costello, "Airlines Find Lost Cellphones Are a Real Hang-Up," *Wall Street Journal*, August 7, 2001, p. B7.

Practical Action Box

a. Study by Impulse Research for *Iconoclast* newsletter, reported in D. Plotnikoff, "E-Mail: A Critical Medium Has Reached Critical Mass," *San Jose Mercury News*, April 4, 1999, pp. 1F, 2F.
b. K. Clark, "At Least the Coffee and Pens Are Still Free," *U.S. News & World Report*, June 7, 1999, p. 70.
c. S. Shostak, "You Call This Progress?" *Newsweek*, January 18, 1999, p. 16.
d. A. Markels, "Don't Manage by E-Mail," *San Francisco Examiner*, August 11, 1996, p. B-5, reprinted from *Wall Street Journal*; "Don't Overuse Your E-Mail," *CPA Client Bulletin*, March 1999, p. 3; B. Fryer, "E-Mail: Backbone of the Info Age or Smoking Gun?" *Your Company*, July/August 1999, pp. 73–76; S. Armour, "Boss: It's in the E-Mail," *USA Today*, August 10, 1999, p. 3B; L. Guernsey, "Attachments" #@%&#@ Are Full #+@&*¢# of Surprises," *New York Times*, July 22, 1999, p. D11.

Chapter 2

1. Graham T. T. Molitor, "Five Forces Transforming Communications," *The Futurist*, September–October 2001, pp. 32–37.
2. Charles Smith, "Ready or Not, Here Comes . . . Ubicomp," *San Francisco Chronicle*, August 11, 2001, pp. 1, 4.
3. Molitor, 2001, p. 33.
4. "Say Hello to Instant Messaging," *Smart Computing*, September 2002, p. 51.
5. Michelle Slatalla, "The Office Meeting That Never Ends," *New York Times*, September 23, 1999, pp. D1, D8.
6. Jeanne Hinds, quoted in Slatalla, 1999.
7. "Egregious Email," *Smart Computing*, October 2002, pp. 95–97.
8. "Spam Levels Still Rising," *ZD Net*, December 13, 2002, *www.nua.com*.
9. Julian Haight, quoted in David Lazarus, "Fan Spam Is Hard to Shake," *San Francisco Chronicle*, February 7, 2000, pp. C1, C2.
10. Elizabeth Weise, "Successful Net Search Starts with a Need," *USA Today*, January 24, 2000, p. 3D; Timothy Hanrahan, "The Best Way to . . . Search Online," *Wall Street Journal*, December 6, 1999, p. R25; and Weise, "Web Changes Direction to People Skills," 2000.
11. Matt Lake, "Desperately Seeking Susan OR Suzie NOT Sushi," *New York Times*, September 3, 1998, p. D1.
12. Megan Doscher, "The Best Way to Find Love," *Wall Street Journal*, December 6, 1999, p. R34.
13. Sharon Cleary, "The Best Way to Find an Old Friend," *Wall Street Journal*, December 6, 1999, pp. R26, R45.
14. William M. Bulkeley, "The Best Way to Go to School," *Wall Street Journal*, December 6, 1999, pp. R18, R22.
15. Bulkeley, 1999; and Faith Bremner, "On-line College Classes Get High Marks Among Students," *USA Today*, November 16, 1998, p. 16E.
16. Ellen Laird, "Internet Plagiarism: We All Pay the Price," *Chronicle of Higher Education*, June 13, 2001, p. B5.
17. Bruce Leland, quoted in Peter Applebome, "On the Internet, Term Papers Are Hot Items," *New York Times*, June 8, 1997, sec. 1, pp. 1, 20.
18. Eugene Dwyer, "Virtual Term Papers" [letter], *New York Times*, June 10, 1997, p. A20.
19. John Yankey, "Cheating, Digital Plagiarism Rise as Tech Hits Classroom," *Reno Gazette-Journal*, July 30, 2001, p. 23E.
20. William L. Rukeyser, "How to Track Down Collegiate Cyber-Cheaters" [letter], *New York Times*, June 14, 1997, sec. 4, p. 14.
21. David Rothenberg, "How the Web Destroys the Quality of Students' Research Papers," *Chronicle of Higher Education*, August 15, 1997.

Chapter 3

1. Alan Robbins, "Why There's Egg on Your Interface," *New York Times*, December 1, 1996, sec. 3, p. 12.
2. Joshua Quittner, "Aqua: The Movie," *Time*, January 31, 2000, p. 82.
3. Irving Wladawsky-Berger, quoted in Deborah Solomon, "Could Linux

Outdo Windows?" *USA Today*, March 9, 2000, pp. 1B, 2B.

Chapter 4

1. Michael S. Malone, "The Tiniest Transformer," *San Jose Mercury News*, September 10, 1995, pp. 1D, 2D; excerpted from *The Microprocessor: A Biography* (New York: Telos/Springer Verlag, 1995).
2. Malone, 1995.
3. Laurence Hooper, "No Compromises," *Wall Street Journal*, November 16, 1992, p. R8.
4. Cade Metz, "Firewire vs. USB," *PC Magazine*, February 25, 2003, pp. 100–106.
5. Edward Baig, "Be Happy, Film Freaks," *Business Week*, May 26, 1997, pp. 172–173.
6. Jefferson Graham, "New Devices Plug the Gap Between Floppy and CD," *USA Today*, September 9, 2002, p. 4D; and Larry Armstrong, "A Keychain Never Forgets," *Business Week*, August 5, 2002, p. 24.
7. Walter S. Mossberg, "How to Buy a Laptop: Some Basic Guidelines in a Dizzying Market," *Wall Street Journal*, October 21, 1999, p. B1.
8. Stephen H. Wildstrom, "How to Shop for a Laptop," *Business Week*, April 3, 2000, p. 25.
9. "The New Laptops," *Consumer Reports*, May 2000, pp. 12–16; Walter S. Mossberg, "Buying Your Next PC? Get the Most Memory, Not the Fastest Chip," *Wall Street Journal*, April 6, 2000, p. B1; and Bill Howard, "Notebook PCs," *PC Magazine*, August 1999, pp. 154–155.

ST1. Henry Norr, "Data Files Need to Be Backed Up," *San Francisco Chronicle*, March 13, 2003, p. E1.

Chapter 5

1. David F. Gallagher, "2 Rooms, River View, ATM in Lobby," *New York Times*, June 6, 2002, p. Eb.
2. John Tierney, "Shop Till Eggs, Diapers, Toothpaste Drop," *New York Times*, August 28, 2002, pp. A1, A14.
3. Stephen H. Wildstrom, "The Liberation of Laptop Design?" *Business Week*, November 25, 2002, p. 24; Stephen H. Wildstrom, "The Microsoft Pen Is a Mite Clunky," *Business Week*, November 13, 2002, p. 20; Janet Rae-Dupree, "Keyless Entry," *U.S. News & World Report*, November 13, 2002, p. 36; Walter S. Mossberg, "Can Tablets Cure PC Industry?" *Wall Street Journal*, November 7, 2002, pp. Bl, B4; and David Pogue, "Tablet PCs: Computing Drawn Anew," *New York Times*, November 7, 2002, pp. Gl, GB.
4. David Pogue, "Scrawl to Screen with a Pen," *New York Times*, February 13, 2003, pp. E1, E6; Edward G. Baig, "What You Write Is What You Get with 'io' Digital Pen," *USA Today*, November 27, 2002, p.6D; Jergen Sundgot, "Everything but the Kitchen Pen," *InfoSync World*, July 16, 2002, *www.infosync.no/news*; David LaGesse, "Writing in Pen, Ink, and Pixels," *U.S. News & World Report*, June 17, 2002, p. 60; and Paula Hancocks, "VPen Promises Write Stuff at CeBIT," *CNN.com/Sci-Tech*, March 15, 2002, *www.cnn.com/2002/ TECH/03/15 /cebit.pen.*

Practical Action Box

a. Marty Jerome, "Boot Up or Die," *PC Computing*, April 1998, pp. 172–186.

Chapter 6

1. "What Does 'Digital' Mean in Regard to Electronics?" *Popular Science*, August 1997, pp. 91–94.
2. *www.csgnet.com*, March 24, 2003.
3. Tony Perkins, quoted in Bill O'Driscoll, "Expert: Business Needs to Tap the 'Always On,'" *Reno Gazette-Journal*, February 12, 2003, pp. 1D, 6D.
4. Daniel R. Mintz, "For a Dad, Video-conferencing Ties That Bind," *New York Times*, June 10, 2001, sec. 3, p. 13.
5. Stephanie Armour, "Telecommuting Gets tuck in the Slow Lane," *USA Today*, pp. 1A, 2A. June 25, 2001; Stephanie Armour, "More Bosses Keep Tabs on Telecommuters," *USA Today*, July 24, 2001, p. 1B; Jim Hopkins, "How Solo Workers Keep from Feeling Deserted," *USA Today*, May 9, 2001, p. 9B; Bonnie Harris, "Companies Turning Cool to Telecommuting Trend," *Los Angeles Times*, December 28, 2000, pp. A1, A6; and Kemba J. Dunham, "Telecommuters' Lament," *Wall Street Journal*, October 31, 2000, pp. B1, B18.
6. David Kline, quoted in W. James Au, "The Lonely Long-Distance Worker," *PC Computing*, February 2000, pp. 42–43.
7. David Perlman, "Satellite Network Captures Volcano Drama in Hawaii," *San Francisco Chronicle*, February 17, 1997, p. A4.
8. Lisa Guernsey, "With Wires in the Walls, the Cyberhome Hums," *New York Times*, March 27, 2003, pp. D1, D7.
9. Yahoo!, cited in Del Jones, "Cyberporn Poses Workplace Threat," *USA Today*, November 27, 1995, p. B1.
10. Lawrence J. Magid, "Be Wary, Stay Safe in the On-line World," *San Jose Mercury News*, May 15, 1994, p. 1F.
11. Peter H. Lewis, "Limiting a Medium without Boundaries," *New York Times*, January 15, 1996, pp. C1, C4.

Practical Action Box

a. Catherine Greenman, "You Want to Be in Pictures? Will You Settle for a Web Page?" *New York Times*, March 16, 2000, p. D9; Chris O'Malley, "Prefab Home Pages," *Popular Science*, September 1999, p. 56; and Deborah Kong, "Building a Web Site," *San Jose Mercury News*, April 1999, p. 1F, 2F.
b. Kim Komando, "Web Site Wizards," *Reno Gazette-Journal*, February 24, 2003, p. 1E.

Chapter 7

1. "IDC Research: Worldwide Net Traffic to Rise," March 3, 2003, NUA Internet Surveys, *www.nua.com/survey*.
2. Ramez Elmasri and Shamkant Navathe, *Fundamentals of Database Systems*, 3rd ed. (Addison-Wesley, 2000), p. 4.
3. Michael J. Hernandez, *Database Design for Mere Mortals*, copyright 1997 by Michael J. Hernandez, Addison-Wesley, Reading, MA: p. 11.
4. Hernandez, 1997, p. 12
5. Elmasri and Navathe, 2000, p. 4.
6. See J. Quittner, "Tim Berners-Lee," *Time*, March 29, 1999, pp. 193–194.
7. "eMarketer: Worldwide B2B Revenues to Pass One Trillion," April 1, 2003, NUA Internet Surveys, *www.nua.com/survey*
8. Sarah E. Hutchinson and Stacey C. Sawyer, *Computers, Communications, and Information: A User's Introduction*, rev. ed. (Burr Ridge, IL: Irwin/McGraw-Hill, 1998), pp. E1.1–E1.3.
9. Jeff Bezos, quoted in K. Southwick, interview, October 1996, *www.upside.com*.
10. "Amazon.com Shows Higher Sales, Lower-Than-Expected Profit," *Pudget Sound Business Journal*, January 23, 2003, *http://seattle.bizjournals.com/seattle/stories/2003/01/20.*
11. Jonathan Berry, John Verity, Kathleen Kerwin, and Gail DeGeorge, "Database Marketing," *BusinessWeek*, September 5, 1994, pp. 56–62.
12. Sarah Reese Hedberg, "The Data Gold Rush," *Byte*, October 1995, pp. 83–88.
13. Cheryl D. Krivda, "Data-Mining Dynamite," *Byte*, October 1995, pp. 97-103.
14. Edmund X. DeJesus, "Data Mining," *Byte*, October 1995, p. 81.
15. U.S. Department of Commerce, "E-Commerce 2001 Highlights," *E-Stats*, March 19, 2003; *www.census.gov/estats*
16. Don Tapscot, "Virtual Webs Will Revolutionize Business," *Wall Street Journal*, April 24, 2000, p. A38.
17. Carolyn Said, "Online Middlemen," *San Francisco Chronicle*, April 10, 2000, pp. C1, C3; William J. Holstein, "Rewiring the 'Old Economy,'" *U.S. News & World* Report, April 10, 2000, pp. 38–40; Claudia H. Deutsch, "Another Economy on the Supply Side," *New York Times*, April 8, 2000, pp. B1, B4; and Kelly Zito, "Online Exchange for Shops," *San Francisco Chronicle*, March 9, 2000, pp. B1, B4.
18. Tapscot, 2000.
19. William Safire, "Art vs. Artifice," *New York Times*, January 3, 1994, p. A11.
20. Cover, *Newsweek*, June 27, 1994; and cover, *Time*, June 27, 1994.
21. Jonathan Alter, "When Photographs Lie," *Newsweek*, July 30, 1990, pp. 44–45.
22. Fred Ritchin, quoted in Alter, 1990.
23. Robert Zemeckis, cited in Laurence Hooper, "Digital Hollywood: How Computers Are Remaking Movie Making," *Rolling Stone*, August 11, 1994, pp. 55–58, 75.
24. Woody Hochswender, "When Seeing Cannot Be Believing," *New York Times*, June 23, 1992, pp. B1, B3.
25. Bruce Horowitz, "Believe Your Eyes? Ads Bend Reality," *USA Today*, April 24, 2000, pp. 1B, 2B.

26. Penny Williams, "Database Dangers," *Quill*, July/August 1994, pp. 37–38.
27. Lynn Davis, quoted in Williams, 1994.
28. David Lazarus, "A Deluge of Credit," *San Francisco Chronicle*, March 7, 2003, pp. B1, B3.

Practical Action Box

a. Kathryn Rambo, quoted in Ramon G. McLeod, "New Thieves Prey on Your Very Name," *San Francisco Chronicle*, April 7, 1997, pp. A1, A6.
b. Rambo, quoted in T. Trent Gegax, "Stick 'Em Up? Not Anymore. Now It's Crime by Keyboard," *Newsweek*, July 21, 1997, p. 14.
c. McLeod, 1997.

Chapter 8

1. Harold Gilliam, "Mind Over Matter," *San Francisco Chronicle*, February 9, 2003, pp. D1, D6.
2. Edmund L. Andrews, "New Scale for Toting Up Lost Freedom vs. Security Would Measure in Dollars," *New York Times*, March 11, 2003, p. A11.
3. Andrews, 2003; and Ann Davis, "Some Colleges Balk at FBI Request for Data on Foreigners," *Wall Street Journal*, November 25, 2002, pp. B1, B5.
4. Andrea L. Foster, "ID Theft Turns Students into Privacy Activists," *Chronicle of Higher Education*, August 2, 2002, pp. A27–A28.
5. John Schwartz, "Professors Vie with Web for Class's Attention," *New York Times*, January 2, 2003, pp. A1, A14; and Ian Ayres, "Lectures vs. Laptops," *New York Times*, March 20, 2001, p. A29.
6. Tamar Lewin, "New Online Guides Rate Professors," *New York Times*, March 24, 2003, p. A9.
7. Florence Olsen, "Internet2's Network Adopts New Protocol for Addressing and Packaging data," *Chronicle of Higher Education*, September 6, 2002, p. A45.
8. Steve Rosenbush, Roger O. Crockett, and Charles Hadad, "What Hath the FCC Wrought?" *Business Week*, March 10, 23003, pp. 38-39.
9. Michael Astor, "Internet to Become More Global," *San Mateo County Times*, April 13, 2004, *www.sanmateocountytimes.com*; Craig Liddell, "ICANN Goes Global," April. 8, 2003, *http:// australia.internet.com*; and Scarlett Pruitt, "ICANN Works on Going Global," *InfoWorld*, March 26, 2003, *www.infoworld.com.*
10. Scott McCartney, "Pilots Go to 'the Box' to Avoid Midair Collisions," *The Wall Street Journal*, July 18, 2002, p. D3; and George Johnson, "To Err Is Human," *New York Times*, July 14, 2002, sec. 4, pp. D1, D7.
11. We are grateful to Professor. John Durham for contributing these ideas.
12. John Allen Paulos, "Smart Machines, Foolish People," *Wall Street Journal*, October 5, 1999, p. A26.
13. Katherine S. Mangan, "Online Medical-School Application Becomes a Nightmare for Students," *Chronicle of Higher Education*, July 13, 2001, p. A33; and Sally McGrane, "Glitches Stymie Medical School Applicants," *New York Times*, July 5, 2001, p. D3.
14. Heather Newman, "Recording Industry Has Warning: File-Sharers Have to Face the Music," *Free Press*, April 5, 2003; *www.freep.com/money/tech/newman5_20030405.htm.*
15. David Lieberman, "Millions of Pirates Are Plundering Satellite TV," *USA Today*, December 2, 2002, pp. 1D, 2D.
16. Associated Press, "Iraq War Souvenirs Selling on eBay," ABC7News, April 11, 2003, *http://abclocal.go.com/kgo/news.*
17. Curt Anderson, "Internet Fraud Reports Triple in 2002," *San Francisco Chronicle*, April 10, 2003, p. B3; and Henry Norr, "Fast-Growing Fraud from Nigeria Uses Internet to Search for Suckers," *San Francisco Chronicle*, September 8, 2002, p. A6.
18. Internet Fraud Complaint Center, reported in Anderson, 2003.
19. Henry Norr, "Vigilance Against Viruses," *San Francisco Chronicle*, September 24, 2001, pp. E1, E2.
20. Tom Gromak, "After 9 Months, Klez Worm Still a Top Viruns Threat," *Reno Gazette-Journal*, July 29, 2002, p. 1E, reprinted from *The Detroit News*; and George Smith, "The Commoner's Virus," *Business Week*, June 11, 2002, *www.businessweek.com/technology/content/jun2002/tc20020610_4372.htm.*
21. John Schwartz, "Worm Hits Microsoft, Which Ignored Own Advice," *New York Times*, January 28, 2003, p. C4; "Net Experts Surprised by Worm Impact," *San Francisco Chronicle*, January 28, 2003, pp. B1, B6; and "Viruslike Attack Slows Much Internet Traffic," *New York Times*, January 26, 2003, sec. 1, p. 17.
22. David Carter, quoted in Associated Press, "Computer Crime Usually Inside Job," *USA Today*, October 25, 1995, p. 1B.
23. Steven Bellovin, cited in Jane Bird, "More Than a Nuisance," *The Times* (London), April 22, 1994, p. 31.
24. Eugene Carlson, "Some Forms of Identification Can't Be Handily Faked," *Wall Street Journal*, September 14, 1993, p. B2.
25. John Holusha, "The Painful Lessons of Disruption," *New York Times*, March 17, 1993, pp. C1, C5.
26. Enterprise Technology Center, cited in "Disaster Avoidance and Recovery Is Growing Business Priority," special advertising supplement in *LAN Magazine*, November 1992, p. SS3.
27. Lee Gomes, "Experts Say Encryption Can't Be Limited, a Setback for Lawmakers Seeking Change," *Wall Street Journal*, September 26, 2001, p. B5.
28. Holusha, 1993.
29. Enterprise Technology Center, 1992.
30. David Lazarus, "Toxic Technology," *San Francisco Chronicle*, December 3, 2000, pp. B1, B4, B8.
31. Andrew Park, "Stemming the Tide of Tech Trash," *Business Week*, October 7, 2002, pp. 36A – 36F; "Cleaning Up E-Waste," editorial, *San Francisco Chronicle*, July 22, 2002, p. B6; Henry Norr, "Group Exposes America's Dirty Tech Secret," *San Francisco Chronicle*, February 25, 2002, pp. E1, E3; John Markoff, "Technology's Toxic Trash Is Sent to Poor Nations," *New York Times*, February 25, 2002, pp. C1, C4; Patrick McMahon, "Where Does the TV Go When It Dies?" *USA Today*, January 22, 2002, p. 3A; Associated Press, "Disposal Is a Problem as LCDs Displace Tube Monitors," *Wall Street Journal*, August 13, 2001, p. B6; Henry Norr, "Drowning in E-Waste," *San Francisco Chronicle*, May 27, 2001, pp. E1, E5; Lawrence Magid, "Don't Be So Quick to Toss Out Your PC," *San Francisco Chronicle*, October 29, 2000, pp. D5, D7; John Yaukey, "Upgrading the Junk Computer Contagion," *Reno Gazette-Journal*, August 28, 2000, p. 4E: and William J. Holstein, "Take My Personal Computer—Please!" *U.S. News & World Report*, June 5, 2000, p. 51.
32. National Safety Council, reported in Norm Alster and William Echikson, "Are Old PCs Poisoning Us?" *Business Week*, June 12, 2000, pp. 78, 80.
33. Kathy Jo Wetter, ETC Group, quoted in Jim Krane, "Risks of Nanotechnology Debated," *San Francisco Chronicle*, September 9, 2002, p. E6.
34. Lutz Erbring, coauthor of Stanford University survey of 4,113 people about internet impact on daily activities, quoted in Joellen Perry, "Only the Cyberlonely," *U.S. News & World Report*, February 28, 2000, p. 62.
35. Study by Robert Kraut, *Journal of Social Issues*, reported in Deborah Mendenhall, "Web Doesn't Promote Isolation, Study Says," *San Francisco Chronicle*, August 22, 2001, p. C3, reprinted from *Pittsburgh Post-Gazette*; and Lisa Guernsey, "Cyberspace Isn't So Lonely After All," *New York Times*, July 26, 2001, pp. D1, D5. Also see study by Jeffrey Cole, UCLA Center for Communication Policy, reported in Greg Miller and Ashley Dunn, "Net Does Not Exact a Toll on Social Life, New Study Finds," *Los Angeles Times*, October 26, 2000, pp. C1, C8.
36. Survey by Microsoft Corp., reported in Don Clark and Kyle Pope, "Poll Finds Americans Like Using PCs, but May Find Them to Be Stressful," *Wall Street Journal*, April 10, 1995, p. B3.
37. Survey by Concord Communications, reported in Matt Richtel, "Rage Against the Machine: PCs Take Brunt of Office Anger," *New York Times*, March 11, 1999, p. D3.
38. Jonathan Marshall, "Some Say High-Tech Boom Is Actually a Bust," *San Francisco Chronicle*, July 10, 1995, pp. A1, A4.
39. Eleena de Lisser, "One-Click Commerce: What People Do Now to Goof Off at Work," *Wall Street Journal*, September 24, 1999, pp. A1, A8.
40. Surfwatch Checknet, cited in Keith Naughton, Joan Raymond, Ken Shulman, and Diane Struzzi,

"CyberSlacking," *Newsweek*, November 29, 1999, pp. 62–65.

41. STB Accounting Systems 1992 survey, reported in Del Jones, "On-line Surfing Costs Firms Time and Money," *USA Today*, December 8, 1995, pp. 1A, 2A.

42. Dan Gillmor, "Online Reliability Will Carry a Price," *San Jose Mercury News*, July 18, 1999, pp. 1E, 7E.

43. Paul Saffo, quoted in Laura Evenson, "Pulling the Plug," *San Francisco Chronicle*, December 18, 1994, Sunday sec., p. 53.

44. Daniel Yankelovich Group report, cited in Barbara Presley Noble, "Electronic Liberation or Entrapment," *New York Times*, June 15, 1994, p. C4.

45. Jon Schwartz, "More Firms Replace Operators with Software," *USA Today*, May 20, 2002, p. 1B.

46. Timothy Aeppel, "Workers Not Included," *Wall Street Journal*, November 10, 2002, pp. B1, B11.

47. Jeremy Rifkin, "Technology's Curse: Fewer Jobs, Fewer Buyers," *San Francisco Examiner*, December 3, 1995, p. C-19.

48. Michael J. Mandel, "Economic Anxiety," *Business Week*, March 11, 1996, pp. 50–56; Bob Herbert, "A Job Myth Downsized," *New York Times*, March 8, 1996, p. A19; and Robert Kuttner, "The Myth of a Natural Jobless Rate," *Business Week*, October 20, 1997, p. 26.

49. Stewart Brand, in "Boon or Bane for Jobs?" *The Futurist*, January-February 1997, pp. 13–14.

50. Paul Krugman, "Long-Term Riches, Short-Term Pain," *New York Times*, September 25, 1994, sec. 3, p. 9.

51. "Bringing a Nation Online: The Importance of Federal Leadership," quoted in John Schwartz, "Report Disputes Bush Approach to Bridging 'Digital Divide,'" *New York Times*, July 11, 2002, p. A16.

52. Ariana Eunjung Cha, "'Digital Divide' Debate Heats Up," *San Francisco Chronicle*, July 3, 2002, pp. A1, A12, reprinted from *Washington Post*; Robert J. Samuelson, "Debunking the Digital Divide," *Newsweek*, March 2002, p. 37; and Yochi J. Dreazen, "White House Takes Aim at Technology Programs," *Wall Street Journal*, February 27, 2002, p. A22.

53. Government Accounting Office study, 2001.

54. Beth Belton, "Degree-based Earnings Gap Grows Quickly," *USA Today*, February 16, 1996, p. 1B.

55. Alan Kruger, quoted in LynNell Hancock, Pat Wingert, Patricia King, Debra Rosenberg, and Alison Samuels, "The Haves and the Have-Nots," *Newsweek*, February 27, 1995, pp. 50–52.

56. Sabra Chartrand, "Software to Provide 'Personal' Attention to Online Customers with Service Untouched by a Human," *New York Times*, August 20, 2001, p. C8.

57. Judith Anne Gunther, "An Encounter with AI," *Popular Science*, June 1994, pp. 90–93.

58. Sara Robinson, "Human or Computer? Take This Test," *New York Times*, December 10, 2002, pp. D1, D4.

59. William A. Wallace, *Ethics in Modeling* (New York: Elsevier Science, 1994).

60. Laura Johannes, "Meet the Doctor: A Computer That Knows a Few Things," *Wall Street Journal*, December 18, 1995, p. B1.

61. Campus Computing Project 1997 survey, reported in Lisa Guernsey, "E-Mail Is Now Used in a Third of College Courses, Survey Finds," *Chronicle of Higher Education*, October 17, 1997, p. A30; and Edward C. Baig, "A Little High Tech Goes a Long Way," *Business Week*, November 10, 1997, p. E10.

62. Student Monitor LLC, cited in Danielle Sessa, "For College Students, Web Offers a Lesson in Discounts," *Wall Street Journal*, January 21, 1999, p. B7.

63. National Center for Education Statistics, in "Internet Access Booms in Schools," *USA Today*, July 17, 2001, p. 1C.

64. Nanette Asimov, "Home-Schoolers Plug into the Internet for Resources," *San Francisco Chronicle*, January 29, 1999, pp. A1, A15.

65. Mary Beth Marklein, "Distance Learning Takes a Gigantic Leap Forward," *USA Today*, June 4, 1998, pp. 1D, 2D; and Godie Blumenstyk, "Leading Community Colleges Go National with New Distance-Learning Network," *Chronicle of Higher Education*, July 10, 1998, pp. A16–A17.

66. Rebecca Quick, "Software Seeks to Breathe Life into Corporate Training Classes," *Wall Street Journal*, August 6, 1998, p. B8.

67. Elizabeth Schatz, "Reaching a Doctor by E-Mail," *Wall Street Journal*, April 15, 2003, p. D4; Lauran Neegaard, "Move to Put Bar Codes on Hospital Drugs," *San Francisco Chronicle*, March 14, 2003, p. A4; Laura Landro, "Why You Can't Find a Doctor for Your Kid," *Wall Street Journal*, January 30, 2003, pp. D1, D2; Randi Hutter Epstein, "Sifting Through the Online Medical Jumble," *New York Times*, January 28, 2003, p. D8; Linda H. Lamb, "Cyber-Savvy Doctors Increase Efficiency," *Reno Gazette-Journal*, January 7, 2003, p. 2F; Evan Ramstad, "Patients Rely on Monitor Implants," *San Francisco Chronicle*, December 23, 2002, p. E5; Tara Parker-Pope, "Finding Someone Who Feels Your Pain: Matching Services Connect Sick Patients," *Wall Street Journal*, December 17, 2002, p. D1; Ann Carrns, "Doctor Online Guidelines Tightened," *Wall Street Journal*, December 4, 2002, p. D3; Unmesh Kher, "Who Needs Doctors?" *Time*, October 28, 2002, pp. 50–51; Avery Comarow, "Under the (Virtual) Knife," *U.S. News & World Report*, October 21, 2002, pp. 65–66; Arlene Weintraub, "Make Your PDA a Health Partner," *Business Week*, October 7, 2002, pp. 138–140;

"Telemedicine, the Easy Way," *New York Times*, October 1, 2002, p. D6; and Rita Rubin, "The Virtual Doctor Will See You Now," *USA Today*, June 10, 2002, p. A1.

68. Myron Magnet, "Who's Winning the Information Revolution," *Fortune*, November 30, 1992, pp. 110–117.

69. Tony Rutkowski, quoted in Patricia Schnaidt, "The Electronic Superhighway," *LAN Magazine*, October 1993, pp. 6–8.

70. Hal Lancaster, "Technology Raises Bar for Sales Job; Know Your Dress Code," *Wall Street Journal*, January 21, 1997, p. B1.

71. Ingred Wickelgren, "Treasure Maps for the Masses," *Business Week/Enterprise*, 1996, pp. ENT22–ENT24.

72. Paul Saffo, quoted in Jared Sandberg, "CyberCash Lowers Barriers to Small Transactions at Internet Storefronts," *Wall Street Journal*, September 30, 1996, p. B6.

73. Denise Caruso, "On-Line Day Traders Are Starting to Have an Impact on a Few Big-Cap Internet Stocks in What Some Call a 'Feeding Frenzy,'" *New York Times*, December 14, 1998, p. C3.

74. Gene Bylinsky, "The E-Factory Catches On," *Fortune*, July 23, 2001, pp. 200[B]–200[H].

75. Charles Bermant, "Musicians Tap Rich Lode of Sheet Music, Sold and Shared," *New York Times*, April 23, 1998, p. D5.

76. Peter Stack, "The Digital Divide," *San Francisco Chronicle*, May 19, 1999, p. E1.

77. Bruce Haring, "Digitally Created Actors: Death Becomes Them," *USA Today*, June 24, 1998, p. 8D.

78. Dan Johnson, "Politics in Cyberspace," *The Futurist*, January 1999, p. 14.

79. *The State of "Electronically Enhanced Democracy": A Survey of the Internet* (New Brunswick, NJ: Rutgers University, Douglass Campus, Walt Whitman Center, Department of Political Science, 1998).

80. Jim Crinkard, "Holes in Punch-Card System Noted Long Ago," *USA Today*, March 7, 2001, p. 6A.

81. California Institute of Technology and Massachusetts Institute of Technology, study reported in Florence Olsen, "MIT and Caltech Researchers Propose Shifts in Voting Technology," *Chronicle of Higher Education*, August 3, 2001, p. A37; Katharine Q. Seelye, "Study Says 2000 Election Missed Millions of Votes," July 17, 2001, p. A17; Richard Winton, "Balloting Study Calls for Updating Equipment," *Los Angeles Times*, July 17, 2001, p. A6; and Florence Olsen, "Computer Scientists and Political Scientists Seek to Create a Fiasco-Free Election Day," *Chronicle of Higher Education*, April 20, 2001, pp. A51–A53.

82. Study by House Government Reform Committee, U.S. Congress, reported in Laura Parker, "Technology Can Reduce Voting Flaws, Study Says," *USA Today*, July 10, 2001, p. 9A.

83. Edward Tenner, "The Perils of High-Tech Voting," *New York Times*, February 5, 2001, p. A27; and John Carey, "Is There Any Help for the 'Hanging Chad'?" *BusinessWeek*, November 27, 2000, pp. 54–56.

84. Associated Press, "Pentagon's E-Voting Test Blasted Over Cost Per Ballot," *San Francisco Chronicle*, August 11, 2001, p. A4.

85. Frank Eltman, "Government of the People, Via the Net," *San Francisco Chronicle*, May 31, 2000, p. D3.

Practical Action Box

a. Nate Stulman, "The Great Campus Goof-Off Machine," *New York Times*, March 15, 1999, p. A25.

b. Robert Kubey, "Internet Generation Isn't Just Wasting Time" [letter], *New York Times*, March 21, 1999, sec. 4, p. 14.

c. Marco R. della Cava, "Are Heavy Users Hooked or Just Online Fanatics?" *USA Today*, January 16, 1996, pp. 1A, 2A.

d. Kenneth Hamilton and Claudia Kalb, "They Log On, but They Can't Log Off," *Newsweek*, December 18, 1995, pp. 60 – 61; and Kenneth Howe, "Diary of an AOL Addict," *San Francisco Chronicle*, April 5, 1995, pp. D1, D3.

e. Stella Yu, quoted in Hamilton and Kalb, 1995.

f. Jonathan Kandell, quoted in J. R. Young, "Students Are Unusually Vulnerable to Internet Addiction, Article Says," *Chronicle of Higher Education*, February 6, 1998, p. A25.

g. American Psychological Association, reported in R. Leibrock, "AOLaholic: Tales of an Online Addict," *Reno News & Review*, October 22, 1997, pp. 21, 24.

h. Hamilton and Kalb, 1995.

i. Keith J. Anderson, reported in Leo Reisberg, "10% of Students May Spend Too Much Time Online," *Chronicle of Higher Education*, June 16, 2000, p. A43.

j. R. Sanchez, "Colleges Seek Ways to Reach Internet-Addicted Students," *San Francisco Chronicle*, May 23, 1996, p. A16, reprinted from *Washington Post*.

k. Sanchez, 1996.

l. Questionnaire adapted from chart, "Characteristics of 'Internet Dependent' Students," from Keith J. Anderson, Rensselaer Polytechnic Institute, in Reisberg, 2000.

m. Ben Gose, "A Dangerous Bet on Campus," *Chronicle of Higher Education*, April 7, 2000, pp. A49–A51.

n. Jeremy Siegel, Wharton School, University of Pennsylvania, quoted in David Segal, "The Minefield of Internet Trading," *San Jose Mercury News*, September 6, 1998, pp. 1F, 6F, reprinted from *Washington Post*.

Appendix

1. Alan Freedman, *The Computer Glossary*, 6th ed. (New York: AMACOM, 1993), p. 370.

2. "How to Use Scripts on Your Site: The Commands That Perform Specific Functions," *Smart Computing*, August 2001, *www.smartcomputing.com/editorial/article.asp?article=articles*.

3. Michael Krantz, "Keeping Tabs Online," *Time*, November 10, 1997, pp. 81–82.

Index

Boldface page numbers indicate pages on which key terms
are defined.

Abandonware, 104
Accelerator board, 157
Access security, 286–287
Active-matrix display, 169, **197**, **205**
Active server pages (ASPs), 276
ActiveX controls, **A27**
Addicts, internet, 292
Address-book feature, 48
Addresses
   email, 47–48
   website, 56, 58–60
AGP (accelerated graphics port) bus, **158**, **170**
Algorithms, **A9**
Amazon.com, 262
American Psychological Association (APA), 292
America Online (AOL), 241
Amplitude modulation, 220
Analog cellphones, 231, **243**
Analog signals, **217**, **243**
   converting into digital signals, 219–220
   modem conversion of, 218–219
Analog-to-digital converter, 220
Analytical graphics, **115**–116, **128**
Analyzing systems. *See* Systems analysis
Anderson, Keith J., 292
Andreesen, Marc, 58
Animation, **68**, **77**, 299
Anonymous FTP sites, 70
ANSI symbols, A12
Antispam software, 54
Antivirus software, **284**, **301**
Applets, **67**–68, **77**, A24
Application service providers (ASPs), 104
Application software, **20**, **28**, **102**–127, **128**
   audio editing software, 125
   buying tips for, 126
   computer-aided design programs, **126**–127
   database software, **116**–120
   desktop publishing programs, **123**–124
   documentation for, **104**
   drawing programs, 124
   file types and, 104–105
   financial software, **122**–123
   installing/reinstalling, 110
   methods for obtaining, 102–104
   painting programs, **124**
   presentation graphics software, **120**–122
   project management software, 125–**126**
   review questions/exercises on, 136–138
   specialty software, 120–127
   spreadsheet programs, **113**–116
   tutorials for, **104**
   types of, 105–106
   video editing software, 124–125
   web page design software, 127, 241
   word processing software, **107**–113
Arendt, Hannah, 216
Arithmetic/logic unit (ALU), **151**, **170**
Arithmetic operations, 151
Artifacts, 125

Artificial intelligence (AI), **294**–297, **301**
   ethics of, 297
   expert systems, **295**
   natural language processing, **296**, A20
   review questions/exercises on, 303–304
   robotics, **294**–295
   Turing test and, **296**–297
Artificial life (A-life), **296**, **301**
ASCII coding scheme, **145**, **170**
ASCII files, 255
Assemblers, **A18**
Assembly language, **A17**–A18
ATMs (automated teller machines), 182, 185, 286
Attachments, email, 50, 51
Auctions, online, 73–74
Audio
   digital sampling of, 220
   output devices for, 201–202
   software for editing, 125
   streaming, **68**
Audio CDs, 220
Audio files, 255
Audio-input devices, **192**, **205**
Audit controls, 288
Automated teller machines (ATMs), 182, 185, 286
Automated virtual representatives (vReps), 294

B2B (business-to-business) commerce, **74**, **77**, 263–264
Backbones, 46, **237**, **243**
Backups
   application software, 103
   importance of, 163
Backus, John, A20
Bandwidth, **38**, **77**, **226**, **243**
Banking, online, 74, 299
Bar charts, 116
Bar-code readers, **189**–190, **205**
Bar codes, **189**–190, **205**
Baseband transmission, 38
BASIC programming language, A21, A22
Batch processing, 256
Batteries, 169
Bays, **146**, **170**
Bellovin, Steven, 286
Berners-Lee, Tim, 56, 261, A25
Beta testing, A15
Bezos, Jeffrey, 262
Bina, Eric, 58
Binary coding schemes, 145
Binary system, **143**–145, **170**, 217
Biological nanocomputers, 8
Biometrics, **195**, **205**, **286**–287, **301**
BIOS programs, 87
Bit depth, 197
Bit-mapped images, 124
Bitmaps, 189
Bits (binary digits), 39, **144**, **170**, **252**, **271**
Blocking software, 242
Blogs, **72**, **77**
Bloom, Benjamin, 34
Bluetooth technology, **233**, **243**
Bookmarks, 62

Boolean operators, 66–67
Booting, **87**, **128**
Boot-sector virus, 283
Bozo filters, 291
Bps (bits per second), **39**, **77**
Brand, Stewart, 293
Brenner, Viktor, 292
Bricklin, Daniel, 113
Bridges, **239**, **243**
Broadband connections, **38**, **43**, **77**, **226**, **243**
Broadband wireless digital services, **232**, **243**
Broadcast radio, **227**, **243**
Browser software. *See* Web browsers
Bugs, software, 280–281
Buses, **151**, 157–158, **170**
Business, online, 73–74, 298–299
    cybercash and, 299
    manufacturing systems and, 299
    third-world countries and, 75
    See also E-commerce
Business graphics, 115–116
Business-to-business (B2B) systems, 74, **263**–264, **271**
Business webs (b-webs), 263
Buying considerations
    for notebook computers, 169
    for personal computers, 143
    for printers, 201
    for software, 126
Bytes, 17, **144**, **170**

C programming language, A21, A22
C++ programming language, A24
Cable modem, **43**, 45, **77**
Cache, **153**–154, **170**
Cache card, 157
Cache folder, 61
CAD programs, **126**–127, **128**
CAD/CAM programs, **127**, **128**
Captchas, 297
Car buying websites, 298
Carrier waves, 217
Carter, David, 284
Caruso, Denise, 299
Cascading menus, **92**, 93, **128**
Case (system cabinet), **15**, **28**, 146, 147
Case control structure, A14
CASE tools, **A5**
CD drive, **17**, **28**
CD-R disks, **165**, **170**
CD-ROM disks, **164**–165, **170**
CD-ROM drive, 165
CD-RW disks, **165**, **171**
Cell pointer, **115**, **128**
Cells
    communication, 231, 232
    spreadsheet, **115**, **128**
Cellular telephones, 3–4, 231–232
    analog, 231
    broadband, 232
    digital, 231–232
Censorship issues, 242
Central processing unit (CPU), 12, **28**, **150**–151, **171**
    data processing by, 150–151
    internal management of, 87–88
CGI scripts, A27
Character-recognition devices, 190–191
Characters, **252**, **271**
Charts, 115–116
Cheating, 76
Chips, **141**, **171**
    CISC, **148**
    CMOS, **153**
    flash memory, **153**

making of, 142
memory, **15**, 152–153
microprocessor, **141**
processor, **15**
RAM, **152**
RISC, **148**
ROM, 153
CISC (complex instruction set computing) chips, **148**, **171**
Civil unrest, 281
Classrooms, online, 73, 298
Clients, **11**, **28**
Client/server LANs, **237**–238, **244**
Clinton, Bill, 279
Closed architecture, 157
Closing windows, 95
CMOS (complementary metal-oxide semiconductor) chips, **153**, **171**
Coaxial cable, **225**, **244**
COBOL programming language, A21, A22
Codec techniques, 234
Coding, **A12**
Collaborative computing, 222
Collaborative Reference Service, 297
Color depth, **197**, **205**
Column charts, 116
Columns
    spreadsheet, 113
    text, 111
Command-driven interface, 90
Comments, inserting, 112
Commerce, electronic. *See* E-commerce
Commercial software, 102–103
Common Gateway Interface (CGI), A27
Communications, 13
    ethical issues in, 242
    practical uses of, 221–224
Communications hardware, 19
Communications media, **224**–235, **244**
    compression methods and, 233–234
    radio-frequency spectrum and, **226**–227
    wired vs. wireless, 225–233
Communications path, 224
Communications satellites, **43**, 45, **77**, **228**, **244**
Communications technology, **3**, **28**, 215–250
    cellular telephones, 231–232
    compression methods and, 233–234
    contemporary examples of, 3–7
    cyberethics and, 242
    fusion with computer technology, 218–219
    Global Positioning System, **229**–230
    home networks, 223
    networks, **235**–240
    overview of developments in, 23–24
    pagers, **231**
    radio-frequency spectrum and, **226**–227
    review questions/exercises on, 248–250
    satellites and, 228
    smart television and, 223–224
    telecommuting, **222**–223
    timeline of progress in, 22–27, 216–219
    videoconferencing, **221**–222
    virtual office, **223**
    wired vs. wireless, 225–233
    See also Information technology
Compilers, **A19**
Comprehension, 34
Compression, 233–**234**, **244**
Computer-aided design (CAD) programs, **126**–127, **128**
Computer-aided design/computer-aided manufacturing (CAD/CAM) programs, **127**, **128**
Computer-aided software engineering (CASE) tools, **A5**
Computer-created search sites, 66
Computer crime, **282**–283, 284–285, **301**
Computer Ethics (Forester and Morrison), 26

Computer operators, A16
Computers, **3**, **28**
 basic operations of, 12–13
 crimes related to, 282–283, 284–285
 custom-built, 12, 14, 21
 digital basis of, 217
 environmental issues related to, 289–290
 guarding against theft, 203
 hardware of, **12**, 14–19
 health issues related to, 203–204
 recycling, 26, 289, 290
 software of, **12**, 20
 types of, 7–11
 See also Personal computers
Computer technology, 3
 contemporary examples of, 3–7
 fusion with communications technology, 218–219
 overview of developments in, 22–23
 timeline of progress in, 22–27, 216–219
Connectivity, **23**, **29**
Content templates, 120
Context-sensitive help, 96
Control structures, A10, **A12**, A14
Control unit, **150**, **171**
Convergence, 24
Conversion
 signal, 219–220
 system, A7
Cookies, 64
Coprocessor board, 157
Copy command, 111
Copyright, **102**, 128
Cost-benefit analysis, 278
CPU. *See* Central processing unit
Crackers, **285**, **301**
Credit bureaus, 269
Critical thinking, 34
Crosstalk, 225
CRT (cathode-ray tube), **197**, **205**
Cursor, **108**, **129**
Custom-built PCs, 12, 14, 21
Cut command, 111
Cyberethics, 242
Cyberspace, 5–**6**, **29**
Cycles, 149

Daisy chains, 154, 156
Data, **12**, **29**
 accuracy of, 266–267
 completeness of, 266–267
 digital vs. analog, 217
 hierarchical organization of, 252–253
 importing and exporting, 105
 manipulation of, 264–266
 permanent storage of, 12, 17–18
 privacy issues and, 267
 protecting, 203, 287–288
 theft of, 282
 transmission of, 38–40
Data access area, 160
Database files, 105
Database management system (DBMS), **257**, **271**
Databases, **116**, **129**, **252–276**, **271**
 accessing data on, 255–256
 accuracy of information in, 266–267
 business-to-business systems and, **263**–264
 data mining and, **262**–263
 data storage hierarchy and, **252**–253
 e-commerce and, 261–**262**
 ethical issues related to, 264–267
 file types and, 254–255
 hierarchical, **258**, 259
 identity theft and, 269

key field in, **253**
 management systems for, 256–258
 network, **258**, 259, 260
 object-oriented, **261**
 privacy issues and, 267
 relational, **117**, **260**
 review questions/exercises on, 275–276
 storing data from, 255–256
 types of, 257–258
Database servers, 238
Database software, **116–120**, **129**
 benefits of, 116–117
 features of, 117–119
 illustrated overview of, 118
 personal information managers, **119**
Data files, **254**, 255, 271
Data flow diagram (DFD), **A4**
Data mining (DM), **262–263**, 271
Data storage hierarchy, **252–253**, **271**
Davis, Lynn, 267
DDR-SDRAM chips, 152
Debugging programs, **A15**
Decimal to binary conversion, 144
Dedicated fax machines, **192**, **205**
Dedicated ports, 156
Default settings, **112**, **129**
Deleting text, 111
Democracy, electronic, 300
Design templates, 120
Desk-checking, **A15**
Desktop, **92**, **129**
Desktop PCs, **9**, **29**
Desktop publishing (DTP), **123–124**, **129**
Desktop scanners, 189
Detail design, A5
Developing information systems. *See* Systems development
Device drivers, 86, **89**, **129**, 255
Diagnostic routines, 87
Diagnostics, A15
Dial-up connection, 40–41, 45
Digital cameras, **193**, **206**
Digital convergence, 216
Digital-data compression, 233–234
Digital divide, 293
Digital environment, 278–279
Digital signals, **217**, **244**
 converting analog signals into, 219–220
 modem conversion of, 218–219
Digital television (DTV), **223–224**, **244**
Digital-to-analog converter, 220
Digital wireless services, **231–232**, **244**
Digitizers, **188**, **206**
Digitizing tablets, **188**, **206**
DIMMs, 152
Direct access storage, **255–256**, **272**
Direct implementation, A7
Directories, web, **64**, **77**
Dirty data problems, 281
Disaster-recovery plans, **288**, **301**
Disk controller card, 157
Diskettes, 160–161
 formatting, **88**, 161
 viruses passed via, 284
Display screens, **196–199**, **206**
 health issues and, 204
 notebook computer, 169
 standards for, 198–199
 touch screens, **187**
 types of, 197
Distance learning, **73**, **77**, 298
Distributed databases, **258**, **272**
Documentation, **104**, **129**, **A15–A16**
Document files, 105
 creating, 108

editing, 110–111
formatting, 111–112
illustrated overview of, 109
inserting comments into, 112
printing, 112
saving, 112
toggling between, 113
tracking changes in, 112
web, 113
Document Type Definition (DTD), A26
Domains, **47**–48, **78**
DOS (Disk Operating System), 97, **129**
Dot pitch (dp), **196**, **206**
Downlinking, 228
Downloading data, **40**, **78**
Dpi (dots per inch), 197, 199, **206**
Draft quality output, 199
DRAM chips, 152
Drawing programs, **124**, **129**
Drive bays, 146
Drive gate, 160
Drivers. *See* Device drivers
Drop-down menu, 92
Drum scanners, 189
DSL (digital subscriber line), **42**, 45, **78**
Dubinsky, Donna, 102
Dumb terminal, **184**, **206**
DVD drive, **17**, 166
DVD-R disks, **166**, **171**
DVD-ROM disks, **165**–166, **171**
DVD zones, 166
Dwyer, Eugene, 76

EBCDIC coding scheme, **145**, **171**
E-commerce (electronic commerce), **73**, **78**, **262**, **272**
databases and, 261–262
money used for, 299
sales and marketing for, 298
See also Business, online
Economic issues, 291, 293–294
Editing documents, 110–111
Education
distance learning and, **73**, 298
income related to, 293–294
information technology and, 297–298
plagiarism issues and, 76
software for, 106
See also Learning
EIDE controllers, 163
Einstein, David, 12, 21
Electromagnetic spectrum, 226
Electromechanical problems, 281
Electronic democracy, 300
Electronic imaging, 189
Electronic spreadsheets. *See* Spreadsheets
Email (electronic mail), **4**–5, **29**, 46–55
addresses, 47–48
attachments, 50, 51
filters for, 53, 54
instant messaging and, **50**, 52
junk, 54
mailing lists, 52
netiquette, **52**–53
privacy issues, 55
remote access to, 48
replying to, 48, 49
sending and receiving, 49
software and services, 47
sorting, 53
tips on managing, 5
viruses passed via, 284
Emoticons, **53**, **78**
Employee crime, 284–285

Employment
contemporary changes in, 293
online resources for, 74
technology issues and, 290–291
Emulator board, 157
Encryption, **287**, **301**
Enhanced paging, 231
ENIAC computer, 22, 140
Entertainment, 73, 299–300
Entertainment software, 106
Environmental Protection Agency (EPA), 289
Erasable optical disk, 165
Erasing files, 180
Ergonomics, 203–204
Ethernet, 233
Ethics, **25**–26, **29**
artificial intelligence and, 297
censorship issues and, 242
information accuracy and, 266–267
media manipulation and, 264–266
online music and, 299
plagiarism and, 76
privacy and, 267
Ethics in Modeling (Wallace), 297
Event-driven program, A24
Executable files, 254
Expansion, **147**, 156, **171**
Expansion buses, 157–158
Expansion cards, **157**–159, **171**
Expansion slots, **16**, **29**, **157**, **171**
Expert systems, **295**, **301**, A23
Exporting data, **105**, **129**
Extensible Markup Language (XML), A26
Extension names, 254
External cache, 153
Extranets, **240**, **244**

FAQs (frequently asked questions), **52**, **78**
Favorites, 62
Fax machines, **191**–192, **206**
Fax modems, 157, **192**, **206**
Federal Bureau of Investigation (FBI), 283, 285, 286
Federal Communications Commission (FCC), 279
Federal privacy laws, 268
Fiber-optic cable, **225**, **245**
Fields, 117, **252**, **272**
File allocation table (FAT), 256
Filenames, **254**, **272**
File-processing system, 257
Files, **104**, **130**, **252**–253, **272**
converting, A7
data, **254**, 255
erasing, 180
exporting, **105**
importing, **105**
managing, 88
program, **254**
types of, 104–105, 254–255
File servers, 238
File virus, 283
Film making, 299–300
Filters
email, 53
spam, 54
Finance, online, 74, 299
Financial software, **122**–123, **130**
Find command, 111
Firewalls, **240**, **245**
FireWire, **156**, **172**
First-generation (1G) technology, 231
Five generations of programming languages, **A16**–A17
Flaming, **53**, **78**
Flash drive, 168

Flash memory cards, **168**, **172**
Flash memory chips, **153**, **172**
Flatbed scanners, **189**, **206**
Flat-panel displays, **197**, **206**
Floating-point operations, 149
Floppy-disk cartridges, **160**, **172**
Floppy-disk drive, **17**, **29**, 161
Floppy disks, **160**–161, **172**
    formatting, **88**, 161
    viruses passed via, 284
Flops, **149**–150, **172**
Flowchart, A12, A13
Fonts, **111**, **130**
Foreign keys, 117
Forester, Tom, 26
Formatting
    disks, **88**, **130**
    documents, 111–112
Formulas, **115**, **130**
FORTRAN programming language, A20, A21
Frames, **64**, **78**
Freeware, **103**–104, **130**
Frequency
    modem technology and, 218, 220
    radio signals and, 226–227
Frequency modulation, 220
Frontside bus, 157
FTP (File Transfer Protocol), **70**, 71, **78**
Function keys, **108**, **130**
Functions, **115**, **130**

Gambling, online, 290, 292
Gates, Bill, 98
Gateways, **239**, **245**
Geostationary earth orbit (GEO), 228
Gibson, William, 5
Gigabits per second (Gbps), **40**, **78**
Gigabyte (G, GB), 17, **144**, **172**
Gigahertz (GHz), 15, **149**, **172**
Gilliam, Harold, 278
Gillmor, Dan, 291
Gilmore, John, 242
Global Positioning System (GPS), **229**–230, **245**
Government
    federal privacy laws and, 268
    information technology and, 300
Grammar checker, **111**, **130**
Graphical user interface (GUI), **90**–96, **130**
Graphics, analytical, **115**–116
Graphics cards, 157, **158**, **172**, 198
Groupware, 105, 222
Gunther, Judith Anne, 296–297

Hackers, **285**, **301**
Hand-geometry systems, 287
Handheld computers, 10
    operating systems for, 101–102
    See also Notebook computers
Handheld scanners, 189
Hardcopy output, **196**, **207**
Hard-disk cartridges, 163
Hard-disk controller, **163**, **173**
Hard-disk drive, **17**, **29**
Hard disks, **162**–163, **172**
    crashing of, 162
    nonremovable, **162**–163
    removable, **163**
Hard goods, 73
Hardware, **12**, 14–19, **29**, **139**–180
    buying, 143
    cache, 153–154
    communications, 19
    computer case, 146
    converting, A7
    CPU, **150**–151
    expansion cards, **157**–159
    health issues related to, 203–204
    input, 14, **183**, 184–195
    memory, 15–16, 152–153
    microchips, 141, 142, 148–149
    miniaturization of, 141
    motherboard, 146–148
    obtaining for systems, A6
    output, 18–19, **183**, 195–202
    portability of, 141–142
    ports, **154**–156
    power supply, **146**
    processing, 15–16, 150–151
    protecting, 203
    review questions/exercises on, 178–180, 212–214
    secondary storage, 17–18, **159**–168
    system unit, 146, 147
    theft of, 203, 282
    transistors, **140**–141
Hawkins, Jeff, 102
Head crash, **162**, **173**
Headers/footers, 112
Health issues
    computer use and, 203–204
    data mining and, 263
    online information about, 73
    telemedicine and, 298
Help command, **95**–96, **130**
Hertz (Hz), 197, 226
Hierarchical databases, **258**, 259, **272**
Hierarchy chart, **A10**, A11
High-definition television (HDTV), **224**, **245**
High-level programming languages, **A18**–A20
High-speed phone lines, 41–43
History list, 62
Home networks, 223
Home page, **58**, 59, **78**
    personalizing, 61
    web portal, 64
Hopper, Grace Murray, A22
Host computer, 237
HTML (hypertext markup language), 56, 57, **78**, A25–A26
HTTP (HyperText Transfer Protocol), **59**, **79**
Hubs, **239**, **245**
Human errors, 280
Human-organized search sites, 65–66
Hybrid search sites, 66
Hyperlinks, 56, 60, 63, A25–A26
Hypertext, **56**, **78**
Hypertext index, 64
Hypertext links, A25–A26
Hypertext markup language (HTML), **56**, 57, **78**, A25–A26
HyperText Transfer Protocol (HTTP), **59**, **79**

ICANN (Internet Corporation for Assigned Names & Numbers), **279**
Icons, **92**, **130**
Identification systems, 286–287
Identity theft, 269–270
Illustration software, 124
Image-editing software, 124
Image files, 255
Impact printers, **199**, **207**
Implementing systems. *See* Systems implementation
Importing data, **105**, **130**
Income gap, 293–294
Individual databases, **257**, **272**
Information, **12**, **29**
    accuracy and completeness of, 266–267
    education and, 297–298

intelligent agents and, 297
  manipulation of, 264–266
  privacy issues and, 267
  See also Data
Information overload, 2, 26–27, 291
Information superhighway, 278
Information technology (IT), **3**, **29**
  business and, 298–299
  contemporary trends in, 21–25
  crime related to, 282–283, 284–285
  economic issues and, 291, 293–294
  education and, 297–298
  entertainment industry and, 299–300
  ethics and, 25–26
  government and, 300
  health/medicine and, 298
  modern examples of, 3–7
  quality-of-life issues and, 289–291
  security issues and, 280–288
  timeline of progress in, 22–27
  See also Communications technology; Computer
    technology
Infrared ports, **156**, **173**
Infrared wireless transmission, **227**, **245**
Initializing disks, 88, 161
Ink-jet printers, **200**, **207**
Input, **12**, 13, **30**, 183
Input hardware, 14, **183**, 184–195, **207**
  audio-input devices, **192**
  biometric devices, **195**
  digital cameras, **193**
  digitizers, **188**
  ergonomics and, 203–204
  fax machines/modems, **191**–192
  health issues related to, 203–204
  keyboards, **184**–185
  light pens, **187**, 188
  pen-based computer systems, **187**–188
  pointing devices, **185**–188
  radio-frequency identification tags, **194**
  review questions/exercises on, 212–214
  scanning/reading devices, 188–192
  sensors, **194**
  source data-entry devices, **188**–192
  speech-recognition systems, **193**–194
  touch screens, **187**
  types of, 184
  webcams, **192**
Inserting text, 110
Insertion point, 108
Installing software, 20, 110
Instant messaging (IM), **50**, 52, **79**, 221
Integrated circuits, 23, **141**, **173**
Intelligence, artificial. *See* Artificial intelligence
Intelligent agents, **297**, **302**
Intelligent hubs, 239
Intelligent terminal, **185**, **207**
Intel-type chips, **148**–149, **173**
Interactive TV, 223
Interactivity, **24**, **30**, 63–64
Interfaces, 86, 89–96
Internal cache, 153
International Data Corporation (IDC), 2
Internet, **6**, **30**, 37–84
  addiction to, 292
  bandwidth and, **38**
  blogs on, **72**
  brief history of, 40–45
  business conducted on, 73–74, 298–299
  censorship issues, 242
  discussion groups, 52
  distance learning via, **73**, 298
  domains on, **47**–48
  email and, 46–55

examples of uses for, 39
FTP sites on, **70**, 71
government resources on, 300
influence of, 6
ISPs and, 44–46
netiquette, **52**–53
newsgroups on, **72**
new versions of, 279
personal uses for, 72–74
physical connections to, 39–44, 45
plagiarism issues, 76
programming for, A25–A27
real-time chat on, **72**
regulation of, 279
review questions/exercises on, 82–84
Telnet feature, **70**, 71, 72
tips for searching, 66–67
veracity of information on, 65, 74
viruses downloaded from, 284
  See also World Wide Web
Internet2, **279**, **302**
Internet Corporation for Assigned Names & Numbers
  (ICANN), **279**
Internet Explorer, 58, 59, 241
Internet Fraud Complaint Center, 283
Internet Service Providers (ISPs), **44**, 46, **79**
  comparison shopping for, 44
  personal websites and, 241
Internet telephony, **69**, **79**
Internet terminal, **185**, **207**
Internet Traffic Report, 46
Internet TV, 223
Interpreters, **A19**
Intranets, **240**, **245**
ISA (industry standard architecture) bus, **158**, **173**
ISDN (Integrated Services Digital Network), **42**, 45, **79**
Isolation, 290
ISPs. *See* Internet Service Providers
Iteration control structure, A14

Java programming language, **68**, **79**, A24
JavaScript, A27
Java Virtual Machines (VMs), A24
Jhai Foundation, 75
Job hunting, 74
JPEG compression standard, **234**, **245**
Junk email, 54
Justification, 111–112

Kandell, Jonathan, 292
KaZaA, 282
Kemeny, John, A22
Kernal, 87–88
Keyboards, **14**, **30**, **184**–185, **207**
  health issues and, 204
  layout and features, 106–108
  notebook computer, 169
  specialty, 184–185
  traditional, 184
Keyboard shortcuts, 108
Keychain memory, 168
Key field, **117**, **131**, **253**, 256, **273**
Keywords, **65**, **79**
Kilobits per second (Kbps), **40**, **79**
Kilobyte (K, KB), 17, **144**, **173**
Kiosks, 182
Kline, David, 223
Knowledge engineers, 295
Krantz, Michael, A26
Kraut, Robert, 290
Krugman, Paul, 293
Kubey, Robert, 292
Kurtz, Thomas, A22

Labels
    mailing, 119
    spreadsheet, **113**, **131**
Languages, programming. *See* Programming languages
Language translators, 86, 146, **A18**
LANs. *See* Local area networks
Laptop computers. *See* Notebook computers
Laser printers, **199**–200, **207**
Last-mile problem, 225
Laws, privacy, 268
Learning
    critical-thinking skills for, 34
    distance, **73**, 298
    information technology and, 297–298
    See also Education
Lewis, Peter, 5, 242
Life
    analog basis of, 217
    artificial, **296**–297
Light pens, **187**, 188, **207**
Lights-out factories, 293
Line graphs, 116
Line-of-sight communication, 227
Links. *See* Hyperlinks
Linux, **100**–101, 102, **131**
Liquid crystal display (LCD), **197**, **207**
LISP programming language, A23
Listserv, **52**, **79**
Local area networks (LANs), **9**, **30**, 223, **237**–239, **246**
    client/server, **237**–238
    components of, 238–239
    operating systems for, 98–101
    peer-to-peer, **238**
    wireless, 233
Local bus, 157
Logical operations, 151
Logic bomb, 283
Logic errors, **A15**
Log-on procedures, **46**, **79**
Long-distance wireless communications, 228–232
Lossless compression, 234
Lossy compression, 234
Low earth orbit (LEO), 228
Lucas, George, 299
Lycos, 241

Machine cycle, **150**, **173**
Machine interfaces, 86
Machine language, **145**–146, **173**, **A17**, A18
Macintosh operating system (Mac OS), **97**–98, 102, **131**
Macros, **108**, **131**
Macro virus, 283
Magid, Lawrence, 242
Magnetic ink character recognition (MICR), **190**, **207**
Magnetic-strip card, 167
Magnetic tape, **166**, 167, **173**
Mail, electronic. *See* Email
Mailing labels, 119
Mailing lists, 52
Mail servers, 46, 238
Mainframes, **9**, **30**
Main memory, 152–153
Maintenance
    program, A16
    system, A7
Make-or-buy decision, A6
Malone, Michael, 140
Management
    database, 256–258
    task, 88
Managers, A3
Maney, Kevin, 6
Manufacturing systems, 299

Marketing
    data mining used in, 263
    online, 298
Mark-recognition devices, 190–191
Markup languages, **A25**–A26
Master file, **255**, **273**
Matchmaking services, 72
Maximizing windows, 95
McCarthy, John, A23
McDermott, Trish, 72
Media manipulation, 264–266
Medical technology, 298
    See also Health issues
Medium earth orbit (MEO), 228
Megabits per second (Mbps), **40**, **79**
Megabyte (M, MB), 17, **144**, **173**
Megahertz (MHz), 15, **149**, **173**
Memorization, 27, 34
Memory, 12, 152
    flash, 153
    main, 152–153
    read-only, 153
    virtual, **154**
Memory bus, 157
Memory chips, **15**, **30**, 152–153
Memory expansion board, 157
Memory modules, 152
Mental-health problems, 290
Menu, **92**, **131**
Menu bar, **94**, **131**
Menu-driven interface, 90
Metalanguage, A25
Metasearch sites, 66
Metropolitan Area Exchanges (MAEs), 46
Metropolitan area networks (MANs), **236**, **246**
Microchips. *See* Chips
Microcomputers, **9**, **30**
    networking, 9
    types of, 9–10
    See also Personal computers
Microcontrollers, **10**, **30**
Microprocessors, 7, 140, **141**, 148–149, **173**
Microsoft Internet Explorer, 58, 59, 241
Microsoft .NET platform, **99**, **131**
Microsoft Pocket PC, **102**, **131**
Microsoft Tablet PC, 187
Microsoft Windows. *See* Windows operating systems
Microwave radio, **227**–228, **246**
MIDI board, **192**, **208**
Midsize computers, 9
Miniaturization, 23
Minicomputers, 9
Minimizing windows, 95
Mintz, Daniel, 221
MIPS, **149**, **174**
Mobile-telephone switching office (MTSO), 231
Mobility, 141–142
Modeling tools, **A4**
Modem cards, 158
Modems, **19**, **30**, **40**, **79**, **246**
    cable, **43**
    dial-up, 40–41, 45
    signal conversion by, 218–219
Modules, **A10**
Molitor, Graham, 38
Money
    online use of, 299
    software for managing, 122–123
Monitors, **18**, **30**, 196–199
    See also Display screens
Moore, Gordon, 148
Moore's law, 148
Morrison, Perry, 26
Mossberg, Walter, 169

Motherboard, **16**, **31**, 146–148
Motorola-type chips, **149**, **174**
Mouse, **14**, **31**, 185–186, **208**
    functions performed by, 90
    variant forms of, 185–186
    See also Pointing devices
Mouse pointer, 186
Movie industry, 299–300
MPEG compression standards, **234**, **246**
Multicasting, 224
Multifunction printers, **201**, **208**
Multimedia, 6, **24**, **31**
    databases for storing, 261
    World Wide Web and, 56, 67–68
Multipartite virus, 283
Multipoint videoconferencing, 221
Multitasking, 2, 27, **88**, **132**
Multiuser databases, 257–258
Music
    online access to, 299
    theft of, 282
My Computer icon, 94

Nanotechnology, 8, 290
Napster, 282
Natural hazards, 281
Natural language processing, **296**, **302**
Natural languages, **A20**
Near-letter-quality (NLQ) output, 199
NEC Earth Simulator, 8
Netiquette, **52**–53, **80**
Netscape Navigator, 58, 59, 241
NetWare, **98**, **132**
Network access point (NAP), 46
Network computers, 185
Network databases, **258**, 259, 260, **273**
Network interface cards (NICs), **158**, **174**, 238
Network operating system (NOS), 238
Networks, **4**, **31**, 235–240, **246**
    benefits of, 235–236
    client/server, 11
    components of, 238–239
    extranets, **240**
    firewalls for, **240**
    home, 223
    intranets, **240**
    local area, 223, **237**–239
    metropolitan area, **236**
    operating systems for, 98–101, 238
    personal-area, 233, 237
    types of, 236–237
    wide area, **236**
Neuromancer (Gibson), 5
Newsgroups, **72**, **80**
Newsreader program, **72**, **80**
Node, 237
Nonimpact printers, **199**, **208**
Nonremovable hard disks, **162**–163, **174**
Nonvolatile memory, 168
Notebook computers, **10**, **31**
    durability of, 203
    guarding against theft, 203
    tips on buying, 169
    See also Handheld computers

Object, **A23**
Object code, A19
Object-oriented databases, **261**, **273**
Object-oriented programming (OOP), **A23**–A24
Office suite, 105
Offline storage, **256**, **273**

One-way communications, 228–231
Online, **3**, **31**
Online classes, 73, 298
Online connections, 45
Online demographics, 36
Online game player, 185
Online intimacy, 72–73
Online secondary storage, 168
Online services, 44
Online storage, 168, **256**, **273**
Online trading, 74, 299
Open architecture, 157
Open-source software, **101**, **132**
Operating systems (OS), 20, 86, **87**–88, 96–102, **132**
    DOS, **97**
    functions of, 87–88
    handheld computer, 101–102
    Linux, **100**–101
    Macintosh, **97**–98
    Microsoft .NET, **99**
    NetWare, **98**
    network, 98–101, 238
    Palm OS, **102**
    researching, 102
    restoring, 110
    Unix, **100**
    user interface of, **89**–96
    Windows, 98–99, 102
    See also System software
Operator documentation, A16
Operators, Boolean, 66–67
Optical cards, **167**, **174**
Optical character recognition (OCR), **191**, **208**
Optical disks, **164**–166, **174**
Optical mark recognition (OMR), **190**–191, **208**
Optical mice, 185–186
Organic light-emitting diode (OLED), 197
Output, **13**, **32**, 183, 195–196
Output hardware, 18–19, **183**, 195–202, **208**
    display screens, **196**–199
    ergonomics and, 203–204
    health issues related to, 203–204
    printers, 199–201
    review questions/exercises on, 212–214
    sound-output devices, **201**–202
    types of, 195–196
    video, **202**
    voice-output devices, **202**

Page description language (PDL), **199**, **208**
Pagers, **231**, **246**
Painting programs, **124**, **132**
Palm OS, **102**, **132**
Palmtops, 10
Parallel implementation, A7
Parallel ports, **154**, **174**
Parisi, Tony, A26
Pascal, Blaise, A22
Pascal programming language, A21, A22
Passive hubs, 239
Passive-matrix display, 169, **198**, **208**
Passwords, **286**, **302**
Paste command, 111
PC cameras, 222
PC cards, **158**, 159, **174**
PCI (peripheral component interconnect) bus, **158**, **174**
PCs. *See* Personal computers
PC/TV terminal, 185
PDAs. *See* Personal digital assistants
Peer-to-peer LANs, **238**, **246**
Pen-based computer systems, **187**–188, **208**
Peripheral devices, **18**, **32**

Perkins, Tony, 221
Perl (Practical Extraction and Report Language), **A27**
Personal-area networks, 233, 237
Personal computers (PCs), 9
    buying, 143, 169
    custom-built, 12, 14, 21
    environmental issues related to, 289–290
    guarding against theft, 203
    health issues related to, 203–204
    main uses of, 4
    recycling, 26, 289, 290
    types of, 9–10
    See also Computers; Notebook computers
Personal digital assistants (PDAs), **10**, **32**, 101, 185
Personal-finance managers, **122**–123, **132**
Personal information managers (PIMs), **119**, **132**, 257
Personalization, 25
Personalized TV, 223
Personal software, 106
Pervasive computing, 2
Pesce, Mark, A26
Petabyte (P, PB), **145**, **174**
Phased implementation, A7
Photolithography, 142
Photo manipulation, 265–266
Physical connections, 39–44, 45
    broadband, 38, 43
    cable modems, 43
    dial-up modems, 40–41
    high-speed phone lines, 41–43
    wireless systems, 43–44
Pie charts, 116
Pilot implementation, A7
PIN (personal identification number), **286**, **302**
Pirated software, **104**, **132**, 282
Pixels, **196**, **208**
Plagiarism, 76
Platform, **96**, **133**
Plug-ins, **67**, **80**
Plug and play, **155**, **174**
Pointer, **89**–90, **133**
Pointing devices, **185**–188, **208**
    mouse and its variants, 185–186
    notebook computer, 169
    pen input devices, 187–188
    touch screens, **187**
Pointing stick, **186**, **209**
Point-of-sale (POS) terminal, 185
Point of presence (POP), 44
Point-to-point videoconferencing, 221
Polymorphic virus, 283
Pop-up menu, **92**, **133**
Portability, 24–25, 141–142
Portable computers. *See* Handheld computers; Notebook computers
Portals, 47
Ports, 16, **154**–156, **174**
Power supply, **146**, **174**
Preliminary design, A5
Preliminary investigation, **A4**
Presentation graphics software, **120**–122, **133**
    templates, 120
    views, 120–122
Previewing documents, 112
Primary key, 117
Primary storage, **12**, **15**, **32**
Printers, **19**, **32**, **199**–201, **209**
    buying, 201
    dot-matrix, 199
    ink-jet, **200**
    laser, **199**–200
    multifunction, **201**
    thermal, **201**

Printing documents, 112
Print Scrn key, 199
Print servers, 238
Privacy, **267**, **273**
    databases and, 267
    email messages and, 55
    federal laws on, 268
    information on guarding, 267
Problem clarification, **A9**
Problem-oriented programming languages, **A20**
Procedural errors, 280
Procedural programming languages, **A18**–A20
Processing, **12**, 13, **32**
    hardware components for, 15–16
    speed of, 23, 149–150
Processor chips, **15**, **32**, 141, 148–149
Productivity software, **105**, 106, **133**
Program design, **A9**–A10
Program documentation, A16
Program files, **254**, **273**
Program flowchart, **A12**, A13
Programming, **A8**–A16
    internet, A25–A27
    languages used for, A12, A16–A23
    object-oriented, **A23**–A24
    steps in process of, A8–A16
    visual, **A24**
Programming languages, **A12**, A16–A23
    assembly language, **A17**–A18
    contemporary examples of, A20–A23
    five generations of, **A16**–A17
    high-level or procedural, **A18**–A20
    history and evolution of, A20
    machine language, **A17**
    markup, **A25**–A26
    natural, **A20**
    scripting, A25, A27
    very-high-level or problem-oriented, **A20**
    See also names of specific languages
Programming process, A8, A9–A16
    clarifying programming needs, A9
    coding the program, A12
    designing the program, A9–A12, A13, A14
    documenting the program, A15–A16
    maintaining the program, A16
    testing the program, A15
Programs, 12, 86, **A7**
    creating, A8–A16
    debugging, **A15**
    utility, 86, 89
    See also Software
Program testing, **A15**
Project management software, 125–**126**, **133**
PROM (programmable read-only memory), 153
Protocols, **59**, **80**
Prototypes, **A5**
Prototyping, **A5**
Pseudocode, **A10**, A11, A12
Public-domain software, **103**, **133**
Pull-down menu, **92**, 93, **133**
Pull-up menu, **92**, 93, **133**
Push technology, **69**, **80**

Quality-of-life issues, 289–291
    environmental problems, 289–290
    mental-health problems, 290
    workplace problems, 290–291
Queries, database, 117
Quittner, Joshua, 261
QXGA (quantum extended graphics array), **199**, **209**

Radio
    broadcast, **227**
    microwave, **227**–228
    web, 69
Radio buttons, **64**, **80**
Radio-frequency (RF) spectrum, **226**–227, **246**
Radio-frequency identification (RFID) tags, **194**, **209**
RAM (random access memory), 15, 152
    See also Memory
RAM chips, **152**, **175**
Range, spreadsheet, **115**, **133**
Rapid application development (RAD) system, A24
Raster images, 124
RDRAM chips, 152
Reading data, 153, 160, **175**
Read-only memory (ROM), 87, 153, 164–165
Read/write head, **160**, **175**
Real-time chat (RTC), **72**, **80**
Real-time processing, 256
Recalculation, **115**, **133**
Records, 117, **252**, **273**
Recycling computers, 26, 289, 290
Reference software, 106
Refresh rate, **197**, **209**
Registers, **151**, **175**
Relational databases, **117**, **133**, **260**, **274**
Relationships, online, 72–73
Releases, software, 103
Removable hard disks, **163**, **175**
Rentalware, **104**, **133**
Replace command, 111
Research, web-based, 76
Resolution, 189, **196**–197, **209**
Restore disk, 110
Review questions/exercises, 34
    on application software, 136–138
    on artificial intelligence, 303–304
    on communications technology, 248–250
    on databases, 275–276
    on hardware, 178–180, 212–214
    on information technology, 34–36
    on the internet, 82–84
    on security issues, 303–304
    on system software, 136–138
Rheingold, Howard, 2
Ribbon cable, 17
Rifkin, Jeremy, 293
RISC (reduced instruction set computing) chips, **148**, **175**
Ritchie, Dennis, A22
Robbins, Alan, 86
Robotics, **294**–295, **302**
Robots, **294**–295, **302**
Rollover feature, **92**, **133**
ROM (read-only memory), 87, **153**, 164–165, **175**
ROM chips, 153
Root record, 258
Rothenberg, David, 76
Routers, **239**, **246**
Rukeyser, William, 76
Runtime libraries, 254

Saffo, Paul, 291, 299
Safire, William, 265
Sales, online, 298
Sampling process, 220
Satellites, communications, **43**, 45, **228**
Saving files, **112**, **134**
Scanners, **189**, **209**
Scanning and reading devices, 188–192
    bar-code readers, 189–**190**
    character-recognition devices, 190–191
    fax machines/modems, **191**–192

mark-recognition devices, 190–191
    optical scanners, 189
Scatter charts, 116
Science, data mining in, 263
Screens. *See* Display screens
Scripting languages, A25, A27
Scripts, **A25**
Scroll arrows, **64**, **80**
Scrolling, **64**, **80**, **108**, **134**
SCSI controllers, 163
SCSI ports, **154**, **175**
SDLC. *See* Systems development life cycle
SDRAM chips, 152
Search command, 111
Search engines, **65**–66, **80**
Searching the internet, 66–67
Secondary storage, **12**, 17–18, **32**, 159–168
    direct access, **255**–256
    offline, **256**
    online, 168, **256**
    sequential, **255**
Secondary storage hardware, 17–18, **159**–168, **175**
    flash memory cards, **168**
    floppy disks, **160**–161
    hard disks, **162**–163
    magnetic tape, **166**
    optical disks, **164**–166
    smart cards, 166–**167**
    Zip disks, **161**
Second-generation (2G) technology, 231
Sectors, **160**, **175**
Security, 280–288, **286**, **302**
    access rights and, 286–287
    broadband connections and, 43
    civil unrest and, 281
    computer crime and, **282**–283, 284–285
    disaster-recovery plans and, **288**
    encryption and, **287**
    errors/accidents and, 280–281
    general procedures for, 287–288
    identification systems and, 286–287
    natural hazards and, 281
    review questions/exercises on, 303–304
    terrorism and, 281
    viruses and, 283–**284**
    WiFi technology and, 250
    worms and, 283–**284**
Selection control structure, A14
Self-scanning checkout, 190, 191
Semiconductors, **141**, **175**
Sensors, **194**, **209**
Sequence control structure, A14
Sequential storage, **255**, **274**
Serial ports, **154**, **176**
Servers, **11**, **32**, 237–238
Service packs, 110
Service programs, 89
Services, theft of, 282
Set-top box, 185
SGML (Standard Generalized Markup Language), A25
Shared databases, **257**–258, **274**
Shareware, **103**, **134**
Sheet-fed scanners, 189
Shortcut keys, 108
Short-range wireless communications, 233
Silicon, 23, **141**, **176**
SIMMs, 152
Simpson, O. J., 265
Sites, **56**, **80**
Slide shows, 120
Smart cards, 166–167, **176**
Smart mobile devices, 2
Smart mobs, 2, 27

Smartphones, 4
Social Security number (SSN), 267, 269
Softcopy output, **195**, **209**
Soft goods, 73
Software, **12**, 20, **32**, 86
    abandonware, 104
    antivirus, **284**
    blocking, 242
    buying tips, 126
    commercial, 102–103
    converting, A7
    documentation, **104**
    errors in, 280–281
    firewall, 240
    freeware, **103**–104
    installing, 110
    make-or-buy decision for, A6
    open-source, **101**
    origins of term, 86
    pirated, **104**, 282
    productivity, **105**
    protecting, 203, 287–288
    public-domain, **103**
    rentalware, **104**
    shareware, **103**
    theft of, 282
    tutorials, **104**
    types of, 105–106
    See also Application software; System software
Software engineering, A8
    See also Programming
Software license, 102–103, **134**
Software Publishers Association (SPA), 285
Solaris, 100
Solid-state devices, **141**, **176**
Sorting
    database records, 117
    email messages, 53
Sound board, **192**, **209**
Sound card, **18**, **32**, 157, **158**, **176**, 201–202
Sound manipulation, 265
Sound-output devices, **201**–202, **210**
Source code, A19
Source data-entry devices, **188**–192, **210**
Source program files, 254
Spam, **54**, **80**
Speakers, **19**, **32**
Special effects, 299–300
Special-purpose keys, **107**–108, **134**
Specialty software, 106, 120–127
Speech-recognition systems, **193**–194, **210**, 296
Speed
    data transmission, 38–40
    processing, 23, 149–150
Spelling checker, **111**, **134**
Spreadsheets, **113**–116, **134**
    creating charts from, 115–116
    features of, 113, 115
    illustrated overview of, 114
SRAM chips, 152
Standard-definition television (SDTV), 224
Start button, 94
Stealth virus, 283
Stock trading, 74, 299
Storage, 12, 13
    direct access, **255**–256
    offline, **256**
    online, 168, **256**
    primary, **12**, 15
    secondary, **12**, 17–18, 159–168
    sequential, **255**
    volatile, **152**
Streaming audio, **68**, **80**
Streaming video, **68**, **80**

Stress, 290
Stroustrup, Bjarne, A24
Structured programming, **A10**
Students
    distance learning for, **73**, 298
    infotech challenges for, 278
    internet addiction among, 292
    plagiarism issues for, 76
Subprograms/subroutines, A10
Subscription services, 69
Supercomputers, **7**–8, **32**
Supervisor, **87**–88, **134**
SVGA (super video graphics array), **198**, **210**
Switching hubs, 239
SXGA (super extended graphics array), **198**, **210**
Syntax, **A12**
Syntax errors, **A15**
Synthespians, 300
System, **A2**
System board. *See* Motherboard
System cabinet, **15**
System clock, **149**, **176**
Systems analysis, **A4**–A5
Systems analysis and design, **A3**
    participants in, A3
    six phases of, A3–A7
    See also Systems development life cycle
Systems analyst, **A3**
Systems design, **A5**–A6
Systems development, **A6**, A8
Systems development life cycle (SDLC), **A3**–A7
    analyzing the system, A4–A5
    designing the system, A5–A6
    developing/acquiring the system, A6, A8
    implementing the system, A6–A7
    maintaining the system, A7
    participants in, A3
    preliminary investigation, A4
Systems implementation, **A6**–A7
Systems maintenance, **A7**
System software, **20**, **33**, 86–102
    components of, 86–87
    device drivers, 86, **89**
    operating systems, **87**–88
    restoring, 110
    review questions/exercises on, 136–138
    service packs, 110
    utility programs, 86, **89**
System testing, A6
System unit, **15**, 143–159

T1 line, **43**, 45, **81**
Tablet PC, 187
Tape cartridges, **166**, 167, **176**
Taskbar, **95**, **134**
Task management, 88
Taxonomy of Educational Objectives (Bloom), 34
Tax software programs, 123
Technical staff, A3
Teenage Research Unlimited (TRU), 7
Telecommunications Act (1996), 242, 279
Telecommunications technology. *See* Communications
    technology
Telecommuting, **222**–223, **247**
Teleconferencing, 221–222
    See also Videoconferencing
Telemedicine, 298
Telephones
    cellular, 3–4, 231–232
    internet telephony and, 69
    line protection for, 218
    modems connected to, 40–41, 45
    smartphones, 4

Television
    contemporary technologies for, 223–224
    manipulation of content on, 266
Telework, 222–223
Telnet, **70**, 71, 72, **81**
Temp files, 89
Templates
    document, **111**, **134**
    presentation graphics, 120
    worksheet, 116
Terabyte (T, TB), 17, **145**, **176**
Terminals, **9**, **33**, 184–185
Term papers, 76
Terrorism, 281
Testing
    information systems, A6
    program code, A15
Text-to-speech (TTS) systems, 202
TFT display, 197
Theft
    hardware, 203, 282
    identity, 269–270
    software, 282
    time and services, 282
Thermal printers, **201**, **210**
Thesaurus, **111**, **134**
Thinking skills, 34
Third-generation (3G) technology, 232
Time, theft of, 282
Title bar, **94**, **134**
Toolbar, 94–95, **134**
Top-down program design, **A10**
Top-level domain, 47
Torvalds, Linus, 100, 101
Touchpad, **186**, **210**
Touch screens, **187**, **210**
Tower PCs, **9**, **33**
Trackball, **186**, **210**
Tracks, **160**, **176**
Transaction file, **255**, **274**
Transceivers, 227
Transistors, 23, **140**–141, 142, 149, **176**
Trojan horse, 283
Tukey, John, 86
Turing, Alan, 296
Turing test, 296–297, **302**
Tutorials, **104**, **135**
TWAIN technology, 189
Twisted-pair wire, **225**, **247**
Two-way communications, 229, 231–232

Ultra ADA controllers, 163
Undo command, 111
Unicode, **145**, **176**
Uninstall utility, 98
Unit testing, A6
Universal Product Code (UPC), 189
Unix, **100**, **135**
Upgrading, **147**, 156–157, **176**
Uplinking, 228
Uploading data, **40**, **81**
URLs (Uniform Resource Locators), **58**–60, **81**
USB hubs, 156
USB ports, **155**–156, **177**
Usenet, **72**, **81**
User ID, 47
User interface, **89**–96, **135**
User name, 47
Users
    participation in systems development by, A3
    training on new systems, A7
Utility programs, 86, **89**, **135**
UXGA (ultra extended graphics array), **198**, **210**

Vacuum tubes, 140, 141
Values, spreadsheet, **115**, **135**
V-chip technology, 242
Vector images, 124
Versions, software, 103
Very-high-level programming languages, **A20**
Video, **202**, **211**
    manipulation of, 266
    software for editing, 124–125
    streaming, **68**
Video cards, **18**, 198
Videoconferencing, **202**, **211**, **221**–222, **247**
Video display terminals (VDTs), 184
    See also Display screens
Video files, 255
Viewable image size (vis), 196
Views, presentation graphics, 120–122
Virtual memory, **154**, **177**
Virtual office, **223**, **247**
Virtual Reality Modeling Language (VRML), **A26**
Viruses, 283–**284**, **302**
    as attached files, 50
    pirated software and, **104**
    protection against, 284
    types of, 283
Visual BASIC, A24
Visual programming, **A24**
Voice-output devices, **202**, **211**
Volatile storage, **152**, **177**
Von Neumann, John, 7
Voting technology, 300
VRML (Virtual Reality Modeling Language), **A26**

Wafers, 142
Wallace, William A., 297
Watermarks, 112
Wavetable synthesis, 158
Web browsers, **58**, **81**
    cache folder for, 61
    development of, 58
    features of, 60–62
    navigating the Web with, 60–64
    rating systems in, 242
Webcams, **192**, **211**, 222
Webcasting, **69**, **81**
Web documents, 113
Web exercises
    on application software, 137–138
    on artificial intelligence, 304
    on communications technology, 249–250
    on databases, 276
    on hardware, 180, 213–214
    on information technology, 36
    on the internet, 83–84
    on security, 304
    on system software, 137–138
    See also Review questions/exercises
Web files, 255
Web pages, **58**, **81**
    designing, 70, 241
    hyperlinks on, 60, 63
    interactivity of, 63–64
    multimedia effects on, 67–68
    software for designing, 127, 241
    See also Websites
Web portals, **64**–65, **81**
Web servers, 59, 238
Websites, **56**, **81**
    addresses for, 58–60
    bookmarking, 62
    creating your own, 241
    history of visited, 62
    tips for finding, 66–67
    See also Web pages; World Wide Web

Web terminal, 185
What-if analysis, **115**, **135**
Whittler, David, 6
Whois database, 279
Wide area networks (WANs), **236**, **247**
WiFi technology, **233**, **247**, 250
Wildcards, 67
Wildstrom, Stephen, 241
Williams, Penny, 266
Window (computer display), **50**, **81**, **95**, **135**
Windows operating systems, 98, 102
    Windows 95/98, **98**, **132**
    Windows 2000, **99**, **132**
    Windows CE, **102**, **131**
    Windows Millennium Edition, **98**, **131**
    Windows NT, **98**–99, **132**
    Windows XP, **99**, 100, **132**
Wintel platforms, 96
Wired communications media, 225
Wireless Application Protocol (WAP), 233
Wireless communications, 226–233
    internet connections and, 43–44, 45
    long-distance, 228–232
    media used for, 226–228
    radio-frequency spectrum and, 226–227
    short-range, 233
    types of, 228–233
Wireless keyboards, 184
Wireless pocket PC, 185
Wirth, Niklaus, A22
Wizards, **111**, **135**
Word processing software, **107**–113, **135**
    creating documents, 108
    formatting documents, 111–112
    illustrated overview of, 109
    printing documents, 112
    saving documents, 112
    shortcut keys, 108
    tracking document changes, 112
    web documents and, 113
Word size, **150**, **177**
Word wrap, **108**, **135**
Workgroup computing, **222**, **247**
Workplace
    contemporary changes in, 293
    technology issues and, 290–291
    See also Employment

Worksheet files, 105, 113
Worksheet templates, 116
Workstations, **9**, **33**
World Wide Web (WWW), **6**, **33**, 55–70
    addiction to, 292
    addresses used on, 56, 58–60
    browser software, **58**, 60–64
    business conducted on, 73–74, 298–299
    censorship issues, 242
    creating sites on, 241
    government resources on, 300
    how it works, 56, 58–60
    HTML and, 56, 57
    hyperlinks on, 56, 60
    multimedia on, 56, 67–68
    navigating, 60–64
    personal uses for, 72–74
    plagiarism issues, 76
    portal sites on, 64–65
    push technology and, **69**
    review questions/exercises on, 82–84
    search engines on, **65**–66
    telephone calls via, 69
    terminology associated with, 56, 58–59
    tips for searching, 66–67
    veracity of information on, 65, 74
    See also Internet; Websites
Worms, 283–**284**, **302**
Write-protect notch, **160**, **177**
Writing data, **153**, 160, **177**
Writing program documentation, **A15**–A16

XGA (extended graphics array), **198**, **211**
XML (eXtensible Markup Language), A26

Yahoo!, 65, 241

Zemeckis, Robert, 266
Zip-disk drive, **17**, **33**, 161
Zip disks, **161**, 166, **177**

Photo Credits

T = top; M = middle; B = bottom; L = left; R = right

*Page 1*TL Chiaki Tsukumo/AP Photo/ Wide World; *1*BL Courtesy of Sun Microsystems; *1*TR Courtesy of Hewlett-Packard; *2* Ed Bock/Corbis; *4* Courtesy of Sanyo Corporation; *8*L Chiaki Tsukumo/AP Photo/ Wide World; *8*R Chiaki Tsukumo/AP Photo/Wide World; *9*T Courtesy of IBM; *9*LM Courtesy of Sun Microsystems; *9*BL Courtesy of Hewlett-Packard; *9*BR, Courtesy of Hewlett-Packard; *10*TL Courtesy of Hewlett-Packard; *10*TR Courtesy of Hewlett-Packard; *10*B Courtesy of Motorola Corp.; *11* Courtesy of Hewlett-Packard; *11* Courtesy of Hewlett-Packard; *15*L Courtesy of Intel; *15*BL Courtesy of Micron; *15*R Courtesy of Motorola; *17*TL Corbis; *17*BL Courtesy of Iomega; *20*TL Courtesy of Microsoft Corporation; *20*BL Courtesy of Adobe Systems Inc.; *20*ML Courtesy of Microsoft Corporation; *20*BR Courtesy of Adobe Systems Inc. *22*TL Courtesy of Unisys Archives; *22*TR Mark Richards/PhotoEdit; *23* Don Mason/Corbis Stock Market; *24* Courtesy of PR NewsFoto; *25*R Elaine Thompson/AP Photo/Wide World; *25*L Linda Spillers/AP Photo/ Wide World; *37* Courtesy of DirectTV; *56* Elise Amendola/AP Photo/Wide World; *58* Richard Drew/AP Photo/ Wide World; *75* Courtesy of The Jhai Foundation; *77* Judy Mason; *92* Yang Liu/Corbis; *98* Chris Farina/ Corbis Sygma; *101*L Mike Blake/Reuters/Corbis; *101*BR Courtesy of Palm Computing; *101*TR Courtesy of Lycoris; *115* Peter Beck/ Corbis; *127* Brand X Pictures/Getty Images; *139*TL Courtesy of Intel; *139* TR Courtesy of Intel; *141* Courtesy of IBM Archives; *142*BL Courtesy of Intel; *142*TL Courtesy of Intel; *142*TR J. Kyle Keener; *142*BR Courtesy of Intel; *148*TL Courtesy of Intel; *148*TR Courtesy of Intel; *148*BL Courtesy of Intel; *149* Courtesy of Motorola; *152*T Courtesy of Intel; *152*B Courtesy of Intel; *155*T Courtesy of Acer Inc.; *155*B Judy Mason; *156*T Courtesy of Adaptec; *156*B Courtesy of Hewlett-Packard; *156*M Courtesy of Hewlett Packard; *157* Brian Williams; *159* John S. Reid; *161*T Brian Williams; *161*M Courtesy of Acer Inc.; *161*B Courtesy of Iomega; *162* Courtesy of IBM; *163*L Courtesy of IBM; *165*L Koji Sasahara/AP Photo/ Wide World; *165*R Brian Williams; *167*TL Courtesy of Hewlett-Packard; *167*BL Photo by ActivCard via Getty Images; *167*TR Courtesy of Hewlett-Packard; *168*T Courtesy of Wolverine Data Corporation; *168*B Courtesy of M-Systems/ DiskOnKey; *169* Courtesy of Hewlett-Packard; *181* Charles Gupton/Stock Boston; *182*R Jon Freilich/AP Photo/ Wide World; *182*L Bell Atlantic/AP Photo/ Wide World; *185*L Ryan McVay/Getty Images; *185*R John Slater/Taxi/Getty Images; *186*TR Courtesy of Logitech; *186*BL Courtesy of IBM; *186*ML Courtesy of Hewlett Packard; *186*BR Courtesy of IBM; *187*TL David Kohl/AP Photo/ Wide World; *187*B Courtesy of Acer Inc.; *187*TR Rich Pedroncelli/AP Photo/ Wide World; *188*T Courtesy of FastPoint Technologies; *188*M Courtesy of Wacom Technology; *188*B Courtesy of Seiko Instruments USA Inc.; *189*L Myrleen Ferguson Cate/ PhotoEdit; *189*R Wenatchee World, Mike Bonnicksen/AP Photo/ Wide World; *189*M Tim Flach/ Getty Images; *191*T Courtesy of NCR Corporation; *191*B Courtesy of Symbol Technology; *191*Top 2 Courtesy of Hewlett-Packard; *192*Bottom 2 Courtesy of IBM; *193*TL Courtesy of Hewlett-Packard; *193*TR Courtesy of Sony Ericsson; *193*B Courtesy of Commodio; *194*TL Courtesy of Tom Burdete/USGS; *194*BL Gilles Mingasson/Getty Images News; *194*BR Gilles Mingasson/Getty Images News; *195*L Mark Peterson/Corbis SABA; *195*R Courtesy of Identix; *196*T Tony Cenicola/New York Times Pictures; *197* Courtesy of Hewlett-Packard; *200*M Brian Williams; *200*B Courtesy of Hewlett Packard; *201* Courtesy of Hewlett Packard; *208*T Corbis; *215*L Sean Gallup/Getty Images; *221*L Jose Luis Pelaez Inc./Corbis; *221*M R. W. Jones/Corbis; *221*R Steve Chenn/Corbis; *222* Javier Pierini/Corbis; *225*T Corbis; *225* 2nd from top Phil Degginger/Getty Images; *225* 3rd from top Eric Myer/Taxi/Getty Images; *225*BL Spike Mafford/PhotoDisc Red; *225*BR Ed Degginger; *228*TR Brian Williams; *228*B Liu Liqun/Corbis; *229* HO/AP Photo/ Wide World; *230*BL Najtah Feanny/Corbis; *230*BR James Leynse/ Corbis Saba; *230*TL Courtesy of Pulse Data; *231*T Corbis; *231*B Courtesy of Blackberry; *232* Corbis; *233*T Courtesy of IBM; *233*B Jacques Brinon/AP Photo/Wide World; *233*M Courtesy of IBM; *235* AFP/ Corbis; *237* Juan Carlos Ulate/Reuters NewMedia Inc./Corbis; *239*TR Judy Mason; *239*M AP Photo/ Wide World; *239*TL Courtesy of Hewlett-Packard; *239*B Courtesy of Microsoft; *239*TL Judy Mason; *240* Courtesy of Check Point Software Technologies; *254* Pierre Schwartz/Corbis; *257* Noboru Hashimoto/Corbis; *262* Brian Williams; *263* Brian Williams; *265* Courtesy of Elastic Reality; *266*B Courtesy of Princeton Video; *266*TL J. W. Burkey/Getty Images; *266*TR Paul Higdon/ The New York Times Pictures; *277* Daniel Hulshizer/AP Photo/Wide World; *281*T Corbis Bettmann; *281*B Liz Gilbert/Sygma/Corbis; *282* Brian Williams; *285*B Corbis; *285*T Fujifotos/The Image Works; *288* Reuters NewMedia Inc./Corbis; *289*T Brian Williams; *289*B Courtesy of Larson, a DMB Company; *289*B Courtesy of Larson, a DMB Company; *293* David M.Russell; *294* Fujifotos/The Image Works; *295*TR Mike Derer/AP Photo/ Wide World; *295*BR Bob Self/Florida Times-Union/AP Photo/ Wide World; *295*TL Bertil Ericson/AP Photo/ Wide World; *299* AFP/Corbis; *300* Marissa Roth/The New York Times Pictures; *A3* Photodisc/Getty Images; *A4* Photodisc/ Getty Images; *A5* Photodisc/Getty Images; *A6* Photodisc/Getty Images.

Additional Art Credits
Page 197 ("Happy") *www.bergen.org/AAST/ComputerAnimation/Graph-Pixel.html; 230* adapted from *San Francisco Chronicle,* Benny Evangelista, "GPS Essential for Success of U.S. Military Effort in Iraq," March 20, 2003, p. W6.

About the Authors

Who are **Brian Williams and Stacey Sawyer**? We live near Lake Tahoe, Nevada, and share an avid interest in seeing students become well educated—especially in information technology.

What best describes what we do? We consider ourselves watchers and listeners. We spend our time watching what's happening in business and society and on college campuses and listening to the views expressed by instructors, students, and other participants in the computer revolution. We then try to translate those observations into meaningful language that can be best understood by students.

Over the past two decades, we have individually or together **authored more than 22 books** (and over 32 revisions), most of them on computers and information technology. Both of us have a commitment to helping students succeed in college. Brian, for instance, has co-authored six books in the college success field: *Learning Success, The Commuter Student, The Urban Student, The Practical Student, The Successful Distance Learning Student,* and *College to Career.* Stacey has an interest in language education and has worked on several college textbooks on information technology, English as a Second Language (ESL), and Spanish, German, and French We thus bring to our information-technology books an awareness of the needs of the increasingly diverse student bodies.

Brian has a B.A. and M.A. from Stanford University and has held managerial jobs in education, communications, and publishing. Stacey has a B.A. from Ohio Wesleyan and Freiburg University, Germany, and an M.A. from Middlebury College and the University of Mainz, Germany. She has taught at Ohio State University and managed and consulted for a number of for-profit and nonprofit health, educational, and publishing organizations.

In our spare time, we enjoy travel, music, cooking, and reading philosophy and history.